T0338891

PROCEEDINGS

OF THE

HARVARD CELTIC COLLOQUIUM

Volume 40, 2021

Edited by

Lorena Alessandrini
Myrzinn Boucher-Durand
Colin Brady
Oisín Ó Muirthile
Nicholas Thyr

Published by
The Department of Celtic Languages and Literatures
Faculty of Arts and Sciences, Harvard University

Distributed by
Harvard University Press
Cambridge and London
by the President and Fellows of Harvard University,
Department of Celtic Languages and Literatures
©2023
All Rights Reserved

ISBN: 978-0-674-27881-3

The cover design is based on the medallion of an
Early Christian belt shrine from Moylough, Co. Sligo.
Drawing by Margo Granfors

Designed and typeset by the Fenway Group
Boston, Massachusetts

CONTENTS

Harvard Celtic Colloquium 40

PREFACE

The annual Harvard Celtic Colloquium originated in a graduate student conference convened in 1980 by students in the Harvard University Department of Celtic Languages and Literatures. Since then the conference has developed into an internationally recognized event, drawing together scholars and students from around the world to present work on all facets of Celtic Studies. The Colloquium is the oldest graduate-run conference in the field of Celtic Studies, and, true to its origins, it remains entirely run and organized by the graduate students of the Harvard Celtic department. The principal organizers of the Colloquium then become the editorial board for the publication of its proceedings.

Papers given at a Colloquium may be submitted for publication following peer review in the journal, *The Proceedings of the Harvard Celtic Colloquium (PHCC)*. The journal is distributed by Harvard University Press, which also handles subscriptions and orders for single volumes. Information on the Colloquium and *PHCC* may be found through the Harvard University Department of Celtic Languages and Literatures web site. The managing editor for *PHCC* may be contacted directly at phcc@fas.harvard.edu.

Acknowledgements

The editors are indebted to Professor Catherine McKenna for her advice and encouragement, and to the Celtic department staff, Ms. Mary Violette and Mr. Steven Duede, for their help with the Colloquium and administrative matters. We also wish to thank the Managing Editor of *PHCC*, and the staff of Fenway Group for their help with the publication of this volume.

Lorena Alessandrini
Myrzinn Boucher-Durand
Colin Brady
Oisín Ó Muirthile
Nicholas Thyr

Organizers of the Harvard Celtic Colloquium 2019, and Editors of *PHCC* volume 40 (2023).

Irish World Annals and Universal Chronicling: Medieval Irish Scholars and their 'Global Turn'

Máire Ní Mhaonaigh

Introduction: the Intellectual Context

For medieval Irish scholars, written history was Christian history, an account of past deeds of relevance to the present, framed within an overarching linear and universal (and so Christian) view of time. Their notion of historical thought was shaped by intense engagement with the Bible, prompting both moral and allegorical interpretations of events, as well as the construction of typological connections between 'then' and 'now'. In this way, in Gabrielle Spiegel's words, "the past becomes an explanatory principle, a way of ordering and making intelligible a relationship between events separated by vast distances of time."[1] Sequences of happenings were thus significant,[2] as was the idea of continuity through time. Early Christian writers presented that ordered continuum in various ways, a number of which were highly influential in medieval Irish learned circles.[3] These include the *Chronici Canones* (Chronological Canons) composed in the early fourth century by the bishop of Caesarea, Eusebius, and later translated into Latin and continued to 378 CE by St Jerome.[4] In

---

[1] Gabrielle M. Spiegel, "Historical Thought in Medieval Europe," in *A Companion to Western Historical Thought*, ed. Lloyd Kramer and Sarah Maza (Malden, MA: Blackwell Publishers, 2002), 78-97, at 84.

[2] Spiegel, "Historical Thought in Medieval Europe," 86-7; for medieval England, see Nancy F. Partner, *Serious Entertainments: the Writing of History in Twelfth-century England* (Chicago, IL: University of Chicago Press, 1977), 59.

[3] Michael I. Allen presents an account of the most influential early Christian writers in his "Universal History 300-1000: Origins and Western Development," in *Historiography in the Middle Ages*, ed. Deborah Mauskopf Deliyannis (Leiden and Boston, MA: Brill, 2003), 17-42.

[4] *Eusebius Werke: die Chronik des Hieronymus: Hieronymi Chronicon*, vol. 7, ed. Rudolf Helm, Griechische Christliche Schriftsteller 47, second revised ed. (Berlin: De Gruyter, 1956). An account of Eusebius's original Chronicle and Jerome's continuation is provided by Allen, "Universal History," 20-6.

Eusebius-Jerome's Chronicle, subsequent writers found a useful system of parallel chronologies, synchronising biblical history with that of other major peoples, including the Greeks. The pivotal place of Rome was indicated by its position in the final column, both Eusebius and Jerome, as well as their successors, Augustine of Hippo and Paulus Orosius, being concerned with highlighting the essentially Roman nature of the emerging Christian world.[5] In this way, Rome was accorded chronological, as well as theological significance, through its ultimate role in God's Christian creation.[6]

Rome's importance was underlined by Orosius whose *Historiae aduersus paganos* (Histories against the Pagans) completed about the year 417 CE towards the end of his life, positioned a Christian Rome as successor to a series of world empires, comprising Assyrians, Medes and Persians in the east, the Carthaginians to the south, and the Macedonians in the north.[7] His focus on geography, most notably in his prologue, ensured that all peoples could find a place in his universal scheme.[8] This was a key factor in the later application of Orosius's historical paradigm to other territories and communities, including Ireland.[9] While Orosius's scheme was structured around

---

[5] Spiegel, "Historical Thought in Medieval Europe," 88.

[6] See, for example, Allen, "Universal History," 24-6.

[7] *Histoires (contre les païens), Orose*, ed. and trans. Marie-Pierre Arnaud-Lindet, 3 vols (Paris: Belles Lettres, 1990-91); an earlier edition is available online, *Paulus Orosius: Historiarum adversum Paganos, libri VII*, ed. Karl Zangemeister (Leipzig: Teubner, 1889) (www.attalus.org/latin/orosius.html, accessed June 14, 2022); and see *Orosius: Seven Books of History against the Pagans*, trans. Andrew T. Fear, Translated Texts for Historians 54 (Liverpool: Liverpool University Press, 2010).

[8] There is an account of Orosius's approach in Allen, "Universal History," 26-9, and a comparison between this and that of Augustine, 29-31. For a detailed account of Orosius and his relationship to Augustine, see Peter van Nuffelen, *Orosius and the Rhetoric of History*, Oxford Early Christian Studies (Oxford: Oxford University Press, 2012).

[9] Elizabeth Boyle discusses the way in which depictions of Babylon in Middle Irish sources are indebted to Orosius in her *History and Salvation in Medieval Ireland*, Studies in Early Britain and Ireland (London and New York: Routledge, 2021), 125-9. Rolf Baumgarten examines the place of Ireland in Orosius's prologue in "The Geographical Orientation of Ireland in Isidore and Orosius," *Peritia* 3 (1984): 189-203.

earthly empires, his contemporary, Augustine, who had prompted Orosius to commence his work, but was ultimately more concerned with sacred than with secular history, structured his writing around the concept of the Six Ages of the World. This system of periodisation underlies Augustine's best-known work, *De civitate Dei* (The City of God), but is set out in more elaborate form in his *De Genesi contra Manichaeos* (Commentary of Genesis against the Manichees), in which the six days of creation (and hence of the week), the six ages of sacred history, and the six ages of human life are co-ordinated.[10] This scheme too proved formative in the medieval Irish construction of their past, particularly as refined and developed by Isidore, seventh-century bishop of Seville, the influence of whose writings in Irish intellectual circles is well known.[11] Bede's articulation of Augustine's temporal categories took place in the same general learned milieu.[12]

---

[10] For a summary of Augustine's scheme (with textual references), including its development by Isidore and Bede, see Michael Clarke and Máire Ní Mhaonaigh, "The Ages of the World and the Ages of Man: Irish and European Learning in the Twelfth Century," *Speculum* 95:2 (April 2020): 467-500 at 472-5, 500 (Appendix).

[11] *Traité de la nature, Isidore de Séville*, ed. and trans. Jacques Fontaine (Paris: Institute d'études augustiniennes, 1960). The focus in scholarship has been on the influence of Isidore's *Etymologiae* in medieval Irish learned circles; see, for example, Rolf Baumgarten, "A Hiberno-Isidorean Etymology," *Peritia* 2 (1983): 225-8; Paul Russell, *'Read it in a Glossary': Glossaries and Learned Discourse in Medieval Ireland*, Kathleen Hughes Memorial Lectures 6 (Cambridge: Department of Anglo-Saxon, Norse, and Celtic, 2008), 6-8.

[12] Bede, *De temporum ratione*, ed. Charles W. Jones, Corpus Christianorum Series Latina 123B (Turnhout: Brepols, 1977); *Bede, the Reckoning of Time*, trans. Faith Wallis, Translated Texts for Historians 29 (Liverpool: Liverpool University Press, 1999). See also Máirín MacCarron, *Bede and Time: Computus, Theology and History in the Early Medieval World*, Studies in Early Medieval Britain and Ireland (London: Routledge, 2019). For the general context, see James Palmer, "The Ordering of Time," in *Abendländische Apokalyptik: Kompendium zur Genealogie der Endzeit*, ed. Catherin Feik, Leopold Schlöndorff, Veronika Wieser, Christian Zolles and Martin Zolles (Berlin: Akademie Verlag, 2013), 607-18.

Bede's scholarship was drawn on by early Irish authors,[13] but he too owed a debt to medieval Irish thinking, particularly in the realm of computus.[14] The intense interest in the ecclesiastical calendar demonstrated by Irish scholars is likely connected to their cultivation of syncretistic historiography, in which the narratives of universal history espoused by Eusebius-Jerome, Augustine and Orosius, and later Isidore, were made to frame the human experience of the Irish, whose past events, real and imagined, were correlated with happenings of the biblical and classical world; whose dynasties were aligned with those of major kingdoms; and whose local terms of reference were punctuated in line with the Six Ages of the World.[15] This type of pseudo-historical, synthetic writing flourished in the eleventh and twelfth centuries,[16] as narratives such as the vernacular Irish adaptation of *Sex aetates mundi*,[17] and the account of Irish origins

---

[13] See, for example, Pádraig Ó Néill, "An Old-Irish Treatise on the Psalter and its Hiberno-Latin Background," *Ériu* 30 (1979): 148-64; Boyle, *History and Salvation*, 92-4.

[14] Immo Warntjes has provided a survey of computistical works produced between the time of Isidore and Bede, which demonstrates the key involvement of both Irish and Anglo-Saxon scholars in the field: "Irische Komputistik zwischen Isidor von Sevilla und Beda Venerabilis: Ursprung, karolingische Rezeption und generelle Forschungsperspektiven," *Viator* 42 (2011): 1-32. See also his *The Munich Computus, Text and Translation: Irish Computistics between Isidore of Seville and the Venerable Bede, and its Reception in Carolingian Times* (Stuttgart: Steiner, 2010). The connection between Bede and contemporary Irish authors is explored, for example, in Dáibhí Ó Cróinín, "The Irish Provenance of Bede's Computus," *Peritia* 2 (1983): 238-42.

[15] Clarke and Ní Mhaonaigh, "The Ages of the World," 475.

[16] For history writing in this period, see Máire Ní Mhaonaigh, "The Peripheral Centre: Writing History on the Western 'Fringe'," *Interfaces* 4 (2017): 59-84 (https://riviste.unimi.it/interfaces/article/view/9469/8994, accessed June 14, 2022).

[17] On this aspect of *Sex aetates mundi*, see Clarke and Ní Mhaonaigh, "The Ages of the World," 475-9; and Patrick Wadden, "*Prímchenéla* and *Fochenéla* in the Irish *Sex aetates mundi*," *Ériu* 66 (2016): 167-78. There are two editions of the text: *The Irish Sex aetates mundi*, ed. and trans. Dáibhí Ó Cróinín (Dublin: Dublin Institute for Advanced Studies, 1983), and *Sex aetates mundi: die Weltzeitalter bei den Angelsachsen und den*

expounded in the various versions of *Lebor Gabála Érenn* (The Book of the Taking[s] of Ireland) show.[18] It is evident at an earlier period also, however, as the biblical underpinning of texts such as the grammatical treatise, *Auraicept na nÉces* (The Scholars' Primer),[19] and the vernacular poem, *Can a mbunadas na nGáedel* (Whence the Origins of the Irish?), plausibly ascribed to the late ninth-century cleric, Máel Muru Othna, make clear.[20] A connection with wandering (chosen) peoples who had spent time in Egypt and Scythia, before taking Ireland from Spain, is highlighted in the latter composition.[21] Earlier texts also allude to

---

Iren, Untersuchungen und Texte, ed. and trans. Hildegard L.C. Tristram (Heidelberg: Winter, 1985).

[18] *Lebor Gabála Érenn: the Book of the Taking of Ireland*, ed. and trans. R.A.S. Macalister, 5 vols, Irish Texts Society 34-35, 39, 41, 44 (Dublin: Irish Texts Society, 1932-42); and see the contributions in *Lebor Gabála Érenn: Textual History and Pseudohistory*, ed. John Carey, Irish Texts Society Subsidiary Series 20 (Dublin: Irish Texts Society, 2009).

[19] The text is composite, but the core has been generally taken to be early eighth-century in date on linguistic grounds: Anders Ahlqvist (ed. and trans.), *The Early Irish Linguist: an Edition of the Canonical Part of* Auraicept na nÉces, *with Introduction, Commentary and Indices* (Helsinki: Societas Scientiarum Fennica, 1983). A later, ninth-century date for the earliest stratum has been proposed by Nicolai Egjar Engesland, based on his reading of the cultural context of the text, "The Intellectual Background of the Earliest Irish Grammar," *Journal of Medieval History* 47:4-5 (2021): 472-84.

[20] The text of the poem is edited and translated by James Henthorn Todd in his *Leabhar Breathnach annso sís: the Irish Version of the Historia Brittonum of Nennius* (Dublin: Irish Archaeological Society, 1848), 220-71; for an account of Máel Muru, see John Carey, "In Search of Mael Muru Othna," in *Clerics, Kings and Vikings: Essays on Medieval Ireland in Honour of Donnchadh Ó Corráin*, ed. Emer Purcell, Paul MacCotter, Julianne Nyhan and John Sheehan (Dublin: Four Courts Press, 2015), 429-39.

[21] See *Leabhar Breathnach*, ed. and trans. Todd, 232-3, lines 92-100. On *Can a mbunadas na nGáedel*, see Máire Ní Mhaonaigh and Elizabeth Tyler, "The Language of History-writing in the Ninth Century: an Entangled Approach," *Journal of Medieval History* 47:4-5 (2021): 451-71, at 462-4; and Katja Ritari, "*Can a mbunadas na nGáedel*: Remembering the Past in Irish Pseudohistorical Poems," *Peritia* 28 (2017): 155-76, at 160-5.

biblical ancestry; in seventh-century genealogical material concerned with Leinster, Labraid Loingsech 'the exiled one', an ancestor-figure, is linked directly to Míl of Spain and through him to Noah and to Adam.[22] Descent of the Irish more generally is traced back to Japheth in the same corpus.[23]

The place of the Irish in universal history was also being discussed in learned contexts elsewhere. Fifty years or so before Máel Muru composed his sequential history, concerned with relating historical happenings in the order they occurred,[24] the author of the *Historia Brittonum* (the History of the Britons), on the other side of the Irish Sea in Gwynedd, considered the origins of the Irish (and the English), when exploring the ancestry of the Britons.[25] It is claimed therein that the Irish were descended from a Scythian nobleman (a common trope in other histories), who was expelled from Egypt. Moreover, this is said to have been related by *peritissimi Scottorum* (the wisest of the Irish).[26] In *Can a mbunadas na nGáedel*, the journey outlined is from Scythia to Egypt. Fénius, illustrious learned forefather

---

[22] *Über die älteste irische Dichtung, I: rhythmische, alliterierende Reimstrophen*, ed. Kuno Meyer (Berlin: Verlag der königlichen Akademie der Wissenschaften, 1913), 27-31, 39-50.

[23] For discussion, see Donnchadh Ó Corráin, "Creating the Past: the Early Irish Genealogical Tradition," *Peritia* 12 (1998): 177-208, at 201-2.

[24] He specifically states that his concern is with *ord senchasa*, 'the order or organisation of *senchas* (historical knowledge),' and with *sreth senchasa mac Míled* 'the arrangement of the *senchas* of the sons of Míl': *Leabhar Breathnach*, ed. and trans. Todd, 224-5, lines 23-4, 27.

[25] The text is edited and translated in *Nennius, British History and the Welsh Annals*, ed. and trans. John Morris (London: Phillimore, 1980); for discussion, see David N. Dumville, "*Historia Brittonum*: an Insular History from the Carolingian Age," in *Historiographie im frühen Mittelalter*, ed. Anton Scharer and Georg Scheibelreiter (Vienna: Oldenbourg, 1994), 406-34; and Thomas M. Charles-Edwards, *Wales and the Britons, 350-1064* (Oxford: Oxford University Press, 2012), 437-47. Ben Guy has put forward cogent arguments in favour of Nennius as the ninth-century author: "The Origins of the Compilation of Welsh Historical Texts in Harley 3589," *Studia Celtica* 49 (2015): 21-56, at 45-54.

[26] *Nennius*, ed. and trans. Morris, 21 and 62 (§15).

of the Irish,[27] first spent time in Scythia whence his son, master of all the world's languages, came to Egypt where Scotta bore him a son, eponymous ancestor of the Irish or the Gaels, Gáedel Glas.[28] According to the vernacular poem, the Irish, having multiplied, eventually came to Spain, from where sons of Míl went on to Ireland, dividing the island between them. It is directly from these first settlers that Máel Muru traces numerous dynasties of his own time.[29] A trio of sons is alluded to in *Historia Brittonum*, in a passing reference to *tres filii militis Hispaniae* (three sons of a soldier of Spain).[30]

Notwithstanding the specific reference in *Historia Brittonum* to Irish scholars,[31] the sources from which the author drew his information could have been of continental rather than Irish provenance.[32] Scholarly comments in ninth-century manuscripts indicate that the biblical origin of the Irish was a topic for discussion further afield as well.[33] Medieval Irish scholars were forging a place for themselves, but also being accommodated by others, within universal Christian history flourishing in scholarly communities in Carolingian Europe, England and elsewhere. The idiom within which individual histories was expressed might vary, but similar points of origin–be they classical or biblical–and the desired common goal of salvation, enabled accounts of different peoples to be articulated within a recognisable frame. This in turn facilitated an understanding of the present as a stage on a universal Christian journey, explicable

---

[27] The name may be a deliberate allusion to Aeneas: see Bart Jaski, "Aeneas and Fénius: a Classical Case of Mistaken Identity," in *Texts and Identities in the Early Middle Ages*, ed. Richard Corradini, Rob Meens, Christina Pössel and Philip Shaw, Forschungen zur Geschichte des Mittelalters 12 (Vienna: Verlag der österreichischen Akademie der Wissenschaften, 2006), 17-33.

[28] *Can a mbunadas na nGáedel*, ed. and trans. Todd, 226-31, lines 41-68.

[29] *Can a mbunadas na nGáedel*, ed. and trans. Todd, 248-69.

[30] *Nennius*, ed. and trans. Morris, 20 and 61 (§13).

[31] *Nennius*, ed. and trans. Morris, 21 and 62 (§15).

[32] See Ní Mhaonaigh and Tyler, "The Language of History-writing," 460.

[33] See Olivier Szerwiniack, "D'Orose au *LGÉ*," *Études celtiques* 31 (1995): 205-17; and Michael Clarke, "The *Leabhar Gabhála* and Carolingian Origin Legends," in *Early Medieval Ireland and Europe: Chronology, Contacts, Scholarship*, ed. Pádraic Moran and Immo Warntjes (Turnhout: Brepols, 2015), 441-79, at 454-6.

by means of interpretative tools–allegorical, moral, typological and the like–linking it to a structured past, and looking forward to a predictable, providential future, in line with the purpose of God.[34]

Among the many forms in which such conceptually interconnected histories were presented were universal chronicles, the Chronicle of Eusebius as revised by Jerome being the most significant model in this regard. Examples include the seventh-century *Chronicon* or Chronicle of Fredegarius which was circulating widely at the ninth-century Carolingian court in which Irish origins were being discussed.[35] A product of the same court and written around the same time the *Historia Brittonum* was composed was the *Historiae* of Frechulf of Lisieux,[36] who drew on both Augustine and Orosius to a significant degree.[37] These texts are also comparable with another rich source in which the history of the Irish is presented in a universal frame. The material in question is referred to as the Irish World Chronicle.[38] A synchronistic account of global and pre-Christian Irish events, it has survived in a number of versions which form part of annalistic compilations.[39] Annal-writing was an important strand of early Irish writing, and references to earlier events were incorporated into collections of annals retrospectively. The Irish World Chronicle, recounting kingdoms and events pertaining to the time before the coming of St Patrick to Ireland in the fifth century, forms a significant

---

[34] See Boyle, *History and Salvation*, Allen, "Universal History," and Björn Weiler, "Historical Writing in Europe, *c.* 1100-1300," in *The Chronicles of Medieval Wales and the March: New Contexts, Studies and Texts*, ed. Ben Guy, Georgia Henley, Owain Wyn Jones and Rebecca Thomas, Texts and Cultures of Northern Europe 31 (Turnhout: Brepols, 2020), 33-67.

[35] Clarke, "The *Leabhar Gabhála*," 463-5.

[36] Frechulf of Lisieux, *Historiarum libri XII*, in *Opera omnia*, ed. Michael I. Allen, Corpus Christianorum Continuatio Mediævalis 169 (Turnhout: Brepols, 2002), 17-724.

[37] For Augustinian influence, see Nicolaus Staubach, "*Christiana tempora*: Augustin und das Ende der alten Geschichte in der Weltchronik Frechulfs von Lisieux," *Frühmittelalterliche Studien* 29 (1995): 167-206; Graeme Ward places more emphasis on his debt to Orosius: "Frechulf of Lisieux, Augustine and Orosius," *Early Medieval Europe* 22:3 (2014): 492-505.

[38] Thomas F. O'Rahilly used this term in his *Early Irish History and Mythology* (Dublin: Dublin Institute for Advanced Studies, 1946), 253-4.

[39] The textual evidence is discussed in what follows.

part of this non-contemporary material, providing an interpretative structure within which later historical happenings could be understood. Its date of composition is difficult to determine, as is its end-point, since it survives as a kind of global preface to interlinked records of historical events. It is often understood as an account of the pre-Patrician period,[40] and there is evidence to suggest that Patrick's coming was deemed an important marker in the relating of events, as we will see. However, in the view of John V. Kelleher, what he termed Irish World Annals–to distinguish his concept from O'Rahilly's pre-Patrician Irish World Chronicle–"entirely replaced the original annalistic texts up to about 590, and from then to 735 fit like a sleeve over what remains of the true annals."[41] He argued that this rewriting took place sometime between the late eighth and late ninth centuries and was politically motivated, on behalf of the most powerful dynasty in Ireland at the time, Uí Néill.[42] My aim in this publication in Kelleher's memory is to explore the content and structure of his Irish World Annals,[43] with reference to the broader framework of history-writing and universal chronicling in which the Irish were engaged, as

---

[40] Thus, O'Rahilly, *Early Irish History and Mythology*; see also Thomas Charles-Edwards (trans.), *The Chronicle of Ireland*, Translated Texts for Historians 44, 2 vols (Liverpool: Liverpool University Press, 2006), I: 2-3. By contrast, both pre- and post-Patrician annals are considered a unity by Daniel P. McCarthy, *The Irish Annals: their Genesis, Evolution and History* (Dublin: Four Courts Press, 2008); this view, aspects of which had been published in earlier articles, is proposed as part of a complex theory about the development of Irish annalistic writing more generally which has not gained widespread acceptance: see Nicholas Evans, *The Present and the Past in Medieval Irish Chronicles*, Studies in Celtic History 27 (Woodbridge: Boydell and Brewer, 2010), 3-6, and Thomas Charles-Edwards, Review of Daniel P. McCarthy, *The Irish Annals*, *Studia Hibernica* 36 (2009-10): 207-10.

[41] John V. Kelleher, "Early Irish History and Pseudo-history," *Studia Hibernica* 3 (1963): 113-27, at 125.

[42] "But everything that deals with the kingship of Tara . . . or with the rise of the identity of the Uí Néill, or with the two chief ecclesiastical centres in Ireland, Armagh and Clonmacnois, can only be regarded with wary suspicion.": Kelleher, "Early Irish History," 122.

[43] Kelleher himself discussed some of its content in his "The Táin and the Annals," *Ériu* 22 (1971): 107-27.

outlined in brief above. To this end, I will set out the textual evidence, and discuss its structure and sources, as well as the interpretative framework it provides. My primary focus here is on the content of the Irish World Annals or Chronicle and what it suggests about medieval Irish attitudes to the construction of their past. Immersed in universal chronicling and acutely aware of their own place in the wider world, medieval Irish scholars reveal a skilful 'global turn'.[44]

The Textual Evidence

Defining the Irish World Annals or Chronicle is difficult, as the various names applied to it and the uncertainty as to its end point make clear. It is in fact a phantom text, the original form of which can only be surmised, since it has been incorporated into longer annalistic compilations in surviving copies, as noted above. The earliest version forms part of the Annals of Inisfallen preserved in Oxford, Bodleian Library, Manuscript Rawlinson B. 503; entries down to the year 1092 were transcribed by a single scribe in the late eleventh century.[45] The material is acephalous, beginning with Abraham, the commencement of the Third Age of the World.[46] After a reference to the Council of Ephesus of 431, the scribe appears to mark the end of a section: "now ends this short writing from the beginning of the world" (*nunc finit haec parua perscriptio a principio mundi*), remarking that it had been "gathered from all sources and based on no exemplar of its own" (*undecunque collecta, id est sine exemplari propria*).[47] A regnal list of Irish kings beginning in the time of St Patrick follows, from Láegaire mac Néill to Máel Sechnaill mac Domnaill in the eleventh century. In this version, therefore, there is a dividing line between the pre-

---

[44] This article originated as the John V. Kelleher Lecture delivered at Harvard University, October 10, 2019. I am grateful to Prof. Catherine McKenna and Prof. Joseph F. Nagy for their hospitality on that occasion, and to the audience for their interest and questions. I am also indebted to Dr. Elizabeth Boyle, Brigid Ehrmantraut, Prof. Ralph O'Connor, and Prof. Erich Poppe who provided perceptive comments on the written draft.

[45] Brian Ó Cuív, *Catalogue of Irish Language Manuscripts in the Bodleian Library at Oxford and Oxford College Libraries, Part I, Descriptions* (Dublin: Dublin Institute for Advanced Studies, 2001), 201-2.

[46] Seán Mac Airt (ed. and trans.), *The Annals of Inisfallen* (*MS. Rawlinson B. 503*) (Dublin: Dublin Institute for Advanced Studies, 1953), 1.

[47] Mac Airt, *Annals of Inisfallen*, 42, and xiv for discussion.

Patrician material and the account of Láegaire's reign which comes after.[48] Notwithstanding this, notice of world events and imperial rulers continue for some time.[49]

The version preserved in another Oxford manuscript, Bodleian, Rawlinson B. 502 is more extensive; it is commonly known as the Annals of Tigernach.[50] It occupies the first twelve folios of this manuscript and was once independent from the second part of the manuscript with which it was brought together by James Ware in the seventeenth century.[51] It has been tentatively dated to the late eleventh or early twelfth century, not least because of the presence in the manuscript of glosses in Hand H of Dublin, Royal Irish Academy Manuscript 1229, Lebor na hUidre (The Book of the Dun Cow).[52] It too is acephalous, beginning a short while before the birth of the founders of Rome, Romulus and Remus, and continuing down to the reign of Antoninus Pius as Roman Emperor in the second century CE.[53] A related version preserved in the fourteenth-century manuscript, Oxford, Bodleian, Rawlinson B. 488 extends further, covering events down to the fourth century, noting the captivity of St Patrick in Ireland towards the end.[54]

An abbreviated version of the material survives in a later manuscript, London, British Library, Cotton Titus A. XXV, referred

---

[48] Mac Airt, *Annals of Inisfallen*, 42-4 (fol. 9r).

[49] The sixth-century succession of Justinian to Justin and on to Tiberius is recorded: Mac Airt, *The Annals of Inisfallen*, 72-3.

[50] Ó Cuív, *Catalogue of Irish Language Manuscripts, Part I*, 164-5.

[51] Ó Cuív, *Catalogue of Irish Language Manuscripts, Part I*, 163.

[52] Ó Cuív, *Catalogue of Irish Language Manuscripts, Part I*, 163 (and 165 for references to a discussion of the H Hand); but see Jürgen Schmidt, "Zu einer Neuausgabe des Annalen-Fragment in der HS. Rawl. B 502 (sog. Tigernach-Annalen, erstes Fragment)," in *Akten des ersten Symposiums deutschsprachiger Keltologen* (*Gosen bei Berlin, 8.-10. April 1992*), ed. Martin Rockel and Stefan Zimmer, Buchreihe der Zeitschrift für celtische Philologie 11 (Tübingen: Max Niemeyer Verlag, 1993), 267-86, at 268-70.

[53] Whitley Stokes (ed. and trans.), "The Annals of Tigernach (Part 1)," *Revue celtique* 16 (1895): 375-419. Thomas Charles-Edwards notes that they begin "at a point corresponding to 2 Kings 15": *The Chronicle of Ireland*, I: 3 n. 3.

[54] Whitley Stokes, "The Annals of Tigernach (Part 2)," *Revue celtique* 17 (1896): 6-33.

to as the Cottonian Annals or the Annals of Boyle.[55] This version has been dated to the late twelfth or early thirteenth centuries;[56] the information it provides on world history is considerably sparser than that in either the Annals of Inisfallen or the Annals of Tigernach.[57] It begins with a reference to the biblical Enos, and this type of 'global' material continues down to 453 CE, as noted by Kari Maund, and so the coming of Patrick is not a significant division, according to this work.[58] By contrast, the coming of Palladius and Patrick is where the Annals of Ulster commence in the sixteenth-century manuscript, Oxford, Bodleian, Rawlinson B. 489.[59] An earlier fifteenth-century manuscript version of this chronicle, Dublin, Trinity College, 1282, includes pre-Patrician material in a series of folios now prefaced to the folio on which material pertaining to the fifth century CE is preserved.[60] It is likely that this was originally an independent manuscript which later became part of MS 1282; thus, the pre-Patrician material in the Annals of Ulster, often labelled 'the Dublin Fragment', may have originally been a separate text.[61] Like many

---

[55] A. Martin Freeman (ed. and trans.), "The Annals in Cotton MS. Titus A. XXV," *Revue celtique* 41 (1924): 301-30; *Revue celtique* 42 (1925): 283-305; *Revue celtique* 43 (1926): 358-84; *Revue celtique* 44 (1927): 336-61.
[56] See Kari L. Maund, "Sources of the 'World Chronicle' in the Cottonian Annals," *Peritia* 12 (1998): 153-76, at 153.
[57] The sources of this material and its relationship to the pre-Patrician annals in other chronicles are discussed by Maund, "Sources of the 'World Chronicle'."
[58] Maund, "Sources of the 'World Chronicle'," 170.
[59] Ó Cuív, *Catalogue of Irish Languages Manuscripts, Part I*, 153-63.
[60] This begins at fol. 16 of the manuscript, fols 12-14 contains the pre-Patrician material, while fol. 15 is blank, apart from some inscriptions: Daniel McCarthy, "The Original Compilation of the *Annals of Ulster*," *Studia Celtica* 38 (2004): 69-95, at 70.
[61] The principal evidence for this takes the form of palaeographical and codicological differences between both parts of the manuscript: see Evans, *The Present and the Past*, 9-10 (*pace* McCarthy, "The Original Compilation," 87-92). Whitley Stokes considered the pre-Patrician portion to be part of the Annals of Tigernach (following earlier scholars) and published it as "The Dublin Fragment of Tigernach's Annals," *Revue celtique* 18 (1870): 374-91. McCarthy presents a useful account of the

other witnesses to this material, it too is acephalous, beginning in the reign of the Emperor Domitian in the first century CE, and concluding with references to the rule of Níall Noígíallach and to the preaching of St Jerome.[62]

The relationship between these various textual witnesses and the sources upon which they and ancestor text(s) drew has been a matter of debate.[63] Their debt to Eusebius-Jerome has been acknowledged, as has the parallelism underlying them, synchronising episodes of Irish history with world events within a global frame. The specifics of this interweaving in many cases remain to be examined, as does the use and influence of this overarching account in a learned milieu.[64] How this world-history material is interconnected with other accounts of Irish origins, particularly *Lebor Gabála Érenn*, is also in need of more extensive exploration.[65] The version preserved in *Chronicon Scottorum* in the hand of the seventeenth-century scholar, An Dubhaltach Mac Fhirbhisigh, and in two other compilations of around the same time, the Annals of the Four Masters, and the Annals of

---

scholarship concerning this fragment, "The Original Compilation," 77-84, while arguing that both sections should be viewed as an original unit, 85-9. This accords with his view that Irish annals are an extension of a late Latin world chronicle and that Irish and non-Irish events were included from at least the sixth century, and so "the hypothesis of a 'world chronicle' ever having been 'prefixed' to these medieval annals is not sustainable" ("The Original Compilation," 85). This is expounded in detail in an earlier article, "The Status of the Pre-Patrician Irish Annals," *Peritia* 12 (1998): 98-152; see also his *The Irish Annals*.

[62] The material is prefaced to their edition of the post-Patrician annals in Seán Mac Airt and Gearóid Mac Niocaill (eds and trans.), *The Annals of Ulster (to A.D. 1131), Text and Translation* (Dublin: Dublin Institute for Advanced Studies, 1983), 2-37.

[63] See, for example, Maund, "Sources of the 'World Chronicle'"; R.A.S. Macalister, "The Sources of the Preface to the 'Tigernach' Annals," *Irish Historical Studies* 4:13 (1944): 38-57; McCarthy, *The Irish Annals*, 118-52.

[64] Kelleher discusses this, in the context of specific entries, in his article, "The Táin and the Annals".

[65] The link between *Lebor Gabála* and the pre-Patrician annals has been noted in passing, but not explored in any detail: see Kelleher, "Early Irish History," 125; O'Rahilly, *Early Irish History and Mythology*, 253-4; Bart Jaski, "The Irish Origin Legend: Seven Unexplored Sources," in *Lebor Gabála Érenn*, ed. Carey, 48-75, at 63-8.

Clonmacnoise, an English-language account by Conall Mac
Eochagáin, commence with the coming to Ireland of Cessair who led
the first settlers to Ireland, according to *Lebor Gabála*.[66] The history
of the world, as set out in these annalistic texts, is punctuated with
reference to the Six Ages, interspersed with other strands of learning
detailed in *Lebor Gabála*. These include the invention of Irish at the
Tower of Babel; the clearing of plains and eruption of lakes in
Partholón's time; and the wandering of Míl through Scythia and Egypt
until his sons and their entourage settle in Ireland. In the summary
version provided in *Chronicon Scottorum*, this is stated to be prefatory
to the *aimsir oile* 'other time' beginning with Patrick's birth.[67]
Moreover, the debt to *Lebor Gabála* is specified at various points:
amail indister a ngapalaib Eirenn ("as it is related in 'The Takings of
Ireland'").[68] In the same way *Lebor Gabála* is acknowledged in the
Annals of the Four Masters, the principal scribe of which, Mícheál Ó
Cléirigh, had copied the former text as well.[69] Many of these same
themes form part of *Can a mbunadas na nGáedel*, Máel Muru's ninth-
century poetic rendering of Ireland's past, as we have seen, and some
are incorporated into the earlier accounts of the Irish World Chronicle
outlined above. But these stand somewhat apart from this seventeenth-
century annalistic grouping for which *Lebor Gabála Érenn* provides a
structuring thread.

Other events accommodated within this global-Irish story are
recorded in sources other than *Lebor Gabála*; many a battle referred

---

[66] William M. Hennessy (ed. and trans.), *Chronicum Scotorum: A Chronicle
of Irish Affairs, from the Earliest Times to AD 1135* (London: Longmans,
Green, Reader and Dyer, 1866), 1-2; John O'Donovan (ed. and trans.),
*Annála Ríoghachta Éireann, Annals of the Kingdom of Ireland by the Four
Masters from the Earliest Period to the Year 1616*, vol. 1 (Dublin: Hodges,
Smith and Co., 1856), 2-3; Denis Murphy (ed.), *The Annals of
Clonmacnoise being Annals of Ireland from the Earliest Period to A.D.
1408* (Dublin: University Press, 1896), 11-12.
[67] Hennessy, *Chronicum Scotorum*, 14-15.
[68] Hennessy, *Chronicum Scotorum*, 8-9, with reference to Parthalón's
occupation of Ireland; the account of Míl is also stated to be *amail gaptur a
ngabalaib Ereann* (as it is recounted in 'The Takings of Ireland'), 10-11.
[69] e.g. a*mhail as follus isin croinic da ngoirther Leabhar Gabhala* 'as is
evident from the chronicle which is called *Leabhar Gabhála*': O'Donovan,
Annals of the Kingdom of Ireland, I: 10-13.

14

to in a synchronising chronicle is related in much greater detail in a tale; shadowy kings whose rules calibrate a continuous world history are seen as fleshed-out characters in narratives revolving around the figures in question. In shaping their universal history, medieval Irish scholars had access to a library of resources out of which an Irish parallel 'column' in a Eusebian-style structure could be formed. Their approach and creativity can be illustrated with reference to a selection of material, as will be shown in what follows. I will focus primarily on the earliest versions of the Irish World Annals/Chronicle, the Annals of Inisfallen and the Annals of Tigernach, examining the structure adopted; the language chosen; and the specific content of the material in turn. In this way, I hope to provide an insight into the thinking of medieval Irish scholars when writing history and to illuminate their 'global turn'.

Structuring History, Language and Sources

The prevailing influence of the Chronicle of Eusebius-Jerome is most apparent in the Annals of Tigernach, which preserves the most extensive version of world-history material, as we have seen.[70] Eusebius is mentioned by name at various points in the narrative,[71] often with reference to specific chronology, and a named Chronicle.[72] Bede is also specified as an authority throughout,[73] as is the first-

---

[70] In examining the material in the Annals of Tigernach, I have benefitted much from access to a draft edition of the material in Rawlinson B. 502 prepared by Roger McClure, to whom I am very grateful. In particular, his presentation of the text of Rawlinson B. 488 alongside that of Rawlinson B. 502 where they overlap has enabled me to compare the two manuscripts directly (see notes 83 and 87 below).

[71] See, for example, Stokes, "Annals of Tigernach (Part 1)," 377: *ut Eusebius ait*; the Annals of Inisfallen preserves a similar entry without specific reference to Eusebius: Mac Airt, *Annals of Inisfallen*, 18 (§§137-8). There are further specific references to Eusebius, including Stokes, "Annals of Tigernach (Part 1)," 383 (with reference to Eusebius' chronological table), 384 (*Eusebius ait*); 409: *ut Eusebio placet*.

[72] e.g. Stokes, "Annals of Tigernach (Part 1)," 383: *iuxta uero Cronicam Eusebi xxxii*; 386: *in libris cronicorum Eusebi*; 409: *iuxta uero Cronicam Eusebii*.

[73] For a typical example, see Stokes, "Annals of Tigernach (Part 1)," 377: *Beda uero refert*.

15

century author of *Antiquitates Iudaicae* (The Antiquity of the Jews), Flavus Josephus, and the third-century historian, Julius Africanus.[74] In addition, citations to Orosius occur.[75] Within material drawn from these and other sources, Irish events are placed. Structuring nodes include biblical figures, the coming of the Fir Bolg to Ireland being situated before the birth of Moses;[76] their opponents, the Tuatha Dé, arrive during the time of Moses, before his sojourn on Mount Sinai and in the desert.[77] The sons of Míl are placed next in the sequence, Éber son of Míl dying before Moses himself died.[78] The division of Ireland into five is said to have occurred during the rule of Eglon, king of Moab and before Deborah's role in the subjugation of Jabin, king of Canaan, as related in the Book of Judges.[79] A further division of Ireland is synchronised with Samson's death.[80] This is preceded by a series of entries concerning classical events, including the reign of Priam, the rape of Helen, the death of Hector and the fall of Troy.[81] These provide a further connecting strand.[82] Finally, time and happenings are measured in relation to the Six Ages of the World. The Annals of Inisfallen include vernacular verses marking the boundary

---

[74] See, for example, Stokes, "Annals of Tigernach (Part 1)," 388: *et Ioseppi atque Affricani scriptis.*

[75] See, for example, Stokes, "Annals of Tigernach (Part 1)," 387-8: *Orosius refert.*

[76] Mac Airt, *Annals of Inisfallen*, 4 (§§24, 29).

[77] Mac Airt, *Annals of Inisfallen*, 5 (§§31-3).

[78] Mac Airt, *Annals of Inisfallen*, 5-6 (§§35, 39).

[79] Mac Airt, *Annals of Inisfallen*, 7 (§§ 49-51).

[80] Mac Airt, *Annals of Inisfallen*, 10 (§75-6).

[81] Mac Airt, *Annals of Inisfallen*, 9-10 (§§60, 65-7, 69, 73).

[82] Imperial reigns provide another chronological anchor; the Fir Bolg, for example, arrived during the rule of the Assyrian king, Armamithres, and the sons of Míl, during that of Mithreus, according to a Middle Irish poem beginning, "Nin mac Bel, roga na rig," edited by Elizabeth Boyle, to whom I am grateful for pointing out the parallel: "Biblical History in the Book of Ballymote," in *Book of Ballymote, Codices Hibernensis Eximii 2*, ed. Ruairí Ó hUiginn (Dublin: Royal Irish Academy, 2018), 51-76, at 22 (stanza 16) and 23 (stanza 19).

lines between the final four ages, followed by a Latin formula signalling the incipit of the new age.[83]

As these intervals between the ages indicate, this universal history is bilingual, Latin being the dominant language throughout. The language adopted is an intrinsic part of the interpretative framework, but as the demarcation of the ages also demonstrates, there is not a simple binary opposition between local and vernacular, on the one hand, and global and Latin, on the other. At first glance, the synchronisation of the cattle-raid of Cooley (*Táin Bó Cuailnge*) with the birth of Mary, mother of Christ might suggest otherwise, with its juxtaposition of the two languages with subject matter: *Maria mater domini nata est*; Slógad Tána bo Cualngi.[84] Much more commonly, however, Latin is the language of chronicling, whatever the subject of the entry: thus the three-year rule of Echu Sálbuide in Emain, followed by the somewhat longer twelve-year rule of his successor, Fergus mac Léti, are noted in Latin, including the additional information concerning Fergus's death: *qui conflixit contra bestiam hi Loch Rudraige & ibi demersus est* (who fought against a monster in Loch Rudraige and drowned there).[85] This pair of regnal entries is followed by a notice of the birth of Cú Chulainn.[86] Significantly, however, there is linguistic variation between the two extant versions of the Annals of Tigernach, the later manuscript, Rawlinson B. 488 occasionally recording in Irish information provided in Latin in Rawlinson B. 502, the Latin words remaining suggesting a deliberate linguistic choice.[87]

---

[83] Mac Airt, *Annals of Inisfallen*, 12 (third to fourth age); 21 (fourth to fifth); 30 (fifth to sixth). The Annals of Tigernach similarly marks the end of the ages still present in the manuscript with vernacular verse: Stokes, "Annals of Tigernach (Part 1)," 382 (fourth-fifth age boundary marked by a single stanza different from the two preserved in the Annals of Inisfallen); 406 (fifth-sixth age boundary, the two vernacular stanzas in the Annals of Inisfallen are preserved in one manuscript version, Rawlinson B. 488, but are not in Rawlinson B. 502).

[84] Stokes, "Annals of Tigernach (Part 1)," 406.

[85] Stokes, "Annals of Tigernach (Part 1)," 404.

[86] Stokes, "Annals of Tigernach (Part 1)," 404: *Natiuitas Con Culainn maic Sualtaim.*

[87] The reference to the drowning of Fergus mac Léti, and to the birth of Cú Chulainn are in Irish in Rawlinson B. 488: a nadaig poeste a lLoch

In the case of shorter narratives with which sparser chronicle entries are frequently interspersed, they are often in the vernacular when Irish events are being described. But linguistic variation is a feature of these episodes also. Thus, the notice of the death of Cú Chulainn commences in Latin: *Mors Con Chulaind fortissimi herois Scottorum*; the names of his slayers are then supplied prefaced by the Irish preposition *la* 'by', and these act as a linguistic bridge leading on to the brief account in the vernacular of the highlights of the hero's life that follows: *Uii mbliadna a áes in tan rogab gaisced. xuii mbliadna dano a aes in tan mboí i ndegaid Tána Bó Cuailgne, xxuii bliadna immorro a aes in tan atbath* (He was seven years old when he took up arms; his age was seventeen years when he was in pursuit of the Cattle-raid of Cooley; he was twenty-seven years of age when he died).[88]

Moreover, narratives concerning world events are also preserved in the vernacular. In the Annals of Inisfallen, for example, an extensive account of the beginning of the kingdom of the Persians is related in Irish. This concerns the release by King Cyrus of the Babylonian captivity, with particular reference to the number and names of some of the captives.[89] It is prefaced by two stanzas from an eleventh-century poem by Flann Mainistrech on world kingdoms, *Réidig dam, a Dé do nim* (Relate to me, O heavenly God).[90] This episode is also of particular interest to the Tigernach annalist, but his amplification is in Latin and dependent on Orosius.[91] His concern was with the layout and structure of Babylon which despite its size and solidity was destroyed by Cyrus who diverted the River Euphrates to do so. The

---

Rudhraidhe & a badudh ann; Genemain Con Culainn herois; similarly the reference to the birth of Mary just noted is also recorded in Irish in Rawlinson B. 488, as McClure's presentation of the text of both manuscripts in his forthcoming edition makes clear.

[88] Stokes, "Annals of Tigernach (Part 1)," 407.

[89] Mac Airt, *Annals of Inisfallen*, 23, 49-50 (§171.4).

[90] Seán Mac Airt (ed. and trans.), "Middle-Irish Poems on World Kingship (*suite*)," *Études celtiques* 7 (1955), 18-45: 28-9 (III.1, lines 325-9); 30-1 (III.4, lines 337-41), the latter is a variant of the stanza.

[91] Stokes, "Annals of Tigernach (Part 1)," 384-5, *Orosius dicit* is given in the margin; cf. Zangemeister, *Paulus Orosius*, 42-3; Fear, *Orosius*, 83-5 (Book 2.6). The debt to Orosius is noted by McClure in his forthcoming edition.

universal moral of the story, expressed by Orosius and repeated here, is the futility of human endeavour; whatever is constructed by labour and skill goes to ruin in the end; this is Babylon symbolising "the transient nature of worldly power."[92] The annalist's reference to the release by Cyrus of Jewish captives is standard, echoing that in Eusebius-Jerome, as well as Bede.[93] It lacks the detail of the Irish version in the Annals of Inisfallen, the list of captives summarising other stanzas of Flann Mainistrech's poem, as noted by Seán Mac Airt.[94]

In the case of this account of Babylon, therefore, it is accorded a different focus in two interlinked universal histories. The language of each may owe something to the source upon which each annalist drew, the Annals of Tigernach citing Orosius explicitly, and the Annals of Inisfallen having recourse to a vernacular poem, as we have seen. What this passage in its various versions exemplifies is the creativity with which medieval Irish scholars constructed their past, as well as the complex layers of history evident in their compositions. In the Annals of Tigernach, Babylon as the embodiment of human destruction is highlighted and in this way the impermanence of secular power is underlined.[95] The author's interest in the construction of the city is to emphasise that even walls of fired brick and bitumen come tumbling down. Nonetheless, its inclusion of Orosius's detail concerning the breadth of the palisade, for example, as well as its exterior gates and interior houses accords with an interest in urban spaces, and specifically Babylon, as noted by Elizabeth Boyle, and which she associates with the growth of larger settlements in Ireland, particularly Dublin, after the coming of Scandinavians.[96] Thus, in his

---

[92] Boyle, *History and Salvation*, 119.

[93] Stokes, "Annals of Tigernach (Part 1)," 385.

[94] Mac Airt, Annals of Inisfallen, 23 n. a; Mac Airt, "Middle-Irish Poems," (*Études celtiques* 7) 30-3 (III.7-11). In her study of Cyrus, Elizabeth Boyle draws attention to the great variety of material circulating about him in Ireland; see, for example, her *History and Salvation*, 126-9, 144-8.

[95] For this reading, see Boyle, *History and Salvation*, 119.

[96] *History and Salvation*, 125-6; the details about the city provided in *Sex aetates mundi*, some of which are said to be *i llebraib antiquitatum* (in the books of Antiquities, presumed to be the work by Josephus) are in large part

embellishment of Babylonian history, the Tigernach annalist may also have reflected these developments.

By contrast, it is the person of Cyrus the Great who is central in the Annals of Inisfallen's augmented text. Moreover, it is Cyrus the Liberator who is extolled, the stanza about him cited celebrating how "he brought the captives from Babylon" (*tuc in brait a Babilóin*).[97] The captives are personified; Zarobabel is their leader (*tuisech*), Jeshua son of Josedek their priest (*sacart*) and Esdras is the prophet (*fáid*). Nehemiah is another leader (*toissech oile*) who rebuilt Jerusalem. The narrative ends with the death of Cyrus, though the circumstances of his death–that he was killed by Tomyris, queen of the Massagetae, seeking to avenge her son–are omitted.[98] This account chimes with an interest in other strands of Babylonian history, reflected in Flann Mainistrech's *Réidig dam*, as well as other sources.[99] As Boyle notes, "it is not difficult to see the attraction of Cyrus as a character: narratives of his career anticipate those of Alexander the Great in terms of their dramatic scope."[100] The annalist's interest in such figures is illustrated elsewhere in the Annals of Inisfallen also, vernacular verses from Flann Mainistrech's poem augmenting his entries on a later Persian king, Ararxerxes II Mnemon,[101] as well on the exemplary Greek ruler, Alexander the

---

identical with those here: a wall, 50 cubits thick, and 200 cubits high and a circumference of 480 stadia. Boyle discusses the influence of Orosius on Middle Irish material concerning Babylon, *History and Salvation*, 127-9.

[97] Mac Airt, *Annals of Inisfallen*, 23, 50.

[98] This detail is included in Flann Mainistrech's poem: Mac Airt, "Middle-Irish Poems," (*Études celtiques* 7) 32-3 (III.11, lines 365-8); see also Boyle, *History and Salvation*, 145.

[99] The Middle Irish interest in Cyrus is elucidated by Boyle, *History and Salvation*, 144-7.

[100] Boyle, *History and Salvation*, 145.

[101] Mac Airt, *Annals of Inisfallen*, 26, 50-1 (§186); see Mac Airt, "Middle-Irish Poems," (*Études celtiques* 7) 39-41 (III.25-9, lines 421-40). Two stanzas marking the end of the rule of the Persians and the beginning of that of the Greeks are also common to both the Annals of Inisfallen and Flann Mainistrech's poem: Mac Airt, *Annals of Inisfallen*, 27, 51 (§191.2) and Mac Airt, "Middle-Irish Poems," (*Études celtiques* 7) 43-5 (III.33-4, lines 453-60).

Great.[102] That his focus is on specific characters is illustrated by the fact that he appears to summarise his poetic source by listing rulers, when discussing the period after Alexander's death, moving swiftly and succinctly onto Cleopatra until her deposition.[103]

Annalists' particular interests and their creative use of sources is illustrated at various points throughout the Irish World Chronicle; universal history appears in many hues. Selective use of Latin and vernacular in turn is part of the complexity; Cú Chulainn may be sketched in Latin, while Alexander is given vernacular dress, as we have seen. Sources, direct and indirect, such as the Vulgate Bible, Orosius, the Chronicle of Eusebius-Jerome, and Bede, provide the warp and weft of the material, as has been noted, but a range of other sources, Latin and vernacular, are drawn upon as well. What the chroniclers present in their world histories are not simply parallel universes, however, or indeed not just a synchronisation of Irish happenings with significant global events (though this is part of it). Rather what the extant redactions provide is a sophisticated structure within which Ireland's past was interpreted as an integral part of a larger whole, as snapshots of the history focussing on Irish events will reveal.

Ireland's Leaders on a World Stage

The focus on world leaders highlighted in the material pertaining to Cyrus and his successors outlined above is paralleled by an interest in Irish kings. The swift summary of rulers after the time of Alexander the Great provided in the Annals of Inisfallen ends with the deposition of Cleopatra who died in 30 BCE. This is followed by further detail in Latin concerning the fourth-/third-century founder of the Ptolemaic dynasty Cleopatra later led, Ptolemy I Soter of Egypt, and his contemporary and ruler of Syria and the east, Seleucus I Nicator, both of whom were generals of and successors to Alexander the Great. This

---

[102] Mac Airt, *Annals of Inisfallen*, 28, 51-2 (§193.2); Seán Mac Airt, "Middle-Irish Poems on World Kingship (*suite*)," *Études celtiques* 8: 98-101 (IV.3-4 and IV.6-7, lines 469-76 and 481-8). The annalist cites a slightly different version of these stanzas.

[103] Mac Airt, *Annals of Inisfallen*, 28, 52; this alludes to some information expanded in greater detail in the remainder of Flann Mainistrech's poem: Mac Airt, "Middle-Irish Poems," (*Études celtiques* 8) 101-8.

material is common both to this compilation and the Annals of Tigernach. Its chronological significance is underlined with reference to the account in the Book of Maccabees of the kingship of the Greeks being reckoned from this time.[104] Furthermore, the first of a list of rulers of Emain Macha, Cimbáeth mac Fintain, is synchronised with the eighteenth year of Ptolemy's reign.[105] Cimbáeth is specified as *primus rex Emna* in the Annals of Inisfallen.[106] Subsequent rulers of Emain punctuate the succeeding timeline, with reference to kings of Tara and occasionally of Ireland as well.

The catalogue of rulers of Emain, beginning with Cimbáeth, is the most complete regnal list in the interrelated Annals of Inisfallen and Tigernach, and is accorded primacy in the compilations, as they have come down to us. Cimbáeth is aligned with a king of Tara, Echu Buadach, in the Annals of Tigernach, though the author expresses uncertainty about this synchronisation, attributing it to others: *tunc Echu Buadach pater Úgaine in Temoria regnase ab aliis fertur.*[107] Moreover, he cast doubt on information before Cimbáeth's time: *omnia monimenta Scottorum usque Cimbaed incerta erant* (all the

---

[104] Stokes, "Annals of Tigernach (Part 1)," 393.

[105] Stokes, "Annals of Tigernach (Part 1)," 394.

[106] Mac Airt, *Annals of Inisfallen*, 29; this additional information is not included in the Annals of Tigernach.

[107] Stokes, "Annals of Tigernach (Part 1)," 394; the annalist continues *liquet praescripsimus ollim Úgaine imperasse* "we have written that Úgaine reigned in the past", alluding to an earlier entry on the burning of Úgaine's son Cobthach at Dind Ríg (Stokes, "Annals of Tigernach (Part 1)," 378. This double entry concerning Echu Buadach's father, Úgaine, and similar doublets involving the legendary kings, Conchobar mac Nessa and Conaire Már mac Eterscéle, were examined by Alice Lyons in 2014, in an unpublished University of Cambridge MPhil dissertation, "Historiographical Evidence from Rawlinson B 502." In the case of Echu, she suggests that connections drawn between him and Cimbáeth in "De Flaithiusaib Érenn", a king-list preserved in the twelfth-century manuscript, the Book of Leinster, may have prompted their presentation as contemporaries here (p. 15); see Richard I. Best, Osborn Bergin and M.A. O'Brien (eds), *The Book of Leinster, formerly Lebor na Nuachongbála*, vol. 1 (Dublin: Dublin Institute for Advanced Studies, 1954), 82-5. I am grateful to Alice Lyons for permission to cite her work.

records of the Irish up to Cimbáeth were uncertain).[108] Accurate chronology, therefore, is said to begin with the first ruler of Emain, Cimbáeth, the period of whose power coincides with the beginnings of the Ptolemaic dynasty in the aftermath of Alexander the Great.

The Ptolemaic dynasty ended with Cleopatra and it is in the year of her death that the rule of the most famous king of Emain Macha, Conchobar mac Nessa, is placed.[109] The division of Ireland into five between Conchobar and four others, including Cairpre Nia Fer and Ailill mac Mágach, is said to have occurred around the same time, the Annals of Tigernach linking it in a vernacular entry with the destruction of Conaire Már mac Eterscélae at Da Derga's hostel.[110] This is immediately followed by the reference to the birth of Mary and the hosting of the Cattle-raid of Cooley, noted above.[111] These events take place around the time of the beginning of the Sixth Age, in the first year of which Christ was born.[112] The deaths of Cú Chulainn and Conchobar are then recorded, embedded among the deaths of King Herod, Archelaus of Cappadocia who defected to the Emperor Augustus/Octavian, Octavian himself and Pontius Pilate. Significantly, the Crucifixion is also fixed at this chronological node.

The death of Conchobar mac Nessa is synchronised with the Crucifixion in other sources. The two events are linked explicitly in the death-tale of this king of Emain Macha, *Aided Chonchobair*, since Conchobar is said to have died when news reached him of Christ's

---

[108] Stokes, "Annals of Tigernach (Part 1)," 394. This information is not included in the corresponding entry in the Annals of Inisfallen.

[109] Stokes, "Annals of Tigernach (Part 1)," 405.

[110] Stokes, "Annals of Tigernach (Part 1)," 405; the reading in Rawlinson B. 488 assigns the fifth part to Ailill, together with his wife, Medb Cruachna. The destruction of Da Derga's Hostel is noted a second time in the Annals of Tigernach during the reign of Claudius in the decades after Christ's birth, the record being attributed to 'others' (*ut alii aiunt*); a gloss in the Hand of H of Lebor na hUidre adds *sed certe falluntur* "but this is certainly false" (Stokes, "Annals of Tigernach (Part 1)," 411. This chronological doublet has also been discussed in detail by Lyons, "Historiographical Evidence," 18-25.

[111] Stokes, "Annals of Tigernach (Part 1)," 406.

[112] Stokes, "Annals of Tigernach (Part 1)," 406.

execution.[113] Moreover, in some accounts this ultimate warrior-king can be seen to undergo a baptism of blood in death.[114] The emphasis in this death-tale is on Conchobar's immediate conversion to Christianity on learning of the evil deed committed against Christ.[115] His precocious belief marked him out as one of only a pair of exceptional men who knew of Christ before Ireland became Christian.[116] He is hailed as the first pagan to enter heaven in another version of the story;[117] his soul having been rescued from hell by Christ himself, according to yet another account.[118] He shares not alone a death-date with Jesus, but also a birthday, according to some recensions in which the identification between king and saviour is given greater emphasis.[119] In the Annals of Tigernach and Inisfallen, a direct connection is not drawn between the slaying of Christ and Conchobar's passing, both obits being placed in close proximity, alongside that of another Christ-like Irish figure, Cú Chulainn, as noted above. An explicit statement was scarcely needed, since by co-ordinating the dying of Conchobar and Christ, the pagan king and by

---

[113] Kuno Meyer (ed. and trans.), *The Death-tales of the Ulster Heroes*, Todd Lecture Series 14 (Dublin: Royal Irish Academy, 1906), 14-15 (Version B), 16-17 (Version C). Meyer was not aware of all manuscript versions of the story when he produced his edition, and subsequently published a further version based on the text in Oxford, Bodleian Library, Laud Miscellany 610: "Mitteilungen aus irischen Handschriften," *Zeitschrift für celtische Philologie* 13 (1921): 3-30. The relationship between these and other extant versions of the tale are discussed by Helen Imhoff, "The Different Versions of *Aided Chonchobair*," *Ériu* 40 (2012): 43-99. A new edition of a number of versions formed part of Chantal Kobel's doctoral dissertation completed in 2015: "A Critical Edition of *Aided Chonchobair*, 'The Violent Death of Conchobar'," unpublished PhD, Trinity College Dublin, available online: http://www.tara.tcd.ie/handle/2262/80099 (accessed July 17, 2022).

[114] Meyer, *Death-tales*, 14-15 (Version B), 16-17 (Version C).

[115] Meyer, *Death-tales*, 8-9 (Version A); 12-13, 14-15 (Version B).

[116] The other was Morann: Meyer, *Death-tales*, 8-11 (Version A).

[117] Meyer, *Death-tales*, 14-15 (Version B).

[118] Meyer, *Death-tales*, 16-17 (Version C).

[119] Meyer, *Death-tales*, 16-17 (Version C), where Christ and Conchobar are presented as *comaltai* (foster-brothers); according to version A, both share a birthday but were born in a different year: Meyer, *Death-tales*, 8-9.

extension his followers, were implicitly elevated through association with a major Christian event.[120]

Conchobar's death is also recorded at an earlier point in the Annals of Tigernach, however, where 'it is said' (*dicitur*) that he rested in the eighth year of Tiberius.[121] This adopted son of Emperor Augustus/Octavian ruled from 14 to 37 CE, and this earlier date of death is the only one recorded in the Annals of Inisfallen.[122] In Conchobar's own death-tale, he is said to undergo two deaths. The first was a type of living death, when he was gravely wounded, having been struck by the calcified brain of a dead warrior, Mess Gegra. Exertion of any kind subsequently would result in his demise. The emotional strain he experienced on hearing of Christ's Crucifixion then brought about his ultimate expiration. A version of this narrative survives in the twelfth-century manuscript, the Book of Leinster.[123] But a connection between Conchobar and Christ's slaying was drawn by Cináed ua hArtacáin in the tenth century in his poem detailing how a series of Emain warriors, including Conchobar, met their end.[124] In fact, the earliest attested association between Conchobar's death and that of Christ is in what is most likely an eighth-century hagiography, *Vita S. Albei*, the Latin Life of Ailbe of Emly, as Helen Imhoff has argued.[125] A poem in which Conchobar expresses anger at Christ's death, but also apparent regret that he should continue to live after him, may also be eighth-century in date.[126] This poem is incorporated

---

[120] The precise dating of the Crucifixion itself was also of concern to the annalists, see Stokes, "Annals of Tigernach (Part 1)," 409; Mac Airt, *Annals of Inisfallen*, 31-2 (§212).

[121] Stokes, "Annals of Tigernach (Part 1)," 408.

[122] Mac Airt, *Annals of Inisfallen*, 31. Lyons, "Historiographical Evidence," 27-8, draws attention to a chronological note in *Chronicon Scottorum* which also places the death of Conchobar before the Crucifixion at about 20 CE (Hennessy, *Chronicum Scotorum*, 20-1); and see 25-9 for her discussion of the evidence relating to the double date of the death of Conchobar.

[123] Meyer, *Death-tales*, 4-11 (Version A).

[124] Kuno Meyer (ed. and trans.), "*Fianna bátar i nEmain*," *Revue celtique* 23 (1902): 303-48, at 304.

[125] Imhoff, "The Different Versions," 68-80.

[126] Johan Corthals (ed. and trans.), "The Retoiric in *Aided Chonchobuir*," *Ériu* 40 (1989): 41-59; Kobel presents linguistic evidence in support of Corthal's proposed date of *c.* 700: "A Critical Edition," 74-6.

into some versions of the death-tale, including B which may have been composed in the eighth or ninth century.[127]

In considering the two dates assigned to King Conchobar's death in the Annals of Tigernach, therefore, it may be that the later death-date (mirroring that of Christ) was influenced by themes that were expanded in *Aided Chonchobair*, though these were well established by the eighth century, as we have seen.[128] Tiberius is specifically mentioned in Version B of the death-tale: Altus, a Roman consul, visited Conchobar frequently "with exchanges of treasure from Tiberius son of Augustus [Octavian], king of the Romans" (*co clōemclōdaib sēt ō Tibir mac Auguist rī[g] Rōmān*).[129] It was this envoy who notified Conchobar of the Crucifixion, according to this version, explaining its significance as well. Bachrach, a druid of Leinster, is given the task in the story as related in the Book of Leinster copy, with Altus as alternative, a tax-collector in this instance, being alluded to as well.[130] Thus, not only is Conchobar a precocious Christian, but he is accommodated within the sprawling structure administered by the stewards of Rome.[131] As Imhoff notes, the Roman setting is reminiscent of accounts in the Gospels,[132] and it also resonates with the biblical and imperial context within which the deeds of pre-Christian Irish are set out in the annalistic material under consideration here. It is scarcely surprising that in Conchobar's case a suggestion that he predeceased Christ was superseded by an account in which the fate of the two leaders became intertwined. After all, in dying in the same year as Christ, Conchobar was anointed as Ireland's first Christian king almost as soon as Christianity had come into being. This meant that Ireland's history was presented as a Christian history from the very start.

---

[127] Kobel, "A Critical Edition," 87-92. Imhoff demonstrates how the poem was understood in different ways in the two versions, A and B, in which it is found: "The Different Versions," 80-95.

[128] See Lyons, "Historographical Evidence," 39-40.

[129] Meyer, *Death-tales*, 12-13.

[130] Meyer, *Death-tales*, 10-11.

[131] Imhoff, "The Different Versions," 70. It notes how the political status of Conchobar, and Ireland, is elevated through this interaction with Rome. She discusses the Altus strand in the tale, 70-3.

[132] Imhoff, "The Different Versions," 69.

Conchobar's successors are subsequently listed in the Irish World Annals/Chronicle, but there is a subtle shift of emphasis in the account to the kingship of Tara. It is from Lugaid Reóderg, king of Tara, that thirty kings of the northern part of Ireland (Leth Cuinn) are reckoned down to the time of Diarmait mac Cerbaill in the sixth century.[133] Lugaid's twenty-six year rule is said to have commenced shortly after Emperor Claudius attacked Britain in 43 CE, and Mark wrote his Gospel in Rome.[134] The activities of Claudius and his imperial successors, Nero and Vespasian, are related in detail, before the Tigernach annalist refers to two alternative accounts of Lugaid's death: that he was killed "by the three Ruadchinn" (*óna tríb Rúadchennaib*) of Leinster; "or he may have thrown himself on his sword, so that he died of grief for his wife, i.e. Derbforgaill, who had died" (*nó commad im claideb dodoleced conn-abbad de chommaid a mná .i. Deirbe Forgaill, nodechsad*).[135] Both traditions are attested elsewhere: a detailed description of how Derbforgaill was mutilated by her female contemporaries, dying as a result and prompting Lugaid's death is recounted in Derforgaill's death-tale which may be tenth-century in date.[136] The version of the Annals of Tigernach in Rawlinson B. 488 provides the additional information, also present in the narrative, that Derbforgaill was "the daughter of the king of Lochlainn" (*ingen ríg Lochlann*), suggesting that for this version of the annalistic record at least, material drawn on by the author of *Aided Derbforgaill*, or that narrative itself, may have been a source. In relation to the account of a later king, Tuathal Techtmar, the brief information provided forms part of a longer eleventh-century

---

[133] Stokes, "Annals of Tigernach (Part 1)," 411-12; Mac Airt, *Annals of Inisfallen*, 32 (§220).

[134] Stokes, "Annals of Tigernach (Part 1)," 411; the reference to Rome is attributed to Bede: *ut Beda ait*.

[135] Stokes, "Annals of Tigernach (Part 1)," 414.

[136] Carl Marstrander (ed. and trans.), "The Deaths of Lugaid and Derbforgaill," *Ériu* 5 (1911): 201-18; a more recent edition is available online, Kicki Ingridsdotter, "*Aided Derbforgaill* 'The Violent Death of Derborgaill': A Critical Edition with Introduction, Translation and Textual Notes," unpublished PhD dissertation, Uppsala University 2009 (https://www.diva-portal.org/smash/get/diva2:213892/FULLTEXT01.pdf; accessed June 20 2022).

composition, *Bórama Lagen*, but is too general for direct textual dependency to be posited in this case.[137]

The Rawlinson B. 502 version of the Annals of Tigernach breaks off during Tuathal Techtmar's rule, Mál mac Rochride being listed as king of Emain at this time, and while Emperor Antoninus Pius (died 161 CE) was in power.[138] The related version in Rawlinson B. 488 continues with a notice of Tuathal Techtmar's slaying by his northern counterpart, Mál.[139] The close relationship between these two manuscript copies when Rawlinson B. 502 remains a witness, suggests that Rawlinson B. 488 represents their common source, but it is the latter fourteenth-century manuscript that is the sole Tigernach witness from this point on. The Annals of Inisfallen provides some of the same information in abbreviated form, as do the Annals of Ulster, and the Cottonian Annals. Much of the focus in this second- and third-century material is on King Conn Cétchathach and his descendants, particularly Cormac mac Airt. The division of Ireland between Conn and his southern counterpart, Mag Nuadat, is placed after the very end of the rule of Antoninus Pius in 161 CE.[140] There is a catalogue of battles,[141] some of which are related in some detail, most notably Cath Chinn Abrat and Cath Maige Mucrama, both involving Lugaid Mac Con.[142] Cormac mac Airt emerges as the main character, his various activities embedded among the deeds of emperors and early Christians, the Annals of Tigernach providing a detailed picture, including an etymological explanation of his epithet Ulfhota "since he

---

[137] Stokes, "Annals of Tigernach (Part 1)," 419: "to him was first pledged and paid the cattle-tribute of the Leinstermen" (*is dó cetaronasced ocus fris roíccad bórama Lagen*); see also Mac Airt, *Annals of Inisfallen*, 34 (§248). An entry under the preceding kalend in the Annals of Tigernach on Tuathal's father, Fiachu Findfholaid, provides supplementary information on his killing also found in the *Bórama*, including that Tuathal avenged his father's slayer in the battle of Aichill: Stokes, "Annals of Tigernach (Part 1)," 418-19; Whitley Stokes (ed. and trans.), "The Bóroma," *Revue celtique* 13 (1892): 32-124, 299-300, at 36-7 (§1).

[138] Stokes, "Annals of Tigernach (Part 1)," 419.

[139] Stokes, "Annals of Tigernach (Part 2)," 6.

[140] Stokes, "Annals of Tigernach (Part 2)," 7; Mac Airt, *Annals of Inisfallen*, 35 (§257).

[141] See, for example, Stokes, "Annals of Tigernach (Part 2)," 13.

[142] Stokes, "Annals of Tigernach (Part 2)," 10-11.

sent the Ulaid a long way away" (*dia rochuir Ultu a fad*).[143] Various alternative accounts of his death are alluded to,[144] followed by less detailed references to the deeds of his son and successor, Cairpre Lifechair;[145] his grandson, Fiacha Sraiptine,[146] and great-grandson, Muiredach Tírech, including conflict with the three Colla.[147] Muiredach Tírech's son was Eochu Mugmedóin, father of the eponymous ancestor of Uí Néill, Níall Noígíallach, whose birth along with that of his brothers is synchronised with Patrick.[148] In the period immediately preceding the coming of Patrick, therefore, it is with the dynasty of Uí Néill that the Irish events in this global structure are predominantly concerned.

Conclusion

In the view of John V. Kelleher, this was the overarching theme of early Irish annals, owing to rewriting on behalf of the Uí Néill, probably some time in the ninth century, as noted above.[149] The concerns of this powerful polity are undoubtedly very well-represented in the annalistic record, including in the retrospective material pertaining to the period before the conversion of Ireland in the fifth century, discussed in outline here. However, the account it presents of Ireland's leaders, kingdoms, happenings, enmeshed within those of other world peoples is not merely directed at a single dynastic line. Broader in concept and focus, it provides an extended, structured history in a familiar learned frame.

Ordering history in this way had a purpose; it furnished a structured archive within which the past could continue to be

---

[143] Stokes, "Annals of Tigernach (Part 2)," 18, following on from a notice of Cormac's banishment of the Ulaid from Ireland to the Isle of Man.
[144] Stokes, "Annals of Tigernach (Part 2)," 20.
[145] Stokes, "Annals of Tigernach (Part 2)," 20-3.
[146] Stokes, "Annals of Tigernach (Part 2)," 23-8.
[147] Stokes, "Annals of Tigernach (Part 2)," 29-32.
[148] Stokes, "Annals of Tigernach (Part 2)," 32.
[149] Kelleher, "Early Irish History," 122, 125; in his vivid, memorable words: "[T]he Uí Néill emerge into history like a school of cuttlefish from a large ink-cloud of their own manufacture."

chronicled and the changing needs of the present served.[150] This mode is not specifically Irish, as comparable texts pertaining to Britain and Carolingian Europe make clear.[151] It had wider application also, as is evident in Fozia Bora's discussion of medieval Islamic historiography, describing a flexible archival framework within which source material was incorporated and interpreted, and evolving power dynamics were embedded.[152] This approach to writing history has a bold recognisable hue. The specific models to which the medieval Irish are indebted, some of which were noted above, form part of what Björn Weiler has termed "a trans-European phenomenon,"[153] learned communities exchanging sources which provided a common structure around which various local histories could be draped. The recurrence of similar textual patterns in a variety of text-types, across a relatively wide geographical area and down through a number of centuries, is testament to a shared literary practice of considerable endurance. The very endurance and universality of this common historical framework

---

[150] See Ní Mhaonaigh and Tyler, "The Language of History-writing"; for Carolingian Europe, see Helmut Reimitz, *Ein karolingisches Geschichtsbuch aus Saint-Amand: Studien zur Wahrnehmung von Identität und Raum im Frühmittelalter* (Vienna: Institut für österreichische Geschichtsforschung, 1999) and his "The Social Logic of Historiographical Compendia in the Carolingian Period," in *Herméneutique du texte d'histoire*, ed. Osamu Kano (Nagoya: Nagoya University, 2012), 17-28, available online https://www.gcoe.lit.nagoya-u.ac.jp/eng/result/pdf/157-170_REIMITZ.pdf (accessed July 24 2022).

[151] For the approach and a discussion of Carolingian and Anglo-Saxon examples, see Ernst Breisach, *Historiography, Ancient, Medieval & Modern* (Chicago IL: University of Chicago Press, 1983), 77-106. For a later period, see the wide range of pertinent texts examined in *Universal Chronicles in the High Middle Ages*, ed. Michele Campopiano and Henry Bainton, Writing History in the Middle Ages 4 (Woodbridge: Boydell and Brewer, 2017). *Historia Brittonum* is often included in such general accounts, but medieval Irish writing of this type is rarely mentioned, despite its richness and abundance, but see now *Origin Legends in Early Medieval Western Europe*, ed. Lindy Brady and Patrick Wadden, Reading Medieval Sources 6 (Leiden and Boston, MA: Brill, 2022).

[152] *Writing History in the Medieval Islamic World: the Value of Chronicles as Archives* (London: I.B. Tauris, 2019).

[153] Weiler, "Historical Writing," 33.

indicates its innate flexibility, as various peoples could situate their own story successfully within it.

In highlighting aspects of the complex annalistic material setting out the history of Ireland before the coming of St Patrick, I have sought to situate the Irish World Annals or Chronicle within that broader framework of history-writing and universal chronicling in which the medieval Irish were skilfully engaged. Manuscript evidence has survived from the eleventh and twelfth centuries, though the themes intertwined in the various chronicle versions were being explored at an earlier period, as we have seen. The intellectual milieu in which this syncretistic history took the forms in which it has come down to us seems broadly similar to that in which texts such as *Auraicept na nÉces* and *Can a mbunadas na nGáedel* were composed.[154] But constructing the past was a significant learned endeavour in medieval Irish scholarly circles, and so any possible date-range must remain broad. The date of the often brief annal entries themselves is difficult to determine, not least because Latin is paramount. But in their use of Latin and vernacular, the authors of these accounts, could add nuance to their history. Their reports might also be refined with reference to narratives and other sources detailing the same event, though the direction of borrowing is not always clear. What is manifest, however, is medieval Irish engagement with world history and the place of Irish kingdoms and events within it; their interpretation of more local history within a biblical, classical, universal whole. As universal chroniclers, medieval Irish scholars proved expert in a 'global turn'.

---

[154] With reference to the chronological data in the interlinked sets of annals, and in other related sources, McCarthy has proposed a very specific and detailed model for the development of the world history material, usefully summarised in his *The Irish Annals*, 150-2. The extant evidence does not in my view allow us to state with confidence that the sixth-century founding abbot of Iona, and his seventh-century successor Adomnán, added entries to a chronicle compiled by Rufinus of Aquilea and continued by Sulpicius Serverus (or one of his circle) which was first brought to Ireland in *c.* 425. My focus here, however, has been on the overarching concept underlying this material.

Ancestors, Gods, and Genealogies

Ruairí Ó hUiginn

One of the areas in which John Kelleher made a significant contribution to our understanding of medieval Ireland was in his study of various aspects of the Irish annals and genealogies.[1] The annals, historical records of events in medieval Irish society, have attracted the attention of many and naturally have formed the bedrock of countless historical studies. They also have been the subject of scholarly research as texts in their own right. The main collections have long been edited and translated and most are now online, and are searchable.[2] While they doubtless have much more to reveal and will continue to require further extensive study, as primary source texts they now are easily accessible.

Genealogies, on the other hand, have proved to be more forbidding and have enticed a much smaller cohort of scholars. In the strictest sense, the genealogies with which we are concerned are the pedigrees and lines of descent of important Irish dynasties and families, of which there were many, and the surviving body of Irish genealogies is very extensive, dwarfing corresponding collections from other West European traditions.[3]

---

[1] See, for instance, "Early Irish history and pseudo-history", *Studia Hibernica* 3 (1963), 113-27; "The pre-Norman Irish genealogies", *Irish Historical Studies* 16 (1968), 138-53; "The Táin and the Annals", *Ériu* 22 (1971), 107-27; "Uí Maine in the annals and genealogies to 1225", *Celtica* 9 (1971), 61-112. This article is an expanded text of the seventeenth annual John V. Kelleher lecture, delivered on line 7 October, 2021.

[2] For a list of the annalistic compilations, editions, translations, and secondary literature, see D. Ó Corráin, *Clavis Litterarum Hibernensium* (Turnhout: Brepols Publishers, 2017, hereafter *Clavis*). Three vols. Vol. II §§699-759. See also, N. Evans, *The Present and the Past in Medieval Irish Chronicles* (Woodbridge: Boydell Press, 2010) and G. Mac Niocaill, *The Medieval Irish Annals* (Dublin: Dublin Historical Association, 1975). Electronic versions of the main collections can be found on the University College Cork CELT website https://celt.ucc.ie/ (accessed 2 January, 2022).

[3] On this, see D. Ó Corráin, "The Book of Ballymote: a genealogical treasure", in R. Ó hUiginn (ed.), *Book of Ballymote. Codices Hibernenses Eximii II* (Dublin: Royal Irish Academy), 1-31, at 2-3.

Therein lies the nub of the matter, for their sheer extent, comprising thousands upon thousands of personal names, the problems inherent in trying to unravel various interlinked strands of descent, the challenge of reconciling differing genealogical accounts, the keen-eyed vigilance required to detect error, or indeed to spot wilful forgery, have proved to be tasks that have deterred all but the most intrepid.

We are fortunate, however, that most of those who have been drawn into their orbit have been scholars of the highest calibre and much of the work they have done in editing tracts or in explicating their contents has stood the test of time and has laid the foundations on which future research will be built.[4] Yet, compared to the annals, the study of the genealogies is still in its infancy, and given the relative lack of attention they have received, it is perhaps no wonder that the title of Nollaig Ó Muraíle's introductory booklet on the subject, *The Irish Genealogies,* carries the subtitle: *Irish History's Poor Relation?* for, in contrast to the annals, many of our surviving genealogical tracts have not yet been edited, let alone investigated and analysed.

Despite this relative lack of attention, the pervasive importance of genealogy in Irish tradition cannot be overstated. A simple indicator of this is afforded us by the fact that most of our earliest surviving MSS written in Irish contain significant swathes of genealogical material. This is true of the two twelfth-century codices, the Oxford Bodleian MS Rawlinson B 502 and the Book of Leinster,[5] as it is also true of the 'Ó Cianáin Miscellany' of the mid-fourteenth century,[6] of Lúcás Ó Dalláin's genealogical tract of roughly the same time,[7] and of

---

[4] Nollaig Ó Muraíle, *The Irish Genealogies: Irish History's Poor Relation?* (London: Irish Texts Society Occasional Lecture Series 3, 2016). This work offers an excellent overview of the genealogies and is replete with references to editions and to secondary literature. See also Ó Corráin, *Clavis II* §§760-1029.

[5] For the genealogies from the Book of Leinster and Rawlinson B502, both of which are of Leinster provenance, see M. A. O'Brien, *Corpus Genealogiarum Hiberniae* (Dublin: Dublin Institute for Advanced Studies, 1962, hereafter *Corpus Gen.*).

[6] On this collection see James Carney, "'The *Ó Cianáin miscellany*'", *Ériu* 21 (1969), 122-147; Ó Muraíle, *The Irish Genealogies*, 33.

[7] TCD MS 1298 (H 2.7)

the other great Connacht codices compiled later in that century: the Book of Uí Mhaine, the Book of Ballymote and the Great Book of Lecan.[8] By my rough estimation, genealogical tracts account for between 25 and 35 percent of each of the three latter compilations. And when we consider that each of these MSS is now incomplete and gapped–especially the Book of Uí Mhaine–we realise that their genealogical content may originally have been considerably more extensive.

These approximate figures I have given refer solely to the tabular genealogical tracts in the MSS, those long lists of names the published forms of which have been characterised by John Kelleher as having "all the charm of an obsolete telephone directory from some small, remote capital".[9] These tables list pedigrees from son to father to grandfather to great-grandfather and so on, tracing lines of descent back to common ancestors, showing how various different families and septs are related and at which nodes in the genealogical trees they are joined.

But extensive though these tables may be, the actual genealogical content of our MSS is far greater than what they encompass, for many of them also contain narratives that serve to elucidate or expand crucial nodes in the genealogical trees. Thus, the tale *Echtra mac nEchach Mugmedóin*, found in the Book of Ballymote and in several other manuscripts[10] is the origin legend of the Uí Néill, the dominant

---

[8] There are as yet no full published editions of these genealogical tracts. For the genealogical contents of the Books of Ballymote, Lecan and Uí Mhaine, see T. F. O'Rahilly et al., *Catalogue of Irish Manuscripts in the Royal Irish Academy* (Dublin: Royal Irish Academy: 1926-70), MSS 536, 535 and 1225 respectively. On the genealogies of the Book of Ballymote and the Great Book of Lecan, see N. Ó Muraíle, "The Books of Ballymote and Lecan: their structure and contents compared", in R. Ó hUiginn (ed.), *Book of Ballymote*, 155-190, at 181-3. For the genealogical contents of the Book of Uí Mhaine, see R. Ó hUiginn, "Ancestors and gods in the Book of Uí Mhaine", in E. Boyle and R. Ó hUiginn (eds), *Book of Uí Mhaine* (Dublin: Royal Irish Academy, forthcoming 2022), 56-78.

[9] "The pre-Norman Irish genealogies", 138.

[10] S. H. O'Grady (ed. and trans.), "Echtra mac [n]Echach Muigmedóin" in *Silva Gadelica. A Collection of Tales in Irish* (London: Williams and Norgate, 1892), vol. 1, 326-30 (text), vol. II, 368-73 (translation) and M.

power in the northern half of Ireland for much of the early medieval period, and explains their relationship with other dynasties.[11] The legend of the three Collas tells of the origin of the Airgialla,[12] prominent affiliates of the Uí Néill, while the legend of the expulsion of the Déisi, of which we have more than one version, purports to explain how a number of people designated *Déisi* (vassal people), came to inhabit the different territories in which they were found in medieval Ireland.[13] Several other texts serve a similar purpose in purporting to explain how different peoples came to occupy the territories in which they were found in the historical period. Many of our genealogical compilations, moreover, are interspersed with poetry or with snippets of narrative, extolling the exploits of significant ancestral figures, be they secular rulers or saints, or recapitulating some of the information presented in the genealogies themselves. And the tentacles of genealogy extend even further into the literary tradition, as we presently shall see, for some of the legendary ancestral figures who populate the prehistoric pedigrees are the self-same characters who feature prominently in the Early Irish sagas and in other literary material.[14]

This keen interest in genealogy and in origins can be seen as part of a wider 'national' project that was concerned with the origins and history of the Irish themselves. The project had as its goal to establish for Ireland a place among the nations of Christendom, a place not accorded them by the all-important Old Testament. Through the

Joynt (ed. and trans.), "Echtra mac Echdach Mugmedóin" (metrical version), *Ériu* 4 (1910), 91-111. For further references, see Ó Corráin, *Clavis* III, §1049.

[11] On origin legends, see M. A. O'Brien, "Early Irish origin legends", in M. Dillon (ed.), *Early Irish Society* (Dublin: Cultural Relations Committee of Ireland, 1954), 36-51.

[12] K. Meyer (ed.) K. Meyer, "The Laud genealogies and tribal histories", *ZCP* 8 (1912), 291-338, at 317-20. For further references, see Ó Corráin, *Clavis* III, §1138.

[13] K. Meyer (ed.) "The expulsion of the Déssi", *Ériu* 3 (1907), 135-42. For other editions and further references, see Ó Corráin, *Clavis* III, §1125.

[14] Note also that several further origin legends are embodied in the important collection of genealogies in the Oxford Bodleian MS Laud 610; see K. Meyer, "The Laud genealogies and tribal histories", *ZCP* 8 (1912), 291-338.

labours of numerous generations of scholars, an Irish national legend was forged and grown as they grafted an Irish branch onto the tree of world history as it was depicted in the Bible.[15] Texts such as the *Sex Aetates Mundi*[16] and *Lebor Gabála Érenn*, in particular,[17] purported to explain the lines of descent of the Irish from Japhet, son of Noah, through figures such as Goídel Glas and Míl Espáine and through a series of invaders and settlements, treating also of the separate colonisations of Ireland by Cessair, Partholón, Nemed, the Fir Bolg and Túatha Dé Danann, all of which were supposed to have taken place prior to the arrival of the Gaels.

This enterprise had to do with creating a history for Ireland and the Irish and to provide them with an *origo gentis*. Those who forged it used a wide variety of materials: Biblical history, antique learning, mythology, dynastic propaganda, and fiction. The long genealogical tracts that have been transmitted to us were a central part of this project, providing for Irish dynasties lines of descent that stretched back into the world of the Old Testament.[18]

The outcome of this was that any Irish king or lord could trace his origins and legitimacy to rule back through the centuries into that world. Take, for instance, Tomaltach Mac Donnchaidh (†1397 AD), *taoiseach* (leader, lord) of a small North Connacht lordship in whose house at Ballymote, Co. Sligo, much of the book that bears that name

---

[15] On the work of the 'synthetic historians', see D. Ó Cróinín, "Ireland 400-800" in id. (ed.) *A New History of Ireland. I. Prehistoric and Early Ireland* (Oxford: Oxford University Press, 2005), 182-234, at 182-6; F. J. Byrne, *Irish Kings and High-Kings* (London: B. T. Batsford, 1973), 9-10.

[16] On the Irish *Sex Aetates Mundi*, see D. Ó Cróinín, *The Irish Sex Aetates Mundi* (Dublin: Dublin Institute for Advanced Studies, 1983) and Ó Corráin, *Clavis I*, §§119-20.

[17] R. A. S. Macalister, *Lebor Gabála Érenn. The Book of the Taking of Ireland*, 5 vols (London and Dublin: Irish Texts Society, vol. 34, 35, 39, 41, 44, 1938-56 (=hereafter *Lebor Gabála*); P. Ó Riain, *Lebor Gabála Érenn. Index of Names* (London, Irish Texts Society, vol. 63); cf further Ó Corráin, *Clavis III*, §1141.

[18] It has been suggested that the genealogical tradition was inspired by the writings of Bishop Isidore of Seville († 636) and that the manner in which it was laid out in the MSS is indebted to the influence of the Old Testament. On this see D. Ó Corráin, "Creating the past: the early Irish genealogical tradition", *Peritia* 12 (1998), 177-208, at 201-206.

was written.[19] The Meic Dhonnchaidh were a minor branch of the dominant Síl Muiredaig dynasty of Connacht, an offshoot of the powerful Uí Briúin. Tomaltach's pedigree as set out in the Book of Ballymote and in other compilations, extends back over very many generations to Míl Espáine, forefather of the Irish. At various nodes in his genealogical tree the lines of different peoples converge. Our Tomaltach was four generations removed from Donnchadh, son of Tomaltach na Carraige mac Diarmada, from whom the Mac Donnchaidh surname derives. Tomaltach was king of the Mac Diarmada lordship of Moylurg, Co. Roscommon (1197–1207 AD) of which the Meic Dhonnchaidh were a subsidiary branch, and the line extends back a further two generations to Diarmaid son of Tadhg Mór who reigned in Moylurg (1124–1159 AD) and who was the eponymous ancestor of that family. Tadhg's line in turn goes back several more generations to Máel Rúanaidh Mór, a brother of Conchobar († 973 AD), king of Connacht, from whom the great Ó Conchobair dynasty of Connacht descended. Conchobar's own line goes back through various different kings of note all the way, to Brïon, a son of Echu Muigmedón, brother to the famous Niall Noíghiallach and the eponymous ancestor of the dominant Connacht dynasty, the Uí Briúin. This line of descent can be traced back a further 38 generations to the legendary high-king Úgaine Már and continues back for yet another 23 generations to Éremón, son of Míl Espáine.[20] Míl Espáine's own genealogy is traced in *Lebor Gabála* all the way back to Japhet, the son of Noah. In this manner was Tomaltach's ancestry, nobility and place in the world established and confirmed. Many other dynasties also claimed descent from Míl Espáine through Éremón but others, such as the Ulaid, traced their pedigrees through Ír, another son of Míl Espáine or through other legendary figures.

The creation and maintenance of such a body of data required a considerable investment of intellectual and material resources over a long period of time. And as it encompassed the whole of Ireland and indeed much of Gaelic Scotland it can be seen as a national project for the Gaelic world. But when we use the term 'national' to designate

---

[19] On Tomaltach Mac Donnchaidh, see R. Ó hUiginn, "The Book of Ballymote: scholars, sources and patrons", in Ó hUiginn (ed.), *Book of Ballymote*, 191-219.

[20] For this section of the pedigree, see O'Brien, *Corpus Gen.*, 172.

this undertaking we should understand it in a cultural rather than in a political sense, for when we look at our earliest written sources for medieval Ireland, we find we are not dealing with a unitary kingdom, much less anything approaching a 'nation' in the modern sense of the word, but with a mosaic of smaller petty kingdoms dispersed throughout the land. While we find a high degree of linguistic and cultural unity, and indeed an understanding that the Irish were a discrete people, we do not find a centralised monarchy or a king with country-wide dominion.[21]

Between the fourth and the tenth centuries, evidence points to an increase in population in Ireland.[22] This was brought about by favourable climatic conditions and improvements in farming methods, introduced from Roman Britain. It coincides in part with the introduction of Christianity, which not only introduced a new religion to the country but had a considerable influence on many areas of material life, including agricultural technology and cereal growing, and thus contributed to an improvement in food production. This period also saw a growth in ringfort settlements, to which the Irish toponymical and archaeological records still attests.[23] Such beneficial developments, however, would also have been partly offset by natural calamities. The 'Justinian' plague came to Ireland in the 540s and the outbreak of another devastating epidemic is recorded in 664. Between these two outbreaks, the adverse climatic conditions of what is known as the late antique little ice age were experienced. Several other outbreaks of pestilence in both people and livestock and instances of

---

[21] Although it is possible such may have been in existence prior to our earliest written records. On this question, see L. Breatnach, "Varia VI: 3 *Ardrí* as an old compound", *Ériu* 37 (1986), 191-93, at 192.

[22] On population, settlement and rural economy in early medieval Ireland, see N. Edwards, "The archaeology of early medieval Ireland, c.400-1169: settlement and economy", in D. Ó Cróinín (ed.), *A New History of Ireland, I.* (Oxford), 235-300, at 296-300; and see further D. Ó Corráin's detailed discussion of settlement and economy at c.800 AD, "Ireland c. 800: aspects of society", in Ó Cróinín (ed.), *A New History of Ireland* 1, 459-608, at 540-74.

[23] On the dating of these constructions, see M. Stout, *The Irish Ringfort* (Dublin: Four Courts Press, 1997).

shortage and famine caused by unfavourable weather are also recorded.[24]

How exactly events such as these would have affected the political landscape we cannot say with certainty. An increase in population would have created a demand for land and would have led to acquisition of further territory by peoples who had the military and economic wherewithal to extend their reach, while natural calamities would have weakened peoples of less resources and may have made them susceptible to colonisation and subjugation. The upshot of this is that the political landscape was dynamic, not static, and subject to change, with larger kingdoms becoming fragmented and sometimes disappearing while new dynasties arose.

The number of population units or petty kingdoms we encounter in our records is considerable. One estimation is that at any time from the seventh to the twelfth centuries there may have been as many as 150 kings, each ruling a separate *túath* (people).[25] There also were over-kings, more powerful rulers, who could claim the allegiance of several lesser kings. Such a political landscape is reflected in Early Irish law, where reference is made to various different grades of king, up to that of a province.[26] But it has been shown that from the seventh century onwards, there was a movement towards the consolidation of larger power blocks and a concomitant decline in the importance of the petty túath, so that by the tenth century there were in existence only about a dozen overkingdoms of any consequence, a number that had declined even further two centuries later.[27]

---

[24] On these, see Ó Corráin, "Ireland c.800", 575-7.

[25] Byrne, *Irish Kings and High-Kings*, 7, but this is questioned by Ó Corráin in "Nationality and kingship in pre-Norman Ireland" in T. W. Moody (ed.), *Nationality and the Pursuit of National Independence*: Historical Studies X1 (Belfast: Appletree Press, 1978), 1-35, at 11. See also Byrne's further remarks in "Tribes and tribalism", 160.

[26] On the different grades of king, see D. A. Binchy (ed.), *Críth Gablach* (Dublin: Dublin Institute for Advanced Studies, 1941), 104-5 and idem, *Celtic and Anglo-Saxon Kingship* (Oxford: Clarendon Press, 1970).

[27] Ó Corráin, "Nationality and kingship", 11. This does not mean that the minor subordinate peoples who were eclipsed by the consolidation of larger power blocks disappeared immediately. The names of many peoples not prominent in our early sources have transferred to the territory they once occupied and have endured to this day as toponyms.

ANCESTORS, GODS, AND GENEALOGIES

In his study of the population groups we encounter in our early texts, Eoin MacNeill, distinguished a number of strata based on the structure of their nomenclature and the use of certain names.[28] To the latest stratum he would assign the sept names formed with *Uí* 'descendants', + eponym, many of which were coined during the time of our historical records and continued to be formed throughout the medieval period.[29] This grouping encompasses designations such as Uí Néill, Uí Briúin, Uí Liatháin etc., the most common form of nomenclature for lordships in the later medieval period. Sept names were otherwise formed with the noun *cenél* 'race', e.g. *Cenél Conaill, Cenél nEógain*, with the terms *cland*, or *muinter*, both of which are borrowings from Latin, (Lat. monis– and planta), e.g. *Cland Cholmáin, Clann Ricaird, Muinter Eóluis, Muintir Birn*; or with *síl* 'seed, progeny', e.g. *Síl Muiredaig, Síl nAnamchada, Síl nAéda Sláine*.[30] Yet another naming practice involves the use of the word *fir* 'men, people' followed by a place-name to designate the inhabitants of that place, e.g. Fir Maige Féne, Fir Bile, Fir Rois, etc. [31]

But beside designations such as these that were being coined well into the historical period, we find older strata of name formation that came into existence before our written records. To these belong broad-based ethnonyms or names that encompass many peoples, designations such as *Ulaid, Érainn, Laigin, Connachta* etc. In their structure they are plural formations, but their origins and etymologies are unclear. In some cases, these names can refer to political over-

---

[28] "Early Irish population-groups: their nomenclature, classification and chronology", *Proceedings of the Royal Irish Academy*, 29 (1911), Section C, 59-114.

[29] See *Electronic Dictionary of the Irish Language* (eDIL) s.v. *úa, óa, ó*. A sept is a familial group claiming common descent, often a subdivision of a larger group claiming descent from a legendary avatar.

[30] "Early Irish population groups", 82-87. *DIL* s.v. *muinter, clann*.

[31] On this, see *DIL* s.v. 1 *fer* (d), and R. Ó hUiginn, "Éireannaigh, Fir Éireann, Gaeil agus Gaill", in C. Breatnach and M. Ní Úrdail (eds) *Aon don Éigse* (Dublin: Dublin Institute for Advanced Studies, 2015), 17-49. This formation also includes the names of earlier population groups that had transferred to the territory they once occupied, as in the case of Fir Manach (whose name survives in modern Fermanagh). On this people, see T. F. O'Rahilly, *Early Irish History and Mythology* (Dublin: Dublin Institute for Advanced Studies, 1946, hereafter *EIHM*), 30-33.

kingdoms (e.g. *Ulaid, Connachta, Laigin*), but in others seem to refer simply to genealogical affiliation (e.g *Érainn, Cruithni*).[32]

Most numerous in our records, however, are the names of smaller, individual population groups or *túatha* 'peoples',[33] the *túath* being the basic political unit in medieval Ireland. Each *túath* had its own name, formed according to a number of well-known structures. The most prominent of these are names formed with the suffixes -*r(a)ige*, e.g. *Ciarraige, Ossraige, Benntraige, Catraige* etc.,[34] or those formed with the suffix -*ne/-na*, e.g. *Conmaicne, Cuircne, Latharna, Delbna* etc.[35] Other prominent formations, consist of the words *Corcu* 'seed, progeny',[36] or *Dál* 'division, share',[37] followed by a noun in the genitive, e.g. *Corcu Mo-Druad, Corcu Laígde, Dál Riata, Dál gCais, Dál Fíatach.*

---

[32] On the Érainn, see T. F. O'Rahilly, *EIHM*, 71-85, and for the Cruithin, ibid. 341-52. It has been noted that formations of this kind are the only type found in the names of peoples listed by Ptolemy (c.150 AD), our earliest source for the names of different peoples in Ireland. On these names, see O'Rahilly, *EIHM,* 1-42; and G. Toner, "Identifying Ptolemy's Irish places and tribes", in P. Sims-Williams and D. Parsons (ed.), *Ptolemy: towards a Linguistic Atlas of the Earliest Place-Names of Europe* (Aberystwyth: Cambrian Medieval Celtic Studies, 2000), 73-82.

[33] Túath (sg,) is sometimes translated as 'tribe', but as this term may carry connotations not implied by túath, I have opted for 'people' as a more neutral translation. MacNeill, used the equally neutral term 'population group'; cf. his discussion of the term túath in "Early Irish population groups", 88-89. Both D. A. Binchy, *Celtic and Anglo-Saxon Kingship* (Oxford, 1970), 8 and F. J. Byrne, "Tribes and tribalism in Early Ireland", *Ériu* 22 (1971), 128-66, at 128-32, however, favour the term 'tribe'.

[34] On names formed with this suffix, see MacNeill "Early Irish population groups", 67-9, and M. Ó Brien "Studien zu irischen Völkernamen 1. Die Stammesnamen auf rige", *ZCP* 15 (1925), 222-237.

[35] On this formation, see MacNeill, 'Early Irish population groups', 69-70. MacNeill's collection contains well in excess of 100 names that end in -*ne/-ni* only 22 of which he could securely identify as the names of population groups. But as he points out, it is possible that many of the other names in his list had a similar origin and once referred to people who had disappeared from the historical record but left their name on the territory they once occupied or on individual toponyms therein.

[36] "Early Irish population groups", 65.

[37] "Early Irish population groups", 66-7.

We cannot now establish how exactly this political landscape came into being. Most of the túatha we encounter in our sources have their origins in the prehistoric period. The origin of the naming patterns used in their formation is also uncertain. While names formed with *-r(a)ige*, appear to be compounds containing the noun *ríge* 'kingship, kingdom', the nature of the first or 'core' element with which it is compounded seems to vary.[38] In some of these formations it may possibly be a personal *name,* e.g. Artraige (< Art).[39] In others, the name of an animal is implied, e.g. Ossraige (< oss 'deer'), Catraige (< catt 'cat') Gaborraige (< 1 gabor 'goat' or 2 gabor 'horse'). In further cases the first element suggests the name of a *craft* or following, e.g. Cerdraige (< cerd 'craftsman, smith'), Semonraige (< seim 'rivet, riveter'), Céchtraige (< cécht 'plough'), Cnámraige (< cnám 'bone'), while in others it may refer to a *colour*, e.g. Ciarraige (< ciar 'dark, dun'), Dubraige (<dub 'black'), Odoraige/Odraige (< odar 'dun'). But in very many instances, the etymology and meaning of the first element is quite obscure, e.g. *Múscraige, Tratraige, Luffraige.*[40]

The suffix *-ne/-na,* appears to have a collective function.[41] In this category, personal names are quite prominent as the core element, e.g.

---

[38] While OIr *ríge* is a neuter noun, the compounded form found in the names of population groups appears to be masculine or feminine in our sources.

[39] As the word *art* 'bear' can also refer to a living creature, *Artraige* might otherwise be consigned to the category of names in which the core element signifies a living creature.

[40] We may note in passing that no name of this structure or of any of the other structures discussed here appears among the 33 names of peoples listed in Ptolemy's geography.

[41] Rudolf Thurneysen, *A Grammar of Old Irish,* rev., enl., ed., and trans. By D. A Binchy and Osborn Bergin (Dublin: Dublin Insitute for Advanced Studies, 1946, reprint 1969, §262. The feminine suffix *-(ai)ne* is normally used in the formation of abstract nouns from other nouns, e.g. *cairddine* 'friendship' (< *carae* 'friend'), but sometimes appears to have a collective function, e.g. *feochuine* 'ravens' (< *fiach*); cf *GOI* §262. This probably is the same suffix that we find in collectives such as *maicne* 'sons, progeny' which appears to have both masculine and feminine gender (eDIL s.v.). As the suffix *-na*, it forms a feminine noun in the name Delbna, as can be seen

Conmaicne (< Conmac), Conaille (< *Conaillne < Conall), Cuircne (< Corc), Cremthainne (< Cremthainn/Crimthainn), Conchuburne (< Conchobar), Latharna (< Lothar/Lathar), Luigne/Luaigne (< Lug). We can assume that the personal name refers to the eponymous ancestor of the people who may have been conceived of as a divine personage.[42] But as with the names formed with -r(a)ige, many of the core elements in the names that have the -ne/-na suffix, are obscure as to their etymology and meaning.

As MacNeill has noted, the core elements of these names can appear in the genitive, following *Dál* or *Corcu*, in an alternative designation for some peoples, e.g. *Dál Cuirc ~ Cuircne, Corcu Bibuir ~ Bibraige*. Similarly, in the Ogam inscriptions and in some early written sources, the use of the term *moccu* with following genitive denotes the affiliation of the person commemorated.[43] Saint Brendan, who was of the Alltraige of Kerry, appears as *Brendenus mocu Alti* in Adomnán's *Vita Columbae*, while the seventh-century poet Luccreth moccu Chíara was of the Ciarraige.[44]

A noteworthy feature in the early political map of Ireland is that we encounter peoples bearing the same name in different parts of the country. In some cases we find what appear to be independent *túatha*

---

from the genitive forms, Delbna Móire and Delbna Bige, listed by Hogan, *Onomasticon* s.n. Delbna ua maine; see also *Historical Dictionary of Gaelic Placenames. Foclóir Stairiúil Áitainmneacha na Gaeilge,* s.n. See note 45 for full reference. It is possible that the suffix originally formed neuter nouns, as the proto-form [*]-*inion*, proposed by MacNeill ("Early Irish population groups" 69), suggests.

[42] On the concept of dynasties being descended from gods, see Ó Corráin, "Nationality and kingship", 5 and G. Mac Niocaill, *Ireland before the Vikings* (Dublin: Gill and McMillan, 1972), 3.

[43] MacNeill "Early Irish population groups", 71-81. On the use of the early form *moccu* and its subsequent confusion with *mac uí*, cf. further MacNeill's article, "Mocu, maccu", *Ériu* 3 (1907), 42-9.

[44] An alternative formation in which the plural form of the eponym is used on its own is also attested; cf. *Hic Fergus mac Rōich condrecat na Cuircc 7 na Cēir 7 na Conmeicc ex maiori parte* "at Fergus mac Rōich the [lines of descent of] the Cuirc, the Ciarraige, and the Conmaicne for the most part converge", *Corpus Gen.* 137. Here, the Cuirc appear to refer to the Corcu Mo-Druad whose origin is traced in some genealogical tracts to Corc, son of Fergus.

bearing the same name in close proximity to each other, e.g. the various branches of the *Ciarraige* found in mid-Connacht (e.g. *Ciarraige Aí, Ciarraige Airtig* and *Ciarraige Áirne*) or in Munster (e.g. *Ciarraige Lúachra, Ciarraige Cuirche*),[45] or the many branches of the *Múscraige* in Munster (e.g. *Múscraige Mittine, Múscraige Lúachra, Múscraige Breogain, Múscraige Tíre*).[46] In others, however, peoples bearing the same name are found at some remove from each other, e.g. the *Cianachta*, who held territories in part of what are now Cos. Derry and Louth,[47] the *Conmaicne*, in West Galway and the midlands,[48] the *Benntraige*, found both in West Cork and in Wexford,[49] or the many branches of the *Calraige*, dispersed throughout the north-west, the midlands and Munster.[50]

We can speculate as to why we find such dispersal of these peoples, and in truth several reasons may be possible. In the first instance, it could be due to the fragmentation of what was a larger population unit. Fragmentation could be caused by external or internal agencies. An existing kingdom could be broken up through invasion, as appears to have happened in the case of the various branches of the Ciarraige in Connacht which suffered initially from the expansion of the Uí Fhiachrach and later of the Uí Briúin dynasty in the eighth and ninth centuries.[51] Otherwise, a more powerful overlord might decide to divide a subordinate people whose power was growing and who

---

[45] For a full list of the different branches of the Ciarraige, see P. Ó Riain, K. Murray and E. Nic Cárthaigh (eds*), Historical Dictionary of Gaelic Placenames. Foclóir Stairiúil Áitainmneacha na Gaeilge* (London: Irish Texts Society, 2003-. hereafter *Dictionary Gaelic PNN*), s.nn.

[46] See *Onomasticon*, s.n.

[47] *Dictionary Gaelic PNN*, s.n.

[48] *Dictionary Gaelic PNN*, s.n.

[49] *Dictionary Gaelic PNN*, s.n.

[50] On the branches of the Calraighe, see D. Ó Corráin, "Lugaid Cál and the Callraige", *Éigse* 13 (1969), 225-6; N. Ó Muraíle, "Some early Connacht population groups", in A. P. Smyth (ed.), *Seanchas: Studies in Early and Medieval Irish Archaeology, History and Literature in Honour of Francis J. Byrne* (Dublin: Four Courts Press, 2000), 161-177, at 162-5. and *Dictionary Gaelic PNN*, s.n.

[51] Byrne, *Irish Kings and High Kings*, 236.

might pose a threat to his rule.[52] Internal dissent, probably in relation to succession rights or claims to sovereignty, could also have been be a catalyst for division. In the later medieval period, we find such fragmentation arising out of internal strife within a lordship, cf. the dominant Uí Chonchobair dynasty of Connacht who by the late fourteenth century had broken into a number of separate groupings due to internal disunion.[53] It is not unlikely that internal division of this nature was a recurring feature of medieval Irish polity.

In other cases, however, dispersal may be due to migration and settlement. We know, for instance, that during the late Roman and early medieval periods Irish peoples settled in different parts of Britain. We have evidence of colonisation of parts of south-west Britain by the Uí Liatháin and the Déisi from Munster;[54] parts of North Wales were colonised from Leinster, while the Dál Riada expansion into Scotland proved to be the most enduring of all these settlements. From later periods we also have evidence that such migration also took place within Ireland, and while tales such as that about the expulsion of the Déisi, or that about the migration of the Corcu Óchae from Ulster to south-west Munster,[55] are fictitious, the movement and resettlement of people within Ireland also had a part to play in shaping a landscape frequently subject to change.

Internal migration may have been caused through people becoming dispossessed and taking 'sword land' elsewhere or migrating to serve as a vassal people to a more powerful unit, but it may otherwise have arisen through settlement of a more benign nature. A connection between some similarly named peoples situated at a

---

[52] This recalls the stratagem Fergus suggests to Ailill and Medb in Táin Bó Cúailnge to disperse the powerful body of Gáilióin throughout the army of the Connachta for fear of them acting in unison against their leaders and seizing land in Connacht. T. Kinsella, *The Tain* (Oxford: Oxford University Press, 1969), 67.

[53] On this, see A. Cosgrove "Ireland beyond the Pale 1399-1460" in idem. (ed.) *A New History of Ireland II. Medieval Ireland* (Oxford, 1987), 569-90, at 576-80.

[54] See T. Ó Cathasaigh, "The Déisi and Dyfed", *Éigse* 20 (1984), 1-33 and Byrne, *Irish Kings and High-Kings*, 183-4.

[55] K. Meyer, "The Laud Genealogies and Tribal Histories", 307-9 and R. de Vries *Two Texts on Loch nEchach. De Causis Torchi Corc' Óche and Aided Echach maic Maireda* (London: Irish Texts Society, vol. 65), 53-141.

remove from each other is established by the fact that the same patron saint was venerated by them.[56] It may have been that founders of churches brought with them adherents from their own people who subsequently settled in the territory where their venerated kinsman had established his church. Yet another possibility is that a people may have wished to ally themselves with a more powerful political entity with which they had no connection by adopting their name.

At any rate, however fragmented the political landscape may have been at an earlier period, the growing tendency to establish larger political groupings and the decline or subsuming of minor polities has resulted in few of these peoples being mentioned in the annals, compilations that were more concerned with the ruling septs or dynasties of their own day than in the records of people whose importance had diminished and who had ceased to be significant players on the political playing field. And where the names of such population groups occur in the annals, we cannot always be certain if reference is being made to a people or if the name has transferred to the territory once occupied by that people.[57]

How accurate a record is the information provided by our genealogies is far from certain. Their prehistoric sections obviously contain very much that is fictional, and, as Kelleher has shown, the genealogies of the various different prehistoric kings who supposedly descended from Ír, Éber and Éremón are quite tangled and do not align with each other in different genealogical collections.[58] But even within the historical period, generations can be skipped or names confused, such being normal problems of transmission. And the further back we go, the greater the likelihood is of encountering error and of entering the realms of pure fiction. We can add to this the fact that those who undertook the preservation and further transmission of the genealogies were not averse to falsifying or altering the record in some other way to suit contemporary political purposes. Kelleher again has shown that

---

[56] On this question, see T. M. Charles-Edwards, "Saints' cults and the early Irish church", *Clogher Record* 1, (2007-2008), 173-184.

[57] On the transference of the names of population groups to the territory occupied or once occupied by them, see, for instance, D. Flanagan, "Transferred population or sept-names: *Ulaid* (a quo Ulster)", *Bulletin of the Ulster Place-Name Society, series* 2.1 (1978) 40-44.

[58] "The pre-Norman Irish genealogies", 144.

the early genealogies bear the sign of being remoulded, perhaps in the eighth century, to reflect the dominant political power in the northern part of Ireland for most of the early medieval period, the Uí Néill.[59] And it can be demonstrated that other sections of the genealogies were altered with similar contemporary motives in mind.[60]

Despite issues such as these, the genealogies do indeed contain much that is old. Although our earliest collections are found in MSS of the twelfth century or later, they contain material that is considerably earlier than the date of these written sources. Some of this material is quite archaic.[61] Certain of the narrative passages embodied in the genealogies are written in Old Irish, and some in quite an early form of it. As such they can present us with layers of history not found in the annals.

Beside the genealogies themselves, we have other texts that are concerned with genealogical or historical matter. These include hagiographies, historical tracts, sagas and poems. Evaluating the evidence of such sources presents other difficulties. While some of these texts are also old, many others were composed during the Middle Irish period or later, and although they may make use of older genealogical material, they are compositions of their own time and we should always be aware of the context in which they were written down. Yet they also can contain information of value, but perhaps

---

[59] "The pre-Norman Irish genealogies", 143.

[60] This serves once again to remind us that in dealing with any medieval Irish text that purports to relate events that happened in the distant past, we can accept as a possibility that the text does indeed contain material that is old. It is also probable that such texts contain much that is fictional. And very often these compositions will have more to tell us about the time in which they were first written and about matters that concerned their authors than about the people and events from the distant past which they purport to describe. Cf. also D. Ó Corráin's comments on alterations made to the genealogies of the Callraige: "Here we come face to face with a common practice of the genealogists: they are quite often prepared to alter the genealogical affiliations of a people to suit political (and doubtless social) purposes." in "Lugaid Cál and the Callraige", 225. Cf. his further discussion "Creating the past", 181-5, and Byrne, "Tribes and tribalism", 147-8.

[61] On the information the genealogies contain about early Irish society, see Ó Corráin's evaluation of the genealogies in a late-fourteenth-century compilation in "The Book of Ballymote". See note 8.

more about the time in which they were written down than about the ancient political entities with which they are ostensibly concerned.

Apart from attempting to explain the dispersal of peoples in Ireland, one of the issues that engaged those who transmitted genealogies and related material was the question of a hierarchy of peoples. Early Irish society, as we know, was highly stratified, a situation reflected in the laws which legislate for the status of individuals from king down to serf.[62] In similar fashion, we encounter a number of terms in our sources that serve to distinguish peoples of different status: *sáerthúatha, fortúatha, aithechthúatha* and *dáerthúatha*. The precise meaning and application of these terms requires much further investigation and we should always reckon with the possibility that their meanings may have changed in the course of time as indeed may the status of the peoples to whom such terms were applied.[63] MacNeill, for his part, distinguished three grades of túatha, namely, *soerthúatha* (lit. noble or free people), a grade not subject to tributes; *fortúatha*, peoples retaining internal autonomy but tributary to an external overking; and *aithechthúatha*, vassal communities paying tribute to local chiefs of free race.[64]

With regard to the individual, both *sáer* 'noble, free' and *dáer* 'base, servile' feature prominently in legal texts where they are used with reference to the status of individuals. A *sáerchéile*, for instance, is a client (*céile*) in a relationship with his lord who is entitled to terminate it at will by returning his fief to the lord, whereas a *dáerchéile* does not enjoy such a privilege.

With reference to the túath, we could surmise with MacNeill that a sáerthúath refers to a people not required to pay tribute to an overlord, be that a *ruiri*, a *rí ruirech* or some more powerful king, whatever else their obligations to him might be. However, as Charles-Edwards has pointed out, the termination of political clientship of this nature was not possible, unlike the 'seigneurial' free clientship of the

---

[62] The classic legal text on status is D. A. Binchy (ed.), *Críth Gablach*. See note 26 above.

[63] See also F. J. Byrne, "Tribes and tribalism", 161.

[64] "Early Irish population groups", 93.

individual.[65] The status of the *dáerthúath*, a term not discussed by MacNeill, must obviously be inferior, most likely in their having to pay tax or tribute to the overking, in having to yield hostages to him in addition to other duties and obligations to which they might be subject but having local autonomy.

The fortúath are defined as being a people not descended from the same stock as the ruling túath and are obliged to pay tribute to them.[66] This status might have been brought about their migration into the territory of the dominant people, or through their being conquered and colonised by the people to whom they subsequently had to pay tribute.

The term *aithech* (first element of aithech-thúatha) originally had the legal meaning 'rent-payer, vassal', and is used sometimes simply to refer to a commoner as opposed to a person of aristocratic standing. It subsequently develops a set of more pejorative meanings: 'boor, churl' and later 'giant, monster'.[67] It is not clear what the status of the *aithechthúatha* is in relation to other dáerthúatha or if the term aithechthúath and dáerthúath are sometimes variant terms used to describe servile peoples.[68] As with the individual, it is not unlikely that there were different classes of subordinate peoples defined by the

---

[65] "*Lebor na Cert* and clientship", in K. Murray (ed.), *Lebor na Cert: Reassessments* (London: Irish Texts Society Subsidiary Series 25, 2013), 13-33, at 22.

[66] See also O'Rahilly, *EIHM*, 27.

[67] See *eDIL* s.v. 1. *aithech*. The word is a derivative of 1 *aithe* 'recompense, payment', the verbal noun of *ad-fen* 'repays'. An alternative etymology for *aithechthúath* is proposed by Kim McCone who suggests they may be equated with the Atecotti, a people some classical writers locate in Ireland; cf. *The Celtic Question: Modern constructs and ancient realities* (Dublin: Dublin Institute for Advanced Studies, 2008), 12-14 and P. Freeman, *Ireland and the Classical World* (Austin: University of Texas Press, 2001), 95-6. Whatever about the exact etymology, popular tradition would almost certainly have understood the first element of the word as the term for 'rent-payer, churl'.

[68] The Bibraige, for instance, are listed as one of the dáerthúatha Caisil in a sixteenth-century tract found in RIA MS C i 2, (40a) while the tracts in the Book of Ballymote and in TCD MS H 3.17 count them among the aithechthúatha. See T. Ó Raithbheartaigh, *Genealogical Tracts*, (Dublin: The Stationery Office, 1932), 107, 119.

nature of their relationship with the dominant polity, a relationship that may have changed with time.[69]

The aithechthúatha formed a subject of particular interest to the genealogists. Separate tracts in the Books of Ballymote, Lecan and Fermoy, in the Trinity College Dublin MS H 3.17 and in other sources provide lists of the people numbered in their ranks.[70] Some of these tracts are also accompanied by a legend that purports to explain why the *aithechthúatha* came to be dispersed throughout Ireland. This tale, of which we have a number of versions in prose and in verse, is known variously as *Bruiden meic Da Reo* "Mac Da Reo's hostel," *Scél ar Chairbre Cinn Cait* "Story concerning Cairbre Cinn Cait," or by the first line of the metrical version, *Sóerchlanda Érenn uili*.[71]

According to this tradition, the *aithig* (vassals), under the leadership of a certain Cairbre Cinn Chait or Cairbre Catchenn had grown weary of the workload imposed on them by the noble families of Ireland and so resolved to kill them.[72] To achieve this aim, they invited the nobles to a feast at Mac Da Reo's hostel in Bréifne.[73] For eight days and nights, they plied them with food and drink, but on the ninth day murdered them *en masse*, leaving alive only three pregnant women who managed to escape and flee to Alba.

The rule of the aithig proved to be disastrous. Crops failed, there was no produce from the land, nor fruit on trees, nor fish in weirs, nor

---

[69] For further discussion of these terms, see Byrne *Irish Kings and High-Kings*, 45-6 and Charles-Edwards "*Lebor na Cert* and clientship".

[70] Edited and translated by T. Ó Raithbheartaigh, *Genealogical Tracts*, 107-132; cf. also D. Ó Corráin, "On the *Aithechthúatha* tracts", *Éigse* 19 (1982), 159-165.

[71] For the different recensions of this legend, see. T. F. O'Rahilly, "Cairbre Cattchenn", in J. Ryan (ed.), *Féil-Sgríbhinn Éoin Mhic Néill* (Dublin: At the Sign of the Three Candles, 1940 [reprinted Dublin: Four Courts Press, 1995]), 101-110, at 105 and Ó Corráin *Clavis* §996.

[72] For this and related texts, see R. Thurneysen, "Morands Fürstenspiegel", *ZCP* 11 (1917), 56-106; Eoin MacNeill, "The revolt of the vassals", *The New Ireland Review* 26 (1906), 96-106; Ó Raithbheartaigh, *Genealogical Tracts*, 122-131 and 108-114. On the possible origin of Cairbre's epithet, understood in tradition to mean 'cat head', see O'Rahilly, "Cairbre Cattchenn", 101-3.

[73] An area in South Ulster and North Connacht, corresponding roughly to the modern counties of Cavan and Leitrim.

milk from cows, nor fine weather, nor peace within that time, but instead great famine for twenty years.[74] So dire did their situation become, that the aithig finally had to send messengers to Alba to implore the children of the women who had fled to return to rule. For this they offered sureties of heaven and earth, of sun and moon and all of the elements and agreed that they and their posterity would do constant service to them in perpetuity. In this manner, the sáerchlanna were reinstated in Ireland and the aithechthúatha, now bound to perpetual servitude, were dispersed throughout the land.

The text dates from the Middle Irish period and reference to it in both of the Middle Irish tale-lists, shows that it was in existence by the tenth century.[75] This was not the only tale to treat of the insubordination of the aithechthúatha, for we have what seems to be a variant of this legend from an earlier period, in a narrative concerning Túathal Techtmar, son of the king Fiachu who had been slain by the aithechthúatha. As a result of their misdeed, God inflicted famine on them as the land failed to yield its produce, cattle failed to produce milk and there was an absence of fish in the waters. As happens in the legend of Cairbre Cattchenn, Túathal the rightful ruler, comes to claim his patrimony and in so doing defeats the aithechthúatha of each province.[76]

Whether there is any basis of fact in legends such as these, as O'Rahilly held, is a matter of conjecture.[77] But it is clear that they were composed to provide a 'historical' account for the existence of classes of variously subordinate or servile peoples who were a feature of societal structure in Ireland in the early and later medieval periods, and to justify their inferior status or their servitude. And there are other texts that testify to this ongoing concern with peoples and their status.

---

[74] Such an outcome is normally reflective of the injustice of the ruler, and indeed the text states that the disasters that befell Ireland had been brought about by the great crime the aithig had committed. On the concept and consequences of unjust rule, see F. Kelly (ed. and trans.) *Audacht Moraind* (Dublin: Dublin Institute for Advanced Studies, 1976), xvii and §§12 ff.
[75] P. Mac Cana, *The Learned Tales of Medieval Ireland* (Dublin: Dublin Institute for Advanced Studies, 1980), 47 and 62.
[76] The legends concerning Túathal are discussed by O'Rahilly, *EIHM*, 154-170.
[77] *EIHM*, 161-70.

The eighth-century *Frithfolaid* text deals with the rights and dues of the kings of Cashel with regard to subject peoples in Munster,[78] while the late eleventh-century *Lebor na Cert* focuses on the tributes due to the provincial kings from their subject peoples.[79]

The lists of aithechthúatha given in the different genealogical tracts are not fully in agreement with each other. In several cases the names given appear to have suffered textual corruption in the course of transmission.[80] Names found on one list are not always present on others and where there appears to be correspondence, the forms of the names are not invariably identical. There would also appear to be a number of doublets, or names repeated in two different forms on the same list. Some of these names are unique to the list on which they are found and do not appear in other sources. It would seem that these lists derive from a much older source or sources which may have been subject to modification and imperfect transmission over a long period of time leading to such variation in the forms of names in the different tracts.

It has been noted that a majority of the names of the aithechthúatha listed in these tracts, are compounded with -r(a)ige and it is possible that the others, all of which have the Dál or Corcu + eponym structure, may also have had alternative forms with -r(a)ige.[81] It is further of note that collective names formed with a word that denoted 'kingship, kingdom' should be used with reference to base or servile peoples. The fact that several of them have as their core element the name of a trade or craft (e.g. *Cerdaige, Semonraige* etc.) which may suggest the craft or trade pursued by the people. Comparing this formation with the small number of attested names in Continental Celtic that contain a derivative of the word for 'king',

---

[78] J. G. O'Keeffe (ed.), "Dál Caladbuig", in J. Fraser, P. Grosjean and J. G. O'Keeffe (eds), *Irish Texts* 1 (London: Sheed and Ward, 1931), 19-21.

[79] M. Dillon (ed. and trans.), *Lebor na Cert. The Book of Rights* (London: Irish Texts Society, vol. 46, 1962).

[80] On this, see the many corrections and amendments suggested by Ó Briain, "Studien zu irischen Völkernamen", to the collection of names in *-r(a)ige* listed by MacNeill, many of which concern various aithechthúatha.

[81] On this see G. Mac Niocaill, *Ireland before the Vikings*, 4. Thus, of the 46 names listed in the Book of Ballymote tract, 28 are formed with *-r(a)ige*, eight have Corcu + eponym, while the remaining ten have Dál + eponym.

MacNeill held that in the use of -*r(a)ige* in the names of Irish petty or subordinate population groups its original meaning has 'degenerated'.[82] But while names of this structure are indeed prominent among the aithechthúatha, the same formation appears in the names of other people who enjoyed some power and prestige in the historical period and are frequently mentioned in the annals, e.g. Ciarraige Lúachra, Múscraige, Osraige, Calraige etc. These may well have been people who were originally subordinate but who subsequently rose to positions of power in the changing political landscape of medieval Ireland or, conversely, some of the peoples listed as aithechthúatha in the genealogical tracts formerly had a higher status which they subsequently lost.[83]

One major development that marked this changing world of medieval Ireland was the rise of the Uí Néill dynasty. While there are many questions about how and where they originated, tradition held them to be the progeny of Niall Noígiallach a king who was believed to have lived in the fifth century.[84] By the seventh century they and their allies dominated much of the northern half of Ireland, the collective being sometimes referred to as Dál Cuinn. This domination was achieved at the expense of other peoples, who lost territory and status in Ulster, Leinster and Connacht.

---

[82] "Early Irish population groups", 90. Given the multitude of túatha in existence, each with its own *rí,* the translation 'king' might give the impression of a more exalted office than was actually the case. It might be better to view the *rí túaithe* as a 'headman, chief, leader' or the like.

[83] Another point that has been noted is that no names with this structure appear among the 33 tribes listed by Ptolemy (150 AD). This list is dominated by plural formations, of which only a few can be identified with anything approaching certainty. A possible explanation for this is that that Ptolemy's list contains only the names of overkingdoms, and that the peoples with which we are concerned were at a level below that. In the course of time, we know that some of the peoples listed by Ptolemy had declined in importance, (e.g. the Érainn, on which see O'Rahilly, *EIHM*, 75-91) while some of the people who then were at a lower level rose to positions of power, others remained at the level of 'free' people, while yet more descended into various levels of servitude, a situation which continued to evolve as reflected in our early sources.

[84] On the rise of the Uí Néill, see F. J. Byrne, *Irish Kings and High-Kings*, 70-86.

ANCESTORS, GODS, AND GENEALOGIES

In the northern part of the country, one of the peoples affected by the rise of the Uí Néill was the overkingdom of the Ulaid. Loss of territory to the Uí Néill and their affiliates, the Airgialla, restricted their dominance to a part of north-east Ireland roughly coterminous with the modern counties of Antrim and Down with part of North Co. Louth. But they formerly claimed sway over much of the northern part of the country where according to tradition they had ruled the land extending from the mouth of the River Boyne (Bōin) at the southern reaches of the modern Co. Louth to the mouth of the River Drowse (Drobaīs) in Co. Donegal.[85] Their former glory is celebrated in the body of heroic saga literature known as the Ulster Cycle, though its make up is not codified.[86] These tales hark back to a time in which their dominance throughout much of the northern part of Ireland was absolute and their king and royal family resided at Emain Macha in the modern county of Armagh. The origins of this body of literature is to be sought among the Ulaid, and in its written form it must have been committed to vellum in one or more of the monastic scriptoria that lay under their control, establishments such as Bangor, Armagh, Louth, Drumsnat and others. Some compositions associated with the Cycle belong to the oldest strata of Irish literature and have been dated to the seventh and eighth centuries. And it is possible that they embody traditions that are yet older.

Cultivation of these tales and traditions, however was not confined to Ulster. Some of these traditions were known and used at a very early stage elsewhere. We also know that certain compositions were redacted or rewritten in various centres in the country, and new compositions, reflecting an interest in the midlands or in Connacht were later added to this body of tales. We will revert to some of these compositions presently.

---

[85] A note entered in the Book of Leinster genealogies states that Conchobar's province (*coicid*) stretches *ó Drobaīs co Bōin*; see O'Brien, *Corpus Gen.*, 422.

[86] Although the designation 'Ulster Cycle' is widely used, we note that not all of the tales associated with this cycle feature the Ulaid, e.g. *Echtrae Nerai* or *Aided Medbae*, the events of which concern members of the Connachta, or *Togail Bruidne Da Derga,* tale that is concerned with the fate of a legendary king of Tara in which a fleeting mention of Conall Cernach is its only connection to Ulster.

54

RUAIRÍ Ó HUIGINN

The Ulster Cycle was an influential body of tradition. It formed part of the national narrative, chronicling as it claimed to do, events in Ireland around the time of Christ, a period of no small importance in the Christian perception of world history. Although it has been suggested that some of these tales may have a historical background,[87] much of what purports to be history quite clearly is fiction. Archaeological excavation and research has shown, for instance, that what is depicted as their royal centre at Emain Macha (Navan Fort, Co. Armagh) never was a royal residence of any kind but apparently was a construction that had a ceremonial function before it was burned c.100 BC.[88] This ruined landmark was appropriated by the framers of the Ulster tales who invested it with a status it quite likely never had in prehistory, in much the same way as the megalithic tomb at Newgrange was deemed by tradition to have been the dwelling place of Óengus, son of the Dagda, or that many of the prehistoric dolmens found in different parts of Ireland had been erected by members of the legendary Fianna.

We have previously noted that the genealogists used figures drawn from the early sagas to populate the prehistoric sections of the various different pedigrees they constructed. The Ulster Cycle was not excluded from this process, for several of the Ulster heroes appear in the lines of descent of various peoples not only in Ulster but also in other parts of Ireland. The Ulster lines of descent are traced back over many generations through an ancestor named Rudraige and the Ulaid, accordingly, are sometimes referred to as *Clanna Rudraige*, (the

---

[87] That is that the warfare between the Ulaid and the Connachta, found in tales such as *Táin Bó Cúailgne*, may embody a memory of the prehistoric warfare between the Ulaid and the Connachta from whom it is believed the Uí Néill emerged. For a discussion of different opinions that have been expressed on the possible historical background to the tales, see J. Carney, "Early Irish literature: the State of Research", in G. Mac Eoin, (ed.), *Proceedings of the Sixth International Congress of Celtic Studies* (Dublin: Dublin Institute for Advanced Studies, 1983), 113-130, at 114-17. Carney himself was of the opinion that Táin Bó Cúailnge was neither fiction nor history but an amalgam of both (p.116).

[88] On Emain Macha, see C. Lynn *Navan Fort. Archaeology and Myth* (Bray: Wordwell, 2003). On the 'historicity' of the Ulster Cycle in general, see N. B. Aitchison, "The Ulster Cycle: heroic image and historical reality", *Journal of Medieval History* 13 (1987), 87-116.

offspring of Rudraige), while their province is on occasion designated *Cóiced Rudraige* (the fifth of Rudraige). The Rudraige from whom they are descended was Rudraige mac Sitraide meic Duib, a prehistoric king who ruled for seventy years according to the traditions of *Lebor Gabála* and the genealogies where it is stated that the people known as Dál nAraidi, who were regarded as the *fír-Ulaid* 'true Ulaid', were descended from him.[89] He is, however, but one of three figures in *Lebor Gabála* who bear this unusual name. Elsewhere in the text it is recorded that Rudraige mac Dela was one of the leaders of the Fir Bolg who had colonised Ireland in prehistoric times and to whom was assigned the province of Ulster.[90] Yet another bearer of the name was Rudraige, the son of Parthalón, the leader of another invasion of Ireland.

The name has every appearance of being in origin the designation of a population group formed with -r(a)ige that had become obsolete by the time of our records, but the memory of which had endured in toponyms such as Dún Rudraige, Loch Rudraige, Fertas Rudraige or Trácht Rudraige, all in the vicinity of Dundrum Bay in the modern Co. Down.[91] Indeed *Lebor Gabála* asserts that Loch Rudraige was named after Rudraige, the son of Parthalón, due to this sea inlet coming into existence as he was being buried, and it elsewhere states that Trácht Rudraige was where Rudraige son of Dela of the Fir Bolg had landed in Ireland.[92] The names of these legendary ancestral figures were most likely abstracted from such toponyms, in accordance with the well-

---

[89] R. A. S. Macalister (ed. and trans.), *Lebor Gabála Érenn,* Part 5, (London: Irish Texts Society, vol. 44, 1956), 290, §593.
[90] On this figure see R. A. S. Macalister (ed. and trans.), *Lebor Gabála Érenn,* Part 3, (Dublin: Irish Texts Society, vol. 39, 1940), §263.
[91] For these toponyms, see Ó Corráin's revised online edition of E. Hogan, *Onomasticon Goedelicum Locorum et Tribuum Hiberniae et Scotiae* (Dublin, 1910, hereafter *Onomasticon*). The core element of the name is possibly a form of the adjective *rúad* 'red' that also appears in other words, e.g. the personal names Rudgal, Rudgus etc. which also have variants with initial Rúad-. For the formation, compare the names Odraige (< odar 'dun') and Dubraige (< dub 'black'). On this see R. Ó hUiginn, "Fergus, Russ and Rudraige", *Emania* 11 (1993), 31-40, and for formations based on the underlying root see D. Stifter, "Study in red", *Die Sprache* 40 (1998), 202-223.
[92] *Lebor Gabála* Part 5, 490, v.14.

established dindshenchas practice of creating heroic figures from already existing place-names.[93]

In populating the prehistoric sections of the genealogies, the genealogists found a place in the tradition of Síl nÍr for Conchobar mac Nessa, the legendary king of Ulster, and his sons; for Lóegaire Búadach, Bricriu mac Carbada, Muinremur mac Geirrcinn, Sencha mac Ailella, Celtchar mac Cuithechair and many of the other characters who appear in this cycle of tales. While some of these figures are simply listed in the lines of descent presented in the genealogical tables, others are highlighted as the ancestors of certain peoples. Two heroes in particular are prominent in this regard, i.e. Conall Cernach, ancestor of the Loígsi, the Uí Echach, Dál nAraide and the various different branches of the Sogain, and Fergus mac Róich, ancestor of several population groups in Connacht and in Munster. It is on the latter of these two ancestral figures we will now focus our attention to see how the strands of genealogical and literary tradition are intertwined.

As in much of the north and east of the country, the province of Connacht in the west also came to be dominated by descendants of Niall Noígiallach. Three dynasties, the Uí Ailello, the Uí Fhiachrach and the Uí Briúin, cast as the progeny of Niall's three brothers, Ailill, Fiachra and Brïon, rose to power in the western province. In the earlier period, the Uí Fhiachrach, centred mainly in the north west, were dominant, but in the course of time were displaced by the Uí Briúin, of which there were several branches.[94] The most prominent branch based in central Connacht were the Uí Briúin Aí, who claimed descendant from Brïon through Muiredach Muilethan (†702 AD), ten generations removed from the eponymous ancestor.[95] Known accordingly as Síl Muiredaig ('the progeny of Muiredach'), under his

---

[93] The name Rudraige was later adopted by the Uí Dhomhnaill lordship and some of their affiliates in the course of the fourteenth century and was to become popular among them. Dindshenchas is the lore of place names.

[94] i.e. the Uí Briúin Aí, the Uí Briúin Umaill, the Uí Briúin Bréifne, the Uí Briúin Seóla. The Uí Ailello never achieved prominence and by the eighth century were no longer of significance. On this eclipse see Byrne, *Irish Kings and High-Kings*, 85, 231.

[95] For these lines of descent, see the tables presented in Byrne, *Irish Kings and High-Kings*, 299-300.

great-great grandson Muirgius (†815 AD) they consolidated their position of power in Connacht, and from Muirgius's lineal descendant Conchobar (†973 AD), five generations later, came the Uí Chonchobair (O'Connor) dynasty that was to extend their grasp on Connacht and in Tairdelbhach (†1156 AD) and Rúaidhrí (†1198 AD) was to provide Ireland with two 'high-kings'.

Below this overlay of Dál Cuinn suzerainty, however, was a stratum of subordinate peoples. It is reasonable to assume that these were people previously occupying territory in Connacht who had lost out to the expanding invaders and had now become their tributaries. While references to such subject peoples are none too plentiful in the annals due to the dominance of the larger overkingdoms, a number of these population groups are mentioned in other sources, some of which are quite early.

Of these peoples, the most prominent were the Ciarraige, of which there were several branches in Connacht and a number in Munster.[96] Another prominent people were the Conmaicne, again with several branches in Connacht, Bréifne and elsewhere in Ireland. The Calraige were dispersed throughout different parts of Connacht,[97] and the Delbna constituted another group with several offshoots.[98] Further south in Connacht were the Sogain, who bordered on the Uí Maine in the south of the province. And there were many other peoples who once may have had power and status but for whom our evidence

---

[96] On the Ciarraige of Connacht, see N. Ó Muraíle, "Some early Connacht population groups" 165-74. They are mentioned in Tírechán's collection of material concerning the Patrician foundations, compiled in the late seventh century, and evidently were of some import at that time. By the time of *Lebor na Cert*, however, both main groupings of the Cíarraige are represented as subject peoples of the kings of Crúachain and of Caisel. The name of the Ciarraige of Connacht survives in the townland Cloonkerry (Cluain Ciarraí) in the Barony of Kilmaine, Co. Mayo. See also Ó Muraíle "Some early Connacht population groups", 173.

[97] For the Calraige, cf. Ó Corráin "Lugaid Cál and the Callraige", Ó Muraíle "Some early Connacht population groups", 162-5 and *Dictionary Gaelic PNN*, s.nn

[98] For the various branches of the Delbna, cf. *Dictionary Gaelic PNN*, s.nn.

is scantier.[99] That these have become subordinate or tributary peoples by the time of our early records is clear, but their exact relationship to the ruling dynasties is not.[100] Several of these people are classed as aithechthúatha in the genealogical tracts, while others may have been subject peoples of higher standing. From our point of view, it is of importance that very many of these subordinate Connacht peoples traced their descent from the ancient Ulaid through the ancestral figure of Fergus mac Róich.[101]

Fergus has a significant role in several tales of the Ulster Cycle. These include the early compositions *Táin Bó Cúailnge*,[102] *Longas mac nUislenn*,[103] *Táin Bó Flidais*,[104] *Aided Fergusa meic Róig*[105] and

---

[99] See the list of minor Connacht peoples compiled by Ó Muraíle, 'Some early Connacht population groups', 74. The Domnainn of North-West of Connacht are frequently mentioned in literary sources, but the term seems to be used as a general ethnonym for a number of peoples rather than as the name of a separate population group. Different branches of this people were also located in Leinster. The name appears to be the same of that of the Dumnonii or Damnonii found in Devon and Cornwall and in Strathclyde. According to the genealogies in the Book of Leinster, Domnainn and Galióin were other names for the Laigin (*Corpus Gen.* 334). On this people, see O'Rahilly, *EIHM*, 92-99.

[100] The subordinate status of the Conmaicne, the Ciarraige, the Delbna, and a number of other Connacht peoples is made clear in *Lebor na Cert*, which counts the Uí Briúin, Uí Fhiachrach, Síl Muiredaig, and Cenél nAéda as free peoples who enjoy equal status with the king. On this, see Dillon (ed. and trans.), *Lebor na Cert*, 46-61.

[101] As did other population groups in Munster.

[102] C. O'Rahilly *Táin Bó Cúailnge. Recension I* (Dublin: Dublin Institute for Advanced Studies, 1976, hereafter *TBC Rec. I*), and by the same author, *Táin Bó Cúalnge from the Book of Leinster* (Dublin: Dublin Institute for Advanced Studies, 1967).

[103] V. Hull (ed. and trans.), *Longes mac n-Uislenn: The exile of the sons of Uisliu*, The Modern Language Association of America 16, (New York: Modern Language Association of America, 1949).

[104] E. Windisch, (ed. and trans.), "Táin bó Flidais", in: E. Windisch and W. Stokes (eds.), *Irische Texte mit Wörterbuch*, 4 vols, vol. 2:2, (Leipzig: Verlag Hirzel, 1887), 206-22.

[105] K. Meyer (ed. and trans.), *The Death-Tales of the Ulster Heroes*, Todd Lecture Series 14, (Dublin: Royal Irish Academy, 1906), 32-35, 45.

the incomplete *Fochann Loingsi Fergusa meic Róig*.[106] He also is alluded to in early genealogical tracts. Presented as a figure of gigantic proportions, the genealogies count Fergus as a grandson of the great Ulster ancestor Rudraige, a descendant of Ír. In addition to his normal patronymic, he is also sometimes called Fergus mac Rossa, or Fergus mac Rossa Róig, and there are good grounds for holding that the legendary king of Ulster, Fergus mac Leite, who drowned in Loch Rudraige is a doublet.[107] His name which can be taken to mean 'manly vigour son of great horse', suggests a divine origin.[108] The main outlines of Fergus's career as found in the Early Irish narratives in which he is prominent can be summarised as follows:[109]

Formerly a king of Ulster, he desired a woman called Ness and she acquiesced to his advances on the condition that her son, Conchobar would be made king for a year. This proves to be a ruse as Conchobar's rule is very successful and Fergus is deprived of the kingship of Ulster forever.

Conchobar proves to be a good ruler initially, but sets his sight on a new-born girl named Deirdre of whom it is foretold that she would grow to be a woman of great beauty but also would bring about the destruction of Ulster. Undeterred, he has her raised in a secluded place until she reaches womanhood. But when she does, she shuns the

---

[106] V. Hull (ed. and trans.), "The cause of exile of Fergus mac Roig", *ZCP* 18 (1930), 293-98.

[107] The Early Irish narrative concerning Fergus mac Leite is embedded in a legal commentary. It has been edited and translated by D. A. Binchy, "The saga of Fergus mac Léti," *Ériu* 16 (1952), 33-48. A later burlesque retelling of the tale without the legal dimension has been edited and translated by S. H. O'Grady in *Silva Gadelica* vol. 1, 238-52 (text), vol. II, 269-85 (translation). On the various different forms of his name, cf. O'Rahilly, *EIHM*, 480 n.3 and Ó hUiginn 'Fergus, Russ and Rudraige', 32-4. See the article in this volume by G. Darwin on this tale.

[108] By this I mean no more than a figure endowed with superhuman qualities and abilities. O'Rahilly goes somewhat further, holding that Fergus and other bearers of this name "represent the Otherworld-deity under different designations", *EIHM*, 68.

[109] A more detailed account can be found in R. Ó hUiginn, "Fergus, Russ and Rudraige"; see also P. Ní Mhaoileoin, 'The heroic biography of Fergus Mac Róich. A case study of the heroic-biographical pattern in Old and Middle Irish literature', unpublished PhD thesis, NUI Galway, 2012.

king for a younger lover named Noísiu whom she forces to elope with her. The couple suffer great hardship while in exile in Britain and in the knowledge that the greatly loved Noísiu was not the instigator of the affair, the Ulaid get Conchobar to agree to let them return to Ulster. Fergus and Conchobar's son Cormac act as guarantors for the safety of the returning couple, but when Conchobar reneges on the agreement and has Noísiu and his brothers killed, the enraged Fergus causes much destruction in Ulster before going into exile in the province of Connacht, where he is welcomed by Queen Medb and her consort Ailill mac Máta. While there, he has a love affair with Medb from which triplets, according to one version, or sextuplets according to another are born. Fergus later departs to stay with another king in Connacht, named Ailill Find, whose wife Flidais he also seduces and takes after killing her husband. While in Connacht with Ailill mac Máta and Medb, Fergus leads the Connacht army into his native Ulster in the quest for the Brown Bull of Cooley, but as an Ulsterman he has a crisis of conscience and does so reluctantly, leading the Connacht army astray on occasion. After the events of Táin Bó Cúailnge Medb's jealous husband Ailill arranges that he is killed while swimming entwined with Medb in a lake in Connacht.

His significant role in the genealogies arises from his love affair with Medb, Queen of the Connachta, for from this liaison several children were born. Their offspring were to become significant ancestors of various different peoples in Connacht and Munster, but as we have noted, tradition does not agree on the number of children born to them. Nor is there total agreement in the genealogies as to the names of these ancestral figures or their genealogical associations. According to the tract in Rawlinson B 502, the three sons born to Fergus and Medb, were Ciar, Corc, and Conmac. Ciar is presented as the eponymous ancestor of the Ciarraige of Munster and Connacht; Corc is cast as ancestor of the Corcu Mo-Druad,[110] while the ancestry of many of the different branches of the Conmaicne in Connacht and Leinster is traced back to Conmac.[111]

Elsewhere in the same tract, however, the ancestry of both the Ciarraige and the Conmaicne, together with that of the Bibraige is

[110] A people located in what is the modern Co. Clare. The name survives in that of the Barony of Corca Mruadh/Corcomroe in that county.
[111] See O'Brien, *Corpus Gen.* 279.

traced to a son of Fergus named Mug Tóeth.[112] Corcu Mo-Druad are traced back to another son named Fer Deoda or Fer Dea, as are the four branches of the Araid,[113] while a son named Eithlenn is presented as the ancestor of the Orbraige and Benntraige[114] and another, named Corbb Aulomm, appears as the ancestor of the Corcu Auloimm.[115] Other peoples in Ireland claimed descent from Fergus through further offspring of his. As O'Rahilly observed, Fergus proved a 'boon' for the genealogists who adopted him as ancestor of many minor septs of 'pre-Goidelic' origin.[116] But there was not full agreement of the lines of descent, for in addition to the Ulster ancestry traced through Rudraige, there were alternative pedigrees which traced his descent from Míl Espáine through Érech, son of Míl, or through Lugaid mac Ítha, ancestor of the Corcu Loígde.[117]

The genealogical dimension, complex though it may be, can help us place some of the early narratives relating to Fergus in context, for these tales served to explain how different people dispersed throughout Ireland claimed racial affinity with the Ulaid. The real reason they did so has probably been lost to us, but the tradition that it came about because an exiled king of Ulster had had a liaison with the Connacht Queen, was widely accepted and became part of the *senchus coitchenn* 'common history'. This was an old and well-established tradition. It is alluded to in a poem by the seventh-century poet Luccreth moccu Chiara embedded in a genealogical tract found in Oxford Bodleian MS Laud 610,[118] and is repeated time and again in

---

[112] *Corpus Gen.*, 254, 321. This name appears in a number of variant forms; cf. *Corpus Gen.* 703, s.n. Mug-Dōet.

[113] *Corpus Gen.*, 321. On the Araid see *Dictionary Gaelic PNN*, s.n.

[114] *Corpus Gen.*, 321. Various branches of the Orbraige were found in Munster and Connacht; cf. Hogan *Onomasticon*, s.n., while the Benntraige were located in West Cork and in Wexford where their name endures in Beanntraí/Bantry, a designation for baronies in both modern counties.

[115] Corcu Auloim/Úloim were a people located near Sliabh Mis in Kerry; see D. Ó Corráin, "Onomata", *Ériu* 30 (1979) 165-80 at 176-8.

[116] *EIHM*, 480.

[117] *Corpus Gen.*, 427-8; cf. also O'Rahilly, *EIHM*, 480-81 and Ó Corráin, "Onomata", 176-7.

[118] K. Meyer, 'The Laud Genealogies and Tribal Histories', 305-7. This tract also states that Fergus's descendants first settled in Tara, then

other compilations as Fergus is presented as ancestor of many peoples in Connacht and Munster. This, however, was not uncontested. The early version of *Táin Bó Flidais* relates that Fergus was loved by Flidais, the wife of Ailill Find, who resided in Áth Fén *hi crích Ciarraigi* (in the territory of the Ciarraige) thus giving us to understand that the Ciarraige were already settled in Connacht at the time of Fergus's sojourn with Medb.[119] Another text we have purports to tell how the Ciarraige migrated from Munster into Connacht under the leadership of a certain Coirbre mac Conaire during the reign of Aed mac Eachach Tirmcharna (†577 AD), a king of Connacht who flourished in the second half of the sixth century.[120]

Vernam Hull, who edited this text, accepted the essence of the tradition that the Ciarraige originated in Munster and thence migrated to Connacht.[121] Further evidence for such a migration has been adduced by Ó Muraíle from the presence in the territories in Connacht occupied by this people of a significant number of Ogam-stone inscriptions.[122] As is well known, the greatest density of Ogam inscriptions is found in modern Co. Kerry, where this tradition and writing system may have originated,[123] and it is possible that those who inscribed the stones in the territory of the Ciarraige in mid Connacht were either new migrants from Munster or were their close descendants.

Other important associations between Munster and mid-Connacht are evidenced in the establishment of a number of midland ecclesiastical foundations in the sixth and seventh centuries by clerics who came from the southern province.[124] These include Brénainn (otherwise known as St Brendan the Navigator) of Clonfert, who was

---

subsequently moved to the south. The name of his son Fer Tlachtga, presented in some tracts as ancestor of the Ciarraige, is of interest in this respect for it would appear to be associated with the toponym Tlachtga, the old name of the Hill of Ward, Co. Meath, not far removed from Tara.

[119] On the location of the Ciarraige, see Windisch, "Táin Bó Flidais", 207-8.
[120] See V. Hull (ed. and trans.), "The migration of the Ciarraige", *Speculum* 25, (1950), 184-189.
[121] The modern county name of Kerry is derived from that of the Ciarraige Lúachra, the dominant branch of this people in Munster.
[122] "Some early Connacht population groups", 173.
[123] See D. McManus, *A Guide to Ogam* (Maynooth: An Sagart, 1991), §4.3.
[124] Byrne, *Irish Kings and High-Kings*, 170-1.

of the Al(l)traige, a subordinate people of the Ciarraige located on the Dingle Peninsula in the modern Co. Kerry.[125] The genealogies provide a pedigree for him that extends back to Fergus mac Róich through his son Mug Tóeth or Ciar, ancestor of the Ciarraige.[126] The founders of many other ecclesiastical establishments, both in the west midlands and elsewhere likewise were provided with genealogies that traced their pedigrees back to the Ulster hero. Among these was St Ciarán the founder of Clonmacnoise, and while not a Munsterman, he was supposedly born at a place called Ráith Crimthann in Mag nAí and furnished with a pedigree that had him descend from Fergus mac Róich, through his son Corc, ancestor of the Corcu Mo-Druad.[127]

With its midland position on the river Shannon, Clonmacnoise enjoyed support and patronage from dynasties both in Connacht and in Leinster.[128] While its abbots were originally drawn from the aithechthúatha in different parts of Ireland,[129] by the late eleventh century it had come under the influence of the dominant Uí Chonchobair (Síl Muiredaig) dynasty of Connacht and by the following century the abbacy was dominated by the Uí Mhaoil Eoin family, who may have been a subaltern branch of the ruling family.[130] As the dominant dynasty in Connacht, the Uí Chonchobair proved to be powerful patrons, [131] but in the aftermath of church reform in the twelfth century they expended much of their largesse on foundations established by the continental religious orders. New ecclesiastical foundations such as Abbeyknockmoy, Boyle Abbey, Tuam Priory, Ballintubber Abbey, Cong, Roscommon Abbey and several others

---

[125] On the Al(l)traige, see D. Ó Corráin, "Studies in West Munster history. II. The Alltraige", *Journal of the Kerry Archaeological and Historical Society* 2 (1969), 27-37.

[126] P. Ó Riain (ed.), *Corpus Genealogiarum Sanctorum Hiberniae* (Dublin: Dublin Institute for Advanced Studies, 198, hereafter Corpus Gen. Sanct.), 22 (§127.1).

[127] *Corpus Gen. Sanct.* 21 (§125.1.2).

[128] On the history of Clonmacnoise, see A. Kehnel, *Clonmacnois: the Church and Lands of St Ciarán* (Münster: Lit Verlag, 1997).

[129] Byrne, *Irish Kings and High-Kings*, 171. For a list of abbots and other ecclesiastical officials at Clonmacnoise and their affiliation, see A. Kehnel, *Clonmacnois: the Church and Lands of St Ciarán*, 246-92.

[130] Kehnel, *Clonmacnois*, 151.

[131] Kehnel, *Clonmacnois* 126-9.

were founded in the twelfth and thirteenth centuries by the Uí Chonchobair or by subsidiary branches of Síl Muiredaig. In addition to their patronage of the church, Síl Muiredaig became significant patrons of Irish literature and learning, providing for the four main branches of native learning: medicine, law, history and poetry. Connacht, as a result, became the major centre of Irish literary production in the later Middle Ages. This period also sees a development in literary practice as activity moves by and large from ecclesiastical to secular settings. While this movement may already have been in progress prior to the advent of reform, it becomes prominent in the thirteenth and fourteenth centuries as literary families such as the Uí Mhaoil Chonaire, the Uí Dhuibhgeannáin, the Meic Fhir Bhisigh, the Meic Aodhagáin and others flourished in the schools of learning they established and from which has been transmitted to us the significant literary legacy of Connacht in this period.[132]

Prior to these later developments, Clonmacnoise had become from its foundation in the sixth century to its demise in the twelfth, one of the most powerful ecclesiastical settlements in the country and a vibrant centre of literary production. By the eleventh century at the latest, tales of the Ulster Cycle were being redacted here. Our earliest surviving compilation of these tales is found in Lebor na hUidre, the

---

[132] On this legacy, see T. Ó Concheanainn "A Connacht medieval literary heritage: texts derived from Cín Dromma Snechtai through Leabhar na hUidhre", *Cambridge Medieval Celtic Studies* 16 (Winter, 1988), 1-40. On the rise of these families, see Robin Flower, *The Irish Tradition* (Oxford, 1947), 67-93 and Proinsias Mac Cana ,"The rise of the later schools of *filidheacht*", *Ériu* 25 (1974), 126-146. As many of these literary families came from the ranks of church officials attached to settlements such as Clonmacnoise, it is likely that they inherited the contents of church libraries. It has been argued, for instance, that Lebor na hUidre entered the possession of the Ó Sgingín family who became hereditary historians to the Ó Domhnaill Lordship of Cenél Conaill (Donegal). See R. Ó hUiginn "Lebor na hUidre: from Clonmacnoise to Kilbarron", in id. (ed.) *Lebor na hUidre. Codices Hibernenses Eximii 1* (Dublin: Royal Irish Academy, 2013), 155-82, at 171-82. For an alternative view, that it was aquired by the Ó Cléirigh family who succeeded the Uí Sgingín as historians to Cenél Conaill, see N. Ó Muraíle "Notes on Lebor na hUidre's later history, including its Connacht sojourn, 1359-1470" in Ó hUiginn (ed.) *Lebor na hUidre*, 183-206, at 186-90.

oldest Irish-language manuscript now extant which is believed to have been written c.1100 AD in this midland settlement.[133]

Clonmacnoise played a crucial role in the transmission of the Ulster tales and of other literary material from the Early Irish period, but its scholars may also have contributed to opening a new chapter in the history of the Cycle. From the twelfth century, we find that a number of early Ulster tales are rewritten and that new compositions are added to the Cycle. Several of these compositions have as their focus not the ancient province of Ulster, but areas in the Irish midlands and west, taking in much of the province of Connacht. The connection between the heroes of Ulster and the kingdom of Connacht is provided by the tradition of Fergus and other Ulster warriors having been in exile there as a result of Conchobar's treachery to Noísiu and his brothers which lead to their death.[134]

An early text in this later phase of the Ulster Cycle is the saga *Bruiden Da Choca* (*BDC*) which is concerned with the killing in Da Choca's hostel of Conchobar's exiled son, Cormac Cond Loinges.[135] Cormac was to become king of Ulster following the death of his father but was killed in the hostel in Co. Westmeath by the Connachta while on his way back to Ulster. The tale has been dated to the early twelfth century and would appear to have been written by a member of the community of Clonmacnoise as the writer shows intimate familiarity with the area in which the settlement was situated.[136]

---

[133] On the provenance, date and contents of Lebor na hUidre, see R. I. Best and O. Bergin, *Lebor na hUidre* (Dublin: Royal Irish Academy, 1929, hereafter *LU*) and R. Ó hUiginn (ed.), *Lebor na hUidre*.

[134] As related in the Early Irish tale, *Longas mac nUislenn*.

[135] G. Toner (ed. and trans.), *Bruiden Da Choca* (London: Irish Texts Society, vol. 56, 2007).

[136] Toner, *Bruiden Da Choca*, 3-6, and D. Ó Corráin, "Early Ireland: directions and re-directions", *Bullán: an Irish Studies Journal* 1, no. 2, Autumn, 1994; 1-15, at 10-11.

While *Bruiden Da Choca* may be based on an earlier tale now lost,[137] its sequel, *Cath Airtig*,[138] is a new composition which deals with the aftermath of Cormac's death at the hostel of Da Choca. The kingship of Ulster passes to Cúscraid, son of Conchobar, who divides the province up between the Ulster warriors. As the land to be divided involved territory contested by the Connachta, a war broke out between the two provinces in which the ancient peoples of Connacht, the Domnainn, the Fir Chraoibhe and the Túatha Taíden join battle with the Ulaid at a place called Airtech.[139] As a result of this battle, the text informs us, the Domnainn are destroyed.

Reference is made to Fergus in both of these tales, but the light in which he is presented is far from heroic. *BDC* states that although the Ulaid considered re-instating Fergus as their king, the memory of his treachery towards them in joining the army of Medb to fight against his native province caused them to baulk at doing so (*BDC* §1). At a later stage in the narrative, as the journeying Ulaid repair to the hostel of Da Choca to spend the night, Dubthach tries to assuage their worries about being attacked there by pointing out that Fergus is behind them guarding the rear. However, Ilann Fionn, Fergus's own son, interjects by saying that it should be easy for anyone to evade him due to his father's poor powers of perception (*BDC* §30). This proves to be the case, for Medb tricks Fergus into letting the Connacht army pass to visit destruction on the Ulaid who overnight at Da Choca's hostel (*BDC* §§38-40).

The reference in *Cath Airtig* simply recounts that the Ulaid made peace with Fergus, and in the ensuing division of the old province he was granted the land of Sualdam mac Róich in an area of Co. Louth and north Co. Meath. Having settled there with his wife Flidais, he was forced to return to Connacht after her death as his householding there was no longer successful. Mention of Fergus being incapable of maintaining a household without the input (*tinchur*) of his wife is

---

[137] The tradition of Cormac's death is referred to in a poem by Cináed úa hArtacáin (†975 AD) and the Early Irish tale-lists contain a tale by the name of *Togail Bruidne Da Choca*. These early references are evaluated by Toner, *Bruiden Da Choca*, 21-5.

[138] R. I. Best, (ed. and trans.), "The battle of Airtech", *Ériu* 8 (1916), 170-90 and Ó Corráin *Clavis* §1001.

[139] Artagh is now an electoral area in Co. Roscommon.

made in greater detail in the revised text of the Old Irish saga *Táin Bó Flidais*, found in Lebor na hUidre, a codex written in Clonmacnoise as we have noted.[140] The unfavourable implications of this reference have been discussed elsewhere.[141]

The negative portrayal of Fergus in these texts, however, pales when compared with that presented to us in the later version of *Táin Bó Flidais* (*TBF²*) The early version of text was expanded and developed as an extensive prosimetrical narrative,[142] a narrative that also appears to embody a modernised version of *Fochan Loingsi Fergus meic Róich*, a tale preserved incompletely in the sole Early Irish version we have, while the tradition found in the related tale *Longas mac nUislenn* is developed and rewritten as *Oidheadh Chloinne hUisneach* (*OCU*).[143] These texts are found together in the

---

[140] *LU*, ll.1632-41.

[141] R. Ó hUiginn, "Adapting myth and making history", in E. Boyle and D. Hayden (eds) *Authorities and Adaptations. The reworking and transmission of textual sources in Medieval Ireland* (Dublin: Dublin Institute for Advanced Studies, 2014), 1-21, at 13-18.

[142] D. Mackinnon (ed. and trans.), "The Glenmasan manuscript", *The Celtic Review* 1 (1904-1905), 3-17, 102-31, 208-29, 296-315; *The Celtic Review* 2 (1905-1906), 20-33, 100-21, 202-23, 300-13; *The Celtic Review* 3 (1906-1907), 10-25, 114-37, 198-15, 294-317; *The Celtic Review* 4 (1907-1908), 10-27, 104-21, 202-19 and M. E. Dobbs, "On Táin Bó Flidais", *Ériu* 8 (1916), 133-49 who supplies the text of passages missing from Glenmasan from RIA MS B IV 1 (seventeenth-century). On the components of this later tale, see C. Breatnach "Oidheadh Chloinne Uisnigh", *Ériu* 45 (1994), 99-112 and R. Ó hUiginn, "Growth and development in the late Ulster Cycle: The case of *Táin Bó Flidais*", in: J. F. Nagy, (ed.), *Memory and the Modern in Celtic Literatures*, CSANA Yearbook 5, (Dublin: Four Courts Press, 2006), 143-61. For further references, see Ó Corráin *Clavis* §1105.

[143] C. Mac Giolla Léith (ed. and trans.), *Oidheadh Chlainne hUisneach* (London: Irish Texts Society vol. 56, 1993 = *OCU*). As the final section of *OCU* and the opening of *TBF²* are missing from the Glenmasan manuscript, it is unclear if they once formed part of a composite tale or if *OCU* was a separate narrative as is the case in the other (later) MSS in which it is found. For a discussion of this issue, see Breatnach "Oidheadh Chlainne hUisneach". It is clear, however, that stylistically and thematically *OCU* and *TBF²* are of a piece and, if they did not form a composite text originally, at the very least can be seen as chapters of a longer tale. For further references, see Ó Corráin *Clavis* §1080.

Glenmasan Manuscript, a manuscript dating to c.1500 AD which is now preserved in the National Library of Scotland.[144] The resulting extended narrative is a tour de force of medieval Irish literature.

OCU, as is well known, is not a modernised version of *Longas mac nUislenn*. It deals with the same tradition, but rather than explaining the background to Deirdre's birth and elopement with Noísiu, as is done in the earlier tale, it focuses on their return from Scotland and the ensuing death of Clann Uisneach. As such the role of Fergus becomes central. His portrayal in this text is not dissimilar to that of *BDC*. He is presented as a person who is gullible and malleable, weak and vacillating. Having been inveigled by Conchobar into guaranteeing the safe return of the lovers from Scotland, he is despatched to accompany them home. However, he fails abjectly in this task and despite the sureties he had given to Clann Uisneach, Conchobar arranges to have Noísiu and his brothers killed. Deirdre's comment to her lover when she realises that their death is nigh: *do fheall Fearghus oraibh, a Naoise* ("Fearghus betrayed you, Naoise"),[145] epitomises the negative light in which he is portrayed.

Worse, however, awaits this character in *Táin Bó Fliodhaise*, which continues the narrative of *OCU*. Having being tricked by Conchobar into leading Clann Uisneach to their death, a vengeful Fearghus ravages Emain Macha, expels Conchobar and re-assumes kingship for a period. But his reign proved to be disastrous. As the text states:

> *Agus adberat aroile go raibhe Ferghus go cenn*
> *secht mbliadhan a righi nUladh ⁊ nár ēirigh grian*
> *tar uillinn laoch-mhúir na hEmhna, gurab dubh-*
> *flaithes Ferghusa ainm na righe si.*

> Some say, however, that Fergus was in the kingship
> of Ulster for seven years and that (during that time)
> the sun did not rise over the edge of the warlike
> rampart of Eamhain, so that that kingship is called

---

[144] NLS 53.
[145] *OCU*, ll.543-4.

"the black reign of Fergus".[146]

The tale continues in a similar vein, detailing Fergus's sojourn with Ailill and Medb in Crúachu and later with Ailill Find and Flidais at Áth Fén. His time with Medb is marked by their affair, where their comical sexual encounter in a hazel tree is observed by her spouse, Ailill. Although moved to kill his rival for violating his honour, Ailill instead removes Fergus's sword from its scabbard and replaces it with a wooden one (*TBF²* §60).[147] Fergus's subsequent liaison with Flidais at Áth Fén brings further indignity as her husband, Ailill Find, defeats him in combat and then subjects him to sexual humiliation by having him bound, naked, to a pillar and allowing firstly the women and then the rabble of the encampment to come and view the vanquished hero (*TBF²* §60). Although Fergus eventually is freed and succeeds in defeating and killing Ailill Find, he subsequently is shunned by Flidais and emerges from the tale as a figure of mockery and derision.[148]

While the Yellow Book of Lecan, (YBL), the earliest manuscript in which it is found dates from the late fourteenth century, the text itself is evidently older. As has been pointed out elsewhere, the H scribe of Lebor na hUidre who rewrote part of the earlier *Táin Bó Flidais* in that codex, appears to have been familiar with a version of the later narrative.[149] The episode in which Ailill removes Fergus's sword from its scabbard, is also alluded to in *Táin Bó Cúailnge*. It would thus appear that an expanded version of *Táin Bó Flidais* was already in existence in the Middle Irish period and that this was used by the person who wrote *TBF²* as the basis for his text. The H scribe was active in the first quarter of the twelfth century, and while it is unlikely that our text dates from this time it may not be very much later.[150]

Questions arise as to who may have composed this tale, what his purpose was and what audience he had in mind. We know that this

---

[146] *Ériu* 8, 140.
[147] Reference is made to this incident in *Táin Bó Cúailnge*. *TBC Rec.* 1, ll.1306-10.
[148] A fuller discussion of this tale and the portrayal of Fergus therein is found in Ó hUiginn, "Growth and development".
[149] On this, see Ó hUiginn, "Growth and development", 155-6.
[150] On the H scribe, see L. Breatnach "Lebor na hUidre: some linguistic aspects" in R. Ó hUiginn (ed.), *Lebor na hUidre,* 53-77.

person was intimately familiar with an area of West Mayo, given the profusion of toponyms from this area that permeate the text. The author also had great interest in the 'legendary' history of Connacht, the ancient peoples of which features prominently in his tale,[151] and he clearly shared the poor view of Fergus mac Róich we see in other compositions. He evidently was a person of some learning who had access to genealogical and other literary material.

Given the period in which he worked and his location, he almost certainly belonged to one of the celebrated literary families of Connacht, the Uí Mhaoil Chonaire, the Uí Dhuibhgeannáin or the Meic Fhir Bhisigh, for instance, all of whom enjoyed the patronage of the dominant Dál Cuinn dynasties in the province, Síl Muireadaig, the Uí Briúin or the Uí Fhiachrach. In light of his familiarity with the Erris district of Mayo, Robin Flower made the reasonable assumption that he came from the ranks of the Meic Fhir Bhisigh, historians to the Uí Fhiachrach Muaidhe, and that he was active in the fourteenth century.[152] Tomás Ó Con Cheanainn has gone further and suggested that its author was the celebrated Giolla Ísu mac Fhir Bhisigh, who

---

[151] On the legendary history of Connacht, see E. Bhreathnach, "Tales of Connacht: *Cath Airtig, Táin bó Flidhais, Cath Leitreach Ruibhe*, and *Cath Cumair*", *Cambrian Medieval Celtic Studies* 45 (Summer, 2003), 21-42, and Ó hUiginn, "Adapting myth and making history". Most of texts concerned with the legendary history refer to the *Sen-Chonnachta*, the 'ancient' peoples of Connacht, included among which are Dál Druithne, Fir Chraoibhe, Túatha Taíden, Catraige, and Ga(r)braige Suca, most of which were counted as aithechthúatha. These people are sometimes assigned to the Domnainn, while in other cases they are considered to belong to the Fir Boilg. On these, see O'Rahilly, *EIHM*, 97, 101 and 407 and P. Walsh "Christian kings of Connacht", *Journal of the Galway Archaeological and Historical Society* 17 (1936), 124-43, at 125-6. The name of the Catraige survives in the Irish toponym, Tuaim Catraí (< Catraige), the English name of which is Kellysgrove, Co. Galway. The Irish name shows that this people existed. On the other hand, several of these texts-and especially *TBF²*-make mention of a people called the Gamhanradh from Erris, a people that had no existence, being a purely literary creation. On this, see R. Ó hUiginn "The Gamhanradh", *Celtica* 27 (2013), 79-94.
[152] R. Flower, *Catalogue of Irish Manuscripts in the British Library. Part 2* (London: the British Library, 1926,reprinted Dublin: Dublin Institute for Advanced Studies, 1992), 347-8.

was responsible for the text of *TBF²* in YBL and who flourished at the end of the thirteenth century and in the first decades of the fourteenth. There are, however, some difficulties with this identification and it is likely that all three manuscript witnesses derive from an earlier exemplar now lost.[153] Whether it was the work of an earlier member of the Meic Fhir Bhisigh or of a different learned family is not certain.

But as much as this composition might have appealed to the writer's patrons, there were others in Connacht to whom it would have been less pleasing. Many of the peoples who had been dispossessed by the rise to power of the Uí Fhiachrach and Uí Briúin had remained in Connacht, albeit as subject peoples. Although their circumstances were reduced, they had not disappeared and were not entirely insignificant. Obituaries and other events concerning the leading family of the Ciarraige, the Uí Cheithearnaigh, are recorded a number of times in the annals,[154] as are those concerned with the foremost families of the Conmaicne, the Meic Raghnaill[155] and the Uí Fhearghail.[156] These people all claimed descent from Fergus mac Róich and in presenting their forefather as incompetent, weak and unheroic, the author of *TBF²* belittles his descendants, now subject peoples of the author's patrons who themselves would doubtless have found much to enjoy in his tale.[157]

---

[153] "A personal reference by Giolla Íosa Mac Fhir Bhisigh", *Celtica* 18 (1986), 34; but as Lára Ní Mhaoláin has pointed out in her forthcoming edition of the text, some of the readings of YBL are inferior to those of the two other MS witnesses. This points to all three being derived from an earlier exemplar, or exemplars, now lost. On Giolla Íosa, see N. Ó Muraíle *The Celebrated Antiquary. Dubaltach mac Fir Bhisigh (c.1600-1671): his lineage, life and learning* (Maynooth: An Sagart, 2002), 16-38.

[154] Cf. W. M. Hennessy (ed. and trans.) *The Annals of Loch Cé*, 2 vols. (London, 1871; rep. Dublin, 1939, hereafter *ALC*), s.a. 1266.1, 1266.17, 1307.5, 1316.2, 1341.6. etc.

[155] *ALC*, s.a. 1196.10, 1237.1, 1247.4, etc.

[156] *ALC*, s.a. 1196.11, 1206.7, 1212.4, 1218.3, 1221.1 etc. The name *Conmaicne* occurs several times in the later annals, but it seems to be used in many of these instances with reference to the territory over which they formerly had ruled rather than to the people.

[157] In the Old Irish version of the tale, Ailill Find's dwelling at Áth Féne is situated in the territory of the Ciarraige Aí. Its relocation in *TBF²* to Erris,

The portrayal of Fergus in later tradition was not totally negative. Among other people who claimed descent from him were the Corcu Mo-Druad of Co. Clare. From two prominent leaders of this people who flourished around the year 1000 AD, Lochlann and Conchobar, issued the Uí Lochlainn and the Uí Chonchobair, lords of Corcomroe, Co. Clare.[158] The latter who styled themselves 'Kings of the Burren' were significant patrons of Irish learning. The law-school at Cahermacnaughten run by the legal family of Dubh Dá Bhoireann (O'Davoren), for instance, enjoyed their support, as did later poets and scribes in the area. One such person was the poet and scribe Aindrias mac Cruitín who in 1727 compiled the manuscript known as the Book of Ó Lochlainn, now housed in the Royal Irish Academy (RIA).[159] This work was written for a member of that family named Brian Ó Lochlainn, who was a doctor of medicine. The manuscript is a miscellany of poetry and prose, much of which is dominated by compositions celebrating the ancient Ulaid and their ancestor Fergus, or bewailing the reduced circumstances of his progeny. And it contains excerpts from the genealogies that outline the pedigrees of the Uí Lochlainn and other families of the area all of whom descended from Fergus mac Róich.

And here, more than a thousand years after Luccreth moccu Chiara composed his poem on the migration of certain Ulster peoples to Munster, we find the same tradition being celebrated in that southern province, testimony yet again to the enduring centrality of genealogy in early Irish society, its learning and its literature.

Co. Mayo, is likely the work of the author who was familiar with the area. On this, see Ó hUiginn, "Growth and development", 158-9.

[158] On these families, see D. Ó Corráin, "The families of Corcumroe", *North Munster Antiquarian Journal* 17 (1975), 21-30.

[159] RIA MS 11 (E iv 3). For its contents, see T. F. O'Rahilly *et al. Catalogue of Irish Manuscripts in the Royal Irish Academy* (Dublin: Royal Irish Academy, 1926-70).

Geoffrey of Monmouth in Medieval Ireland? Cambro-Norman Identity, Political Prophecy, and an Irish Sea Network

Georgia Henley

In studying the 'matter of Britain' and its antecedent, Trojan history, in the manuscript traditions of fourteenth-century Wales and Ireland, we find no shortage of material from medieval Wales. Stories of Arthur and other Galfridian figures can be found in all manner of native tales and triads, as well as in Middle Welsh romances translated from French.[1] The Welsh translation of Dares Phrygius's *De excidio Troiae historia*, called *Ystorya Dared*, was popular as well, circulating in over forty manuscripts.[2] Broadly speaking, medieval Welsh genealogies, histories, and prophecies are pervaded with the influence of Geoffrey of Monmouth's *De gestis Britonum*, which traces the royal line of British kings from Troy through Brutus and Arthur down to Cadwaladr. *Brut y Brenhinedd*, the Welsh translation of Geoffrey's history, is frequently paired with *Ystorya Dared*, which offers a prequel of sorts for Brutus's settlement of Britain after the Trojan war. This pairing is reflected in Welsh genealogies, which trace the ancestry of Welsh kings and princes back to Troy, providing evidence for sustained Welsh interest in their Trojan heritage throughout the medieval period and beyond.

In medieval Ireland, however, Geoffrey and his literary characters, namely Arthur, are a bit more difficult to find. Key studies of Arthur in Irish sources have unearthed his presence in a smattering

---

[1] For recent discussion, see *Arthur in the Celtic Languages: The Arthurian Legend in Celtic Literatures and Traditions*, ed. Ceridwen Lloyd-Morgan and Erich Poppe (Cardiff: University of Wales Press, 2019).

[2] See Helen Fulton, "History and *Historia*: Uses of the Troy Story in Medieval Ireland and Wales," in *Classical Literature and Learning in Medieval Irish Narrative*, Studies in Celtic History, 34 (Cambridge: D.S. Brewer, 2014), 40-57; Erich Poppe, "The Matter of Troy and Insular Versions of Dares's *De Excidio Troiae Historia*. An Exercise in Textual Typology," *Beiträge zur Geschichte der Sprachwissenschaft* 19, no. 2 (2009): 252-98; B.G. Owens, "Y Fersiynau Cymraeg o Dares Phrygius (*Ystorya Dared*)," unpublished MA thesis, University of Wales, 1951.

of genealogies and annals, as well as *Acallam na Senórach* and a handful of fifteenth- and sixteenth-century romances.[3] The figure of Arthur in Irish genealogical sources is limited to the use of 'Arthur' as a name, without any explicit connection to the mythical hero or to a specific textual source.

The situation is complicated by the question of whether Geoffrey's Latin history circulated in Ireland, which is difficult to ascertain. There is just one confirmed copy of *De gestis Britonum* in medieval Ireland (Dublin, Trinity College, 11500, s. xiv, from the Cistercian abbey of St Mary's in Dublin) and no extant translations of the history into Irish.[4] TCD 11500 is, as far as I know, the only example of a manuscript of *De gestis Britonum* of Irish provenance. The text is preceded in the manuscript by Dares Phrygius and followed by Gerald of Wales' works on Ireland, the *Topographia* and *Expugnatio Hibernica*. This lack of evidence for the circulation of *De*

---

[3] See, for example, John Carey, ed., *The Matter of Britain in Medieval Ireland: Reassessments* (Dublin: Irish Texts Society, 2017); Aisling Byrne, "The Circulation of Romances from England in Late-Medieval Ireland," in *Medieval Romance and Material Culture*, ed. Nicholas Perkins (Cambridge: D.S. Brewer, 2015), 183-98; Joseph Falaky Nagy, "Arthur and the Irish," in *A Companion to Arthurian Literature*, ed. Helen Fulton (Malden: Wiley-Blackwell, 2009), 117-27; and Ann Dooley, "Arthur of the Irish: A Viable Concept?" *Arthurian Literature* 21 (2004): 9-28. The texts in question, ranging from medieval to early modern, are *Lebor Breatnach*; *Acallam na Senórach*; various genealogies (particularly of the Dál Ríata and Dál Fíatach); a surviving tale title, but lost tale, *Aigidecht Arthúir* (Hosting of Arthur); *Lorgaireacht an tSoidhigh Naomhtha* (Quest of the Holy Grail); stories about the death of Mongán Mac Fiachna of the Dál nAraidi; *Eachtra an Mhadra Mhaoil* (Adventure of the Cropped Dog); *Céilidhe Iosgaide Léithe* (Visit of Iosgaid Liath); *Eachtra Mhacaoimh an Iolair* (Adventure of the Eagle Boy); *Eachtra an Amadáin Mhóir* (Adventure of the Big Fool); and *Eachtra Mhelóra agus Orlando* (Adventure of Melóra and Orlando).

[4] For discussion of this manuscript, see Georgia Henley, "Transnational Book Traffic in the Irish Sea Zone: A New Witness to the First Variant Version of Geoffrey of Monmouth's *De gestis Britonum*," *North American Journal of Celtic Studies* 4, no. 2 (2020): 131-62; Bernard Meehan, "A Fourteenth-Century Historical Compilation from St Mary's Cistercian Abbey, Dublin," in *Medieval Dublin XV*, ed. Seán Duffy (Dublin: Four Courts Press, 2016), 264-76.

gestis Britonum in Ireland is surprising when one considers the popularity of the history throughout Europe, as well as the influx of Norman settlers in Ireland in the late twelfth century at precisely the time that Geoffrey's history was becoming popular in francophone communities, both insular and continental.[5] As is well known, strong political and ecclesiastical links between Ireland and the Welsh Marches developed in the late twelfth century because most of the invaders came from the marcher lordships of Wales and the borderlands.[6] This resulted in strong communication networks between the two regions and, one can assume, a high likelihood of transmission of texts and manuscripts between these communities, aided particularly by ecclesiastical networks.[7] *De gestis Britonum* was

---

[5] For Geoffrey's early reception, see Jaakko Tahkokallio, "Early Manuscript Dissemination," in *A Companion to Geoffrey of Monmouth*, ed. Georgia Henley and Joshua Byron Smith, Brill's Companions to European History, 22 (Leiden: Brill, 2020), 155-80; and Françoise Le Saux, "Geoffrey of Monmouth's *De gestis Britonum* and Twelfth-Century Romance" in the same volume, pp. 235-56.

[6] These individuals include Richard fitz Gilbert de Clare, William Marshal, Robert fitz Stephen, Maurice fitz Gerald, Meilir fitz Henry, Robert and Philip de Barry, Raymond le Gros, Walter de Lacy, Maurice de Prendergast, and the Bloet family of Striguil. See Marie Therese Flanagan, *The Transformation of the Irish Church in the Twelfth and Thirteenth Centuries* (Woodbridge: Boydell, 2010); Steve Flanders, *De Courcy: Anglo-Normans in Ireland, England, and France in the Eleventh and Twelfth Centuries* (Dublin: Four Courts Press, 2008); John Gillingham, *The English in the Twelfth Century: Imperialism, National Identity, and Political Values* (Woodbridge: Boydell, 2000), 145-60; Marie Therese Flanagan, *Irish Society, Anglo-Norman Settlers, Angevin Kingship* (Oxford: Oxford University Press, 1989); R.A. Stalley, *The Cistercian Monasteries of Ireland: An Account of the History, Art, and Architecture of the White Monks in Ireland from 1142 to 1540* (New Haven: Yale University Press, 1987); David H. Williams, "The Welsh Cistercians and Ireland," *Cistercian Studies* 15 (1980): 17-23; Geraldine Carville, "The Cistercian Settlement of Ireland," *Studia Monastica* 15 (1973): 23-41.

[7] Monasteries in Ireland with mother houses in Britain include Abbeylara, Abington, Ards, Ballybeg, Comber, Downpatrick, Dunbrody, Graiguenamanagh, Grey, Inch, Nendrum, North and South Youghal, St Mary's Dublin, Tintern Minor, and Tracton.

very popular in Britain–can we extrapolate that it would have been read in Anglo-Norman Ireland as well? One also suspects that the lack of copies of Geoffrey's history of Irish provenance may be a result of the high bar of evidence required to locate a Latin manuscript's provenance more precisely than features that indicate a manuscript is 'British' or 'insular.' In other words, there may be more copies of Irish provenance buried in the catalogue of *De gestis Britonum* manuscripts than we know. It may prove useful to examine whether any of the Irish texts that mention Arthur (in footnote 3 above) show any contact with Geoffrey's history specifically, or if they are more broadly indicative of Irish interest in Arthuriana. Concerning these allusions to Arthurian romance in Irish romance and poetry, Aisling Byrne writes, "these references, though intriguing, do not necessarily expand our knowledge of which romances were known in medieval Ireland. It is quite clear the Irish translation of the *Queste* [*de Saint Graal*] could, potentially, have been the source for all of them."[8] That is to say, Geoffrey was not necessarily the source underlying references to Arthur in Irish texts.

Evidence for knowledge of the story of Troy in Ireland is comparatively much more secure (and more widely studied than *Ystorya Dared*, for that matter). The Irish manuscript record shows sustained interest in Troy, from *Togail Troí*, the Middle Irish adaptation of Dares Phrygius, and *Imtheachta Aeniasa*, the Middle Irish adaptation of the *Aeneid*, to the twelfth-century poem *Clann Ollaman Uaisle Emna* (The Children of Ollam are the Nobles of Emain) and *Stair Ercuil ocus a Bás*, a late medieval Irish adaptation of the first two books of Caxton's *Recuyell of the Histories of Troie*. To this list we can add other mentions of the destruction of Troy in Irish poetry. These texts show a particular engagement by Irish speakers with the story of Troy, which some have interpreted as part of an overall interest in world history.[9] As Michael Clarke and Brent Miles have shown, *Togail Troí* (which is more of a set of adaptations

---

[8] Byrne, "Circulation of Romances," 187.
[9] See, for example, Brent Miles, "Togail Troí: The Irish Destruction of Troy on the Cusp of the Renaissance," in *Fantasies of Troy: Classical Tales and the Social Imaginary in Medieval and Early Modern Europe*, ed. Alan Shepard and Stephen D. Powell (Toronto: Centre for Reformation and Renaissance Studies, 2004), 81-96, at 83.

of Dares than a single text) was reworked in the fourteenth and fifteenth centuries to reflect new Latin and French source material.[10] As will be shown further below, these centuries are precisely the time during which interest in Merlinic prophecy comes into focus in Ireland.

Further engagement with the broad narrative of Trojan and British history is evident when we consider the reading habits of francophone communities in South Wales and Ireland from the twelfth century onward. These communities were seeded and governed by Cambro-Norman families (including the De Clares, Geraldines, De Lacys, Marshals, and Mortimers) who held lands in both Ireland and Wales and whose associates traveled between the two countries frequently. For the purposes of this article, I refer to these communities as "Cambro-Norman" and "Hiberno-Norman," clumsy identity terms, neither of which was in contemporary usage, but which do reflect the hybrid, in-between nature of these communities, linked across the Irish Sea by marcher families with ties to both places.[11] A better term of ethnic identity is Gerald of Wales's term *marchiones* "marcher lords," the group he refers to in the *Descriptio Kambriae* as *gens in Kambriae marchia nutrita*, people who have lived all their

---

[10] Michael Clarke, "International Influences on the Later Medieval Development of *Togail Troí*," in *Adapting Texts and Styles in a Celtic Context*, ed. Axel Harlos and Neele Harlos (Münster: Nodus Publikationen, 2016), pp 75-102; Brent Miles, *Heroic Saga and Classical Epic in Medieval Ireland* (Cambridge: Brewer, 2011); Miles, "Togail Troí." See also Ralph O'Connor, ed., *Classical Literature and Learning in Medieval Irish Learning* (Cambridge: Brewer, 2014); Uáitéar Mac Gearailt, "*Togail Troí*: An Example of Translating and Editing in Medieval Ireland," *Studia Hibernica* 31 (2000-2001): 71-86.

[11] For "Cambro-Norman" identity and identity terms, see discussion in Marie Therese Flanagan, "Strategies of Distinction: Defining Nations in Medieval Ireland," in *Nations in Medieval Britain*, ed. Hirokazu Tsurushima (Donington: Shaun Tyas, 2010), 104-21; James F. Lydon, "Nation and Race in Medieval Ireland," in *Concepts of National Identity in the Middle Ages*, ed. Simon Forde, Lesley Johnson, and Alan V. Murray, Leeds Texts and Monographs, New Series, 14 (Leeds: University of Leeds, 1995), 103-24; Robin Frame, "'Les Engleys Nées en Irlande': The English Political Identity in Medieval Ireland," *Transactions of the Royal Historical Society* 3 (1993): 83-103.

lives in the Marches and who are best suited to the challenge of Welsh warfare tactics.[12]

In this article, I track whether such a sense of marcher identity, as defined by Gerald of Wales, persisted among the Cambro-Normans in Ireland, particularly through evidence of interest in Galfridian and Trojan history. Generally speaking, I consider the matter of Britain as a prism through which one can identify key aspects of national identity, due to its strong ideological associations with themes of rulership and conquest, and its pervasive use in political discourse in a range of medieval contexts. First, I will briefly demonstrate engagement with the 'matter of Britain' and the British past on the part of the Cambro-Norman invaders of Ireland, as well as by their later relatives and counterparts in the March of Wales. I will then turn to developments in interest in Dares Phrygius and Geoffrey of Monmouth in later Hiberno-Norman Ireland, and discuss whether and how such interest differs from engagement with the same texts in the March of Wales.[13] Overall, I demonstrate that while there is keen interest in Dares, Geoffrey, and associated prophecies of Merlin on the part of the francophone communities of Ireland, their interpretation of those histories is a bit different than in the Welsh Marches.[14]

---

[12] Gerald of Wales, *Descriptio Kambriae* II.viii, ed. J.F. Dimock, *Giraldi Cambrensis Opera*, 6 (London: Longmans, Green, Reader, and Dyer, 1868), 220; Gerald of Wales, *Expugnatio Hibernica* II.xxxviii, ed. J.F. Dimock, *Giraldi Cambrensis Opera*, 5 (London: Longmans, Green, Reader, and Dyer, 1868), 395.

[13] For a full account of francophone literature in and about medieval Ireland, see Keith Busby, *French in Medieval Ireland, Ireland in Medieval French: The Paradox of Two Worlds*, Medieval Texts and Cultures of Northern Europe, 27 (Turnhout: Brepols, 2017); Evelyn Mullally, "Hiberno-Norman Literature and its Public," in *Settlement and Society in Medieval Ireland: Studies Presented to F. X. Martin, o.s.a.*, ed. John Bradley (Kilkenny: Boethius Press, 1988), 326-43; Matthieu W. Boyd, "The source of enchantment: the marvels of Rigomer (Les Mervelles de Rigomer) and the evolution of Celtic influences on francophone storytelling," Ph.D. diss. Harvard University archives: Dissertations, 2011.

[14] I will not discuss the Irish reception of the *Historia Brittonum*, because as far as I know the *Lebor Breatnach* did not circulate among the Normans of Ireland; see David N. Dumville, "The Textual History of Lebor Bretnach: A Preliminary Study," *Éigse* 16, no. 4 (1975-1976): 255-73.

CAMBRO-NORMAN IDENTITY

I will begin with the keen interest in the matter of Britain and Troy among the Cambro-Norman invaders of Ireland, who came from the March of Wales, as mentioned above. The first port of call is Gerald of Wales, who offers a very precise articulation of Cambro-Norman identity and background. At the outset of this article I mentioned that medieval Welsh nobility traced their descent from Troy through Aeneas and Brutus, who founded the kingdom of Britain according to the standard narrative of Welsh history. Belief in this line of descent is well-documented in medieval Welsh history and genealogy and had long-lasting resonance in Wales and the Marches. According to Gerald, as early as the late twelfth century the marcher families involved in the invasion of Ireland had adopted this identity. In the *Expugnatio Hibernica*, he articulates the 'hybrid' descent of his people from both Norman and Welsh stock. Placing words in the mouth of Robert fitz Stephen in a speech to his soldiers, he writes,

> *Troiano partim ex sanguine linea descendimus*
> *originali. Ex Gallis quoque propaginem ex parte*
> *trahimus et naturam. Hinc nobis animositas, illinc*
> *armorum usus accedit.*

> In part we come of Trojan stock [blood] by direct line of descent. But we are also partly descended from the men of Gaul, and take our character in part from them. From the former we get our courage, from the latter our skill in the use of arms.[15]

Citing their descent from the men of Troy and the men of Gaul seems to rule out the possibility that Gerald is referring to the Trojan descent of the Franks, who had a similar Trojan origin legend as the Welsh. In this passage, Victoria Flood sees "the influence of the Trojan narrative of Geoffrey's *Historia*: the conquest of Ireland is re-imagined as the British foundation legend in miniature. In this framework of imaginative engagement, Ireland is a second Britain, its conquest prophetically ratified as was the first."[16] It is perhaps ironic that the

---

[15] A.B. Scott and F.X. Martin, ed. and trans., *Expugnatio Hibernica. The Conquest of Ireland* (Dublin: Royal Irish Academy, 1978), 48/49.
[16] Victoria Flood, *Prophecy, Politics and Place in Medieval England: From Geoffrey of Monmouth to Thomas of Erceldoune* (Woodbridge: D.S. Brewer, 2016), 50.

idea of the Britons' Trojan descent is popularized in this era by Geoffrey's *De gestis Britonum*, a source Gerald otherwise criticizes, but of course he is no stranger to using source material with some degree of subterfuge. Nevertheless, this passage indicates that there was a perception in the late twelfth century that the group of Normans who settled in the March of Wales, intermarried with Welsh nobility, and then came to Ireland, had a sense of Trojan lineage.

The concept is carried forward in time by the example of the Middle English translation of the *Expugnatio Hibernica*, the *Conquest of Ireland*:

> Of the folke of Troy we ben kyndlych y-come, on þat oon half, fro þe first begynnyge; of ffraunce, we haue kynde on other half. Throgh kynd of Troy, we owe to be hardy; throgh kynd of ffraunce, we ben vsed in wepene…[17]

This translation was made, Aisling Byrne has argued, for the Geraldine earls of Kildare, descendants of some of the participants in the twelfth-century invasion of Ireland.[18] One can imagine the Geraldines of the fifteenth century identifying with their conquering Trojan forebears who came from Britain to Ireland just as Arthur did when he conquered Ireland in *De gestis Britonum*. With this concept of Trojan ancestry comes a tremendous amount of ideological baggage and a broad, accompanying political discourse, not least of which is the exceptionalism of the Fitzgerald family who can brag of this dual descent and their unique qualifications as inheritors of Brutus' kingdom. The Galfridian argument allows Gerald, and later the English translator of *Expugnatio Hibernica*, to frame the Norman conquest of Ireland as mirroring King Arthur's earlier conquest of the same island, and therefore justified.

This ideology is evident in Gerald's quotation of Geoffrey's *Prophetiae Merlini* to justify the conquest of Ireland. In a passage in *Expugnatio Hibernica*, in which Gerald explains a prophecy, Henry II

---

[17] Frederick J. Furnivall, ed., *The English Conquest of Ireland, A.D. 1166-1185* (London: Kegan Paul for the Early English Text Society, 1896), 22.
[18] Aisling Byrne, "Family, Locality, and Nationality: Vernacular Adaptations of the *Expugnatio Hibernica* in Late Medieval Ireland," *Medium Ævum* 82, no. 1 (2013): 101-18.

is implicitly identified as the sixth king mentioned in *Prophetiae Merlini*, a king who will conquer Ireland: *Quinque porciones in unum redigentur, et sextus Hiberniae moenia subvertit,* "The five parts will be reduced to one, and the sixth will overthrow the walls of Ireland."[19] Geoffrey's depiction of conquests of Ireland, first by Arthur and later by the sixth king, is a plausible explanation for why Geoffrey was not popular among the Gaelic Irish. The Cambro-Norman settlers are a different case.

In the March of Wales, Cambro-Norman engagement with their Trojan ancestry through Brutus, and with the ancient British past as outlined by Geoffrey, is not limited to Gerald of Wales, but appears to be sustained across the medieval period, particularly in sources from Glamorgan and Shropshire.[20] This interest encompasses a range of materials, including Mortimer genealogies which present the male line as descending from both Locrinus and Camber; the use of *De epitome historiae Britanniae*, a short adaptation of Geoffrey's history continued to the fourteenth century, as a preface to the Ludlow Annals, which are interested in the activities of marcher lords; copies of Anglo-Norman, Latin, and Middle English Prose *Brut* texts from the Marches; and copies of Geoffrey's Latin history from the Marches. Collectively, these texts provide evidence that marcher belief in descent from Troy and the kings of Britain was sustained across the Middle Ages. Further west in Ireland, families like the Marshals, the Mortimers, and the de Lacys held lands in Wales, Ireland, and England and traveled back and forth between their various lands. If the Cambro-Norman families saw themselves as descendants of Troy and as inheritors of the kingdom of Britain through Brutus, the circulation of Dares and Geoffrey in those regions can be seen in a different light.

The main question is whether this aspect of marcher identity–this belief in descent from Troy and Britain–is sustained in the Hiberno-Norman communities of aristocrats gradually assimilating to Irish culture, to varying degrees, during the late medieval period.

---

[19] Scott and Martin, ed. and trans., *Expugnatio Hibernica*, 96/97; see discussion in Victoria Flood, "Prophecy as History: A New Study of the Prophecies of Merlin Silvester," *Neophilologus* 102, no. 4 (2018): 543-59 at 553.

[20] See Georgia Henley, *Reimagining the Past in the Medieval Anglo-Welsh Borderlands* (forthcoming, Oxford University Press).

Additional pressing questions include: is there a sense of identity in the Hiberno-Norman communities that fuels a particular interest in Geoffrey, Dares, and the prophecies of Merlin that is discernable in the manuscript record? Was the ideology and political discourse of Geoffrey's history further used to justify the conquest of Ireland in the generations after Gerald? Given that Geoffrey, Dares, and the prophecies are everywhere in medieval Europe, do they have special resonance for these marcher communities in Ireland? These questions can be addressed through the following survey of materials. The impression that emerges from this survey is that interest in Geoffrey and Dares in Ireland is centered at Waterford and Dublin, towns at the heart of the English settlement in Ireland (though this may just be an accident of survival), and that engagement with the 'matter of Britain' in Anglo-Norman Ireland takes a different shape than in the Welsh Marches.

British History in MS Trinity College Dublin, 11500

The first item under consideration is TCD 11500, mentioned above as the *De gestis Britonum* manuscript of Irish provenance. In the fourteenth century, this manuscript was owned by St Mary's Abbey in Dublin, a Cistercian abbey with close ties to Buildwas in Shropshire, St Werburgh's in Chester, and Basingwerk in Flintshire. Its links to these abbeys would have permitted traffic in Latin books across the Irish Sea. The book may not have been created in Ireland, but some texts and annotations seem to have been added to it when it was there. Its contents are as follows:

- Unidentified religious poem (f. 1r)
- Aristotle, *De natura animalium* (ff. 3–14v)
- Dares Phrygius, *De excidio Troiae historia* (ff. 15r–27r)
- First Variant Version of Geoffrey of Monmouth's *De gestis Britonum* (ff. 27v–111r)
- Commentary on Prophecies of Merlin (ff. 111v–117v)
- Miscellaneous texts (ff. 118–123)
- Gerald of Wales, *Topographia Hibernica* (ff. 124–162v)

- Gerald of Wales, *Expugnatio Hibernica* (ff. 162v–207r)
- Miscellaneous texts (ff. 207–208)

When taken as a codicological whole, a compilatory argument emerges. In the *Expugnatio Hibernica*, Gerald of Wales argues for the conquest of Ireland and promotes the actions of his relatives taking part in the invasion. He justifies Henry II and the Geraldines' presence there and asks King John not to neglect the country. Most of all he praises the role of his own family members, and seeks to correct some perceived wrongs in the historical record. With Dares and Geoffrey in this manuscript as well, the significance of some of Gerald's comments about the invaders of Ireland is heightened. The conquerors come from Britain; they are the descendants of the people described in Geoffrey and Dares. Gerald presents them as such in the speech by Robert fitz Stephen, as discussed previously, reminding the soldiers of their descent from Troy. In short, the narrative in *De gestis Britonum* reinforces the argument being made in the *Expugnatio*.

What makes this manuscript particularly interesting, and not just another manuscript that simply reflects contemporary interest in these texts, is its readerly interpretation, specifically the miscellaneous texts that are added to blank pages after the manuscript was put together. These include the short prophetical poem *Regnum Scotorum*, or "Song on the Kings of Scotland," and a preliminary version of the Ordinances of 1311. These miscellaneous texts were added to the very end of quire 11 and the beginning of quire 12, each in a different hand (see Figure 1).[21] The prophetical poem *Regnum Scotorum* is written in one column following the conclusion of the commentary on the *Prophetiae Merlini* at the end of quire 11.[22] The Ordinances of 1311 begin the next quire, quire 12, which consists of miscellaneous short texts that do not seem to be part of the original design of the manuscript.

---

[21] For a full codicology, see Henley, "Transnational Book Traffic," 143.
[22] For digital images of ff. 117v and 118r, see the digitized manuscript, *Digital Collections: The Library of Trinity College Dublin*, accessed December 7, 2021, https://digitalcollections.tcd.ie/concern/works/ft848s23x?locale=zh.

Quire 11, ff. 105–117
- End of First Variant Version of *De gestis Britonum* (ff. 105–111r, main hand 5)
- Short commentary on the *Prophetiae Merlini* (ff. 111v–117va, main hand 5)
- *Regnum Scotorum* / Song on the Kings of Scotland (f. 117vb, marginal hand A)

Quire 12, ff. 118–123
- Ordinances of 1311 (ff. 118r–120r, marginal hand B)
- Verses on the Sybils (f. 120va, marginal hand C)
- Blank folios (ff. 120vb–123r)
- Quotes from Statius, Ovid, and Juvenal pulled from the first preface of *Topographia Hibernica* and annotated (f. 123v, marginal hand D)

Figure 1: Contents of quires 11 and 12

The Topographia Hibernica begins on the next folio, at the beginning of Quire 13. Marginal hand D has pulled quotes of classical authors from the text on f. 124r and written them on the previously blank f. 123v.

An important question to address before interpreting these marginalia as part of an Irish Cistercian readership is: can we prove they were written into this manuscript while it was in Ireland? It is unclear whether the manuscript itself was written in Ireland–it could have been brought over from Britain. It was at St Mary's Dublin in the fourteenth century, when the contents list on f. 2v and the *ex libris* mark on f. 210r was were made, and in the fifteenth century, when an additional *ex libris* mark was added to f. 2v. Its next known owner after St Mary's Dublin was Redmond O'Gallagher, bishop of Killala from 1545–69. The book was brought to England after the Dissolution and was bound together in the seventeenth century in the library of James Ley (1550–1629).[23]

Regnum Scotorum would have been added to quire 11 (by marginal hand A) in the fifteenth century, possibly when it was still at St Mary's, and very probably while still in Ireland, because the book

---

[23] For list of owners, see Meehan, "Fourteenth-Century Historical Compilation," 272.

is not known to have left Ireland until after the Dissolution. But it is not clear when quire 12 was written and bound into the manuscript. The texts written in marginal hands B–D do not appear in the fourteenth-century contents list from St Mary's Dublin, suggesting they were not there at that time, which is consistent with the dates of the hands, or that they were not important enough to be listed. Marginal hands B–D are fifteenth century, so one is tempted to assume that they (and quire 12) were added while the manuscript was at St Mary's, or perhaps somewhere else in Ireland before it was owned by Redmond O'Gallagher, bishop of Killala, in the mid-sixteenth century.[24] But we cannot be certain that quire 12 was added to the book any time before the date of the seventeenth-century binding. A possibility remains open, therefore, that quire 12 was created outside of Ireland, the most likely alternative being England. This skepticism reveals the very high bar of proof, in manuscript studies, required to place Latin texts' point of origin in Ireland. Without the presence of a Celtic vernacular language or Irish minuscule script, England is often the default provenance for Latin texts written in gothic or Anglicana hands–despite the fact that people trained in those hands did reside in monastic houses and lay households in Anglo-Norman Ireland. For the purposes of this article, therefore, I will entertain the possibility that the marginal texts in quire 12 were added to the manuscript in Ireland. At the very least, discussion of *Regnum Scotorum* and the preliminary version of the Ordinances of 1311 will help us gain a better understanding of a contemporary reader's interpretation of Geoffrey and Gerald in this manuscript.

Regnum Scotorum, the prophetic poem that follows the commentary on the *Prophetiae Merlini* in TCD 11500, was composed in 1307 shortly after Edward I died.[25] It appears in manuscripts mostly

---

[24] For fifteenth-century hands, see Jean F. Preston and Laetitia Yeandle, *English Handwriting, 1400-1650: An Introductory Manual* (Binghamton: Medieval & Renaissance Texts & Studies, 1992).

[25] It is edited by Thomas Wright, ed., *The Chronicle of Pierre de Langtoft in French Verse, from the earliest period to the death of King Edward I*, 2 vols. (London: Longmans, Green, Reader, and Dyer, 1868), II.448-50 and William F. Skene, ed., *Chronicles of the Picts, Chronicles of the Scots, and other early memorials of Scottish history* (Edinburgh: H.M. General

from northern England and the March of Wales, often with Geoffrey of Monmouth or the anti-Scottish chronicle of Pierre Langtoft. It prophesies a time when the Scots and Britons will band together to defeat the English, in the manner of Welsh prophetical poems like *Armes Prydain Fawr*, and uses animal imagery and other concepts from Prophecies of Merlin to encourage rebellion against Edward II. It makes sense that this poem would be added to a manuscript already containing Geoffrey of Monmouth's *De gestis Britonum* and *Prophetiae Merlini*. The poem *Regnum Scotorum* is written in the same vein as, perhaps even in imitation of, the *Prophetiae Merlini*, and indeed fulfills Merlin's prophecy by describing the Saxons being overcome by the Celtic peoples they had conquered:

> *Sanguine saxonico tincta rubebit humus*
> *Regnabunt Britones Albane gentis amici*
> *Antiquuum nomen insula tota feret*
> *Ut prefert aquila veteris de terre loquta*
> *Cum Scottis Britones regna paterna regent*
> *Regnabunt patria in prosperitate quieta*
> *Hostibus expulses iudicis usque diem* (ll. 36–42).

> The ground will grow red, stained with Saxon blood; the Britons will rule, friends of the Alban race; the whole island will lament the ancient name; as the eagle of the ancient land demonstrates by his word, the Britons, with the Scots, shall rule their native kingdom. They will rule their native land in peace and prosperity, having driven out all their enemies, until the Day of Judgement.[26]

Lesley Coote has interpreted this poem as anti-Scottish, arguing that the unification of Britain and Scotland is actually a message about the English ruling over Scotland: "The English believed they were the Britons, and the new overlord of the united Britain was not to be the

---

Register House, 1867), 117-18. Neither of these editions use all of the extant manuscript witnesses, and a new edition would be useful particularly due to the amount of variation between versions.

[26] Text from manuscript; translation by Lesley Coote, *Prophecy and Public Affairs in Later Medieval England* (Woodbridge: Boydell & Brewer, 2000), 72.

king of Scotland, but the king of England," because at this stage the English had fully adopted belief in Trojan descent from Brutus through Locrinus, and Edward I was supposed to unite the kingdoms.[27] Helen Fulton has connected *Regnum Scotorum* to Owain Glyn Dŵr, arguing that he may have been thinking of this very poem when he writes in a letter to Robert III of Scotland about the Welsh and the Scots banding together to be released from Saxon oppression.[28] But how would the poem be interpreted by a fourteenth- or fifteenth-century clerical audience in Dublin? Did they see themselves as English, rightfully ruling over their territory as descendants of Brutus? Or did they see themselves as oppressed by English royal power? Is there a sense of affinity with the Britons who are also being targeted by the English and therefore a worthy ally? Or, a more remote possibility, would they recognize of the common ancestry of Normans in Ireland and Wales, both of whom are feeling the overreach of the Edwards? If one entertains the possibility that the poem was present in the manuscript while it was in Dublin, its presence suggests that readerly engagement with the prophecies of Merlin in this context was very much focused on politics in Britain. The poem's view is eastward, even as the manuscript is of Irish provenance.

In TCD 11500, *Regnum Scotorum* faces a preliminary version of the Ordinances of 1311 on the following folio, a set of reforms that sought to limit Edward II's power. Michael Prestwich argues they were inspired by resentment about taxation and favoritism of Piers Gaveston, who was sent into exile and made the Lord Lieutenant of Ireland in 1308.[29] They were repealed in 1322 by the Statute of York but seem to have had lasting political relevance, having been written in TCD 11500 in the fifteenth century. It makes sense that this text, too, would be written here in the manuscript because like *Regnum*

---

[27] Coote, *Prophecy and Public Affairs*, 72.

[28] Helen Fulton, "Owain Glyndŵr and the Prophetic Tradition," in *Owain Glyndŵr: A Casebook*, ed. Michael Livingston and John K. Bollard (Liverpool: Liverpool University Press, 2013), 475-88, at 481.

[29] Michael Prestwich, "The Ordinances of 1311 and the Politics of the Early Fourteenth Century," in *Politics and Crisis in Fourteenth-Century England*, ed. John Taylor and Wendy Childs (Wolfeboro Falls, NH: A. Sutton, 1990), 1-18.

Scotorum it opposes the overreach of English royal power, though in a more practical sense than the verse prophecy.

Another interesting piece of marginalia in this manuscript is a passage from the *Topographia Hibernica* that has been added immediately after the end of the *Expugnatio* on ff. 207rb–207va.[30] This version of *Expugnatio Hibernica* ends with Gerald of Wales' letter to King John, in which he exhorts John to remember Ireland and the courageous Fitzgeralds who conquered it, but are being unfairly misremembered by their enemies. The paragraphs added after the end of the *Expugnatio* are, specifically, *Topographia* iii.39–40, describing the conquest of Ireland by Gurmundus and the death of Turgesius. In this passage in the *Topographia*, Gerald is once again using Geoffrey of Monmouth as a source, taking information from *De gestis Britonum* XI.8:

> *UNDE IN HIBERNIAM VEL BRITANNIAM GURMUNDUS ADVENERIT. In Britannica legitur historia, Gurmundum ab Affrica in Hiberniam advectum, et inde in Britanniam a Saxonibus accitum, Cirecestriam obsidione cinxisse: qua tandem capta, et passerum, ut fertur, maleficio igne succensa, ignobili quoque tunc Britonum rege Keredicio in Kambriam expulso, totius regni dominium in brevi obtinuisse. Sive ergo Affricanus, seu, quod verius esse videtur, Norwagiensis fuerit, vel in Hibernia nunquam fuit, vel, relicto ibidem Turgesio, modici temporis in ea moram fecit.*

> WHENCE GURMUNDUS CAME INTO IRELAND OR BRITAIN. In the British history, we read that Gurmundus came to Ireland from Africa, and thence, having been summoned by the Saxons, besieged Cirencester and took it. Kedericius, then the unworthy king of the Britons, was driven to Wales, and in a short time Gurmundus came to rule the whole

---

[30] For digital images of ff. 207r and 207v, see the digitized manuscript at *Digital Collections: The Library of Trinity College Dublin*, accessed December 7, 2021, https://digitalcollections.tcd.ie/concern/works/ft848s23x?locale=zh.

kingdom. Whether, then, Gurmundus was an African, or, as is more probable, a Norwegian, either he never was in Ireland, or was there for a short time only and left Turgesius behind him.

QUALITER, INTERFECTO IN GALLIA GURMUNDO, TURGESIUS IN HIBERNIA DOLO PUELLARUM DELUSUS OCCUBUIT. Gurmundo itaque in Galliarum partibus interfecto, et barbarorum jugo a Britannicis collis ea occasione jam depulso, gens Hibernica ad consuetas artis iniquae decipulas non inefficaci molimine statim recurrit. Cum igitur ea tempestate filiam regis Medensis, scilicet Omachlachelini, Turgesius adamasset, rex ille, virus sub pectore versans, filiam suam ipsi concedens, ad insulam quamdam Mediae, in stagno scilicet Locherino, illam cum quindecim puellis egregiis ei missurum se spopondit. Quibus et Turgesius gavisus, cum totidem nobilioribus gentis suae, statuto die et loco obviam venit. Et inveniens in insula quindecim adolescentes imberbes, animosos, et ad hoc electos, sub habitu puellari dolum palliantes, cultellis, quos occulte secum attulerant, statim inter ipsos amplexus Turgesius cum suis occubuit.

HOW [WITH] GURMUNDUS HAVING BEEN KILLED IN GAUL TURGESIUS DIED IN IRELAND, HAVING BEEN DECEIVED BY WHAT APPEARED TO BE GIRLS. When Gurmundus, therefore, was killed in Gaul and as a result the yoke of the barbarians was removed from British necks, the Irish people immediately had recourse once again to its accustomed practices in the evil art of deceit–and not without success. Turgesius happened at the time to be very much enamoured of the daughter of Omachlachelinus, the king of Meath. The king hid his hatred in his heart, and granting the girl to Turgesius, promised to send her to him with fifteen beautiful maidens to a certain island in Meath, in the lake of Lochver. Turgesius was delighted and went to the rendezvous on the appointed day with fifteen nobles of his people. They encountered on the island, decked out in girls' clothes to practise their deceit, fifteen young men, shaven of their beards, full of spirit, and especially picked for the job. They carried knives hidden on their persons, and with these they killed Turgesius and his companions in the midst of their embraces.[31]

Of course, the entire *Topographia* also appears in this manuscript, but these two chapters have been copied onto this page and the following page. This decision seems random, but at closer examination reveals a potential purpose.

At this point in the *Topographia*, Gerald is engaging in a larger survey of the successive invasions of Ireland: first by the Norwegians, led by Turgesius; then Gurmundus; later the Norwegians again; and finally by Henry II. Gerald is justifying Henry II's actions in the 1170s by showing he is just one of many invaders of Ireland throughout history. Gerald is also trying to reconcile the fact that Geoffrey says that Gurmundus conquered Ireland, while Irish sources say that Turgesius conquered Ireland, and neither mentions the other. Gerald then describes the death of Turgesius at the hands of treacherous Irishmen dressed as maidens. I would guess that a scribe has included this passage immediately after the conclusion to the *Expugnatio* because of the thematic similarities to that text. The scribe may have wanted to sketch out the broader historical context of invasions of Ireland next to the *Expugnatio*, rounding out the information it provides about the Norman invasion specifically. Gurmundus's invasion from Britain provides further precedent for and parallels to the Norman invasion detailed in the *Expugnatio*. In sum, the evidence of TCD 11500 suggests keen interest in British and Trojan history on the part of readers at or for St Mary's Abbey in Dublin, combined with

---

[31] Gerald of Wales, *Topographia Hibernica* iii.39-40, ed. J.F. Dimock, *Giraldi Cambrensis Opera*, 5 (London: Longmans, Green, Reader, and Dyer, 1868), 184-85; translated by John J. O'Meara, *The History and Topography of Ireland* (New York: Penguin Books, 1982), 120-21. The additions from *Topographia Hibernica* conclude two-thirds of the way down column a of TCD 11500, f. 207v. Column b is filled with hymns to St Catherine in marginal hand E.

a dislike of royal power that is rooted in an understanding of British and Irish exceptionalism.

British and Trojan History in Francophone Ireland

To turn to the broader landscape of francophone Ireland's interest in the "matter of Britain": further interest in Trojan and British history on the part of Hiberno-Norman colonists is evident in the late thirteenth- or early fourteenth-century translation into French of Dares Phrygius' *De excidio Troiae* by Jofroi of Waterford, whom Keith Busby has recently argued was working in Waterford, not Paris as previously thought.[32] This translation, *La gerre de Troi*, survives in a single manuscript contemporary to the author (France, Bibliotheque nationale, fr. 1822) alongside his other translations, which were for a patron.[33] Jofroi was a Dominican of St Saviour's or possibly a Franciscan working in Waterford, "a centre of Francophone culture."[34] Busby demonstrates that *La gerre de Troi* is a fairly direct translation from a Latin text, and Louis Faivre D'Arcier has worked out that it is most similar to an English group of *De excidio* manuscripts.[35] This makes sense because such a copy could easily travel from England to Waterford across the Irish Sea. In the absence of secure Irish provenance of any of the Latin manuscripts of Dares other than TCD 11500, this is an important attestation of interest in the story of Troy in Hiberno-Norman Ireland. To this we can add the fifteenth-century list of books from the library of the earls of Kildare, recently studied by Aisling Byrne.[36] Their library, now completely lost, apparently contained copies of Raoul Lefèvre's *Le recueil des histoires de Troyes*

---

[32] Keith Busby, ed., *The French Works of Jofroi de Waterford* (Turnhout: Brepols, 2020); Busby, *French in Medieval Ireland*, 152-67; see also Mullally, "Hiberno-Norman Literature and its Public," 330-32.

[33] For digitized manuscript, see https://gallica.bnf.fr/ark:/12148/btv1b8425997k/f16.item, accessed 7 December 2021.

[34] Busby, ed., *French Works of Jofroi de Waterford*, 12.

[35] Louis Faivre d'Arcier, *Histoire et géographie d'un mythe: la circulation des manuscrits du De excidio troiae de Darès le Phrygien (VIIIe-XVe siècles)*, Mémoires et documents de l'Ecole des chartes, 82 (Paris: École des Chartes, 2006).

[36] Aisling Byrne, "The Earls of Kildare and their Books at the End of the Middle Ages," *The Library* 14, no. 2 (2013): 129-53.

and Lydgate's *Siege and Destruction of Troy*, as well as Chaucer's *Troilus and Criseyde*, a romance (*Lancelot du Lac*) and possibly Malory's *Le Morte d'Arthur*. Gaelic readerly communities in Ireland were also interested in the story of Troy in the fourteenth century in the form of *Togail Troí*, as previously discussed, and reworked it at this time to accommodate Guido delle Colonne and Benoît de Sainte-Maure as sources.[37]

Unlike Gerald of Wales, Jofroi de Waterford does not make any explicit connections to the Trojan ancestry of the Normans in Ireland, and there are no marginalia in BNF fr. 1822 other than ownership inscriptions. Because of this, we cannot make any definite conclusions that the text's Hiberno-Norman readers sustained the interest in their Trojan heritage that had been expressed by Gerald of Wales. I suspect that the translation reflects interest in the story of Troy comparable to elsewhere in Europe. Erich Poppe has said similarly:

> In the book of Leinster, [*Togail Troí*] serves as an extended analogue and as a mirror image to events in Irish pre-history. In contrast to the situation particularly in Wales . . . where the destruction of Troy had some relevance for contemporary national and individual history, the story of Troy remained an event in classical antiquity and basically unrelated to the myths of Irish origins, and it therefore did not acquire a narrative continuation connecting it to medieval Irish history.[38]

That said, Hiberno-Norman communities exhibited keen interest in the politics of Britain. Given the Galfridian ideologies that medieval British politics sometimes included, such engagement may have fueled their interest in prophecies of Merlin.

An additional attestation of interest in Troy at Waterford in the fourteenth century is the appearance of short excerpts from the concluding paragraph of Dares' *De excidio Troiae* in London, British Library, Harley 913, a miscellany from fourteenth-century Waterford

---

[37] Clarke, "International Influences," 81-83.
[38] Poppe, "Matter of Troy," 271.

known as the 'Kildare Lyrics.'[39] This manuscript is similar in thematic interest and multilingualism to the miscellanies created by the Harley scribe in Ludlow, Shropshire, between 1314 and 1349.[40] The Harley 913 miscellany, probably written by a Franciscan, contains a wide range of texts in English, Latin, and French, including the important French poem composed in Ireland called "The Walling of New Ross" and the Middle English poem "The Land of Cockaygne."[41] The excerpts from Dares in this manuscript (ff. 40r–40v) consist of the concluding sentences of *De excidio Troiae* and a list of Trojan and Greek characters and casualties. The paragraph from Dares reads,

---

[39] This miscellany is rather better studied than some of the other materials discussed here. See Deborah L. Moore, "Medieval *convivium*, Anglo-Irish Style in London, British Library, MS Harley 913," *Early Middle English* 1, no. 2 (2019): 73-81; Deborah L. Moore, *Medieval Anglo-Irish Troubles: A Cultural Study of BL MS Harley 913* (Turnhout: Brepols, 2016); Thorlac Turville-Petre, ed., *Poems from BL MS Harley 913, 'The Kildare manuscript'*, Early English Text Society, o.s. 345 (Oxford: Oxford University Press for Early English Text Society, 2015); Alan John Fletcher, "The Date of London, British Library, Harley MS 913 (the 'Kildare Poems')," *Medium Ævum* 79, no. 2 (2010): 306-10; John J. Thompson, "Mapping Points West of West Midlands Manuscripts and Texts: Irishness(es) and Middle English Literary Culture," in *Essays in Manuscript Geography: Vernacular Manuscripts of the English West Midlands from the Conquest to the Sixteenth Century*, ed. Wendy Scase, Medieval Texts and Cultures of Northern Europe, 10 (Turnhout: Brepols, 2007); Neil Cartlidge, "Festivity, Order, and Community in Fourteenth-Century Ireland: The Composition and Contexts of BL MS Harley 913," *Yearbook of English Studies* 33 (2003): 33-52; Mullally, "Hiberno-Norman Literature and its Public," 332-33.
[40] For discussion, see *Studies in the Harley Manuscript: The Scribes, Contents, and Social Contexts of British Library MS Harley 2253*, ed. Susanna Fein (Kalamazoo: Medieval Institute Publications, 2000).
[41] For "The Walling of New Ross," see Busby, *French in Medieval Ireland*, 107-27; Diane Peters Auslander, "The Walling of New Ross, 1265: Multilingualism, Ethnicity, and Urban Politics in Post-Invasion Ireland," in *Multilingualism in the Middle Ages and Early Modern Age: Communication and Miscommunication in the Premodern World*, ed. Albrecht Classen, Fundamentals of Medieval and Early Modern Culture, 17 (Berlin: De Gruyter, 2016), 85-102.

Pugnatum est annis .x. mensibus. vii. diebus .xii. ad Trojam, ruerunt ex Argivis, sicut acta diurna indicant, quae Dares Phrygius scripsit, dccc.lxxxvi. hominum, et ex Troianis ruerunt, usque ad opidum proditum circiter dc.lxxvii. hominum opido prodito, cc.lxxvii. Eneas nauibus profectus quibus Alexander in Graeciam ierat, numero .xxii., quem omnis etas circiter .iii.cccc. sedita est. Antenorem secuti sunt .ii. quingenti. Andromachen et Helenum .i.cc. hucusque historia Daretis scripta est.

The war against Troy lasted for ten years, seven months, and twelve days. According to the journal which Dares Phrygius wrote, 886,000 Greeks were killed, and up until the forfeiture of the city, 678,000 Trojan men were killed, and with the city forfeited, 278,000. Æneas departed with the ships which Alexander had sailed to Greece, twenty-two in number, with around 3,400 people of all ages. Antenor was followed by 2,500, Andromache and Helenus by 1,200. Up to this point the history of Dares was written.[42]

The passage has a heading, *Troia*, at the top of the page. It is preceded by a poem on the Crucifixion and followed by a list of Franciscan houses in Ireland, and there are no marginalia. In other words, the manuscript context does not reveal much about what the Trojan war meant to the scribe or to the reader. The manuscript also contains an excerpt of the prophetic poem *Regnum Scotorum* discussed above, on f. 53v in a marginal hand. The excerpt in Harley 913 is just interested in the part of the poem where the Scots and British are banding together to expel the English. This correlates intriguingly with the appearance of the poem in TCD 11500. The fact that this poem appears in one monastic manuscript from Dublin and one lay manuscript from Waterford suggests at the very least that English settlers in Ireland were very much interested in political events in

---

[42] London, British Library, Harley 913, f. 40r; my transcription and translation.

Britain. Whether these readers were identifying with the Saxons in this poem or with the Welsh and Scots is an open question.

The Prophecies of Merlin in Ireland

I will conclude this article with a few examples of prophecies of Merlin from Ireland (the genre, not the actual *Prophetiae Merlini* in *De gestis Britonum*). First, a copy of the *Prophecy of the Six Kings to Follow John* survives in Cambridge, Corpus Christi College, 405, another fourteenth-century manuscript from Waterford, owned by the Knights Hospitaller. This manuscript is a composite, with an eclectic range of contents, including a monastic calendar and liturgical offices, Latin documents relating to the borough of Waterford, and a number of Anglo-Norman French texts, such as a translation of the *Vision of Paul*.[43] It has been speculated that some parts of it were copied in south-east England and then brought to Waterford, specifically to the Knights Hospitaller community, or perhaps it was created in Waterford entirely.[44] *Six Kings to Follow John* was a very popular set of prophecies in medieval Britain, found in Latin, Middle English, Welsh, and French versions.[45] The text was written in the late fourteenth century in Northern England and supported the stepping down of Edward II and the accession of his son.[46] Victoria Flood argues that it was popular in Northern England due to the perception that Edward II was not adequately containing the Scottish threat at the

---

[43] For discussion, see Busby, *French in Medieval Ireland*, 146-51; Colmán Ó Clabaigh, "Prayer, Politics, and Poetry: Cambridge, Corpus Christi 405 and the Templars and Hospitallers at Kilbarry, Co. Waterford," in *Soldiers of Christ: The Knights Templar and the Knights Hospitaller in Medieval Ireland*, ed. Martin Brown and Colmán Ó Clabaigh (Dublin: Four Courts Press, 2016), 206-17; Mullally, "Hiberno-Norman Literature and its Public," 335-38; Keith V. Sinclair, "Anglo-Normans at Waterford: The Mute Testimony of MS Cambridge, Corpus Christi College 405," in *Medieval French Textual Studies in Memory of T.B.W. Reid*, ed. Ian Short, Anglo-Norman Text Society, Occasional Publications Series, 1 (London: Anglo-Norman Text Society, 1984), 219-38.
[44] See discussion in Ó Clabaigh, "Prayer, Politics, and Poetry," 211-12.
[45] A copy of this text from London, British Library, Harley 746 is edited by Rupert Taylor, *The Political Prophecy in England* (New York: Columbia University Press, 1911), 160-64.
[46] Flood, *Prophecy, Politics and Place*, 87.

border.[47] The version in this manuscript is French, suggesting an upper-class lay audience.[48] Robert the Bruce's flight to Ireland in 1306 may have increased the significance of this political prophecy for readers in Ireland.

Second, the *Prophecies of John of Bridlington* survives in Cambridge, University Library, Add. 3392, another manuscript owned by St Mary's Abbey Dublin.[49] This is a fourteenth-century manuscript interested in history: it also contains Gerald's *Expugnatio*, Henry of Huntingdon's *Historia Anglorum*, Higden's *Polychronicon*, and other materials. The *Prophecies of John of Bridlington* is also a widely popular prophetical text, written in Latin, originally from Yorkshire, that refers to events from the reign of Edward III, prophesying who his successor will be. The presence of the *Prophecies of John of Bridlington* at St Mary's Abbey indicates contemporary, eastward-facing interest in royal politics on the part of this religious institution. This manuscript also contains a short chronicle that details the landing of Edward the Bruce in Ireland until his death in 1318, which perhaps puts the prophecies into context.

Conclusion

In sum, my short survey of Dares, Geoffrey, and the prophecies of Merlin in Irish manuscripts reveals interest not only in the historic 'matter of Britain' but in popular, contemporary prophecies about the Edwardian kings of England and the Anglo-Scottish wars, suggesting that Hiberno-Norman readers were very engaged in conflicts of the day. Their interest in prophecies and in Trojan and British history more generally corresponds to the same interest on the part of readers in the March of Wales, at least to a certain extent. There are many attestations of similar interests in Merlinic prophecies and in British and Welsh history in Anglo-Welsh manuscripts from the Welsh Marches, such as in London, British Library, Royal 12 C. xii (written

---

[47] Flood, *Prophecy, Politics and Place*, 94.
[48] Flood, *Prophecy, Politics and Place*, 88.
[49] This text is edited by Thomas Wright, *Political Poems and Songs relating to English history, composed during the period from the accession of Edw. III. to that of Ric. III.*, 2 vols. (London: Longman, Green, Longman, and Roberts, 1859-61), I.128-211.

by the Harley Lyrics scribe in Ludlow) or Aberystwyth, National Library of Wales, Peniarth 50 (a collection of Welsh prophecies and other texts).

But there is one key difference: in the Welsh Marches, interest in Trojan and Galfridian history was stimulated by marcher aristocrats' belief in their own Trojan and British ancestry, which elevated them and made them exceptional as continuers of the line of British kings, with a right to rule over their conquered Welsh and Irish territories. The engagement, in Anglo-Norman Ireland, with prophecies of Merlin and associated texts, and with the histories of Geoffrey and Dares, is consistent with the circulation of these texts in the March of Wales, but perhaps with a different overall view. The presence of these materials in Waterford and Dublin, occurring in both monastic and personal lay miscellanies, suggests that reading communities in francophone Waterford and Dublin were indeed interested in the broader political scene in fourteenth-century Britain. They were "eastward facing" in their interest in Merlin's prophecies and engaged in the Anglo-Scottish politics of their day. This engagement must have fostered a network of transmission, an Irish sea network of sorts, between communities in Ireland and Britain. But the textual examples surveyed here do not indicate that Hiberno-Norman readers had any special relationship with British or Trojan history that set them apart from other populations. In this, the Hiberno-Norman community differs from its counterpart in the March of Wales, where francophone aristocrats sustained a keen interest in Galfridian history throughout the Middle Ages. In other words, the political discourse, ideology, and rhetoric offered by Geoffrey's tales of Arthur and Gurmundus' conquests of Ireland may have propelled the ideological arguments for the initial Anglo-Norman colonization of Ireland, but an understanding of Trojan and British origins was not sustained by later generations of Hiberno-Norman families, in the same way it was in the Welsh Marches, where being descended from the kings of Britain was conceptually much more important. This small sampling of Dares, Geoffrey, and prophecies of Merlin in Ireland has begun to answer some questions about the differences between Hiberno-Norman identity and Cambro-Norman identity, as shown by their engagement with popular history in the fourteenth and fifteenth centuries.

GEORGIA HENLEY

Acknowledgements

I am very grateful to the audience of the 40th Annual Harvard Celtic Colloquium on October 9, 2021, for their helpful and interesting comments on a version of this paper, to Patrick Wadden and Lindy Brady for answering preliminary questions I had about the topic, and to Paul Russell for discussions of TCD 11500. All errors are my own.

'Cronnack an hager dhu'
Sign of a flourishing language? Efforts to Advance Cornish by the Cornish Language Community in the COVID-19 Pandemic

Kensa Broadhurst

Previous studies of the history of the Cornish language[1] in education notably include MacKinnon for the Government Office of the South-West, and Sayers et al, for the European Research Centre on Multilingualism and Language Learning.[2] Ferdinand examined public views on the status of the language in education in the twenty-first century, and Cornwall Council produces both five-year strategic and annual operational plans.[3] This paper aims to report on the most up-to-date position of formal and informal teaching of Cornish, including the expansion made possible through the movement to online classes necessitated by national lockdowns implemented in the United Kingdom brought about by the onset of the COVID-19 pandemic in the Spring of 2020, and the introduction of a new undergraduate course. It also aims to describe efforts to professionalise the language community through training and the creation of new resources. Finally, it outlines issues to consider in both the immediate and longer-term future, including what needs to occur for the language to gain a greater presence in schools, further and higher education.

---

[1] 'Ugly black toad', an insult supposedly used by Dolly Pentreath, the so-called last speaker of the Cornish language. Reported in William Bottrell, *Traditions and Hearthside Stories of West Cornwall*, vol. 1. (Penzance: Bottrell, 1870), 184. It is also the symbol of a badge used to indicate the wearer is a Cornish speaker.

[2] Ken MacKinnon, *An Independent Academic Study on Cornish* (Plymouth: Government Office for the South-West, 2000).
Dave Sayers, Merryn Davies-Deacon, and Sarah Croome, *The Cornish Language in Education in the UK* (Mercator: European Research Centre on Multilingualism and Language Learning, 2018).

[3] Siarl Ferdinand, *Introducing Cornish in Education,* https://www.researchgate.net/publication/344464261_Introducing_Cornish_in_education/ (Skians Conference, online, 2020).

The Cornish revival dates from the publication of Jenner's *Handbook of the Cornish Language* in 1904.[4] Classes were established in Cornwall and London, and key figures such as Robert Morton Nance and A.S.D. Smith began producing teaching materials.[5] In 1967 the *Kesva an Taves Kernewek* (Cornish Language Board) was established.[6] This undertook the examination of Cornish at three levels, the highest at a level just above O Level.[7] By the 1980s there were around twenty adult classes in Cornwall, the correspondence course *Kernewek Dre Lyther* (Cornish by letter) had been established, and examination results reflected increasing numbers of proficient speakers. In 1989 examinations were extended to a fourth-grade equivalent to A level and by 2000, the number of classes had risen to thirty-six.[8]

At the end of the 2020/21 academic year, the Cornish Language Office of Cornwall Council carried out a survey of adult education in the Cornish language through questioning class teachers.[9] One of the aims of this survey was to discover how classes and teachers had dealt with the challenges of the COVID-19 pandemic; whether they had continued in an online or hybrid fashion for example. The survey was split into four main sections: class information, student information, venue, and class administration. A survey of this kind was last undertaken at the end of the 2013/14 academic year, which makes some direct comparisons possible, although sadly a direct comparison with figures for the final pre-pandemic academic year, 2018/19, is not feasible. In 2021 responses were received from thirty-two classes, compared with twenty-three in 2014.[10] There were 217 students in 2021 taught by twenty-two different teachers, a growth compared with

---

[4] Peter Beresford Ellis, *The Cornish Language and its Literature* (London: Routledge & Kegan Paul, 1974), 153.

[5] Dee Harris, *The Cornish History Notebook* (Pool: An Kylgh Kernewek and Ors Sempel, 2016), 42.

[6] Sayers et al, *The Cornish Language in Education*, 7.

[7] MacKinnon, *Study on Cornish*, 42.

[8] MacKinnon, *Study on Cornish*, 44.

[9] Mark Trevethan, Cornish Language Class Survey: 2021 Report (Truro: Cornwall County Council, 2021).

[10] Trevethan, *Cornish Language Class Survey*, 4.

the twelve teachers surveyed in 2014.[11] This shows a positive trend in both the availability of classes and people willing to teach Cornish which will hopefully continue. Classes were based at fifteen different locations around Cornwall, as well as in London.[12] These referred to the physical locations which teachers would have used, had in-person teaching been possible for the academic year, or where they were able to return to some level of face-to-face sessions. Of the 217 students in the 2021 survey, eighty-five were beginners and sixty-five learning at an intermediate level. There were fifty-four students at a high level and twenty-three students were fluent speakers who continue to attend classes.[13] Whilst this breakdown shows healthy numbers both beginning to learn the language, and continuing with their studies, the breakdown of student ages is less healthy for the future of the language. Of the 217 students, eighty were aged over 60, sixty aged 41-60, thirty-three aged 25-40 and only nine aged 17-25; however, not all classes reported the information for this question. This places 65 percent of all reported learners over the age of 41.[14]

Overall numbers of students show a marked increase from the 2014 survey, which reported forty-four beginners and thirty intermediate students. There is less change in numbers of advanced students from 2014, which reported thirty-nine, and the twenty-seven fluent speakers who continued to attend classes was actually a higher number than the figure for 2021.[15] What is not evident from the figures is anecdotal evidence that as classes moved online, some higher-level students preparing to sit exams took the opportunity to attend more than one class during the week. By doing so, these particular students were able to make the move to online learning benefit them, perhaps as a way of counter-acting any perceived impairment from the loss of face-to-face teaching. Student numbers did fluctuate over the 2020/21 academic year and teachers were asked to cite reasons for this. Some students started later in the academic year, often after deciding to take up the language following taster sessions at special events.[16] In the

---

[11] Trevethan, *Cornish Language Class Survey*, 7.
[12] Trevethan, *Cornish Language Class Survey*, 4.
[13] Trevethan, *Cornish Language Class Survey*, 7.
[14] Trevethan, Cornish Language Class Survey, 7.
[15] Trevethan, Cornish Language Class Survey, 7.
[16] Trevethan, *Cornish Language Class Survey*, 8.

summer of 2020, a concerted effort was made by, amongst others, teachers from *An Kylgh Kernewek* (The "Cornish Circle") [a teaching group based around Redruth] and the Cornish Language Office to run online taster sessions after concerns that those usual events where classes could be promoted, through having an informational stall at feast days and agricultural shows for example, had all been cancelled due to the ongoing health crisis. These taster sessions were a new initiative created in direct response to the challenges the on-going pandemic brought with regards to promotion of classes and recruitment of students. These online taster sessions were promoted through the use of social media, especially Facebook pages dealing with Cornish topics. This meant taster sessions were available to potential students both within and without Cornwall. Perhaps one possible area for future research is asking those students who took up online Cornish lessons during the pandemic why they did so. Possible reasons might include: a specific link to Cornwall, being of Cornish heritage, usually being unable to access in-person classes due to geographical location, or a wish to use the extra time created by the national lockdowns for an educational purpose. Further research on whether or not online attendance in classes dropped once the United Kingdom came out of lockdowns would also be of great interest and relevance.

That numbers of actual students did fluctuate over the course of the academic year, and the difficulties of teaching large numbers together in the same online session provides an argument for extra beginners' classes starting in January in addition to September, the traditional start of the academic year, to deal with demand. Staggering start dates would help both teachers and students by avoiding the need to accommodate beginners at different stages in the same class. Students also left classes, citing reasons such as time commitments, difficulty in dealing with online learning, and confidence issues.[17] Teachers were also asked to report if they had had initial enquiries from people looking for a class which did not translate into enrolments. Reasons given for not enrolling included a lack of space within the class and attempts to enroll mid-year. This once again

---

[17] Trevethan, *Cornish Language Class Survey*, 8.

strengthens the argument for provision of classes with a January start date.[18]

Although most classes occur in the evenings, six classes were held during the daytime, compared with just two in 2014.[19] Anecdotally, some classes were offered during the day to accommodate overseas learners located in time zones to the east of Great Britain, including a cluster of new students based in Australia. Learners based in time zones to the west of Great Britain, such as the United States, were more easily able to join evening classes. Most classes take place in school term time, with only nine carrying on all year round. This has changed from 2014, where the split between term-time and all year round was 10:13.[20] There were twenty-one classes taught using the Standard Written Form (SWF) spelling system, up from six in 2014. *Kernewek Kemmyn* (Common Cornish) was used in nineteen classes, the same as in 2014, and classes were also taught in *Kernewek Unys* (Unified Cornish) and *Kernowek Standard* (Standard Cornish); one class in each spelling system in both 2014 and 2021). No classes were reported as using the pre-SWF Revived Late Cornish orthography down from two in 2014 and reported in the survey under the name Kernowek Bew.[21] However, the language group which teaches this form, *Cussel an Tavas Kernowek* (The Cornish Language Council), believes that its class has been included in the general figures for classes using the SWF orthography. Teachers were asked to report if any of their students had requested help to cover any additional needs they might have. The surveys report requests for help that include consideration of hearing loss, fatigue, arthritis, and the need for larger print.[22] The number of students asking for additional support fell from thirteen in 2014, to six in 2021. The online nature of classes made them more accessible for certain students with particular needs, especially those with mobility issues. However, provision for students with further needs remains an issue which language teachers will need to address, and for which they require additional support and training themselves. Indeed, the Kesva

---

[18] Trevethan, *Cornish Language Class Survey*, 8.
[19] Trevethan, *Cornish Language Class Survey*, 5.
[20] Trevethan, *Cornish Language Class Survey*, 6.
[21] Trevethan, *Cornish Language Class Survey*, 6.
[22] Trevethan, *Cornish Language Class Survey*, 9.

an Taves Kernewek committee has received a request from the Royal National Institute for the Blind to allow them to reproduce a recent textbook in braille.[23]

It can be argued that the switch to online learning necessitated by the national lockdowns in the United Kingdom which began in March 2020 benefitted the teaching of the Cornish language. Although Cornish teaching provision had been available outside Cornwall prior to this date through both the long-standing London Cornish class, the correspondence course Kernewek Dre Lyther and occasional classes held elsewhere, such as those in Bristol and Cardiff, widespread access to the teachers based in Cornwall (and elsewhere) was now available to those residents anywhere in the world. Although as classes such as my own initially moved online to accommodate those students who had previously attended in-person, soon it became apparent that there was a demand for students from outside Cornwall to access these. In my own class this began when a correspondence course student based in London, for whom I was acting as tutor, asked if she could join my zoom classes. Not long after this, I was contacted by an acquaintance of Cornish heritage, resident in the United States, who asked if her sister (also resident in the United States), who was already learning Cornish, could join my class. This particular student took advantage of the new access to Cornish lessons available to her to join two zoom classes based in Cornwall each week. As seen above, many of the new students now accessing online classes were based in countries traditionally associated with the Cornish Diaspora, that is, the countries to which Cornishmen emigrated during the nineteenth century, primarily because their hard rock mining skills were in demand.

Teachers were also asked to report on their intentions for the academic year 2021/22. This question was included in the survey because of the on-going uncertainty in the United Kingdom as to whether or not in-person teaching would be possible under any potential legislation put in place to respond to the on-going pandemic. Anecdotally, some teachers were also wary about returning to face-to-face teaching due to health concerns of their own. A meeting was held in the late spring of 2021 in part to discuss the issue of higher numbers

---

[23] Kesva an Taves Kernewek, *unpublished email to committee members,* October 2021.

of students from outside Cornwall taking part in classes as they moved online. In this meeting, attended by a majority of language teachers, teachers discussed which levels they would be teaching in the following academic year, and whether they were sticking to online classes or aiming to return to in-person teaching. This allowed for informal arrangements to be made in which teachers then passed students that they would no longer be able to teach for either geographical or level reasons on to other teachers, in order that all current students could be accommodated for the up-coming academic year. Nine classes were aiming to return to in-person teaching, eleven were due to stay online only, and twelve would be blended, for example teaching online for three sessions a month and meeting in person for a fourth session. [24]

With regards to the results of the teacher survey of the proposed in-person classes, eleven would teach multiple levels of students within one room, but ten of these would have multiple teachers to deal with this. In only one class would one teacher be teaching multiple levels of student simultaneously.[25] Twenty-one of the thirty-two classes surveyed are affiliated with a language organisation.[26] According to the Go Cornish website, forty-one adult education classes at all levels, and eleven *yeth an werin* (conversation classes) were being offered in the 2021/21 academic year.[27] As not all class teachers who were contacted completed the class survey in the spring of 2021, this perhaps reflects a more accurate picture of the current position with regards to the number of classes being taught.

In 2019 eighty-two candidates took language examinations across the four grades.[28] After deciding not to offer examinations in 2020 due to the uncertainty surrounding the COVID-19 pandemic and what provision might be possible, in 2021 Kesva an Taves Kernewek did offer students the chance to sit examinations once more, in their

---

[24] Trevethan, *Cornish Language Class Survey*, 10.

[25] Trevethan, *Cornish Language Class Survey*, 12.

[26] Trevethan, *Cornish Language Class Survey*, 14.

[27] "Klassow ha Bagasow (Classes and Groups)," Go Cornish website, accessed September 30, 2021, https://gocornish.org/all-learners/classes-groups/.

[28] Kesva an Taves Kernewek, *Derivas Blydhenyek 2019/ Annual Report 2019,* (Truro: Kesva an Taves Kernewek, 2020), 9.

own homes with an invigilator provided by the candidate. This relied on a level of trust in both the candidate and invigilator to run the examination in the proper format in terms of time allowed, use or otherwise of dictionaries and other prompts, and outside assistance. Oral examinations took place through the use of Zoom. The third-grade oral exam asked students to prepare a presentation on a topic released a few weeks before the examinations. There was one instance of a student putting the presentation on social media and asking for feedback; this issue needs to be addressed and provision made for alternative papers with new content or a disciplinary procedure as examinations will continue in this fashion in 2022. Eighty-three students sat examinations.[29] It is a little surprising that this number is so similar to 2019, given that candidates were unable to sit an examination in the intervening year. A possible explanation is that candidates by-passed the examination grade they might have sat in 2020 and moved on to sit the examinations for the next grade. An analysis of the numbers at each grade reveals that forty-two, or half of all candidates, sat first-grade examinations. This correlates to the reported rise in numbers of students learning Cornish as classes moved online and access to attend classes became easier for students outside Cornwall. Sixteen students sat the fourth-grade examinations, a rise on the six candidates at this level in 2019.[30] This can be ascribed to the lack of examination in 2020 causing a backlog in candidate numbers and can be regarded as a key indicator of the effect of the Coronavirus pandemic on Cornish language learners. Cornish leaners who continue with their studies are often keen to obtain their fourth-grade qualification as it is one of the pre-requisites for becoming a language bard of *Gorsedh Kernow* (the Cornish Gorsedh).

Turning to examine the status of Cornish in formal educational settings, the teaching of Cornish to pre-school children began when particular families involved in the language revival movement brought

---

[29] Kesva an Taves Kernewek, *unpublished examiner paperwork*, February - July 2021.
[30] Kesva an Taves Kernewek, *unpublished examiner paperwork*, February-July 2021.

up their children speaking Cornish at home.[31] However, momentum within the educational establishment to support these initiatives was limited. In 1979 the organisation *Dalleth* (Beginning) was founded to support both these efforts, and also those families known to be bringing up their children as bilingual. In 1980 Dalleth introduced a children's magazine, *Len ha Lyw* (Read and Colour).[32] The *Movyans Skolyow Meythrin* (Nursery Schools Movement), established the *Skol dy-Sadorn Kernewek* (Cornish Saturday School) at Cornwall College in Pool in 2010, providing a Saturday morning session for children aged two to five, and child-based Cornish lessons for parents. In 2017 the *Skol Veythrin Kerenza* (Love Nursery School) became an Ofsted-registered fully Cornish-medium day care centre for children aged up to eight, and a new location was due to open at Easter 2020.[33] Unfortunately, this did not happen due to the coronavirus pandemic, and a change in the circumstances surrounding the anticipated premises for the day care centre. Currently new premises are being adapted to host the centre, which will instead provide a bilingual nursery. In the meantime, efforts have been concentrating on providing bilingual events for families when these have been possible under the health regulations such as walks and a beach clean.[34]

Meanwhile, the Tregenna Nursery Group which owns two early years sites in St Ives and St Erth, has introduced Cornish into its daily routines.[35] A Cornish learner herself, the owner decided to introduce the language due to the importance of passing the language on to the next generation. Cornish has been embedded into the daily routine

---

[31] For a further discussion of the progress of the new initiatives in early years education see: Kensa Broadhurst, Forthcoming, "Cornish: Can an Indigenous Language become a Fixture in the Local Primary Curriculum?" in *'Other' Voices in Education-(Re)stor(y)ing Stories: Stories as an Analytical Tool*, ed. C. Blyth (Singapore: Springer Nature).

[32] MacKinnon, *Study on Cornish,* 21.

[33] Esther Johns, Trustee Movyans Skolyow Methrin, email to author, July 2020.

[34] Esther Johns, Trustee Movyans Skolyow Methrin, email to author, August 2021. This centre is due to open in September 2022.

[35] "An Mis 48," Pellwolok an Gernewegva video channel, https://www.youtube.com/watch?v=bE_Q7gYLzD8, accessed 30th August 2021.

with the use of greetings, *mar pleg* (please) and *meur ras* (thank you) at the lunchtime meals, and the inclusion of stories with key phrases in Cornish each day. These include both pre-existing stories and new ones adapted by the owner. In addition to this, sessions are held for smaller groups across the term. At each session the children produce something Cornish to take home, such as paintings with the words in Cornish, and newsletters for parents include Cornish vocabulary. In recognition of their learning children are awarded certificates in Cornish at the end of the school year at a special ceremony attended by a former Grand Bard of Gorsedh Kernow. During the national coronavirus lockdowns in 2020, videos of the stories were produced for parents to use with their children at home. The feedback from parents is positive overall. As most staff are not Cornish speakers, displays within the nursery also include phonetic spelling of the Cornish vocabulary. In the summer term 2021, thirty-five children were receiving these Cornish sessions.[36]

Before the 1980s, Cornish was reportedly taught in a handful of schools. A 1984 report on the state of the language found it was being taught in seven primary, and two secondary schools.[37] However, the introduction of the national curriculum confined any Cornish language provision to lunchtime and after school clubs. This relied on either volunteer provision or a keen teacher who was able either to speak Cornish or use the resources available. During its existence the former Cornish Language Partnership, Maga, run by Cornwall Council, sent three language learning packs to all primary schools across Cornwall. In 2012 their two part-time education officers worked with around twenty schools.[38] Maga also delivered training to teachers, providing teaching materials and some taster sessions, usually in the form of workshops. Since 2016, the company Golden Tree has been contracted by Cornwall Council to develop and support the teaching, learning, and use of Cornish. Their task has been to embed Cornish into the general curriculum across a core group of primary schools, rising from five to fifty within a five-year period.[39] In 2019 this programme ran at

---

[36] Sue Davies, owner, Tregenna Nursery Group, zoom conversation with author, September 2021.
[37] MacKinnon, *Study on Cornish*, 44.
[38] Sayers et al, *The Cornish Language in Education,* 11.
[39] Sayers et al, *The Cornish Language in Education,* 19.

eighteen schools in Penzance and Liskeard.[40] For Cornish to succeed at primary level, it needs both the support of headteachers and a teacher who is able either to speak Cornish, or to run the sessions. As yet, Cornish does not have enough of a stronghold within the primary system in Cornwall either within curriculum time, or as part of a club, due to inadequate manpower provision. However, if school staff become more willing and confident to deliver the language, and less reliant on outside providers, uptake should continue to grow. A key marker of the success of Cornish in primary schools will be the acceptance of Cornish as a language in terms of adherence to the national curriculum stipulation that "teaching may be of any modern or ancient foreign language."[41]

With the advent of the first national lockdown in March 2020, Golden Tree decided to switch and redevelop its focus with regards to supporting the use of Cornish in primary schools. Rather than concentrating on geographical clusters of primary schools, they have developed a framework "to celebrate the language in fun and immersive ways" and help schools to embed use of the language across the entire school, from curriculum topics to daily communication.[42] This framework will be offered at three levels: bronze, silver, and gold, through which schools can either work progressively or choose to stay at the initial bronze level. These require differing levels of commitment to embed Cornish within the curriculum and are designed for initial delivery by teachers or teaching assistants with no prior knowledge of the language. Support and resources are all provided for free via a secure members' website. By September 2021, twenty-nine schools had signed up to the project, which is already more than the number of schools reached by the cluster initiative.[43]

---

[40] Mark Trevethan, Cornish Language Officer, Cornwall Council, personal communication with author, September 2020.
[41] Department for Education, *Languages Programme of Study: Key Stage 2. National Curriculum in Englan,* London: DFE-00174-2013, 2013, 2.
[42] "Go Cornish for Primary Schools," Go Cornish website, accessed 20th September, 2021, https://gocornish.org/primary-schools/.
[43] Will Coleman, Artistic Director and Vicki Kent, Company Manager of Golden Tree, zoom communication with author, September 2021.

One of the key aspects Golden Tree is considering in the delivery of this project over the next eighteen months is demonstrating its sustainability. This includes dedicated Cornish language training for teachers and schools aiming to complete the silver and gold levels and embed more of the language throughout their provision. Golden Tree also aims to ask those schools signed up to the programme for feedback on what is, or is not, working within the curriculum. Through the use of tracking surveys, it will be far easier to collect and monitor data from the schools.[44] Golden Tree hopes that in comparison with the previous cluster model, this programme can be delivered in schools without direct input from Golden Tree staff members.

At secondary level, it was possible to study Cornish General Certificate of Secondary Education (GCSE) until 1996, when forty-two candidates took the examination. However, it became no longer commercially viable and was scrapped.[45] In 2000 Cornish was being taught at four secondary schools as part of a club, but as with the primary curriculum, finding space for Cornish within the secondary curriculum is all but impossible.[46] Within the national curriculum, the teaching of a modern foreign language is compulsory to the age of fourteen, with the proviso that this provides the basis for further study.[47] How, therefore, do we define Cornish within these parameters? The provision of Cornish at secondary level would require a vast increase in resources and teacher training, both of which currently rely heavily on the voluntary sector within Cornish adult education.[48] For Cornish to succeed within the state education system, it requires status, a place within the school day, properly resourced and paid peripatetic teachers, or resources and retraining for existing teachers within schools. For Cornish to be attractive to both students and teachers at a secondary level it needs to have a purpose beyond

---

[44] Will Coleman, Artistic Director and Vicki Kent, Company Manager of Golden Tree, zoom communication with author, September 2021.
[45] MacKinnon, *Study on Cornish*, 46.
[46] MacKinnon, *Study on Cornish*, 4.
[47] Department for Education, *Languages Programme of Study: Key Stage 3*. National Curriculum in England. London: DFE-00195-2013, 2013, 1.
[48] Mark Trevethan, *Strateji an yeth Kernewek Towl Oberansek 2017/18-Derivas Penn an vledhen/ Cornish Language Strategy Operational Plan 2017/18-End of Year Plan*. (Truro: Cornwall County Council, 2018), 4.

the classroom. This could include creating opportunities either for examination success or for further use beyond secondary education–within higher education or the workplace.

In the autumn of 2021, Exeter University introduced an undergraduate module, "Cornish for Beginners". Completion of this module will allow students to work towards graduating with proficiency in the Cornish language. The course is very much shaped towards teaching Cornish as a living language, fit for everyday use, although it also includes elements such as place name derivations, the history of the language, and culture in a wider context.[49] The university has also introduced an online Cornish evening class aimed at the wider staff and student population. This has proved so popular that it has been necessary to run two classes to accommodate all those who have enrolled.[50] All of the foundation work and staff meetings to develop this new module took place, by necessity, online. As these meetings involved a team of staff based at the university's campuses which are approximately one hundred miles apart, there were many benefits to this medium. Meetings could be shorter and more frequent, as necessary, rather than requiring staff members to travel. In addition to this new module, an increasing number of research students within the Institute of Cornish Studies at Exeter are now concentrating on language-based research which has not always been the case. It is hoped that this will generate even greater expansion of the language as an academic subject. There are also PhD students elsewhere, who are researching aspects of the language, often coming under the umbrella of Celtic Studies departments.

In 2018 WJEC [formerly known as the Welsh Joint Educational Committee], introduced Entry Level and Level 1 examinations in Cornish. These are pre-GCSE level qualifications also offered in other languages. These examinations were taken in 2019 by a pilot group of students attending Cornish adult education classes: twenty-six at Entry

---

[49] "Cornish for Beginners," University of Exeter website, accessed 20th September, 2021, http://humanities.exeter.ac.uk/flc/modules/PLC1130/.
[50] "Learn Cornish in your own home as part of an exciting new online course," University of Exeter website, accessed 20th September, 2021, https://www.exeter.ac.uk/news/staff/title_870214_en.html.

Level, and four at Level 1.[51] Examinations were put on hold in 2020, which has stalled the programme, but the hope is that further students will sit these and that a Level 2 Cornish qualification will be developed. Understandably, the WJEC priority has to lie with those qualifications aimed at schoolchildren and necessary for their life progression. Although this work is co-ordinated by the Cornish Language Office of Cornwall Council, the development of teaching and exam materials, and the teaching of adult education classes, is all carried out by volunteers. Most teachers are language bards of Gorsedh Kernow, who have passed the highest level of the Cornish Language Board examinations, and many are current or former teachers, although not necessarily in languages.

The year 2020 witnessed a concerted effort to support those teaching Cornish within adult education, both by providing training, especially in online teaching prompted out of necessity due to the switch to this format, and through the production of high-quality, modern resources which have been made freely available.[52] The legacy of the Cornish language revival is that many of the teaching books and resources were produced by people lacking modern pedagogical training in languages. These teaching materials were based on their memories of the language teaching received at school. This old-fashioned approach is highly skewed towards the teaching of grammar and does not consider more recent developments in the teaching of languages, including the teaching of listening and speaking skills and the use of modern technologies. As the 2021 class survey results showed, one of the reasons students gave up learning Cornish was a lack of confidence. This is certainly something I have seen in the beginner classes I teach. Students arrive reporting that they hated languages at school, and were no good at them, therefore they were already expecting to do badly at Cornish. If they are then taught in a manner and with materials which remind them of their school experience this is only going to exacerbate their lack of confidence.

---

[51] Mark Trevethan, *Strateji an yeth Kernewek Towl Oberansek 2019/20-Derivas Penn an vledhen/ Cornish Language Strategy Operational Plan 2097/20-End of Year Plan* (Truro: Cornwall County Council, 2020), 8.
[52] "Dyskans/ Learning", Kesva an Taves Kernewek/ Cornish Language Board website, accessed 21st September, 2021, https://kesva.org/learning.

Thus, the modernisation of Cornish language teaching and teaching resources could also serve to break this negative cycle of expectation.

An internet search of resources for independent Cornish study does result in many options. However, for someone with no prior knowledge of the language, there are no obvious means of judging the quality of these resources, their provenance in many cases, and which orthography they use. Therefore, someone could select poor quality resources, or resources which use different spelling systems and become easily put off or confused. Steps are being taken to rectify this by introducing a branded Learn Cornish range of websites linked both physically and visually to aid those looking for information. This grouping will hopefully include websites hosted by the principal language organisations and the Cornish Language Office.[53]

How can the language community support the future growth of Cornish in formal education? Efforts are currently underway to modernise and professionalise the teaching of Cornish in adult education, to increase the availability of the language at the pre-school level, and to provide some availability at primary level. The language movement now needs to consider what benefits it can offer to secondary, further, and higher education. If the number of candidates taking the WJEC examinations continues to rise, a new GCSE might be possible, which in turn could lead to A Level provision. This could be an attractive proposition to adult learners, as well as schools. However, the availability of teachers capable of teaching at these levels and the quality of educational resources remains one of the biggest problems. Remedying this would necessitate the provision of a training programmes for teachers and a wide variety of language materials. Learning a language solely through the medium of grammar books and dictionaries only gives an artificial flavour of the range of use in a particular language. Through seeking to provide as diverse a range of education, and educational materials, it should be possible to preserve the language as a living being, fit for purpose in everyday situations and to better reflect the purposes for which it was originally used. None of these issues will be resolved overnight. Whereas adults do learn new subjects as a hobby, students in formal educational settings do not necessarily have the leisure time to study a subject just

---

[53] Gemma Goodman, An Rosweyth Project Officer, zoom communication with author, August 2021.

for the fun of it; their qualifications need to provide a positive outcome for their future educational or employment plans. Where Cornish could be introduced as a subject worthy of academic study is at tertiary level, where Celtic Studies and languages have a long academic tradition. Successful introduction of a subject at university level makes it attractive at secondary level. Here, once more, the issue of sourcing people able to teach the language and access to appropriate resources is key, combined with the necessity for any such provision to be economically viable for the institution. Perhaps one way for Cornish to be introduced more widely within higher education is to examine the possibility of cross-institution partnerships with the aim of providing teaching in Cornish to Celtic studies students at several institutions. This approach could not only provide a large enough cohort of students to make such a course economically viable, but such collaborations might also be able to attract funding from outside the institutions themselves.

The advent of the Coronavirus pandemic forced the Cornish language community to adapt in order to continue the provision of classes (in both formal and community educational settings) and other activities. Initially this meant finding new ways to continue with pre-existing classes, but as the potential of communication mediums such as Zoom to facilitate teaching became apparent, it was clear that a much wider geographical audience were now within easy reach. Running in parallel with this use of technology to reach new audiences, was the use of technology to reach existing language learners in new ways, such as the video recordings of Cornish stories made by the Tregenna Nursery Group to continue routines already established within the school. The training provision offered to language teachers, out of necessity focussed on ways to adapt teaching to the online environment. Of course, the pandemic has also had a negative effect, delaying the launch of the Movyans Skolyow Meythrin nursery and the new Go Cornish programme in primary Schools. A positive outcome was the use of online meetings between academics based at the Penryn Campus of the University of Exeter with colleagues at the main Exeter campus to initially discuss the possibility of creating an undergraduate module in Cornish, through all the development stages of this module and acceptance as a course. Had these meetings needed to occur in a face-to-face format, fewer meetings would have been possible, and it is feasible the module would not have been developed in time for the start of the 2021/22 academic year. The Cornish language community now needs to ensure that the momentum it has created during the pandemic and necessary switch to online learning is not allowed to disappear, but rather is used as a springboard to facilitate parallel streams of both online and in-person activities and as a means to bring together both new and existing speakers of the language.

KENSA BROADHURST

Bibliography of additional sources on Cornish

Courtney, J.S. "Chronological memoranda, Relating to the Town of Penzance." *Report of the Royal Cornwall Polytechnic Society,* 7 (1839): 22-57.

Cornish Language Partnership. *Strateji an Yeth Kernewek 2015-2025/ Cornish Language Strategy 2015-2025.* Truro: Cornwall County Council, 2015.

Crystal, David. *Language Death.* Cambridge: Cambridge University Press, 2004.

Dixon, R.M.W. *The Rise and Fall of Languages.* Cambridge: Cambridge University Press, 2008.

Dunbar, Robert. "Is There a Duty to Legislate for Linguistic Minorities?" *Journal of Law and Society,* 33, 1 (2006): 181-198.

Dunbar, Robert. "Language Legislation and Policy in the UK and Ireland." *International Journal on Minority and Group Rights,* 23 (2016): 454-484.

Fishman, Joshua A, ed. *Can threatened languages be saved? Reversing language shift revisited: an 21st century perspective.* Clevedon: Multilingual matters Ltd, 2001.

Harrison, K. David. *When languages die: The extinction of the World's languages and the erosion of human knowledge.* Oxford: Oxford University Press, 2007.

Hinton, Leanne, Huss, Leena and Gerald Roche, eds. *The Routledge Handbook of Language Revitalisation.* New York & London: Routledge, Taylor & Francis, 2018.

Kandler, Anne, Unger, Roman and James Steele. "Language shift, bilingualism and the future of Britain's Celtic languages." *Philosophical Transactions: Biological Sciences,* 365, 1559 (2010): 3855-3864.

Kesva an Taves Kernewek. *Derivas Blydhenyek 2019/ Annual Report 2019,* Truro: Kesva an Taves Kernewek, 2020.

Kesva an Taves Kernewek. *Unpublished examiners' paperwork,* Truro: Kesva an Taves Kernewek, 2021.

Kohn, Marek. *Four Words for Friend.* Yale: Yale University Press, 2019.

Nettle, Daniel and Suzanne Romaine. *Vanishing Voices: The Extinction of the World's Languages,* Oxford: Oxford University Press, 2000.

Pellwolok an Gernewegva. "An Mis 48," accessed 30th August 2021. https://www.youtube.com/watch?v=bE_Q7gYLzD8.

117

'CRONNACK AN HAGER DHU'

Sutherland, Margaret B. "Problems of Diversity in Policy and Practice: Celtic Languages in the United Kingdom." *Comparative Education,* 36, 2 (2000): 199-209.

Swadesh, Maurice. "Sociologic Notes on Obsolescent Languages." *International Journal of American Linguistics,* 14, 4 (1948): 226-235.

Timm, Lenora A. ""On va Parler Breton a Bruxelles?" The Impact of the European Union on Celtic Cultural and National Identities." *Proceedings of the Harvard Celtic Colloquium,* 22 (2002): 203-225.

Callan and the Cosmos

Neil Buttimer

This paper investigates, summarily, an Irish-language geographical compendium attributable to Co. Kerry native, Amhlaoibh Ó Súilleabháin (*anglicé* Humphrey O'Sullivan, d. 1838). He was a resident when compiling it of the south Co. Kilkenny town the title here mentions.[1]

My interest in the author stems from the same motivation as that of most other commentators who consider him. This is the importance attaching to Humphrey's famous diary of 1827-35, a major report on Gaelic-speaking Ireland before the Great Famine devastated the island during 1845-52, together with mass migration from it.[2] The resulting portrait of his country would be enriched by the range of perspectives

---

[1] See, for helpful overviews of him, <https://www.ainm.ie/Bio.aspx?ID=1227>, web site of "Beathaisnéisí Gaeilge," and <https://www.dib.ie/biography/o-suilleabhain-amhlaoibh-osullivan-humphrey-a7077>, web site of *Dictionary of Irish Biography*. The writer employs the Irish-language and English-language versions of his name throughout his documentation. Consequently, both will be used interchangeably here. I am indebted to an anonymous peer reviewer for suggested improvements to the text of the article, and also to this journal's editorial team for their thorough consideration of it. I am especially indebted to Nicholas Thayer for his painstaking copy-editing, and to the editors at *PHCC* for accommodating last-minute alterations. Any remaining errors of fact or interpretation are my sole responsibility.

[2] The journal is printed, with accompanying English translation and occasional annotation, by Michael McGrath (ed.), *Cinnlae Amhlaoibh Uí Shúileabháin: the Diary of Humphrey O'Sullivan*, I-IV (London and Dublin: Simpkin, Marshall, Ltd. and the Educational Company of Ireland, for the Irish Texts Society, 1936-37). References to, or citations from it, are given here as *CL*, with date (day, month and year, where applicable), relevant volume numbers in roman, accompanied by the pages on which any Irish-language extracts commence. Standardized selections from McGrath's copy, including further analysis of them, appear in Tomás de Bhaldraithe (eag.), *Cín Lae Amhlaoibh* (Baile Átha Cliath: An Clóchomhar, 1970), those passages rendered into English by the same scholar in his *The Diary of an Irish Countryman 1827-1835: a Translation of Cín Lae Amhlaoibh* (Cork and Dublin: Mercier Press, 1979).

from which O'Sullivan's varied engagements as teacher, trader or participant in public affairs enabled him to observe it and its activities. Amhlaoibh became in turn a chronicler of private life as much as its social side. Representation of his own conduct and character proves equally intriguing, to the extent he allowed himself to reveal them. There are few similar accounts of the Irish past for which profiles of the personalities of those who produced such records may be outlined as a control on the evidence they generated, or how it was shaped.[3] Hence the opportunity Ó Súilleabháin's case affords to delve more deeply into his extant writings as entities in themselves, while also taking the measure of the man responsible for them.

Amhlaoibh provided no statement which appears to survive clarifying why he began his journal or sustained it during upwards of a decade toward the end of his life. There is speculation about his undertaking the task in emulation of English-medium diary drafting.[4] I am not minded to dismiss that opinion, except to argue it may not be the sole explanation of its genesis. Neither does the conjecture deal comprehensively with other dimensions to the piece, such as certain strands of data detectable in it, or the modalities of its composition. The search for an *Ursprung* in his *Cín Lae* tends to overlook a key contextual factor. This is the realization that Ó Súilleabháin had been a writer of Irish for the greater part of twenty years before launching into his systematic journal entries. Rather than resorting to hypotheticals, therefore, it would appear incumbent on us to commence, as he did, with earlier phases of his output. An approach of that nature to Amhlaoibh's sizeable *Nachlaß* leads us to see what

---

[3] Lesa Ní Mhunghaile, "Gaelic Literature in Transition, 1780-1830," in Connolly, Claire (ed.), *Irish Literature in Transition, 1780-1830* (Cambridge: Cambridge University Press, 2020), 36-51; and Nicholas Wolf, "Antiquarians and Authentics: Survival and Revival in Gaelic Writing," in Campbell, Matthew (ed.), *Irish Literature in Transition, 1830-1880* (Cambridge: Cambridge University Press, 2020), 199-217. Both consider conditions affecting composition in the Irish language on dates coinciding with those of Humphrey O'Sullivan's journal.

[4] Breandán Ó Madagáin, "Cinnlae Amhlaoibh Uí Shúileabháin: a Nature Diary," in Ó Murchú, Liam P. (ed.), *Cinnlae Amhlaoibh Uí Shúileabháin: Reassessments*, Irish Texts Society Subsidiary Series 14 (London: Irish Texts Society, 2004), 67-78.

he created in the round, appraising its components as integral to, rather than isolated from, each other.

What is ventured accordingly in the present brief report is one of a set of steps requiring to be taken to meet that objective. The enquiry will comprise the following sections. At its core lies a preliminary exploration of the short but compelling tract proposed for analysis. We shall deal firstly with its structure, and give some flavour of the item's contents. The latter is attempted with the assistance of sample citations from it, offered in the original together with my accompanying English translations. An overview of the compilation's background then follows, to the degree that ingredients in its making can at all be identified. The third topic consists of general pointers to be derived both from this testimony and reflection on it, with reference to Amhlaoibh Ó Súilleabháin himself and what he authored. The wider backdrop, relating to anything which could be encompassed or expressed in Irish writing by that stage in this vernacular's history, is reviewed in conclusion.

The work and its world

Ó Súilleabháin's geography text is found in Maynooth University, Ms. **C** 115 (d), henceforth **C**.[5] It occupies twenty-six pages. Upwards of six of that number of pages are either fully or partially blank. The item dates to December 1, 1811. It claims the Earth (*Domhan*) is divided into four main continents (*prímhRanna*),

---

[5] Pádraig Ó Fiannachta, *Lámhscríbhinní Gaeilge Choláiste Phádraig Má Nuad: Clár Fascúl VI* (Má Nuad: An Sagart, 1969), 86, describes the source. Its cataloguer's pagination is given in citations in square brackets. Page breaks are flagged by a vertical line I introduce into the Irish text, but not in my translations. Manuscript compendia or contractions will be supplied silently, as also a modicum of punctuation features like full stops, the latter invariably omitted from Amhlaoibh's original. Further discussion of such issues as scribal corrections, or the writer's provision of paratextual matter, generally overlooked in the paper's extracts, awaits the type of editorial work mentioned below, particularly at n. 26. De Bhaldraithe, *Cín Lae*, xxiii-iv, discusses **C** briefly, citing (xxiv, n. 40) in a conflated manner portions of its descriptions of the city of Copenhagen, Denmark, occurring slightly apart from each other in the source (**C**, p. [9]). My particular thanks to Susan Durack, Special Collections and Archives, Maynooth University for permission to cite from **C** for this article.

Europe, Asia, Africa, and America (**C**, p. [1]). There are five principal oceans, the northern, the western or Atlantic, the Southern Sea, the Pacific (*an sithAigein*), and the eastern. Europe has nineteen divisions (**C**, pp. [2]–[3]). Those territories are numbered and named, together with their capitals, or, occasionally, the cities' main rivers. The remainder of the document is taken up with an excursus on various of the latter regions (**C**, pp. [3]–[26]). That more expansive segment commences with Denmark (**C**, p. [3]). Its surrounding seas are spoken of, those including, among others, the Kattegat, the North Sea, and the Baltic. Provinces within the country are presented in tabular form, almost, as follows:

- Albourg air Abheis Limford
- Uisberg
- Ripen
- Arthus
- Slesmhic. (**C** p. [3])

The foregoing entries concentrate on locations in Jutland.[6] No description of Zealand appears, although what could be read as a retrospective jotting, added transversely to the lower outer margin, mentions Denmark having islands (*Oilenn*, **C**, p. [3]), on which further elaboration is nonetheless absent.

Norway comes next (**C**, pp. [4]–[7]). It is treated similarly in part, in that the land's major subdivisions are identified, and the seas adjacent to them named. However, as the foregoing pagination suggests, greater quantities of data are furnished about this realm than for Denmark. The extract to follow exemplifies those added elements (where an explanatory gloss will be found after the second asterisk below, enlarging on the text preceding the first asterisk):

> *Is amhla ata an Righe-so o cenn go cenn lionta le sleibhte arda siocamhla uim gleannta dorcha dubh- | nelacha 7 Aimhne trena borb ag titimt o Aill go h-Aill 'na dTonnta mora torntren curbhan air a cuirter* [*m-bi* cancelled] *crainn guise ag triall go*

---

[6] Localities mentioned are the northern city of Aalborg (and the nearby sea inlet, Limfjord), the western towns, Esbjerg and Ribe (probably), the eastern urban centre, Aarhus, and the Schleswig region further south.

Cuanta na Criche ₇ as sin do gach Crich do'n Domhan. Fasan begán Coirce ₇c in sa taebh thes ach ni mar sin do'n Imel thuagh oir ni'l ag fas an ach caenach noch a ithenn na Agh-allta. Is e Ainm is coitena don taebh thuagh do'n T.S. R [sic] *Tír na Lap in a m-bi Cine Daine isella toirtamhla Cennmora noch a deacha chum Cath na Coinbhlîcht | Mairid ar a gCuid Agh-Allta enlaith ₇ Iasg.** | **bid lethbhliaghain air selg, air enlaigh ₇ air íasga. ₇ lethbleaghain | an geimhredh an uamhnaibh dorcha datamhuil mar bhinn cheithre mhi d'Oidche aca in sa geimhredh ₇ an fad cedna. do lo 'san samhradh.* (**C**, pp. [5]–[8])

This is how that kingdom is from end to end full of high frosty mountains surrounding dark black-clouded valleys and strong vigorous rivers falling from cliff to cliff in huge vigorously resounding white-foamed waves upon which pine trees are sent to the country's harbours and from thence to each land on earth. A little oats etc. grows in the south but that is not so for the northern border, as nothing grows there except moss which wild deer eat. The commonest name for the country's northern part is Lappland, in which exists a race of small stout people with large heads who did not engage in battle or conflict. They live on their wild deer, birds and fish. They spend half a year hunting birds and fish and the winter half-year in dark painted caves, because they have four months of night in winter and the same length in the day during summer.

Issues focused on in the above include the region's climatology, its productivity and a theme resembling ethnography.[7] Treatment of the

---

[7] For an instance of how Sámi culture, at issue in the extract, across its northern hinterland generally, may have been known about and perceived in areas within Ó Súilleabháin's ambit and timescale, see Linda Andersson Burnett, "Translating Swedish Colonialism: Johannes Schefferus's

ethnic aspect to Norway's population means this account differs from that of other societies described, for which equivalent coverage is not furnished. One might suggest as reason for its inclusion the obvious inference that its compiler must have been taken by the nomadism of the people in question. This practice was infrequent by then in Europe, and since, but retained possible echoes among customs like 'booleying,' still practiced in Ireland during Ó Súilleabháin's time, and especially in contiguous Gaelic-speaking districts.[8]

The rest of the compendium makes an otherwise unheralded switch subsequently from prose to verse, almost exclusively (**C**, pp. [9]–[26]). Denmark, Norway and Sweden, first described via the former mode, are treated again, but now through the latter. Metrically based accounts of regions introduced briefly only at a previous point, such as Russia, Scotland, Ireland and Italy, follow. The last-mentioned we find described in two poems, with a prose passage interposed between them (**C**, pp. [24]–[26]). Italy's second verse element is given thus:

Naples

Ta ceithre Sleibhte Tinntech
in san Euroip; Ecla Miltech
Mhesumhius, Etna na n-Glám
*Stramboli sán Muir Menn.*1*

Féc anis an Tinsliabh-so
Nélta dubha air a sliasda
fuaim is fothrum, gair is glam
*tinnte trena astig ann.*2*   *[cf. note 9]

Titenn tennbhailte trena
ta an Talamh tirm a Raebadh
Aimhne iair [?] derglasad a buitredh
O'n tine chnoc garbh a bhruchtadh.

Lapponia in Britain c. 1674-1800," *Scandinavian Studies* 91, No. 1-2 (Spring/Summer 2019): 134-62.
[8] Eugene Costello, *Transhumance and the Making of Ireland's Uplands, 1550-1900* (Woodbridge: Boydell Press, 2020), 107-32, gives an account of that activity in the Galtee Mountains in Cos. Tipperary and Limerick down to the mid-1800s.

Ca bhf-huill Pompí, Cathir bregh
nó Eracleum, mor le radh !! —
ni'll le fail, ach mo buare
taid muchta fa sliabh luathre. (**C**, p. [26])

There are four fiery mountains in Europe, injurious Hecla, Vesuvius, bellowing Etna, Stromboli in the Mediterranean Sea.

Look now at this volcano, dark clouds on its slopes, sound and noise, cries and roaring, strong fires within it.

Solid strong towns fall, the dry ground is being torn up, rivers burned red are roaring from the rough fiery mountain overflowing.

Where is Pompeii, a fine city, or celebrated Herculaneum! Neither is to be found, but, alas, they are smothered under an ashen mountain.

Once more, as with Norway and the comparatively unusual make-up of its communities, Ó Súilleabháin is likely to have emphasized Italian vulcanology for its distinctiveness in European terms. Shortly after completing his geographical treatise, Amhlaoibh would press into service lines from the extract just supplied here, in slightly altered ways, within a further composition of his. That was a lengthy, almost epic, poem on the biography of Ireland's patron saint,

including, particularly in the present context, clerical training Patrick is said (by some authors) to have received while in Italy, prior to his leaving the continent to convert the Irish people from paganism.[9] O'Sullivan used certain of the Maynooth tract's features in an apparent burst of inventive re-adaptation, intending to give an element of local colour and vividness to his portrayal of the national apostle's risk-laden sojourn overseas. In that regard, Amhlaoibh probably

---

[9] See Neil Buttimer, "A Late Life of Patrick," in Carey, John, Máire Herbert and Kevin Murray (eds.), *Cín Chille Cúile: Texts, Saints and Places:Essays in Honour of Pádraig Ó Riain* (Aberystwyth: Celtic Studies Publications, 2004), 1-43, for a discussion of that borrowing (7). Stanzas 1 and 2 in the passage on volcanoes cited above from **C** under review for transposition into this text were marked there as *.

responded to a dramatic element characterising virtually all moments of the Patrician career, from the holy man's abduction down to his Christianization campaign. This step in itself seems to be an early instance of the type of textual interdependence linking various of the author's compositions, both over time and across the different genres of writing he cultivated. The geography work breaks off abruptly while tackling Italy.[10] Whether that gap results from a chasm in the manuscript occasioned by factors like the conditions in which the piece was transmitted is uncertain. This position is reminiscent of frequent disjunctures occurring throughout Amhlaoibh Ó Súilleabháin's other writings. Thus, his diary comes to an unexpected close during mid-1835, although there may be a hint that he picked it up again at some stage prior to his own death three years later. Amhlaoibh provides no overt rationale for any such hiatus throughout all of his documentation. We shall reflect further below on similar anomalies after a precis of how others of **C**'s strata might have been constructed or laid out.

Inputs

What were his sources? Ó Súilleabháin names none specifically. There are different possibilites to assess when tracking them down. One is that the material was eclectic rather than singular in its provenance. Derivation from various categories of illustrative matter, like an atlas, or map, cannot be discounted. O'Sullivan was attracted to, and a practitioner of, visual representation. For the first month with which his journal commences, he went on outings to sites in the local countryside, sketching its antiquities (*CL* i 1827; I, 4). *Cairt*, a name for a notepad used, might invoke the term implicit in 'cartography.' In that connection, a verbal account of what looks like an islet in a body

---

[10] That the text could have dealt with other aspects of this country may be seen from additional references to it surviving residually, perhaps, in the diary, such as mention of Italy's Alpine mountain range (*CL*, 20 iv 1827; I, 26) or other heights (*CL*, 1 viii 1827; I, 102), its produce, like marble (*CL*, 12 iv 1827; I, 17), and the like. Yet more parts of the world could have been treated in it too, if the journal's noting of specific topics such as climate in Asia or the Middle East (*CL*, 27 iv 1827, 7 viii 1827; I, 37, 108), for example, embodies data from components of **C** not now available, had they existed in the first place.

of water near Callan compares the feature from its shape to North and South America, divided by the isthmus of Panama (*CL*, 25 ix 1828; II, 18), a visualisation almost certainly redolent of mapping.[11] It may not be the sole representational aid of the kind considered here to be attested in that work. Amhlaoibh lost a night's sleep on a certain evening when wind caused a shop sign across from his Callan dwelling to creak. The object in question is described as *comhartha an chruinne* (*CL*, 22 iv 1827; I, 28). Its translator takes the latter to depict a "globe,'" if it does not in fact comprise the globe itself. This suggests such a device, its mechanism or what could be outlined in it, was not unfamiliar to him.[12]

Given that the Maynooth tract is narrative-based, that truncated work is most likely to be dependent on one textbook or another, at whatever remove. The issue then becomes that of delineating its source's contours, in the hope of pinning down likely candidates. I do not have a specific list of possibilities to suggest, but propose, rather,

---

[11] If Ó Súilleabháin took his maps from printed works, the scale of the project involved in identifying his choice may be seen from the quantum of such illustrations in near contemporary publications, as detailed by the likes of Barbara Backus McCorkle: (https://kuscholarworks.ku.edu/bitstream/handle/1808/5564/CARTO-BIBLIOGRAPHY.PDF?sequence=3&isAllowed =y), her *A Carto-Bibliography of the Maps in Eighteenth-Century British and American Geography Books* (University of Kansas, 2009). For thought-provoking comments on the balance between pictorial versus word-based accounts of geographical features in works from another European tradition, see Nicholas Verdier, "The Spread of Maps and the Affirmation of Geographical Knowledge in France: the Paradox of Implementing the Use of Geographical Maps during the Eighteenth Century," *L'Espace géographique* 44, Issue 1 (2015): 38-56.

[12] That this type of commercial signage was known in Ireland may be seen from Máire Kennedy, "At the Sign of Shakespeare: Bookshop Signs in Eighteenth-Century Ireland": (<https://mairekennedybooks.wordpress.com/2020/11/15/at-the-sign-of-shakespeare-bookshop-signs-in-eighteenth-century-ireland/comment-page-1/>), which lists no fewer than seven globes, singly or with other items, in Dublin stores for the period, often bookshops. For their wider usage, see David Garrioch, "House Names, Shop Signs and Social Organization in Western European Cities, 1500-1900," *Urban History* 21 No. 1 (April 1994): 20-48. The origin and development of the object itself is explored by Sylvia Sumira, *The Art and History of Globes* (London: British Library, 2014).

to speak to coordinates in the quest. One of these is chronological. The proposed item (or items) must post-date the 1720s. To take one nation in the tract mentioned previously here, Denmark had regained control by that stage of Schleswig, a territory whose borders and governance it disputed regularly with neighbouring German statelets.[13] If this supplies a helpful *terminus a quo*, and there may be others, the self-described timing of the treatise's own completion (i.e., December 1, 1811) gives us a temporal limit at the opposite end. One might envisage a *terminus ante quem* prior to 1811. If **C** is indebted to Amhlaoibh's father, Donnchadh, for certain of its contents, that parent's death in 1808 (*CL*, 17 viii 1827; I, 114) suggests a dating before the latter event for those components (or, indeed, for the type of discourse present in Amhlaoibh's geography, if this too was influenced by his father). The younger Ó Súilleabháin followed Donnchadh into the teaching profession, seemingly working alongside him, as the junior assistant master later recalled (*CL*, 14 v 1827; I, 54). It cannot be discounted that their evident collaboration might have seen a transfer of instructional matter from the O'Sullivan elder to his better-known son, papers or printings which the former had accumulated over many years beforehand.

Should Amhlaoibh Ó Súilleabháin's compilation derive from an eighteenth-century compendium, this is no guarantee that his text does not depend for some of its entries on material from even earlier moments in time. One is struck in that connection by the Callan document's Nordic emphasis. That focus could reflect nothing other than a point of view now commonplace: seeing the world from the perspective of north, south, east and west, in that sequence. Few viewpoints are more deceptive than what may be regarded as conventional, however. By way of contrast, *mappa mundi* material from the Middle Ages could align matters differently, often on grounds of religious belief, with east on top, for instance, where Paradise was thought to repose.[14] Those and other similar culture-

---

[13] For this protracted affair and its wider ramifications, see Jeremy Black, *European International Relations 1648-1815* (Basingstoke: Palgrave, 2002), 103-48.
[14] David Woodward, "Medieval Mappaemundi," in J. B. Harley and David Woodward (eds), *The History of Cartography Volume One: Cartography in*

centred factors probably account for the type of directional adverbial expression, *thuas sa Spáinn*, appearing in the renowned poem, *Mac an Cheannaí*, by the celebrated Aogán Ó Rathaille (d. *ca* 1729). The country in which an unnamed hero expired, who might have been able, had he survived, to rescue Ireland from recent adversity, as discussed momentarily, is situated by this *aisling* (vision poem) 'above,' rather than 'below,' in southern Europe, as one might envisage Spain's location in current parlance.[15]

The Harvard scholar whose lectures first drew my attention to orientation in cartography from the era in question claimed, with reference to yet more antique compilations, like genealogies or regnal lists, from the Middle Ages, that he was suspicious of vast stretches of "question-begging" certainty in them.[16] Applying a parallel scepticism to Ó Súilleabháin's geography, rather than it being of no untoward or unusual consequence, does his compendium's commencing with Scandinavia embody a memory of this region's influence on its home continent during the 1600s, for example, in the course of the Thirty Years' War (1618–48)? The latter episode in Europe's history produced traumatic reflexes in Ireland by the 1640s and 1650s, when former contributors to that transnational inter-faith conflict re-surfaced as protagonists in military campaigns against the Irish insurgency of those decades. Leaders attempting to quell the latter included the Scottish General Robert Monroe (d. 1680). Formerly a commander in the Swedish army under the Lutheran King Gustavus Adolphus (d. 1632), the Scotsman was due to be granted safe passage when defeated at the Battle of Benburb in Co. Tyrone in 1646, one of

---

Prehistoric, Ancient, and Medieval Europe and the Mediterranean (Chicago: University of Chicago Press, 1987), 286-370, treats the evolution and character of cartography in the period.

[15] For a convenient modern copy of this text, see Breandán Ó Buachalla (eag.), *Aogán Ó Rathaille Filí 1* (Baile Átha Cliath: Field Day Publications, 2007), 30-31, with the placename at the piece's l. 30. Clarification regarding matters of direction in the adverbial expression at issue is also forthcoming in the electronic *Dictionary of the Irish Language* (*eDIL*), s.vv. *túas, thúas*, <http://dil.ie/42228>. That lemma also contains references to related terms for direction or orientation in the language. I thank Professor Diarmuid Ó Giolláin for discussing this point with me.

[16] John V. Kelleher, "Early Irish History and Pseudo-History," *Studia Hibernica* 3 (1963): 113-27 (124).

the few notable victories won by Gaelic aristocrat and champion of the Catholic interest, Owen Roe O'Neill (d. 1649).[17] What of other interventions from the European mainland, such as happened in the so-called 'Glorious Revolution' of the 1690s, which saw the arrival of a Dutch prince, William of Orange (d. 1702), on England's throne, not to mention the Hanoverian dynasty's transfer from Germany to Britain and Ireland by 1714 following the coronation of King George I (d. 1727)?[18] Amhlaoibh's own diary looks back often to various forms of destruction in Ireland from the mid-seventeenth century onwards and the British government of the period which carried out the despoliation (*CL*, 13 v 1827; I, 52).

Other entries in Amhlaoibh's geography might help to retrieve and date an *Urtext*. Take the case of how Scotland appears in Ó Súilleabháin's compilation. It is located with reference to the country's surrounding seas and external territorial borders. Internal boundaries are also addressed (**C**, pp. [16]–[17]). These number thirty-three. The text uses the term, *Mír*, to denote those divisions. Does the word designate a shire or a county? If the former, what profile of shire-formation is implicit in it? Might the inventory take account of a reconfiguration or redistribution of local governmental operations consequent on the 1745 Rebellion, and offer, thereby, a different dating criterion?[19]

---

[17] For one foundational diary-like Gaelic text on the events of the 1640s in Ulster, see Tadhg Ó Donnchadha (ed.), "Cín Lae Ó Mealláin," *Analecta Hibernica*, No. 3 (September, 1931): 1-61, where preparations for the Benburb encounter, the event itself and its aftermath are reported in this near contemporary account (40-4). Michelle O Riordan, *Poetics and Polemics: Reading Seventeenth-Century Irish Political Verse* (Cork: Cork University Press, 2021), treats alternative Irish-language and ancillary evidence relating to the transformational epoch at issue, including participants in it and responses to its outturn.

[18] Breandán Ó Buachalla, *Aisling Ghéar: na Stíobhartaigh agus an tAos Léinn, 1603-1788* (Baile Átha Cliath: An Clóchomhar, 1996), is a *locus classicus* in the study of Irish sources' reaction to these developments. See also Éamonn Ó Ciardha, *Ireland and the Jacobite Cause, 1685-1766: a Fatal Attachment* (Dublin: Four Courts Press, 2001).

[19] Alexander Joseph Murdoch, "'The People Above': Politics and Administration in Mid-Eighteenth-Century Scotland," PhD thesis (University of Edinburgh, 1978), examines this evolving situation.

The trawl for material from which Humphrey O'Sullivan drew for this compendium will be aided greatly by a more thorough review than can be conducted here of recent scholarship on eighteenth- and nineteenth-century geography manuals.[20] That enterprise should benefit also from ongoing study of access to reading matter in Ireland specifically during that period.[21] In this connection, some comment may be made about the possibility of Ó Súilleabháin himself having encountered geographical textbooks. His documentation appears to indicate that there was a circulating library in his adoptive Callan (*CL*, 5 i 1828; II, 198). Such a library could well have been a provider of works underlying the tract we have been discussing,[22] while Amhlaoibh may have acted as his own supplier of the relevant sources also. One of his occupations, as we have seen, was that of retail merchant. His journal notes multiple out-of-town trips for stock of various types, perhaps calling to vendors in Dublin for school texts (*CL*, 9 iii 1828; II, 236, to cite one of his visits to the capital), this being related, no doubt, to his other activity as instructor. The likelihood that geographical treatises featured among such requisitioning deserves to be considered.

---

[20] Matthew H. Edney and Mary Sponberg Pedley (eds.), *The History of Cartography Volume Four: Cartography in the European Enlightenment* Part I (Chicago: University of Chicago Press, 2020), consider such material.
[21] See J. R. R. Adams, *The Printed Word and the Common Man: Popular Culture in Ulster, 1700-1900* (Belfast: Institute for Irish Studies, Queen's University Belfast, 1987); Niall Ó Ciosáin, *Print and Popular Culture in Ireland, 1750-1850* (Basingstoke: Macmillan); Garret FitzGerald, *Irish Primary Education in the Early Nineteenth Century: an Analysis of the First and Second Reports of the Commissioners of Irish Education Enquiry, 1825-6* (Dublin: Royal Irish Academy, 2013). Evidence on schooling, not entirely unrelated although generally later in date, derived from both Gaelic and English-language sources, is presented in Caoimhe Máirtín, *An Máistir: An Scoil agus an Scolaíocht i Litríocht na Gaeilge* (Baile Átha Cliath: Cois Life, 2003).
[22] K. A. Manley, *Irish Reading Societies and Circulating Libraries founded before 1825: Useful Knowledge and Agreeable Entertainment* (Dublin: Four Courts Press, 2018), traces the background to these facilities as well as the categories of reading they made available.

CALLAN AND THE COSMOS

Outcomes

The foregoing enquiry leads us back gradually in the direction of broader issues mentioned at the start of this paper. Among those topics is the question of what predisposed Amhlaoibh to an absorption with geography as a discipline, or how it influenced him. Its origins in his own lived experience might be adduced, over and above a later involvement with pedagogy. When not much more than ten years of age, O'Sullivan relocated from Killarney via Waterford to Kilkenny (as recalled in *CL*, 14 v 1827; I, 52), travelling, perhaps, along parts of north Cork where there may have been family ties, or possibly by the banks of Munster's Blackwater river, well known as a routeway from west to east. Itineraries of different kinds remained an aspect of his circumstances thereafter. The opening pages of his diary commence, as we have seen, with strolls for leisure, or for the purpose of attending communal events like funerals (*CL*, 1 iv 1827; I, 6). A couple of years later, he would set out on a bitter winter horseback ride from Callan to Waterford city (*CL*, 27 xii 1829; II, 214), hoping, unsuccessfully as it transpired, to secure a new spouse following the death of his wife.[23] In each instance, specified locations traversed are recorded in considerable detail. That is done not alone by naming them but through deliberate reiteration of the prepositions, *tre* or *tar*, as though in the latter case mirroring usage of this speech element during movement in early Irish saga. What I am concerned with here is not so much any echoes from an older literature within the phraseology, or ensuing concatenation of places, as the mindset of the person employing the expressions in settings as they were listed. Spatial awareness manifest throughout prior stages of Amhlaoibh's life and consistently thereafter is likely to have left him with an abiding geographical predilection. Formal contact with that domain to which

---

[23] The prospective partner was the sister of a Co. Kilkenny priest scribe, Síomón Breathnach (for whom see
<https://www.ainm.ie/Bio.aspx?ID=1046>). If, as it would appear, Amhlaoibh engaged also with him in matters relating to the Irish language, that interaction may be one of a number of forms of personal contact mentioned in this paper which could have been instrumental in motivating Humphrey to write in that vernacular and sustain his commitment to the same effort.

the Maynooth document bears early testimony probably nurtured this sensibility, imbuing his later written records with a similar outlook.

That tendency is particulary evident in his diary, if in an unstated manner. Topography is ubiquitous here. Amhlaoibh has references to flooding in Derry (*CL*, ii 1827; I, 6) and cholera in Belfast (*CL*, 27 iii 1832; III, 124). We drop by London for a notice of difficulty arising during construction of the Thames Tunnel (*CL*, 26 v 1827; I, 64), together with an inundation which impacted it afterwards (*CL*, 15 i 1828; II, 208). He takes us to Kirkaldy in Scotland's county and royal burgh of Fife to describe a recent lethal church building collapse (*CL*, 21 vi 1828; II, 287). The Kerryman is steadfast in his fascination with a prolonged eastern Mediterranean standoff between Turks and Greeks as the 1820s ended, leading to the latters' independence. He had been tracking that development from the year the diary began (*CL* 6 viii 1827; I, 108). He recorded a Belgian rebellion against Dutch control in the next decade (*CL*, 5 x 1830; II, 344). We accompany him to Montserrat to learn about descendants of Irish people banished to the Caribbean during and after the Cromwellian settlement (*CL*, 1 iv 1831; III, 32). The departure of close relatives of his to Newfoundland in an era of economic depression in Ireland was noted as well (*CL*, 20 iv 1830; II, 266). That insert reflects direct personal contact, but others of the foregoing journal pieces most likely incorporate contemporary newspaper reportage. In no instance among the ones just invoked for sampling purposes does the diarist appear to feel the need to expand on where the locations in question are actually to be found. Information as to their siting is assumed, as though part of his existing knowledge base.

Aspects of the Maynooth handbook permit one to presuppose that Ó Súilleabháin had indeed applied himself systemically, by and large, to the acquisition of geographical information, and, no doubt, to imparting it. A comparative regularity is seen from the treatise's keeping Europe and its components together as a unit. The compiler adhered substantially to the arrangement in which the first five countries, at least, were set down by his prefatory listing of the continent's states when it came to treating them in greater depth farther into the document. There is also an element of randomness to the item, however. Revisiting citations from it presented above, certain entries seem ample, with others clearly short. No necessary correlation is apparent between those parameters and the area or extent of the territories they describe. The skeletal outline of its initial data on Denmark, for example, may indicate that strand was prepared, partially, as an *aide mémoire*. Those placename pointers could have been entered to meet their author's immediate, possibly urgent, need for notes only. The work's verse element gives it a mnemonic feel. One wonders whether this facet might not have been for his pupils' benefit, if the tract were to be employed in class as a learning aid. A not insignificant number of unfilled pages suggests Amhlaoibh intended to supplement the text, should an opportunity to gather more detail on the subject have arisen afterwards. Did the demands of attending to other obligations or requirements imposed on him by those in his charge impede Humphrey's liberty to seek out or access missing facts? It is noteworthy that analogous constraints–multiple duties at home and in the workplace–can be shown arguably to have governed the writing of his *Cín Lae* during the decades to come,[24] much as exigencies like them might affect any reading he was yet to complete, so as to augment the geographical account.[25] The latter text perhaps demonstrates, therefore, that variability which would emerge in due course as a constant in Amhlaoibh's literary endeavours was already visible even as such efforts got underway in earnest in the 1810s, if not sooner.

Variety of a different sort is encountered in the last element of the work explored here, namely, C's language. A satisfactory study of that topic awaits the complete edition not only of this text but also the remainder of O'Sullivan's considerable written corpus. That enquiry might be conducted best by taking research on other extensive collections of writing from his own approximate time and place as model.[26] Until such work has been done, a handful of key linguistic

---

[24] Neil Buttimer, "Amhlaoibh Ó Súilleabháin's Writings," in Ó Murchú, *Cinnlae Amhlaoibh*, 79-110, discusses the interplay involved.

[25] For a comparative study of factors influencing that work, see Christina Lupton, *Reading and the Making of Time in the Eighteenth Century* (Baltimore: Johns Hopkins University Press, 2018).

[26] One such exemplary investigation I would cite is Barra Ua Cearnaigh, *Amhail Fuaim Chogair Bhig: Teangeolas Shéamais Uí Scoireadh*. Dán agus Tallann, 17 (An Daingean: An Sagart, 2011), a work which analyses comprehensively the issues of Irish-language usage, whether with regard to normalization or the

features in the tract can be highlighted. The latter is presented, in terms of orthography and morphology, essentially in the type of Early Modern Irish which provided a bedrock for rendering the language during its immediate post-Classical phase.[27] Amhlaoibh is likely to have acquired a competence in such usage from his aforementioned scribal father, Donnchadh. Potential archaisms could be apparent when employing the epithets, *Ce* and *braenach* (both in **C**, p. [1], and as he spells them) to qualify the Earth.[28] Any potentially value-laden attitude of a negative kind towards the world implicit in each might reflect an age antecdent to Ó Súilleabháin's own, during which geography seemed as much a moral as a mental science.[29] In that connection, there appears little doubt but that the writer is unhappy with the prevailing dispensation, one where foreign interference, as he would have seen it, imposed unprecedented regulatory layers (*Ranna nua*, **C**, p. [22]) on Ireland and its ancient territorial divides, a cause of sadness. His text includes a virtual prayer for the overthrow of those responsible for that unwelcome reconfiguration:

---

retention of colloquial or other features, in the considerable spread of translations or original writings by Kilkennyman, James Scurry (d. 1829). Ó Scoireadh's output was known to Humphrey O'Sullivan (see *CL*, 16 vii 1827; I, 90). Amhlaoibh may have been encouraged also in his own employment of Irish through his apparent familiarity with another advocate for the vernacular, the east-Cork poet, and later a well-read author of letters to Ireland from his exile in the United States, Pádraig Phiarais Cundún (d. 1857). Contact between them is looked at by Neil Buttimer, "Comhfhreagras Corcaíoch," in Ó Coileáin, Seán, Liam P. Ó Murchú, Pádraigín Riggs (eag.), *Séimhfhear Suairc: Aistí in Ómós don Ollamh Breandán Ó Conchúir* (An Daingean: An Sagart, 2013), 1-38 (especially 25-32).

[27] The transitional stage involved here is the subject, partially, of Nicholas Williams, "Na Canúintí a Theacht chun Solais," in McCone, Kim, Damian McManus, Cathal Ó Háinle, Nicholas Williams, Liam Breatnach (eds), *Stair na Gaeilge in Ómós do P[h]ádraig Ó Fiannachta* (Maigh Nuad: Roinn na Sean-Ghaeilge, Coláiste Phádraig, Maigh Nuad, 1994), 447-78.

[28] For explorations of the first term's denoting the "present" world rather than the next, see the relevant entry on it in *eDIL*, s.n., 1. *cé*, <http://dil.ie/8419>, and the same source for its treatment of "moisture-laden" in *bráenach*, <http://dil.ie/6471>.

[29] David N. Livingstone, The Geographical Tradition: Episodes in the History of a Contested Discipline (Padstow: Routledge, 2006), 105-25.

A Dhia thuas os na Nelta
do chúm an Cruinne is na srértha [sic–*spéartha*]
cuir Techtaire do chruagh dhioltuis
da ruagadh uain lucht an leirsgrîs. (**C**, pp. [22]–
[23])

O God above over the clouds,
who created the universe and the skies,
send the messenger of your harsh vengeance
to banish from us that destructive crew.

Politicization seen almost everywhere afterwards throughout his
Cín Lae was thus already well anchored in his consciousness during
Amhlaoibh's younger years.[30]

Dialect looks traceable here as well, as shown by consonant
metathesis in *Brenthach* (**C**, p. [3]), this adjective obviously standing
for *Breatnach*, the 'British' Sea, west of Denmark, by which the
English Channel was known previously. Examination of other aspects
of the piece's nomenclature shows Amhlaoibh engaged in more
innovative practices as far as this element is concerned. He designates
some lands by their expected names, like *Alba*, for Scotland or *Eire*
(as the source spells that word) for Ireland (**C**, p. [2]). Conversely,
others are calques, typified by his giving "Norway" as *Tuaigh-shligh*
(**C**, p. [2]), as though segmenting the placename into its key parts
(North + way). Similarly *Germanith* (**C**, p. [2]), where the
compound's second element comprises an older term, *iath (*country,
territory). [31] As with other aspects of the analysis to date, usage here
already anticipates by a good stretch of time a pseudo-etymologizing
trend widespread in diary entries. One prominent example which we
have seen already may suffice to illustrate the approach in the journal,
his calling the imperial capital, London, *Longdun*, (ship fort), (*CL*, 26
v 1827: I, 64; cf. the alternative *Lunnduin, CL*, 2 xii 1827; I, 168). The
form, *Longdún*, is a not improbable explanation in a certain sense,
given the town's maritime history, but scarcely reflective of the

---

[30] Gearóid Ó Tuathaigh, "Amhlaoibh Ó Súilleabháin as Historical Witness: an
Historiographical Perspective," in Ó Murchú, *Reassessments*, 1-24, provides a
succinct analysis of the diarist's politics.
[31] For this lexeme, see *eDIL*, s.n.1. *íath*, <http://dil.ie/27115>.

toponym's attested Celtic roots. That had also been its form when the same metropolis was listed in the text under discussion (**C**, p. [2]).

Other tendencies in Ó Súilleabháin's presentation of the names of places deserve notice. Some of these, though Gaelic in origin, occur in a spelling which does not capture their original attestations or underlying elements, such as the Co. Fermanagh settlement, *Iniscillín* (**C**, p. [19]), for *Inis Ceithleann* (anglicised as Enniskillen), or the Co. Meath town, *An Uaimh*, which he gives as *Namhan* (**C**, p. [23]). The latter appears as though heard colloquially in everyday Hiberno-English (Navan nowadays).[32] Each usage combines to raise questions about his abilities in Irish: whether Amhlaoibh was essentially bilingual, or to what degree,[33] if his command of the vernacular might be estimated as restricted, not to say deficient, in certain technical respects.[34] To the extent that the Maynooth geography manual could have been directed at a wider audience, like students, linguistic analysis of it might well also shift focus to include language competence among his speech community rather than any such study concentrating on Amhlaoibh Ó Súilleabháin himself solely. If intended for classroom purposes, it seems reasonable to infer that Irish still enjoyed at least a modicum of currency among those younger cohorts. This may point to the Ó Súilleabháin writings as a resource for appraising in greater depth what levels of acculturation were like across his locale's age-related and social strata, or any combinations of those strands.[35]

---

[32] Authorative toponomic and topographic data on the two locations in question, their background and orthography over time, will be found in respective entries about them in the web site of the Placenames Database of Ireland, <https://www.logainm.ie/en/s?txt=Inis+Ceithleann&str=on> and <https://www.logainm.ie/en/37598?s=An+uaimh>.

[33] Louis Cullen, "Humphrey O'Sullivan's Callan," in Callan Heritage Society, *Callan 800 (1207-2007): History & Heritage* (Naas, Co. Kildare: Naas Printing Ltd, 2013), 60-76, includes perceptive comments on this aspect of his subject's capabilities (68-69).

[34] His access to earlier eighteenth-century dictionary work is broached in Proinsias Ó Drisceoil, "Amhlaoibh Ó Súilleabháin (1783-1838) agus Foclóir Uí Bhriain (1768)," *An Linn Bhuí* 23 (2019):179-88.

[35] For a treatment of the composition of that society, see Pierce A. Grace, *The Middle Class of Callan, Co. Kilkenny, 1825-45,* Maynooth Studies in Local History No. 120 (Dublin: Four Courts Press, 2015).

CALLAN AND THE COSMOS

Envoi

Given the occurrence of "cosmos" as the final word in the paper's title, one might expect that the Ó Súilleabháin tract would discuss the Earth's positioning in the universe. However, a presentation of that kind does not appear within the document's extant portion. Amhlaoibh was certainly aware of planets, like Jupiter (*CL*, 1 v 1828, 2 vi 1829; I, 278, II, 164), or Mars (*CL*, 6 and 28 viii 1828, 21 x 1828; I, 316, 332, II, 40), or other nearby celestial phenomena such as cloud movements. These displacements he calculates and illustrates with geometric nicety (*CL*, 24 iv 1827, 18 v 1827; I, 28, 58). "Cosmos" in my rubric is thus largely metaphorical, put there to convey openess to the environment in which he found himself, insofar as he could gain knowledge and an understanding of it. Ó Súilleabháin was no Medici, entering the renowned map room, La Stanza della Guardroba, on the second floor of the Palazzo Vecchio, by the banks of Florence's river Arno. Its sixteenth-century denizens gazed up from opulent images of horizons they had painted on the chamber's ornate walls, past the surrounding belt of Tuscany's Appenine hills, outward to the roadways of their mercantile fortunes. No such vistas awaited Amhlaoibh so long as Ossory's hovels intruded on its finer manors in his line of sight. Nevertheless, that author, albeit constricted in both setting and circumstances, did reside in the self-same world. As **C** and his other sources confirm, the world also resided in him.

I raise the last-mentioned topic because of its concluding implications. Ó Súilleabháin belongs to a period still characterized, as far as (some of) Irish-speaking Ireland is concerned, by a resonant descriptor associated with the musings of his fellow Munsterman (albeit of a later generation), Daniel Corkery (1878–1964).[36] The term suggests an isolated and inward-looking domain. That the Callan inhabitant's society did experience marginalisation, introspection and disadvantage is undisputed.[37] However, recent scholarship shows its ongoing dynamism and an openess to externality. The Post-Classical Irish phase at issue is book-ended by this Maynooth geographical tract

---

[36] See his classic, *The Hidden Ireland: a Study of Gaelic Munster in the Eighteenth Century* (Dublin: M. H. Gill & Son, 1924).

[37] Ian McBride, *Eighteenth-Century Ireland: the Isle of Slaves* (Dublin: Gill and Macmillan, 2009).

from early in the nineteenth century, and, earlier still, around the beginning of the 1700s, by an even more inclusive treatise devoted to the same topic. This is the Dublin-based Ó Neachtain learned family's adaptation of the bestselling *Geography Anatomiz'd* (1693, and later editions), by a Briton, Patrick Gordon.[38] As that work's Irish-language subtitle reveals, in being grounded on dialogue between a scribal father and son, it might be held to resemble **C**, if Amhlaoibh's parent can be posited as having augmented the latter. Verse is also interspersed throughout the prose in *Eólas ar an Domhan*. It celebrates the Irish past and its glories, decrying a reduction in the country's status. Entries of the latter variety suggest Gordon's work must have been filled out (presumably by Seán and Tadhg Ó Neachtain) with data unavailable to the original author, much as the Ó Súilleabháin piece could have been susceptible to amplification of its own from time to time.[39]

Further comparison between **C** and *Eólas* confirms that they diverge almost entirely otherwise in size, structure, ordering, or the contents entered about the regions treated. Accordingly, the former cannot derive from the latter. Quite clearly, therefore, each must have arisen independently of the other. However, they share the same identity and ethos as part of a continuum and continuity of interests and their expression in the vernacular they hold in common. That language remained capable, even as the 1800s commenced, of conveying the functionality and practicality of the subject on which Amhlaoibh's text expounds. The Maynooth tract did so, like its metropolitan predecessor, while absorbing its own creative age-old

---

[38] Meadhbh Ní Chléirigh (eag.), *Eólas ar an Domhan i bhFuirm Chomhráidh idir Sheán Ó Neachtain agus a Mhac Tadhg* Leabhair ó Láimhsgríbhinnibh XII (Baile Átha Cliath: Oifig an tSoláthair, 1944). The scholarly circles in which the treatise was refashioned are examined by Liam Mac Mathúna, *The Ó Neachtain Window on Gaelic Dublin, 1700-1750* Cork Studies in Celtic Literatures 4 ([Cork]: Cork Studies in Celtic Literatures, 2021).

[39] See Ní Chléirigh, *Eólas*, 2-15, for instances of how Ireland was handled, as well as the prosimetric dimension to that treatment. A rapprochement between *Eólas* and **C** was already implicit in comments on the latter made by de Bhaldraithe, *Cín Lae*, p. xxiii-xxiv.

aesthetic, coupled with a fairly frank stance.[40] Thus, the story of modern Irish which the Callan writer's work reflected was not yet one of absolute impairment, neither a *terra nullius* nor an untilled field.

[40] Although differing obviously in scale from the capital, Callan was also primarily an urban setting. For its influence as such on a writer so closely associated with that town, see Proinsias Ó Drisceoil, "Amhlaoibh Ó Súilleabháin: *Habitus* agus Gort," in Mac Mathúna, Liam, Regina Uí Chollatáin (eag.), *Saothrú na Gaeilge Scríofa i Suímh Uirbeacha na hÉireann, 1700-1850* (Baile Átha Cliath: Ollscoil Náisiúnta na hÉireann, 2016), 165-78.

A Celtic epic for Galicia: The influence of Ossian in *Os Pinos*, by Pondal and Veiga

Javier Campos Calvo-Sotelo

Introduction

In March 1890, the composer Pascual Veiga proposed to the poet Eduardo Pondal the creation of a Galician march. Pondal wrote *Os Pinos* (The Pines)[1], an extensive poem reflecting strong Ossianic influence, greater than is generally assumed.[2] In 1984, *Os Pinos* was officially declared the anthem of Galicia, with music by Veiga. The main source for Pondal's Celtic inspiration was Paul Christian's 1867 French translation of the poems by James Macpherson and John Smith, although, in Pondal's estimation, the sole author was the bard Ossian.[3] *Os Pinos* constitutes the essence of his Galician-Ossianic

---

[1] Galician original; hereafter GO. In this paper all the translations into English are by the author. Regarding the cited works by Pondal, the reference is the 1972 complete edition: Eduardo Pondal, *Queixumes dos Pinos e Outros Poemas* (Vigo: Castrelos).

[2] Isidoro Montiel, *Ossián en España* (Barcelona: Planeta, 1974); Ricardo Carballo Calero, *Historia da Literatura Galega Contemporánea 1808-1936* (Vigo: Galaxia, 1981 [1975]); Manuel Ferreiro, *Eduardo Pondal, o Cantor do Eido Noso* (Santiago de Compostela: Laiovento, 2017). Some general studies on the national symbols of Galicia deserve attention, such as Xosé R. Barreiro and Ramón Villares (eds.), *Os Símbolos de Galicia* (Santiago de Compostela: Consello da Cultura Galega; La Coruña: Real Academia Galega, 2007) and Baldomero Cores, *Los Símbolos Gallegos* (Santiago de Compostela: Velograf, 1986).

[3] Paul Christian, *Ossian, barde du IIIe siècle. Poëmes gaéliques recueillis par James Mac-Pherson* (Paris: Hachette, 1867 [1842]). Macpherson (1736-1796) was a Scottish writer who, in the late-eighteenth century, created the figure of the remote bard Ossian as the purported author of an epic cycle of narratives in Scottish Gaelic. Macpherson claimed to have translated the cycle into English-when the real author was himself-and had many imitators, among whom Reverend John Smith (1747-1807) stood out. The Ossianic controversy has been intense ever since Macpherson's first publication in 1760, as there were serious doubts about authenticity. However, the legend was successful and influential: "Ossianism developed

141

epic, a personal synthesis of local semiology and alleged Gaelic elements, such as pines, harps, and bards. The personification of nature, obsession with the past, overabundance of adjectives, and phonetic resonance obey the same principle: in *Os Pinos* there is not a single stanza without Ossianic echoes. Interestingly, Pondal's Celticness owes more to James Macpherson than to John Smith, against the pervasive belief,[4] making him the most relevant Ossianic author of nineteenth-century Spain. Thanks to a permission granted by the Real Academia Galega, I have examined the correspondence between Veiga and Pondal concerning *Os Pinos* and other original manuscripts that reveal Pondal's feverish elaboration. This paper also analyses Veiga's music for the poem, which lacks most of the formal traits from the so-called 'Ossianic manner' but shares with it an ethos of pastoral peacefulness, thus becoming an atypical anthem.[5]

Situated in the northwest corner of the Iberian Peninsula, Galicia is the most Atlantic region of Spain, with a long-standing Celtic tradition supported by an elite group of intellectuals and writers since the outbreak of local identity awareness in the nineteenth century. For these reasons, this region has been frequently twinned with the 'Celtic Fringe'.[6] However, "in Galicia, the popular grassroots of Celticness were enormous [. . .] but the recognition of this fact by the rest of

---

into a phenomenon that transcended the boundaries of literature." (Tim Worth, "Ossianism in Britain and Ireland, 1760-1800," Master's thesis, Aberystwyth: Aberystwyth University, 2012, 6).

[4] Howard Gaskill, "Introduction: 'Genuine poetry ... like gold'," in *The Reception of Ossian in Europe*, ed. Howard Gaskill (London and New York: Thoemmes Continuum, 2004), 1-20, at 16-18; Montiel, *Ossián en España,* chapter xii; Ricardo Carballo Calero, "John Smith e Eduardo Pondal," *Grial* 15, no. 55 (1977): 121; Xerardo Muñoz, "Os temas ossiánicos na poesía de Ramón Cabanillas," *Grial* 14, no. 54 (1976): 451-64, at 452.

[5] The "Ossianic manner" is discussed below.

[6] The "Celtic Fringe" is a geocultural entity referring to the regions of the Celtic League (see below). It has been strongly contested by authors like David Cornick ("Iona, Glastonbury and Anfield. Aspects of a common tradition?," *The Expository Times* 109, 1997: 42-7) and Daniel G. Williams ("Another lost cause? Pan-Celticism, race and language," *Irish Studies Review* 17/1, 2009: 89-101).

Celtic cultures was negligible."[7] Galician Celticness gave rise to suspicion due to the lack of Celtic linguistic roots (Galician is a Romance language) and for historiographical reasons.[8] In 1987, these factors led the Celtic League to exclude Galicia and the neighbor region Asturias as members of the association in a controversial decision.[9] Moreover, many Galician historians and intellectuals have rejected the Celtic theory over the last century, claiming that it misrepresents and trivializes the actual Galician culture.[10] Nonetheless, we are witnessing a resurgence of this theory in the notion of "Atlantic Celts" or "Celtic from the West," which aims to re-Celticize Galicia and other regions involved in recent archeological

---

[7] GO. Ramón Villares Paz, "Bretaña na cultura galega: conexións e semellanzas," *Grial* 55, no. 215 (2017): 14-21, at 16.

[8] For an explanation of Galician Celticness in history and differences with the Celtic Fringe, see Ramón Villares Paz, *Historia de Galicia* (Vigo: Galaxia, 2004) and Javier Campos Calvo-Sotelo, *Fiesta, Identidad y Contracultura. Contribuciones al Estudio Histórico de la Gaita en Galicia* (Pontevedra: Diputación Provincial, 2007). For northern Celts, Galicia belongs to the Spanish-Mediterranean stereotype, which also includes seeing it as a Catholic monarchy and a colonial empire, and with the absence of a Celtic language.

[9] Peter Berresford Ellis, *Celtic Dawn: The Dream of Celtic Unity* (Talybont: Y Lolfa, 2002). The Celtic League is a pan-Celtic association founded in 1961 and headquartered in Bodmin (Cornwall). It promotes Celtic nationalist culture in the "six Celtic nations" (Alba-Scotland, Breizh-Brittany, Cymru-Wales, Éire-Ireland, Kernow-Cornwall, and Mannin-Isle of Man), arguing their linguistic and historical otherness.

[10] On Galician "Celtophobia," see Beatriz Díaz Santana, *Los celtas en Galicia. Arqueología y política en la creación de la identidad gallega* (La Coruña: Toxosoutos, 2002). For example, at the Conservatory of Vigo (the largest city of South Galicia), if a student currently shows inclination towards any kind of 'Celtic music,' teachers will immediately deter him/her, as the Celtic myth is no longer credible for them (Xaquín Xesteira, teacher at this conservatory. Personal communication, December 2012; cited with permission).

research on the Bronze and Iron Age;[11] this trend is led by the archaeologists John Koch and Barry Cunliffe.[12] On the other hand, the Celtic roots of the 'Celtic Fringe'–the canon of Celticness worldwide– are being called into question (or just demolished) in the critical works of historians like Simon James, John Collis and Caoimnhín de Barra.[13]

Far from the main centers of development, virtually autarchic in the management of its resources, and anchored in the past, Galicia lived for centuries apart from modernity and progress, to the point that Ramón Otero–a prominent local writer–coined the metaphor of Galician insularity.[14] In the words of Galicia's most beloved poet, Rosalía de Castro (1837-1885): *"Galicia, ti non tes patria / Ti vives no mundo soia"* (Galicia, you have no homeland / you are alone in the world).[15] However, isolation helped the region to preserve a rich traditional culture of its own. It is at the intersection of Galicia's rural background with avant-garde literature that we can locate the figure of Pondal.

Eduardo González Pondal (1835-1917) belongs to a second generation of Galician Romantic authors, following pioneering

---

[11] Javier Campos Calvo-Sotelo, "In the name of Ossian: Celtic Galicia and the 'brothers from the north'," *Social Identities. Journal for the Study of Race, Nation and Culture* 25, no. 6 (2019): 828-42.

[12] Koch and Cunliffe were the editors of three consecutive volumes published in 2012, 2013 and 2016 under the generic title *Celtic from the West* (Oxford, UK: Oxbow Books).

[13] See, for example, Caoimnhín de Barra, *The Coming of the Celts, AD 1860. Celtic Nationalism in Ireland and Wales* (Notre Dame, Indiana: University of Notre Dame Press, 2018); F. L. Vleeshouwer, "Imagining the Celts: The Celtic image as known from historical, linguistic and archaeological sources, compared to the view on the Celts in the British (popular) media of the last five years (2010-2015)" (Master's thesis, Amsterdam: University of Leiden, 2015).

[14] Ramón Otero Pedrayo, *Ensaio Histórico sobre a Cultura Galega* (Vigo: Galaxia, 1982 [1930]). Along with several allusions to isolation, Otero underlined an ethnic alterity in the metaphor: "The Spanish differential character [. . .] cannot be applied to Galicia. Of Aryan, Atlantic, and Western lineage, the inner nature of Galician history can be assumed as insular . . . ." (GO, at 16).

[15] GO. Rosalía de Castro, "A Gaita Gallega," in her collection of Galician poems *Cantares Gallegos* (Vigo: Compañel, 1863), 125-29, at 127.

promoters of 'Galician Celticness' such as José Verea and Benito Vicetto. He completed a degree in Medicine at the University of Santiago de Compostela, but his wealthy upbringing afforded him the opportunity to devote his life to literature. Pondal remained in his birthplace in the small village of Ponteceso (North Galicia) his entire life, except for a few stays in nearby localities. He mastered classical Greek and Latin, as well as French (especially), Italian, Portuguese, and other languages. Very slow and self-critical in his work, he wrote little, completing only two brief books and some other poems throughout his lifetime. However, the quality of this work is beyond doubt, well above almost any other Galician writer from his time. Tightly linked to the *Rexurdimento* (local 'resurgence' movement), he became a patriarch for Galician nationalism, despite his limited involvement in practical politics.[16] The historian Manuel Murguía (1833-1923) exerted a strong influence during his youth, and they would become great friends for the rest of their lives. Murguía understood Galicia from an organicist perspective as a 'Celtic' country whose race was superior to the rest of Spain, and thus set the basis for the construction of Galician alterity.[17] Although Murguía's Celtic-oriented Galician-ness was uncritical in many ways (an "ethno-historical fancy" according to Leerssen),[18] it turned out to be far-reaching in the collective imagination of his regionalist followers. Pondal received his Celtic baptism from him, and the impact on his

---

[16] *Rexurdimento*: a Galician pre-nationalist tendency involving cultural revival; it was particularly intense in the second half of the nineteenth century.

[17] Murguía was influenced by authors such as Ernest Renan (especially his volume *La Poésie des Races Celtiques*. Paris: J. Claye et cie, 1854), Gobineau, and Thomas Carlyle, and their notion of a distinctive racial Celticness, as can be seen in his seminal volume *Los Precursores* (Coruña: Latorre y Martínez, 1885). On the notion of "nation-as-family," theorized by Steven Grosby, see Peter McQuillan, "The Conceptualization of Nationhood in Early-seventeenth Century Irish: A Frame-Semantic Approach," in *Proceedings of the Harvard Celtic Colloquium 39: 2019*, eds. Myrzinn Boucher-Durand, Shannon Parker, Elizabeth Gipson, and Nicholas Thyr (Cambridge, MA: Harvard University Press), 229-57.

[18] Joep Leerssen, "Gods, heroes and mythologists: Romantic scholars and the pagan roots of Europe's nations," *History of Humanities* 1, no. 1 (2016): 71-100, at 91.

work would be decisive after reading Paul Christian. When Murguía married Rosalía de Castro, the three writers formed a unified group which proved to be fundamental for the formation of Galician modern language and cultural identity.

With respect to the enthusiastic Ossianic fashion that spread in Europe and the Americas since the first publications by James Macpherson in the early 1760s, Spain was certainly a peripheral territory. This circumstance has led scholars to consider every Spanish writer as irrelevant to the trend, underestimating Pondal.[19] First of all, when he started writing under its influence, Ossianism was already in decline and did not attract the same attention.[20] Secondly, Pondal only borrowed five Ossianic names: Tura (city); Ullin (bard); Erin (Ireland); Cairbar (hero); and Lugar (warrior).[21] Additionally, Pondal mentioned Ossian only twice in his complete works.[22] Therefore, his Ossianic legacy was apparently minimal, but the trace of Ossian is key to understand his motivation and work, including most notably *Os Pinos* and its consequences for Galician history. As stated by Clark,

---

[19] Isidoro Montiel, "La primera traducción de Ossián en España," *Bulletin Hispanique* 70, no. 3-4 (1968): 476-85; Isidoro Montiel, *Ossián en España*; Andrew Ginger, "The Suggestiveness of Ossian in Romantic Spain: The Case of Espronceda and Garcia Gutierrez," in *The Reception of Ossian in Europe*, 335-50. Montiel's 1974 referential book remains the only comprehensive study of Spanish Ossianism.

[20] Furthermore, the image of Spain as an exotic reflection of the inner 'Other' within Europe was then experiencing a renewal process towards an alleged primitive and passional pathos of Spanish people, modeled on the Andalusian culture, its legendary bandits and female black-eyed dancers, rather than on the Celtic fringe. Jean Canavaggio, *Les Espagnes de Mérimée* (Madrid: Centro de Estudios Europa Hispánica, 2016); Michael Christoforidis and Elizabeth Kertesz, *Carmen and the Staging of Spain. Recasting Bizet's Opera in the Belle Epoque* (New York: Oxford University Press, 2019).

[21] Montiel presents an extensive list, although most of the names he displays are not literal copies (*Ossián en España*, 189-94).

[22] With respect to key terms, in his entire repertoire Pondal mentioned "Celtic" frequently, but only twice "Galicia," which is a bit surprising. Conversely, Macpherson cited "Scotland" many times, and barely used "Celtic," probably because in the eighteenth century the 'Celtic myth' was only beginning to take shape in the literary imaginary of the islands (Caoimnhín de Barra, *The Coming of the Celts*).

"Pondal's debt to Macpherson is enormous,"[23] to the extent that the Galician writer embodied the ideals that he was reflecting in poetry, as a symbiosis of art and existence. Pondal retired from modern life and took refuge in his birthplace, far from noise and rush, going for long walks, admiring the peace and beauty of Galicia, hearing the voice of nature, and enjoying the *pazo* of his family.[24] He liked to be called *o bardo* (the bard)–as in the meetings of the Cova Céltica in Coruña–and so was he named by his neighbors and Galician media.[25]

The creation of Os Pinos

Pascual Veiga was the father of the anthem of Galicia. *Os Pinos* was born when he organized a music contest to be held in Coruña by late August 1890. Veiga was at the peak of his career as a composer and director of choral societies, and planned a magnificent competition, with several categories and great awards. For the category of "Best Regional March," lyrics were necessary, and thus Veiga sent a letter to Pondal–whose career was also thriving after the successful publication of *Queixumes dos Pinos* in 1886–proposing to him that he write the verses. Pondal probably sensed the historical importance of the occasion and accepted immediately. One of the major features he had adopted from Ossian was the aim of immortality, of surviving over time in the memory of the people, a true

---

[23] David M. Clark, "Sons and daughters of Breogán. Scottish and Irish influence on Galician Language Literature," in *What country's this? And whither are we gone?*, eds. J. Derrick McClure, Karoline Szatek-Tudor and Rosa E. Penna (Newcastle: Cambridge Scholars, 2010), 8-22, at 13.

[24] *Pazo*: from Italian *palazzo* (palace). In Galicia it indicates the house of a noble family, quite more ample and refined than those of the countrymen. *Pazos* are distinguished by a tower-relic of old times-and a large garden, and so is the Pazo Pondal in Ponteceso.

[25] Coruña was the largest and most important city of Galicia. Situated in the north seashore, it had an active trade abroad, and became the entrance gate of cultural and scientific novelties. Veiga lived in Coruña and Pondal visited the city frequently, especially the bookstore of his friend Eugenio Carré Aldao, who provided him with the latest publications of interest. In the back room of his store, Carré organised periodical meetings of intellectuals and artists that would receive the name of "Cova Céltica" (Celtic cave). In those meetings Pondal rose as a leader, and was named *o bardo* due to his exaltation of Celtic culture.

147

obsession that could be fulfilled by authoring an everlasting anthem in collaboration with Veiga. Pondal wrote *Os Pinos*, an extensive poem, over a rather short period of time. Original manuscripts evince his feverish elaboration of multiple drafts, with altered, and even undecipherable passages, in small, tight handwriting. This marked an unprecedented effort in his life, especially during the first days of composition.

Pondal left four groups of drafts identifiable as progressive layers according to the contents.[26] The last one shows the initial poem–of only seven stanzas–that Pondal sent to Veiga on April 5, 1890. The title was not *Os Pinos*, but *Breogán*.[27] Veiga noticed problems in the distribution of accents and inner rhythm for a choir performance, and required specific changes (April 7). Pondal modified the accents and extended the poem to nine stanzas (April 14); he also changed the title, which became the definitive *Os Pinos*, although Breoghan remained the referential figure–all the stanzas finishing with his name except for the first and third.[28] Veiga expressed his complete satisfaction for the outcome in the last letter between them (April 22), and this marked the end of Pondal's contribution to the future anthem of Galicia. Only in 1910 the Galician emigrant in Havana José Fontenla Leal, who had been the driving force for its premiere in 1907, did write a letter to Pondal requiring the original manuscript of the lyrics. Pondal responded in 1913, adding a new stanza; hence, the final poem has ten stanzas and eighty verses.[29]

Despite the rush, Pondal was able to create a little masterpiece, condensing both the aesthetic and the ideological principles that had guided his career. *Os Pinos* constitutes the quintessence of Pondal's

---

[26] Manuel Ferreiro Fernández, *De Breogán aos Pinos. O texto do Himno Galego* (Santiago de Compostela: Laiovento, 2007).

[27] Breogán (Breoghan) was the Pondalian replica to Ossian. His figure is explained below.

[28] This concluding reiteration lends the anthem a remarkable thematic and rhyming cohesion.

[29] Fontenla was a key figure not only for the official premiere and dissemination of the Galician anthem, but for the foundation of the Real Academia Galega (in 1905), the consolidation of the Galician flag, and as a tireless promoter in the task of taking in, instructing and providing employment for the massive Galician emigration in Cuba.

Galician-Ossianic epic and his culmination as a writer, in a personal synthesis of local culture and Irish-Scottish legends.

A Celtic epic for Galicia

As said above, Pondal's Ossianism derived from a French translation by Paul Christian, which gathered the narrations by Macpherson and Reverend John Smith as belonging to a unique bard Ossian.[30] After reading it, the 'Celtic dream' revived in him, with immediate impact on his work. In *Canto de las vírgenes celtas* ("Song of the Celtic virgins," 1868), Pondal explicitly cited the name of Ossian, in a direct translation of the initial passage "Daughter of beauty" (*fille de la beauté*) from *Fingal III* (see Table 1 below). He wrote *Cantos Célticos* (Celtic chants) around 1869, but his greatest tributes to Ossian were the volumes *Rumores de los Pinos* (Rumors of the pines, 1877, in Spanish) and *Queixumes dos Pinos* (Laments of the pines, 1886), and culminated in *Os Pinos* (1890), the latter two in Galician.[31] In these works, Pondal created the character of Breoghan

---

[30] Paul Christian, *Ossian, barde du IIIe siècle*. Between 1842 and 1910, Paul Christian (pseudonym for Christian Pitois) published eight editions of this work, which, in Paul Van Thieghem's critical evaluation (*Ossian en France*, Paris: F. Rieder, vol. 2, 1917 [1910], 315), was a *succédané* (substitute) for Hill (pseudonym for David de Saint-Georges and Antoine Gilbert Griffet de Labaume), *Poésies d'Ossian et de quelques autres Bardes, pour servir de suite à l'Ossian de Letourneur* (Paris: Gueffier, 1794). According to Howard Gaskill, the volume by Christian was "a modest reworking of Le Tourneur" ("The Homer of the North," *Interfaces* 27, 2008: 13-24, at 19), referring to Pierre Letourneur and David Saint Georges (trans.), *Ossian, fils de Fingal, barde du troisième siècle* (Paris: Musier, 2 vols., 1777). Hill's version was written after Le Tourneur, and both translations were more appreciated than Christian's, which became, nonetheless, very popular. Pondal purchased the 1867 edition shortly after it was released in Paris. Contrary to his custom, he did not write a single note or underline any word in the book, as perhaps it was like a Bible for him, to be preserved unspoiled.

[31] It is very common to consider *Os Pinos* as a poem contained in *Queixumes dos Pinos*. Although the former was very much inspired by the latter, it is a completely new composition, longer and more complex than any other in the book.

as an "Ossianic ethnotype"[32] in the process of construction of Galician cultural otherness. Breoghan, originally taken from the medieval Irish text *Lebor Gabála Érenn* (commonly known as The Book of Invasions), became Galicia's national hero; since his descendants occupied Ireland and Scotland in the Milesian legend, Galicia was now associated with the Celtic nations from the north.[33] There were good reasons for this appropriation process, as Galician literature scholar Ricardo Carballo outlines:

> Bergantiños was in Galicia what Morven [was] in Scotland. Breoghan, our Fingal. But while the ancient Irish epic and Gaelic chants provided Macpherson with abundant names of heroes [. . .] no Celtic epic tradition was preserved in Galicia.[34]

Galicia had few heroes, glorious events, and deeds to rely upon from real history. Hence, Pondal resorted to the Celtic mythological universe, which was an overflowing source of motifs and characters, additionally building a literary alliance with the pan-Celtic brotherhood.[35]

An important question is whether he created exactly an 'epic.' Important features of this complex and imprecise genre–"on the verge of orality and literacy"–are present.[36] As Macpherson did for Scotland, Pondal re-wrote Galician history in a long narration, chronicling (inventing) great feats that were meant to be significant to the local identity. It was a decision which went beyond literary purposes; as

---

[32] Joep Leerssen, "Celticism," in *Encyclopedia of Romantic Nationalism in Europe*, ed. Joep Leerssen (Amsterdam: Amsterdam University Press, 2018). Available online: https://bit.ly/3NB0Ekh. Accessed August 13, 2021.
[33] Campos, "In the name of Ossian."
[34] GO. Carballo, *Historia da Literatura Galega Contemporánea*, 270-1. Bergantiños is a small region within Galicia, in which Ponteceso is located.
[35] 'Pan-Celtic brotherhood' and similar expressions can be defined as the communal belief of belonging to a historical and cultural unity derived from sharing Celtic ancestry, advocating solidarity and cooperation between the so-called Celtic nations, and containing pastoral and magical connotations. They have been widely promoted in recent decades by 'Celtic' musicians like Enya and Alan Stivell.
[36] Andrew Ford, *Homer. The Poetry of the Past* (Ithaca: Cornell University Press, 1993), 14.

Bohlman states: "[t]he epic was a bridge from the past to the future," which in the nineteenth century "would assert itself as the musical and poetic genre of the nation and of nationalism."[37] Ferreiro approaches Pondal as the creator of a national epic for Galicia (*épica nacional*).[38] Conversely, Muñoz and Carballo believe that Pondal had not enough foundations to create a complete epic, and therefore he just "Celtified" regional toponyms and elements of the vegetation and landscape.[39] Clark esteems that Pondal generated:

> [A] unique literary tradition [. . .] Pondal's work provides a creation which encompasses a series of mythical characters made up of warriors, bards, pilgrims and shepherds against a physical backdrop of pines, mists, snows and winds.[40]

Definitely, Macpherson and Pondal were not traditional oral epic singers, but *artists* in the modern sense of the term, and the divergence between these dichotomic conceptions is radical.[41] Whereas traditional oral epic singers in non-literate societies narrate/reframe powerful symbols and myths by and for the community, in the artist we hear the voice of the poet as himself, an omniscient narrator who recreates the voices of the characters that he reinvents and reshapes from oral tradition. However, these Romantic reifications can still be considered from a "metageneric"[42] approach to Celtic cycles as a new

---

[37] Philip V. Bohlman, "Herder's Nineteenth Century," *Nineteenth-Century Music Review* 7, no. 1 (2010): 3-21, at 15-6.

[38] Ferreiro, *Eduardo Pondal, o cantor do eido noso*, 96. *Os Eoas* (the children of the dawn, in Greek) was a late and unfinished attempt by Pondal within the epic genre.

[39] Muñoz, "Os temas ossiánicos"; Carballo, *Historia da Literatura Galega Contemporánea*, 270-1.

[40] Clark, "Sons and daughters of Breogán," 13.

[41] Ford, *Homer. The Poetry of the Past* (especially chapter 2, pp. 57-89). See also Corinna Laughlin, "The Lawless Language of Macpherson's 'Ossian'," *Studies in English Literature, 1500-1900* 40, no. 3 (2000): 511-37; and James Mulholland, "James Macpherson's Ossian Poems, Oral Traditions, and the Invention of Voice," *Oral Tradition* 24, no. 2 (2009): 393-414.

[42] Beyond the constraints of a specific genre.

interpretive framework for the literary epic that may help to revitalize interest in this canon.[43]

The influence of Ossian

There has been some debate about whose influence was more determining in Pondal: Macpherson or Smith. In southern Europe, the legend of Ossian was mostly known via the combined translations of both authors and, therefore, Smith was as accessible as Macpherson to the Spanish audience, increasing his potential impact there.[44] This fact was strengthened by the popularity of Antonio Chocomeli's Spanish translation of Smith's poem "Gaul," published in 1874.[45] However, the Ossianism of Pondal owes much more to Macpherson than to Smith, drawing especially from the following works included in Christian's translation (in this order):[46]

- "Carthon"–16
- *Fingal* (the six books)–1
- "The Songs of Selma"–8
- "Carric-Thura"–7

---

[43] Barry Weller, "The Epic as Pastoral: Milton, Marvell, and the Plurality of Genre," *New Literary History* 30, no. 1 (1999): 143-57.

[44] Howard Gaskill, "Ossian in Europe," *Canadian Review of Comparative Literature* 21, no. 4 (1994): 643-678, especially p. 658 ff. See also Clark, "Sons and daughters of Breogán." During the nineteenth century, José Ortiz, Pedro de Montengón, Abbot Marchena, Nicasio Gallego, and Antonio de Chocomeli partially translated the poems of Ossian, but the most comprehensive attempt was a rendering in verse by Lasso of Christian's 1867 French version (Ángel Lasso de la Vega, *Ossian Bardo del Siglo III. Poemas Gaélicos*. Madrid: Biblioteca Universal, 1883, 3 vols.). Pondal had a volume of Lasso in his library, but the pages were unopened (as I found out personally), so it should not be considered one of his sources. The writers José de Espronceda, García Gutiérrez, A. de Saavedra, López Soler, Vicente Boix, and G. A. Bécquer left some Ossianic passages, but little seems to be their influence on Pondal, who maybe adopted some ideas from Espronceda's poem "Oscar and Malvina" in 1837 (Elena Catena, "Ossian y España," *Cuadernos de Literatura* 10/11/12, 1948: 57-95; Montiel, *Ossián en España*, especially p. 118).

[45] Antonio Chocomeli Codina, *Gaul. Poema de Ossian* (Madrid: Victoriano Suárez, 1874).

[46] Each title includes the respective number in Christian's edition.

- "Comala"–2
- "The Battle of Lora"–5

Therefore, it looks as though Pondal was especially drawn to the first texts; this could explain, at least partially, why Smith was less influential on the Galician writer (his tales are the last fourteen items in Christian's volume–numbers 26 to 39). A close analysis also reveals that Pondal integrated more elements from the beginnings (and endings) of those initial chapters into his Ossianic poems. For instance, there is a direct influence from the first lines of each of the six books of *Fingal*–the first chapter in Christian's *Ossian, barde du IIIe siècle*.

Importantly, besides some coincidences between Scotland and Galicia,[47] and besides their common admiration towards Homer and rejection of Roman ambition, there was probably a particular affinity between Macpherson and Pondal stemming from the similarities of their personalities. Pondal was harsh, misanthropic, and preferred vigorous and dramatic images for poetry, either lyrical or epic, like the robust and tall pine. According to Filgueira, Pondal's inclination was towards toughness, virility, and strength:

> He didn't want [. . .] a weak or tearful page [. . .]
> 'to put the boy to sleep.' He said it many times [. . .]

---

[47] Mostly coming from the pan-Celtic collective imagination, where the twinning of both regions is taken for granted as part of a shared ethnogenesis despite evidence (see above the "Introduction" to this chapter). However, some common elements can be outlined, like the green landscape, rainy weather, ruralism (scattered settlement), rich folklore and cultural heritage, Atlantism, peripheral status as remote and isolated regions far from the respective capital (London, Madrid), and an emerging consciousness of historical recovery. But it was not until the first Celtic revivals that these elements began to be assumed as a common ethos and cultural destiny. See Tudi Kernalegenn, "The differentiated imagination of the region in Brittany, Galicia and Scotland," in *Regions in Europe. Administrative structures and territorial identity issues,* ed. Elisabeth Károlyi (Budapest: L'Harmattan, 2016), 206-218; Javier Campos Calvo-Sotelo, "*Don't say Celtic!* Recent research around Celtic music in Scotland, Galicia, and Ireland," presentation at *The Society for Ethnomusicology 2021 Annual Meeting* (Atlanta, October 28-31).

And he would settle it in the anthem itself: 'Esteem is not reached / with a vile soft moan.'[48]

Gaskill puts forward the different personality of Smith compared to Macpherson, and the former would fall far from Pondal's temperament:

[B]y comparison with Macpherson Smith tends to accentuate the tender as against the heroic, his pathos is gentler, his sentimentality sweeter, the love interest more pronounced. As Van Tieghem observes, his poetry displays a more personal, already quite romantic melancholy.[49]

Nevertheless, in Pondal there are also elements adopted from Smith's *Galic Antiquities*; as Montiel detected: "The siege that Gairbar [Cairbar] and Gundariz imposed on Tura [Pondal, *Queixumes dos Pinos*] is [. . .] a motif or scene taken from the story told in "The Fall of Tura," an Ossianic poem [. . .] by John Smith."[50]

The trace of Ossian is immediately apparent in the obsession with the past, Romantic emotion and overabundance of adjectives. The poetic pantheism and personification of nature (a true animistic cosmology) is deeply rooted in the socio-cultural milieu of its time.[51]

---

[48] GO. José Filgueira Valverde, *O Himno Galego: da "Marcha do Reino de Galicia" a "Os Pinos" de Veiga e Pondal* (Pontevedra: Caixa de Pontevedra, 1991 [1978]), 16-7. Filgueira quotes *Os Pinos*, ninth stanza, lines 1-2.

[49] Howard Gaskill, "Introduction," 18.

[50] Spanish original. Montiel, *Ossián en España*, 184. John Smith, *Galic Antiquities: Consisting of a History of the Druids...* (Edinburgh: MacFarquhar and Elliot, 1780).

[51] This literary pantheism reflects a deep sociological phenomenon that followed the rationalism of Enlightenment and the first wave of the industrial revolution. Old and new myths spread in countless reifications to compensate the disenchantment of the world, as the outstanding case of Ossian and Celticness illustrates (Javier Campos, "New Gods, New Shrines. Identity and De-secularization Processes in Young Followers of Celtic Music," in *Holy Crap! Selected Essays on the Intersections of the Popular and the Sacred in Youth Cultures*, eds. Antti-Ville Kärjä and Kimi Kärki, 15-24. Turku: International Institute for Popular Culture, 2016. Available online at https://bit.ly/3OlUR23).

Other features transferred from Macpherson are: the desire of immortality; the "joy of grief";[52] the lack of story/plot (there is hardly any action); a particular musicality;[53] and an uncritical Celticness blurring fantasy and reality, the Iron Age and the Middle Ages, the human and the supernatural, and so on. The Ossianic footprint is also clear in concrete elements, like the revered pines, harps, and roe deer.[54] The same happens with specific characters, like the heroine, the warrior, and the bard.[55] Some local names (either anthroponyms or toponyms) are transformed into characters, echoing an Ossianic resonance, as in the case of "Ousinde"–a young heroine in *Os Pinos*, the name coming from a north-Galicia surname, and probably inspired by 'Ossian' phonetics; "Maroñas"–a hamlet near Ponteceso, and the name of another Pondal heroine–may evoke "Ma-ronnan/

---

[52] "A species of emotional ambivalence that releases the subject from despair and instead conveys a kind of dignity" (James Porter, *Beyond Fingal's Cave: Ossian in the Musical Imagination*. Rochester: University of Rochester Press, 2019, 4). In "Carric-Thura," Fingal exclaims: "Pleasant is the joy of grief!", probably borrowing the expression from Edmund Burke, and the message conveyed is clear in Homer's *Odyssey*. The sense of a "joy in/of grief" became a true Romantic motto, also for Pondal.

[53] This is another outstanding feature in Pondal, who emphasizes the accents, prosody, resonance in the names of personages and locations, and general phonetic effect.

[54] The pines are the central subject of the Galician anthem, but a rather secondary tree species in Galicia, although abundant in Bergantiños. Quite more representative of the regional flora and literary tradition is the oak, which shows how much Pondal was committed to the Celtic cause as a renewing cultural capital. Moreover, Pondal chose the Spanish denomination (*pinos*) ignoring the Galician word (*piñeiros*), and this raises some questions. Concerning the de-contextualization of characters, the figure of Ossian as a bard who plays the harp was an invention: "[t]he picture of the Ossianic bard [. . . .] in no way corresponded to the historical reality in Ireland, Scotland, or Wales" (Porter, *Beyond Fingal's Cave*, 29).

[55] These were also rather alien figures to Galician culture. Pondal's replicas of the heroines Inibaca and Oithona (*Fingal*), Utha ("Carric-Thura"), and Colmal ("Calthon and Colmal"), are the beautiful Maroñas, a warrior virgin *de majestuoso andar* ("of majestic gait," GO); the sweet Maimendos, a poetess who plays the harp; and Ousinde.

Maronnan."[56] As in Homer and Macpherson, the literary architecture of Pondal includes lengthy descriptive epithets indicating the predominant feature of the character; for instance: *Cairbar* [. . .] *como esbelto y alto pino* ("Cairbar [. . .] like slender and tall pine").[57] Other specific passages, names, and expressions molded upon Macpherson undergo a similar practice of transduction in Pondal's poems, like the beginning of "Carthon" (which will be analyzed below).

In any case, Pondal was not a Galician mirror of James Macpherson. He developed a particular interpretation of the Ossianic epic, and there are relevant differences with the style of the Scottish writer:

> [The] procedures of the poems recast by Macpherson and those by Pondal are quite different. In the Gaelic poems there is literary dramatization, sustained scenes, a long work of systematized sensibility [. . .] In Pondal [there is] the fast, accurate, evocative impression [. . .], with borderlines that bring to the spirit the scene and the drama that the poet unfolded.[58]

Pondal was extremely ambiguous and vague, even more than the Ossianic source. As José Luis Varela explains, the Galician poet went further than his model in this regard:

> Pondal is not the author of Ossianic epic stories, but of Ossianic scenes and notes. Pondal narrates minimally; He does not describe, properly, either: he supports with fragile elements a scene or an object that will serve him for a sentimental escape or an

---

[56] A warrior chief, "Ma-ronnan" in "The battle of Lora" and "Conlath and Cuthona"; "Maronnan" in *Temora*. In Christian, we only find "Maronnan." Smith also uses this character in "The Fall of Tura."

[57] In *Queixumes dos Pinos*, poem *En turbia noche de invierno* ("On a murky winter night)", lines 52-53. With regards to these descriptive epithets, the list in Macpherson is extensive. Pondal uses, for example, Gundariz, *el prudente* (the cautious) or Tomil, *bardo de nobre andar* (bard of noble gait, GO), and those of the heroines mentioned above.

[58] GO. Ramón Otero Pedrayo, "Romantismo, saudade, sentimento da raza e da terra en Pastor Díaz, Rosalía Castro e Pondal" [Induction speech by Otero at the Real Academia Galega] (Santiago de Compostela: Nós, 1931), 141.

invocation. From Ossian he retains the elegiac and lyrical tone, the invocation, the melancholic soliloquy of the bard. He discards [. . .] all "history", all "adventure", all argument.[59]

An important divergence comes from the native sources dealt with in each case. In Macpherson, the 'translation' was based upon elements coming from Gaelic oral epic poetry, developing "a pioneering fieldwork methodology for Gaelic culture," and making "Gaelic poetry, old and new, a marketable commodity."[60] Instead, Pondal ignored many components of his own culture, and adopted the Celtic legend in the search for an entirely new semiology. His abstraction of Galicia is such that Breoghan is never described, nor he does ever participate in the events of the poems–another meaningful difference with the Ossian of Macpherson. Breoghan is an essence, fundamental as a patriarch of Galicia, but limited to modify the nouns that he redeems in *Os Pinos* ("land, harps, daughters, . . . of Breoghan").[61]

Text comparison

The following comparative tables show how the material process of 'Ossianizing Galicia' took place in the poetry of Pondal after his 'conversion' in 1868. His first poem that year was "Canto de las vírgenes celtas," whose headwords consisted of a literal translation of a passage from *Fingal III* in the French version by Christian (Table 1). Pondal wrote "Ossian" under the headwords as its author; this was the first time he mentioned Ossian explicitly.[62]

---

[59] Spanish original. José Luis Varela, "Un capítulo del ossianismo español: Eduardo Pondal," in *Estudios dedicados a Menéndez Pidal*, vol. 6 (Madrid: CSIC, 1956), 556-590, at 564.

[60] Thomas A. McKean, "The fieldwork legacy of James Macpherson," *Journal of American Folklore* 114/454 (2001), 447-463, at 460.

[61] Line 8 of stanzas 5, 7 and 8 respectively.

[62] The second (and last) one occurred in *Rumores de los Pinos* (1877), in the title of the poem *El Recuerdo de la Pátria (Sobre motivos de Ossián)* [The Memory of the Fatherland (On Ossian's motifs)].

Macpherson 1773 (1762)[63]	Christian 1867	Pondal 1868. Headwords for "Canto de las vírgenes celtas" 1868
"Daughter of beauty," calm I said, "what sigh is in thy breast? Can I, young as I am, defend thee, daughter of the sea? My sword is not unmatched in war, but dauntless is my heart."	Fille de la beauté, lui dis-je avec amour, pourquoi pleures-tu? Puis-je te protéger, puis-je te défendre, ó vierge de la mer? Mon glaive peut voler en éclats sur le bouclier d'un ennemi; mais mon cœur n'a point de rival.	Hija de la belleza, díjele con amor, ¿por qué lloras tú? ¿Puedo yo protegerte, puedo yo defenderte, oh virgen del mar? Mi espada puede volar en astillas sobre el escudo de un enemigo; pero mi corazón no tiene rival.

Table 1. *Fingal*, book III

At a simple glance it becomes clear how Christian tends to ornament the text; Macpherson is, despite his literary exuberance, more concise. This fact influenced the richness of images in Pondal. In his translation into Spanish, every single word as well as the punctuation are modeled upon the French rendering. We can conclude that, in this early period of influence, Pondal was a 'Frenchified' Ossianic author. However, the fact that he did not rely on the English originals prevented him to access the richness and the nuances intrinsic to the language. For example, one of the crucial (perhaps the most crucial) words of his poetry, pine, was modeled on the French *sapin/pin*; as a result, Pondal missed the additional semantics evoked

---

[63] For this study I have used the edition of James Macpherson, *The Poems of Ossian. Translated by James Macpherson* (London: Strahan and Becket, 1773, 2 vols.).

by Macpherson (to pine as to languish).[64] He continued working on the same French basis in the future, but instead of literal translations, Pondal would undertake the core task of 'Galicianizing' Ossian or, to be more precise, 'Ossianizing' Galicia, in the creation of an epic destined to legitimize its nationalist aspirations as a proud and free homeland.[65]

Table 2 compares the English and French beginning of "Carthon" with *Os Pinos* and *Queixumes dos Pinos* (*QP*). I have indicated in bold type the passages common to the three texts, in order to highlight how Pondal reworked his source; I have underscored the additions by Christian which were incorporated by Pondal (not present in Macpherson). "Carthon" is a relevant hymn ascribed to Ossian himself; it starts and ends with the exclamation "A tale of the times of old!" and consists of an epic narration, replete of war, love, mythological characters, and an animistic nature, all elements which

---

[64] Among other divergences due to the linguistic and cultural translation, the pivotal position of the harp in Macpherson hid a subtle political intention, which most certainly went unnoticed by both Christian and Pondal (Tim Worth, *Ossianism in Britain and Ireland*).

[65] However, although Pondal is the cornerstone of Galicianism in poetry, he subordinated regionalism to the idea of Spain at some crucial moments. In his letter to Veiga on April 5, 1890, the poet declared his rejection of political *separatismo* (separatism) and advocated to continue to be part of *nuestra grande y gloriosa España* ("our great and glorious Spain"; Spanish original), and only under these terms he accepted to write the text for the anthem. In this sense, his figure has been politically instrumentalized, at the expense of his strictly literary merits.

Macpherson 1773 (1762)	Christian 1867	Pondal 1890, *Os Pinos* / 1886, *QP*[1]
A tale of the **times of old**! The **deeds of days of other years.**	**Splendeurs des siècles passés, gloire des héros décédés, revivez dans mes chants**	*Splendor dos pasados tempos* (*QP*)[2] – "Times of old"
The **murmur of thy streams**, O Lora! Brings back the **memory of the past**. The **sound of thy woods**, Garmaller, is lovely in mine ear. Dost thou not behold Malvina, a rock with its head of **heath! Three aged pines** bend from its face; **green is the narrow plain** at its feet; ….	Le **murmure de tes ruisseaux**, ô Lora, rappelle la **mémoire desjours** qui ne sont plus. Le **frémissement de tes forêts**, ô Germallat, est doux à mon oreille comme le bruit de **cent harpes**. Malvina, ne vois-tu pas ce rocher couronné de **bruyères? Trois vieux pins** se détachent de son front sourcilleux, et à ses pieds s'étend une **vallée verte**. ….	**Rumorosos** (1st ST) – "Murmur" *Non des a esquecemento … os tempos son chegados* (2nd/4th ST) – "Memory of the past" *Os Pinos* (title); *Teus soantes pinos* (6th ST) – "Aged pines" *Escuro arume arpado … arpas de Breogán* (1st/8th ST) – "Cent harpes" *Verdecente … amor da terra verde, da verde terra nosa* (1st/7th ST) – "Green" *Uces* (*QP*)[3] – "Head of heath"
The deer of the mountain avoids the place, for he beholds a **dim ghost** standing there. **The mighty** lie, O Malvina! In the narrow plain of the rock. ….	**Le chevreuil** de la montagne s'en fuit à l'aspect du **fantôme** qui garde ce lieu sacré. Deux **guerriers** fameux, ô Malvina, reposent dans cette vallée. ….	*Corzo* – "Chevreuil"; *Fantasma, esprito* (*QP*)[4] – "Ghost" *Galegos sede fortes* (10th ST) – "The mighty"
Bard of the times to come!	**Bardes futurs**	*Bardos das edades* (4th ST) – "Bard of the times"

Table 2. Beginning of "Carthon"

[1] In this Table all the texts by Pondal are GO from *Os Pinos*, except for a few from *QP* (as indicated). ST: stanza/s.
[2] From "En turbia noche de invierno" (cited above), line 67.
[3] Elsewhere.
[4] Elsewhere.

proved to be especially ideal to inspire Pondal. One by one the key motifs of these (French) first lines are mimicked in *Os Pinos*. "Carthon" contains, within itself, the seeds of the anthem of Galicia.

It is significant how Pondal removes the initial "e" in the word *splendor*, which either in Spanish or in Galician is *esplendor*; probably with the purpose of stressing the resonance of the sound "s" from the French text. The term comes exclusively from Christian, as Macpherson did not use it.[66] The locution *bards futurs* (bard of the times to come) does not appear until the middle of the tale, and seemingly Pondal is closer to Macpherson than to Christian in the Galician rendering (*bardos das edades*), but Christian uses elsewhere in his book either *bards des temps anciens* or *bards des temps passés*. However, in cases like this it is plausibly an interference originating from a different source.[67]

For a better understanding of the structure, phonetics and content of *Os Pinos*, Table 3 displays the two first stanzas, with the translation

---

[66] Other interesting elisions and contractions stemming from French can be consulted in the editors' initial note to Eduardo Pondal, *Queixumes dos Pinos*, 7-12. More subtleties from Macpherson's English-that went logically unnoticed by Pondal-can be read in Giuliana Bertipaglia, "Ossian and Cesarotti: Poems and Translations," *Studies in Scottish Literature* 32, no. 1 (2001): 132-139, especially 135.

[67] Carballo suggests that Pondal accessed other Celtic sources, like *Les bardes bretons, poème du VI siècle* by Theodor H. de La Villemarqué, first published by Renouard in Paris, 1850 (*Historia da Literatura Galega Contemporánea*, 258-9). I think there is a probable literary borrowing from Melchiorre Cesarotti's 1772 celebrated Italian translation of Ossian (*Poesie di Ossian*. Padua: Comino, 4 vols.) in the use of *verdecente* (green); from Italian *verdeggiante*; there are no French, Galician or Spanish equivalents) in the first stanza of *Os Pinos*. Other secondary influences are quite possible, like the early translation by Montengón into Spanish (Pedro Montengón, *Fingal y Temora: poemas épicos de Osian antiguo poeta céltico*. Madrid: Benito García, 1800). Overall, Pondal's work shows undeniable traces of the legacy from Virgil, Tasso, Camoes, Milton, and French contemporary poetry, as well as from Spanish literary neo-classicism-clearly visible in the rhyme scheme.

in English.[68] The vague, Romantic, and pastoral atmosphere of Ossianism pervades the whole text, as well as concrete elements. The term *rumorosos* (murmuring) represents the pines; in this case, the adjective replaces the noun, a Pondalian frequent rhetorical device that forces the reader to rebuild the absent parts of the narration. The poet supposedly asks the pines about the history and future of Galicia (first stanza), and the response comes from Galicia herself through the animistic symbol of the trees, in a discourse addressed to all Galicians (second stanza onwards).

Galician	English
¿Que din os rumorosos	What do the murmurers say
na costa verdecente,	on the green coast
ao raio transparente	under the clear beam
do prácido luar?	of the serene moonlight?
¿Que din as altas copas	What do the lofty treetops
de escuro arume arpado	of harped dark pine twigs say
co seu ben compasado	in their harmonious
monótono fungar?	monotonous hum?
Do teu verdor cinguido	Girded by thy greenness,
e de benignos astros,	and by benign stars,
confín dos verdes castros	bound of the green hill forts
e valeroso chan,	and O brave land,
non des a esquecemento	Let not thyself into oblivion
da inxuria o rudo encono;	the harsh grudge of scorn;
desperta do teu sono	awaken from thy slumbers,
fogar de Breogán.	O hearth of Breoghan.

Table 3. Os Pinos, Galician original and English. First two stanzas.

Many other passages could be fruitfully compared, as the Pondalian production is flooded with Ossianism. In Table 4 there are some complementary examples of interest, concerning the elements of sound and color, from the English original text to the French one, and eventually the transition to the poetry of Pondal in *Os Pinos*. Bold is for relevant coincidences.

---

[68] The official lyrics of the anthem of Galicia (which are not exactly the verses Pondal wrote in 1890) can be read at https://bit.ly/3NEG16w (accessed May 14, 2021). The complete poem and further changes have been analyzed by Manuel Ferreiro in different works.

Macpherson 1773 (1760/2)	Christian 1867	Pondal 1890, *Os Pinos*
'Moonbeams' (elsewhere; also Smith) '**He pierced her white side!**' (*Fingal I*) '**Breast of snow**' (*Fragments ...*) '**white besomed daughter / white as the driven snow**' ("Songs of Selma")	'**Rayons de la lune**' (elsewhere) '**[Ducomar frappe] ... le beau sein de la vierge**' (*Fingal I*) '**Sein de niege**' ("Comala") '**Beau sein**' (elsewhere)	'**Raio transparente do prácido luar**' (1st stanza) '**Os doces e albos peitos / Das fillas de Breogán**' (7th stanza)
'Cuthullin sat by Tura's wall: by the **tree of the rustling sound**' (*Fingal I*, first sentence) '**What murmur rolls along the hill ... ?**' (*Fingal I*) Fingal, on the death of Erragon: '**O stranger ... Listen to the sound of his woods!**' ("The Battle of Lora")	'Cuchullin se reposait près des murs de Tura, sous **arbre au tremblant feuillage**' (*Fingal I*) '**Quel est, dit-il, ce murmure qui vient roulant le long des collines ...?**' (*Fingal I*) '**Étranger, prête l'oreille au bruit de ses forêts**' ("La Bataille de Lora")	'**Qué din os rumorosos ... Qué din as altas copas?**' (First verses; 1st stanza). '**Robustos ecos ... das sonorosas cordas / das arpas de Breogán**' (8th stanza)
The voice of the spirit of Loda is '**like distant thunder**' ("Carric-Thura")	'**Comme un écho lointain du tonnerre**' ("Carric-Thura")	'**Xigante a nosa voz pregoa**' (4th stanza) [Our voice is] '**rumor gigante**' (9th stanza)

Table 4. Color and sound

A CELTIC EPIC FOR GALICIA

In Macpherson's *Ossian*, paleness reflects the then dominating canon of female beauty, and a strong eroticism is present in the three authors. The interrogation to elements of nature (forest, wind), and their pantheistic personification is clear in Pondal. *Rumorosos* (murmuring) has also aural connotations, as a secret whisper coming from the heart of the land. The power of voice forms part of a general aesthetics of musicality adopted by Pondal from Macpherson, as outlined above. Pondal captured the musical dimension of Ossian, and his Galician replica is not inferior to the model, as in his poems the combination of prosody accents with verbal images of sound is deep and masterful.[69] In *Os Pinos*, the verses *Robustos ecos* [. . .] *das sonorosas cordas / das arpas de Breogán* (Robust echoes [. . .] of the sonorous strings / of the harps of Breoghan)[70] evince that trait, but also the important nuance of amplification, with loud and powerful sounds, since harps are not potent instruments.

This preeminence of sonic elements put into question the epistemological shift in Western civilization towards the hegemony of visuality and visibility, typical of the industrial era.[71] Instead, in the Ossianic kingdom sound reigns supreme, and not only the harp, but a whole stormy nature, voices and laments, challenge the visual paradigm. Indeed, in this literature the thunder of the waves and the roar of the wind are assiduous, just like the harp is described as half-viewless–dimly perceived, and therefore barely visible. The dominant colors are gloomy: black and stormy green. Shadows and darkness abound. Furthermore, Ossian is blind, and his main means of expression are the voice and the harp. In Pondal,

> [T]he auditory element is always a priority. It is
> this lyrical voice that listens more than it sees, which

---

[69] Benito Varela Jácome, "La métrica de Eduardo Pondal," *Cuadernos de Estudios Gallegos* 45 (1960): 63-88; Amado Ricón, "Algunos ejemplos del 'Axis Rítmico' en la poesía de Pondal," *Boletín de la Real Academia Gallega* 30, no. 350 (1968): 3-16; Manuel Forcadela, *A Poesía de Eduardo Pondal* (Vigo: Edicións do Cumio, 1995).

[70] Lines 5-8, eighth stanza.

[71] Richard Leppert, "The Social Discipline of Listening," in *Aural Cultures*, ed. Jim Drobnick (Toronto: YYZ Books 2004), 19-35.

constructs his analysis of the world upon the most subtle, most immaterial, most spiritual perceptual element.[72]

In this sense, the Ossianic poetry carries out a regression to predominantly aural stages of Western culture, prior to the visual and logocentric explosion of the contemporary era. It is a major semantic field of aesthetic and ideological renewal that Ossianism conveyed, and with which Pondal pervaded his works.

The music by Veiga for Os Pinos

The history of the music Pascual Veiga Iglesias (1842-1906) composed for *Os Pinos* is convoluted and cannot be summarized here. The main question for the present study is whether it can be considered 'Ossianic music' or not. There are some locutions coined around the cultural stereotypes that stemmed from the myth of Ossian, like "Ossianic mode" for painting (Boime);[73] "Ossianic ethnotype" for nationalism (Leerssen);[74] and "Ossianic manner" for music. The latter was introduced in 1984 by Todd's study on Mendelssohn, which was followed by Daverio's focus on Schumann in 1998, and, more recently, by the works of Smith, Moulton, and Porter.[75] In the field of music, there is consensus in separating the 'literal' imitation of the formal parameters that identify that Ossianic manner from a general ethos of peacefulness and Arcadian nostalgia that is related to the pastoral topic and its long tradition in Western art music. The latter is more subtle, based on abstract/dematerialized imitation, and recalls

---

[72] GO. Forcadela, *A Poesía de Eduardo Pondal*, 72.

[73] Albert Boime, *Art in an Age of Bonapartism, 1800-1815* (Chicago: University of Chicago Press, 1990).

[74] Leerssen, "Celticism."

[75] R. Larry Todd, "Mendelssohn's Ossianic Manner, with a New Source-*On Lena's Gloomy Heath,*" in *Mendelssohn and Schumann: Essays on their Music and its Context*, eds. Jon W. Finson and R. Larry Todd (Durham: Duke University Press, 1984), 137-60; John Daverio, "Schumann's Ossianic Manner," *19th-Century Music* 21 (1998): 247-73; Christopher Smith, "Ossian in Music," in *The Reception of Ossian in Europe*, 375-92; Paul Moulton, *Imagining Scotland in Music: Place, Audience, and Attraction* (Tallahassee: Florida State University Libraries, 2008); James Porter, *Beyond Fingal's Cave*.

the essence of program music. The former group may include elements like 6/8 time, F or G major tonality, pentatonic scales, peasant melodies, drone accompaniment, presence of harps, onomatopoeic effects, and occasional brushstrokes of musical primitivism/exoticism. Todd mentions "beginning in the low strings, frequent octave doublings, disjunct lines, and open spacings [. . .] sequential bare fifths," as an attempt "to capture the primitive, the unconventional" in Mendelssohn's *Scottish Symphony*.[76]

Veiga lacked the influence of the Ossianic manner detectable in Mendelssohn, Le Sueur, Niels Gade, Schubert, and other composers. Quite surely, he was unaware of those sophisticated innovations. However, Ossian was widely read, and its repercussions went far beyond the boundaries of literature, affecting the formation and development of such a fertile repertoire as it was Romantic music– whose echoes would reach regions as remote as Galicia.[77] Thus, the influence of Ossian in Veiga was probably indirect, but real and tangible.

The idea of a misty Celtic past, wrapped in pastoral beauty, weighed heavily on Veiga's imagination. Porter defines this style as of "gentle melancholy"[78] and it perfectly fitted within the aesthetic orientation of Galician regionalism, thus making the anthem a singular piece in the genre. However, it is not a "folk anthem" either, as defined by Boyd.[79] *Os Pinos* is possibly based on one or more Galician popular melodies;[80] this has not been convincingly demonstrated, but the piece does have a distinctive local gist, with its smooth-flowing melody based on conjunct motion. Interestingly, it starts with the G major tonic chord in first inversion, instead of the root position (the normal

---

[76] Todd, "Mendelssohn's Ossianic Manner," 152-153.

[77] For instance, it is unlikely that Wagner could have written *Der Ring des Nibelungen* without the inspiration of Ossian. At least there is evidence of his knowledge of the poems and concrete reflections in some of his operas, loosely projected on the Norse sagas (Porter, *Beyond Fingal's Cave*, 300).

[78] Porter, *Beyond Fingal's Cave*, 4.

[79] Malcolm Boyd, "National anthems," in *The New Grove Dictionary of Music & Musicians*, ed. Stanley Sadie (London: Macmillan, 1980, vol. 13), 46-75, at 47. Boyd assumes folk anthems as typical of colonized countries, possibly including indigenous instruments and specific gestures.

[80] Filgueira, *O Himno Galego*.

one to begin an anthem). This musical anomaly provokes an initial sensation of instability, lacking the martial vigor and assertive impulse that characterizes the genre, but raising an expectation in the listener, who perceives a question to be answered; therefore, the music syncretically mirrors the text by Pondal, which begins with a question from the poet. As in most national anthems, *Os Pinos* repeats unvaried each stanza–with the resource of modal alternation between G major and minor–changing only the conclusion in the last one. The structure, polyphony, meter, and timbre are also as simple and plain as in most pieces from this particular genre. Veiga made some technical mistakes, due to his limited formation as a composer, but those flaws amazingly resulted in a more popular and understandable piece of music to the intended audience.

In summary, the music of *Os Pinos* constitutes a pastoral trope with the addition of a strong nationalist dimension (although only a few formal parameters are clear in both directions), by means of a native-inspired texture translated into semi-classical music. Comparatively, it becomes more accessible to the people of Galicia than the sophisticated and abstract lyrics by Pondal, which are, nonetheless, a step above in terms of art quality.

Conclusion

The assessments by Varela and Montiel about the superficiality of Pondal's Ossianism need revision.[81] Rather, according to his literary evolution, the epic tales of Ossian released his creative talent ahead of any other influence with the remarkable result that "Pondal was unique in Galician and indeed in European poetry."[82] The legend of the Irish-Scottish bard actually became the epicenter of his literature and private life It was both an aesthetic and political choice: in front of Homer, the bard of the Mediterranean-Latin world–who represented Classicism–Ossian (re-epitomized as Breoghan) emerged as the capital figure of the Atlantic-Romantic realm, the Celtic challenge to Western cultural hegemony. It was this challenging dimension of Ossian that seduced Pondal; in his poems, Celtic Galicia

---

[81] José Luis Varela, "Un capítulo del ossianismo español: Eduardo Pondal"; Montiel, *Ossián en España*, chapter xii.
[82] Clark, "Sons and daughters of Breogán. Scottish and Irish influence on Galician Language Literature," 13.

turns into a self-referential land, as it encompasses a holistic explanation of its origins, patriarchs, heroes/heroines, and *máxicos destinos* (magical destinies, *Os Pinos*).[83] The Celtic epic became thus a core commitment for the subsequent nationalist thought, changing the cultural and political history of Galicia, and its trace is currently well visible. After Pondal, "the Celtic myth, the Breoghan myth, remained forever in the history of Galicia,"[84] and his collaboration with Veiga gave the country a remarkable and original anthem.

---

[83] Sixth stanza, line 7.

[84] GO. Xosé Ramón Barreiro, "A recreación do mito celta," *A Nosa Terra* 7 (special issue: *Pondal, hombre libre, libre terra*, 1986): 27-29, at 29.

The Destruction of Archives in Brittany

Yves Coativy

The study of the history of medieval Brittany is faced with a
rather large obstacle, a difficult one to overcome, that is the lack of
archives. Compared to other French regions such as Burgundy or
Savoy, and to other countries such as Belgium and England, this
observation is indisputable. There is almost nothing left before the
beginning of the thirteenth century, documentation was very scarce
before the 1420s, and until the sixteenth century, many sectors
(accounts for example) were damaged. In addition to the usual causes
(fire, humidity, wars, etc.), there are other reasons that explain the
extent of the gaps, 'the sorting', which is probably ancient, as we shall
see, but which happened most especially from the time of the French
Revolution. All historians of the Middle Ages have to address this
issue, as was the case for Jean Kerhervé in 1986 when he stated that:

> *Il faut dire que l'état actuel de la documentation ne
> facilite pas l'approche de la question [les finances
> ducales à la fin du Moyen Âge] puisqu'elle est à la
> fois dispersée, inégale et insuffisante à bien des
> égards. Les détournements anciens, les transferts, les
> vicissitudes de l'histoire expliquent qu'il faille
> aujourd'hui rechercher nombre de document
> financiers, parfois d'un grand intérêt, hors de
> Bretagne dans les dépôts parisiens et dans plusieurs
> centres départementaux d'archives.*

It must be said that the current state of documentation
does not make approaching the question [of ducal
finances at the end of the Middle Ages] easy since the
surviving documents are scattered, uneven, and
insufficient in many respects. The old detours,
transfers, and the tribulations of the past would
explain why it is necessary, nowadays, to begin
searching for a number of financial documents,
sometimes of great interest, outside of Brittany, in the

DESTRUCTION OF ARCHIVES

Parisian repositories and in several departmental archive centers.[1]

It should be noted that another difficulty is added to this one, that of the unequal distribution of archives. In the four 'Breton' archive centers of modern-day administrative Brittany: Archives départementales des Côtes d'Armor (Saint-Brieuc), du Finistère (Quimper), d'Ile-et-Vilaine (Rennes), and du Morbihan (Vannes), there is little about, and from, the Middle Ages outside of urban and ecclesiastical archives. The Loire-Atlantique departmental archives (Pays de Loire region) hold the most important archival collections, including the Treasury of the Charters of the Dukes of Brittany. It is the history of these archives that we will explore in this paper.

Ancient destruction

As many other regions have, Brittany has been the victim of ancient destructions of archives. The Viking raids of the ninth and tenth century caused a lot of destruction, in particular of charter books from coastal abbeys,[2] then these damages were aggravated by the war of Succession of Brittany, a civil war which bloodied the duchy in the middle of the fourteenth century. It is, for example, at this time that the castle of Suscinio, a ducal residence, was burnt and we know that it is on that occasion that its archives disappeared. The War of Independence of Brittany at the end of the fifteenth century and the Wars of Religion in the following century finalized the loss of the remaining documentation.

One specific case we will look into suggests a first period of sorting. When making the inventory of chancery registers (which keep track of the decisions made by the ducal powers before 1491), one notices that the volumes that remain correspond exactly to the periods of tension or war between Brittany and the kingdom of France. The

---

[1] Jean Kerhervé, *L'Etat breton au 14e et 15e s. Les ducs, l'argent, les hommes*, (Paris: Maloine, 1986), 7.

[2] In a charter, Louis the Pious (814-840) mentions, for example, the burning of the charters of the abbey of Saint-Méen by the Vikings. Sophie Le Goff, *Transcription, traduction et analyse de la Chronique anonyme de Saint-Brieuc* (thèse de doctorat, Brest, 2022), 438-439. At the same time, the Vikings destroyed the abbey of Landévennec, forcing the monks to rewrite their cartulary from memory fifty years later.

others have disappeared into the past, as is suggested by the inventories of archives from the sixteenth century. They prove that from that time on, there are important gaps in the preserved archives. This suggests that the volumes may have been sorted out by the royal power after the end of the war in 1491, as part of what might be called a 'witch hunt', attested elsewhere against the servants of Francis II and Anne of Brittany, between 1491 and 1498. It might have been a way for the royal power to keep track of the names of those who had worked with the duke and duchess and therefore against the king of France. The archival situation was thus degraded on the eve of the French Revolution, but in a way that was quite normal for the time. There were already large gaps of documentation, but as was the case elsewhere, except that the sorting of chancery registers that we have mentioned seems to be a rather unusual phenomenon in late medieval France.

Breton archives during the revolutionary period: an eventful period[3]

The 1789 revolutionaries began a period of destruction following a very clear ideology:

> *Lorsque les statues des tyrans sont précipitées, lorsque la lime et le ciseau n'épargnent aucun emblème de la monarchie et de la féodalité, les républicains ne peuvent voir qu'avec indignation dans les collections de manuscrits les traces de tant d'outrages faits à la dignité de l'homme (. . .). Ce ne sont à la vérité que des ossements desséchés et sans vie, mais qui, de la poussière des tombeaux, paraissent attendre qu'une voix puisse les rassembler et les ranimer.*

---

[3] The basis of the developments in Ille-et-Vilaine comes from Jacques Charpy, "Les Archives en révolution. Les premières années des Archives départementales d'Ille-et-Vilaine (1789-1802)", (*Bulletins et mémoires de la Société archéologique d'Ille-et-Vilaine*, tome XCIII, 1991), 33-60. You can also read Michael Jones, "*Membra disjecta* of the Breton *Chambre des Comptes* in the Late Middle Ages: Treasures revisited and rediscovered", Christopher Allmand (éd.), *War, Government and Power in Late Medieval France*, (Liverpool: Liverpool University Press, 2000), 209-220 which traces the dispersion of these sources among several archives and libraries.

DESTRUCTION OF ARCHIVES

> When the statues of tyrants are thrown down, when
> the file and the chisel spare no emblem of monarchy
> and feudalism, the republicans can only see with
> indignation, in the collections of manuscripts, the
> traces of so many outrages done to the dignity of man
> (. . .). They are, in truth, only dry and lifeless bones,
> but which, from the dust of the tombs, seem to wait
> for a voice to gather them and revive them.[4]

The revolutionary regime took several measures to organize the
archives, that had, until then, been the responsibility of aristocratic
families or institutions such as the Church. It was decided that the
founding texts of the new regime and the patrimonial documents
would go to the national archives as well as the rest to the departments
and districts, with the transfer, to the latter, of religious and aristocratic
collections. Sorting was then undertaken to know where to send the
documents but also to determine which ones to keep and which ones
to destroy, since, at the same time, the new regime chose to make a
'clean sweep of the feudal past', so to say.

It was decided, at first, to burn the documents relating to the
reformations of nobility, which was done in Rennes on August fifth,
1792. On June 25th, 1794, the sorting took a systematic turn and the
new archivist, Duval Pineu, agreed to take things into his own hands.
Four other men joined him, and Gicquel des Touches agreed to help
them out. It was thus decided to destroy confessions, rentiers,
judgments or decrees relating to feudal rights, but also documents
deemed useless, both on paper and on parchment, which, one must
admit, is quite a vague decision. Ninety-one percent of the bundles
thus created were originally destined to be destroyed, including the
archives of all the parishes of Rennes, but in the end only eight percent
were effectively destroyed so.

The government also ordered the departmental directories to burn
the accounts of the old administrations prior to 1762 branded as
"useless". In Loire-Inférieure, 10,000 pounds, about five tons, of old
documents disappeared. Instead of having them all burnt, old papers
and parchments were sold at auction in Nantes on February fourth and

---

[4] Léon de Laborde quoted by François Souchal, *Le vandalisme de la
Révolution*, (Paris: Nouvelles éditions latines, 1993), 266.

fifth, 1793, for a total of 3478 £ 4 s 9 d (French pounds). The five Breton departments were concerned by this measure. In Côtes-du-Nord, the two bishoprics were treated in different ways. The sorters first processed the archives of the diocese of Saint-Brieuc and then those of Tréguier, but in between those two, the sorting stopped. The result can thus be measured quantitatively: there are 292 bundles left for the archives of the diocese of Saint-Brieuc and 567 bundles for that of Tréguier, which was noticeably smaller and poorer. In the department of Loire-Inférieure, no less than 10,000 books of documents were burnt in 1792.

But the power also quickly sought a means of using this resource, particularly for war purposes. The Convention[5] sent commissioners to renew the sorting operations because:

> [L]es directoires des départements qui ont des
> dépôts de papiers et parchemins dans leur
> arrondissement, laisseront aux préposés du ministre
> de la marine toute la liberté pour procéder sans
> délai au triage et à l'enlèvement de ceux qu'ils
> jugeront propres au service de l'artillerie.

> [T]he directories of the departments which have
> deposits of papers and parchments in their district,
> will leave to the officers of the minister of the navy
> all the freedom to proceed without delay to the sorting
> and the removal of those which they will judge
> suitable for the service of the artillery.

It is even reminded that: *les départements de la guerre et de la marine ayant un besoin pressant de parchemins inutiles pour faire des gargousses et autres usages* (the departments of war and the navy having a pressing need of useless parchments to make gargousses,[6]

---

[5] The National Convention is both the French political regime and the Parliament that governed France from September 21st, 1792 to October 26th, 1795 during the French Revolution. The Convention engaged the country in a very violent revolutionary phase.

[6] Those usually are bags used by the artilleryman to contain the powder used to project cannonballs. When arming his gun, he would put in the gunpowder, the wadding, the cannonball into the tube, stabilize the material with a new layer of wadding and the gun would be ready to fire.

and for other uses). The sorters were thus backed up by the main power:

> *[C]ette opération est urgente par les demandes journalières que fait à l'administration du département le directeur de l'artillerie, commandant du château, pour obtenir des papiers nécessaires à la formation des cartouches dont il se fabrique 200 000 par décade*

> [T]his operation is urgent due to the daily requests that the director of the artillery, commander of the castle, makes to the administration of the department to obtain papers necessary for the fabrication of the cartridges, 200,000 of which are manufactured per decade.

Such a line of work was not easy and the citizens Etienne and Fourage complained of a task at hand *immense par son étendue, ingrate par son objet, pénible par son genre de travail et dangereuse par l'air infect qu'on y respire* (immense by its extent, thankless by its object, painful by its kind of work and dangerous by the foul air which one breathes there). One may notice in the lists of objects chosen to be destroyed, the accounts, correspondences, registers of jurisdiction and the hymnal of the cathedral. Those hymnals (35), made of parchment, were considered to be particularly useful for the making of artillery cartridges ('gargoyles').[7]

The Departmental Archives of Ille-et-Vilaine nevertheless possess the most astonishing objects of these 'gargoyles' collections, including fourteen artillery gargousses that can be dated back to the revolutionary or imperial period. *L'encyclopédie* of Diderot and D'Alembert provides a valuable article regarding these objects:

> *Le parchemin seroit assez bon pour faire les cartouches : mais c'est une matiere trop chere, difficile à manier, & qui se tourmente aisément ; il vaut donc mieux se servir de carton ou de bon papier (...). Les gargouges sont de papier, parchemin, ou toile : les meilleures & les plus sûres sont celles qui*

---

[7] Le baron de Wismes, "Le Trésor de la rue des Caves à Nantes", (*Revue de Bretagne et de Vendée*, t. V, 1859), 152-161 and 311-335.

sont faites de parchemin, parce que le feu ne s'y attache point; le parchemin ne fait que griller, sans s'attacher à la piece. Le papier & la toile ont cette incommodité, qu'ils laissent presque toûjours quelque lambeau accroché au métal de l'ame de la piece avec du feu; ce qui a souvent causé de fort fâcheux accidens, & ordinairement ces malheurs arrivent quand on est près de l'ennemi & pressé : car quand il faut servir une piece, les canoniers négligent d'écouvillonner; la nouvelle gargouge que l'on fourre dans la piece rencontrant ce papier ou cette toile allumée, prend feu, & en ressortant de la piece, brise avec la hampe de la lanterne ou de l'écouvillon les bras & les jambes de ceux qui chargent, & les tue fort souvent (. . .). Lorsque l'on sera obligé de se servir de papier ou de toile dans l'occasion, il ne faut pas oublier d'écouvillonner à chaque coup, & pour celles de parchemin, de trois coups en trois coups. La longueur des gargouges sera de quatre calibres de la piece où elles devront servir, dont un demi-calibre servira à fermer le cul, & un autre pour fermer le dessus quand la poudre y sera ; cette poudre doit être charge ordinaire. Celles de parchemin ne feront qu'un tour, avec un peu plus de largeur pour la couture : elles seront trempées dans le vinaigre, afin de les coudre plus facilement. A celles de toile la largeur de la couture doit être en-dedans la gargouge; les ourlets seront froncés avec de la ficelle.

Parchment would be good enough to make cartridges: but it is too expensive, difficult to handle, and easily damaged; it is therefore better to use cardboard or good paper (. . .). The cartridges are made of paper, parchment, or canvas: the best and safest are those made of parchment, because the fire does not attach itself to it; parchment only burns, without attaching itself to the piece. Paper and canvas have this inconvenience, that they almost always leave some flap attached to the metal of the core of the piece with fire; this has often caused very unfortunate accidents, and usually these misfortunes happen when one is close to the enemy and in a hurry: because when it is necessary to serve a piece, the gunners neglect to swab; the new cartridge that one stuffs in the piece meeting this paper or this lit fabric, takes fire, and while leaving the piece, breaks with the staff of the lantern or the swab the arms and the legs of those who charge, & kills them very often (. . .). When one is obliged to use paper or canvas on occasion, one must not forget to swab at each shot, and for those of parchment, from three shots to three shots. The length of the cartridges will be of four calibers of the piece where they will have to be used, of which a half-caliber will be used to close the bottom, & another to close the top when the powder is there; this powder must be ordinary load. Those of parchment will make only one turn, with a little more width for the seam: they will be soaked in vinegar, in order to sew them more easily. To those of fabric the width of the seam must be inside the cartridge; the hems will be gathered with string.[8]

In a letter dated December 23, 1794, the Arms and Powder Commission of Nantes specified the size of parchment most suitable to making cartridges: the ball of 36 (162 mm in diameter) required a sheet of 24 by 19 ¼ inches; the ball of 3 (about 70 mm) required a sheet of 14 by 8 ½ inches, plus 8 intermediate calibers. The hymnals of the cathedral of Nantes, made of parchment, were considered particularly useful for the making of cartridges. In Finistère, Pierre-Jean Le Breton recounts his engagement to deliver *les parchemins inutiles pour le service des ports et des arsenaux* (the useless

---

[8] Denis Diderot and Jean Le Rond d'Alembert, *Encyclopédie ou Dictionnaire raisonné des sciences, des arts et des métiers*, (Paris: André Le Breton, Laurent Durand, Antoine-Claude Briasson and Michel-Antoine David, 1751-1765), s.v. Cartouche.

parchments for the service of the ports and the arsenals).[9] He placed there the documents of seigniorial management, the documents of justice, the confessions, and specifically mentions files from the priory of Benedictines of Locmaria.[10]

The accounting books of the city of Quimper also deserve a special mention:

> *[C]e dépôt nous a fourni une quantité de parchemin propre au service de l'artillerie (. . .). Nous ferons peser les liasses de parchemin que nous délivrerons pour le service de l'artillerie et nous vous en ferons passer le montant. Les feuilles de parchemin trop petites pour faire des gargousses nous sont demandées par le directeur de la mine de charbon de terre de Quimper pour faire de la colle. Nous lui avons déjà délivré cent livres de papiers pour faire des cartouches dont il se sert pour faire jouer la mine.*

> [T]his deposit has provided us with a quantity of parchment suitable for the service of the artillery (. . .). We will have the bundles of parchment that we deliver for the artillery service weighed and we will pass on to you the amount. The sheets of parchment too small to make gargoyles are requested from us by the director of the Quimper coal mine to make glue. We have already delivered to him one hundred pounds of paper to make cartridges which he uses to make the mine 'play'.[11]

---

[9] Jacques Charpy, "Les premiers archivistes du Finistère et la formation des archives départementales (1790-1851)", (*Bulletin de la Société Archéologique du Finistère*, 1967), 223.

[10] A twelfth century manuscript of Bede bearing the mark of the priory of Locmaria de Quimper is in the Schoyen collection, Oslo-London, under the number 2036. It is not unreasonable to suspect that it was salvaged from the lost Quimper library. Jean-Luc Deuffic, "Notes de bibliologie bretonne. Un manuscrit de Bède d'une abbaye bretonne oubliée: Locmaria de Quimper", (*Pecia. Ressource en médiévistique*, 2004), 104.

[11] Jacques Charpy, Les premiers archivistes du Finistère et la formation des archives départementales (1790-1851)", 225-226; "faire jouer la mine" i.e.

DESTRUCTION OF ARCHIVES

While that type of sorting officially ceased in 1796, the destruction continued for quite some time, until the spring of 1798. In Rennes, the archivists Estin and Le Page continued to provide parchment for *munitions et artifices de guerre nécessaires pour la descente en Angleterre* (ammunition and artifices of war necessary for the invasion of England). The former archivist at Rennes, Gicquel des Touches, declared that it was *mieux faire des gargousses pour nos canons et en terrasser nos ennemis plutôt que de les bruler* (better to make cartridges for our cannons and to knock down our enemies than to burn them). All was not destroyed, in the end. In 1815 in Ille-et-Vilaine, the archivist Le Mintier had a large box of parchment removed from the arsenal and returned to the archives. It is quite likely that the gargousses still kept in Rennes come from this rescuing effort.

The same happened in Finistère, where two men, Pierre-Jean Le Breton and Le Gallic de Kerisouët, set out to work sorting, in 1795, with three main objectives: the sorting–both to keep interesting items and destroy those considered useless–of state titles, useful for the maintenance of national or private properties; the conservation of historical documents; the annihilation of any monarchic or feudal vestiges.[12] In Morbihan, the operations took place amidst an atmosphere of civil war. It was in the archives of the districts that the titles and charters of the suppressed religious communities and the emigrants were found. The 'brigands' (the Chouans)[13] also destroyed the archives of the district of La Roche-Sauveur and La Roche-des-Trois, for example, burnt in 1793. In 1820, in a report addressed to the Ministry, the archivist Armand Le Bobinnec described "le nombre des lacunes qu'on y rencontre".[14] In Brest, the important sorting

---

to make explosives for use in the mine. Editors note. The sources show a variety of terms for artillery cartridges but we have used the general term in the English translations.

[12] Jacques Charpy, "Les premiers archivistes du Finistère et la formation des archives départementales (1790-1851)", 215-272.

[13] The Chouans were men who armed themselves to fight against the Revolution and demanded the return of a king as well as the Catholic religion. The phenomenon primarily took place in the West of France.

[14] Armelle Sentilhes, "La formation des archives du Morbihan, 1790-1884", (*Mémoire de la Société d'Histoire et d'Archéologie de Bretagne*, 1985), 493.

operations led to the disappearance of an important dictionary that was being produced by the Académie.[15]

The situation was more or less identical in the Côtes-du-Nord and the year 1790 began as it did elsewhere with the handing-over of the papers. On August 7, 1792, the department gave its assent to the burning of the genealogical titles that existed in the chamber of accounts in Nantes. In a letter by the department dated March 11, 1797 it is reminded that the people in charge of the old chief towns of district: *si le triage n'a pas été effectué, vous devez nous envoyer tous les papiers ; il se fera ici et nous transmettrons à chaque canton ce qui le concerne* (if the sorting has not been carried out, you must send us all the papers; it shall be done here and we will hand over to each canton what concerns it).[16] As was done in Morbihan, the Chouans destroyed the archives of Rostrenen in January 1800.

On October 26, 1796, a law put a temporary stop to the sorting. Before that, archives of the various districts flowed into Quimper by carts.[17] Beyond the regulatory aspect of archives, this sorting crisis was of relative importance: the archivists were poorly paid and without suitable means, their funds were poorly housed, the sorting begun was not completed, and yet parts of the parchments and large size papers were delivered to the artillery, and transfers were done at random. Archives were destroyed both by the revolutionaries themselves and also by the Chouans, and that is assuming they were not also looted. Once peace had been restored, a period that Jacques Charpy describes as "sleepy" and unstable, ensued. The archivists were not trained to do their job properly and at least two out of the five that operated in Brittany were suspected of being "sellers of parchment".[18] It was not until the middle of the nineteenth century that things were put back in order and inventory work began.

---

[15] Prosper Levot, *Histoire de la ville et du port de Brest. Le port depuis 1681*, (Brest: chez l'auteur, 1865, t. II), 252.

[16] Régis de Saint-Jouan, "Histoire des archives de Côtes-du-Nord", (Bulletin de la Société d'Emulation des Côtes-du-Nord, 1981), 11.

[17] Jacques Charpy, "Les premiers archivistes du Finistère et la formation des archives départementales (1790-1851)", 215-272.

[18] Jacques Charpy, "Les archivistes bretons face à leur temps", (*Kreiz 4. Etudes sur la Bretagne et les pays celtiques*, 1995), 51-52.

DESTRUCTION OF ARCHIVES

Not everything was destroyed, and some scraps were returned to the archives in the nineteenth and twentieth centuries. In Rennes, some documents were sent to salvage stores–where parchment could be sold to make shoes and bindings–but most others were kept in bulk at the archives. They were found during a move in 1886. Some collections managed to escape the disaster in spite of everything.[19]

Le trésor de la rue des Caves (The treasure of Cellar Street)

The cast-offs of the Nantes archives suffered another fate, which is told to us in a fascinating article by Baron de Wismes.[20] Passing rue des Caves in Nantes, around 1857, in front of the store of a parchment maker, supplier of bindings and cardboard, he saw three men busy washing parchments.

> *Un jour, il y a de cela deux ans environ, je passais par la rue des Caves* [Nantes] *quand, à travers la porte toute grande ouverte d'une assez vieille maison, j'aperçus deux ou trois individus accroupis près d'un puits situé dans l'angle de la cour de cette maison et occupés à laver des piles de vieux parchemins. Piqué de curiosité à cette vue, je m'arrêtais, m'avançais doucement de quelques pas dans la cour et bientôt, voyant qu'on ne semblait point se formaliser de ma présence peut-être indiscrète, je fus près des parcheminiers et ne tardai pas à tomber dans un muet étonnement d'abord, puis dans une expansive admiration, en reconnaissant dans l'objet de leurs manipulations plus ou moins dégoutantes au premier aspect, soit de précieux fragments d'anciens manuscrits, soit des titres et des documents historiques du plus haut intérêt.*

> One day, about two years ago, I was passing through the rue des Caves [in Nantes] when, through the wide-open door of a rather old house, I saw two or three

---

[19] See what Gaël Chenard writes on this subject in the directory of the series 2 G, Archives départementales des Côtes d'Armor, http://archives.cotesdarmor.fr/pdf/FRAD022_2G.htm, accessed February 19, 2018.

[20] Le baron de Wismes, "Le Trésor de la rue des Caves à Nantes", p. 152-156.

individuals squatting near a well, located in the corner of the courtyard of this house and busy washing piles of old parchments. Piqued with curiosity at this sight, I stopped, advanced slowly a few steps into the courtyard and soon, seeing that they did not seem to take any notice of my, perhaps indiscreet presence, I was close to the parchment-makers and did not delay in falling into a mute astonishment at first, then into an expansive admiration, by recognizing in the object of their manipulations, more or less disgusting at first sight, either precious fragments of ancient manuscripts, or titles and historical documents of the highest interest.

Gaëtan de Wismes visited the house with two brothers, which was full of parchments that had been, or were being, processed, and the two men offered him a deal: *à deux francs la livre, tous ces parchemins sont à vous.–Tous c'est trop mais j'en prendrais volontiers quelques dizaines de kilos à mon choix* ("At two francs a pound, all these parchments can be yours.–All of them would be too much, but I would gladly take a few dozen kilos of them of my choice"). He then began his shopping and the next day, he informed Arthur de La Borderie. Between them, they explored the whole of the stock and found elements of the ducal accounts, straight from the archives of the Chambre des Comptes de Bretagne (which had been sorted during the Revolution). *En effet, ce n'était rien moins qu'une partie des archives de la Chambre des Comptes de Bretagne que nous avions découvertes* ("Indeed, it was nothing less than a part of the archives of the Chambre des Comptes de Bretagne that we had uncovered").

He appealed to his friend La Borderie for help, writing to him: *Rue des Caves, il existait un trésor, le nom seul de la rue pouvait le faire soupçonner ; ce trésor, je l'ai trouvé, mais il s'agit de l'enlever, la cassette est lourde, venez me donner un coup de main, nous partagerons en frères.* ("Rue des Caves, there was a treasure, the name of the street alone could make one suspect it; this treasure, I found it, but it is a matter of removing it, the cassette is heavy, come and lend me a hand, we will divide it up as brothers"). La Borderie replied: *Vous pouvez compter sur moi, j'ai l'épaule solide* ("You can count on me, for I have a strong shoulder").[21]

The oldest documents dated back to the thirteenth century. They were the archives of the Chamber of Accounts of Brittany.[22] The bookbinders had bought them at low price, washed them up and offered them to the town halls, to bind the *Bulletin des lois* and the registers of the civil status, at low prices. The names found on the labels of bookbinders in the funds of the Departmental Archives of Ille-et-Vilaine made it possible to find the counterparts of the Alsatian brothers of the rue des Caves, such as J.-B. Huart, bookseller and printer in Dinan; Blondel, bookbinder and gilder, rue de Bourbon; and the citizen Robiquet, rue impériale n° 4, Rennes. We were even given prices: *Les deux Registres coutant pour papier, façon signature et depose de l'ancien quatre livres cinq sols* ("The two Registers costing for paper, way signature and deposit of the former four livres five sols").[23]

Through the fragments, we can spot some lost medieval Breton manuscripts such as *Le songe du vieil pèlerin* (The Dream of the Old Pilgrim) by Philippe de Mézières (circa 1327-1405), scattered among the Departmental Archives of Morbihan, Loire-Atlantique and the Municipal Archives of Nantes.[24] The Rennes library has one of the oldest French manuscripts of Arthurian stories. A detached sheet of the *Conte de la charrette* was used as a folder for property titles; it reads: *Acquêt de la pièce et du pré de la Chapelle, de la Vigne, des Ruiseaux* (sic)*, de la Grange, du Loraux, par René Ribault, ainsi que quelques pieces . . . 1845* ("Acquisition of the piece of land and the meadow of the Chapel, the Vine, the Ruissaux, the Barn, the Loraux,

---

[21] Baron de Wismes, "Le trésor de la rue des caves", 154.

[22] Michael Jones and Philippe Charon published the oldest fragments in *Comptes du duché de Bretagne. Les comptes, inventaires et exécution des testaments ducaux, 1262-1352*, (Rennes, Presses universitaires de Rennes, 2017).

[23] Archives départementales d'Ille-et-Vilaine, bookbinding archives.

[24] Yves Coativy, 'Un "lieu de mémoire breton" : les fragments du *Songe du viel pelerin* de Philippe de Mézières', *actes du colloque du Mans, mai 2016, Philippe de Mézières et l'Europe. Nouvelle histoire, nouveaux espaces, nouveaux langages*, édité par Joël Blanchard et Renate Blumenfeld-Kosinski, (Paris: Droz, 2017), 295-308.

by René Ribault, as well as some pieces . . . 1845").[25] In the Departmental Archives of Morbihan, we also find fragments of Aristotle's *De politica* and the *History of Rome before Caesar* or the *Roman de Mélusine et Grande Dent* found in the bindings of parish registers of the seventeenth century of Moustoir-Remungol, probably prior to 1387.[26] Finally, we recall that one of the oldest Breton documents was found by chance by Michel Maréchal and Éric Joret in Saint-Germain-en-Coglès in November 1992. It is a ducal act from the middle of the eleventh century reused in the binding of a land registry volume.[27] But there are also numerous texts or fragments that relate to the management of the seigneury or the life of the parishes, not to mention numerous pages of antiphonaries or law books and palimpsests, parchments that have been so well washed that they have been reused without the original text being known. It can be seen in the places where the washers have not done their job properly.

The archive is like a treasure trove for the historian. When opening a bundle, one never knows if one will find something interesting or if one will have to wait for the last collection to finally find something useful. In the multitude of boxes, some of them conceal a part of the unknown, especially the 'bindings' resources we have just discussed. They reflect the hazards of a particularly tormented period in the history of France, and they also leave the historian a little bitter in front of the extent of the losses. These collections are very rich and have often been neglected by historians. We must now hope that someone will delve into these bundles to make a detailed inventory and allow us to better measure their richness.

---

[25] Sophie Cassagnes-Brouquet, *Les romans de la table ronde. Première images de de l'univers arthurien*, (Rennes: Presses universitaires de Rennes, 2005), 8.

[26] Archives Départementales du Morbihan 37 J 1 and Louis Rosenzweig, "Fragments manuscrits d'un roman de chevalerie", (*Bulletin de la société polymathique du Morbihan*, 1871), 53-59.

[27] Michel Maréchal, "Une journée particulière", *Talabardoneries ou échos d'archives offerts à Catherine Talabardon-Laurent*, (Rennes: Société d'histoire et d'archéologie de Bretagne sd.), 51-59.

The Deaths of Fergus mac Leite

Gregory Darwin

For some time, I have been preparing a new critical edition and translation of the Early Modern Irish saga *Imthechta Túaithe Luchra ocus Aided Fergusa* (hereafter *ITLAF*).[1] Over the course of reviewing the relevant literature, I encountered many statements which summarily identified this text as a 'version,' 'retelling,' 'redaction,' etc. of the Old Irish *Echtra Fergusa maic Leite*.[2] This present discussion is a reassessment of this received wisdom that the Early Modern Irish saga is a later 'retelling' of the Old Irish one. In particular, I wish to challenge the implicit assumption that, when there are surviving Early Modern Irish and Old or Middle Irish texts reflecting a common story or narrative tradition, that the Early Modern Irish texts are derived from the *extant* Old or Middle Irish texts. On the contrary, I argue that more careful attention to such later texts has the potential to yield insights into the development of the narrative tradition as a whole, and to inform debates regarding earlier narrative texts within the tradition. Before turning to the question of the relationship between the Early Modern Irish *ITLAF* and the Old Irish *Echtra Fergusa*, I will begin with an overview of the existing material surrounding the eponymous Fergus mac Leite and his death.[3]

---

[1] Rather than modernizing the spelling of the title, I have opted to follow the conservative orthography of the primary manuscript witness, British Library MS Egerton 1782. Further information on this text, the manuscript witnesses, dating, and previous critical work is given below, pp. 194-197. I am grateful to Ariana Malthaner for looking over an early draft of this paper, as well as to the anonymous reviewer for their many helpful suggestions. Any remaining mistakes or omissions are, of course, to be blamed on leprechauns.

[2] D. A. Binchy, "The Saga of Fergus mac Léti," *Ériu* 16 (1952), 33-48. On the title of this text, and the spelling of the patronymic as *Leite* vs *Léite*, see the next note and note 7.

[3] I follow Ruairí Ó hUiginn in taking Fergus' patronymic to be *mac Leite*, with a short <e> on the basis of the rhyme *Leite* / *bice* in the Early Modern Irish *ITLAF* (item 26 in the author's forthcoming edition of this text, p. 252 in O'Grady's edition, where it is silently emended to beice). The second

Fergus mac Leite was a legendary king of Ulster who, according to the historical tradition, reigned during the pre-Christian period; different sources identify him as a contemporary of either Conn Cétchathach or of Congal Cláiringnech.[4] He is often confused or conflated with his better-known namesake, Fergus mac Róich, as both figures play an important role in the genealogies of the Ulaid, both possess an excessive virility and libido which provide them with no end of trouble, both are said to possess the sword Caladcholg, and both suffer violent deaths in bodies of water: mac Róich by his foster-brother Lugaid, who was tricked into doing the deed by a jealous Ailill, and mac Leite by a sea-monster dwelling in Loch Rudraige, modern-day Dundrum Bay.

Fergus mac Leite's death is recounted in multiple Irish literary sources. The earliest account occurs within the opening sections of *Di Chethairshlicht Athgabálae*, the opening tract of the Senchas Már legal collection, which Binchy dated to the seventh century.[5] These

---

word, the feminine genitive singular of *bec* "small," has a short vowel, and <c> represents a voiceless stop /g/; rhyme with this word indicates that Leite has both a short vowel and a voiced dental stop /d/, Leide in Modern Irish orthography. Ruairí Ó hUiginn, "Fergus, Russ and Rudraige: A Brief Biography of Fergus mac Róich," *Emania* 11 (1993), 31-40, at 35-6. Also see his article in this volume, p. 62. Although he did not provide his reasons for thinking so, D. A. Binchy earlier called attention to the vowel length in his contribution to Myles Dillon's *Irish Sagas*: "I have an idea that the *e* was short and that we should really call our hero Fergus mac Leti (pronounced 'leddy')". D. A. Binchy, "Echtra Fergusa maic Léite," in *Irish Sagas*, ed. Myles Dillon (Dublin: The Stationary Office, 1959), 42.
[4] Ó hUiginn, "Fergus, Russ and Rudraige," 35-8.
[5] Daniel A. Binchy (ed.), *Corpus iuris Hibernici: ad fidem codicum manuscriptorum* (Dublin: Dublin Institute for Advanced Studies, 1978), ii:352.26-31, 353.26-8, 354.8, 12-14, also v:1897.16-26. A restored text and translation appear in Neil McLeod, "Fergus mac Léti and the Law," *Ériu* 61 (2011), 1-28, at 8-10.
On the dating of the text, Binchy remarks "I do not think that we are justified in dating the poem earlier than the seventh century" (Binchy, "The Saga of Fergus mac Léti," 45). Although he did not propose a specific date, Calvert Watkins implied that this account was older with his description of it as "archaic poem," a term he also used to describe verse from the sixth

sections are in alliterative unrhymed verse, and provide very few details, but we are told that Fergus *ferglethech* (the manly warrior (?)) seized cattle which had belonged to Conn *cétchorach* (of the hundred treaties (?)) in atonement for the slaying of Eochu Bélbuide, who was under his legal protection. A woman named Dorn was also brought into captivity, presumably as part of Fergus' compensation, and she "perished on account of the truth which she uttered in Fergus' face" (*do-cer inna fírinni / seiches i ngnūis Fergusa*). Following this:

> *Ferais Fergus ferfechtas*
> *finech i lloch Rudraige*
> *dia-marbad i mārchinta.*

> Fergus made a manly incursion
> into the tribal (?) loch of Rudraige
> as a result of which he was killed for [his] grave wrongdoing.[6]

A fuller account of Fergus' death is given in *Echtra Fergusa maic Leite*, translated by Daniel Binchy as "The Saga of Fergus mac Léti."[7] This text, which has attracted some attention for being the earliest mention of leprechauns in Irish literature, was dated to the eighth century by Binchy on linguistic grounds, although Jacobo Bisagni has more recently suggested that the text cannot be assigned a date more

---

century. Calvert Watkins, "Indo-European Metrics and Archaic Irish Verse," *Celtica* 6 (1963), 194-249, at 223. Watkins was, presumably, the "American Celtic scholar who has taken [Binchy] to task" for not dating the prose *Echtra* to the late seventh century, which would make the verse earlier. Binchy, "Echtra Fergusa," 50. McLeod agreed with Binchy's dating, referring to the "seventh- and eighth-century versions" (i.e. the verse and prose versions) of the saga. McLeod, "Fergus mac Léti and the Law," 24.

[6] McLeod, "Fergus mac Léti and the Law," 9-10.

[7] D. A. Binchy, "The Saga of Fergus mac Léti," The title *Echtra Fergusa maic Lēte* was first assigned to this text by Rudolf Thurneysen, *Die irischen Helden- und Königsage bis zum siebzehnten Jahrhundert* (Halle: Niemeyer, 1921), 539. Donnchadh Ó Corráin gives the text the title *Echtrae Fergusa meic Leite*, with short <e>, presumably for the same reasons given by Ó hUiginn as discussed in note 3. Donnchadh Ó Corráin, *Clavis littterarum Hibernensium: Medieval Irish Books and Texts (c. 400-c. 1600)* (Turnhout: Brepols, 2017), § 1044.

specific than to the Old Irish period in general.[8] The text survives in two sixteenth-century legal manuscripts as an extended gloss on the section of *Di Chethairshlicht Athgabálae* discussed above. The text has no title in either witness; the current title was supplied by Rudolf Thurneysen from one of the medieval Irish tale lists.[9]

As in the account in Senchas Már, Eochu Bélbuide is slain by Asal son of Conn Cétchathach, the four sons of Buide mac Ainmirech, and Foitline, the son of Dorn and a foreigner (*mac deoraid*), in violation of Fergus' protection.[10] In response to this, Fergus visited Conn's territory, accompanied by an armed host, and in recompense for the violation of his protection received lands and cattle. As Foitline had no recognized paternal kin, his mother Dorn entered servitude with Fergus in exchange for his life. Some time after this, Fergus and his charioteer visited the sea and fell asleep by the shore. There, Fergus was seized by a group of *luchorpáin*, supernatural beings which can be identified with the *leipreacháin* or leprechauns of later folklore.[11] Fergus awoke and overpowered his supernatural attackers and, in exchange for their lives, they granted him herbs to put in his ears (or, according to an alternate tradition, a mantle to wrap around his head), which would grant him the power to travel underwater, and warned

---

[8] Jacopo Bisagni, "Leprechaun: A New Etymology," *Cambrian Medieval Celtic Studies* 64 (2012), 47-84, at 52. See note 5.

[9] "Dieser Titel nur in Sagenliste B." Thurneysen, *Die irische Helden- und Königsage*, 539n5; cf. Ariana Malthaner, "The Intersection of Literature and Law: The Saga of Fergus mac Léti," *Studia Celtica Fennica* 16 (2019), 90-106, at 94-5.

[10] The son is not named in the text of TCD MS H 3 18 (1337), which was translated by Binchy, but it appears as (nominative) *Fotline* in the British Library MS Harleian 432 text, and (genitive) *Foitline* in the manuscript in a gloss on the line *"bretha Dorn i ansoīre"* (Dorn was brought by him into captivity) in *Di Chethairshlicht Athgabálae* in the same manuscript. Binchy, *Corpus iuris Hibernici*, ii:353.38, 354.35. See also Binchy's summary of the tale. Binchy, "Echtra Fergusa Maic Léiti,"43-48.

[11] The various Old and Middle Irish names for these beings, as well as their characterization and possible derivation from Latin *Luperci* are discussed at length in Bisagni, "Leprechaun: A New Etymology." For a discussion of the leprechaun in later tradition, see Diarmuid Ó Giolláin, "The *Leipreachán* and Fairies, Dwarfs and the Household Familiar: A Comparative Study," *Béaloideas* 52 (1984), 75-150.

him never to go under the surface of Loch Rudraige. Predictably, Fergus eventually does just this, and encounters a monster referred to as a *muirdris* living within the lake.[12] After this encounter, Fergus' face was permanently distorted in terror, a fact which his subjects kept concealed from him for seven years. One day, when Dorn was bathing Fergus, he grew impatient and struck her for being too slow; in response, she taunted him for his blemish. Fergus struck her dead with his sword, and then returned to Loch Rudraige to confront the muirdris again. He prevailed over the monster, and lived long enough to utter "I am the survivor" (*meise is tiugba*) before succumbing to his wounds.

Fergus' death is mentioned in a historical poem attributed to the tenth century poet Cináed Úa hArtacáin, preserved in the Book of Leinster:

> *(Fer)gus macc Léite ba laech*
> *luid cosin mbéist, ba bidg baeth*
> *(co) torchratar [im]malle*
> *for Fertais ruaid Rudraige.*

> Fergus son of Léite was a hero:
> he went to the monster–'twas a
> silly start–so that they have
> fallen together on the red Fertais Rudraigi.[13]

His death is also mentioned in the early Irish World Chronicle section of the Annals of Tigernach, preserved in Rawlinson B. 502, taking place between the assassination of Julius Caesar and the birth of Cú Chulainn: *"Fergus mac Leti, qui conflixit contra bestiam hi Loch Rudraige et ibi demersus est, regnauit in Emain annis .xii."* (Fergus mac Leti who fought against the beast in Loch Rudraige, and was there drowned, reigned twelve years in Emain).[14]

Fergus mac Leite's death features in *ITLAF*, a much longer Early Modern Irish prosimetrum in which the *luchorpáin*–referred to here as the eponymous *Tuath Luchra ocus Lupracánach*–figure prominently.

---

[12] See note 35 for a discussion of this word.

[13] Whitley Stokes, "On the deaths of some Irish heroes," *Revue Celtique* 23 (1902), 303-48, 438, at 304-5.

[14] Whitley Stokes, "The Annals of Tigernach [part 1]," *Revue Celtique* 16 (1895), 374-419, at 404. Translated by the author.

The text is preserved in a single independent manuscript witness, British Library MS Egerton 1782, dating to the early sixteenth century, along with a mid-eighteenth-century copy, TCD MS 1384 (H 5 12); one of the poems in the text, incipit "Ingnad echtra," is also preserved within the Book of the Dean of Lismore.[15] The only complete edition and translation of the text is that of Standish O'Grady, published in 1892 in *Silva Gadelica*, although several passages, mainly of a sexual nature, were omitted from his translation.[16] One of the poems, incipit "Arocal fil acam-sa," was translated by Kenneth Jackson as "Iubhdhán's Fairy House" in *A Celtic Miscellany*.[17] A heavily bowdlerized Modern Irish translation, based on O'Grady's edition, was published by Peadar Ua Laoghaire as *Eisirt*.[18]

The text has been dated to the thirteenth or fourteenth century by Thurneysen, Myles Dillon, and Seán Ó Catháin, and I see no reason to disagree with this assessment.[19] William Gillies and the late

---

[15] An edition and translation of the poem from the Book of the Dean of Lismore, along with a transcription of the poem given in Egerton 1782, was published as William Gillies, "A Poem on the Land of the Little People," in *Fil súil nglais - a Grey Eye Looks Back: A Festschrift in Honour of Colm Ó Baoill* ed. Sharon Arbuthnot and Kaarina Hollo (Ceann Drochaid: Clann Tuirc, 2007), 33-52.

[16] Standish O'Grady, *Silva Gadelica: A Collection of Tales in Irish*, 2 vols (London: Williams and Norgate, 1892), i:238-52 [text], ii:269-85 [translation]. One of the censored passages, involving the captive Iubhdán laughing at a gullible husband, was translated in Robin Flower, review of *The Vita Merlini*, edited by J. J. Parry, *Review of English Studies* 2 (1926), 230-32, at 231-2.

[17] Kenneth Jackson, *A Celtic Miscellany: Translations from the Celtic Literatures* (London: Routledge & K. Paul, 1951), 193. On the spelling of this name, see note 26.

[18] Peadar Ua Laoghaire, *Eisirt* (Dublin: Brún agus Ó Nualláin, 1900).

[19] "13-14. Jh.?" Thurneysen, *Die irische Helden- und Königsage*, 541. "c. 1300" Myles Dillon, "Nominal Predicates in Irish," *Zeitschrift für celtische Philologie* 16 (1927), 313-56, at 328. "The proportion of -*s*- to -*r*-endings . . . would correspond to a position in the Annals midway between the periods 1251-1300 and 1301-1378 . . . also from an examination of the state of the infixed an independent pronoun, the conclusion was come to that the earliest period to which the text could be assigned was 1200-1250."

Donnchadh Ó Corráin, on the other hand, have suggested an early thirteenth or late twelfth-century date of composition, on the grounds that a poem by Muireadhach Albanach Ó Dálaigh, dated to 1224, appears to reference this text.[20] I am not convinced by this argument: while the similarities are enough to show that some version of the *story* was extant by the early thirteenth century, they are not close enough to demonstrate conclusively that our poet drew upon the extant *text* of *ITLAF*.[21]

This saga has received very little critical attention as a literary text in its own right and, as noted above, scholars have tended only to

---

Seán Ó Catháin, "Some Studies in the Development from Middle to Modern Irish, Based on the Annals of Ulster," *Zeitschrift für celtische Philologie* 19 (1933), 1-47, at 34. Ó Catháin elsewhere notes (pp. 16-17) that the proportion of preverbal *ro* to *do* suggests a slightly earlier date for this text, although this is the least reliable of the three features chosen as a dating criterion. It should be noted that Ó Catháin made use of O'Grady's text for this study; in the process of preparing my edition, I observed that O'Grady often silently emended preverbal *do* to *ro*. When the correct numbers are supplied, this feature also points to a late thirteenth or early fourteenth-century date.

Both Dillon and Ó Catháin's discussions are based on features of the prose of this text, rather than the verse; some of the poems do show linguistic features which would point to an earlier date of composition, while others appear to be contemporary with the prose.

[20] Gilies, "A poem on the Land of the Little People," 33; Ó Corráin, *Clavis litterarum Hibernensum*, § 970; see also Liam P. Ó Caithnia, *Apalóga na bhFilí* (Dublin: An Clóchomhar, 1984), 79. The poem in question, incipit "Fada in chabair a Cruac[h]ain" was edited and translated by Gerard Murphy, "Two Irish poems written from the Mediterranean in the thirteenth century," *Éigse* 7:2 (1953), 71-9, at 74-9.

[21] The *ITLAF* refers to Iubhdán mac Abhdáin, while Ó Dálaigh's poem refers to an Abhdán mac Ihbdán. Murphy stated that Ó Dálaigh was "doubtless following a different version of the story" in presenting this variant genealogy; however, as the reviewer has pointed out, the order of the names in Ó Dálaigh's poem is not metrically fixed and might reflect an unintentional scribal transposition. In the poem "Beir mo ghó" contained in the *ITLAF*, Iubhdán offers a wide range of gifts with various magical qualities, including a *cris* 'belt' with the power to protect the wearer from disease. Ó Dálaigh's poem only mentions the cris without mentioning any particular qualities.

mention it in passing as a 'version' or 'retelling' of the Old Irish 'saga' of Fergus mac Leite.[22] Marie Henri d'Arbois de Jubainville referred to the *ITLAF* as a "rédaction"; Thurneysen stated that "ein junger Bearbeiter der Sage hat sie nämlich in Märchengestalt umgeformt" and Robin Flower described it as "a late expanded retelling" of the Old Irish text.[23] Binchy elsewhere stated that "in the late Middle Ages some enterprising redactor got hold of the saga and blew it up into a very Rabelaisian fairy tale."[24] More recently, Neil McLeod referred to this text as a "Modern Irish version" of the earlier account, and Ó Corráin described it as "a facetious, somewhat bawdy, reworking of *Echtrae Fergusa meic Leite.*"[25] These statements all suggest that the redactor of the Early Modern Irish text drew directly upon the Old Irish one published by Binchy as the "saga" of Fergus mac Leite. In the remaining space, I wish to reassess the relationship between these two texts. I argue that it is unlikely that the Early Modern Irish text is derived directly from the extant Old Irish one, and suggest that the *ITLAF* ultimately derives from a version of the story which existed

---

[22] Notable exceptions include Vivian Mercier, *The Irish Comic Tradition* (Oxford: Oxford University Press, 1962), 27-31, 188; as well as Gerard Murphy, *The Ossianic Lore and Romantic Tales of Medieval Ireland* (Dublin: Three Candles, 1955), 31-2, where the text is presented as a paradigmatic example of what Murphy saw as a decline in the quality of Irish literature in the later Middle Ages. The text's depiction of the Tuatha Luchra ocus Lupracánach has, however, attracted the interest of some scholars of folklore: John J. Winberry, "The Elusive Elf: Some Thoughts on the Nature and Origin of the Irish Leprechaun," *Folklore* 87 (1976), 63-75; Ó Giolláin, "The *leipreachán*"; Michael Chesnutt, "On Hidden Treasure, Useless Shoes, and Gullible Husbands: A Postscript to a Comparative Study," *Copenhagen Folklore Notes* 1 (2000): 1-8.

[23] Marie-Henri D'Arbois de Jubainville, "La morte violente de Fergus mac Lete," *Zeitschrift für celtische Philologie* 4 (1903), 456-61, at 461; Thurneysen, *Die irische Helden- und Königsage*, 541 ("a later redactor of the saga had evidently molded it into the form of a Märchen"); Robin Flower (ed.), *Catalogue of Irish Manuscripts in the British Museum*, vol 2. (London: British Museum, 1926), 272.

[24] D. A. Binchy, "Echtra Fergusa maic Léite," in *Irish Sagas*, ed. Myles Dillon (Cork, Mercier Press, 1968), 51.

[25] McLeod, "Fergus mac Léti and the law," 1; Ó Corráin, *Clavis litterarum Hibernensum,* § 970.

prior to the composition of the *Echtra* as we have it. First, I offer a summary of the Early Modern Irish tale.

The Early Modern Irish saga begins with a description of a feast in the court of Iubhdán mac Abhdáin, the king of the diminutive Tuath Luchra and Lupracánach.[26] After the king boasts about the power of his court, his poet, Eisirt, laughs. When asked to explain himself, Eisirt claims that he knows of a people, the Ulaid, a single warrior of whom would be more than a match for all of Iubhdán's kingdom combined. Eisirt is seized for this insult and, before he can be punished, he is given leave to voyage to Ulster in order to find proof of his claim. After visiting Fergus mac Leite in Emain Macha, he returns with Aodh, the court dwarf who is a giant among the Tuath Luchra, and places *geasa* (obligations) on Iubhdán to visit Emain Macha and steal the porridge from Fergus' cauldron. Iubhdán and his wife, Bé Bhó, attempt this but become stuck in the porridge and are caught and imprisoned by Fergus. After he spends some time in captivity, and several episodes occur which are passed over in the interests of space, Iubhdán convinces Fergus to allow him home in exchange for one of his treasures. Fergus chooses Iubdhán's shoes, which allow the wearer to travel freely underwater.[27]

The narrative then shifts back to an unspecified point in time when Fergus first encountered the *sínech* or *péist* (monster) dwelling in Loch Rudraige.[28] As in the Old Irish account, Fergus' face is distorted and his people conceal this fact from him. Later, he becomes impatient with his wife while bathing and strikes her; she responds by stating that it would be better for him to avenge himself upon the beast that had distorted him than to strike a woman. Fergus orders a mirror

---

[26] This name is consistently spelled Iubdán or Ibdán in Egerton 1782. I have normalized to Iubhdán and Abhdáin on the grounds of the spelling Vdane in the Book of the Dean of Lismore (Gillies, "A poem on the land of the little people," 40) and Ibhdán in Muireadhach Albanach Ó Dálaigh's poem (Murphy, "Two Irish poems," 77).

[27] The obvious difficulties posed by the diminutive Iubhdán and the gigantic Fergus wearing the same shoes are passed over in silence; cf. the earlier episode where Fergus seduces Bé Bhó, in which the discrepancies in size are discussed at great length.

[28] While this word is spelled with a short <i> in O'Grady's edition, it is consistently written with a long vowel in Egerton 1782. See note 36.

be brought to him, sees his blemish, and acknowledges the truth of what his wife has said. This is stated to be why Fergus chose the shoes. The narrative returns to the present, as Fergus returns to Loch Rudraige, enters the lake to do battle with the monster, and emerges victorious but dies of his wounds.

In addition to being much later in terms of language, the *ITLAF* is considerably longer than the Old Irish *Echtra* and contain a large amount of material with no parallel in any of the older texts.[29] This unique material, roughly comprising the first two thirds of the text, is predominantly concerned with the Tuath Luchra: the proceedings of Iubhdán's court, Eisirt's initial visit to Emain Macha, Iubhdán's failed porridge heist, and his period of captivity in Emain Macha. Only the final third of the text, which relates Iubhdán's liberation and Fergus' encounters with the lake monster, can be said to parallel the *Echtra*, and there are several significant differences between these two accounts.

One major difference is in the chronology of Fergus' supernatural encounters: in the Old Irish account, he is first attacked by the luchorpáin and receives the mantle or herbs from them, and then later comes upon the muirdris when he ignores their warning not to travel under Loch Rudraige. In the Early Modern Irish text, on the other hand, the initial encounter with the lake monster occurs before he is visited by Eisirt and Iubhdán, and there is no logical connection between these events. The Old Irish account presents a satisfying progression of the imposition of a taboo, the violation of said taboo, and supernatural retribution; this progression is absent in the Early Modern account. This altered chronology raises further questions, such as why neither Eisirt (who reveals several uncomfortable truths about Fergus' court) nor Iubhdán (who has never spoken a lie) mentioned Fergus' blemish, as well as how Fergus was able to seduce both his steward's wife and (despite obvious anatomical difficulties) Bé Bhó in his grossly distorted state.

These inconsistencies can be explained by positing that the extant Early Modern Irish text is a compilation of what were originally two separate texts: the *Imthechta Túaithe Luchra*, consisting of Iubhdán and Eisirt's adventures, and the *Aided Fergusa*, consisting of Fergus'

---

[29] The *ITLAF* is about 6,400 words long in my edition, compared with roughly 800 words in the text of H 3 18, as edited by Binchy.

encounters with the monster living in Loch Rudraige. While the language of these two sections seems to be roughly contemporary, there are marked differences in style and tone between them. Vivian Mercier has already called attention to the incongruity between the sexual and slapstick humour of the early sections and the tragic ending of the tale; I may also note that the early sections make extensive use of direct dialogue and rather terse narration, whereas the closing sections are marked by elaborate rhetorical descriptions.[30] On the whole, the *Imthechta* section seems later in terms of style and structure, characterized by the "less grand tone, an unrealistic background, and a diffuse structure characterised by the piling of incident on incident" which Murphy identified as typical of later medieval narrative.[31] In addition to such differences of style, there is very little narrative overlap between the two sections: only Fergus, Iubhdán, and the poet Aodh appear in both sections; both Iubhdán and Aodh play very minor roles in the *Aided* section, and the characterization of Fergus is markedly different in the two sections.

The *Imthechta* sections shows signs of being composed in the post-Norman period, either as an independent story or with the intention of being grafted onto an extant *Aided*. Whatever sources the author of the *Imthechta* drew upon, be they now-lost texts or oral tradition, these sources are distinct from the traditions regarding the death of Fergus discussed above, and need not concern us here.[32] The relationship between the Old Irish *Echtra* and the Early Modern Irish *Aided* now needs to be assessed. The primary differences between these two narratives can be summarized as follows:

---

[30] Mercier, *Irish Comic Tradition*, 28-9. We may also note that the poems in the first section of the text are written in a wide variety of metres, including relatively uncommon metres with non-heptasyllabic lines or stanzas with lines of variable length. In contrast, the poems in the second section are in *roscad, deibide* and *rannaigecht bec*, the most commonly-encountered metres in prosimetric saga.

[31] Gerard Murphy, *The Ossianic Lore and Romantic Tales of Medieval Ireland* (Dublin: Three Candles, 1955), 31.

[32] The episode in which the captive Iubhdán laughs on several occasions at the ignorance of his human captors shows strong parallels with Irish, Scottish, and Icelandic folk tradition; see Chesnutt, "On hidden treasure." Other parallels with oral tradition will be discussed at greater length in the introduction to my forthcoming edition of *ITLAF*.

1) The early sections of the *Echtra* have no parallel in *ITLAF*. There is no mention of the rivalry between Eochu Bélbuide and Conn Cétchorach, the murder of Eochu in violation of Fergus' protection, or of the compensation awarded to Fergus for that violation.

2) In the *Echtra*, a group of luchorpáin attack Fergus when he falls asleep by the shore. Fergus overpowers them, and immediately receives their magical gift and warning in exchange for sparing them. In *ITLAF*, Iubhdán is a solitary invader, who unsuccessfully tries to steal Fergus' porridge. He is captured by Fergus, and grants him a gift in exchange for his freedom after a long period of captivity.

3) In the Old Irish account, the luchorpáin offer Fergus herbs to place in his ears so that he may travel freely underwater; the text provides an alternate tradition stating that they offered him a cloak with the same ability.[33] In the later account, it is Iubhdán's shoes which have this power, although he offers several other gifts, including his cloak.

4) The H 3 18 text of the *Echtra* alludes to Fergus' servant Ogma and his dog, and claims that the luchorpáin introduced the custom of sucking a man's breast as a sign of submission.[34] These references are absent in the Early Modern Irish text.

5) The *Echtra* identifies the monster as a muirdris and a péist, and describes it as "alternately inflating and contracting

---

[33] Binchy, "The Saga of Fergus mac Léti," § 4-5.
[34] Note also the gloss on *Di Chethairshlicht Athgabálae* §2 in the same manuscript: *aibinn ainm in gilla ⁊ ogma ainm in con* (Aíbinn is the name of the servant, and Ogma the name of the dog), Binchy, *Corpus Iuris Hibernici*, 881.41-882.1,
The phrase *iss esside abac dide a cichesom fergusa ⁊ gaba(i)s a gruaide i nnairide a anacuil* (this was the dwarf who sucked his, Fergus', breasts and caught hold of his cheek as a token of [asking] quarter from him) § 5, is occasionally been interpreted as a parallel to St. Patrick's refusal to *suggere mammellas eorum* in his *Confessio* (Ludwig Bieler (ed.), *Libri Epistolarum Sancti Patricii Episcopi: Introduction, Text and Commentary* (Dublin: Royal Irish Academy, 1993): §18). See *ibid.*, ii: 139-40; M. A. O'Brien, "Miscellanea Hibernica," *Études Celtiques* 3 (1938), 362-373, at 372-3.

itself like a smith's bellows" (*ala nuair rosraiged in uair naili nosnimairced amal bolg ngobenn*).[35] In the later text, the beast is described as a sínech and, although it is described extensively with elaborate rhetorical passages, the image of the inflating and contracting bellows is absent.[36] It is also the monster's noxious breath, rather than

---

[35] Binchy, "The Saga of Fergus mac Léti," § 6. *Muirdris* is a *hapax legomenon*, apparently a compound of *muir* 'sea' and *dris*. Regarding the second element of this word, Binchy notes (43) that "I have not met this word elsewhere. The second element may be identical with *dris-* in *drisiucc* (a hypocoristic form of *dris* + *cú*, cf. gen. *driscon*). *Muirgris* (gen.) in the gloss AL i. 68. 25 is doubtless a mistake." Calvert Watkins suggests that the second element is "a cognate of the Greek word δράκων 'dragon, serpent'. The zero-grade of the root is common to both **dr̥k-* -> Greek *drak-*, Celtic *drik-.* A suffixed form **dr̥k-si* (or feminine **dr̥k-sih₂*) would yield precisely Primitive Irish **drissi*, Irish *dris*." Calvert Watkins, *How to Kill a Dragon: Aspects of Indo-European Poetics* (Oxford: Oxford University Press, 1995), 447. These explanations are by no means mutually exclusive; it is not inconceivable that a word meaning "name of a poetic grade; a low satirist or lampooner" (*eDIL* s.v. 1 *drisiuc*) might contain an element originally referring to a destructive supernatural force. That the meaning of the word was obscure for the glossator is suggested by the fact that it is immediately followed by the description *peist uiscide uathmar* "a fearful water-monster." The term *smeirdris*, which occurs in *Acallam na Senórach* to describe an aquatic monster, is no doubt related (*eDIL* s.v. *smeirdris*).

[36] As noted above, *sínech* is consistently spelled with a long <í> in Egerton 1782, although O'Grady printed the word as *sinech,* with a short vowel. Dative and accusative *sinig* appears in the Harleian 432 glosses on *Di Chethairshlicht Athgabálae* (Binchy, *Corpus Iuris Hibernici*, ii:354.17-18). Both Thurneysen and D'Arbois de Jubainville understood this word as a derivative of *sine* "teat," and as originating in misunderstanding of the adjective *finech* "tribal (?)" in the *Di Chethairshlicht Athgabálae* poem. Thurneysen, *Die irische Helden- und Königsage*, 541; D'Arbois de Jubainville, "La morte violente de Fergus mac Lete," 461. As the name is consistently spelled with a long <í> in Egerton 1782, and marks of length are absent in this section of Harleian 432, a derivation from *sín* 'storm' also seems possible.

For Thurneysen and D'Arbois de Jubainville, the presence of this name in both glosses on *Di Chethairshlicht Athgabálae* and in the *ITLAF* indicated that the latter text was based on the Old Irish *Echtra*, preserved as an

the sight of it, which causes Fergus to become distorted in the Early Modern Irish text.

6) In the Old Irish text, it is the enslaved woman Dorn who reveals Fergus' blemish to him by taunting him after he struck her. Fergus murders her with his sword, necessitating later compensation to her kin. In *ITLAF*, the blemish is revealed by Fergus' anonymous wife, who does not suffer the same violent fate.[37]

7) The Early Modern Irish *Aided* contains hints of an alternate tradition in which a woman is responsible for Fergus' death. The poem incipit "Uchbadhach mo chraidhi i-nocht" contains the lines *Aillin ingen Echdach uill / dom-rad a n-āit n-écomlainn* (Aillin daughter of great Eochaidh has brought me into a place of peril, 4ab), and the following poem, "Claídter lib fert Fergusa" mentions the death of Fergus *tre bríathraib bāethmná bice* (through the words of a small, foolish woman, (1cd)).[38] This Aillin is not mentioned elsewhere in the *Aided*; it is conceivable that she played a role in an earlier portion of the text which was

---

extended gloss on this legal text. As the term *sínech* is only preserved in connection with Fergus in two sources-the *ITLAF* and the glosses in Harleian 432 (a sixteenth-century manuscript)-I propose another explanation: the scribe responsible for this section of glossing (whether we imagine it to be contemporary with Harleian 432, or copied from an earlier manuscript) was familiar with the *ITLAF* or a related text, and borrowed the term *sínech* from it in order to explain the now-obscure *finech*.
On Sinech with short <i> as a personal name, see Aogán Ó hIarlaithe, "Sinech Cró, an mháthair chíche agus an t-altramas in Éirinn sa Mheánaois," *Celtica* 29 (2017): 55-75.
[37] In the Early Modern Irish text, Fergus strikes his wife with his fist (go t*uc* in rí **dorn** di g*ur* br*is* fíaccuil ina cinn,), although the similarity between the name *Dorn* and the common noun *dorn* here is almost certainly a coincidence. The text here is item 23 in the forthcoming edition of *ITLAF*. In O'Grady *Silva Gadelica,* vol. 1, p. 250 (text), vol. 2, 285 (translation).
[38] The texts and translations given here are from the author's forthcoming edition of *ITLAF*. "Uchbadhach mo chraidhi i-nocht" is item 25 in his edition. "Claidter lib fert Fergusa" is item 26. For the O'Grady text and translations of these poems, see *Silva Gadelica,* vol. 1, p. 252 (text); vol. 2, p. 283 (translation). See also the discussion in note 3 above.

removed in order to accommodate *ITLAF*. Except for Dorn, there are no women mentioned in the Old Irish text.

8) The *Echtra* closes with a discussion of restitution paid for the murder of Dorn, and of the return of the land which was paid to Fergus in compensation for the murder of Eochu.[39] These concerns are absent in *ITLAF*; instead, the dying Fergus tells the Ulstermen to keep his sword safe for another Fergus, mac Rosa Rúaid, who is to come.

When all of the differences between the two texts are considered as a whole, it seems highly unlikely that the *Aided* section is in fact a 'retelling' or 'modernized' form of the extant Old Irish *Echtra*. One possible explanation for these discrepancies is that the Old Irish *Echtra* circulated beyond its legal context, perhaps even entering oral tradition, that the details of the narrative were altered in the process of transmission, and that the closing sections of *ITLAF* are descended from a now-lost intermediary version. A second possibility is that the *Echtra* in its present form and these sections of *ITLAF* both share a common and now-lost source, a narrative tradition which predates the legal setting of the extant *Echtra*.[40] For reasons which I will now discuss, the latter possibility seems more likely to me.

Many of the differences between the Old Irish *Echtra* and the Early Modern Irish saga relate to details which Neil McLeod saw as demonstrative of specific points of early Irish law.[41] The later text does not mention the conflict among the Féni over the kingship of Tara, the murder of Eochu Bélbuide, the compensation paid to Fergus for the violation of his protection, the servitude of Dorn, and the

---

[39] Binchy did not consider this section to be part of the "saga," as it was not included in his edition. The text and translation of this section is available in McLeod, "Fergus mac Léti and the Law," 25-28.

[40] As noted above, the title *Echtra Fergussa Maic Lete* is found in Tale List B, but not in either manuscript witness for the Old Irish saga itself. This may be taken as a reference to the posited original saga although, as the tale list is later than both *Di Chethairshlicht Athgabálae* and the prose account, this title may refer to our extant Old Irish account, or to a text derived from it it. As Malthaner noted, the extant Old Irish account does conform to the echtra tradition, so it not inconceivable that a later author applied the generic term *Echtra* to this text. Malthaner, "The Intersection of Literature and the Law," 98-100.

[41] McLeod, "Fergus mac Léti and the Law."

compensation paid for her murder. It is, of course, possible that these legal elements of the narrative were a feature of *ITLAF*'s ultimate source, but were lost over the course of transmission as they were of less interest to redactors than Fergus' various supernatural encounters were. If this were the case, however, one might expect to see traces or echoes of these earlier details in the text, in the same way that the stray reference to "Aillin daughter of Eochaidh" suggests that she played a role in an earlier stage of transmission. To the best of my knowledge, there are no such echoes of these legal details. A more likely explanation is that such elements were added by the redactor of the extant *Echtra* in order to press an already-existing narrative into service in order to demonstrate the legal procedure of distraint.[42]

Additionally, some features of the extant *Echtra* text suggest that the author or redactor had access to multiple versions of the story at the time of writing, and did not compose it out of whole cloth himself. The saga states that the leprechauns gave Fergus herbs to place in his ears, but also that "some say that the dwarf gave him his cloak" (*asberat araile iss int abac dorat(a) a brat do*).[43] The phrase *asberad araile* "some say" is later used in the H 3 18 text to introduce a brief reference to Fergus' servant Ogma and his hound, who are otherwise not mentioned in this text.[44] A gloss on *Di Chethairshlicht Athgabálae* §1, on the other hand, identifies Ogma as the hound and Aíbinn as the servant.[45] Yet another gloss on the legal tract states that Fergus killed Dorn with a stone rather than his sword.[46]

---

[42] For some examples of such "leading cases," see Myles Dillon, "Stories from the Law Tracts," *Ériu* 11 (1932), 42-65.

[43] Binchy, "The Saga of Fergus mac Leti," § 5.

[44] Binchy states that "obviously there was a different version of the meeting between Fergus and the *lúchorpáin*, but there is no trace of this in the L recension nor in the later expansion of the story known as Aided Fergusa." Binchy, "The Saga of Fergus mac Léti," 42.

[45] See note 34.

[46] "is and sin romarb Fergus durn don chloich fothraicthe re ndul fon loch" (Binchy, *Corpus iuris Hibernici*, ii:354.11). In his notes on the text, Binchy interprets *cloch fhothraicthe* as "one of the stones used for heating the water." Binchy, "The saga of Fergus mac Léti," 44. The language of this section of glossing appears somewhat later than the body of the narrative, and may therefore indicate a tradition postdating the Old Irish account. See note 36.

Scholarly consensus on the origin of the Old Irish account is divided. Binchy suggested that the story was already known from native tradition and had been "pressed into service" by legal scholars in order to demonstrate the law of distraint.[47] The same opinion has been repeated by Calvert Watkins and Jacqueline Borsje in their studies of the text.[48] Thurneysen and D'Arbois de Jubainville, on the other hand, suggested that the prose 'saga' had been invented by legal glossators in order to explain some of the difficult legal poetry in *Di Chethairshlicht Athgabálae*.[49] Most recently, McLeod has argued that the legal verse and gloss tell the same story, one which was "devised by lawyers" rather than adapted by them, in order to demonstrate the finer points of the procedure of distraint.[50]

None of these scholars have taken the *ITLAF* into consideration in their discussions of the Old Irish saga and, as I have mentioned above, have tended to dismiss it as a mere late retelling. The relationship between these two texts, however, has clear implications for discussions concerning the origins of the extant Old Irish saga. If, as I have suggested, the *ITLAF* derives (albeit indirectly) from a source anterior to the *Echtra*, this would support the view that the Old Irish text that we have was not invented out of whole cloth by lawyers, but that it reflects an adaptation of a pre-existing narrative tradition. At the very least, this presents a possibility which has not been considered by those scholars who have argued for the *Echtra* saga as pure legal invention.

The later medieval Irish text, *Imthechta Tuaithe Luchra ocus Aided Fergusa* is understudied in comparison to the Old Irish account of Fergus' death, and most discussions of the Old Irish text give the *Imthechta*, at best, a cursory mention. In spite of this, as I have hopefully demonstrated, this later text has implications for ongoing questions regarding the composition and origin of the Old Irish 'saga'.

---

[47] Binchy, "The Saga of Fergus mac Léti," 48.
[48] Watkins, *How to Kill a Dragon*, 441; Borsje, *From Chaos to Enemy*, 19-20. Malthaner also suggests that the text may be "an authentic retelling of a saga text with legal influence." Malthaner, "The Intersection of Literature and Law," 103.
[49] D'arbois de Jubainville, "La morte violente de Fergus mac Lete," 460-1; Thurneysen, *Die irische Helden- und Königsage*, 539-40.
[50] McLeod, "Fergus mac Léti and the law," 24-5.

In this defense, if not of *rómánsaíocht*, certainly of later medieval Irish literature, I hope to have provided a cautionary tale which has methodological implications for the study of Irish saga in general, and not just the cluster of texts which have formed the subject of my discussion.[51] These later versions, reworkings, or recensions of Irish saga, while frequently neglected, are potentially quite relevant for questions of composition, origin, and textual history, especially in the case of early Irish literature which only survives in much later manuscripts.

---

[51] For a defense of the literary merits of these Early Modern Irish productions, as well as an explanation of my rather torturous joke, see Joseph Falaky Nagy, "In defense of *Rómánsaíocht*," *Ériu* 38 (1987), 9-26.

The Deeds of the House: Rethinking the *Duanaire* – A Material and Tangible Element of Irish Nobility and Legitimacy

Emmet de Barra

Mo dhuanaire tabhair ret ais
don Ghaoidheilg fhíoruasail
fhorais,
go bhfionnam fréamha gach
sgeoil,
géaga goile agas glaineóil.

Bring with thee my verse-book
of noble classic Gaelic,
that I may learn the roots of
each tale,
branches of valour and fair
knowledge.

Go ngabhainn fíorlaoidhthe
feasa
glainiuil na ccraobh
ccoimhneasa,
géaga gionalaidh gach fir,
éachda iongantais is aisdir.

That I may recite learned lays
of the clear knowledge of
kindred stocks,
each man's family tree,
exploits of wonder and travel.[1]

The Dictionary of the Irish Language defines *duanaire* as "(a) maker or reciter of verses: rhymer, chanter, poet, bard" and "(b) song-book, poem-book, collection of poems."[2] This paper will investigate the composition of the bardic poem book, or *duanaire*, of Cormac Ó hEadhra of Luighne, establishing its role as a legitimising object of nobility and right to rule within Gaelic Ireland, and stems from research conducted for a MA thesis at the University of Connecticut.

The most comprehensive published account of the *duanaire* is Brian Ó Cuív's 1973 lecture "The Irish Bardic Duanaire or poem-book." Ó Cuív defines the *duanaire* as "a collection of poems," and when applied to poems in their written form it may be translated

---

[1] Osborn Bergin, *Irish Bardic Poetry: Texts and Translations, Together with an Introductory Lecture*, ed. David Greene and Fergus Kelly (Dublin, 1970), pp. 175-6, 295-6. All translations in this article are the author's unless otherwise indicated.

[2] Electronic Dictionary of the Irish Language (eDIL), s.v. duanaire. Accessed September 30, 2021. http://dil.ie/18971.

"poem-book."[3] Ó Cuív continues to delineate the various types of *duanaire*; miscellaneous anthologies of bardic poetry such as The Book of the O'Conor Don.[4] Another type is a *duanaire* comprising the poems of a single poet or poetic family such as the *duanaire* of the Í Uiginn family within the Yellow Book of Lecan.[5] The final type of *duanaire* is that which contains poems addressed to a single nobleman or family:

> The term *duanaire* when applied to family material can be used to refer to poems composed in honor of one man or, in a slightly wider sense, in honor of one man and his immediate relations and household. In a far more extended sense it can refer to members of a family spread over several generations or even over several centuries.[6]

The oldest surviving autograph duanaire is Leabhar Méig Shamhradháin from the fourteenth century.[7] Many noble families have surviving duanaireadha such as the Uí Eadhra, Uí Néill, Uí Bhroin (the Leabhar Branach, a copy of which is now held in Harvard), and many more.[8] Pádraig de Brún has brought attention to a now lost duanaire

---

[3] Brian Ó Cuív, *The Irish Bardic Duanaire or "Poem-Book"*, The R.I. Best Memorial Lecture Delivered by Professor Brian Ó Cuív to the National Library of Ireland Society in the National Gallery of Ireland on 10th May 1973 (Dublin, 1973), 7.

[4] Ibid., 9-10.

[5] Ibid., 19-20. See also the discussion of the Seifín Duanaire in Ó Cuív, p. 22, and in Mícheál Hoyne, *Fuidheall Áir: Bardic Poems on the Meic Dhiarmada of Magh Luirg c. 1377 - c.1637* (Dublin, 2018), 119-20.

[6] Ó Cuív, 25.

[7] Lambert McKenna, *The Book of Magauran. Leabhar Méig Shamhradháin* (Dublin, 1947). Earlier still, Pádraig Ó Macháin has argued that a composite manuscript in the National Library of Scotland contains a portion of a duanaire to Maghnas Ó Conchobhair, King of Connacht from 1288-93 see Pádraig Ó Macháin, "Maghnus Ó Conchubhair, Rí Connacht (1288-1293): Blogh Dá Dhuanaire," in *Séimhfhear Suairc : Aistí in Ómós Don Ollamh Breandán Ó Conchúir*, ed. Seán Ó Coileáin, Liam P. Ó Murchú, and Pádraigín Riggs (Dingle 2013), 679-704, at 681.

[8] Tadhg Ó Donnchadha, ed. *Leabhar Cloinne Aodha Buidhe* (Dublin, 1931); Lambert McKenna, ed., *The Book of O'Hara. Leabhar Í Eadhra* (Dublin,

of the FitzMaurices that existed in the early seventeenth century.[9] Similarly Brian Ó Cuív has pointed out a reference to a now lost duanaire of the Mac Cárthaigh Riabhach found in the Book of Lismore or Leabhar Mheic Cárthaigh Riabhaigh.[10] Based on the sheer number

---

1951); Seán Mac Airt, *Leabhar Branach, The Book of the O'Byrnes* (Dublin, 1944); David Greene, *Duanaire Mhéig Uidhir* (Dublin, 1972). See the discussion in Pádraig Ó Macháin, *Téasc agus Údar i bhFilíocht na Scol* (Dublin, 1998), 20-23, on the "duanaire" of Cú Chonnacht Mág Uidhir (d.1691) RIA MS C iv 1; Book of the De Burgos: TCD MS 1440 (F.4.13); Tomás Ó Cléirigh, "A Poem Book of the O'Donnells," *Éigse* 1 (1939), 51-61; Bodleian Library MS. Rawl. B. 514, James Carney, ed., *Poems on the O'Reillys.* (Dublin, 1950); E. C. Quiggin, "A Book of the O'Reillys," *Ériu* 6 (1912), 125-29; James Carney, ed., *Poems on the Butlers of Ormond, Cahir and Dunboyne (A.D. 1400-1650)* (Dublin, 1945); Duanaire na nDíolmhaineach, Royal Irish Academy, MS A v 2; The Book of Fermoy, RIA MS 23 E 29; *Leabhar Chlainne Suibhne* (RIA MS 24 P 25) is discussed in Pádraig Ó Macháin, "Three Early Poems by Fearghal Óg Mac an Bhaird, with Notes on the Duanaire of Domhnall Mac Suibhne," *Celtica* 27 (2013): 38-54, at 43. Paul Walsh edited a large prose portion of the manuscript in 1920, see Paul Walsh, *Leabhar Chlainne Suibhne: An Account of the Mac Sweeney Families in Ireland with Pedigrees* (Dublin, 1920). Seán Ó Foghlú also edited four poems from the same manuscript, see Seán Ó Foghlú, "Four Bardic Poems from Leabhar Chlainne Suibhne," unpublished MLitt thesis (Trinity College Dublin, 1992). Pádraig Ó Macháin, "Two Nugent Manuscripts: The Nugent Duanaire and Queen Elizabeth's Primer," *Ríocht Na Midhe: Records of the Meath Archaeological and Historical Society* 23 (2012), 121-42. Ó Cléirigh, Tomás. "A Poem Book of the O'Donnells." *Éigse - A Journal of Irish Studies* 1 (1939): 51–61.

[9] Pádraig de Brún, "A Lost FitzMaurice Duanaire," *Journal of the Kerry Archaeological and Historical Society* 15 & 16, no. 83 (1982), 58-60.

[10] Brian Ó Cuív, "A Poem for Fínghin Mac Cárthaigh Riabhach," *Celtica* XV (1983): 96-110, at 100. My thanks to Pádraig Ó Macháin for this reference. Another "lost" (non- or late bardic?) duanaire is that compiled in honour of Sir James Cotter (d.1705), see Brian Ó Cuív, *Párliament na mBan* (Dublin, 1977), xxxviii.

of surviving examples or references, one could speculate that nearly every noble family held a duanaire.[11]

Duanaireadha were the principal material repository for bardic poetry of the nobility which served a special role within Gaelic Ireland. As Marc Caball has written:

> It is clear that the primary professional function of *fileadha* [poets] was to provide political and social validation for the ascendant elite. Invoking a series of motifs and conventions sanctioned by long usage, bardic poets established the validity of a ruling or potential lord before fellow noblemen and the inhabitants of his territories. In this sense, the poetry projects the key ideological precepts which underpinned conventional notions of lordship and its exercise.[12]

Bardic poetry was used to legitimise the position of rulers in Gaelic Ireland, but one must ponder what happened to the poems after their composition and first recitation. How were they used and *reused* to legitimise the nobility of Ireland? What motivated the creation of these duanaire and how were they viewed by those who held them? What did they say?

Ó Cuív has argued that they were compiled in the patron's honour and were perhaps a "formal presentation" of the available poems.[13] Marc Caball has argued that "poem-books are by their very essence instruments of contemporary local propaganda" and that "bardic expressions of lordship and self-image underlines the functional focus of these poem-books."[14] Pádraig Ó Macháin has argued that the duanaireadha were "statements of identity and noble ancestry on the

---

[11] For a discussion of the word duanaire in the Annals, the work of Seathrún Céitinn, and within the corpus of poetry itself see, Emmet de Barra, "The Deeds Of The House; A Study In The Materiality, Structure And Content Of The Irish Bardic Duanaire And Its Role As An Object Of Legitimacy In Late Medieval And Early Modern Ireland.," an unpublished MA thesis (University of Connecticut, 2021), pp. 19-25, 28.

[12] Marc Caball, *Poets and Politics: Continuity and Reaction in Irish Poetry,* 1558-1625 (Cork, 1998), 2.

[13] Ó Cuív, *Irish Bardic Duanaire,* 29.

[14] Caball, *Poets and Politics,* 24.

part of some of the Gaelic and long-naturalised Anglo-Norman families in the face of Elizabethan aggression" and were status symbols of Gaelic Ireland amongst the nobility.[15]

Building on the work of other scholars, there is scope for further discussion by investigating the manuscripts themselves and crucially recognising the agency of both scribes and patrons in the compilation of these duanaireadha. I do not believe that the measure of one's duanaire was simply that the more poems within the better or that they were written in a haphazard or piecemeal manner as poems were received from poets. They were not merely status symbols, displaying the wealth of the patrons. That is not to say that the duanaire did not have a creative afterlife. They most certainly did, and duanaireadha were extended upon or bound with other manuscripts. However, at their first compilation they were conscious works of synthesis. These poems and duanaireadha were read and were *expected* to be read; Lords were expected to be able read them as evidenced by the numerous references to the erudite intelligence of Irish Lords within the corpus of poetry itself.[16] Drawing attention to the focus on written

---

[15] Pádraig Ó Macháin, "The Emergence of the Gaelic Paper Manuscript: A Preliminary Investigation," in *Paper and the Paper Manuscript: A Context for the Transmission of Gaelic Literature*, ed. Pádraig Ó Macháin (Cork, Cló Torna, 2019), 21-43, at 40.

[16] See, for example, a poem to Uilliam Burc entitled "Beannocht ar anmuin Uilliam" from RIA MS 3 23 L 17, 148a. Translation mine. For a diplomatic edition and discussion, see Pádraig Ó Macháin, "A Crosántacht for Uilliam Búrc," *Celtica* 25 (2007), 175-94.

Ba file é budh fer dána	He was a poet, a man of the arts,
budh fer brégtha bandála	He was a man of the charming of
do thuill gnaoi dhá ghné roghluin	assemblies of women
budh saoi é "sna healadhnaibh.	He earned fame for his pure appearance
	He was a scholar of the arts
	He was a reader of dark books [i.e.
Budh léaghthóir leabhar ndorcha	faded, old]
ag sin cuid dá chomhortha	They are some of his characteristics
rug an fithleóir geall an ghrinn	The chess player? has taken – [?*geall an ghrinn*?]
sgribhnneóir dob fherr a nÉirinn.	The best writer in Ireland.

word, it is worth mentioning a quatrain from a poem addressed to Cú Chonnacht Mág Uidhir by Muiris Ó hEodhusa.

Mág Uidhir re hénfhéchain Maguire understands the
tuigidh fháth gach éneolaigh; composition of every scholar
luas Í Cholla ar **caoillínibh** at a single glance;
cruas a rolla réidheobhaigh.[17] his speed in reading **narrow**
lines will simplify the
difficulty of his genealogy.

As mentioned above, Ó Cuív speculated that the family duanaire was a "formal presentation of available material" and stated that "an analysis of these duanaireadha would, I think, illustrate my theory."[18] This present paper builds on the theory advanced speculatively by Ó Cuív by analysing a family duanaire with specific focus on its structure and content as evidenced by the materiality of the manuscript combined with close textual readings while drawing on the historical context of composition. It pushes back against the theory advanced by James Carney that the duanaire was analogous to a "modern photo album," that poems were entered into the duanaire "about the time of the event it commemorates," or that family duanaireadha constituted samples of verse that the poet had left behind in return for hospitality that he had received such as was argued by E. C. Quiggin.[19]

See also, Katharine Simms, "Literacy and the Irish Bards," in *Literacy in Medieval Celtic Societies*, ed. Huw Pryce (Cambridge: Cambridge University Press, 1998), 238-58.

[17] David Greene, *Duanaire Mhéig Uidhir* (Dublin, 1972), 200-1 (emphasis mine): The imagery used by the poet is quite ingenious. While praising Maguire for his learning he mentions the "narrow" lines of his genealogy. These narrow lines imply a page in a manuscript that is full to the brim with his genealogy. Maguire's genealogy is so long and illustrious that it is difficult to read. The point at play here, however, is that the focus is on reading both the poems (compositions) and the genealogy from the manuscript and not listening to a recitation of them aloud. The implied possession of an illustrious manuscript is also apparent.

[18] Ó Cuív, 29.

[19] Carney is quoted in Ó Cuív, 32. E. C. Quiggin, "Prolegomena to the Study of the Later Irish Bards 1200-1500," *Proceedings of the British Academy* V (1911): 1-55, at 14.

DEEDS OF THE HOUSE

Leabhar Í Eadhra

The Leabhar Í Eadhra or "The Book of O'Hara" NLI MS G 1303 is a vellum manuscript containing 37 poems addressed to the various members of the Í Eadhra, the majority of which are to Cormac mac Céin Ó hEadhra. The manuscript was edited and translated by Lambert McKenna S.J. and published in 1951.[20] The Í Eadhra Buidhe were lords of Luighne, an area within modern County Sligo. By the late sixteenth century, Luighne was under the control of Cormac Ó hEadhra. He participated in the Nine Years' War in support of Ó Néill and Ó Domhnaill.[21] Pardoned in 1602, Ó hEadhra controlled the territory until his death in 1612.[22] His son Tadhg succeeded him and died in 1616.

The manuscript was written by a variety of different hands, but for most part by Tuathal Ó hUiginn who died in 1625.[23] David Greene and McKenna identify him as scribe of all but 5 of the 37 poems in the manuscript, including 23 of the 24 poems addressed to Cormac Ó hEadhra and also the genealogy and introduction (see below) on page v.[24] His hand is quite legible and the *mise-en-page* is well laid out. The only scribal note which connects him to Leabhar Í Eadhra occurs on page 34 of the manuscript following a short anonymous poem:

Isam Sgítheach aniu a nGleann Fhiadha a
mBaoidhiollchaibh. Ag sin doid a Chormuic Í
Eadhra ogus sgoth leis ód chaomh ód charoid

---

[20] Lambert McKenna, ed., *The Book of O'Hara. Leabhar Í Eadhra* (Dublin: Dublin Institute for Advanced Studies, 1951). McKenna lists 38 poems but Poems XXVI and XXVII are actually the same poem. For a discussion on this see Pádraig Ó Macháin, "Tadhg Ó Rodaighe and His School: Aspects of Patronage and Poetic Practice at the Close of the Bardic Era," in *Princes, Prelates and Poets in Medieval Ireland: Essays in Honour of Katharine Simms.*, ed. Seán Duffy (Dublin, 2012), 538-51, at 542-3.

[21] J.S. Brewer and William Bullen, eds., *Calendar of the Carew Manuscripts, Preserved in the Archi-Episcopal Library at Lambeth*, vol. 3, [1589-1600] (London, 1869), 300.

[22] *Leabhar Í Eadhra*, xxii-xxv.

[23] Eleanor Knott, *A Bhfuil Againn Dár Chum Tadhg Dall Ó hUiginn*, vols. XXII, XXIII Irish Texts Society: Main Series (London: Irish Texts Society, 1922), XXIII, 300-1.

[24] *Leabhar Í Eadhra*, xxviii; David Greene, "The O'Hara MS.," *Hermathena*, no. 60 (1942), 81-86, at 81.

208

Tuathal Ó hUigintt, 7 ní fheadar cia do-ríne an dán beagsa ro sgríobhus daoibhsi go fóill.

I am tired out today in Gleann Fiadha in Baoigheallaigh. This is for thee O Cormac Ó hEadhra and good wishes (?) with it from thy comrade and friend Tuathal Ó hUiginn. I do not know who composed this little poem which I have just written out for you.[25]

Upon analysis of scribal hands, the *mise-en-page* such as dry-point ruling, line fillers, and the use of the *ceann faoi eite*, attribution of authorship and patron of the poem, and continuities of stylistics approaches, three distinct sections and a poem without links to other parts of the manuscript become clear, revealing the original structure of the duanaire.[26]

One example of this is the use of what has been called a 'line filler' at the end of a line of text in order to present the text as justified. I have not been able to find any research on the use of 'line fillers' in medieval and early modern Irish manuscripts although it could be the case that they are so common that they have been overlooked as a 'feature' worth noting.[27] The scribe(s) of the poems on leaves which have been dry-point ruled use two distinct line fillers. Style A which is the same symbol as that used for the *ceann faoi eite* which might be represented as "⅌⅌⅌" and Style B which might be represented as such //.//.//.//.[28] What is remarkable in this instance is the division between the use of Style A and Style B. The scribe(s) do(es) not mix

---

[25] Ibid., 242-3.
[26] The poem, "Féch, a Chríosd, ar crích Luighni" (*Leabhar Í Eadhra*, 2-7, Poem I), occurs on a separate and distinct folio now placed at the start of the manuscript (NLI MS 1303, pp. i, ii). It does not share any stylistic or paleographic similarities with the rest of the manuscript. For further discussion, see Emmet de Barra, "The Deeds Of The House," 47-52. The *ceann faoi eite* is a common scribal notation to mark a line that continues into space left in the line above.
[27] Chantal Kobel has noted their use in her descriptive catalogue of TCD MS H 3. 18 (1337). Chantal Kobel, "A Descriptive Catalogue of TCD MS H 3. 18 (1337), Vols 2-4, Pp. 1-87: "Máel Íosa's Book," *Celtica* 32 (2020), 187-215.
[28] NLI MS G 1303 pp. 13, 65.

the styles in any instance throughout the manuscript. All the poems with the exception of two addressed to Cormac Ó hEadhra (see below) use Style A.[29] The poems which use Style B are addressed to various members of the Í Eadhra, the earliest of which is addressed to Fearghal Mór Ó hEadhra who died in 1390, and the latest to Tadhg mac Cormaic Í hEadhra who died in 1616.[30]

Another point of difference between Poems in Style A and Style B is the attribution of authorship to all but one of the poems in Style A (20 out of 21), while poems in Style B lack attribution of authorship in three of the eight poems present. The presence or lack thereof of attribution of authorship is not necessarily significant in and of itself, and its practice was certainly varied throughout medieval and early modern Ireland.[31] While the poems in Style B that are without attribution are addressed to figures who were definitely deceased by the end of the sixteenth century and might explain the gap in knowledge on the part of the scribe, the only poem in Style A without attribution is directly followed by a scribal note from Tuathal Ó hUiginn in which he states "I do not know who composed this little poem which I have just written out for you."[32] In my opinion, this is not an unremarkable statement and reveals that Tuathal Ó hUiginn was consciously thinking about authorship of the poems he had scribed. It also further serves to enhance the consistency of practice with the poems in Style A.

Two poems that are addressed to Cormac Ó hEadhra do not follow Style A (nor Style B) or the ruling practices of the manuscript. Poem XVII, "Fada re huaisle Clann Chéin," by Diarmuid Dall Mac an Fhir Léighinn, immediately follows Poem XVI on page 28 of the manuscript. McKenna, in his edition, identified the hand as that of Tuathal Ó hUiginn.[33] Upon further inspection of the hand, it is clear

---

[29] Poems II-XVI, XVIII-XXIII. Poems XVII and XXIV are also addressed to Cormac but do not follow this pattern.

[30] Poems XVII and XXIV.

[31] I am unaware of any dedicated study to this practice.

[32] *Leabhar Í Eadhra*, 242-3, Poem XXII.

[33] *Leabhar Í Eadhra*, xxviii, McKenna's incorrect attribution is understandable as he was mainly working from RIA MS 3 B 14, a transcription of the manuscript made by Mícheál Óg Ó Longáin for the

that it is not that of Tuathal Ó hUiginn. The scribe in this instance uses different scribal abbreviations where Tuathal has been quite consistent.[34] The scribe is also unusual in not making use of any marks of lenition and instead inserting a *h* following the lenited letter. This discrepancy, unfortunately, does not provide any definite answers to the provenance of the poem but merely points out its oddity within the manuscript as a whole. One is tempted to conclude that it did not form the original composition and was composed sometime between 1597 and 1612.[35]

The second poem is simpler to explain. "Fáth cumadh ar crích Luighne" was written by Fearghal Óg Mac an Bhaird, a poet who has other poems within the Style A section of the manuscript. It is written quite haphazardly, does not follow any of the scribal conventions preceding it and is written in a very different hand. The poem's attribution of author and subject matter further confirm that it is separate:

> *Fearghal Mhac an Bhaird do-roighne an dánso ar cclos Í Eadhra .i. Cormac mhac Céin do bheith tinn.*

> Fearghal Mac an Bhaird wrote [lit. made] this poem on hearing that the Ó hEadhra, Cormac son of Cian was sick.[36]

The poem itself discusses how sad the people of Luighne are now that Cormac is at death's door and precedes to celebrate his exploits in the past tense.[37] It is clear this was not a poem composed before

---

Royal Irish Academy in 1826, and viewed from photostats of what is now NLI MS G 1303, only briefly examining the original. See ix-x.

[34] In particular, compare Tuathal's use of the *rr* compendium to that of the scribe of XVII.

[35] The poem follows a poem composed by Domhnall Óg Mhac Aodha Meic Dhomhnoill Chaim Í Uiginn (XVI) and is followed (although not confirmed by the pages of the same folio) by two poems by Maghnus Óg Mhac Aodha Meic Dhomhnoill Chaim Í Uiginn, the brother of Domhnall Óg.

[36] *Leabhar Í Eadhra*, 250. Translation mine.

[37] *Guais bháis do bheith ar Chormac/mhac Céin barr na mbogroshlat/ tuar mímheannma druim ar dhruim/ do chloinn ríEadhra ó Fhréamhuin* (That Cian's son, whose hair is in wavy plaits, is in danger of death, causes anxiety to the whole race of royal Eadhra from Fréamhuinn,) Ibid., 250-1.

1597 when Cormac was in full health and taking part in the Nine Years' War.

Textual arrangement of poems in the manuscript

[See appendix A chart]

Section A can be firmly identified as a duanaire compiled on the behalf of Cormac Ó hEadhra in 1597 by Tuathal Ó hUiginn. What statement does this *duanaire* make and what motivated its creation? The duanaire begins with a genealogy and preface, followed by 21 poems by various authors finishing with a poem by the scribe of the duanaire, Tuathal Ó hUiginn. Tuathal Ó hUiginn consciously grouped the poems based on patron and poet. That other poems to other Ó hEadhra patrons by the same authors exist within the manuscript but *not* in this section further confirms that Section A should be analysed as the duanaire of Cormac Ó hEadhra. The following section of this article will analyse the genealogy and preface, poems, and final poem separately.

Genealogy and Preface

The duanaire begins with a genealogy tracing Cormac Ó hEadhra's back through (pseudo)history.[38] Cormac is styled as *the* Ó hEadhra Buidhe, i.e. Chief of his Name. We are told he is related to Eadhra "a q*uo* Ó hE*adra*" ("from whom the Í Eadhra"), and to Tadhg mac Céin, who fought at the pseudohistorical battle of Crionna in

---

[38] See appendix B for full text.

226 AD and received the territory of Magh Breagh for his efforts,[39] culminating in the figure of Éibhear Fionn, mac Míl Easbáine.[40]

Tuathal Ó hUiginn was not undertaking any radical departure in creating this genealogy, nor was he "inventing" a genealogy for Ó hEadhra, he was merely tapping into a long and well-established tradition.[41] Genealogies tied the nobility of Ireland to a common framework interwoven with a deep and rich corpus of historical texts. The effect on a reader of the duanaire cannot be overstated. Not merely giving his ancestry, the genealogy serves as a reference point to

---

[39] For the Battle of Crionna see, Annals of the Four Masters 226.1 *Ferghus Duibhdhedach, mac Iomchadha, 'na righ ós Erinn fri ré m-bliadhna, co t-torchair, h-i c-cath Crionna, la Corbmac ua Cuind, do laimh Logha Lagha. [. . .] I sochraide Corbmaic tainic Tadhg mac Céin & Lughaidh don chath h-ishin, & ba i tir-focraic an chatha do-rata o Chorbmac do Thadhg an feronn forsa t-tá Ciannachta, i Muigh Bregh, amhail as erdheirc i leabhraibh oile.*

Fearghus Duibhdeadach, son of Imchadh, was king over Ireland for the space of a year, when he fell in the battle of Crinna, by Cormac, grandson of Conn, by the hand of Lughaidh Lagha. [. . .] In the army of Cormac came Tadhg, son of Cian, and Lughaidh, to that battle; and it was as a territorial reward for the battle that Cormac gave to Tadhg the land on which are the Ciannachta, in Magh Breagh, as is celebrated in other books. John O'Donovan, ed.*, Annála Ríoghachta Éireann: Annals of the Kingdom of Ireland, by the Four Masters, from the Earliest Period to the Year 1616*, trans. John O'Donovan, second ed., 7 vols. (Dublin, 1856), 111.

See also, "This Tadhg made large conquests in Leath Cuinn afterwards. For Tadhg son of Cian, son of Oilill Olom, had two sons, namely, Connla and Cormac Gaileang. From Iomchaidh son of Connla comes O Cearbhaill, and from Fionnachta son of Connla comes O Meachair. From Cormac Gaileang son of Tadhg, son of Cian, comes O Eadhra and O Gadhra and O Conchubhair Ciannachta. The following are the territories they acquired, namely: Gaileanga, east and west; Ciannachta, south and north; Luighne, east and west." Geoffrey Keating, *Foras Feasa Ar Éirinn: The History of Ireland by Geoffrey Keating D.D*, ed. David Comyn, vol. I (1901), 291.

[40] The Milesians are named for Míl Easpáine of Spain; a central figure in Irish mythology and national identity. For an introduction see, John Carey, "Did the Irish Come from Spain? The Legend of the Milesians," *History Ireland* 9, no. 3 (2001), 8-11.

[41] See for example another Ó hEadhra genealogy in The Great Book of Lecan RIA MS 23 P 2, f. 223 r.

213

understanding who Cormac Ó hEadhra is. From *whom* is his nobility. Any individual in Gaelic Ireland would have been intimately acquainted with the figures mentioned within the genealogy and would have understood their significance. It directs the focus of the reader entirely on him as the direct heir to a noble ancestry and thus the rightful ruler or Ó hEadhra Buidhe. It serves as an impressive introduction to Cormac Ó hEadhra.

Immediately following the genealogy, Tuathal Ó hUiginn includes a long piece of text identifying the *causa scribendi* of the book and its patron.

> *Is e O hEadhra Buide .i. Cormac mac Céin mheic Oilill .i. an fear dhar sgriobhadh an leaphursa, aoinneach as **úaisle dh'fuil** agus **as sáoire modha agus béasa** ogas as **lia airrgheana ríogh agus flatha** agas **as oirrdhearca a n-ilghníomhradhoibh uaisle ionnsoightheacha** ogas fós **as lía rocheannoigh dh'fíon, d'eachaibh ogas d'ealadhain.***
>
> *Ro dhearsoigh Cormac O hEadhra seach uaislibh oile a chomaimsire fein isna hilcheimionnoibhsi. As se fós **as mhó báigh agus connailbhe ré tróghaibh agus bochtaibh** ar son Dé agas **lía ro fhurtoigh d'aighilgneachaibh an Choimhdheagh.***
>
> *Is **d'uaisle** fos Chormaic Í Eadhra teachta o (?) cuigeadh Ol nÉagmacht a n-éinchleith chogaidh do chongnomh ris O Néill agas ris O Domhnaill do chomhdha a dhuithche ar Ghalloibh agus ar ghradh a anma agus a choguis.*
>
> *Is an bhliadhoin ro sgriobhadh an leauarsa tangadar Goill agus maithe Connacht agus Muimhneach morshluaighiodh go Sidh Aodha Easa Ruaidh i gConallchaibh agus athchuirthear iad dá n-aimhdheoin tar Duibh tar Drophais as sin go Sligeach tar a n-ais.*
>
> *As ro tionnsgnadh an leauarsa dho sgriobhadh laimh re ....*

EMMET DE BARRA

*A nGleann Fiadha i mBaoidhiollchaibh ro
gcriochnuigheadh .... blíadhna deag agus ceithri
fichitt agus .u.c. agus m...*[42]

Ó hEadhra Buidhe .i. Cormac son of Cian son of
Oilill, is the man for whom this book is written, a man
of **highest lineage**, of **noblest manner and ways**, of
most **numerous kingly and princely qualities**, a
man most famous for **noble and venturesome
achievements, most lavish in buying wine and
steeds and works of art.**
In all these ways Cormac Ó hEadhra excelled other
chieftains [nobles] of his age. He excelled too in
**loving and caring for the poor and destitute for
God's sake,** and **in aiding the subjects of the Lord.**
It was owing to his nobility, too, that Cormac Ó
hEadhra left the Province of Ol nÉagmacht in a war-
league to aid Ó Néill and Ó Domhnaill in defending
his country against the Goill [Foreigners, the English]
and to satisfy his soul and conscience
In the year in which this book was written the Goill
and nobles of Connachta and of the men of Mumha
came on a great hosting to Síodh Aodha of Eas
Ruaidh in Conallaigh.[43] They were forced back over
the Dubh and the Drobhais and thence back to
Sligeach.
The writing of this book was begun near . . . It was
finished in Gleann Fiadha in Baodheallaigh 159-.[44]

Tuathal Ó hUiginn identifies the book as an object in itself "an
leaphur**sa**" and closely ties Cormac Ó hEadhra with its creation.
Tuathal Ó hUiginn begins to describe Cormac Ó hEadhra in what
might be seen as hyperbolic praise. However, Tuathal lays out the key
requirements for rule in medieval and early modern Ireland as

[42] *Leabhar Í Eadhra,* 10. Emphasis mine.
[43] Assaroe, Co. Donegal.
[44] *Leabhar Í Eadhra,* 11. Emphasis and insertions in brackets are mine. It is
unfortunate that the manuscript is damaged at the very end.

understood by the Irish literati and used extensively by bardic poets. Cormac is portrayed as being:

(1) "of highest lineage/noblest of blood" (*as úaisle dh'fuil*);

(2) "of noblest manner and ways" (*as sáoire modha agus béasa*), "of most numerous kingly and princely qualities" (*as lia airrgheana ríogh ogas flatha*);

(3) "a man most famous for noble and venturesome achievements" (*as oirrdhearca a n-ilghníomhradhóibh uaisle ionnsoightheacha*);[45]

(4) "most lavish in buying wine and steeds and works of art"[46] (*as lía rocheannoigh dh'fhíon, d'eachaibh ogas d'ealadhain*);

(5) "in loving and caring for the poor and destitute for God's sake, and in aiding the subjects of the Lord" (*fós as mhó báigh agus connailbhe ré tróghoibh agas bochtoibh ar son Dé agus lía ro fhurtoigh d'aighilgneachaibh an Choimhdheagh*).

This is the argument developed by Tuathal Ó hUiginn. Cormac Ó hEadhra is *the* man who should be ruling over Luighne. This is not only due to his noble birth and lineage but also to his kingly and lordly actions and behaviour, his martial prowess, his generosity to poets, and his religious commitment. These are the criteria upon which to judge Cormac Ó hEadhra's right to rule but what evidence does Tuathal Ó hUiginn give for these statements? For that, one must turn to the poems themselves.

"As uaisle dh'fuil"

The first poem to Cormac Ó hEadhra is an 84 stanza long poem by the famed Tadhg Dall Ó hUiginn entitled "An áil libh Seanchus Síol gCéin." This poem recounts the history of the 'seed' (*síl*) of Cian,

---

[45] This should really be translated with an emphasis on the martial qualities; s.v. Ionnsaigidh "approach, attack," accessed March 7, 2021, https://léamh.org/glossary/ionnsaighidh/.

[46] Read 'poetry.'

the ancestors of Cormac Ó hEadhra. Tadhg Dall begins with Éibhear son of Míl.

1. An áil libh seanchus síl gCéin *Go mbeirthior iad go héinfhréimh* *Ar ghlainchineadh Éimhir Fhinn* *Caithfidhear déinimh díchill*	Do you wish for the history of seed of Cian, until they are all traced to a single root? For the bright race of Eber the Fair one must do the utmost.[47]

Ó hUiginn continues to tell of the history of the race of Míl. Tadhg mac Céin, the famous warrior of Crionna is celebrated. Following the exposition of Cormac Gaileangach who first settled Luighne, Tadhg Dall recounts all the kings of Luighne and the lengths of their reigns.[48] Finally in stanza 65, he introduces Cormac Ó hEadhra, taking "possession in place of his forefathers."[49] "Wrongs are repealed, strongholds are erected."[50] He renews his charter over Luighne through his military prowess. Now Luighne is a "restful fairylike plain; without pain, without enmity, without wrath, without desire of plundering of conflict."[51] This is as it should be as "for nine hundred and four years Leyney [has] been under the tribe of Cian."[52] That they are both sons of a Cian cannot have been lost on Tadhg Dall and he finishes by comparing Cormac to Tadhg mac Céin;

79. Ní tháinig ó Thadhg mhac
    Céin
go mac Úna dá fhírfhréimh –
clú a shean ón ghasroidh dho
    ghlac –
fear budh casmhoil re Cormac.
	Never has there been of his true race from Tadhg, son of Cian, to the son of Úna–the fame of his forefathers he has inherited from the warriors–a man comparable to Cormac.

Tadhg Dall is clearly fixing Cormac within the historical record of the Í Eadhra and within the wider Irish historical tradition. He is

---

[47] *Leabhar Í Eadhra*, 25.

[48] Interestingly stanza 64 of the poem which concerns Conn mac Ruaidhrí, Cormac's predecessor as Ó hEadhra Buidhe is left out of the version of the poem found in the manuscript. See, Eleanor Knott, *A Bhfuil Againn Dár Chum Tadhg Dall Ó hUiginn*, vol. I (London, 1922), 229-42.

[49] *Leabhar Í Eadhra*, 43.

[50] Ibid., 43.

[51] Ibid., 47.

[52] Ibid., 45.

displaying the 'nobility' of Cormac's ancestors and therefore Cormac's inherent nobility and right to rule. This theme is replicated consistently by other poets. Tadhg Mac Giolla Bríghde Meic Bruaidheagha in his poem "Cionnus fríth fearann Luighne" recounts the history of Luighne from Tadhg mac Céin.[53]

4. Tadhg mhac Céin céidfhear do ghlac Luighne a gcath Crionna ó Chormac ar son a eadrána air ar ccor theagmhála um Theamraigh.	Tadhg, son of Cian was the first to receive Luighne from Cormac [mac Airt] in the battle of Crionna because, when fighting the battle about Teamhair, he had defended Cormac.[54]

Fearghal Óg Mac an Bhaird continues this theme in his poem "Sona sin a Chlanda Cuinn" in which Cormac is again compared to Tadhg mac Céin as the rightful inheritor of the land.[55] Irial Ó hUiginn, in his poem "Creach ag Luighne ó Leith Modha," also evokes this imagery:

21. Gnáth airrghi ríogh 'n-a ríoghfhuil Síol an Taidhgsi 's dá ttréidhibh, maicne fa dhíol do dheoiraibh síol leomhain d'aicmi Éimhir.	The marks of a king were ever to be found in their royal blood. they were among the characteristics of this race of Tadhg; the lion-seed of Éibhear's race is worth lamenting
22. Sé dá mheas le mac Úna meadh chosmhoil mar do-chuala lorg Taidhg ar ghníomh do-ghébha sgéla ríogh ós aird uadha.	Compared with Úna's son (i.e. Cormac) Tadhg will–I am told–be found like him; thou shalt find an imitation of Tadhg in Cormac's deeds, thou shalt find coming to light stories worthy to be told of any king.
23. Beith dána a dheaghbhloidh dlighidh	Ó hEadhra's fine name makes it his duty to be valiant and sets

---

[53] *Leabhar Í Eadhra,* 88.
[54] Ibid., 91. Insertion in brackets mine.
[55] Ibid., 130-43.

Ó hEadhra tar chách cuiridh,
teisd cháigh ós aird do fhoiligh
oighir Taidhg re ndáimh
nduiligh.

him above other men; this scion of Tadhg, even in his dealings with the exigent poets, throws all other princes into the shade.[56]

The emphasis throughout the duanaire is clear. Cormac Ó hEadhra possesses noble blood and his inheritance is like that of Tadhg mac Céin, his direct ancestor; control of Luighne.

"As sáoire modha agus béasa ogas as lia airrgheana ríogh ogas flatha"

That Cormac possessed kingly or princely qualities is repeatedly addressed by the poets within the duanaire.[57] Maol Muire Ó'n Cháinte speaks of his princely character:

9. *Tig ann **d'airrgheanoibh***
   flatha
nach díoghoil a dheacracha
le féin gcrannruaidh cláir
   Luighne
d'anbhuain cháigh dho
chomairghe.

His **princely character** prevents him from avenging troubles by getting the bloody-speared troop of Luighne Plain to spread turmoil everywhere as a way of protection for himself.[58]

Another common motif used to describe Cormac's rule over Luighne as just and proper is that of nature overflowing with abundance and that Luighne is as it should be as a result of Cormac's kingly rule.[59] Fruit trees touch the ground because they are so full of fruit. Tadhg Dall eloquently portrays the beauty and fertility of Cormac's reign, a paradise on Earth.

30. *Fuaighidh re teann teasbuch*
   bhfaoilligh
fioghruidh bile re bun bhfeoir;
fágbhoidh cnuas d'ísle san
   fhiodhbhaidh

The warmth of the early spring joins the branches of great trees to the roots of the sward; the fruits bend tress so low that

---

[56] Ibid., 168-9.
[57] Ibid., pp. 168, 174-5.
[58] Ibid., 228-9. Emphasis mine.
[59] For a discussion see, Damian McManus, "'The Smallest Man in Ireland Can Reach the Tops of Her Trees': Images of the King's Peace and Bounty in Bardic Poetry," in *Memory and the Modern in Celtic Literatures*, ed. Joseph Falaky Nagy, CSANA Yearbook 5 (Dublin, 2006), 61-117.

nar dhísle thuas d'iomghaidh
eoin.

there would not be more safety on top for the bird's nest.

31. Feadha lúbtha, lindte
tiorma,
tobuir mhillsi ós mhoighibh túir,
mil fan gcongal re headh
n-uaire
ag donnadh sreabh n-uaine
a húir.

Bending woods and shallow pools, sweet springs over pasture plains, honey ... (?) tincturing green streams from the earth throughout an hour (?).

32. Tearc a leithéid re lind
gCormuic
*acht **clár Parrthois** na bport*
sídh;
ar ibh do shreabhoibh learg
Luighne
beanoidh do leanb cuimhne
chígh.

Scarcely is there anything to equal it in the days of Cormac, save the peaceful havens of **Paradise**; what he drank of the waters of Leyney's plain takes from the child the remembrance of the breast.[60]

"As oirrdhearca a n-ilghníomhradhoibh uaisle ionnsoightheacha"

Fearghal Óg Mac an Bhaird develops Cormac's martial prowess in his poem "Táinig san chluiche ag Cormac."[61] Cormac has been victorious in the game of war and now holds the land of Luighne. From childhood he has performed dangerous deeds at the head of his host.[62] Mac an Bhaird introduces Fionn mac Cumhaill, leader of Na Fianna, and describes his martial prowess and how like Cormac, he lost his father at a young age and overcame his enemies by strength of arms in battle.[63]

26. Do éiridh d'aindeoin gach
fhir;
ar ó nEadhra do imthigh
dála flatha na Féine,
brágha chatha Choirrshléibhe.

He grew up in spite of all men; to Ó hEadhra, the vanguard of the troop of Corrshliabh, there happened what happened to the Prince of the Fian (i.e. Fionn).[64]

---

[60] *Leabhar Í Eadhra*, 84-5.
[61] Ibid., 112-29.
[62] Ibid., 112.
[63] Ibid., 118-9. For the use of apologues in Bardic Poetry, see Liam P. Ó Caithnia, *Apalóga na bhFilí, 1200-1650*. (Dublin, 1984).
[64] *Leabhar Í Eadhra*, 118-9.

Not stopping there, he compares him to the numerous valiant heroes of the Irish literary tradition and history. Mac an Bhaird repeatedly uses the word *oirbheart* (valour/gallantry) across each of the stanzas to drive home his point.[65] Mogh Nuadhat received half of Ireland by his gallantry, Murchadh son of Brian Bóroimhe achieved fame/glory above all other by his gallantry, Cú Rí won fame and glory by his gallantry, Lugh succeeded in defeating the Lochlannaigh on account of his great valour in battle.[66]

48. Dá nós súd–ní saobh in reacht–
fuair tusa inmhe a hoirbheart,
a bhláth craobh Thighe an Teampla,
a bhile saor soidheargtha.

Following their example–a wise principle!–thou didst win wealth[67] by gallantry, O choice here of the branches of Teach an Teampla, O noble blushing hero.

49. Dá bhfaghtha a bhfuarudar sin
ní thiobhartha, a thuir Uisnicch,
geall ar oirbheart d'aon oile,
a ghoirmdhearc shaor hseabhcoidhe.

O lord of Uisneach, blue eyed hawk-like hero, wert thou to get all that was got by the heroes I have mentioned, thou wouldst not be found inferior to any of them in gallantry.

50. Ní dóith d'aonduini hoighriocht;
ní déntar ód dheaghoirbheart
dóith chogoidh do chloinn

O blooming vine, no man dare claim thy inheritance. owing to

---

[65] *oirbheart* "prowess. valour, courage." eDIL s.v. airbert, accessed September 30, 2021, http://dil.ie/1622.

[66] *Leabhar Í Eadhra*, 124-5. Mogh Nuadhat was the (pseudo-historical) king of the southern half of Ireland, which was subsequently known as Leath Mogha or Mogh's half. Murchadh was the son of Brian Bóroimhe, High-King of Ireland who 'defended' Ireland against a 'Viking Invasion' in 1014 and the progenitor of the Uí Briain (O'Briens). Cú Raoi mac Dáire was a king of Munster in the Rúraíocht Cycle. Lugh fought at the famous Battle of Maigh Tuaireadh against the Fomorians and Fir Bolg. It is perhaps noteworthy that these heroes with the exception of Lugh are from the south of Ireland echoing the Uí Eadhra's southern origins.

[67] *Inmhe* could be glossed as "wealth, heritage; state, rank, condition"; eDIL s.v. indme, accessed September 30, 2021, http://dil.ie/28492.

Eadhra,
a chroinn abaidh fhíneamhna.

great gallantry no man dare
contend with Ó hEadhra.

51. Tugsad cách–ní claon in
reacht!–
*geall ar uaisle 's ar **oirbheart***
doit, a chéile cláir Eamhna;
*cóir na **tréidhe tighearna.***

All men have always– 'tis a just
principle!–yielded to thee in
nobility and gallantry, O
spouse of the plain of Eamhain;
by the right has thou those
lordly qualities.

52. Táinig dhíot díon do
*   shleachta;*
*fuair tusa a hucht t'**oirbhearta***
mar nar fhaláir, a bharr Breadh,
anáir Ghall agos Gaoidheal.

Thou hast succeeded in
defending thy race; by thy
gallantry thou hast got honour
from both Goill and Gaoidhil;
it had so to be, O Lord of
Breagha.[68]

Irial Ó hUiginn echoes this in his poem, "Ceanglam re chéile, a
Chormuic," comparing Cormac to Mogh Nuadhat and Lugh.[69] Tadhg
Dall in his poem "Fiodhbhaidh a chéile clú deise" speaks of Cormac's
supremacy on the field of battle.[70]

"As lía rocheannoigh dh'fíon, d'eachaibh ogas d'ealadhain"

Cormac's generosity to poets and in general is emphasised
repeatedly throughout the poems by multiple authors. Many of these
poems take the form of an address from the poet discussing the
relationship they have with Cormac.

7. Ó hEadhra Buidhe, bas dil,
fáth mo ghráidh dá ghruiadh
*   chrithrigh–*
bíd do hsíor ag cleith Chabha
fíon is eich is ealalgha.

The reason I love the
sparkling face of Ó hEadhra
Buidhe, Staff of Cobha,
whose hand I love to grasp, is
that he always possesses **wine
steeds and poetry**.

*8. **Ar sdéduibh uaisle**, ar eallach,*
gnáth leis dán do
***   dheighcheannach,***

Often does this Griffin from
Caiseal's pleasant home
purchase poetry cheap with

---

[68] *Leabhar Í Eadhra,* 124-7. Emphasis mine.
[69] Ibid., 159.
[70] Ibid., 83.

's fíon do dhaoicheannach mar dhigh,
gríobh ó chaoimhtheallacha Caisil

his noble steeds and his expensive purchases of banquet-wine.[71]

In fact, Irial Ó hUiginn composed an entire poem to Cormac asking for a horse.[72] Cormac is the only one in whom Irial has hope that he will grant him his request. Irial offers to compose Cormac a poem in return for a horse–a brilliant bargain according to Irial as a horse's life will be shorter than that of a poem in Cormac's honour.

11. Girre ná sin saoghul h'eich
buaini an laoidh 's ní mar leithbhreith;
cóir iarruidh séad ar a son
dá chéad bliaghoin
do-bhéradh.

Shorter shall thy horse's life be than that of any poem to thee which will live longer, and this is no biased judgement; 'tis right to ask for wealth in return for a gift that will bring thee two hundred years of life.

12. Ní móide go mairfeach heach
a gcionn bliadhna, a bhláth Muimhneach
ós dó a-tám, a ghruadh ghairthi
dán na suadh ní sochaimhthe.

O Flower of the men of Mumha, O blushing cheek, thy horse can hardly live a year while a poet's work is, I assure thee, imperishable.[73]

Tadhg Dall continues the theme of the perpetuity of poetry and its value to Cormac. Cormac is praised for his understanding of the value of poetry. He is a "good merchant" who has exchanged worldly wealth for "the sincerest of fragrant, lasting panegyric."[74] The symbolism of a good merchant is used to represent Cormac's generosity to the arts in the poem "Is maith an ceanduighe Cormac."

---

[71] *Leabhar Í Eadhra*, 152-3. Poem XI; "Grádh mo chroidheisi Cormuc," by Fearghal Óg Mac an Bhaird

[72] Ibid., 178-83. See also the discussion in Pádraig Ó Macháin, "Maoilín Óg Mac Bruaideadha and the Decline of Patronage," *Celtica* 32 (2020): 217-35, at 230, 230, n. 13a.

[73] *Leabhar Í Eadhra*, 180-1.

[74] Ibid., 60-61.

4. Féach an fearr iomlaoid
oile
ná in mhoirn tsuthoin
tsíorruidhe
téid don fhlaith ionfhuair
fhaoilidh
ar mhaith diombuain
díomhaoinigh.

Behold is there any better exchange than the lasting, enduring honour that goes to the pleasant kindly chieftain in return for vain transitory wealth?

5. Gearr do mhairfeadh na
maoine
bronntar le flaith Formaoile
's pudh buain na molta ar
marthoin
dá ghruaidh chorcra
chomharthoigh.

Not for long would the riches given by Fermoyle's lord remain, but the praises of his noble ruddy countenance shall endure eternally.

6. Ní mhairfeadh bleidhe ná
brat
dá bhfaghoid cách ó Chormac
ná arm áigh craoibhlíne cuir
aoinmhíle a-bháin do
bhliadhnaibh.

None of the goblets or cloaks which all receive from Cormac, not the .... (?) engrave battle-weapon for even a single thousand years.

7. Ní mhairfeadh éideadh ná
each
ná feilm loinnearrdha líneach
ná beirt mhaothghorm tsróill
ngloin
ná saorchorn óir ildealbhoigh.

Neither armour nor horse nor shining, carven, helmet, not tunic of soft, blue, sheeny satin nor valued drinking-cup of variously wrought gold would endure.[75]

These instances all re-enforce the image of Cormac as a generous and distinguished patron of the arts.

"As mho báigh agus connailbhe ré tróghoibh agus bochtoibh ar son De agas lía ro fhurtoigh d'aighilgneachaibh an Choimhdheagh"

Cormac's Christianity and loyalty to God is directly addressed in a poem by Maol Muire Ó'n Cháinte, "Dia do chongnamh le

---

[75] *Leabhar Í Eadhra*, 58-61.

Cormac."[76] Maol Muire extolls Cormac's virtues as a man who is favoured by God. Cormac has power over his land as he has "put his trust in God the Father" and "owing to God's grace keeping him from sin."[77] Maol Muire even extolls Cormac's protection of the weak even though he says it is an unusual princely trait.

11. Tuilltear leis a láibh feadhma– *gen gur thréidhe tighearna–* *clú teagmhála fa chlár Cuinn* *lámh eadrána gach anbhfaintt.*	This man so famous on battle-day for fighting on behalf of Conn's Plain deserves to be called "arm of protection for the weak"–though this is not a (common) princely trait.[78]

Final Poem: "Díoghrais chomainn ar Chormac"

The final poem in the duanaire to Cormac Ó hEadhra is a poem by the scribe of the manuscript himself, Tuathal Ó hUiginn. That this is the final poem of the duanaire is indicated not only by its current place in the manuscript but also by the scribal note on the preceding page, placing Tuathal Ó hUiginn in the location where the duanaire was finished.

At first glance, "Díoghruis chomainn ar Chormac" reads like a sycophantic address by Tuathal Ó hUiginn to his patron. However, it serves as a fitting conclusion to the duanaire and serves to recapitulate the reasons he and others love Cormac. Tuathal begins by outlining the reasons for his love for Cormac: his bright cheek, his wavy hair, his care for him and generosity. But! Had Cormac not these features Tuathal would still love him as he is the choice of every man of Luighne.[79] Everybody loves him for multiple reasons:

8. Do thabhoigh Cormac mhac Céin *ar foghloidhibh fuinn tsaoir Néill* *barr ionmhoine nach iarr sin* *a ngrian iorghoile is éigin.*	On the field of fight and stress Cormac son of Cian always gets from the warriors of the land of noble Niall an extreme of Love–more than he expects
9. Más ar tharbha téid an grádh *ar mhuirn nó ar chion nó ar*	Whether love be the fruits of interest or affection or respect

---

[76] Ibid., 226-31.
[77] Ibid., 227.
[78] Ibid., 229.
[79] Ibid., 244-5.

chomhrádh,
filidh cláir naomhthabhuig Néill,
is cóir aoncharuid eiséin [;]

or talk, "tis right that the **poets**
of the holy generous land of
Niall should have it for him
above all[;]

10. *nó ar teasdaibh nó ar*
  tréidhibh ríogh
nó ar díochor uilc nó ainbhfíor
nó ar cléir nduasoirrdhreic do
  dhíol–
as céim uasoilmheic airdríogh–

So too if it be given for good
name or **kingly qualities**, or for
**the banishment of evil or
unfairness** or **for supporting
prize-famous poets**–as is **the
way of a noble high-king's
son.**

11. *nó ar **bhriathraibh tearca***
  ***tromdha**,*
*nó ar **mhaith** nó ar **mhéd***
  ***mbaromhla**,*
nó ar buaidh ndealbha mar
  dhleaghar,
fuair Ó hEadhra a uaisleaghadh,

or (if 'tis) for **rare and weighty
speech** or for **goodness or for
power of prophecy**, or for
exceeding beauty that Ó
hEadhra has been duly
ennobled,

12. *nó **ar clú** nó **ar uaisle** a*
  fhola
a-táid cách dhá chomhthogha,
*nó **ar chor gcliachdha** um*
  chrích a shean
nar iartha a díth do dhéineamh,

or (if 'tis) **for fame or for
nobility of blood** that all men
choose him, or **for fighting of
battles** for ancestors' land
whose loss no man desires,

13. *ionann charoid a chruth nár*
an chaor charud nó an compán,
nó mná seangleabhra gruadh
  nglan,
nó sluadh feidhmfhearrdha
  foghludh.

the close friend, the
companion, the tall graceful
fair-cheeked ladies,
the troop of manly fighting
soldiers–all alike love his
modest form.[80]

---

[80] Ibid., 246-7. Emphasis mine. Quatrain 15 of the poem might add to
Tuathal's comprehension; *Luach ar n-annsa dh'Ó Eadhra / fríth uaidh
dh'aoibhneas oireaghdha; / díol luaidh an bronnadh do-bheir / nach fuair
ollamh a aithghein* which McKeanna has translated as "The full value of
my love in the form of great pleasure (i.e. reading poems) Ó h'Eadhra has
got: worthy of praise is the generosity he shows whose like no other ollamh

These remarkable quatrains close the arc that was begun in the preface and serve as a reminder to the reader (or listener) as to what they have read (or heard). This provides a firm and distinct end to the duanaire of Cormac Ó hEadhra.

As has been outlined, the agentive act of a scribe can be recovered through a combination of material and manuscript analysis and close textual reading of the poems and the texts surrounding them. Tuathal Ó hUiginn, and arguably Cormac Ó hEadhra, sought to create a document that served to exemplify Cormac Ó hEadhra and legitimise his rule. Key motifs of legitimacy are replicated throughout the duanaire and are reenforced by multiple poets. It did not serve to have a single poem on a topic, but a multitude of voices together could strengthen Cormac's nobility and legitimacy. This duanaire is an example of the soft power of culture and literature and specifically bardic poetry being developed and utilised for further political legitimacy.

Conclusion

To conclude this exploration of a duanaire in late medieval and early modern Ireland, one must take stock of the answers this approach has provided. By reading the manuscript itself, it is clear that duanaireadha were compiled in a conscious manner and not in a piecemeal fashion without regard for structure, order, or content. This shines light on the agency of Irish scribes and patrons, and gives a crucial glimpse at their intelligence and capacity to engage and interact with the written word, and furthermore, pushes back against conceptions of the orality of Gaelic Ireland. There is huge scope for further research, but it is evident that the nobility as well as the literati were incredibly comfortable with the written word, utilising it with distinct social and political motives.

---

has ever experienced" (p. 249). However, P. A. Breatnach has stated that the "editor's interpretation of the first couplet is unsound" and offers a different translation "The price of my love for Ó hEaghra has been obtained from him in wonderful enjoyment; worthy of mention is the bounty he bestows, the like of which an ollamh has not received." See Pádraig A. Breatnach, "The Chief's Poet," *Proceedings of the Royal Irish Academy*. Section C: Archaeology, Celtic Studies, History, Linguistics, Literature 83C (1983), 37-79 at n. 178.

DEEDS OF THE HOUSE

The duanaireadha were not merely status symbols of the nobility. A status symbol can be purchased and display the wealth of the patron. The duanaireadha and the poems within them represent far more than the wealth of the patron. These manuscripts provide a history and genealogy, a rooting of person, family, and place, situated within the Irish historical tradition while demonstrating that their patron had fulfilled the requirements to rule in Gaelic Ireland. This is all *verified* by the truth-makers of Ireland, the *filidh*. The duanaireadha provided a tangible object of legitimacy that could be displayed at the courts of the nobility. The duanaireadha were read and expected to be read. They were in every sense the deeds of the house.

Moving further from duanaireadha as objects of legitimacy, how does one begin to *read* the individual statements of each duanaire. A comparative study of all surviving duanaireadha would provide the appropriate framework to begin to answer such questions. However, one is tempted to speculate that this duanaire can provide some tentative indications. The central thrust of the Leabhar Í Eadhra is on Cormac Ó hEadhra himself. His pride and confidence shine through the duanaire. He is intimately aware of his ancestry and history, yet not beholden to it, completely in control. Ultimately, further studies are necessary, but the potential for studies of types of duanaireadha to allow access to the mentalities and perceptions of the nobility in Gaelic Ireland is tantalising.

It is hoped that this research has contributed to the collective understanding of manuscript culture in Gaelic Ireland and to the recognition of the use and *reuse* of bardic poetry that fill their pages in a conscious and deliberate manner to legitimate the rule of the nobility of Gaelic Ireland. It is also hoped that this will enable a wider recognition of the agency and intelligence of Irish patrons, poets, and scribes in the construction of the wider Irish historical tradition.

Acknowledgements

I would like to thank Brendan Kane, Natasha Sumner, Sherri Olson, Kenneth Gouwens, Eoin Mac Cárthaigh, Chantal Kobel, the editors of the *Proceedings of the Harvard Celtic Colloquium*, and the anonymous reader for their helpful suggestions and improvements. All errors are my own.

Appendix A: Textual arrangement of poems in the manuscript

Following the evidence left by the scribe(s) of this manuscript, different sections of the manuscript become apparent. A revised order is below. Breaks in the table indicate where the order is uncertain.

Section A

McKenna	MS p.	Title/First Line	Patron	Poet	Scribe
	v	Genealogy			Tuathal Ó hUiginn
II	3,4,5,6	An áil libh seanchas Síol gCéin	Cormac Ó hEadhra	Tadhg Dall Ó hUiginn	Tuathal Ó hUiginn
III	6,7	Ag so an chomairce a Chormaic	Cormac Ó hEadhra	Tadhg Dall Ó hUiginn	Tuathal Ó hUiginn
IV	8,9, 10	Maith an ceannaighe Cormac	Cormac Ó hEadhra	Tadhg Dall Ó hUiginn	Tuathal Ó hUiginn
V	10, 11, 12	Fiodhbhaigh a chéile clú deise	Cormac Ó hEadhra and Brian (mac Céin) Ó hEadhra	Tadhg Dall Ó hUiginn	Tuathal Ó hUiginn
VI	12, 13, 14	Cionus frith fearann Luighne	Cormac Ó hEadhra	Tadhg mac Giolla Bhrighde meic Bruaigheadha	Tuathal Ó hUiginn
VII	14, 15, 16	Anam gá chéile a Chormaic	Cormac Ó hEadhra	Tadhg mac Giolla Bhrighde meic Bruaigheadha	Tuathal Ó hUiginn
VIII	16, 17, 18	Táinig san chluiche ag Cormac	Cormac Ó hEadhra	Fearghal Óg Mac an Bhaird	Tuathal Ó hUiginn
IX	18, 19, 20	Sona sin, a chlanda Cuinn	Cormac Ó hEadhra	Fearghal Óg Mac an Bhaird	Tuathal Ó hUiginn

X	21	As fiacha ar neach an ní gheallas	Cormac Ó hEadhra	Fearghal Óg Mac an Bhaird	Tuathal Ó hUiginn
XI	21, 22	Grádh mo chroidheisi Cormac	Cormac Ó hEadhra	Fearghal Óg Mac an Bhaird	Tuathal Ó hUiginn
XII	22, 23	Ceanglam re chéile, a Chormuic	Cormac Ó hEadhra	Irial mac Aonghusa Í hUiginn	Tuathal Ó hUiginn
XIII	23, 24	Creach ag Luighne ó Leath Mhodha	Cormac Ó hEadhra	Irial mac Aonghusa Í hUiginn	Tuathal Ó hUiginn
XIV	24, 25	Ag so chugad, a Chormuic	Cormac Ó hEadhra	Irial mac Aonghusa Í hUiginn	Tuathal Ó hUiginn
XV	25, 26	Cionnaim anois cia ar gcara	Cormac Ó hEadhra	Irial mac Aonghusa Í hUiginn	Tuathal Ó hUiginn
XVI	26, 27, 28	Frémh na fíoruaisle fuil Chéin	Cormac Ó hEadhra	Domhnall Óg mac Aodha meíc Dhomhnoill Chaim Í Uiginn	Tuathal Ó hUiginn
XVIII	30, 31	Beiríodh easaonta d'fhuil Chéin	Cormac Ó hEadhra	Maghnus Óg mac Aodha meíc Dhomhnoill Chaim Í Uiginn	Tuathal Ó hUiginn
XIX	31, 32	Na bíodh athtuirse ar fhiul Chéin	Cormac Ó hEadhra	Maghnus Óg mac Aodha meíc Dhomhnoill Chaim Í Uiginn	Tuathal Ó hUiginn
XX	32, 33	Dia do chongnamh le Cormac	Cormac Ó hEadhra	Maol Muire Ó'n Cháinte	Tuathal Ó hUiginn
XXI	33, 34	Mithidh déanamh cuairte ag Cormac	Cormac Ó hEadhra	Maol Muire Ó'n Cháinte	Tuathal Ó hUiginn
XXII	34	Gabh mo chosaoid a Chormaic	Cormac Ó hEadhra	Unknown	Tuathal Ó hUiginn

EMMET DE BARRA

XXIII	35	Díoghruis chomainn ar Chormac	Cormac Ó hEadhra	Tuathal Ó hUiginn	Tuathal Ó hUiginn

Other Poems to Cormac

XVII	28, 29	Fada re huaisle Clann Chéin	Cormac Ó hEadhra	Diarmuid Dall Mac an Fhir Léighinn	Unknown
XXIV	36, 37	Fáth cumadh ar crích Luighne	Cormac Ó hEadhra	Fearghal Óg Mac an Bhaird	Unknown

Section B

IA	1, 2	An Cian céadna a gConnachtaibh	Cian (mac Oiill) Ó hEadhra	Tadhg Óg mac Maoil Mhuire Í Uiginn	Tuathal Ó hUiginn (?)
XXVIII	61, 62	Truagh mo dháil re deich laithibh[1]	Brian (mac Céin) Ó hEadhra and Domhnall (mac Tadhg Buidhe) Ó hEadhra	Tadhg Dall Ó hUiginn	Tuathal Ó hUiginn (?)
XXIX	62, 63, 64	Anois Bréagnoighther Bricne	Seaán Buidhe (mac Eoghain) Ó hEadhra	Tadhg Dall Ó hUiginn	Tuathal Ó hUiginn (?)
XXX	64, 65	Bráidhe ón Éigse a nEas Dara	Ruaidhrí (mac Seaáin Bhuidhe meic Thaidhg) Ó hEadhra	Diarmuid mac an Bhacaigh Í Chlumhain	Tuathal Ó hUiginn (?)

---

[1] This is not the correct first line for this poem. See *Leabhar Í Eadhra*, 401.

XXXII	66, 67	Comhla ratha rún Fearghoil	Fearghal Mór Ó hEadhra	Unknown	Tuathal Ó hUiginn (?)
XXXIII	68, 69	Tuile rabharta rath deise	Domhnall (mac Oilill mheic Mhaghnuis) Ó hEadhra and Onóra (inghean Oilill mheic Mhaghnuis) Ní Eadhra	Unknown	Tuathal Ó hUiginn (?)
XXXIV	69, 70, 71	Ní baodhal feasda fian Luighne	Tadhg (mac Cormaic) Ó hEadhra	Domhnall Óg mac Aodha meic Dhomhnoill Chaim Í Uiginn	Tuathal Ó hUiginn (?)
XXXV	71, 72	A Thaidhg cuimhnigh an comann	Tadhg (mac Cormaic) Ó hEadhra	Domhnall Óg mac Aodha meic Dhomhnoill Chaim Í Uiginn	Tuathal Ó hUiginn (?)
XXXVI	72	Sgitheach sinn a chlanna Cuinn	Unknown	Unknown	Tuathal Ó hUiginn (?)

Section C

XXV	38, 39, 40	Malairt Chrotha ar chrích Luighne	Oilill (mac Cormac Óig mheic Cormaic) Ó hEadhra	Maol Muire Ó hUiginn	Unknown
XXVI	40, 41	Clú gach féadhma ar fhuil Chéin	Ruaidhrí (mac Cormaic Óig mheic Cormaic Óig mheic Cormac) Ó hEadhra	Pádraig Óg Mac an Bhaird	Unknown

| XXXI | 65 | Damh féin do choigleas Oilill | Oilill (mac Cormac Óig mheic Cormaic) Ó hEadhra | Tomás Ó hUiginn | Unknown |
| XXXVII | 72, 73, 74 (?) | Cóir aitreabhadh ar ... | Oilill (mac Cormac Óig mheic Cormaic) Ó hEadhra | Maol Muire (mac Taidhg) Ó hUiginn[2] | Unknown |

Unlinked Poem

| I | i, ii | Féch, a Chríosd, ar crích Luighni | Tadhg (mac Céin) Ó hEadhra | Unknown | Unknown |

[2] McKenna identifies this poet as (Uílliam) Mhac Ruaidhrí Í Uiginn. However, having examined the manuscript digitally on Irish Script on Screen, it is clear that the attribution reads "Maolmuire *mac* Taid*h*g Í Uigin*n cecinit,*" NLI MS G 1303, p. 72.

Appendix B: Genealogy of Cormac Ó hEadhra[81]

D'O Eadhra Buidhe .i.
Cormac mac Cein
m. Oilill
m. Mhadhnuis
m. Ruaidhri
m Sheain Bhuidhe
m. Thaidhg
m. Fhearghoil Mhóir
m. Dhomhnoill
Chleirigh
m. Airt na gCapoll
m. Dhiarmuda
Riabhaigh
m. Aodha
m. Chonchobhair
m. Aodha
m. Thaithligh
Urmumhan
m. Mhuircheartoigh
m. Mhadhnusa
m. Eadhra *a quo* O
hEadhra
m. Shaorghusa
m. Bheic
m. Fhlaitheasa
m. Bhrenoinn
m. Nadfhraoich
m. Fhidheinn
m. Fhiodhchoire
m. Sheisgnein
m. Sheisgeadhseangfhada
eadhon Luighdeach
m. Mhodha Corb
m. Nia Corb[82]
m. Airt Corb
m. Laoich *a quo* Luighni
m. Chormaic Gaileang
m. Thaidhg
m. Cein
m. Oilill Oluim

m. Eoghain Mhoir
eadhon Modh
Nuadhatt
m. Mhodha Neid
m. Dheirg
m. Dheirg
theineadh
m. Enna Moncaoin
m. Loích Mhóir
m. Mho Fheibheis
m. Mhuireadhaigh
Mhuchna
m. Eachaidh
Ghairbh
m. Dhuach Dhuinn
m. Chairbre
Basgleathoin
m. Luighdeach
Luaighnigh
m. Ionnaoimhair
m. Sheadhamhain
m. Niashedh-
damhuin
m. Adhamhair
Fholtchaoin
m. Fhir Chorb
m. Mhodha Corb
m. Chobhthaigh
Chaoimh
m. Reachtoigh
Righdheirg
m. Luighdeach
Láighe
m. Eachoidh Aibhne
m. Oiliolla Find
m. Airt
m. Luighdeach
Laimhdheirg
m. Eachaidh
Uaircheas

m. Luighdeach
Iarrdhuinn
m. Shedhna Dheirg
m. Dhuach Find
m. Shéadhna
Fhinnairmh
m. Bhreis Riogh
m. Airt Imligh
m. Fhéilimb
m. Rothachtaigh
m. Ronáin Roailbhigh
m. Fhailbhi
Iolchorthaigh
m. Cais
Cheadchuimhnigh
m. Ailldeargóid
m. Mhúineamhóin
m. Cais Chlothaigh
m. Fhir Aird
m. Rochochtoigh
m. Rosa
m. Glaisfhearrdha
m. Nuadhatt
Deaghlaimh
m. Eochaidh
Faobharghlais
m. Conmhaoil
m. Eimhir Fhinn
m. Mhilidh Easbainne

EMMET DE BARRA

Notes to Appendix B.

[81] National Library of Ireland MS G 1303, page v. I have returned the genealogy to a format closer to that present in the MS. The transcription is that of McKenna except m. here = meic. For a translation see *Leabhar Í Eadhra*, 8-11.

[82]McKenna has "meic Mhocorb," however it reads "meic Nia Corb" as per the manuscript; c.f. Dubhaltach Mac Fhirbhisigh, *Leabhar Mór na nGenealach: The Great Book of Irish Genealogies, Compiled (1645-66) by Dubhaltach Mac Fhirbhisigh.* Edited with Translation and Indexes by Nollaig Ó Muraíle, 5 vols (Dublin, 2003). Vol. 3, 654, §665.5.

Champions of the Irish Language in America: Daniel Magner, Thomas D. Norris, and their Contributions to "Our Gaelic Department" in the *Irish-American*, 1878-1900

Matthew Knight

On 25 July 1857, the New York *Irish-American* newspaper introduced "Our Gaelic Department," the world's first weekly column printed in the Irish language.[1] For nearly forty cumulative years, "Our Gaelic Department" provided a public forum for readers in America and Ireland to discuss issues of the Irish language, nationalism, and politics; further, the Irish lessons, poetry, folklore, and commentary included in these columns helped to strengthen the bond between home and immigrant communities by facilitating the development of

---

[1] The argument could be made for this being the world's first regular Irish-language department. Patrick Lynch's *Bolg an t-Solair* (1795) lasted for one issue, and Philip Barron's *Ancient Ireland: A Weekly Magazine* (1835) was in fact a monthly and ceased after five issues. Similarly, the weekly *Dublin Penny Journal* had scattered pieces in Irish between 1832-1833, but no dedicated Irish department. In the United States, the New York *Shamrock* ran occasional pieces in the Irish language (1810-1824), as did the Philadelphia *Globe and Herald* (1824), Boston *Emerald* (1836), and New York *Irish Shield and Monthly Milesian* (1829), but none of these offered weekly columns in Irish. See Regina Uí Chollatáin, "Newspapers, Journals, and the Irish Revival," in *Irish Journalism Before Independence,* ed. Kevin Rafter (Manchester: Manchester University Press, 2016), 160-173, at 162; Regina Uí Chollatáin, "'Thall is Abhus,' 1860-1930: The Revival Process and the Journalistic Web between Ireland and North America," in *Language Identity and Migration*, ed. Vera Regan, Chloe Diskin and Jennifer Martyn (Oxford: Peter Lang, 2015) 353-78, at 364-65; and Kenneth E. Nilsen, "The Irish Language in New York, 1850-1900," in *The New York Irish*, ed. Ronald H. Bayor, and Timothy Meagher (Baltimore & London: The Johns Hopkins University Press, 1996), 252-74, at 259-73 for discussion of rare appearances of the Irish language in America before 1857. "Our Gaelic Department" was published, with significant gaps, up to 1896, after which time original Irish material only appeared sporadically until the newspaper shuttered in 1915.

a transatlantic Irish identity.[2] The success of "Our Gaelic Department" encouraged the creation of similar Irish-language columns and bilingual journals in the United States and Ireland; inspired students to become teachers, poets, and advanced scholars; and offered a shared space for readers to contribute material in the Irish language.[3] Despite all this, "Our Gaelic Department" is frequently overlooked in the scholarly record, as are the many Irish-language societies formed in the United States that relied on its columns for educational material.[4] The labor of individuals and societies to cultivate the Irish language not only preceded the formation of the Gaelic League (1893) by decades but also greatly influenced its philosophy and platform: even co-founder Eugene O'Growney freely admitted that "The League has simply adopted the methods of the American societies."[5] Although seldom noted in the literature, in many ways the Irish in America were

---

[2] Uí Chollatáin, "Thall is Abhus," 354-55; Fiona Lyons, "Chaos or Comrades? Transatlantic Political and Cultural Aspirations for Ireland in nineteenth century Irish American print media," *Proceedings of the Harvard Celtic Colloquium* 39 (2019): 191-212, at 208. From the outset, the Gaelic department provided the equivalent of a six-page booklet each month, which was an impressive amount of Irish material available for readers given the relative dearth of printed works in Irish at the time, especially in the United States. There are reports that students in the Philo-Celtic Societies would finish class, fold up their *Irish-Americans* and put them in their pocket for closer study at home. See *Irish-American* (hereafter *IA*), 22 June 1878.

[3] See Matthew Knight, "Our Gaelic Department: The Irish-Language Column in the New York *Irish-American,* 1857-1896" (PhD diss., Harvard University, 2021.

[4] Kenneth E. Nilsen, "Irish Gaelic Literature in the United States," in *American Babel: Literatures of the United States from Abnaki to Zuni,* ed. Marc Shell (Cambridge, MA: Harvard University Press, 2002), 177-218, at 202. Just in terms of poetic compositions, in its 40 years of publication, 'Our Gaelic Department' printed nearly 1500 verses, of which seventy percent are unindexed elsewhere. However, greater attention has been paid to the first bilingual Irish journal, Brooklyn's *An Gaodhal*, which, while extremely important to the story of the Irish language in America, did not appear in print until 1881, nearly twenty-five years after the first Irish column in the *Irish-American.* For a full study see Knight, "Our Gaelic Department."

[5] *IA,* 14 March 1898, 8.

leaders in what became known as the Gaelic Revival in Ireland; and, while the present paper cannot correct all of these notable historiographical omissions, it will highlight two previously undervalued men who dedicated their lives to the cultivation of Irish: Captain Thomas D. Norris and Daniel Magner.

Thomas David Norris was born near Killarney, Co. Kerry in 1827, and emigrated to New York in 1851. Shortly after his arrival Norris enlisted in the Ninth New York Regiment of "Irish Volunteers," the first Irish-American military company recognized by the State of New York.[6] Although this regiment was organized to agitate for a future revolution in Ireland, Norris and other Irish immigrants, like the original editors of "Our Gaelic Department" John O'Mahony and Michael Doheny, had more than just physical force nationalism on their minds.[7] In 1859 the New York Branch of the Dublin Ossianic Society was founded, whose main objects were to fund the Dublin parent society and to promote the study of Irish-language literature.[8] The New York branch had a membership of more than sixty individuals, and, although it was primarily a literary organization, at least ten of these were sworn members of the Fenian Brotherhood.[9] This society, composed mainly of native speakers of

---

[6] *IA,* 20 January 1900, 1. This unit later became a part of the legendary "Fighting 69th" Regiment, of which Captain Norris was an original member.

[7] Kerby A. Miller, *Emigrants and Exiles: Ireland and the Irish Exodus to North America* (Oxford: Oxford University Press, 1985), 335.

[8] *IA,* 8 September 1860, 1; *Pilot* (Boston), 8 September 1860, 2. The Dublin Ossianic Society had been founded on 17 March 1853 for the "publication of Irish manuscripts relating to the Fenian period of our history, and other historical documents, with the literal translation and notes" and had issued four volumes by this time. See *Transactions of the Ossianic Society, for the year 1856,* vol. IV (Dublin: Printed Under Direction of the Council, 1859), viii. The columns of "Our Gaelic Department," edited by O'Mahony and Doheny, were also useful materials for the New York society and read overseas by members of the Dublin group. See *IA,* 17 July 1858, 4.

[9] See *IA,* 23 November 1878, 4, which lists Michael Corcoran, Michael Doheny, Thomas Francis Meagher, Denis Galvin, Patrick O'Dea, John O'Mahony, Patrick O'Leary, Michael Cavanagh, Michael Hannon, Edward J. O'Daly, Thomas D. Norris, and James Roche among others. Members ranged from New York to the Nebraska Territory, Texas, Pennsylvania,

Irish, started what was likely the first organized Irish-language class in New York City, with John O'Mahony offering commentary and anecdotes from his collection of unpublished Irish manuscripts at bi-weekly meetings.[10] Any progress made towards the cultivation of the Irish language and its literature was soon halted, however, as the onset of the Civil War caused the New York Ossianic Society to disband, and Captain Norris marched with the Sixty-ninth Regiment to the defense of Washington and the Union.[11]

During the War, Norris was promoted to the rank of captain for gallantry in the field and was twice severely wounded in action.[12] After recovering from his injuries and taking up work as a storekeeper, he returned to his Irish-language pursuits, assisting in the formation of the New York Philo-Celtic Society (NYPCS) in Manhattan's Bowery neighborhood in 1878.[13] Norris was elected Corresponding Secretary

---

New Orleans, Massachusetts, and California. It was also said that "Irish born men, whether republicans or monarchists, Catholics, Protestants, or Heathens, if any of the latter yet survive, can meet here upon neutral ground." See *Pilot* (Boston), 23 June 1860, 2; *Phœnix* (New York), 18 August 1860.

[10] *Pilot* (Boston), 23 June 1860, 2. See also Séamus Ó Casaide, "Seán Ó Mathghamhna's Irish MSS," *The Irish Book Lover*, 18 (1930), 82. The first evidence I have found of an organized club in America for the study of Irish was formed by Cornelius O'Mahoney in Milwaukee, WI, in 1857. See *IA*, 7 November 1857, 2. Interestingly, John O'Mahony remarked that the scarcity of elementary books was the principal reason why he had not himself started an Irish class years before, and other members of the New York Ossianic Society offered to teach a class if the pupils could provide their own books. See *Pilot* (Boston), 23 June 1860, 2. This dearth of Irish-language material soon made "Our Gaelic Department" a crucial educational resource for language scholars and students.

[11] *IA*, 20 January 1900, 1.

[12] *IA*, 14 May 1894, 4; *Irish World*, 27 January 1900, 11.

[13] The first Philo-Celtic Society was founded in Boston in April 1873, and Brooklyn followed suit in February 1876. See *Irish World*, 10 May 1873, 6; *Boston Globe*, 25 March 1901, 2; *IA*, 3 May 1873, 2; *IA*, 12 February 1876, 5. See also Matthew Knight "Forming an Army of Vindication: The *Irish Echo* and the Irish Language Revival in America," in *North American Gaels: Speech, Story, and Song in the Diaspora*, ed. Aidan Doyle and Natasha Sumner (Montreal: McGill-Queen's University Press, 2020), 217-69.

of the NYPCS, contributing colorful weekly reports to "Our Gaelic Department" that served as effective propaganda to increase membership in the Philo-Celtic Societies, while encouraging other readers to found local Irish classes of their own. In fact, 1878 was a busy year for the study and cultivation of the Irish language in America, with membership reports from nascent Irish schools showing impressive numbers.[14] For example, the first meeting of the Eleventh Avenue school in Manhattan filled a 350-capacity hall, with hundreds being turned away while many remained in the avenue, despite the rain, awaiting an opportunity to gain admission.[15]

At the same time that Captain Norris joined the New York Philo-Celtic Society at the Bowery in 1878, Daniel Magner joined the Ft. Washington branch at 185th Street in Manhattan. A native speaker of Irish from Fermoy, County Cork, Magner became interested in the grammar of the language at a young age when he discovered an old manuscript in a neighbor's home. Although his family had hopes that he would become a priest, he instead resisted and sought his fortune overseas.[16] Magner emigrated to New York and was naturalized in 1874; however, while Captain Norris was a war hero and successful businessman, Magner found himself among the lower classes in

---

[14] Bowery, NY: 400 members; Ft. Washington, NY: 75; Elmira, NY: 75; Hoboken, NJ: 125; Oil City, PA: 50; Jersey City, NJ: 75; Hoboken, NJ: 125; Brooklyn, NY: 300. See *IA,* 9 November 1878, 6; 3 May 1879, 8. These totals do not include the New York Society for the Preservation of the Irish Language, the 'Uptown' Irish class, or the Boston, Alabama, and Louisville societies. Membership numbers are difficult to corroborate, and many attendees at events and meetings were not members, and some members did not regularly attend. See Úna Ní Bhroiméil, *Building Irish Identity in America, 1870-1915: The Gaelic Revival* (Dublin: Four Courts Press, 2003), 37.

[15] An elderly gentleman in attendance noted: "I can speak in Irish, sing in Irish and pray in Irish: that will do me for the short time I have to live. But, he added, reverentially, I thank God for having let me live to see this night, to see the young women and young men here to learn their own old language. It is to encourage the young people that I join." *IA,* 7 December 1878, 8.

[16] *United Irishman,* 7 May 1898, 3.

America, taking up work as a street sweeper.[17] A reporter who learned of his reputation as an Irish scholar described in a published exposé how, with hands raw and blistered from his job cleaning streets, Magner "spent many lonely hours poring over discolored and moth-eaten manuscripts" given to him by other Irish immigrants in a "home haunted by the ever-present spectre of poverty."[18] Prominent Fenian and Nationalist Jeremiah O'Donovan Rossa attested to Magner's excellent command of Irish, noting that he "would occasionally come into my office, sit down and talk Irish–talk it as *slachtmhar* [in as polished a style] as only a few other men in New York could talk."[19]

Like Norris, Magner took to the popular press for the cause of Irish, and admonished those Irish immigrants who remained aloof from efforts to cultivate their language: "Look at the Germans, French, or Italians: no matter where they are found, they will be seen united as one person speaking their language . . . But, how do we find Irishmen? Either totally ignorant of their language, or else arguing about whose Irish is the genuine. Then you will find them, when moving among people of wealth and affluence, denying any knowledge at all of it."[20] Messages like these often concluded with an invitation to attend the free Irish classes offered in Manhattan and Brooklyn. The efforts of Magner, Norris, and others to promote the study and propagation of Irish paid dividends, and, by the mid-1880s, there were more than fifty Irish-language societies across America. Whether styling themselves Philo-Celtic Societies, Gaelic Societies, or Societies to Preserve the

---

[17] Magner's surname is often spelled "Magnier," and he is variously known as "Domhnall Magnaer." For his naturalization record, see Familysearch, "Daniel Magnier", accessed March 1, 2022, https://www.familysearch.org/ark:/61903/1:1:QPTM-6RZX. Users must create a free account to access this record.

[18] *Fall River Daily Globe,* 9 July 1885, 4. According to the article, Magner was entirely self-taught in Irish grammar. He was not yet forty-five years old at this time. Even Gaelic League co-founder Thomas O'Neill Russell, who seldom had a kind word for anyone in the press, noted in this same article that Magner could be the equal of Eugene O'Curry if only allowed more time for study.

[19] *United Irishman,* 7 May 1898, 3. O'Donovan Rossa also recommended that Magner be made Irish-language professor when the Chair of Gaelic was established at the Catholic University of America in 1896.

[20] *IA,* 4 October 1879, 8.

Irish Language, organizations sprang up in Boston, Lawrence, and Malden, MA; Louisville, KY; San Francisco, CA; Galveston, TX; Baltimore, MD; Providence, RI; Philadelphia, Scranton, and Oil City PA; Hartford and New Haven CT; Charleston, SC; St. Louis, MO; Mobile, AL; and Chicago, IL.[21] Significantly, even though many of these Irish societies affiliated themselves with the Dublin Society for the Preservation of the Irish Language, the Irish in America were not merely funding a language movement in Ireland; these immigrants looked to develop a revivalist consciousness to reintegrate that part of their past that was either lost to them or never fully explored–it was as much about their future as that of Ireland itself.[22]

As the variations in name suggest, these societies and their individual members failed to work in an organized, concerted fashion, often holding their own philosophies regarding spelling, grammar, pronunciation, and provincialisms.[23] There was no disagreement, however, with the assertion that the Irish in America were part of a storied heritage and culture, possessing a rich literary tradition that needed to be honored and preserved; nor would any deny that the language was the heart of this cultural inheritance and that Irish needed to be cultivated and regularly utilized in order to protect the distinct nationality of Ireland in America.[24] This prompted spokesmen like Norris and Magner to continually complain that the Irish language was not on the platform of Home-Rulers, Land-Leaguers, or physical-force nationalists, and they taunted the men and women who felt shame in speaking Irish around nativists who might think they did not know English, or who came to a few Irish classes and then only

---

[21] *An Gaodhal,* January 1886. See also *Irish World,* 12 April 1884; 17 May 1884. Many thanks to Fiona Lyons (UCD) for sharing her notes on the formation of these societies from the *Irish-American, Irish World, An Gaodhal,* and the *Irish Echo.*

[22] Fionntán de Brún, *Revivalism and Modern Irish Literature: The Anxiety of Transmission and the Dynamics of Renewal* (Cork: Cork University Press, 2019), 87.

[23] Despite the occasional documented quarrel, it seems the Irish schools attempted to handle dialectical differences amicably. There is simply not enough evidence to suggest that the reason for various societies and titles was mainly due to tensions over dialect in instruction, although it is a tempting conclusion.

[24] *IA,* 19 September 1857, 4.

attended special anniversary entertainments thereafter. Especially sharp derision was aimed at those Irish immigrants who achieved a high level of Irish-language ability in the schools but refused to assist the movement by becoming teachers in the very societies that trained them.[25] Whether in agreement or at odds with one another, however, the Irish societies continued to report their individual progress to "Our Gaelic Department," and the Irish material consistently filled between two-thirds and one full page of the *Irish-American* in the early 1880s.[26] In this way, a bilingual public forum was enjoyed by readers from Ireland, Canada, and throughout the United States, some of whom contributed to the newspaper's columns each week.

Norris and Magner were two of the major contributors to the Irish-language columns in "Our Gaelic Department" over the following two decades. They variously submitted transcribed, original, and translated poetry; narrative prose from manuscripts; and social commentary in the correspondence section.[27] Norris went on to

---

[25] For every Irish expatriate committed to the cultivation of Irish, there were many who were content to utilize the English language exclusively in their new lives in America. Some felt shame in being associated with a nation and language that nativists in America equated with poverty; others believed that English provided more opportunity for upward economic and social mobility; even sympathetic immigrants who spoke Irish from their youth expressed insecurity about their ability to become literate in the language, and resented occasions of elitism among the chief proponents of the cultivation of Irish; and some were simply indifferent to learning Irish for various reasons. See Gillian Ní Ghabhann, "The Gaelic Revival in the U.S. in the Nineteenth Century." *Chronicon* 2, 6 (1998), 1-34.

[26] The editors of "Our Gaelic Department" realized that they needed to take on an additional pedagogical role, for many Irish immigrants were illiterate in the Irish language. To respect their diverse readership of students and scholars with varying degrees of Irish-language competence and literacy, "Our Gaelic Department" offered a range of content each week, effectively creating a nexus of discussion regarding the study of Irish in the U.S.

[27] Both men also submitted original 'occasional' verse, like Magner's *Dán do Scolairibh Gaodhailge an Bhomhraoi* ("Poem for the Bowery Gaelic Scholars)" in which he praised the efforts and linguistic abilities of members of the class at 214 Bowery, or Norris's poem chastising absences from that very school ("Acht ná tréig do sgoil air mhuir na air abhain"*). See

contribute more than thirty poems, the majority original and patriotic compositions, as well as several narrative transcriptions from old manuscripts given to him by fellow Irish immigrants.[28] He was also active in promulgating the Irish language nationally; he delivered a congratulatory Irish address presented to Grover Cleveland in the White House the day after Cleveland's inauguration on 5 March 1885 and later offered an Irish poem celebrating the President's marriage in 1886.[29] For his part, between 1880 and 1894, Magner contributed fifteen Irish poems and twenty-three narrative transcriptions from manuscripts. The prose selections were considerable and took up more than 115 columns over as many weeks in "Our Gaelic Department."[30] In addition to these historic texts, Magner would occasionally offer original translations, like his Irish version of the Declaration of Independence, "Foirghiol Neimhspleádhachda na Stád Aontuighthe," to commemorate the Fourth of July in 1884.[31]

Notwithstanding their participation in the same cause to cultivate and preserve the Irish language, Magner and Norris became bitter adversaries in the popular press. Their feud began in February 1882, after Michael J. Logan, editor of *An Gaodhal,* published a new

---

IA, 30 October 1880, 3; 18 July 1885, 3. This type of verse was quite common in "Our Gaelic Department," Magner's *Dán Air Pósadh Dhomhnail Uí Crimhin* / "On the Marriage of Daniel Crimmin", being another example, *IA,* 4 June 1881, 3.

[28] See Appendices for verse and prose submissions which are not indexed elsewhere. Some of Norris' manuscript effort can be seen in the Patrick Ferriter Manuscript Collection at University College Dublin. See Patrick Ferriter Manuscripts, University College Dublin Special Collections, accessed March 1, 2022, https://www.ucd.ie/specialcollections/archives/patrickferriter/.

[29] *IA,* 21 March 1885, 3; 10 July 1886, 3.

[30] Several of the manuscripts Magner utilized can be found in the *Catalogue of Irish Manuscripts in the University of Wisconsin-Madison,* but the provenance and location of others remain unknown, and many texts are unpublished elsewhere. See Cornelius G. Buttimer, *Catalogue of manuscripts in the University of Wisconsin-Madison* (Dublin: Dublin Institute for Advanced Studies, 1989), 25-28; Kenneth E. Nilsen, "Mícheál Ó Broin agus Lámhscríbhinní Gaeilge Ollscoil Wisconsin," *Celtica* 22 (1991), 112-18.

[31] *IA,* 5 July 1884, 3.

bilingual frontispiece to the journal, which read: "*An Gaodhal*: Leabhar-aithris míosamhal, tabhartha chum an Teanga Ghaedhilge a chosnadh agus a shaorthughadh agus chum Féin-riaghla Chinidh na h-Éireann / *The Gael*: A Monthly Journal Devoted to the Preservation and Cultivation of the Irish Language and the Autonomy of the Irish Nation."[32] Magner and Norris–and many others–criticized Logan's Irish on the title page, and offered their own 'improved' versions.[33] Although the header was not twenty words in length, disagreements over this title page and arcane points of grammar continued in "Our Gaelic Department" from February 1882 through December 1882.[34] In the end, Norris shifted to the side of Logan on these issues, and the two men became convenient targets for Magner and other Irish scholars in the coming years whenever grammatical, philological, or dialectical matters arose.

As petty as the underlying issues might seem, poetic contentions soon became commonplace in the pages of the *Irish-American*, as students and advocates of the language joined a growing list of readers contributing original verse, often under pseudonyms, to "Our Gaelic

---

[32] The header, with the English translation, first appeared in the February 1882 issue; the journal's first issue was published in October 1881.

[33] *IA*, 6 May 1882, 5. Norris suggested "Irisleabhar Míosamhuil Bronnta chum cosnadh agus saothrúgadh do'n teanga Gaedhilge agus chum Féin-riaghlúghadh cíneadh na h-Éirean." He once even wagered an oyster supper with wine on whether 'teanga' was masculine or feminine, and whether 'chum' governed the genitive. See *An Gaodhal*, March 1882; *IA*, 8 April 1882, 5; 15 April 1882, 5. For clarity I give the Irish in the roman typeface throughout this article, although the original was printed in the Gaelic font.

[34] *An Gaodhal,* March 1882; *IA,* 8 April 1882, 5; 15 April 1882, 5. In this lengthy contention, Magner inadvertently fired the first volley in the great 'chum' and the genitive case debate, which would be waged in the pages of the Irish and the Irish-American press intermittently over the next seven years, and which saw Magner and Norris on opposing sides. Magner's letter to the *IA* is clear proof that Irish-language students and scholars now participated in a wider public sphere given this new bilingual journal. In fact, this ongoing contention over 'chum' and the genitive case came to feature such notable combatants as David O'Keeffe, Thomas O'Neill Russell, John Fleming, and William Russell. See also Brian Ó Conchubhair, "The Gaelic Font Controversy: The Gaelic League's (Post-Colonial) Crux," *Irish University Review*, 33 (2003), 46- 63.

Department" in response to the work or opinions of others. Although some individuals took offense at this practice, a handful of scholars looked to emulate the centuries-old *iomarbhánna fíli* (bardic contentions) where poets "showered their darts of satire at each other, and received, in turn, every reply to their linguistic assaults," but eventually concluded to "call the matter a fairly divided issue."[35] The purpose of these good-natured poetic contentions was ultimately the survival of the language and customs of Ireland, and seemed a fitting model for the students and scholars of Irish in America to emulate; however, one of the major themes in these contentions was the fundamental argument over exactly *what* Irish should be cultivated and preserved. Magner and like-minded advocates were convinced that Irish schools should be teaching a literary standard, if not the ancient language of Keating; on the other hand, Norris, Michael Logan and others believed that the language currently spoken by the people should be favored, otherwise the entire movement would lose support.[36]

By the latter half of the 1880s, assisted in part by the continued use of pseudonyms, poetic contentions in "Our Gaelic Department" had turned into bitter disputes which debased and humiliated those who purportedly shared the same overarching goal of cultivating and preserving Irish. More often than not, Captain Norris stood on one side and Daniel Magner on the other. For example, in one bitter feud, "Domhnal Criminn" (whom Norris alleged was Magner under a *nom-*

---

[35] *IA*, 4 December 1886, 5. See also Joep Leersen, *The Contention of the bards (Iomarbhágh na bhFileadh) and its Place in Irish Political and Literary History* (London: Irish Texts Society, 1994), 65, and Nicholas M. Wolf, "Antiquarians and Authentics: Survival and Revival in Gaelic Writing," in *Irish Literature in Transition, 1830-1880*, ed. Matthew Campbell (Cambridge: Cambridge University Press, 2020), 199-217, at 199.

[36] This transatlantic debate extended nearly forty years, although it is important to recognize that the Irish in America were much earlier combatants in the pages of the popular press than has been generally noted. See Philip O'Leary, *The Prose Literature of the Gaelic Revival 1881-1921: Ideology and Innovation* (Pennsylvania: The Pennsylvania State University Press, 1994), 10-12, where discussions of *cainnt na ndaoine* versus the "Keating" standard begin more than a decade after the debates in the American popular press.

MATTHEW KNIGHT

de-plume) submitted *Comhairle Do'n Taoiseach de Norradh* / Advice for Captain Norris," in which he stated that Norris should not write in Irish anymore while pillorying Michael Logan in the process. He wrote:

Ní mían liom sgolairidhe do bheith magadh fút,
'S ag có-mheasgadh d'anma annso 'gus annsúd;
Le ainm an daoi dána' eagaireas an "Gaedhal,"
A g-canamhuin budh dhorcha d'Ardeasbog Mhac h-
Eil.
[. . .]

Tá móran scolairidh na Gaedhilge san tír,
Theagasgas an teanga go díreach 's go fíor;
Teidh fá n-a lamhaibh air feadh bliadhna no dó,
A's beidh graimeur na Gaedhlge chó glan duit le ló.

Achd má leanfair go fóil an cumhaing droich-
shlighe,
Air a bh-fuilir a nois, beidh gach iarradh gan
bhrighe,
'S deirfidh Spioraid na Gaedhilge, "Nach cruaidh
mo dhán,–
Cuir Lógan a's Norradh a n-aon phruclais
amháin."[37]

I do not wish for scholars to be mocking you,
And confuse your name here and there,
With the name of that audacious dunce who edits An Gaodhal,
In a dialect that would be obscure to Archbishop MacHale.
[. . .]
There are many scholars of Irish in this country,
Who teach the language exactly and truly;

---

[37] *IA,* 23 July 1887, 3. Despite Norris' contention, "Domnall Criminn" was likely Thomas O'Neill Russell. Here, and with all Irish material, translations are mine.

247

Go under their authority for a year or two,
And your Irish grammar will be just as pure one day.
But if the narrow part of a bad path is still followed,
As it is now, every effort will be in vain,
And the Spirit of Irish will say, "Isn't my poem harsh,–
Bury Logan and Norris in a single burrow."

After Norris attempted to defend himself, none other than *Spioraid na Gaedhilge* ["The Spirit of Irish"] wrote wishing that Norris and Logan would give up their efforts studying Irish altogether:

Mo chreach! Mo leun!–cad deunfad feasda
Má leanann an dís seo fós mo sgríobhadh?
A m-beagán ama ní aithneochaidh fear mé
Ó teangain cleachda a measg na Sineach.

Saoraidh mé! Saoraidh mé! Saoraidh bhur d-teanga
Ó mhilleadh na n-daoineadh atá gan fhoghluim!
Tá eagla báis ag teacht air m'anam!
Saoraidh mé 'nois ó Lógan a's Norra![38]

Woe is me! Alas! What will I do henceforth
If these two continue to write me further?
In a short time no one will recognize me
From the language practiced among the Chinese.

Save me! Save me! Save your language
From destruction by people without learning!
The fear of death is coming upon my soul!
Save me now from Logan and Norris!

Using his own name, Daniel Magner contributed a short poem addressing both Fionn mac Cumhaill and Oisín, which concluded:

Och! A Oisín, a fhili bhinn,
Do chan gaisgideachd fear n-Éirionn,
Dá léighfá leitir Nórradh
Ba borb binbeach tú dá h-aoradh.[39]

---

[38] *IA,* 20 August 1887, 3; 27 August 1887, 3.
[39] *IA,* 23 July 1887, 3.

Oh, Oisín, sweet poet,
You sang of the valor of Irishmen,
If you were to read Norris's letter
Your satire of it would be sharp and venomous.

Beneath these verses, Magner added a final cut, declaring that Norris spoke the Irish language like a pig and should simply be ignored.[40]

Despite this animosity, both Magner and Norris continued to offer original and edited manuscript material to "Our Gaelic Department." Eventually, however, scholars of Irish began to criticize Magner for his submissions. He was asked by one reader to "give up the Fionn mac Cumhaill business" and avoid archaic language, while another complained that "to digest and assimilate such literary food" without the aid of extensive dictionaries, a "scholar would need to be endowed with the digestive powers of an ostrich."[41] Even the president of the Bowery NYPCS declared, "We are far more anxious to be able to read and speak the language of the living present than of the dead past," and begged Magner to stop poring over worn manuscripts and instead publish short tales from his "boyhood days" to better serve students in the schools.[42] Renowned Irish scholar and Gaelic League co-founder Thomas O'Neill Russell sympathized with Magner's determination to share the storied literary past with readers, noting that, "the trouble with such men as Magner is that they live ahead of the epoch in which their labors would be appreciated . . . As soon as Irishmen begin to have pure, just and sentimental ideas about what constitutes nationhood they will begin to appreciate the worth of such

---

[40] In a jocular twist, Irish student Daniel Criminn wrote to the column to ask that his name not be used as another's pseudonym in future: *"Ní h-áil liomsa m'anim a bheith curtha le h'aon nídh cam / 'S beidh súil agam feasda go leigfhidh mo chómharsainn dham."* [I don't wish my name to be associated with anything crooked / And I will hope in future that my neighbors will leave me alone.] *IA,* 24 September 1887, 3.

[41] *IA,* 6 September 1884, 8.

[42] *IA,* 25 December 1886, 5. This would be an ongoing issue for editors of "Our Gaelic Department": how can you satisfy the broad range of competencies in Irish, the literate and non-literate speakers of the language as well as the absolute beginners?

a man as Daniel Magner."[43] Regardless of this kind of recognition, and without prior notice, Magner ceased publishing Irish material in the popular press in 1892.[44]

Given Magner's absence from the Irish columns, Captain Norris began to submit more frequently, offering manuscript transcriptions and the occasional poem to "Our Gaelic Department." Some of the latter were quite successful; his rendering of "My Country 'Tis of Thee" as *Mo Thír is Ortsa Tá*, for example, was sung with a choral accompaniment at an NYPCS outing, and his *Creud Dhéanfaidh Tú, a Ghrádh* / "What Will You Do, Love?" found a place in Euseby D. Cleaver's reprinted *Duanaire na Nuadh-Ghaedhilge*.[45] Norris also found inspiration in unlikely places, penning a mock-bardic poem addressing Lord Dunraven, who had built the yacht "Valkyrie" to vie for the America's Cup, only to be soundly and fairly defeated by the American ship "Vigilant" in the race.[46] Another touching poetic departure for Norris was the elegy he wrote for a pet blackbird that an NYPCS student had brought over from Ireland; Norris concludes the poem by asking God to please send a beautiful woman with a voice like the bird's and hair as black as its feathers to the young man.[47]

Norris soon assumed a more solemn and historically significant designation, becoming the unofficial eulogist for many leaders of the Irish-language movement in Ireland and America. After the death of Euseby D. Cleaver in November 1894, Norris penned *Dán Bróin* / "A Poem of Grief," which he dedicated to the "bereaved widow of our

---

[43] *Fall River Daily Globe,* 9 July 1885, 4. According to the article, Magner was a native speaker but entirely self-taught in Irish grammar. The writer of this article heard of his reputation as a scholar at a meeting of the NYPCS and sought him out for an interview. He was not yet forty-five years old at this time. O'Neill Russell was interviewed for the article as well.

[44] His final submission to "Our Gaelic Department" was *Beatha Naoimh Stanislais* / "Life of St. Stanislaus," a four-part series on a Polish saint that must have puzzled his critics even more.

[45] *IA,* 28 May 1892, 3; *An Gaodhal,* July 1892; *IA,* 7 July 1888, 3; 9 January 1892, 3; 16 September 1895, 8; Cleaver, *Duanaire na Nuadh-Ghaedhilge,* 52-53.

[46] *IA,* 13 November 1893, 8. The poem, as might be imagined, was more political than a true celebration of American sailing prowess.

[47] *IA,* 1 October 1894, 8.

lamented friend."[48] He apologized for the delay in publishing his contribution, referencing "a severe accident" that delayed its composition. This was in fact an attack of apoplexy from which he never fully recovered. After suffering a second stroke in December 1897, Norris visited a priest, who asked what caused it. He told him, "The doctors said I had overtaxed my brain; for, besides the duties and labors of life, I spent every moment I could spare in trying to do something towards the resuscitation of my native language, the Irish."[49] His physical condition notwithstanding, Norris refused to back down from his life's pursuit.

When Daniel Magner passed away in April 1898, it was noted by the Gaelic Society president that an abler Gaelic scholar "had never been laid to rest in American earth; and he did not think that he had a superior on the other side of the Atlantic." And O'Donovan Rossa lamented, "I am sorry I can never speak to him again; but a more serious sorrow to me abides in the thought that some thoughts and words of Irish that he had may be dead in the grave with him."[50] Norris forgave old wounds and dutifully penned an elegy for Magner, which also celebrated the late John Fleming and David O'Keeffe, bemoaning the "havoc that death has been making on the cause of our dear native language:"

> Bu mhór mo dhóthchus seal ó shoin,
> Go m-beidheadh ár d-teanga féin,
> D'a labhairt airís, go bín, aguinn,
> A n-Éirinn glas na bh-Fian;
> Mar bhí fad ó, a n-gair 'sa n-gleó,
> Gan bac, gan cosg, gan srian.

> Do bhí sí ag teachd air aghaidh go beachd,
> Aimeasg na saoi 's na g-cliar;
> A's áthas ceart, í bheith gan smachd,
> Faoi meas, orruinn go léir,
> Go d-tainigh diachair a's míodhágh,
> Do ghoirtigh sinn faraor!

---

[48] *IA*, 14 January 1895, 8.
[49] *IA*, 4 June 1898, 8.
[50] *United Irishman*, 7 May 1898, 3.

A bháis! A bháis! Do shlad na treoin,
túis an domhain go n-diu,
Do thigeas chughainn go moch, air neoin,
'San oídhche dhiamhar dubh,
Ná creach sinn fós as aon d'ár n-duas,
Tá 'cur na Gaodhailge a g-cruth.
[. . .]

A Thigearna Dhia, bí páirteach linn;
Tabhair cobhair dúin ann gach beart,
Do réir do tholá naomhtha grin;
'S ná leig an Gaodhailge thart,
Gan fuargailt ó na namhadaibh síor',
A's déan a teagasg ceart.[51]

My hope was great in times past,
That our own language would be
Spoken again, harmoniously, by us,
In green Ireland of the Fianna;
As it was long ago, their cry in battle,
Unbending, unrestrained, unbridled.

It was progressing perfectly,
Among the scholars and the societies,
And we all felt real joy, unbounded,
It being held in esteem,
Until sorrow and misfortune arrived
To injure us, alas!

O Death! Death! Who destroyed warriors,
From the beginning of the world until now,
Who came to us early and late,
In the dark, black night,

Do not plunder us of any of our spoils,
Irish is taking shape.
[. . .]

---

[51] *IA,* 14 May 1898, 8. Norris' poem is dated 22 April 1898, so it can be inferred that Magner died in April. I can find no death record.

O Lord God, be partial to us,
Give us help in every deed,
By your will, your holy clear desire,
And do not let Irish pass,
Without unending redemption from its enemies,
And make its teaching correct.

Norris continued his solemn duties with his "Lines on the Death of M. J. Logan" in February 1899, and, noting that "it looks as if fate is against the cause of the dear old tongue," he composed a memorial verse for Eugene O'Growney months later.[52] This was to be his final contribution to the cause of the cultivation of Irish: on 20 January 1900 the Gaelic Society noted that "the Death of Captain Norris removes from our ranks one of the oldest and most earnest of the Gaelic workers," and the NYPCS dispensed with the entertainments of the "Pleasant Hour" long enough to mention that "he was an old and staunch supporter of our Society in times when it was not as flourishing as it is today, and when those who advocated the Irish language were looked on as mere enthusiasts who were doomed to disappointment and failure."[53] While Norris, the last survivor of the New York Ossianic Society, lived to see the day when a true international movement to revive the Irish language had finally begun to flourish through the efforts of the Gaelic League, the tradition of memorializing Irish scholars in "Our Gaelic Department" passed away with him. His Irish elegy was never composed.

Thomas D. Norris and Daniel Magner are prime examples of why efforts to cultivate the Irish language in the United States failed: individuals and societies were united in one singular purpose but were hopelessly divided on the necessary process to achieve it. Distinct personalities and their fundamental philosophical differences over orthography, pronunciation, and grammar had only grown more entrenched and unwavering after the Philo-Celtic Societies began in 1873. This failure to unite under one leader or cohesive strategy eventually transformed the cultivation of the Irish language from a nationalistic ideal into just one of many planks in the platform of a

---

[52] *IA,* 11 February 1899, 8; *IA,* 4 November 1899, 8. On O'Growney see Ní Bhroiméil, *Building Irish Identity,* 51-52.
[53] *IA,* 20 January 1900, 8, 1.

developing Irish cultural identity in America. Further, while Irish immigrants initially attempted to forge a hybrid identity in America,[54] with the study of the Irish language at its core, members of the Gaelic societies eventually preferred a hyphenated identity, with Irish joining the music, literature, and history of Ireland as points of pride, if not intellectual pursuit. Certainly, Magner and Norris wished otherwise; but given their refusal to put aside petty differences and unite under one organization for the cause, they had inadvertently fostered a small, scattered and disunited group of societies who just happened to be focused on the same goal.[55]

Still, the virtual absence of personalities like Magner and Norris in the historiography reveals a systemic underestimation of the role of the Irish in America in the Gaelic Revival and deserves a correction. Their influence on the movement to cultivate Irish on both sides of the Atlantic was significant, and the tendency to begin studies of the Gaelic revival with Douglas Hyde and the formation of the Gaelic League not only demeans the legacy of men like Norris and Magner but obscures the importance of the Irish language to the Irish in America. It cannot be overstated how difficult life was for many Irish immigrants to the United States after the Famine in particular: the powerful forces of anti-immigrant nativism and anti-Catholic discrimination were widespread and exerted brutal suppression on the daily lives and livelihoods of Irish expatriates. Debasing the Irish for their poverty, their religion, their language, and their many imagined social and intellectual deficiencies became normalized in American society.[56] Championing the inherent value of their native tongue and, in turn, the worthiness of the history and culture it preserved, was a psychological lifeline for men like Magner and Norris. The story of the Irish in America, and of *Irish* in America, speaks to the universal

---

[54] Uí Chollatáin, "Thall is Abhus," 374.

[55] Úna Ní Bhroiméil, "Worlds Apart-The Gaelic League and America, 1906-1914," in *Explorations: Centenary Essays,* ed. L. Irwin (Limerick: Mary Immaculate College, 1998), 146-57, at 147.

[56] See Kevin Kenny, *The American Irish* (Harlow: Pearson Education Limited, 2000), 158-160; Ní Bhroiméil, *Building Irish Identity,* 25-27; Cian McMahon, *The Global Dimensions of Irish Identity: Race, Nation, and the Popular Press, 1840-1880* (Chapel Hill: University of North Carolina Press, 2015), 147-150.

struggle for identity that represents a common thread of the immigrant experience. If the loss of one's native tongue is, as Thomas Davis lamented, "a chain on the soul," who should wonder that tired and blistered hands that swept streets each day would, at night, strive to set it free?[57]

---

[57] Thomas Davis, "Our National Language," *Nation,* 1 April 1843.

Appendix A: Index of First Lines of Poetry submitted by (or about) Thomas D. Norris and Daniel Magner to "Our Gaelic Department," 1881-1900

A Chaiptín, a Chaptín do throid inns a' chogadh: T.: *"Comhairle Chairdeamhuil do'n Chaiptín"* / "Friendly Advice for the Captain": P.: "Caraid an Chaiptín": N.: Written to Thomas D. Norris after his scathing letters about other correspondents: (24 May 1890).[58]

A cháirde dhílse, táim a m-baoghal mór: P.: "Spioraid na Gaedhilge": N.: Another poem addressing the feud between Thomas D. Norris and others: (27 August 1887).

A cháirde, is dúbhach dúinn 's is cúis ár n-déara: T.: "Dán Bróin": P.: Thomas D. Norris: Poem lamenting the passing of Rev. E.D. Cleaver: (14 January 1895).

A chómharsana, gallántacha ghrádhuigheas an Gaodhailge: P.: Thomas D. Norris: N.: In a letter discussing the achievements of the Irish school of the Hudson St. Philo-Celtic Society: (3 December 1887).

A chómharsana, machtnuighidh a's tagaidh le chéile: T.: *"An Ath-Chuinghe"* / "The Request": P.: Thomas D. Norris: (19 September 1885).

A chriosduidhe ghrádhmhar, a chairdeas, guidhim tú: T.: *Air Lá Breitheamhnais Deigionaigh* / "On the Day of the Last Judgement": Tr.: Daniel Magner: (11 December 1886, 18 December 1886, 25 December 1886, 1 January 1887, 7 January 1887, 15 January 1887, 28 January 1887, 5 February 1887, 12 February 1887, 19 February 1887, 26 February 1887).

Acht ná tréig do sgoil air mhuir na air abhain: P.: Thomas D. Norris: N.: 4 Lines. Written in a letter chastising absences from the Bowery Irish School: (18 July 1885).

A Dhia, tabhair fóirighthin air mo chroídhe: P.: Thomas D. Norris: N.: Written on the death of Daniel Magner: (14 May 1898).

---

[58] In the appendices the following abbreviations are used T(itle), P(oet), N(ote). Titles of poems and pericopes appear in quotation marks, and italics if followed by English translation.

A Dhonnchadh, is leun liom an sgeul so dha ínsint: T.: "David O'Brien's Advice to Denis O'Sullivan": N.: Submitted by Thomas D. Norris: (27 August 1881).

A éigse an t-seanchuis aicim bhar n-guidhe go fras: T.: "Dán Greannmhar": P.: Séamus Ua Caoindhealbhan: N.: Transcribed and submitted by Daniel Magner. Poem on the death of Séamus Ua Caoindhealbhan's cat: (9 March 1889, 16 March 1889, 23 March 1889, 6 April 1889).

Ag an ringce 's an m-baile budh ead-trom do chois-si: T.: "Mairgréadh Ní Cealleadh": P.: Edward Walsh: Tr.: Daniel Magner: N.: With English original and notes: (14 August 1880).

Aire dhuit, a ógáin fhin: T.: "An Fear Ceadna ag Teagasg na bh-Fea"r: P.: Muiris Mc Daibhí Dubh Mac Ghearailt: N.: Submitted by Daniel Magner from a manuscript of Timothy McCarthy: (5 May 1883).

Air maidin a nae cois gaorthaibh cuain: T.: "Air Fhághail Forálaimh a Chathamh as a Thigh aig Sacsanach ": P.: Seághan O'Muláin: N.: Transcribed by Thomas D. Norris from a manuscript of William Hogan: (26 September 1891).

Aisling do ghéar chéas mé tharbár amach: T.: "Air Bás Phádraic Mhic Dáith Uí Iarluighthe": P.: Conchubhar O'Ríghthordáin: Tr.: Thomas D. Norris: (29 January 1894).

A Logalán, an ghleanna domhain: T.: *"Oidhe Chaithlín"* / "The Fate of Kathleen": P.: Gerald Griffin: Tr.: Daniel Magner: N.: Revised from version published 11 December 1880: (17 January 1886, 23 January 1886, 30 January 1886, 6 February 1886, 13 February 1886).

Ann Lagalan, an ghleanna domhain: T.: *"Óidhe Chaitlín"* / "The Fate of Kathleen": P.: Gerald Griffin: Tr.: Daniel Magner: (11 December 1880, 1 January 1881, 8 January 1881, 15 January 1881).

Aontuighím leat, a ógánaigh, chum an rúnaire bhearradh: T.: "Faoiscríobhadh Chum an Ruinchleirigh do Bearradh": P.: Thomas D. Norris: N.: Poem accompanies Norris' contribution to the Bartholdi pedestal fund: (11 July 1885).

A phlúr na bh-fear! Áigh cuirim chúghat beagan línte: P.: Thomas D. Norris: N.: Written for Michael C. O'Shea, who had recently paid him compliments: (28 February 1891).

A réir a's mé go h-uaigneach faoi bhuaidhreamh am luídhe am shuan: P.: Thomas D. Norris: (3 March 1888).

A Righ na n-aingeal, na aspalna bh-faidh 's na g-clír: T.: "Dán Naomhta": N.: Transcribed by Daniel Magner: (3 April 1886, 10 April 1886, 17 April 1886, 24 April 1886).

A Sháir-fhir ró áluin, gan bhéim, de árd fhuil na h-Éirionn gan gó: P.: Thomas D. Norris: N.: Poem in address given to Father Eugene O'Growney at a meeting of the Philo-Celtic Society of New York: (3 December 1894).

A shaoi dhíl, goirim thú airis, : P.: Thomas D. Norris: N.: Poem delivered at the marriage of Grover Cleveland, 2 June 1886: (10 July 1886).

A Shaoithe eáladhantacha, creididh gur fíor mo sgeul: P.: Thomas D. Norris: (29 October 1887).

A Thaoisigh, A Thaoisigh, glac mo chómhairle anois: T.: "Comhairle Do'n Taoiseach de Norradh": P.: "Domhnal Criminn": N.: Poem in reply to Thomas D. Norris criticizing his Irish and his antagonistic attitude: (23 July 1887).

Beir mo bheannacht leat a sgríbhín: T. *"Dán do Scolairibh Gaodhailge an Bhomhraoí"* / "Poem for the Bowery Gaelic Scholars": P.: Daniel Magner: (30 October 1880).

Bhídheas sealad go seunmhar, 's gan leundubh am' inntinn: T.: "Breathnughadh air Stáid Láithreach na h-Éireann": P.: Thomas D. Norris: (30 April 1894).

Bidheann áthas mór air m' aigne, agus sólás ann mo chroidhe: P.: Thomas D. Norris: N.: Written in reply to "Pádraic" [Patrick O'Byrne] and his poem "Banks of the Lee": (11 April 1885).

Bídhmís ann ár n-Éireannaithibh fíor: P.: Thomas D. Norris: N.: Reply to Thomas O'Neill Russell. Two stanzas: (2 July 1887).

Bíos sealad dom' shaoghal gan spéis a n-dochar na g-cam: T.: "Loch Léin": P.: Thomas D. Norris: (16 June 1888).

Chaitheas tréimhse mhaith do 'm shaoghal, níos mó na fiche bliadhain: T.:"Éire, Tír mo Dhuthchais": P.: Thomas D. Norris: (3 August 1889).

Cómhchruinníghidh le chéile a's saorthúighidh an Gaedhilge chóir: P.: Thomas D. Norris: N.: Written to encourage attendance at Irish schools. 4 lines: (10 September 1887).

Creud dhéanfaidh tú, a ghrádh, 'nuair bheidheadsa 'gluaiseachd: T.: "Abhrán": Tr.: Thomas D. Norris: (7 July 1888, 9 January 1892, 16 September 1895).

Cuirimís le chéile, a Ghaodhala, le neart a's brigh!: T.: "Cuirimís Le Chíle": P.: Thomas D. Norris: (6 July 1896).

Cuirim slán leat, a cheapadh dánta: T.: "Ulick Kearn's Reasoning with His Wife": P.: Ulick Kearn: N.: Submitted by Thomas D. Norris: (15 October 1898).

Dar m-fhallaing, a thighearna, gur mór í do cháil: P.: Thomas D. Norris: N.: Written after the American "Vigilant" defeated the British "Valkyrie" in the America's Cup race: (13 November 1893).

Do b' áil liom féin beagán do rádh: P.: Thomas D. Norris: (17 April 1886, 24 April 1886).

Dob' uaibhreach iad, ceannurraídhe crích Innse Fáil: T.: "Lament for the Milesians": P.: Thomas Davis: Tr.: Thomas D. Norris: (9 September 1895).

Do dhearch mé ó'n b-port, air fhiollsiúghadh na maidne: T.: "I Saw from the Beach": P.: Thomas Moore: Tr.: Thomas D. Norris: N.: Written in reply to David O'Keeffe's translation of the same poem, who asked that, if anyone had issues with his translation, they should submit their own: (22 March 1884).

Dúbhach, sheas meisi, anns an tráth: T.: "Paradise and the Peri": P.: Thomas Moore: Tr.: Thomas D. Norris: (29 March 1884, 5 April 1884, 12 April 1884, 19 April 1884, 26 April 1884).

CHAMPIONS OF THE IRISH LANGUAGE

Eag na d-triath le taobh na bh-flatha do bheir lucht léighin tréith gan mheabhair: T.: "An t-Athair S. O'B. Do Athair Eoghan O'Caoimh": N.: Submitted by Thomas D. Norris: (19 February 1894).

Éisdígh liom-sa sealadh, 'gus nósaid díbh cia a cialleadh: T.: "Seaghan Uí Duibhir an Ghleanna": Tr.: Thomas D. Norris: (23 July 1881).

Gaibh, a Chéin, go caomh mo theagasg uaim-se: T.: "Comhairle Bráthar Bhoichd Do Chian Ua Mathghamhna": N.: Contributed by Daniel Magner: (28 April 1883).

Guilimís, guilimís, agus guilimís: T.: "Lines on the Death of M. J. Logan": P.: Thomas D. Norris: (11 February 1899).

Is áil linn ceart 'san n-Gaedhilge líomhtha: P.: Thomas D. Norris: N.: Written in reply to poem addressed to him by Thomas O'Neill Russell. 8 lines: (10 February 1883).

Is brónach mis' air maidin 'nuair a dhúisighim ar mo neul: T.: "Dán Beag Air Fhaillighe Muintire na h-Éireann 'nna d-Teangain bhreágh agus 'nna d-Tír": P.: Thomas D. Norris: (22 June 1889).

Is dúbhach a bhídhim gach oidhche a's ló: T.: "Focail ó'm Chroidhe do Thír Mo Grádh": P.: Thomas D. Norris: (9 May 1885).

Is dúbhach an sgéul 's is geur le h-innsint: P.: Thomas D. Norris: N.: Elegy written for Rev. Eugene O'Growney: (4 November 1899).

Is fada táir tar bhrághaid na d-tonn: T.: "Chum Eibhlinn Ann Éirinn": P.: Daniel Magner: (25 April 1885).

Is tearc 's is saidhbhir cuach, mo ghrádh: T.: "Bríghidín Bán Mo Stór": Tr.: Daniel Magner: N.: With accompanying English original and notes: (4 September 1880).
Is truagh liom tír mo shinsear, faoi smacht a's smúit mar tá: T.: "Smuainte Cruadha": P.: Thomas D. Norris: (9 July 1894).

Má's míorbhilídhe do nochd' tá uainn: T.: "Freagra Míorbhuileach, Naoimh Antonaoi Phadua": Tr.: Thomas D. Norris: (4 June 1898).

MATTHEW KNIGHT

Mo Thír, is Ortsa Tá: T.:" My Country 'Tis of Thee": Tr.: Thomas D. Norris: (28 May 1892).

Ná déanaidh baillsgeige de 'n teangain is áilne: P.: Thomas D. Norris: N.: Poem in reply to recent criticism by Domhnal Criminn: (20 August 1887).

Ná staon, ná staon 'san t-somhradh theit: P.: Thomas D. Norris: N.: 4 lines encouraging attendance at Bowery school: (12 June 1886).

Ní cheilim na bearta do charas a n-aois m-óige: P.: Conchúbhar Ua Ríordáin: N.: Transcribed by Thomas D. Norris: (26 February 1894).

Níl grián geal Ibh-rathaigh ag soilsiughadh go lónrach: T.: *"Nuaill Chaoint Air Ua Suilleamhán Beara"* / "Dirge of O'Sullivan Beare": P.: J. J. Callanan: Tr.: Daniel Magner: N.: With English original and notes: (24 July 1880).

Ní raibh nidh luachmhar air an saoghal: P.: Thomas D. Norris: (8 May 1886).

Och, a Fhinn na m-bán-ghlach: P.: Daniel Magner: N.: Poem in reply to Thomas D. Norris criticizing his Irish: (23 July 1887).

O! tig liom féin, a mhathair, tig; tar uisge ghlas an t-sáile: T.: *"Inghian an Imircidhe"* / "The Immigrant's Daughter": P.: Denis Florence McCarthy: Tr.: Daniel Magner: (27 March 1886).

Sguir do 'd shuirighe, lean do 'd leas: T.: "Teagasc Chum na m-Ban Óg": P.: Muiris Mc Daibhí Dubh Mac Ghearailt: N.: Transcribed by Daniel Magner from a manuscript written by Timothy McCarthy. Corrected version printed the following week: (28 April 1883, 5 May 1883).

Táim turseach, tréith, lag; ní 'l neart am ghéagaibh: P.: Thomas D. Norris: N.: Written for Michael Cronin, whose Irish blackbird recently died: (1 October 1894).

Tig arduigh suas mé, a leinbh, tóg mé suas beagán níos mó: T.: "Dán Beag Lae Phádraic, anns na Stáidibh Aontuighthe": P.: Thomas D. Norris: (8 June 1889).

Tigídhidh re deagh chroidth' le chéile: P.: Thomas D. Norris: N.: 8 Lines. Poem in a letter to editor urging attendance at the Bowery Irish school: (6 March 1886).

Tráthnóna Earaigh 's mé 'taisdeall cois taoide: P.: Thomas D. Norris: (30 September 1895).

Truagh sin a aoinmhic Aoife, do thuisg do'n chríoch so Ulladh: T.: "Cúchullainn Tar Éis Marbhtha ChonLaoich": N.: Submitted by Thomas D. Norris from a 1732 manuscript: (7 May 1894).

Appendix B: Prose Selections from Thomas D. Norris and Daniel Magner in "Our Gaelic Department," 1881-1896

Manuscript Transcriptions

T.: "Caith Cluana Tairbh": Ed.: Daniel Magner: N.: [Wisc 178, 157-175] See Buttimer, *Catalogue of Irish Manuscripts in the University of Wisconsin-Madison,* 27; Nilsen, *Mícheál Ó Broin,* 117: (5 March 1881, 12 March 1881; shortened version also appears 3 September 1892, 10 September 1892, 17 September 1892, 24 September 1892).

T.: "Oileamhuin Cuchullainn": Ed.: Daniel Magner: N.: [Wisc. 178, 1-38] See Buttimer, *Catalogue of Irish Manuscripts in the University of Wisconsin-Madison,* 26; Nilsen, *Mícheál Ó Broin,* 117: (28 January 1882, 4 February 1882, 18 February 1882, 25 February 1882, 4 March 1882).

T.: "Oidhe Chonnlaoch Mac Cuchullainn": Ed.: Daniel Magner: N.: [Wisc 178, 77-100] See Buttimer, *Catalogue of Irish Manuscripts in the University of Wisconsin-Madison,* 26-27; Nilsen, *Mícheál Ó Broin,* 117: (18 March 1882, 25 March 1882, 1 April 1882, 8 April 1882, 15 April 1882).

T.: "Coimh-Rioth Bhodaigh an Chóta Lachtna agus Cnámh an Irinn": Ed.: Daniel Magner: (10 February 1883, 17 February 1883, 24 February 1883, 3 March 1883).

T.: "Brisleach Maighe Muirtheamhne": Ed.: Daniel Magner: N.: [Wisc. 178, 176-216] See Buttimer, *Catalogue of Irish Manuscripts in the University of Wisconsin-Madison,* 27; Nilsen, *Mícheál Ó Broin,* 117: (7 July 1883, 14 July 1883, 21 July 1883, 28 July 1883, 4 August, 11 August 1883, 18 August 1883, 8 September 1883).

MATTHEW KNIGHT

T.: "Ag So Trachd Air Bheatha Dala Meirlino Maligno (agus a Chompanaigh)": Ed.: Daniel Magner: N.: Due to a postal error, the first portion of the tale appears in the 10 November issue: (13 October 1883, 20 October 1883, 27 October 1883, 3 November 1883, 10 November 1883).

T.: "Comhrac Firdiadh agus Cuchullainn": Ed.: Daniel Magner: N.: [Wisc. 178, 39-75] See Buttimer, *Catalogue of Irish Manuscripts in the University of Wisconsin-Madison,* 26; Nilsen, *Mícheál Ó Broin,* 117: (8 December 1883 15 December 1883, 22 December 1883, 12 January 1884, 19 January 1884, 26 January 1884, 2 February 1884, 16 February 1884, 23 February 1884).

T.: "Cath Cnocha": Ed.: Daniel Magner. N.: Damaged copy. [Wisc 178, 101-156] See Buttimer, *Catalogue of Irish Manuscripts in the University of Wisconsin-Madison,* 27; Nilsen, *Mícheál Ó Broin,* 117. Magner notes that this MS was loaned to him by Dr. Joseph Cromien: (4 October 1884, 11 October 1884, 18 October 1884, 22 November 1884, 29 November 1884, 6 December 1884, 13 December 1884, 20 December 1884, 27 December 1884, 3 January 1885, 10 January 1885).

T.: "Eachtra Cloinne Righ na h-Iorruaidhe": Ed.: Daniel Magner: (24 January 1885, 31 January 1885, 7 February 1885, 14 February 1885, 21 February 1885, 28 February 885, 7 March 1885, 14 March 1885, 21 March 1885, 18 April 1885, 2 May 1885, 30 May 1885, 6 June 1885, 20 June 1885, 4 July 1885).

T.: "Stair air Aitightheoiribh Eirinn, Reimh Teachd Mac Mileadh": Ed.: Daniel Magner (?): N.: From *Foras Feasa ar Éirinn* / History of Ireland, and submitted by Daniel Crimmins. With glossary: (31 December 1887, 21 January 1888, 28 January 1888, 11 February 1888, 18 February 1888, 25 February 1888).

T.: "Eachtra Giolla na g-Croiceann, Mar Inistear é le Cormac Óg Mac Diordal": Ed.: Daniel Magner (?): N.: Prof. Natasha Sumner has identified this as "Eachtra Chéadaigh Mhóir": (16 June 1888, 23 June 1888, 30 June 1888, 11 August 1888, 18 August 1888, 25 August 1888).

CHAMPIONS OF THE IRISH LANGUAGE

T.: "Bruighean Caorthainn an Oileain": Ed.: Daniel Magner (?): (12 October 1889, 19 October, 25 October 1889, 2 November 1889, 16 November 1889, 23 November 1889).

T.: "Eachtra Uillin Airmdheirg, Mic Rígh na Gréige": Ed.: Daniel Magner: N.: From a manuscript translated by John Scanlan of Cork, living in New York. (7 June 1890, 21 June 1890, 28 June 1890, 5 July 1890, 12 July 1890, 19 July 1890, 2 August 1890, 9 August 1890).

T.: "Eachtra Lomnochtáin Sléibhe Riffi": Ed.: Thomas D. Norris: (20 November 1893, 27 November 1893, 4 December 1893, 11 December 1893, 18 December 1893).

T.: "Bruigheann Chéise an Corruinn": Ed.: Thomas D. Norris: (5 March 1894, 12 March 1894).

Translated Literature

T.: *Foirghiol Neimhspleadhachda na Stad Aontuighthe* / Declaration of Independence of the United States: Tr.: Daniel Magner: (5 July 1884).

T.: "*Sliabh na Truaigh bh-Eile* / The Mountain of Miseries": A.: Joseph Addison: Tr.: Daniel Magner: (13 March 1886, 20 March 1886).

T.: "*Beatha Naoimh Stanislais* / Life of St. Stanislaus": Tr.: Daniel Magner: (20 February 1892, 27 February 1892, 5 March 1892, 12 March 1892).

Assorted Texts

T.: "An t-Eagluis Caitliocach": N.: MacCauley's apostrophe to the Catholic Church translated by Daniel Magner: (19 August 1882).

T.: "Address to President Cleveland": N.: Full text of the Irish address of congratulations presented by Thomas D. Norris to Grover Cleveland after his inauguration, 5 March 1885: (21 March 1885).

T.: "La Feile Choluim-Cille": Ed.: Daniel Magner: N.: Taken from the Annals of the Four Masters: (20 February 1886, 27 February 1886, 6 March 1886).

MATTHEW KNIGHT

T.: "Félire Dún na n-Gall" (Extracts): Ed.: Daniel Magner: N.: Includes Brenainn, Colman, Barrfhionn, and Donall Finn: (12 June 1886, 19 June 1886).

T.: *Eachdra Labhrais De Roisde, agus an Fheardha-Cait* / "The Adventures of Larry Roche and the Tom-Cat": Ed.: Daniel Magner: (23 April 1887, 30 April 1887, 14 May 1887, 21 May 1887, 28 May 1887).

T.: *Oraid Sochraide* / "Funeral Oration": A.: Matt Harris: Tr.: Thomas D. Norris: N.: Irish translation of Matt Harris' undelivered funeral oration for John O'Mahony: (22 February 1890, 1 March 1890, 8 March 1890).

T.: "Address of welcome to Father Eugene O'Growney": N.: Speech given by Thomas D. Norris to the New York Philo-Celtic Society on the occasion of O'Growney's arrival in New York City: (3 December 1894).

Medieval Irish Land Law as an Alternative Justice System in Nineteenth- and Twentieth-Century Ireland, Denmark, and Norway

Ciaran McDonough

Introduction

The project to translate the corpus of medieval Irish law in the nineteenth century meant that, for the first time, the contents of the various tracts were widely accessible to those without specialist knowledge of medieval Irish or access to the repositories where the manuscripts were held. The project, which ran from 1852 to 1901, attracted a lot of attention from within and outside Ireland, mainly as the law tracts were considered to be of great use to philologists, but also in anticipation of the insights into Irish society–both medieval and modern–the translations would bring. As the tracts were published under the title *Ancient Laws and Institutes of Ireland*, a popular picture emerged of a more egalitarian and just society, which resulted in frequent appeals to 'Brehon law', as early Irish law was popularly termed, to remedy injustice in contemporary society. Even as more tracts dealing explicitly with the regulation of status in society appeared, this image endured. This article will focus on the ways in which laws relating to land and land tenure were appealed to and examined in the nineteenth and twentieth centuries in Ireland, and how discussions of some of the land laws were printed in newspapers in Denmark and Norway in the 1880s. It will begin by outlining the project to translate the corpus of early Irish law and the role of the Commission appointed to superintend the translation and transcription of the Ancient Laws and Institutes of Ireland and will discuss the publications of the legal tracts. This will also include a brief discussion of other translations of medieval law being carried out at the same time to demonstrate how this was part of a larger trend in European antiquarian research, especially in the Nordic countries. The second half will focus on the modern circulation of the laws relating to land. It shall cover discussions around the potential influence of Land League ideals on the way certain terms were translated and how contemporaneous commentators interpreted them. The article will

CIARAN MCDONOUGH

conclude with the presentation of a discussion of early Irish land law in the pages of some Danish and Norwegian newspapers in the 1880s.

The Translation of the Law Texts

After the topographical project of the Ordnance Survey of Ireland came to a premature end in 1842, the antiquarians John O'Donovan and Eugene O'Curry were employed by James Henthorn Todd to catalogue the Irish manuscripts in the library of Trinity College Dublin.[1] This ultimately led O'Donovan and O'Curry to think about the corpus of medieval Irish law and a potential project in translating it. This idea was received well by Todd and his fellow Church of Ireland clergyman, Charles Graves. They submitted a request for funding to the Government in 1852, along with O'Curry's transcription and translation of the *Book of Acaill*,[2] and were subsequently awarded £5000 to set up and maintain a commission to oversee the project and £500 per annum afterwards.[3] As is well known and documented, the work was beset with problems. This included the initial promotion of O'Donovan over O'Curry at the first meeting of the Commissioners, though this was rescinded at the second.[4] There were also accusations of incompetency in English levelled at the two, which saw their replacement as editors in favour of the Queen's College Belfast Professor of Jurisprudence William Neilson Hancock

---

[1] For a biography of John O'Donovan, see *Dictionary of Irish Biography*, s.v. "John O'Donovan," accessed March 22, 2022, https://www.dib.ie/biography/odonovan-o-donnabhain-john-sean-a6718; For a biography of Eugene O'Curry, see *Dictionary of Irish Biography*, s.v. "Eugene O'Curry," accessed March 22, 2022 https://www.dib.ie/biography/ocurry-curry-o-comhrai-eugene-eoghan-a6664; George Sigerson, ed., "Eugene O'Curry's Statement" by Eugene O'Curry in *Journal of the National Literary Society of Ireland* vol. 1, pt. iii (1902), 147-59 at 148-49.
[2] Ibid.
[3] Minute book of the 'Commissioners appointed to superintend the publication of the Ancient Laws and Institutions of Ireland.' Dublin, Royal Irish Academy MS 24 O 39/CG/BL/1, 33, 17.
[4] First meeting held on 7 December 1852; second on 10 December 1852. RIA 24 O 39/CG/BL/1, 8; 11-12.

and his assistant Thomas Busteed in 1860.[5] With regard to the allegations of incompetency levelled at O'Donovan and O'Curry, Éamon De hÓir suggests that:

> *[B']fhéidir gur dheacair leo glacadh leis an Donnabhánach agus le hEoghan Ó Comhraí, clan fheirmeoirí beaga Caitliceacha gan léann ollscoile, mar scoláirí; ba mhaith ann iad, b'fhéidir leis na 'curious tracts' a bhí le fáil i nGaeilge a mhíniú do na fíorscoláirí, ach ba shin an méid. Má bhí an garbhthiontú a bhí déanta roinnt aisteach anseo is ansiúd – agus bí cinnte go raibh – is é is dóichí gur mheas an Coimisiún nach é deacracht an bhuntéacs ba chuis leis ach easpa Bhéarla lucht an tiontaithe.*

[P]erhaps they found it difficult to accept O'Donovan and O'Curry, the children of Catholic small farmers and lacking university education, as scholars; they might have been good enough to explain the 'curious tracts' in Irish to genuine scholars, but that was all. If the rough translation that had been done was rather strange in places–and no doubt it was–the Commission probably ascribed this not to the difficulty of interpreting the original text but to the translators' inadequate English.[6]

However, the main problem was the simple fact that the task was enormous and resulted in several years' work. O'Donovan died in 1861 and O'Curry in 1862, setting back the project further, though they were replaced by scholars such as William Maunsell Henessy. Their deaths meant that their original translations were revised by the

---

[5] As Graves's draft reports and letters to the Treasury in 24 O 39/CG/BL/1 demonstrate, one of the frequent justifications for the amounts spent on O'Donovan and O'Curry's salaries is their workload. It is interesting to note that whenever Graves and Todd are called to account for spending by the Commissioners or Treasury, they always outline how many pages of transcription and translation O'Donovan and O'Curry have produced.

[6] Éamon De hÓir, *Seán Ó Donnabháin agus Eoghan Ó Comhraí* (Dublin: An Clóchomhar Teo, 1962), 101. My gratitude to Nollaig Ó Muraíle for help with the translation.

later editors, Hancock, Thaddeus O'Mahony, and Alexander George Richey, with aid from Irish scholars, such as the aforementioned Hennessey. The first volume, published by the State Paper Office, was brought out in 1865; volume two in 1869; volume three in 1873; volume four in 1879; and volume five, with a separate volume containing a glossary, in 1901.

The translation of the corpus of medieval Irish law in the mid-nineteenth century was by no means unique and was one series of many different medieval legal translations. Some of these included the *Norges Gamle Love* series edited by P. A. Munch and R. Keyser. Volumes one, two, and three of this series appeared in 1846, 1848, and 1849 respectively. H. S. Collin and C. J. Schlyter edited the series *Corpus iuris sueo-gotorum antiqui. Samling af Sweriges gamla lagar* (The Collection of Sweden's old laws), and volume one appeared in 1822. In 1853, the first volume of the collection of laws relating to medieval Iceland, *Lovsamling for Island*, was published by Jón Sigurðsson and Oddgeir Stephensen. Vilhjálmur Finsen's edition of one of the manuscript witnesses of the law book of the Icelandic Commonwealth, *Grágás*, was published in 1852. Of course, the *Ancient Laws and Institutes of Ireland* followed in the series of the publication of translations of English and Welsh legal material. *Ancient Laws and Institutes of England* was produced by Benjamin Thorpe in 1840 and *Ancient Laws and Institutes of Wales* by Aneurin Owen in 1841. While, based on the name alone, the production of the *Ancient Laws and Institutes of Ireland* certainly followed its English and Welsh predecessors, it is worth mentioning the other European translation projects occurring at the same time, as they were also influential in the publication of the Irish material. Irish antiquarians were certainly aware of research being carried out in other countries, for example, several Irish antiquarians were members of *Det Kongelige Nordiske Oldskriftelskab* (The Royal Society of Antiquaries of the North–a Danish antiquarian society based in Copenhagen) and corresponded with several of their Danish counterparts.[7]

---

[7] For more, see Ciaran McDonough, "'Ireland and Denmark Are Specially to Be Named': The Connections Between Irish and Danish Antiquarians in the Nineteenth Century" in *Ireland and the North*, ed. Fionna Barber et al (Oxford: Peter Lang, 2019), 17-39.

James Henthorn Todd and Charles Graves were certainly aware of the work being carried out on the Icelandic legal material, writing in the *Suggestions with a View to the Transcription and Publication of the MSS of the Brehon Laws, now in the Libraries of the British Museum, the University of Oxford, the Royal Irish Academy, and Trinity College Dublin* that "more recently, the Danish Government furnished the means of publishing the Icelandic laws,–documents remarkably similar in their nature to the ancient laws of Ireland."[8] As a small country within a larger empire, Iceland was in a similar political situation to Ireland, making the translation of the corpus of medieval law of particular relevance to the above-named countries. Like Ireland, Iceland also lost its parliament in 1800, coming under direct rule from Copenhagen, though it was restored as an advisory body in 1845.[9] The status of the vernaculars in both countries was also commented upon in the early nineteenth century: the Danish linguist Rasmus Rask predicted in 1815 that Icelandic would be extinct within two hundred years,[10] whereas in 1851, John O'Donovan gave Irish another few generations before its disappearance of it and the other "Celtic dialects of the British Isles."[11] Like Ireland and Iceland, Norway had also been part of empires during the nineteenth century. In the early sixteenth century, Norway became part of the Danish realm, holding the status of a territory. This lasted until 1814 when Norway was ceded to Sweden after the Napoleonic Wars. While there is no mention of the Norwegian compilation of the corpus of its medieval law, it may possibly have influenced the decision to translate the Irish corpus and may also partly explain why there was an interest in early Irish law later on in the nineteenth century, as discussed below.

---

[8] [Charles Graves], *Suggestions with a View to the Transcription and Publication of the MSS of the Brehon Laws, now in the Libraries of the British Museum, the University of Oxford, the Royal Irish Academy, and Trinity College Dublin* (London: Macintosh, 1851), 6.

[9] Gunnar Karlsson, 'Icelandic Nationalism and the Inspiration of History', in *The Roots of Nationalism: Studies in Northern Europe*, ed. Rosalind Mitchison (Edinburgh: John Donald Publishers Ltd, 1980), 77-89, here 78.

[10] Ibid.

[11] Letter John O'Donovan to John Windele, dated 6th February 1851, Dublin, Royal Irish Academy, MS 4/B/10/117 (ii).

CIARAN MCDONOUGH

Though the project began in 1852, plans for the Irish material began as far back as 1843, when the minutes of a meeting of the Irish Archaeological Society, prefaced to John O'Donovan's edition and translation of *The Tribes and Customs of Hy Many* stated that "the difficult and laborious work of editing our ancient Brehon Laws, Annals, &c" is soon to be underway and that in preparation, it needed to be ascertained what, if any, materials were stored in repositories in Britain and on the continent, as these would need to be consulted before any real work could get underway.[12] Charles Graves and James Henthorn Todd worked behind the scenes in collaboration with the Treasury and Lord Lieutenant of Ireland to secure funding for preliminary work, including O'Curry's sample of an edition and translation of a portion of the *Book of Aicill*, a manuscript witness of which was in the hands of Lord Ashburnham.[13] As his letters to O'Donovan show, Graves always had him and O'Curry in mind for the project he described as "the most important that Irish scholars could be engaged in" even if at the first meeting of the Commissioners in 1852, they first decided to hold an open competition for translators, which was revised at the second meeting.[14]

The Idea of Early Irish Law

Funding for the project to translate the corpus of early Irish law was granted based on an appeal by Graves and Todd to the Government for funding. As has already been mentioned, they submitted a pamphlet called *Suggestions with a View to the Transcription and Translation of the MSS of the Brehon Laws*. As might be expected, the proposal focused mainly on the philological value of the legal material, yet when it came to a report submitted to

---

[12] John O'Donovan, trans., *The Tribes and Customs of Hy Many, Commonly Called O'Kelley's Country* (Dublin: For the Irish Archaeological Society, 1843) p. 7.
[13] Letter Charles Graves to John O'Donovan, dated 9 May 1855, Dublin, Royal Irish Academy MS 24 O 39/JOD/124 (vi).
[14] Letter Charles Graves to John O'Donovan, dated 4 August 1851, Dublin, Royal Irish Academy MS 24 O 39/JOD/124 (i); Minute book of the 'Commissioners appointed to superintend the publication of the Ancient Laws and Institutions of Ireland.' RIA 24 O 39/CG/BL/1, 9; 12. See n. 5 above for the dates of the meetings.

the House of Commons on 17 May 1852, outlining the work carried out so far and requesting more funding for the project, the focus shifted slightly. The *Report of the Commissioners* mentioned instead the urgency of the project, as the scholars able to carry it out would not be around for much longer, and that some observations about contemporary Ireland would be provided by the translation of its ancient laws. It was mentioned above that the publication of the laws was greatly anticipated for the insights into Irish culture it would give. This is repeated in the *Report*, yet with a somewhat negative focus. It is worth repeating the comments of Todd and Graves here in full:

> There are some circumstances which would render the publication of these ancient laws peculiarly interesting in the eyes of the politician. It is not improbable that the habits of thought and action prevailing amongst the native Irish are reflected in the laws which they framed for themselves before they were affected by foreign influences, and to which they continued to cling with obstinate tenacity, even for centuries after they had been compelled to submit to British rule. The Brehon Laws were actually appealed to so late as the reign of Charles I. We must not, therefore, be surprised to find some traces yet remaining of their effect upon society. We would also suggest that good results would be obtained by exhibiting the real state of this country at a remote period of its history. It would then be found that false or exaggerated notions have been entertained of the well-being of society and the advancement of civilisation in early times. Ireland never enjoyed a golden age. It would be more true to say, that she suffered for many ages under an iron feudalism, which administered essentially different laws to the rich and to the poor. Ignorance on this head has certainly created in some minds an unreasonable dissatisfaction with the present order of things, and a perverse disposition to thwart the efforts of those who are doing their utmost to ameliorate it. Nothing could be more efficacious in dispelling such morbid

national prejudices than a complete publication of the
ancient Irish laws.[15]

This extract certainly demonstrates that there was something to
be feared in translating the medieval laws and that the laws had to
demonstrate clearly that any references to better conditions in early
medieval Ireland were "false or exaggerated notions have been
entertained of the well-being of society and the advancement of
civilisation in early times." The phrase "Ireland never enjoyed a
golden age" certainly seems to have been inserted to allay fears of any
nationalist insurrections, as were the last two sentences of the extract.
One vital point that can be gleaned from this extract is that it is the
idea of early Irish law which is powerful and attractive, often more so
than the actuality of early Irish law. Since the late eighteenth-century
early Irish law was discussed outside of scholarly circles, for example
in articles by Tobias Smollett in *The Critical Review: Or, Annals of
Literature* where he is able to mention certain tracts and legal concepts
by name.[16] This also featured outside of the Anglo-phone realm: in
1864 in a newspaper published in Vienna–the *Ost-Deutsche Post*- in
an article called "Das weibliche Kriegsheer", the concept of a Brehon
is applied to a kingly adviser with the explanation that "Brehon
Richter–Brehon ist ein irisches Wort und bedeutet einen nach
ungeschriebenen Gesetzen, also nach dem herkommen urtheilenden
wandernden Richter."[17] The announcement of the project to translate
the corpus in 1852 was met with a fanfare of praise from people who
had an idea of what early Irish law was and why it was important. The
idea of early Irish law became an important cultural point–frequently
connected with the idea of a golden age or as a remedy to a modern

---

[15] The Report of the Commissioners appointed to Inquire and Report
concerning the Ancient Laws and Institutes of Ireland (1852), 3.
[16] See, for example, his anonymous review articles of 'The History of
England from the Accession of James I to the Elevation of the House of
Hanover by Catherine Macaulay', *The Critical Review: Or, the Annals of
Literature* 23 (1767), pp. 81-88 and 'The History of Ireland from the
Invasion of Henry II by Thomas Leland', *The Critical Review: Or, the
Annals of Literature* 36 (1773), 1-14.
[17] *Ost-Deutsche Post*, October 17, 1864, 1. "Brehon judge-Brehon is an
Irish word and means one of the unwritten laws and also comes from the
judging wandering judges." My translation.

grievance–which was frequently referred to. This can be seen in such headlines as this "Divorce … Ancient Irish Style" from the *Evening Herald* in 1982.[18] The first line of the article reads: "any takers, girls, to reinstate the Brehon laws?" Here the idea of early medieval Ireland, when early Irish law, or Brehon law as it is here referred to, is part of the golden age narrative, highlighting the difference between 1982 when divorce was illegal and early medieval Ireland when divorce was permitted under the law. The idea and the actuality of early Irish law can be used to address a wrong when official channels fail to satisfy an individual, providing a sense of alternative justice.

In the twentieth century, early Irish law was cited in two court proceedings on fishing rights in tidal waters in Ireland in the 1920s, 1930s, and 1940s.[19] The first hearing was in 1924. The so-called River Erne trial concerned six salmon fishermen who had been arrested for poaching from Erne fisheries. They counteracted that it was their right to take salmon, as that stretch of river should not be privately owned. In their defence, they cited the Magna Carta, and then early Irish law. The scholars Eoin Mac Néill and Daniel Binchy came to the aid of the defence, firstly by proving that early Irish law was still being enacted in Donegal in the seventeenth century; secondly by demonstrating that English kings had no power in that county before 1184, therefore Irish law was the only one recognised then; and thirdly by citing the following passages from the law tracts, arguing against private ownership based on the rights of a people to "the salmon of the place."[20] I will point out that this was not the only time when medieval laws were upheld in courts of law; in 1862 the laws attributed to the tenth-century king Hywel Dda were cited in a court case over foreshore access in Anglesey, Wales.[21] Even as late as 2017, the thirteenth-century law code *Grágás* was cited in a legal case involving

---

[18] *Evening Herald*, February 11, 1982, 8.
[19] "Days of Brehon Law recalled in Foyle Case", *Irish Independent*, 17 December 1947, 3.
[20] For a full account of the case see Thomas Mohr, "Salmon of Knowledge", *Peritia* 16 (2002), 360-95; here 366-7.
[21] Huw Pryce and Gwilym Owen, 'Medieval Welsh law and the mid-Victorian foreshore', *Journal of Legal History*, 35, no. 2 (2014), 172-99.

a Mixed Martial Arts fighter in Iceland.[22] It could reasonably be concluded that the translations of medieval law texts reminded people that they once had been functioning law codes and they served as inspiration for a recourse to justice when it was denied by contemporary legal channels. For reasons of space, it is not possible to fully discuss the dual nature of the legal sphere in Ireland during the sixteenth and seventeenth centuries, but it is important to note that the long implementation of medieval law codes in Ireland resulted in the idea of alternative legal spaces, which were perhaps more accessible to Irish people than in other countries during the nineteenth century.

The Recirculation of Land Law

As was mentioned previously, the publication of the medieval law tracts in *Ancient Laws and Institutes of Ireland* made the texts far more accessible than they had been before. Naturally, this drew many commentators on the topic and, as the project was of such long duration, this attention lasted across the second half of the nineteenth century. Such was the interest that even a Finnish newspaper in 1852 covered some of the debate in the House of Lords on the costs of financing the project.[23] Naturally, early Irish land law was a component of this and volumes two and four of *Ancient Laws and Institutes of Ireland* cover tracts relating to the ownership and division of land. The project to translate the laws began in 1852, which was after the formation of the Tenant Right League and their demands, later echoed by the Land League, of the so-called three F's: Free sale, fixity of tenure, and fair rent. It can easily be understood why the publication of tracts relating to land would be of interest to politically minded commentators. Many of the arguments were centred around the way the word *túath* was translated and what was implied by it.[24] To many commentators, the land owned by the *túath* was common land, which was divided up and apportioned according to the need of

---

[22] "13th century body of law used in case against MMA fighter", *Iceland Monitor*, April 12, 2017, accessed February 3 2021, https://icelandmonitor.mbl.is/news/news/2017/04/12/13th_century_body_of _law_used_in_case_against_mma_f/.
[23] "Storbritannien", *Finlands Allmänna Tidning*, August 28, 1852, 2.
[24] *Electronic Dictionary of the Irish Language* (*eDIL*), s.v. túath (people, tribe, nation) accessed March 22, 2022, http://www.dil.ie/42241.

the individual for the benefit of the group. In his letters to Karl Marx and in notes for a history of Ireland, Friedrich Engels saw the land as being in communal ownership up to as late as 1600; therefore did not see the importance of personal possession of land in Ireland.[25] In his unfinished "History of Ireland", Engels refers to the deaths of O'Curry, O'Donovan, Todd, and Petrie as hindering the progress of the publication of the law tracts, meaning that he was aware of the project. He cited from the first two volumes, referring to them both as "the *Senchus Mor*" and discussed the text's value in re-creating conditions in early Irish society.[26] These views were later echoed by Joseph Fisher in an article called "The History of Landholding in Ireland", published in 1877. In this article he argued that *Cáin Sóerraith* and *Cáin Aicillne* being translated with the word 'tenure', as they were in *Ancient Laws and Institutes of Ireland* was incorrect, stating that:

> These arrangements did not in any way affect that which we understand by the word 'tenure', that is, a man's farm, but they related solely to cattle, which we consider a chattel. It has appeared necessary to devote some space to this subject, inasmuch as that usually acute writer Sir Henry Maine has accepted the word 'tenure' in its modern interpretation, and has built up a theory under which the Irish chief 'developed' into a feudal baron. I can find nothing in the Brehon laws to warrant this theory of social Darwinism, and believe further study will show that the Cáin Saerrath and the Cáin Aigillne relate solely to what we now

---

[25] Friedrich Engels *The Origin of the Family, Private Property and the State* (Lawrence and Wishart, London, 1977), 194. See also Thomas Mohr, "Law in a Gaelic Utopia: Perceptions of Brehon Law in Nineteenth and Early Twentieth Century Ireland" in *Errinern und Vergessen/Remembering and Forgetting: Yearbook of Young Legal History* eds. Oliver Brupbacher et al (Munich: Martin Meidenbauer, 2007), 247-276.

[26] Friedrich Engels, "History of Ireland" in *Marx and Engels on the Irish Question*, ed. R. Dixon (Moscow: Progress Publishers, 1974), 263-302 at 285-86.

call chattels, and did not in any way affect what we
now call the freehold, the possession of the land.[27]

According to Fisher, "The land system is called Tanistry, from
the Tanist, an officer elected to succeed the chieftain, whose main
office was to divide the land of the tribe among the living members
thereof; he was, in fact, a trustee and heir to the land of each of the
sept or clan, and made such a division as suited the circumstances of
the case."[28] Seeing the matter in the same way as Engels, Fisher argued
that:

> The tanistry system seems to have been based upon
> the idea expressed in Sir John Davis's description,
> lineage; the land had been the possession of some
> remote ancestor and all his lineage were provided for
> out of it. The Caen finny and tanist appear to have
> held the same office, and its main function was the
> equitable division of the land among the lineage of the
> far-away original chieftain. It may sound trite to say
> that even now every man has only a life possession or
> life estate, for all love to think that they can exercise
> a sort of ownership over their lands after death has put
> them out of possession. This right had no place in the
> tanistry system, a man enjoyed the land allotted to
> him while he lived, but when he died the living dealt
> with it as they deemed best for their own interests. But
> this system went further. 'Land was to them perpetual
> man,' the staple of his existence, therefore every one
> of the lineage possessed his share for life. The lands
> of the chief did not descend to his children, they, with
> his office, went to the tanist, the lands of the tanist to
> his successor. All the other lands of the sept were
> divided among the members; there was no tenancy in
> the sense in which we use the word; there was no rent,
> no eviction, none of the powers claimed under the

---

[27] Joseph Fisher, 'The History of Landholding in Ireland', *Transactions of
the Royal Historical Society*, vol. 5 (1877), 228-326+424 at 248-249.
[28] Ibid, 233; See Electronic Dictionary of the Irish Language (eDIL), s.v.
"tánaise," accessed March 22, 2022, http://www.dil.ie/40018.

feudal system by the tenants in fee. This system of tanistry was essentially republican in its character, the land vested in the people, not in the Crown; its division was arranged by the elected officer of the sept or lineage; all its members were joint owners of the common estate, which was strictly settled in tail to the whole of the lineage. No man could sell the inheritance of his children, and there were neither landlords nor tenants. The two administrative officers, the chief and the tanist, had their own official demesnes, which did not descend to their children, but went like church land, or clerical income, to him who succeeded to the office.[29]

Fisher's claims can be seen as possibly being influenced by the increase in land-related tension, which would lead to the Land War in 1879. Certainly, his portrayal of access to land can be seen in light of the demands of the Tenant Right League and, as was explained above, his depiction of Ireland under the Brehon laws seems to be viewing it as a golden age. His views were refuted by Sir Henry Maine, who argued instead that private ownership of land was actually in place during the early medieval period. He wrote that:

The Brehon law-tracts prove, however, that it can only be received with considerable qualification and modification, and they show that private property, and especially private property in land, had long been known in Ireland at the epoch to which they belong, having come into existence either through the natural dis-integration of collective ownership or through the severance of particular estates from the general tribal domain.[30]

The impact of contemporary affairs on the translation of the tracts is emphasised by the Irish nationalist Laurence Ginnell, who took umbrage with the translation of *ciss* in *Ancient Laws and Institutes of*

---

[29] *Ibid*, 240.
[30] Sir Henry Summer Maine, *Lectures on the Early History of Institutions* (New York: Henry Holt and Company, 1875), 98.

Ireland as rent, arguing instead that it should be tribute and that the translators were influenced by the political events of their day.[31]

Fergus Kelly attributes the belief that early medieval Ireland was more egalitarian than the nineteenth to a misleading translation made by the editors of the *Ancient Laws and Institutes of Ireland*. He writes that "the 1865-1901 edition of the *Ancient Laws and Institutes of Ireland* almost always translates *fine* as 'tribe' rather than 'kin-group'. This misled Engels and other modern political thinkers into thinking that land was held in common by all members of the *túath* in early Ireland."[32] For those who supported Land League ideals and who wanted to see greater tenant rights, it is understandable why early Irish law should prove to be such an attractive concept. One such commentator was the Liberal MP Sir Rowland Blennerhassett and it is to the recirculation of one of his works in Scandinavia that we now turn our attention.

Irish Land Law in Scandinavia

It has not yet been possible to trace Blennerhassett's original text. In both the Danish and Norwegian newspapers, the text is simply called "Irland". It is footnoted throughout with references to secondary material on early Irish law, like Maine's *Lectures on the Early History of Institutions* and O'Curry's *Manners and Customs of the Ancient Irish*, so it is unlikely to have originally been a speech and was most likely a pamphlet. The text was serialised over the course of a week in February 1882 in the newspaper *Fædrelandet*, which was originally liberal until Denmark's defeat in the Schleswig-Holstein war of 1864, after which it turned conservative. The original source for *Fædrelandet* is given as V.P. with the subtitle "af Sir Roland Blennerhassett,"[33] which I have also been unable to trace. The extract, referred to as number II, published on February 10, 1882 contains a discussion of early Irish land law. While the current space limitations

---

[31] Laurence Ginnell, *The Brehon Laws: A Legal Handbook*, third ed. (Dublin: P. J. O'Callaghan Ltd, 1894), 69; Electronic Dictionary of the Irish Language (eDIL), s.v. "cís" accessed March 22, 2022, http://www.dil.ie/9231.

[32] Fergus Kelly, *A Guide to Early Irish Law* (Dublin: Dublin Institute for Advanced Studies, 1988, revised 2016), 105.

[33] "Irland", *Fædrelandet*, February 9, 1882, 1.

279

of this article do not allow for close analysis of the laws themselves, it serves our present purpose to present this discussion of laws relating to land. Like Joseph Fisher and many of the commentators mentioned above, this text focused on the division of land among the túath, claiming that individual members had rights to portions of land. Though the translator attempted to convey what a túath was for the readers, it is clear that they were not certain, as in some instances there are examples of code-switching in phrases such as *Tuathafgrændsninger* (the boundaries of a túath).[34] The unknown tract was serialised over the course of a fortnight in the Norwegian newspaper *Christiania Intelligentssedler*, at that time owned by an orphanage in what is now called Oslo.[35]

As a former part of the Danish realm, the text is in Danish rather than Norwegian, but the fact that it is reproduced in Norway as well suggests that it might have had some significance there. The first extracts of this text in both the Danish and Norwegian newspapers were not introduced in any way, so it is not possible to definitively state why this text was translated and reproduced, but we might make some suggestions as to the interest in the recirculation of medieval Irish land law in the late-nineteenth century. As was mentioned above, Norway was in two different empires during the nineteenth century, so there may have been an interest in the situation of similarly situated countries. In examining mentions of Ireland in both Norwegian and Danish newspapers in the ten years before this text was published there, there are many mentions of political events in Ireland, as there had been all across the nineteenth century in newspapers in many European countries.[36] It may be that this is another example of other nations being interested in Irish political affairs, yet without being able to correctly situate the original English text by Blennerhassett, it is hard to say this with certainty. It is most likely a reversal of a statement

---

[34] "Irland", *Fædrelandet*, February 10, 1882, 1.
[35] *Christiania Intelligentssedler*, February 21-March 4, 1882, p. 2.
[36] See, for example, Hugo Vallentin's series of letters in the Swedish newspaper *Aftonbladet* in 1893, titled 'Breve från Homerule-landet' (From Home Rule Land). See Andrew Newby, 'A Swedish View of Galway in 1893: Hugo Vallentin's "Letters from Home-Rule Land"', *Journal of the Galway Archaeological and Historical Society*, 70 (2018), 1-16 for English translations of these.

made in the *Wexford People* in 1880, which captured the interest that the inhabitants of countries in similar political situations had in each other. On the occasion of the restoration of the Icelandic Parliament in 1874, the anonymous author wrote that:

> Ireland cannot fail to feel a profound interest in the efforts of countries similarly circumstanced as herself, when they struggle for that birthright freedom of downtrodden nations which has ever been that daydream of her people, since the "Iron Lords from Normandy with the Saxons in their train," came to despoil her of her most prized gem. And equally profound must be the esteem which she entertains for the men who labour for that great and exalted end, particularly if they be men of genius as well of truth, capable of leading a nation through the wilderness of slavery.[37]

It is just as likely that other countries looked to Ireland for inspiration in their struggles against imperialism as Ireland looked to them. In this case, "Iceland's dearest son" was the nationalist politician and editor of the medieval Icelandic laws Jón Sigurðsson, who had used the laws to argue for greater political and financial autonomy for Iceland, resulting in the restoration of the Icelandic Parliament in 1874.[38] Possibly other scholars had similar intentions in translating their corpus of medieval law and were interested in what would happen with the Brehon Law Project.

Conclusion

This article has demonstrated that, while the publication of the translation of the corpus of medieval Irish law made it more accessible in the nineteenth century, sometimes it was the idea of what the law tracts contained rather than the actuality which was far more attractive and useful to people. Even though an interpretation of the laws had been provided in the translations made, sometimes modern commentators needed to interpret these interpretations to suit their

---

[37] "Iceland's Dearest Son: Her Sword and Her Shield", *Wexford People*, January 3, 1880, 7.
[38] Karlsson, "Icelandic Nationalism and the Inspiration of History", 87.

arguments. As has been argued in this article and elsewhere by Kelly, a mistranslation of a single word could change a whole society into the more egalitarian one that nineteenth-century commentators might have wished to see around them. In a time when land was at the centre of political debates, the access to previous laws relating to land provided commentators with an alternative legal space in which to find what was lacking for them.

Acknowledgements

The research for this article was carried out under the project 'Antiquarianism, Politics, and Sectarianism in Nineteenth-Century Ireland: A Study of *Ancient Laws and Institutes of Ireland* (1852-1901)', funded by the Irish Research Council (GOIPD/2020/676).

Cnoc an Áir: The Hill of the Slaughter in Fenian Tradition

Síle Ní Mhurchú

Hills named Cnoc an Áir (The Hill of the Slaughter) feature in a number of Fenian (Finn Cycle) texts that range in time from *Acallam na Senórach (AS)*, which may date to the early thirteenth century, through lays and a prose tale found in manuscripts of the seventeenth to the nineteenth centuries, to folklore gathered in the twentieth century.[1] In this paper, I investigate links between these texts as well as offering some reflections on the potentialities offered by reading Finn Cycle texts across time: essentially, I argue that tracing the development of the narratives in question alerts us to the rich inspiration provided by the world of Fionn mac Cumhaill and to the considerable creative capacities of those who composed and recomposed the texts under discussion.[2] Other matters touched upon

---

[1] For Cnoc an Áir in Irish literature, see: Brian Ó Cuív, "Varia II," *Celtica* 1/2 (1950): 328-86 at 381; Máirtín Ó Briain, "Some material on Oisín in the Land of Youth," in *Sages, Saints and Storytellers: Celtic Studies in Honour of Professor James Carney*, ed. Donnchadh Ó Corráin, Liam Breatnach, and Kim McCone (Maynooth: An Sagart, 1989), 181-199, at 192-3. For references to texts (all discussed below), see *Historical Dictionary of Gaelic Placenames Fascicle 5 (Clais an Chairn-Cnucha)*, ed. Pádraig Ó Riain, Diarmuid Ó Murchadha, and Kevin Murray (London: Irish Texts Society, 2013), 161-2. On the date of the first recension of *AS*, see: Kevin Murray, *The Early Finn Cycle* (Dublin: Four Courts Press, 2017), 24-8; Caoimhín Breatnach, "The transmission of the earliest recension of *Acallam na Senórach*," in *Lorg na Leabhar: A Festschrift for Pádraig A. Breatnach*, ed. Caoimhín Breatnach, Meidhbhín Ní Úrdail, and Gordon Ó Riain (Dublin: National University of Ireland, 2019), 197-219; Gregory Toner, "The dating of the *Acallam*," in *The Gaelic Finn Tradition II*, ed. Sharon J. Arbuthnot, Síle Ní Mhurchú, and Geraldine Parsons (Dublin: Four Courts Press, 2022), 15-23.

[2] From here on, I use *AS* when referring to *Acallam na Senórach* in general, *AS1* when referring to the first recension, and *AS2* for the second recension, also known as the Reeves *Agallamh*. On the different recensions, see: Nollaig Ó Muraíle, "*Agallamh na Seanórach*," in *An Fhiannaíocht*, Léachtaí Cholm Cille XXV, ed. Pádraig Ó Fiannachta (Maynooth: An

283

include: the use of placenames in the Finn Cycle; the depiction of emotion in the texts; the themes of battle and mourning; and the role of female characters in a male-dominated heroic world.

Cnoc an Áir in two episodes from *Acallam na Senórach*

There are two separate episodes in *Acallam na Senórach* that feature places called the Hill of the Slaughter. I will start with looking at these episodes as they are in Whitley Stokes' edition and then I will look at some other versions that contain details that allow for further interpretation.[3] The two Hills of the Slaughter in *AS1* are clearly distinct locations: one is in Ros na Ríg, north-east of Tara and the another is in Dál nAraide in the north-east of Ulster.[4] The Ros na Ríg episode begins with two questions from Patrick: did the Fianna believe in God and did they know of his existence?[5] Caoilte responds with an affirmative: *"Rofitir in flaithféinnid,"* ar Cáilte, *"ór ba drai ₇ ba fáidh*

Sagart, 1995), 96-127; and for the Reeves *Agallamh* specifically, see: Joseph J. Flahive, "Revisiting the Reeves *Agallamh*," in *In Dialogue with the Agallamh: Essays in Honour of Seán Ó Coileáin*, ed. Aidan Doyle and Kevin Murray (Dublin: Four Courts Press, 2014), 164-84. In this paper, I mostly use Modern Irish forms of placenames and characters when not quoting from the work of others, but in some cases, for names found mostly in earlier literature, I use earlier spellings.

[3] *"Acallamh na Senórach,"* ed. Whitley Stokes, in *Irische Texte mit Übersetzungen und Wörterbuch*, fourth series, volume 1, ed. Whitley Stokes and Ernst Windisch (Leipzig: S. Hirzel, 1900), 1-438.

[4] See: Stokes (ed.), *"Acallamh,"* ll. 1453-84 and ll. 2970-3042; and Ó Cuív, "Varia II," 381. The second of Ó Cuív's references to Stokes' edition should read l. 2990. Two places named Cnoc an Áir are recorded in the "Placenames Database of Ireland": one, anglicized Knockanare, is in the civil parish of Buttevant, Co. Cork, and the other, anglicized Knockanade, in the civil parish of Killeedy, Co. Limerick, is as yet unvalidated. See "The Placenames Database of Ireland," logainm.ie, s.nn, accessed December 20, 2021, https://www.logainm.ie/. Another Knockanare referred to by Ó Cuív and noted by him to lie north of Dripsey, Co. Cork is also recorded in the Database, but the preferred Irish name for this place is now An Coinigéar: see Ó Cuív, "Varia," 381 and "Placenames," s.n, accessed December 20, 2021, https://www.logainm.ie/en/11462. There is further discussion of placenames in the section on folklore below.

[5] This episode is named "How the Fiann knew that God existed" by Stokes (*"Acallamh,"* iv).

284

₇ ba flaith é, ₇ do thuiceamar-ne uili cu raibhi Dia ann tré urchra aenoidche adconncamar" ("The chief and warrior [i.e. Fionn] knew, said Cáilte, for he was a wizard, a seer, and a prince. And we all understood from the destruction that we saw one night that there was a God").[6] Caoilte relates that two hundred men of the household of Cormac mac Airt, each the son of a king and a queen, all of whom were staying in a royal hall at Ros na Ríg, died suddenly and unexpectedly in their sleep one night after a feast there, along with two hundred women. The first to see the dead was Binde Bóinde, the chief steward of Tara, who was sent to the hall to speak to Cormac's son who was among the revellers. It is not explained how or why the Fianna were summoned to the scene but the mass killing indicated to them *go raibi in fírDhia forórdha ann .i. in nech aca raibe comus ₇ cumachta orainn uili* (that there was indeed a True God, someone who had direction and power over us all).[7] In the lay that accompanies this tale, Caoilte emphasises that this was destruction unlike any other he had seen: *"Ní faca urchra mar soin"* (I have not seen ruin like this).[8] He explains that the mound in which the dead royals were buried was known thereafter as the Hill of the Slaughter (*Cnoc an áir*).[9]

The reason why God singled out the revellers of Ros na Ríg for slaughter is not specified, but it might be assumed that they sinned prior to their death: the presence there of an equal number of men and women might hint at sexual misconduct. Caoilte states that the wood in which the hall was located was one of great abundance, containing a thousand of every type of tree and that, after the slaughter, it was swallowed by the earth in front of the Fianna. This brought the Fianna to an understanding of God: *"Ro thuicsem rí[g] nime ₇ talman trít sin"* (We became aware through this of the existence of the King of Heaven and Earth).[10] Through two signs–a mass killing and a landslide–God has revealed that he holds the power of life and death over human beings and that he can alter the landscape at will: his actions bring to

---

[6] Stokes (ed.), *"Acallamh,"* ll. 1455-8; translation from Ann Dooley and Harry Roe, *Tales of the Elders of Ireland* (Oxford: Oxford University Press, 1999), 45.
[7] Stokes (ed.), *"Acallamh,"* ll. 1472-4; Dooley and Roe (trans.), *Tales*, 45.
[8] Stokes (ed.), *"Acallamh,"* l. 1479; Dooley and Roe (trans.), *Tales*, 46.
[9] Stokes (ed.), *"Acallamh,"* l. 1482.
[10] Stokes (ed.), *"Acallamh,"* l. 1484; Dooley and Roe (trans.), *Tales*, 46.

mind Biblical stories such as the destruction of Sodom and Gomorrah and the Parting of the Red Sea.

The second *ASI* tale featuring a place called the Hill of the Slaughter is recounted by Caoilte during his sojourn at Loch Daim Deirg in Dál nAraide in the company of two priests of St Patrick, Colmán Eala and Eoghanán.[11] Colmán asks Caoilte how Tipra in Bantrachta or the Well of the Women got its name. Caoilte tells that Niamh, daughter of Aengus Tírech, the king of the two provinces of Munster, eloped with Oisín to this well. Aengus was less than pleased and sent five battalions after her. These men came upon Niamh one day as she and her retinue of women were washing at the well. Niamh and the women responded as follows to the sight of the soldiers:

> *"Truag sin!" ar-si in ingen: "mogenar do gébad bás*
> *7 aidhed," ar sí, "sul do chífed a oidi 7 a athair 7 a*
> *tri derb[b]raithri, 7 maith[i] da cóicid Muman*
> *amlaid sin hí!" Is annsin tuc inn ingen a gnuis re*
> *lár, 7 fuair bás ann in tricha ban ro boi, 7 ro chuir a*
> *craide ina lia f[h]ola tar a bél amach.*[12]

> "Sad is that!" said Níamh. "Happy the one who would find death and slaughter, rather than that her foster-father and her father, her three brothers and the nobles of the two provinces of Munster would see her thus." She then put her face to the ground and died there together with her thirty women. Her heart came out through her lips in a gush of blood.[13]

Caoilte explains that the hill on which they stood was henceforth called *Cnoc ind áir*[14] and recites a quatrain in which it is indicated that Niamh and the women were buried there. But, the story does not end there. Aengus blamed Fionn, Oisín and the Fianna for his daughter's death and sought to give battle to them. Fionn agreed to this and the

---

[11] This episode is named "The story of the Well of the Women" by Stokes (*"Acallamh,"* v) and it runs from ll. 2970-3042. On the historical saints Colmán Eala and Eoghanán, see Pádraig Ó Riain, *A Dictionary of Irish Saints* (Dublin: Four Courts Press, 2011), s.nn.

[12] Stokes (ed.), *"Acallamh,"* ll. 2983-90.

[13] Dooley and Roe (trans.), *Tales*, 91.

[14] Stokes (ed.), *"Acallamh,"* l. 2990.

Fianna prepared themselves for the fight, but Fergus Fínbel, the poet of the Fianna, declared that it would be an unjust battle as Fionn was responsible for the death of the king's daughter. This disagreement was resolved by recourse to external authority: the judges at Tara ordered that Niamh's corpse be exhumed and weighed, that her body weight in gold and silver be given as compensation to the king, and that compensation also be paid out for all the other women buried in the hill. Evidently, Fionn's initial instinct to accept the challenge issued by the king of Munster was a poor decision.

This tale is an *aithed* (elopement), a tale type in which a woman compels a man to run away with her, often with deadly consequences.[15] Proinsias Mac Cana notes that elopements would not have been approved of in medieval Ireland and it is near certain that the author of *AS1* would have been of this view, given his evident preoccupation with following correct marriage procedures.[16] Indeed, the author of *AS1* seems to take a particularly moralizing approach to this aithed. Whether he composed it himself or whether he was adapting an existing tale is unknown, but he does not describe the meeting of Niamh and Oisín nor does he provide us with any romantic

---

[15] See "*Acallamh*," l. 2975. The title "Athad ingine ríg Muman le hOissin" ("The elopement of the daughter of the king of Munster with Oisín") is given in the margin of the text in Oxford, Bodleian Library, MS Laud Miscellaneous 610: "*Acallamh*," l. 2973.

[16] See Proinsias Mac Cana, *The Learned Tales of Medieval Ireland* (Dublin: Dublin Institute for Advanced Studies, 1980), 74; and also Lisa M. Bitel, *Land of Women: Tales of Sex and Gender from Early Ireland* (Ithaca and London: Cornell University Press, 1996), 53-4. I use the word author here, following Geraldine Parsons, to designate the person who created the work from which the manuscript witnesses to *AS1* derive: Geraldine Parsons, "The Structure of *Acallam na Senórach*," *Cambrian Medieval Celtic Studies* 55 (2008): 11-39, at 15. It is generally assumed that this was the work of one person (see also, for example: Anne Connon, "The Roscommon Locus of *Acallam na Senórach*," in *In Dialogue*, ed. Aidan Doyle and Kevin Murray, Dublin: Four Court Press, 2014, 21-59, at 56-9; and Murray, *The Early Finn Cycle*, 22) but it may also have been a work of joint or multiple authorship such as is modelled in the text itself which emerges from the interactions and conversations of Patrick, Caoilte and others. Whatever the case may be, *AS* certainly places importance on the sanctity of marriage: see Murray, *The Early Finn Cycle*, 36-7.

scenes from their time together in the wilderness and thus, it is clear that his interest is in the grave consequences of the elopement.[17] Oisín spends the time hunting, giving the impression that Niamh is something of a medieval golf widow! Niamh is untroubled by her elopement whilst in the company of Oisín and her womenfolk: Oisín, belonging to the Fianna, is outside of society and the women are her intimates. It is only when confronted by her male kin and the men at their command, representing the patriarchal public order, that Niamh becomes conscious of her wrongdoing: her shame is a public emotion.[18] In the editions of Stokes and O'Grady, Niamh's emotion is not named.[19] Interestingly, in another manuscript witness to *AS1*, that of Dublin, University College, OFM, MS A4, Niamh's father states that his daughter died of shame: *fuair bás do naire* (she died of shame).[20] It is likely that early audiences would have inferred the cause of Niamh's death even when it is not stated overtly: Philip O'Leary notes that death from shame is commonly found in abduction tales.[21] Furthermore, Kicki Ingridsdotter observes that death by shame and other strong emotions in early Irish literature can be expressed overtly or merely implied, so it is not unusual that Niamh's shame is

---

[17] Lisa M. Bitel notes that, in other aitheda, coupling provides "one of the dramatic highpoints" (*Land of Women*, 45).

[18] See the comments of Philip O'Leary, "The Honour of Women in Early Irish Literature," in *Ériu* 38 (1987): 27-44 at 35-6; Bitel notes that the aitheda turn "private passion into a public event" (*Land of Women*, 53).

[19] For O'Grady, see *Silva Gadelica (I-XXXI): A Collection of Tales in Irish with Extracts Illustrating Persons and Places*, ed. Standish H. O'Grady, 2 vols. (London: Williams and Norgate, 1892), i, 160-1; ii, 178-9. O'Grady's edition is based on the Book of Lismore witness to *AS1*; Stokes's source for this section of the text is Laud Misc. 610. On the manuscript sources used by O'Grady and Stokes, see Kevin Murray, "Editing *Acallam na Senórach*: A Test Case Based on the Mucc Shlánga Episode," in *The Gaelic Finn Tradition II*, ed. Arbuthnot, Ní Mhurchú, and Parsons, 24-38, at 24-7.

[20] UCD-OFM, MS A4, 41, col. b, l. 31; translation from Dooley and Roe, *Tales*, 91. The lethal emotion is named in Dooley and Roe's translation, which is based on multiple manuscript witnesses: *Tales*, xxxi-xxxii. Here and in many other Cnoc an Áir texts, there may be punning on the similar-sounding words *ár* (slaughter) and *náire* (shame).

[21] O'Leary, "The Honour of Women in Early Irish Literature," 41.

not named in all manuscript witnesses to *AS1*.[22] However, this added detail is very useful to modern readers and scholars who approach the tale at great remove, and it indicates the value of consulting multiple manuscript witnesses when interpreting *AS*.[23]

Niamh is not the only one to die from shame in *AS1*: elsewhere, Patrick asks for heaven for the soul of the young man Airnélach, who died of shame after receiving a threat of satire from a poet.[24] Such posthumous salvation is not granted to Niamh. While men and women are both depicted as experiencing shame in *AS1*, women pay a greater cost.[25] Because of the lack of detail about Oisín and Niamh's relationship, it is difficult to estimate how painful it is for him to lose Niamh and he does not appear to be punished for his part in the elopement. However, the Fianna as a whole cannot be said to escape unscathed from this episode: they narrowly avoid a battle that would inevitably have led to loss of life and the *éraic* (compensation) they are required to pay for the dead women, the only one ever paid by Fionn, places a heavy financial burden upon them. It is no wonder that they would wish to remember the lessons learned here: naming the hill makes it less likely that these lessons will be forgotten.

There are quite a few scenes of slaughter in *AS1* and the use of the name Cnoc an Áir to describe two of them might just be a

---

[22] "Death from Emotion in Early Irish Literature," *Ulidia 3: Proceedings of the Third International Conference on the Ulster Cycle of Tales*, ed. Gregory Toner and Séamus Mac Mathúna (Berlin: Curach Bhán, 2013), 87-95, at 89.

[23] For discussion of differences between the manuscript witnesses to *AS*, see Breatnach, "The Transmission," and Murray, "Editing *Acallam na Senórach*." Murray's statement that "further editorial work may substantially change our viewpoint" of *AS* is an important one: *The Early Finn Cycle*, 23.

[24] Stokes (ed.), "*Acallamh*," 30-1.

[25] Two other examples to be considered are the case of the innocent Fithir, who dies of shame when she learns that she has married her sister's husband while her sister is still alive ("*Acallamh*," 117-8), and the men of Mórna, whose shameful lack of vigilance leads to the Meadow of Shame (Clúain Imdergtha) being named as such but who themselves are unharmed ("*Acallamh*," 183-4). On shame as a gendered emotion in the early literature, see O'Leary, "The Honour of Women in Early Irish Literature," 41.

coincidence. They may simply be two scenes of carnage that happen to have taken place on hills. On the other hand, it may be that the author of *AS1* is signalling to readers that the two episodes can be read in light of one another.[26] A feature both episodes have in common is a combination of sudden mass death and revelation of truth, but their consequences differ. Niamh's revelation leads to death, but the knowledge of God acquired by Fionn and the Fianna after seeing a macabre sight grants them the possibility of eternal life. The Fianna thus stand out from Niamh and from other inhabitants of the pagan past.

The Ros na Ríg episode and the episode of the Well of the Women are also found in *AS2*, thought to date to the thirteenth or fourteenth century.[27] In the Ros na Ríg episode, some details are changed without affecting the overall narrative, but one difference draws out an interesting nuance.[28] Oisín, who is the one who narrates this episode in *AS2*, describes the emotion felt by the Fianna when they first learned about God:

> *"Tuiccamair-ne," ol Oisīn, "Fíana Éireann, in tan*
> *ad-chualamair-ne an sgéul sgainner-bhorbh*
> *sgannradhach sin, go raibh an fír-Dhia forórdha ōs*
> *ar ccionn a ccomhachtuibh ₇ ōs cionn na cruinne go*
> *comh-choitchionn."*[29]

> "We, the Fianna of Ireland," said Oisín, "when we heard that terrifying tale of [the] fierce attack, understood that the true and glorious God was above us in powers and above the world in general."[30]

---

[26] For an overview of the thoughts of scholars on whether *AS* is a coherent text or not and for a strong argument that it is indeed a carefully structured text with rich intratextual resonances, see Parsons, "The Structure."

[27] On dating, see *Agallamh na Seanórach*, ed. Nessa Ní Shéaghdha, 3 vols., Leabhair ó Láimhsgríbhnibh 7, 10, 15 (Baile Átha Cliath: Oifig an tSoláthair, 1942-5), i, xxiv-xxxi.

[28] The Ros na Ríg episode in *AS2* is in Ní Shéaghdha (ed.), *Agallamh*, i, 141:20-144:2. The end, which in *AS1* describes the swallowing of the wood by the earth, is missing here: *Agallamh*, 144.

[29] *Agallamh*, 142: 22-7.

[30] Translations from *AS2* and elsewhere are my own unless otherwise specified.

Geraldine Parsons stresses the significance of the Ros na Ríg episode as "the first articulation of Finn's precocious theism" in *AS*.[31] While learning through fear might be seen as undesirable in modern times, the idea that fear of God is the beginning of wisdom is stated on multiple occasions in the Bible.[32] This mention of fear shifts slightly our reading of this episode: the terrifying attack seems less like a sudden interruption and more like a carefully designed first step to learning about Christianity. The question of how or whether this insight changes our reading of *AS1*, where the idea of fear is not conveyed directly, is a complex one. Might we read between the lines and come to understand that the Fianna must have felt great fear in *AS1* too? Or would we be falling into anachronism, letting our reading be coloured by a text that did not exist when *AS1* was composed? I will not venture to give a definite answer to these questions here, but I will suggest that *AS2*, as well as being an intrinsically interesting text in its own right, is a valuable companion to reading *AS1*. The author of *AS2* can be seen as an insightful literary critic of *AS1* and comparison of *AS1* and *AS2* can generate useful questions and ideas.

The *AS2* version of the Well of the Women episode provides us with more details about the death of Niamh.[33] When she is confronted by her father and his men, she expresses regret, imagining in vivid detail the future destruction of her kinspeople as a result of her actions:

> *"Monúar," ol sí, "nach bás fuaros sul do-chífinn*
> *m'athair cona thríar mac, m'oide, mo dhá*
> *chomhdhalta, ꝼ maithe Mumhon ol-cheano 'gā*
> *cciorbhadh ꝼ 'gā ccnāimh-ghearradh gan choiccill*
> *acc curadhaibh calmo coimhneartmhora Fhían*
> *Éireann trēm fhochonn ꝼ trēm acois budhdhéin."*[34]

---

[31] Parsons, "The Structure," 33. For more discussion of the precocious theism of Fionn, see Sìm Innes, "Fionn in Hell," *Scottish Gaelic Studies* 29 (2013): 21-53.

[32] For discussion and Irish examples, see Emma Nic Cárthaigh, "*Tús na heagna omhan Dé*: Penance and Retribution in a Poem by Aonghus Fionn Ó Dálaigh", in *Sacred Histories: A Festschrift for Máire Herbert*, ed. John Carey, Kevin Murray and Caitríona Ó Dochartaigh (Dublin: Four Courts Press, 2015), 269-90, at 272-3.

[33] This episode is found in Ní Shéaghdha (ed.), *Agallamh*, ii, 118:20-125: 5.

[34] *Agallamh*, 119:27-120:3.

"Alas," she said, "that I did not die before seeing my
father with his three sons, my foster-father, my two
foster-brothers, and the nobles of Munster hacked and
cut to the bone mercilessly by the brave, equally
strong warriors of the Fianna of Ireland because of
me."

The emotion that caused Niamh's death is then named:

> *[T]ucc a haghaidh re lár ₇ re lán-talmhuin ionnus go
> ffuair bás fō chéadōir d'fhéle ₇ do náire, ₇ nocha
> déarna aoinbhean don bhanntracht gan bhāsughadh
> fān ccuma chēadna.*[35]

She put her face to the ground and to the very earth so
that she died immediately of shame and humiliation
and no woman of the retinue went without dying in
the same fashion.

The words *féle* and *náire* used in the line above are synonymous,
both meaning shame: such pairing is a common stylistic feature of
Early Modern Irish prose. The emotional cause of Niamh's death is
brought out more in *AS2* than in *AS1*: here, the emotion of shame is
named at the moment of death, whereas in the manuscript witnesses
to *AS1* (discussed above), it is mentioned later on by Niamh's father
when he enters into dispute with the Fianna, or not at all. In *AS1*,
Niamh vomits blood when she dies: it is possible that this is a medical
detail that indicates a fatal imbalance of the bodily humours in
Niamh.[36] It is impossible to say whether this detail was left out
deliberately in *AS2* or not, but any loss of drama caused by its absence

---

[35] *Agallamh*, 120:4-8.

[36] Ranke de Vries has recently drawn attention to scenes in *AS1* that indicate
the author's familiarity with medieval medical practice: "Medieval
Medicine and the Healing of Caílte in *Acallam na Senórach*," *North
American Journal of Celtic Studies* 5, no. 1 (2021): 49-82. She notes that
vomiting is seen as unnatural: de Vries, "Medieval Medicine," 61. It is also
possible to read Niamh's death scene as containing an unstated pun based
on another Irish word for shame, *imdergad*, the literal meaning of which is
"making red": Niamh is both shamed and possibly made red (covered in
bloody vomit). See *Electronic Dictionary of the Irish Language* (*eDIL*), 3rd
ed. (2014-2019), s.vv. "imdergad" and "imm-derga," accessed December
20, 2021, dil.ie/27464 and dil.ie/27806.

is made up for by Niamh's vision of her relatives being hacked to death. The author of *AS2* seems to take more of an interest in the battle that could have been: we get a brief glimpse of it in Niamh's vision, and another scene in which the Fianna prepare for the battle is more detailed than in *AS1*. In *AS1*, we are simply told that the Fianna arrayed themselves for battle, whereas *AS2* devotes thirteen lines to a description of their preparations.[37] It must be noted, however, that we also find an extended description of the battle preparations in the UCD-OFM, MS A4 witness to *AS1*.[38] Battles do feature in all Cnoc an Áir-related narratives that belong to the later Finn Cycle, as we shall see.

Cath Chnoic an Áir: A Lay on the Battle of the Hill of the Slaughter

The next Finn Cycle text to feature a place called the Hill of the Slaughter is the lay known as *Cath Chnoic an Áir* (The Battle of the Hill of the Slaughter, henceforth referred to as CCÁ1) or *Laoi Thailc mhic Treoin* ("The Lay of Tailc mac Treoin"). The earliest copies date to the seventeenth century. One of these is in Adv. MS 72.1.48, a Scottish manuscript associated with the MacMhuirich family of poets and written by an unidentified scribe after 1660.[39] The earliest copy by an Irish scribe is in the Giessen Irish MS written by Domhnall Ó hEidirsceoil in Louvain in 1684.[40] The language of the lay does not contain archaic features and it may even have been composed in the

---

[37] Stokes (ed.), "*Acallamh*," ll. 3014-5 (drawing here on Laud Misc. 610); Ní Shéaghdha (ed.), *Agallamh*, ii, 122.11-23.

[38] UCD-OFM, MS A4, 41, column b, l. 51-41[a], column a, l. 5.

[39] A digitized copy and a catalogue description by Ronald Black are available on Irish Script on Screen, accessed December 20, 2021, https://www.isos.dias.ie/. The text is printed in *Reliquiae Celticae: Texts, Papers, and Studies in Gaelic Literature and Philology Left by the Late Rev. Alexander Cameron, L.L.D.*, ed. Alexander Cameron, Alexander MacBain, and John Kennedy, 2 vols. (Inverness: Northern Chronicle, 1892-4), i, 137-9.

[40] See Ludwig Christian Stern, "Notice d'un Manuscrit Irlandais de la Bibliothèque Universitaire de Giessen," *Revue Celtique* 16 (1895): 8-30. This copy of the lay is incomplete. For an early and complete Irish copy, see that of RIA MS 23 M 29 written by Eoghan Ó Caoimh in the years 1684-1707.

seventeenth century. There is little difference between early Scottish and Irish copies of the lay.[41]

At the beginning of *CCÁI*, Oisín tells Saint Patrick that the hill to the west of them is known as Cnoc an Áir and that this name was given for good reason. Oisín tells the tale as follows. A beautiful woman named Niamh Nuachrothach came one day to Fionn and the Fianna, asking them to protect her.[42] She has been betrothed against her will by her father, the king of Greece, to the monstrous Tailc mac Treoin who has two ears, a tail, and a cat's head. Soon after Fionn promises to protect Niamh, Tailc arrives and seeks battle. The Fianna send hundreds of men to fight him, but they are all killed. Oscar asks for Fionn's permission to engage in single combat with Tailc. They fight nonstop for five days and five nights until Oscar finally slays Tailc. When Niamh sees the extent of the slaughter, she is filled with shame and dies, falling among the other dead. The hill is then named the Hill of the Slaughter by the Fianna.

CCÁI is clearly an independent composition, and not a reworking of material from *AS*, but I will argue here that the composer of *CCÁI* took inspiration from *AS*. The Well of the Women episode in *AS*, in particular, seems to have had some influence on *CCÁI*: in both narratives, we have a woman named Niamh who is experiencing marriage-related troubles (a socially unsanctioned coupling/an unhappy match), dying of shame in front of a group of military men (the King of Munster and his troops/Fionn and the Fianna) after gaining awareness of the consequences of her actions (elopement/fleeing from marriage), and a scene of mass killing on a hill which becomes subsequently a memorial toponym.

Another episode in *AS* which portrays the death of a woman named Niamh on a battlefield and thus, may also be linked to *CCÁI*, is one which Stokes named "The Story of Oscar's First Battle."[43] Here, Caoilte sits on a mound near Lough Croan (in present-day Co. Roscommon) with Patrick and tells him of the battle which took place on a plain there. It was fought over Niamh, daughter of the king of Ulster, who was promised to the son of the king of Connacht. Caoilte

---

[41] A later, longer version of *Cath Chnoic an Áir* which I discuss below is found in Irish manuscripts only.

[42] She is called Niamhan Nuachrothach in Adv. MS 72.1.48.

[43] Stokes (ed.), "*Acallamh*," ll. 1020-64.

recites a poem attributed to Fionn in which he incites Oscar to action and then another poem that gives details of some of the warriors killed by Oscar, including both Niamh's father and her husband to be. Niamh's death on the battlefield is also mentioned:

> *Tainic d'féchain in chatha/Niamh an éduigh ildatha,*
> *mebhuis in cath ana cenn/marbhthar in ríghun*
> *roithenn.*[44]

> To view the battle Niamh of the many-coloured
> vesture came:
> the battle's rout bursts full upon her, and the tenacious
> queen is slain.[45]

We are told little else about Niamh's death: the focus in this episode is on Oscar's heroism rather than on her fate. In UCD-OFM, MS A4, on the other hand, more details are given of Oscar and Niamh's relationship and the cause of the battle: *Leandān d'Oscur mac Oisīn hí, 7 tuc rí Condacht tar a sārughadh hí 7 ba hé sin adhbhar in chatha* (She was a darling of Oscar son of Oisín and the king of Connacht took her against her will and that was the cause of the battle).[46] *AS2* similarly places more emphasis on Oscar's love of Niamh:

> *"Searc adhbhal-mhór tuccustar Osccar do Néimh*
> *inghine Dhuinn mheic Fhearghusa Finn .i. d'inghin*
> *rí Uladh," ol Oisín, "₇ tucc Aodh mac Finn mhic*
> *Fhionntain, .i. mac rí Connacht, hí tar thoil*
> *Osccair."*[47]

> "Oscar gave great love to Niamh, the daughter of
> Donn son of Fearghus Fionn, that is to say to the
> daughter of the king of Ulster," said Oisín, "and Aodh
> son of Fionn son of Fionntan, that is to say the son of
> the king of Connacht, took her against Oscar's will."[48]

---

[44] *"Acallamh,"* ll. 1055-6.

[45] O'Grady (ed.), *Silva Gadelica*, ii, 127.

[46] I am quoting here from Ní Shéaghdha (*Agallamh*, i, 20.7-20.9) where material from UCD-OFM, MS A4 is used to fill a lacuna in RIA MS 24 P 5.

[47] Ní Shéaghdha (ed.), *Agallamh*, i, 84.5-84.9.

[48] Oisín is the narrator in *AS2*.

Looking at the Well of the Women episode and Oscar's First Battle together, one might wonder whether there is any significance to the fact that both Oisín and Oscar, father and son, have tragic love affairs with women named Niamh: it might lead us to consider the similarities between them, but, if *CCÁ1* took inspiration from both episodes, this distinction is elided there.[49] The two *AS* narratives could not be said to be doublets as their structures are different: the story of Oscar's First Battle is closer to that of CCÁ1 than the aithed structure of the Well of the Women episode. Dooley and Roe describe the tale of Oscar's First Battle as "one of the many tragic betrothals" in *AS* and this theme is common in the later lays as well.[50] In terms of details, the main differences between Oscar's First Battle and *CCÁ1* are that:

1. Oscar has an affective bond with Niamh in *AS* but not in *CCÁ1*;

2. in *AS*, the opponents of the Fianna are human and Irish, whereas Tailc is a monster from a foreign land;

3. more attention is paid to the death of Niamh in *CCÁ1* than in the *AS* episode; and

4. the tone of the *AS* episode with its focus on Oscar's heroism is triumphal, whereas the lay, despite presenting Oscar as a hero, dwells also on the heavy loss of life.

The latter two differences–the emphasis on Niamh's death and the mournful tone–might have been influenced by the Well of the Women episode. Dáithí Ó hÓgáin suggested that the composer of *CCÁ1* drew on another *AS* episode, one named "The Story of the Ridge of the Dead Woman," which features a woman who comes from overseas to the Fianna fleeing a man she does not wish to marry.[51] Ó

---

[49] The fame of Niamh Chinn Óir who stars in the eighteenth-century *Laoi Oisín ar Thír na nÓg* ("The Lay of Oisín in the Land of Youth") has now outshone that of all other literary Niamhs. Máirtín Ó Briain argues that this character was modelled on Niamh Nuachrothach of *CCÁ1*: "Some Material on Oisín in the Land of Youth," 193.

[50] Dooley and Roe (trans.), *Tales*, 232.

[51] Dáithí Ó hÓgáin, *Fionn mac Cumhaill: Images of the Gaelic Hero* (Dublin: Gill and Macmillan, 1988), 222-4; Stokes (ed.), "*Acallamh*," ll. 5917-6082.

hÓgáin also suggests that the cat's head of Tailc mac Treoin may have been inspired by the dog-headed invaders that feature in the separate Finn cycle tale of *Cath Fionntrágha*.[52] *CCÁ1* is thus a good example of an author combining elements from separate narratives from *AS* and possibly elsewhere in an imaginative way, creating a new and original poem in the process.

I will turn now to the main features of *CCÁ1*. In common with the narrative of Oscar's First Battle, Oscar's heroism is to the forefront in *CCÁ1*. In the lay *Eirigh suas, a Oscair* ("Rise up, Oscar"), which forms part of Oscar's First Battle in *AS*, Fionn expresses great confidence in his grandson's martial abilities.[53] In contrast, Fionn in *CCÁ1* grants Oscar permission to engage in single combat with Tailc but worries that he will be killed.[54] Concision is a feature of *CCÁ1* as we see with the combat between Tailc and Oscar, which, despite lasting five days and nights, is covered in the space of a single quatrain.[55] Similarly, the killing of a thousand of the Fianna by Tailc is noted but not described in any detail.[56] The devastating nature of the battle is portrayed less through the depiction of violence and more through the emotional responses of witnesses. The strongest reaction is that of Niamh, who dies of shame at the sight of the destruction:

> *Niamh Nua-chruthach, mór an scéal*
> *nuair dochonnairc méid an áir,*
> *gabhas náire an ghruadh-dhearg-ghlan*
> *is tuiteas marbh ameasc cách.*[57]

---

[52] Ó hÓgáin, *Images*, 224.

[53] Stokes (ed.), "*Acallamh*," ll. 1032-43. This lay appears as an independent poem in Duanaire Finn: *Duanaire Finn: The Book of the Lays of Fionn*, ed. Gerard Murphy, vol. 2, Irish Texts Society 28 (London: Irish Texts Society, 1933), poem lii.

[54] *Laoithe na Féinne*, ed. Pádraig Ó Siochfhradha [An Seabhac] (Dublin: Clólucht an Talbóidigh, 1941), 31, quatrain 75. Ó Siochfhradha's edition represents the longer version of the lay *Cath Chnoic an Áir* discussed below, but as all quatrains from the short version are found in the longer version, I refer to his edition here.

[55] *Laoithe na Féinne*, 31, quatrain 79.

[56] *Laoithe na Féinne*, 31, quatrain 72.

[57] *Laoithe na Féinne*, 31, quatrain 81.

Niamh Nua-chruthach, a great tale,
when she saw the extent of the slaughter,
the lady of the fair rosy cheeks was seized with shame
and she fell dead among all the rest.

The response of the Fianna, in contrast, is far more moderate:

Tógaimíd trí gártha ós árd
tar éis an chomhraic ba gharbh gleac –
gáir chaointe tré a ndeachaidh den Fhéinn
is dhá gháir mhaoidhte tré éag Thailc.[58]

We give three loud cries
after the combat of the rough struggling–
a mourning cry for all the Fianna who died and two
vaunting cries over the death of Tailc.

Some of the difference in the emotions of the Fianna and Niamh
is due to plot reasons: Niamh can be seen as a wrongdoer because she
has disobeyed her father by refusing the match made by him for her
(even if the audience might be sympathetic to her wish not to marry a
monster), whereas the Fianna are doing their duty by aiding Niamh
and fighting Tailc on her behalf. The Fianna would not be expected to
feel shame in this context: indeed, it would be shameful for them to
refuse to help Niamh. But, a more interesting difference is the
regimented way the Fianna regulate their emotions: their sorrow,
potentially a debilitating emotion, is expressed in unison in a
controlled and contained manner; furthermore, it is outweighed by
their joy at defeating their enemy, but this emotion again is not
excessive. The contrast between the Fianna, men and soldiers, and
Niamh, a woman not trained in military activities, is striking. There
are hints in this lay that the Fianna's emotional discipline takes hard
work to maintain and they are clearly not impervious to disquieting
emotion: we see this in Fionn's fear at the thought of Oscar's death
and again, at the end of the lay, when Oisín states that the Fianna were
greatly affected by Niamh's death.[59] While *CCÁ1* is short and
entertaining, it features a number of weighty themes: anxieties about
women and marriage; emotional responses to death and slaughter;

---

[58] *Laoithe na Féinne*, 31, quatrain 80.
[59] *Laoithe na Féinne*, 31, quatrain 82, ll. 1-2.

ambivalence about heroism and fighting; the problem of excessive loss of life on the battlefield. There are many copies in the later manuscripts, attesting to its enduring popularity. It also inspired engagement by tradition bearers, many of whom expanded on the narrative it contains: all texts discussed in the rest of this article derive to some extent from CCÁ1.

The Cnoc an Áir Narrative Strand in *Agallamh Oisín agus Phádraig*

A longer version of the lay *Cath Chnoic an Áir* (henceforth *CCÁ2*) is found in Irish manuscripts dating from the end of the eighteenth century. *CCÁ2* is usually embedded within a version of *Agallamh Oisín agus Phádraig* (The Dialogue of Oisín and Patrick), the earliest copy of which is in Royal Irish Academy MS 23 C 15 written by Risteárd Ó Ciosáin, seemingly in Co. Kerry, in the years 1775–81.[60] In fact, the events at the Hill of the Slaughter and their aftermath can be described as forming the central narrative strand of this particular version of *Agallamh Oisín agus Phádraig*.

CCÁ2 is made up of the same quatrains as *CCÁ1*, with extra material added, including a prelude to the battle. *CCÁ2* begins with the Fianna at leisure on a hilltop.[61] One of them, referred to as *Draoi Teamhrach* (The Magician of Tara), tells Fionn that he has seen bloody clouds in the sky, indicating that destruction lies ahead. The Fianna observe the clouds: some of the men are unperturbed whilst

---

[60] See Síle Ní Mhurchú, "*Agallamh Oisín agus Phádraig*: Composition and Transmission," in *The Gaelic Finn Tradition*, ed. Sharon J. Arbuthnot and Geraldine Parsons (Dublin: Four Courts Press, 2012), 195-208. There are other versions of *Agallamh Oisín agus Phádraig* where the story of the battle at Cnoc an Áir and related events do not feature or feature to a lesser degree.

[61] *Laoithe na Féinne*, 24. The best-known editions and translations of CCÁ1 and CCÁ2 are discussed in Ní Mhurchú, "*Agallamh*: Composition," 206-8. More information on editions and translations can be found by consulting: Risteárd de Hae and Brighid Ní Dhonnchadha, *Clár Litridheacht na Nua-Ghaedhilge, 1850-1936: 1. Na Leabhra* (Dublin: Oifig Dhíolta Foillseacháin Rialtais, 1938); Risteárd de Hae, *Clár Litridheacht na Nua-Ghaedhilge, 1850-1936: 2. Filidheacht i dTréimhseacháin* (Dublin: Oifig Dhíolta Foillseacháin Rialtais, 1939); Richard Sharpe and Mícheál Hoyne, *Clóliosta: Printing in the Irish Language, 1571-1871* (Dublin: Dublin Institute for Advanced Studies, 2020).

others fall into gloom. Oscar is confident that the Fianna are strong enough to defeat any threat and Conán taunts those who are fearful. Some of the Fianna are less supportive of Fionn than might be expected. Oscar, for example, says he will watch for the arrival of the enemy, but questions the appropriateness of Fionn's desire to sleep at this time: Fionn must explain to him that he expects to gain knowledge of the coming peril while he sleeps. Other men state that they will help Fionn, but on condition that they are not sent to work alone. When Fionn sleeps, he does indeed dream of the enemy: he sees two men of the Fianna, Aodh Beag mac Finn and Goll mac Mórna, beheaded by Tailc mac Treoin. The Magician interprets his dream for him: Aodh and Goll will not die, but the Fianna will face a dreadful attack. Shortly afterwards, an enemy is glimpsed. But first, Niamh Nuachrothach arrives on the scene, as in *CCÁ1*, and the account of the battle with Tailc is identical.

This prelude draws out a theme that appears briefly in the Well of the Women episode from *AS*: potential disunity within the Fianna when some are less keen than others to engage in fighting. This is a common theme, however, and its appearance here does not necessarily derive from *AS*.[62] Fionn is shown to be at the mercy of other members of the Fianna: the warriors do not obey his orders unquestioningly and the character of Draoi Teamhrach seems to be a more effective prognosticator than he is; the Fianna are also divided in their reaction to the sight of the bloody clouds. Some of this prelude seems to have been inspired by yet another episode from *AS*: a tale told by Caoilte which explains why a particular hill is known as *Cnoc in Eoluis* (The Hill of Knowledge).[63] Caoilte relates that a magician named Coinnillsciath was with Fionn on this hill and that at the sight of three

---

[62] I omit from this discussion some details of CCÁ2, such as comedy based around the character of Conán and stanzas of dialogue between Oisín and Patrick.

[63] This narrative features in an episode named "The Story of Cnocc ind eolairi or Cnocc in eolais" by Stokes ("*Acallamh*," ll. 7559-96). Cnoc an Eolais, also known as Cnoc an Eolaire, lies to the northwest of Rathcroghan in present-day Co. Roscommon. No other reference to a hill of either these names is noted in Pádraig Ó Riain, Diarmuid Ó Murchadha and Kevin Murray, *Historical Dictionary of Gaelic Placenames Fasc. 5 (Clais an Chairn-Cnucha)* (London: Irish Texts Society, 2013), s.nn.

noxious clouds in the sky, one clear, one grey, one red, he foretold of future destruction, grief and bloody battle at the site of a bruiden made by Fothad Canainne.[64] Draoi Teamhrach corresponds to Coinnillsciath of *AS*: other common features of the two scenes are coloured clouds spotted on a hill, Fionn's dependence on a magician for their interpretation, and the prediction of future slaughter.[65] It might be tempting to see here an equivalence being made between two enemies of Fionn–Fothad Canainne and Tailc mac Treoin–but this would be anachronistic, as Fothad Canainne (or Fatha Canann as he is called) is a member of the Fianna in the later tradition.[66]

AS does not depict the slaughter predicted by Coinnillsciath: the purpose of the episode of the Hill of Knowledge is to explain a placename, and when that explanation is provided, the text moves on elsewhere. Indeed, this battle narrative may never have existed: Rolf Baumgarten proposed that the idea of the slaughter may be based on a misunderstanding of a verbal form in the earlier tale *Bruiden Átha Í*, which treats of the longstanding feud between Fionn and Fathad Canann.[67] A curious feature of Coinnillsciath's verse interpretation of the clouds is that it features the names of Niamh and Tailc, in the form of the noun *niamh* (lustre, brilliance) and the adjective *tailc* (strong):[68] these are relatively rare words, and one wonders if their presence in that poem might have inspired the composer of *CCÁ2* to borrow

---

[64] The word *bruiden* can refer to a banqueting hall or a quarrel. See *eDIL*, s.vv. "1 bruiden" and "2 bruiden," accessed December 20, 2021. Rolf Baumgarten reads this as being a hostile encounter: "Placenames, Etymology, and the Structure of *Fianaigecht*," *Béaloideas* 54/55 (1986/1987): 1-24, at 11.

[65] On cloud prognostication in Irish literature, including *AS*, see Mark Williams, *Fiery Shapes: Celestial Portents and Astrology in Ireland and Wales 700-1700* (Oxford: Oxford University Press, 2010), 40-51. Draoi Teamhrach does not appear in any other lay, to my knowledge, apart from a brief appearance in *Laoi Mheargaigh na Lann*, which continues the narrative begun in *CCÁ2*: see discussion below and Ó Siochfhradha, *Laoithe*, 32, quatrain 7.

[66] See Murray, *The Early Finn Cycle*, 157-9.

[67] Baumgarten, "Placenames, Etymology," 12. Kevin Murray dates *Bruiden Átha Í* to the late eighth or early ninth century: *The Early Fenian Corpus* (Cork: Cork Studies in Celtic Literatures, 2021), 4.

[68] See Stokes (ed.), "*Acallamh*," l. 7588 and l. 7590.

elements of this scene of cloud prognostication. Overall, this prelude is a very effective addition, as it provides a sense of foreboding to the events that follow.

After Niamh's death in *CCÁ2*, Meargach na Lann comes to avenge the death of Tailc mac Treoin in a lay which is called *Laoi Mheargaigh na Lann* (henceforth *ML*).[69] The encounter between the Fianna and Meargach mirrors their encounter with Tailc. As at the beginning of *CCÁ2*, Fionn must negotiate with the men before the battle and some of them are hesitant to offer him their full support. There is a great deal of fighting in *ML*: a single combat between one Caoinléith of the Fianna and one of Meargach's men takes up some ten quatrains, and an account of single combat between Oscar and Meargach is fifty-one quatrains long.[70] After Meargach is killed, two of his sons turn up and kill many of the Fianna before they are defeated in turn. This is followed by two more single combats between Faolán of the Fianna and two of Meargach's men. The slaughter only stops when Áille Shnua-Gheal, Meargach's wife, arrives on the scene and demands to know what happened to her husband and two sons. When she finds their corpses on the battlefield, she appears to be in the throes of death. Unlike Niamh, however, she regains her composure and sings a lament for her dead. The composer of *ML* clearly had an interest in combat: perhaps there is an effort here too to compensate for the lack of detail in the account of the fight between Tailc and Oscar. The effect of this sequel to the first battle at the Hill of the Slaughter is that it introduces a cycle of revenge: more characters are drawn into conflict with the Fianna, and the number of killings increases greatly.

The next section of the Cnoc an Áir narrative strand, often given the title *Laoi Mhná Mheargaigh* ("The Lay of Meargach's Wife") or *Caoineadh Áille Shnua-Gheal* ("The Lament of Áille Shnua-Gheal"),

---

[69] Edited in Ó Siochfhradha, *Laoithe na Féinne*, 32-53. In the earliest copies of *Agallamh Oisín agus Phádraig* in which the Cnoc an Áir narrative strand appears, the whole text is written continuously without titles: there is discussion of how it was presented in some manuscripts in Síle Ní Mhurchú, "*Agallamh Oisín agus Phádraig*: Léamha ón bParaitéacs," *ComharTaighde* 2 (2016), § 12.

[70] Ó Siochfhradha (ed.), *Laoithe na Féinne*, 37-8, quatrains 62-71; 43-7, quatrains 121-72.

is unusual in that two female characters are given a prominent role: Áille, the widow of Meargach, and Gráinne, who is presented here as defending the honour of the Fianna.[71] We frequently find scenes of lament (most often by men) in Finn Cycle texts, but Áille's lament is unusual because the dead men were enemies: it can be interpreted as a sign of the magnanimity of the Fianna that they allow the widow to speak. The lament runs to some thirty-four quatrains: Áille praises the dead men, expresses her sorrow, recalls the signs that showed her their death was imminent, and condemns the treachery of the Fianna.[72] This lament is similar in content to the *caointe* (laments) of historical women, except that it is in syllabic metre rather than the accentual *caoineadh* (lament) metre.[73]

Áille's lament is interrupted by Gráinne, who cannot countenance her reproach of Fionn. Gráinne's sudden appearance at Cnoc an Áir may seem surprising as she is not mentioned before then, but there is good reason for it when we consider that conflict between women was a feature of the lamenting tradition.[74] Gráinne can dispute Áille's words, whereas the men of the Fianna doing the same might come across as abnormal or brutish behaviour. Consideration of the wider lamenting tradition enrichens our understanding of Áille's lament. Another example is a brief description of Áille pulling out her hair when she reaches the bodies of the dead:[75] female keeners are consistently depicted as having their hair in disarray and thus, a culturally-aware reader or listener can see here that Áille has entered

---

[71] This lay is edited in Ó Siochfhradha, *Laoithe na Féinne*, 54-63.

[72] *Laoithe na Féinne*, 54-7, quatrains 1-28 and 31-6.

[73] See, for example, the *caointe* of the seventeenth-century Caitilín Dubh of County Clare: "Courts and Coteries II: c. 1500-1800", ed. Máirín Ní Dhonnchadha, in *The Field Day Anthology of Irish Writing, Volume IV: Irish Women's Writings and Traditions*, ed. Angela Bourke et al. (Cork: Cork University Press, 2002), 358-457, at 399-405; for further background, see "Lamenting the Dead," ed. Angela Bourke, in *The Field Day Anthology of Irish Writing*, 1365-97.

[74] See discussion in Sorcha Nic Lochlainn, "A Pan-Gaelic Perspective on the Oral Lament," in *Lorg na Leabhar*, ed. Breatnach, Ní Úrdail, and Ó Riain, 447-80, at 455.

[75] *Laoithe na Féinne*, 53, quatrain 34b.

into a state of mourning.[76] A further useful insight from the lamenting tradition is the idea that interruptions, and often mockery, of a lamenting woman could be protective, in that it could help her move from a potentially dangerous level of grief towards a different emotion, anger.[77] This would seem to be the case in our lay, as Gráinne's intervention stops Áille dwelling on her grief and leads to an argument between the two women about whether the Fianna killed Meargach and his sons justly.[78]

Because Áille will not relent, a third battle takes place on the Hill of the Slaughter. In its initial stages, this battle is led by Áille and Gráinne: they each call out thirty warriors, most of whom are subsequently killed. Gráinne offers to let Áille and her surviving soldiers leave unharmed, but Áille refuses. Fionn declares an all-out battle: the Fianna are victorious, but they lose some six hundred men. Gráinne and Fionn are shown to be more reasonable than Áille: they both offer to drop the conflict, but Áille is determined to fight to the end. When the battle is over, she leaves the scene with the three of her soldiers that survived. Oisín states that this was the hardest battle they ever fought and, echoing the end of *CCÁ1*, states that this is why the hill was called the Hill of the Slaughter.

In the next part of this narrative strand, Oisín, at the request of Patrick, names some of the warriors of the Fianna who were killed at the Hill of the Slaughter: this lay is often called *Anmanna na Laochra a Thit ar Chnoc an Áir* ("The Names of the Warriors who Fell on the Hill of the Slaughter") or similar.[79] Oisín names nearly fifty warriors, mentioning the heroic traits of many of them. These are, of course, only a small proportion of the hundreds of men killed on the Hill of the Slaughter, and Oisín concludes with a statement to that effect. These warriors are, to borrow a term from Star Trek fandom, "red shirts," that is to say stock characters who die soon after their appearance (or, in this case, have already died by the time they are named). They do not have backstories or distinguishing traits. The inclusion of this list of names may have different purposes: first of all,

---

[76] See Angela Partridge, "Wild Men and Wailing Women," *Éigse* 18, no. 1 (1980): 25-37, at 29-30.

[77] See Nic Lochlainn, "A Pan-Gaelic Perspective," 456-7.

[78] *Laoithe na Féinne*, 57-59, quatrains 37-59.

[79] Edited in Ó Siochfhradha, *Laoithe na Féinne*, 64-5.

it provides some balance to Áille's lament of three enemies; secondly, it conveys the destruction of the slaughter, even if it is impossible to depict it fully; and thirdly, the heroic traits associated with the dead reflect the values of the Fianna. While the Cnoc an Áir narrative strand under discussion here devotes a great deal of attention to combat, it also shows a preoccupation with mourning and memorialising the dead.

There is one more lay that deals with the repercussions of the events at the Hill of the Slaughter: *Seilg Sléibhe Fuaid* ("The Hunt at Sliabh Fuaid").[80] Here, Áille attempts to avenge herself on the Fianna once more. She and her brother Draoidheantóir trap the Fianna in a magical fortress. This is a long lay with many twists and turns: suffice to say that, at the end, Áille dies of fright when Conán frees the Fianna from the spell that has kept them in a debilitated state, and Draoidheantóir is beheaded by Oscar soon afterwards. While the battles at Cnoc an Áir can be said to be less fantastical, in that the Fianna draw on their strength and military know-how rather than magic, most of the action of *Seilg Sléibhe Fuaid* takes places in a strange, otherworldly realm, giving it a different atmosphere. Oisín states that the Fianna never recovered fully from the spell that was put on them.[81] The cycle of revenge that began with the first Battle at the Hill of the Slaughter is linked here to the very demise of the Fianna: the events at the Hill are more than a painful memory or an example from which a lesson can be learned, and we see the existential danger posed by inordinate thirst for violence and retribution. Oisín's statement here does not necessarily contradict the widespread tradition that associated the demise of the Fianna with another great battle, the

---

[80] For an edition of *Seilg Sléibhe Fuaid*, see: Ó Siochfhradha, *Laoithe*, 93-110. In the context of *Agallamh Oisín agus Phádraig*, this lay is set apart from the other lays just discussed: see Ní Mhurchú, "*Agallamh*: Composition," 196-7; 199-200. Other lays are more loosely associated with the Cnoc an Áir sequence of battles. For example, the lay *Seilg Locha Léin* ("The Hunt at Loch Léin") takes place after the Fianna leave Cnoc an Áir, but there is no specific connection between the events of that lay and the battles: Ó Siochfhradha (ed.), *Laoithe na Féinne*, 66-73.

[81] *Laoithe na Féinne*, 110, quatrain 195.

Battle of Gabhair:[82] it can be understood that the Fianna's weakness meant that they were not as strong in that battle as they might otherwise have been.

The version of *Agallamh Oisín agus Phádraig* that contains the Cnoc an Áir narrative strand was popular: there are over eighty manuscript copies of it, dating from the late eighteenth and the nineteenth centuries and mostly belonging to Munster. Judging by their language and metrical features, the Cnoc an Áir-related narratives do not seem to be very old and may indeed have been composed in the eighteenth century.[83] There is no doubt but that the person or people who composed this narrative strand were inspired by *CCÁ1*, engaging with it and expanding it in order to make it the first event in a longer series of events that would threaten the very existence of the Fianna. While the dramatic potential of combats and other struggles is very much realised in these lays, this is balanced by depictions of sorrow and mourning, and the enemies' insatiable hunger for revenge is shown to be deleterious to all concerned.

A Prose Version of *Cath Chnoic an Áir*

Munster was not the only place where *CCÁ1* inspired further composition: we also have an expanded version from Ulster in the tale known as *Eachtra Thailc mhic Thréun go hÉirinn agus Tóruigheacht na Callaigh as Innse Toirc* ("The Adventure of Tailc mac Tréun to Ireland and the Pursuit of the Hag from Inis Toirc," henceforth *ETT*).[84] The beginning of this tale is similar to *CCÁ1*, but wordier and with extra details added. For example, the single combat between Oscar and Tailc, which is depicted in one stanza in *CCÁ1* (see above), runs to thirty-eight lines of prose in *ETT*.[85] Before this combat, Niamh mentions that it pains her to see so many dead men and that there are

---

[82] See Anja Gunderloch, "The Cath Gabhra Family of Ballads: A Study in Textual Relationships," 2 vols. (PhD thesis, University of Edinburgh, 1997).

[83] Some material in this version of *Agallamh Oisín agus Phádraig* is older: see Ní Mhurchú, "*Agallamh*: Composition," 201-2.

[84] Edited in *Sgéalta Rómánsuíochta*, ed. Máire Ní Mhuirgheasa and Séamus Ó Ceithearnaigh (Dublin: Oifig an tSoláthair, 1952). For some discussion, see Ó hÓgáin, *Images*, 267-9.

[85] Ní Mhuirgheasa and Ó Ceithearnaigh (eds.), *Sgéalta*, 249-51, ll. 6748-85.

streams in her native land that can revive the dead. As in the lay, Niamh dies after Oscar's victory. The corpses of the dead are piled together with Niamh on top and fragrant plants and herbs are placed on them to preserve them: Cnoc an Áir is the name given to this place. The titular Hag from Inis Toirc then arrives and demands to know who killed Tailc, whom we later learn was her foster-son (*dalta*). She places a magical injunction (*geasa*) on Oscar and the other men of the Fianna who were injured in the battle to follow her to her own home, so that she can avenge Tailc's death. This is made more complicated by the fact that the Fianna do not know her name or where she lives. They go on a long expedition overseas during which they meet Niamh's parents who, after Oscar proves his valour to them, are happy for him to marry her. Niamh and the dead Fianna are revived, and the Hag is found and defeated. The Fianna return home with Niamh, and there the tale ends.

ETT did not make as great an impact as the Cnoc an Áir lays: only one manuscript copy exists, MS Ó Tuathail 1, held in St. Malachy's College, Belfast.[86] This manuscript was written by Arthur Bennett (1793-1879) of Ballykeel, Forkhill, Co. Armagh for Éamann Mac Aonghusa (c.1821-1877), a baker and businessman of Newry, Co. Down.[87] In a colophon written before *ETT*, Bennett stated that he was copying from a manuscript written by Arthur Brownlow in 1729, which cannot be correct as Brownlow died in 1712.[88] Ruairí Ó hUiginn suggests that Bennett may have found a copy of *CCÁ1* in an old manuscript and that he himself may have composed the prose

---

[86] See Ní Mhuirgheasa and Ó Ceithearnaigh (eds.), *Sgéalta*, vii-viii; Breandán Ó Buachalla, *I mBéal Feirste Cois Cuain* (Dublin: An Clóchomhar, 1968), 289, no. 17; Pádraig de Brún, *Lámhscríbhinní Gaeilge: Treoirliosta* (Dublin, Dublin institute for Advanced Studies, 1988), 9 and 48, fn. 80.

[87] See Ó Buachalla, *I mBéal Feirste*, 289, and *An Bunachar Náisiúnta Beathaisnéisí Gaeilge* (*ainm.ie*), s.n., accessed December 20, 2021, https://www.ainm.ie/Bio.aspx?ID=1104.

[88] See discussion in: Ní Mhuirgheasa and Ó Ceithearnaigh (eds.), *Sgéalta*, viii-ix; and Ruairí Ó hUiginn, "An Nua-Rúraíocht," in *Diasa Díograise: Aistí i gCuimhne ar Mháirtín Ó Briain*, ed. Mícheál Mac Craith and Pádraig Ó Héalaí (Indreabhán: Cló Iar-Chonnachta, 2009), 387-412, at 394-5.

version.[89] Another indication of our tale's late date may be a fight scene which has elements in common with the Welsh *Hanes Taliesin* ("The Tale of Taliesin"): I suggest that the composer of *ETT* may have read the translation of Charlotte Guest.[90]

Hanes Taliesin features a transformation chase in which Gwion Bach and Ceridwen change themselves into different animals:[91] Gwion transforms into a hare, and Ceridwen becomes a greyhound in order to chase him; the chase continues in a river, with Gwion transforming into a fish and Ceridwen into an otter, and then in the sky, with Gwion transforming into a bird and Ceridwen becoming a hawk. Finally, when Gwion transforms into a grain of wheat, Ceridwen becomes a hen, eats the grain, and becomes pregnant. The child that Ceridwen gives birth to nine months later grows up to become the poet Taliesin. This transformation chase can be compared with the fight scene between the Fianna and the Hag in *ETT*.[92] A female magician gives three peas to Goll mac Mórna, Oscar, and Diarmaid, which they are to use to defeat the Hag and two giants who live with her. They go to the Hag's island, and Goll fights the first giant. When Goll is about to kill the giant, the giant turns himself into a salmon and jumps into a lake. Goll throws his pea where the giant last stood and an otter appears who eats the salmon. Oscar fights the second giant, who turns himself into a deer. Oscar throws his pea, and a hound appears who kills the deer. Diarmaid fights the Hag and she turns herself into a dove to escape. A hawk appears where Diarmaid throws his pea, and that hawk kills the dove. These two scenes from *Hanes Taliesin* and *ETT* tell of very different events–conception and

---

[89] Ó hUiginn, "An Nua-Rúraíocht," 395, 400. Compare this to Ní Mhuirgheasa and Ó Ceithearnaigh's view that this tale is older than ML and *Laoi Mhná Mheargaigh* (discussed above): *Sgéalta*, xiii.

[90] Guest's translations of the *Mabinogi* and related material, including *Hanes Taliesin,* appeared in a number of volumes, beginning in 1835: Rachel Bromwich, "*The Mabinogion* and Lady Charlotte Guest," in *The Mabinogi: A Book of Essays*, ed. C.W. Sullivan III (New York: Garland, 1996), 3-18, at 7-8. Modern editions and translations of the *Mabinogi* do not usually include *Hanes Taliesin.*

[91] See Charlotte Guest, *The Mabinogion: From the Welsh of the Llyfr Coch o Hergest (The Red Book of Hergest) in the Library of Jesus College* (London: Bernard Quaritch, 1877), 472-3.

[92] Ní Mhuirgheasa and Ó Ceithearnaigh (eds.), *Sgéalta*, 282-8.

combat–but the similar transformations and the magical pea/grain may point to some line of influence of the former on the latter.[93] This apparent borrowing from a Welsh text may reveal pan-Celtic sentiment on the part of the Irish author, or it may simply be that he recognised the dramatic potential of the transformation chase when he saw it.

Another theme found in *ETT* which appears in some of the other Cnoc an Áir narratives is Fionn's lack of authority: at the beginning, he is confident that the Fianna will be victorious, but some of the members of Clanna Mórna are skeptical. Conflict between Fionn and Clanna Mórna is common, of course, but here, Fionn's usually loyal hound, Bran, also undermines him: after Fionn declares that he will protect Niamh, Bran gives a hard tormented scream (*sgread chruaidh chráidhte*).[94] Overall, however, the role of Fionn is marginal in this tale, as he does not take part in the overseas adventure. Oscar is the hero, and in the second part of the tale, Clanna Mórna and Clanna Baoiscne are mostly cooperative. The Cnoc an Áir narratives discussed up to this point might be seen as presenting a negative view of women who often cause trouble for the Fianna, but this tale is different. While the Hag is a ferocious enemy, the Fianna twice benefit from the wisdom of women in *ETT*: first, from Niamh, who informs them of the possibility of reviving the dead men, and secondly, from a female magician who is able to reveal the Hag's identity and location after a group of male magicians fail to do so. The possibility of reviving the dead means that *ETT* is less gloomy the lays.[95] *ETT* is a rollicking and enjoyable read, and the different strands of the narrative

---

[93] Transformation combats are found elsewhere in Irish literature and folklore, of course: see Tom Peete Cross, *Motif-index of Early Irish Literature*, Folklore Series 7 (Bloomington: Indiana University Publications, 1952), 113-4. However, I know of none that has as much in common with the fight scene of *ETT* as the chase of Ceridwen and Gwion in *Hanes Taliesin* does.

[94] Ní Mhuirgheasa and Ó Ceithearnaigh (eds.), *Sgéalta*, 244, l. 6609.

[95] Revival of the dead occurs in some Finn Cycle texts: see Pádraig Ó Héalaí, "Trí Scéal Fiannaíochta ó Thomás Ó Criomhthain," *Irisleabhar Mhá Nuad* (2015): 195-245, at 239. More often than not, however, death is final.

are woven together adeptly, suggesting that its author was a skilled writer.

Cnoc an Áir Narratives in Irish Folklore

Cnoc an Áir narratives are richly attested in the folklore collections: twenty-three separate items are categorised as "Cath Chnoc an Áir/Eachtra Thailc mhic Thréun go hÉirinn" in Natasha Sumner's "Catalogue of Fenian Folklore", and a further eight items are categorised as "Meargach na Lann/Laoi Mheargaigh na Lann".[96] I mentioned above that *CCÁ2* and *ML* are not always separated in the manuscripts and the same applies to the folklore sources: in some cases, both narratives or elements of both are combined in one text.[97] The lays *Laoi Mhná Mheargaigh*, *Anmanna na Laochra a Thit ar Chnoc an Áir* and *Seilg Sléibhe Fuaid* are not found in the folklore collections, but Áille's encounter with the Fianna, which belongs to the first of these lays, does appear at the end of some folklore versions of *CCÁ/ML*. The folklore versions display creative divergence and they are a testament to the vitality of the tradition at the time of collection.[98] Most of the folklore items are in prose form and some are in English; some are comprehensive accounts of the events at the Hill of the Slaughter, whilst others take the form of shorter anecdotes.[99] In

---

[96] Natasha D. E. Sumner, "A Catalogue of Fenian Folklore/Supplement to a Dissertation Titled 'The Fenian Narrative Corpus, c.600-c.2000: A Reassessment'" (Harvard University: Graduate School of Arts and Sciences, 2015), items 370-391, 2488 (*CCÁ*) and items 2410-17 (*ML*). In my discussion, I continue to use the acronyms *CCÁ1*, *CCÁ2* and *ML* for folklore versions; I also use the abbreviation *CCÁ* when not referring specifically to *CCÁ1* or *CCÁ2*.

[97] Sometimes, material from other Finn Cycle narratives is added but I omit discussion of such additions here. The twentieth-century folklore sources are in the form of manuscript notebooks but in my discussion here, I use the word manuscript to refer to the scribal manuscripts of the nineteenth century and earlier.

[98] I limit my discussion to the Irish folklore items as I have not been able to access the three Scottish versions of *CCÁ*: Sumner, *Catalogue*, items 389-91. I have also been unable to view two Irish items: 378 and 2417, versions of *CCÁ* and *ML* taken from the poet and storyteller Mícheál Ó Gaoithín.

[99] Sumner's *Catalogue* provides information on the language and form (poetry or prose) of each item.

some cases, the Hill is said to be in a specific place, usually not far from the location of the informant. A great deal of the folklore material comes from Co. Kerry. All *ML* items are from Kerry, with the exception of one from Co. Donegal and one from the Cork side of the Bearra peninsula. We have twelve *CCÁ* items from Kerry and one each from counties, Cork, Donegal, Clare, Limerick, Cavan and Leitrim. It is not possible to discuss all items in detail here, so I will focus on the following matters: real-world places associated with Cnoc an Áir; the treatment of the two female characters, Niamh and Áille; and the depiction of combat.[100]

Item 373 (NFC 353, 642–56) was collected in 1937 from Nóra Ní Mhaoilmhichíl from Ballylongford in North Kerry. The narrative follows that of *CCÁ1* but it is more expansive in style, with extra details about the thoughts of the characters, the manners of the Fianna, and more conversation between the characters. The portrayal of the battle is more elaborate and, while the heroism of the Fianna is stressed, so is the sorrow caused by the loss of so many men. Niamh dies of distress–shame is not named as the cause of her death here. The burial of Niamh and all the dead men is also depicted in more detail than usual, and the fact that the Fianna bury their enemies as well as their own men is said to be a sign of their gentility (*uaisleacht*).[101] It is surmised that, although the Fianna were not Catholics, they must have said some sort of prayer over the dead: "Is dócha go raibh a saghas paidreacha féin aco ó's cionn na marbh, ach níorbh Chaitlaicaidhthe a bhí ionnta an tam san d'réir seanchaídheachta."[102] This item is unusual in that the informant reflects more on the values and manners of the Fianna than in other renditions, both literary and

---

[100] I hope to take a more in-depth look at these folklore sources in a separate article. Sometimes, the names of the characters are changed or they are not named at all: I refer to the characters by the names they have in the earlier lays to avoid confusion. Items are referred to first by their number in Sumner, *Catalogue*, and then the source is given in brackets. NFC stands for the National Folklore Collection, University College Dublin. Manuscript volumes and page numbers are given for each of these. Manuscripts with an appended S (e.g., NFC S399) belong to the Schools' Collection compiled in Irish schools in the late 1930s.

[101] NFC 353, 652.

[102] NFC 353, 654: "They probably had their own sort of prayers above the dead, but they were not Catholics at that time according to the old stories."

oral. As in many folklore versions, the tale is connected to the local landscape. The Fianna placed a memorial stone above Niamh's grave and wrote "Lacka" on it: this monument, the informant states, still stands, and its location is the Hill of the Slaughter, a hill between Ballybunnion and Ballylongford that is now mistakenly called *Cnoc an Óir* (The Hill of Gold).[103] This is a reference to a local hill called *Cnoc an Fhómhair* (The Hill of the Harvest, anglicized Knockanore).[104]

References to Knockanore are also found in some other folklore versions collected in North Kerry. Item 380 (NFC S399, 39-40) was collected from an unnamed informant in the townland of Leansaghane in the parish of Kilconly, north of Ballybunnion, in 1938. It is a summary in English of *CCÁ2,* ending with the death of Niamh, the exact cause of her death remaining unspecified. An extra detail given, similar to Item 373, is that the top of the Hill of the Slaughter where the dead were buried is known as *Leac* ("flagstone"). Item 381 (NFC S400, 68-69) was taken from an unnamed informant in the same parish, Kilconly, and specifies that the hill is near Ballybunnion. Item 383 (NFC S401, 20) was taken from an unnamed informant in Killehenny, Ballybunnion. Here, the Hill of the Slaughter is northeast of Ballybunnion (as Knockanore is). There is mention of a cave ending in the local townland of Moohane, which Tailc entered when he landed in Ireland. The tradition linking Knockanore to the Hill of the Slaughter is clearly of long standing: we find mention of it in a poem by Seán Ó Braonáin (c.1784–c.1843) of Ballymacandrew, which is some twenty km to the south of Ballybunnion. In the opening verse of this poem, he is travelling "re ciúis Chnoic an Fhómhair,/san mbealach mar aithrisid údair/go raibh leadairt na lúithreach i ngleo/idir Mheargach mheanmnach lúthmhar/is an flaithbhile fionn, Oscar óg."[105] We also find the Hill of the Slaughter identified with places outside of Munster in folklore: an example is item 376 (NFC 1257,

---

[103] NFC 353, 654-6.

[104] See "Placenames," s.n., accessed December 20, 2021, https://www.logainm.ie/ga/1165819.

[105] *Filíocht Sheán Uí Bhraonáin*, ed. Pádraig de Brún (Dublin: Cló Bhréanainn, 1972), 122, ll. 2-6: "By the edge of Cnoc an Fhómhair,/along the way where authors say/there was hacking of sinews/between spirited agile Meargach/and the fair noble champion, young Oscar."

130-134), collected from Willie Kinsey of Kiltubbrid, Co. Leitrim in 1894, which is a prose telling in English which corresponds to *CCÁ1*, *ML* and *Caoineadh Áille*. Niamh dies of a broken heart on the Hill of Kildare when she sees all the slain men: this probably refers to the Hill of Allen in Co. Kildare, well-known as the home of Fionn. Áille's death is depicted here: when she sees the bodies of her husband and sons, she falls "on the body of her husband with a wailing keen" and expires.[106]

Tomás Ó Criomhthain, author of the first Blasket Island autobiography, *An tOileánach*, wrote Item 370 (NFC 34, 294a-294e) himself in 1928, with the expectation that it would be published.[107] Some of the lines correspond to CCÁ1 and, in Pádraig Ó Héalaí's edition, these are arranged as verse.[108] Here, when Tailc is killed, he transforms into a handsome man and Niamh, now feeling guilty for having caused his death, throws herself on one of the swords of the Fianna. Her death, then, is a suicide. The next section of this tale is unusual. Half of the Fianna are dead and Fionn is concerned. He chews his thumb and learns that there is a magic boar in west Kerry who sleeps every night at Baile an Chaladh, and that three drops of its blood could revive all the men. This seems to be Baile an Chalaidh on the mainland, not far from the Great Blasket Island: thus, we see in this item again a location in the narrative grafted onto a place in the informant's locality.[109] A quest to revive the dead is only found in this item and in *ETT* discussed above, but Ó Criomhthain's account of the quest only runs to a few lines, whereas the overseas expedition in *ETT* is nearly fifty pages long in the printed edition. It is possible, however, that both reflect a development of the narrative that is otherwise not attested. While the quest is successful in Ó Criomhthain's telling, Fionn decides not to revive Niamh, as he thinks she would only endanger the Fianna again. The posthumous transformation of Tailc from monster to handsome man is mentioned in a quite a few of the folklore sources and also in a colophon to a manuscript copy of *CCÁ2* in BL MS Add. 27,946, which was written by Eoghan Caomhánach in

---

[106] NFC 1257, 133.
[107] Ó Héalaí, "Trí Scéal Fiannaíochta," 200.
[108] Ó Héalaí, "Trí Scéal Fiannaíochta," 239.
[109] See "Placenames," s.n., accessed December 20, 2021, https://www.logainm.ie/en/22586.

1828 in counties Limerick and Clare, showing that this feature of the tale was also known in the early nineteenth century.[110]

We have two versions of *CCÁ2/ML* from Valentia Island that have some features in common with Ó Criomhthain's one. Item 374 (NFC 505, 304-315) was collected from Mícheál Ó Conchubhair in 1938. There is emphasis on the Fianna's fear of Tailc after he kills seven hundred of them. Tailc is transformed after death here too, and when Niamh sees how handsome he is, it frightens the life out of her. In this version, Oscar fears that Meargach has magic which would allow him to win the fight: this is a common concern in Kerry versions. Áille comes to Ireland hoping to make peace with the Fianna before Meargach is killed, but she is too late. It is interesting that Áille is represented as a peacemaker, in contrast to the lays discussed above where she is vengeful to the last. Item 385 (NFC S479, 35-39) was collected from an unnamed informant in Valentia c. 1934. This tale has some features in common with Item 374, such as Áille's desire to make peace with the Fianna. There are also some differences: for example, Tailc's posthumous transformation and Niamh's death are not depicted. In another Kerry source, Item 2488 (NFC S433 101-108), which was written by a teacher named Séamas Ó Luain (Callanafersy, Milltown), Tailc undergoes a posthumous transformation and Niamh stabs herself in the heart with a sword when she sees him. Thus, we find another depiction of Niamh killing herself. The idea of keeping Meargach from sleep being the key to defeating him is found in this telling, as in some other Kerry versions of *ML*.

The final items to be discussed are a number of those items classified as *ML* in Sumner's catalogue. We have three separate renditions from Mícheál Ó Cathaláin from An Gabhlán Ard, near Lispole, Co. Kerry. Items 2410 (NFC 14, 225-230) and 2411 (NFC 215, 66-74) were both collected c. 1933 and are very similar. These begin with Draoi Teamhrach warning of a bloody sign in the sky as in *CCÁ2*. Oscar fears that Meargach has supernatural powers, and Fionn later discovers that he must be prevented from sleeping if Oscar is to defeat him, a motif already met with above. When Áille arrives to lament Meargach, Oscar prevents Conán from killing her, cutting him.

---

[110] See Standish Hayes O'Grady, *Catalogue of Irish Manuscripts in the British Library [Formerly British Museum]*, vol. 1 (Dublin: Dublin Institute for Advanced Studies, 1992), 677.

Áille then mocks Conán and he attacks her.[111] The single combat between Meargach and Oscar is the focal point of this item and the events of *CCÁ1*, on the other hand, are only briefly alluded to. Item 2414 (NFC 376, 490-499) was collected from Mícheál Ó Cathaláin in 1937 and is slightly different to the other two versions of this narrative taken from him. For example, at the end of this text, when Meargach's wife arrives, Oscar protects her from Conán. Comparing this version with the other two from Ó Cathaláin allows us to see how storytellers can alter their tales by adding or removing elements and also reminds us that, in cases where we only have one telling from an informant (as is usually the case), the fact that a certain feature of tale is missing does not mean that the storyteller did not have it in his/her memory. We can also see how depictions of characters can change from telling to telling: Conán's attacking or killing of Meargach's wife in two versions from Ó Cathaláin is a cruel act going against the honour code of the Fianna, but this is absent in the third version.

Many of the oral versions of *CCÁ/ML* focus on combat, but while fighting allows for the Fianna to display their heroism and fortitude, it is clear that Tailc and Meargach's bloodlust is frowned upon. Niamh's death is covered in detail in some versions and glossed over in others, but generally she is treated with sympathy. Tomás Ó Criomhthain's version where Fionn decides not to revive Niamh is unusual, but it is in keeping with the idea, expressed sometimes in the Finn Cycle, that women cause strife and disunity among the men. Áille also emerges as sympathetic figure in the form of a tragic peacemaker in some oral versions, but we only find fragments of *Caoineadh Áille* in the folklore sources. Indeed, while all the Cnoc an Áir lays were common in the manuscripts, only some of them are attested in folklore. It is not surprising that a lay like *Anmanna na Laochra a Thit ar Chnoc an Áir*, which is a long list of names, might not be popular, but it is harder to explain why other lay narratives with plenty of action, such as the combats between Gráinne and Áille and then between Áille and all of the Fianna in *Caoineadh Áille* are not attested in oral sources. Perhaps the idea of women leading a battle did not appeal. *Seilg Sléibhe Fuaid* is a long lay in which dialogue between the characters preponderates over action, and that may be the reason why it is not represented in the folklore collections. This is informed speculation, but it is possible that

---

[111] Or possibly kills her: both texts are unclear here.

further investigation of the folklore sources will be able to shed further light on the question of why some lays from the manuscripts survived in oral tradition while others did not.

In folklore, there was clearly interest in placing Cnoc an Áir in a specific location. This was easily done as the minimum that is required is a hill. Donald Meek has discussed the "transferable toponomy" of the Fionn lays, that is to say the process by which a narrative, when transferred from one location to another, can graft its placenames onto the new location.[112] This process is clearly seen in the folklore versions. The association of Cnoc an Áir with Knockanore near Ballybunnion was certainly strong in Kerry, and while this is not usually mentioned in the manuscripts, it is notable that many of the early copies of *Agallamh Oisín agus Phádraig* featuring the Cnoc an Áir narrative strand were written in that county. It is possible that this narrative strand was composed in Kerry in order to build on an existing tradition associating Cnoc an Áir with Knockanore and to enhance the significance of this part of the country within the wider Finn Cycle. Here, again, we see the value of combining evidence from folklore and traditional manuscript sources, as the evidence for this is less forthcoming in manuscript sources alone.

Conclusion: Reading Finn Cycle Texts Across Time

This paper has looked at a range of Finn Cycle texts spanning some eight hundred years and all featuring places called Cnoc an Áir, many of which were shown to be linked to one another. Reading these makes for a fruitful experience, as we see themes that are merely hinted at in one text become prominent in a later one, or old stories on taking entirely new forms and styles. These narratives were composed in a great variety of circumstances, intended for audiences as different as the "lords and commons of later times" whom Patrick imagines would be entertained by the tales of *AS1*,[113] to the bourgeois

---

[112] Donald E. Meek, "Place-names and Literature: Evidence from the Gaelic Ballads," in *The Uses of Place-names*, ed. Simon Taylor (Edinburgh: Scottish Cultural Press, 1998), 147-68, at 164.

[113] In *AS1*, Patrick famously asked that the stories of the Fianna be preserved as entertainment (do dronguibh 7 do degdáinibh deridh aimsire:) Stokes (ed.), "*Acallamh*," l. 301; translation above from Dooley and Roe, *Tales*, 12.

nineteenth-century businessman Éamann Mac Aonghusa of Newry for whom our one extant copy of *ETT* was written, to the relatively modest and often marginalised communities from which much of the twentieth-century folklore was collected. While details of *tempus, locus, persona* and *causa scribendi* are unknown for many of the narratives discussed in this paper, it would be mistaken to see them all as being of a kind. Instead, they demonstrate the versatility and flexibility offered by the world of Fionn mac Cumhaill and his Fianna, which allowed people in a wide variety of social and historical circumstances to find meaning and enjoyment in it. In some of the cases discussed above, I have pointed out the value of reading Finn Cycle texts diachronically: *AS1*, for example, can be read without concern as to what came after, but comparison with *AS2* has the potential to generate new insights into both recensions. The connections I discussed between *AS* and *CCÁ1/CCÁ2* demonstrate the power of *AS* to inspire creativity in centuries long after it was first written. Looking at the lays of the manuscripts and their folklore equivalents also generated new thoughts about both traditions. While many of the texts discussed were transmitted carefully over time down to our own age, we also see new narratives emerging that are not the product of degeneration or misunderstanding of earlier tradition, but rather conscious artistic efforts that pick and choose from older material in an imaginative fashion, building on it, changing it, reflecting on it, or disregarding certain features of it, as new creators see fit. Comparative reading of Finn Cycle texts over time allows us to see continuities and changes in the tradition and is a generative process leading us to ask new questions about texts old and (relatively) new.

Distribution patterns of imperfect and preterite forms of perception verbs in Middle and Early Modern Welsh prose texts

Elena Parina and Luciana Cordo Russo

A grammar fact which often happens to be learned very early in the course of acquaintance with Middle Welsh is that perception verbs tend to be marked differently from action verbs in the narrative. The default past tense for action verbs in Middle Welsh prose is the preterite (marked on the verb or in the *gwneuthur*-construction), but perception verbs are often used in the imperfect tense. Thus, in a sentence found on the first page of the text of the First Branch of the *Mabinogi*, we read how Pwyll encounters the stag that is being chased by a pack of hounds:

> (Example 1) *Ac ual y byd yn ymwarandaw a llef yr erchwys, ef a glywei* [imperfect, 3. sing.] *llef erchwys arall, ac nit oedynt unllef, a hynny yn dyuot yn erbyn y erchwys ef. Ac ef a welei* [imperfect, 3. sing.] *lannerch yn y coet, o uaes guastat; ac ual yd oed y erchwys ef yn ymgael ac ystlys y llannerch, ef a welei* [imperfect, 3. sing.] *carw o ulaen yr erchwys arall.*[1]

> And as he was listening for the cry of his pack, he heard the cry of another pack, but these had a different cry, and they were coming towards his own pack. And he could see a clearing in the forest, a level field; and as his own pack was reaching the edge of the clearing, he saw a stag in front of the other pack.[2]

Glywei occurs once and *welei* twice in this sentence, and, as can be seen, they are translated in different ways in Sioned Davies's

---

[1] R. L. Thomson, ed., *Pwyll Pendeuic Dyuet* (Dublin: Dublin Institute for Advanced Studies, 1957), p. 1, lines 11-14.

[2] Sioned Davies, *The Mabinogion* (Oxford: Oxford University Press, 2007), 3. Unless otherwise stated, all translations of the *Mabinogion* tales are taken from this book; references are made to page numbers.

translation: *glywei* is rendered by "heard" while the two verbal forms *welei* are translated first by "he could see" and then by "saw."

However, when we look at Middle Welsh texts translated from other languages, such as Latin or French, we often find preterite forms of perception verbs in main clauses, as in the following examples:

(Ex. 2) *Odyna y g6elas* [preterite, 3. sing.] *pa6l g6yr a g6raged yn noethon.*[3]

Then Paul <u>saw</u> men and women naked.

Et <u>vidit</u> Paulus in alio loco viros et mulieres nudos.[4]

And Paul <u>saw</u> in another place naked men and women.

The verb *clywed* 'to hear' shows a similar behaviour to *gweled* 'to see', as the next example from *Cân Rolant* illustrates:[5]

(Ex. 3) *Ac ar hynny Oliuer a <u>giglev</u>* [preterite, 3. sing.] *t6ryf y pagannyeit. ac a'e menegis y rolond val hynn.*[6]

And then Oliuer <u>heard</u> the commotion of the pagans and expressed it to Rolond thus.

---

[3] *Breuddwyd Pawl*, LlA: 130v. All translations of the Welsh texts of the Book of the Anchorite and their Latin source texts are our own.

[4] Lenka Jiroušková, *Die Visio Pauli: Wege und Wandlungen einer orientalischen Apokryphe im lateinischen Mittelalter unter Einschluss der alttschechischen und deutschsprachigen Textzeugen* (Leiden, Boston: Brill, 2006), L7, 778.

[5] We refer to the lexemes by the forms of the verbal nouns as they appear in *Geiriadur Prifyscol Cymru* (GPC) entries.

[6] Diana Luft, Peter Wynn Thomas, and D. Mark Smith, eds., *Rhyddiaith gymraeg / Welsh prose 1300-1425*, http://www.rhyddiaithganoloesol.caerdydd.ac.uk, Peniarth 4, fol. 107v, col. 194, lines 30-32. The translation is our own. Although there is no equivalent line in the French-language source text, there is nonetheless a verb of hearing in the preterite attributed to the Franks: *Granz est la noise, si l'oïrent Franceis* (The noise is great and the Franks heard it). Ian Short, ed. and trans., *La Chanson de Roland* (Paris: Le Livre de Poche, 1990), line 1005; translation from Glyn Burgess, *The Song of Roland* (London: Penguin, 1990), line 1005.

DISTRIBUTION PATTERNS

Therefore, this paper will explore the distribution of imperfect and preterite forms of the perception verbs *gweled* 'to see' and *clywed* 'to hear' in Middle and Early Modern Welsh prose texts, both 'native' and translated (from Latin, French, and English source texts). First, we will briefly introduce the research on the language of texts translated into Welsh. Second, we will present our corpus and the data from native prose and various kinds of translated texts, and third, we will offer some interpretations and conclusions.

Linguistic features of translated texts

The particular distribution of preterite and imperfect forms of *gweled* and *clywed* in translated texts may be considered within the broader issue of the grammar of translated compositions. In the edition of the texts from *Llyfr yr Ancr*, the Book of the Anchorite, John Rhys states: "The texts, being translations, cannot be regarded as the best models for Welsh prose."[7] A further elaboration on this view of translations as 'second class literature' is found in the problematic concept *ôl cyfieithu* or "traces of translation" coined by Henry Lewis in 1925 and since then used by many scholars to refer to "externally motivated and arguably 'foreign' features"[8] (usually negative, in terms of 'faults') which flag the text as a translation, as opposed to those which characterise 'native' prose.[9]

---

[7] John Morris-Jones and John Rhŷs, *The Elucidarium and other tracts in Welsh from Llyvyr agkyr Llandewivrevi A.D. 1346 (Jesus college ms. 119)*, Anecdota Oxoniensia, Mediaeval and Modern Series 6 (Oxford: Clarendon Press, 1894), v.

[8] Elena Parina and Erich Poppe, *Translating devotion in medieval Wales. Studies in the texts and language of Llyfr Ancr Llanddewibrefi* (in preparation).

[9] On the style of translated and 'native' texts see also Diana Luft, "Awdur neu Dyallwr Ystoriau: Theori a Chyfieithiadau Cymraeg yr Oesoedd Canol," *Llenyddiaeth mewn theory* 1 (2006): 15-39, and "Tracking ôl cyfieithu: Medieval Welsh translation in criticism and scholarship," *Translation Studies* 9:2 (2016): 168-82, https://doi.org/10.1080/14781700.2015.1118404; Brynley Roberts, "Testunau Hanes Cymraeg Canol," in *Y Traddodiad Rhyddiaith yn yr Oesau Canol*, ed. Geraint Bowen (Llandysul: Gomer, 1974), 274-302, esp. at 289.

Diana Luft has brought together different lists of such traces of translation and the most frequently mentioned are:[10]

- verb-subject agreement: non-canonical plural agreement of verb and plural noun subjects
- agreement patterns and position of adjectives: high proportion of pre-posed adjectives and plural agreement noun-adjective.
- use of the pronouns *yr hwn, yr hon, y rhai* as relative pronouns,
- agreement patterns between antecedent and verb in relative clauses: non-canonical agreement of plural antecedents and verbs in the relative clause
- adjectives ending in *-edic* and derived abstract nouns in *-edigaeth* from the forms in *-edic*

Regarding the first feature, Plein (2018) examined verb-subject agreement and noticed that many texts, some of them translations, feature a higher frequency of non-canonical verbal agreement in relative clauses.[11] However, this variety in verb-subject concord patterns showed variation within the grammatical system of Middle Welsh and is not necessarily a "trace" of translation. She argued that it is associated with a specific, learned, or high register.

Regarding agreement patterns between nouns and adjectives and the position of adjectives, Meelen and Nurmio recently concluded that "no clear difference between native and translated texts appears from the comparison of absolute numbers of plural agreement examples. Instead, we see considerable variation between the texts, but not according to a clear-cut native vs. translated distinction."[12] Their study therefore suggests that translated texts should not be considered a uniform group.[13] This is true even within one manuscript: in the study of the texts in Llyfr yr Ancr, the Book of the Anchorite, Erich Poppe

---

[10] Luft, "Tracking *ôl cyfieithu*."

[11] Kerstin Plein, *Verbalkongruenz im Mittelkymrischen* (Hagen/Westf: Curach Bhán, 2018).

[12] Marieke Meelen and Silva Nurmio, "Adjectival Agreement in Middle and Early Modern Welsh Native and Translated Prose," *Journal of Celtic Linguistics 21* (2020): 1-28, at 11, https://doi.org/10.16922/jcl.21.2.

[13] As was also Luft's contention in "Awdur neu Dyallwr Ystoriau."

and Elena Parina witness a great variation between individual texts in the distribution of several traces of translation. They suggest that "traces of translation" should be considered with a neutral understanding of the term, as characterising a special register of translation between replication and transformation of the source text and as an expression of linguistic competence and creativity of medieval Welsh translators and redactors.

The use of 'native' narrative conventions is as important in the analysis of the translated texts as that of the 'foreign' features. Meelen analysed word-order patterns in native and translated texts.[14] She identified significant differences between individual translated texts, and although she did not find a clear-cut divide between native and translated texts in terms of word order patterns, she could demonstrate that there is more variety in basic word-order patterns among native prose tales than among translated texts, i.e. some options available in the language are rarely used in translated texts. With this background in mind let us now turn to a feature which has not yet entered these lists of differences between 'native' and translated texts: the tense marking of perception verbs.

Text corpus for this study

The corpus that we will discuss here consists of so-called 'native' and translated texts. The 'native' texts selected are the *Pedeir Keinc y Mabinogi* (*PKM,* the *Mabinogion*), *Peredur*, *Breuddwyd Macsen* (Macsen's Dream), and *Breuddwyd Rhonabwy* (Rhonabwy's Dream). Except for the latter, which is only extant in Oxford, Bodleian Library, Jesus College MS 111 (the Red Book of Hergest), dated to c. 1382- c. 1425, all the other texts are taken from Aberystwyth, National Library of Wales, Peniarth MS 4 (c. 1350).[15] We are well aware of the

---

[14] Marieke Meelen, *Why Jesus and Job spoke bad Welsh. The origin and distribution of V2 orders in Middle Welsh* (Utrecht: LOT, 2016), and "Comparing word order and information structure patterns in native and translated Middle Welsh prose," in Parina and Poppe, *Translating devotion in medieval Wales.*

[15] Our source for the Peniarth 4 texts is the Rhyddiaith Gymraeg website: Luft, Thomas, and Smith, *Rhyddiaith gymraeg.* The dates of the manuscripts are taken from Daniel Huws, *Medieval Welsh manuscripts* (Cardiff: University of Wales Press, 2000).

complex and hybrid nature of *Peredur*.[16] We have included a number of texts from the *Mabinogion* as defined by Lady Guest and Sioned Davies's translations, to ensure variation in our sample.

The translations examined are the texts from Llyfr yr Ancr or Book of the Anchorite, the Charlemagne cycle, and the *Gesta Romanorum*. Oxford, Bodleian Library, Jesus College MS. 119, better known from its colophon as Llyfr Ancr Llanddewi Brefi, the Book of the Anchorite of Llanddewi Brefi (henceforth LIA), It is a heterogeneous collection of religious texts, all of them translations with possibly one exception, the mystical *Ymborth yr Enaid* "The sustenance of the soul."[17] The scribe who compiled the manuscript in 1346 probably did not translate the texts himself, for they show signs of copying, and some are attested in earlier manuscripts. The Charlemagne cycle is composed of four texts: the Welsh *Ystorya Durpin* (Turpin's Chonicle), *Otuel, Cân Rolant* and *Pererindod Siarlymaen*. *Ystoria Durpin* is a translation of the Latin *Historia Turpini* or *Pseudo-Turpin Chronicle* and frames (in the majority of the extant manuscripts) the rest of the tales, which are renditions of French-language epic poems: the story of *Otinel, La Chanson de Roland* (of which only an incomplete Welsh version survives), and the *Pèlerinage de Charlemagne*, respectively. Most of the translations were produced in the thirteenth century except *Otuel*, which was probably composed early in the fourteenth century. The tales are preserved in seven medieval manuscripts: Aberystwyth, National Library of Wales, Peniarth MSS 8i, 8ii, 7, 9, 10, 5, and the aforementioned Red Book of Hergest.[18] Our examples are drawn from

---

[16] For a recent discussion of *Peredur* see Ceridwen Lloyd-Morgan, "*Historia Peredur ab Efrawg,*" in *Arthur in the Celtic Languages. The Arthurian Legend in Celtic Literatures and Traditions*, ed. Ceridwen Lloyd-Morgan and Erich Poppe (Cardiff: University of Wales Press, 2019), 145-56.

[17] See Idris Llewelyn Foster, *The Book of the Anchorite*. Sir John Rhŷs memorial lectures 1949 (London: Geoffrey Cumberlege for the British Academy, 1950).

[18] For an overview of the Welsh Charlemagne cycle see Erich Poppe, "Charlemagne in Ireland and Wales: some preliminaries on transfer and transmission," in *Rittersagas: Übersetzung - Überlieferung - Transmission,*

Peniarth MS 5 which, together with MS 4, forms the well-known White Book of Rhydderch.

One text in our sample lies beyond the Middle Welsh period and represents Early Modern Welsh. The *Gesta Romanorum*, a collection of tales with a moralizing purpose, is found in Welsh in one manuscript, Aberystwyth, National Library of Wales, MS 13076 B (Llanover B 18), dated to the end of the sixteenth or beginning of the seventeenth century.[19] This collection of narratives, ultimately of Latin origin, was translated into Welsh from English at some point in the sixteenth century, the exact source remaining unclear, since it shows affinities to both the Wyncyn der Worde editions published from 1510 to 1557, as well as to the new Protestant version published by Richard Robinson in 1595.[20]

The data

For our study we have searched for all the third person singular forms of *gweled* and *clywed* in the imperfect, *gwelei* and *clywei* respectively, and the preterite forms *gwelas*, *gweles*, and *gwelodd*, and *kigleu* and *clywas*, taking into account all possible orthographical variants and mutated forms. We have then provided for the examples containing these forms information on the type of clause in which the form is used (main clause vs. subordinate clause). Where possible, we have included the corresponding passage in the supposed source text.[21]

The distribution of the forms in *PKM* is clear-cut: the imperfect forms of gweled are predominantly used in main clauses (17 tokens against 1), whereas preterite forms prevail in subordinate clauses (10 tokens against 1), as the following table shows:

---

ed. Jürg Glauser and Susanne Kramarz-Bein (Tübingen: Francke, 2014), 169-190, and Annalee Rejhon, ed. and trans., *Cân Rolant. The Medieval Welsh Version of the Song of Roland*, University of California Publications in Modern Philology, 113 (Berkeley and Los Angeles: University of California Press, 1984).

[19] We follow Williams's edition: Patricia Williams, *Gesta Romanorum* (Cardiff: University of Wales Press, 2000).

[20] Elena Parina, "The 'Glamorgan School of Translation': A No Politics Phenomenon?" in *Politiken des Übersetzens*, ed. Antje Flüchter, Andreas Gipper, Susanne Greilich and Hans-Peter Lüsebrink (Stuttgart: J. B. Metzler, in preparation).

[21] The full dataset is available at https://doi.org/10.17192/fdr/84 .

PKM	Main clause	Subordinate clause	Total
imperfect	17	1	18
preterite	1	10	11
Total	**18**	**11**	**29**

Table 1: Distribution for *gweled* in *Pedeir Keinc y Mabinogi*

We provided an example of the use of the imperfect in main clauses at the beginning of this article (Ex.1). Illustrative cases for the three other contexts are given next [1-3].

Preterite in subordinate clause [1: Ex. 4]:

(Ex. 4) *a phan 6elas ẏ meichat lli6 ẏ dẏd. ef a deffroes 6ẏdẏon. a chẏuodi a 6naeth g6ẏdẏon a guisca6 amdana6 a dẏuot ẏ·gẏt a seuẏll 6rth ẏ creu.* (Fourth Branch, 27v, 107, 9-14)[22]

When the swineherd <u>saw</u> daylight he woke Gwydion, and Gwydion got up and dressed and went with him and stood beside the pen. (p. 62)

The following cases are exceptions to this tendency (the use of the imperfect in main clauses);

Imperfect in subordinate clause [2: Ex. 5]

(Ex. 5) *ac ẏ aber alau ẏn talebolẏon ẏ doethant ẏ'r tir. ac ẏna eisted a 6naethant a gorfo6ẏs. Edrẏch oheni hitheu ar i6erdon ac ar ẏnẏs ẏ kedẏrn a 6elei ohonunt. Oẏ a uab du6 heb hi guae ui o'm ganedigaeth. da a d6ẏ ẏnẏs a diffeith6ẏt o'm acha6s i a dodi ucheneit ua6r a thorri ẏ chalon ar hẏnnẏ. a g6neuthur bed petrual idi a'e chladu ẏno ẏ glan ala6.* (Second Branch, 15r, 57, 25–36)

---

[22] All the examples are quoted, with minor editorial modifications, from Luft, Thomas, and Smith, *Rhyddiaith Gymraeg*; references are to text, folio, column and line numbers.

> They came ashore at Aber Alaw in Talebolion. And
> then they sat down and rested. She looked at Ireland
> and at the Island of the Mighty, what she <u>could see</u> of
> them. "Oh son of God," she said, "woe that I was ever
> born. Two good islands have been laid waste because
> of me!" (p. 33)

This particular case could be explained by the strong modal semantics of the context in which the imperfect form appears: Branwen cannot see the whole island but only a part of it from her viewpoint–hence, possibly, the selection of the non-default verbal tense in the subordinate clause.

Preterite in main clause [3: Ex. 6].

> (Ex. 6) *a chan ỳ geir h6nn6 mynet allan. ac ỳ tra6s ỳ*
> *managassei ef uot ỳ g6r a'r gaer kỳrchu a 6naeth*
> *hitheu Porth ỳ gaer a 6elas ỳn agoret nỳ bu argel*
> *arnei. ac ỳ mý6n ỳ doeth ac ỳgỳt ac ỳ doeth arganuot*
> *prỳderi ỳn ỳmauael a'r ca6c a dỳuot atta6.* (Third
> Branch, 18r, 70, 33-18v, 71, 5)

> And with those words out she went, going in the
> direction he had told her Pryderi and the fort could be
> found. She found [<u>saw</u>] the gate of the fort open–it
> was ajar–and in she came. As soon as she entered she
> discovered Pryderi gripping the bowl, and she went
> up to him. (p. 40)

The use of the imperfect and preterite of gweled in *Peredur* also agrees with the pattern found in *PKM*. This text has the highest number of gweled tokens in the corpus due to the character of story.

Peredur	Main clause	Subordinate clause	Total
imperfect	52	1	53
preterite	2	3	5
Total	**54**	**4**	**58**

Table 2: Distribution of *gweled* in *Peredur*

A short passage from the text will suffice to show the widespread employment of the imperfect in main clauses to introduce the many things that *Peredur* sees in his travels:

(Ex. 7) *ac ar diben ẏ mẏnẏd ef a <u>welei</u> dẏffrẏn cr6n. a gororeu ẏ dẏffrẏn ẏn goeda6c karrega6c. a g6astat ẏ dẏffrẏn oed ẏn weirglodeu. a thired ar. ẏr6g y g6eirglodẏeu a'r coet. ac ẏ mẏnwes ẏ coet ẏ g6elei tei duon ma6r anuana6l eu g6eith. a disgẏnnu a wnaeth ac arwein ẏ varch tu a'r coet ac am talẏm o'r coet. ef a <u>welei</u> ochẏr carrec lem. a'r fford ẏn kẏrchu ochẏr ẏ garrec. a lle6 ẏn r6ẏm 6rth gad6ẏn ac ẏn kẏscu ar ochẏr ẏ garrec. a ph6ll d6fẏn athrugar ẏ veint a <u>welei</u> dan ẏ lle6. a'e loneit ẏnda6 o escẏrn dẏnẏon ac anifeileit.* (37r, 145, 26-146, 5)

At the far end of the mountain he <u>could see</u> a round valley, and the edges of the valley were wooded and stony, and on the floor of the valley were meadows, and ploughed land between the meadows and the forest. In the heart of the forest he <u>could see</u> large, black houses, roughly built. He dismounted and led his horse towards the forest. And at some distance in the forest he <u>could see</u> a steep rock, and the road leading to the side of the rock, and a lion tied to a chain, sleeping by the rock. He could see a deep pit, of huge proportions, below the lion, filled with the bones of men and animals. (p. 82)

In addition, the two dreams, *Breuddwyd Macsen* and *Breuddwyd Rhonabwy*, display the same distribution of imperfect and preterite forms: the predominant use of imperfect forms in main clauses and the employment of preterite forms in subordinate clauses. As the table below shows, *Breuddwyd Macsen* is, not surprisingly, particularly rich in gweled forms, due to the character of the text.[23]

---

[23] For a recent discussion of these two dreams in the context of medieval Welsh dream literature see Xiezhen Zhao, "Dreams in Medieval Welsh Literature" (PhD diss., Cardiff University, 2021), esp. 64-86.

DISTRIBUTION PATTERNS

Breuddwyd Macsen	Main clause	Subordinate clause	Total
imperfect	25	1	26
preterite	3	7	10
Total	28	8	**36**

Table 3: Distribution for *gweled* in *Breuddwyd Macsen* (Macsen's Dream)

Imperfect forms of gweled in main clauses cluster mostly in the first part of the tale, in Macsen's Dream, as the following cases illustrate:

> (Ex. 8) *ac velly y kysc6ys maxen. ac yna y g6elei vreid6yt. Sef breid6yt a welei. Y vot yn kerdet dyffryn yr auon hyt y blaen. ac y vynyd uchaf o'r byt y deuei. ef a tebygei uot y mynyd yn gyfuch a'r awyr.* (45v, 179, 22–8)

> and so the emperor slept. And then he had a dream [he could see a dream]. This was his dream [This was the dream he could see], that he was travelling along the river valley to its source until he came to the highest mountain he had ever seen, and he was sure that the mountain was as high as the sky. (p. 103)

As expected, preterite forms appear in subordinate clauses:

> (Ex. 9) *6ynt a welynt g6ladoed ma6r g6astat. a phrif auonyd ma6r tr6ydunt yn kerdet. Ilyma heb 6ynt y tir a welas yn hargl6yd ni. (46v, 184, 29-33)*

> As they crossed over that mountain they saw great, level plains and great, wide rivers flowing through them. Then they said, "This," they said, "is the land that our lord saw." (p. 106)

The three preterite forms in main clauses pose an interesting question, since they all appear in the context of the actual journey following Macsen's vision and the arrival at Eudaf's court:

(Ex. 10) *Pẏ watwar a wne6ch i amdanaf i. Na wna6n argl6ẏdes un g6atwar amdanat. Namẏn amhera6dẏr rufein a'th <u>welas</u> tr6ẏ e hun.* (47r, 185, 36-40)

"Why are you mocking me?" "Lady," they said, "we are not mocking you at all. But the emperor of Rome <u>saw</u> you in his sleep." (p. 107)

(Ex. 11) *ac ẏ doeth racda6 ẏ'r gaer ac ẏ'r neuad. ac ẏ <u>g6elas</u> ẏno kẏnan vab eudaf ac adeon vab eudaf ẏn g6are ẏr 6ẏdb6yll.* (47r, 186, 38-47v, 187, 1)

He came into the castle and into the hall, and there he <u>saw</u> Cynan son of Eudaf and Gadeon son of Eudaf playing gwyddbwyll, (pp. 107-8)

(Ex. 12) *ac a <u>welas</u> eudaf vab carada6c ẏn eisted ẏ mẏ6n kadeir o asc6rn ẏn torri g6erin ẏr 6ẏdb6yll.* (47v, 187, 2-4)

and [he <u>saw</u>] Eudaf son of Caradog sitting in a chair of ivory, carving pieces for the gwyddbwyll. (p. 108)

The contrast between imperfect and preterite forms in main clauses makes us wonder whether there is a marked difference between seeing in a dream and seeing in the 'real life' of the narrative. However, the last instance of gweled seems to contradict this idea:

(Ex. 13) *Y vor6ẏn a welas tr6ẏ e hun ef a'e <u>g6elei</u> ẏn eisted ẏ mẏ6n ẏ gadeir eur.* (47v, 187, 5-7)

The maiden he had seen in his sleep, he <u>could see</u> sitting in a chair of red gold. (p. 108)

Furthermore, *Breuddwyd Rhonabwy* fits nicely into the pattern described for the 'native' prose tales, as the following table demonstrates:

Breuddwyd Rhonabwy	Main clause	Subordinate clause	Total
imperfect	10	0	10
preterite	0	1	1
Total	10	1	**11**

Table 4: Distribution for *gweled* in *Breuddwyd Rhonabwy*

DISTRIBUTION PATTERNS

One instance of the use of the imperfect in main clauses will suffice to illustrate the ten examples found:

(Ex. 14) *Ac odyna y g6elei vydin a g6isc purdu am bop un onadunt. A godreon pob ỻenn yn purwynn. ac o penn eu d6ygoes a thal eu deulin y'r meirch yn purwynn. (136v, 562, 12-15)*

Then Rhonabwy could see a troop, and each man wearing a pure black garment with pure white fringes, and from the tops of the horses' forelegs and their kneecaps downwards, they were pure white. (p. 219)

The single example of the preterite appears in a subordinate clause:

(Ex. 15) *ac ual yd oedynt yn dechreu y symut kyntaf ar y g6are. Sef y g6elynt ruthur y 6rthunt pebyll brychuelyn m6yhaf o'r a welas neb a del6 eryr o eur arna6. a maen g6erthua6r ym penn yr eryr. (137r, 565, 27-32)*

As they were beginning the first move in the game, they could see a short distance from them a mottled yellow tent, bigger than anyone had ever seen [saw], with an image on it of an eagle made of gold, and precious stones in the eagle's head. (p. 221)

Data from Llyfr Ancr Llanddewi Brefi

In the whole corpus of LlA, 35 examples of third singular forms of *gweled* in imperfect or preterite are found.[24]

Llyfr Ancr LB	Main Clause	Subordinate Clause	Total
imperfect	10	5	15
preterite	10	10	20
total	20	15	35

Table 5: Distribution for *gweled* in the whole Llyfr Ancr Llanddewi Brefi

---

[24] The examples were checked on morphologically annotated files: Elena Parina, Raphael Sackmann, Marieke Meelen, and Erich Poppe. "PoS-Tagged Middle Welsh Texts from Oxford, Jesus College MS. 119." (2018) https://data.uni-marburg.de/handle/dataumr/5.2.

In contrast to the distribution found in native texts discussed above, the number of preterite forms used in main clauses is equal to that of imperfect forms–if one counts the examples from the whole manuscript together. We know, however, from the study of other grammatical phenomena (structure of relative clauses, use of derivatives in -edig, verb-subject agreements),[25] that texts in LlA vary significantly. It therefore makes sense to evaluate some of them separately. Some texts behave similarly to native texts: for example, *Marwolaeth Mair* (one of the Welsh versions of the *Transitus Mariae*, the text on the Assumption of the Virgin Mary), in which the imperfect is used once in a main clause and preterite twice in subordinate clauses:

Transitus	**Main Clause**	**Subordinate Clause**	**Total**
imperfect	1	0	1
preterite	**0**	2	2
total	**1**	2	**3**

Table 6: Distribution for *gweled* in *Marwolaeth Mair (Transitus Mariae)*

(Ex. 16) *Ac yna y g6elei yr ebestyl y heneit yn gynn gannheidyeit ac na allei nep ry6 dyn mar6a6l datkanu a'e daua6t y thecket. (Marwolaeth Mair, (72v, 25-73r, 2)*[26]

And then the apostles saw/could see her soul of such whiteness that no mortal man could discuss with his tongue its beauty.

Viderunt autem apostoli animam eius tanti candoris esse, ut nulla mortalium lingua digne possit effari[27]

---

[25] See Parina and Poppe, *Translating devotion in medieval Wales.*

[26] Quotations from LlA are also drawn from Luft, Thomas, and Smith, *Rhyddiaith Gymraeg*; references are to text, folio number, and lines.

[27] Haibach-Reinisch, Monika, *Ein neuer "Transitus Mariae" des Pseudo-Melito: textkritische Ausgabe und Darlegung der Bedeutung dieser urspruenglicheren Fassung für Apokryphenforschung und lateinische und deutsche Dichtung des Mittelalters,* Bibliotheca Assumptionis B. Virginis Mariae 5 (Rome: Pontificia Academia Mariana Internationalis, 1962), 76.

The apostles <u>saw</u> how her soul was of such whiteness that no mortal tongue could worthily describe [it].

(Ex. 17) *A phann <u>weles</u> hi ef wylya6 a oruc o le6enyd. A dy6edut vrtha6 val hynn.* (*Marwolaeth Mair,* 71r, 1-3)

And when she <u>saw</u> him she wept from joy and said to him like this.

Videnseque eum Maria, coepit prae gaudio flere et dicere[28]

As Maria saw him, she started weeping from joy and saying

Other texts differ significantly. As can be expected from the genre, a dream (*visio*), the text in which *gweled* is most frequently employed is *Breuddwyd Pawl*, a Welsh translation of *Visio Pauli*. In this text *gweled* is used in 3sg form only in main clauses, five times in imperfect form and seven in preterite.

(Ex. 18) *Ac edrych a oruc pa6l o bell y vrtha6, ac ef a 6elei eneit pechadur yn r6ym gann seith gythreul 6edy'r d6yn yr a6r honno o'r corff, ac ynteu yn g6eidi ac yn vda6. (Breuddwyd Pawl, 131r, 5-8)*

And Paul looked afar off, and he <u>saw/could see</u> a sinner's soul bound by seven devils newly taken, at that hour, from the body, while he shrieked and howled.[29]

Post hoc asspexit longius, <u>vidit</u> animam peccatricem inter septem diabolos ululantem et exeuntem de corpore eo die.[30]

After that he looked far off and <u>saw</u> a sinner soul between seven devils howling and coming out of the body this day.

---

[28] Haibach-Reinisch, Ein neuer *"Transitus Mariae"*, 70.

[29] Robert Williams, Selections from the Hengwrt Mss. Preserved in the Peniarth Library, vol. II, with the assistance of G. H. Jones (London: Bernard Quaritsch, 1892), 636.

[30] Jiroušková, *Die Visio Pauli*, L[8], 784.

(Ex. 19) *Ac yna y g6elas pa6l y nef yn kyffroi.*
(*Breuddwyd Pawl*, 131v, 16)
And there Paul <u>saw</u> the heavens stir.[31]
Et tunc Paulus <u>vidit</u> celum subito moveri.[32]
And then Paul <u>saw</u> the sky suddenly stir.

Interestingly, there is manuscript variation among the three codices in which the text is preserved: Peniarth 3 and Llanstephan 27 feature the imperfect, while Peniarth 14 agrees with LlA in the use of the preterite in this sentence:[33]

> *Ac yna y <u>gwelei</u> Bawl y nef yn kyfroi* (Peniarth 3, part ii, p. 28, 32-p. 29, 1)
> *ac yna y <u>g6elei</u> pa6l y nef yn kyffroi* (Llanstephan 27, p. 54r, 14-15)
> *Ac yna y <u>gweles</u> y nef yn kyffroi* (Peniarth 14, p. 159, 9-10).

Unfortunately, we do not have enough information on the relationship of the versions, so we cannot state which form, imperfect or preterite, was used in the Ur-translation.

The relevant forms of the verb clywed, however, are found in *Breuddwyd Pawl* only in imperfect in main clauses (three times):

> (Ex. 20) *Ac yna y <u>kly6ei</u> pa6l llef mil o viloed o engylyon yn lla6enhav 6rtha6. Ac yn dy6edut.*
> (*Breuddwyd Pawl*, 131r, 20–22)

> And then Paul <u>heard</u> the voice of thousands of thousands of angels rejoicing over/could hear him, and saying:[34]

> Et <u>audivit</u> vocem milium angelorum letancium pro ea et dicencium:[35]

> And <u>heard</u> the voice of thousands of angels rejoicing about it and saying:

---

[31] Williams, *Selections from the Hengwrt Mss.*, 637.
[32] Jiroušková, *Die Visio Pauli*, L8, 822.
[33] The next examples are also taken from Luft, Thomas, and Smith, *Rhyddiaith Gymraeg*.
[34] Williams, *Selections from the Hengwrt Mss*, 637.
[35] Jiroušková, *Die Visio Pauli*, C5, 800.

DISTRIBUTION PATTERNS

The data of LIA show us, therefore, that while translated texts might exhibit some deviations from the distribution observed in native prose, they vary considerably in the extent to which they follow the Latin patterns of their models. In this sense, we can see a continuum of prose texts, at the one end of which are native texts, and at the other translated texts which follow Latin patterns.

The Charlemagne cycle

The distribution of preterite and imperfect forms of the verb *gweled* in the Charlemagne cycle is similar to what we observe in LIA. Of 32 total tokens, we find almost the same number of preterite and imperfect forms in main clauses (3 vs 4 respectively), whereas in subordinate clauses we find more examples of the preterite, 16, against 10 of the imperfect. It should be noted, however, that 14 of the 16 examples of gwelas/gweles appear in a very specific context: following the conjunction of time *pan*, 'when.' In all our sample we have not found a single example of the imperfect following this conjunction, thus we can probably claim that the temporal semantics of pan (y) triggers the use of preterite forms.

Charlemagne Cycle	Main clause	Subordinate clause	Total
imperfect	4	10	14
preterite	3	16	19
total	7	26	33

Table 7: Distribution for *gweled* in the Welsh Charlemagne cycle

The following examples are illustrative of the distribution of these verbal forms in the corpus:

Imperfect form in subordinate clause

(Ex. 21) *Ac ar y geirev hynny yny colomen yn ehedec val y g6elei charlys. a'e holl niuer.* (*Otuel*, 84r, 104, 27-30)[36]

---

[36] Quotations are taken from Peniarth MS 5 in Luft, Thomas, and Smith, *Rhyddiaith gymraeg*; references are to text, folio, column, and line numbers. Translations are our own. Regarding the use of "yny" here see Evans, *A Grammar of Middle Welsh*, 245, §278, note.

And with these words a dove comes flying so that Charles and all his host <u>could see</u> it.

A <i>ces paroles vient un columb volant / si ke Charles le <u>vit</u> e tute sa gent.[37]

With these words a dove comes flying, / Where Charles and all his people <u>see</u> it.[38]

Preterite form in subordinate clause after the conjunction *pan* 'when'

> (Ex. 22) *A phan <u>6elas</u> rolon samson yn var6. dolur a gymerth y·gyt a llit.* (*Cân Rolant*, 112v, 214, 27-29)

And when Roland saw Samson dead, he felt grief together with anger.

Li quens Rollant, quant il <u>veit</u> Sansun mort, / Podez saveir que mult grant doel en out[39]

Count Roland, when he <u>sees</u> Samson dead, / Was full of grief, as you may well believe.[40]

Preterite form in main clause

> (Ex. 23) *a thri a <u>6elas</u> abraham ac ef a adoles vn.* (*Ystorya Durpin,* 74v, 66, 9-10)*[41]*

---

[37] Jean-Baptiste Camps, "La *Chanson d'Otinel*: édition complète du corpus manuscrit et prolégomènes à l'édition critique," (PhD diss., Université Paris-Sorbonne, 2016), vol. 2, p. 180, lines 517-518, https://halshs.archives-ouvertes.fr/tel-01664932.

[38] Susanna Fein and David Raybin, trans., "The Anglo-Norman Otinel," in *The Roland and Otuel romances and the Anglo-Norman Otinel*, ed. Elizabeth Melick, Susanna Fein, and David Raybin (Kalamazoo, MI: Medieval Institute Publications, 2019), lines 517-18, https://d.lib.rochester.edu/teams/publication/melick-feinraybin-roland-and-otuel-romances.

[39] Short, *La Chanson de Roland*, lines 1580-81.

[40] Burgess, *The Song of Roland*, lines 1580-81.

[41] The text in *Rhyddiaith Gymraeg* lacks the "vn," which is found in the manuscript. The Red Book of Hergest reads "A thri a welas Yvreham, ac vn a adoles," also supported by Peniarth 8i: "A thri a weles euream ac vn a adoles" (Luft, Thomas, and Smith, *Rhyddiaith Gymraeg*, Peniarth 8i, folio 43, lines 4-5).

And Abraham <u>saw</u> three and he worshiped one.

et Abraham tres <u>vidit</u> et unum adoravit[42]

and Abraham <u>saw</u> three and worshiped one.

The *Gesta Romanorum*

For this study we have analysed a sample of 10.000 words from the Early Modern Welsh *Gesta Romanorum*. The distribution in this sample is similar to that of the 'native' texts discussed earlier. In main clauses, imperfect forms of gweled are mostly used, as in (Ex. 24), while in subordinate clauses the preferred tense is the preterite.

Gesta Romanorum	Main clause	Subordinate clause	Total
imperfect	5	1	6
preterite	1	5	6
Total	6	6	12

Table 8: Distribution for *gweled* in the *Gesta Romanorum*

(Ex. 24) *Ag yno i <u>gwelai</u> ef vaen kaerbwnkl, yr hwnn a oedd yn roi gole i'r holl dŷ.*[43]

And there he <u>saw/could see</u> a carbuncle stone, which was giving light to the entire house.

He helde ferder and sawe a carbuncle in a wall that lyghtened all the house.[44]

(Ex. 25) *A chwedy marw yr amherawdr, ef aeth y mab i gerdded llawer o ynysoedd ag ef a <u>welas</u> llawer o ffolaid.*[45]

---

[42] *Historia Karoli Magni et Rotholandi ou Chronique du Pseudo-Turpin*, ed. Cyril Meredith-Jones (Geneva: Slatkine, 1972 [1936]), chapter xvii, p. 155, lines xx-xxi. The translation is our own.

[43] Williams, *Gesta Romanorum*, 4; NLW 13076 B 10r. All quotations are taken from this edition, and reference is made to page number. Translations are our own.

[44] *Gesta Romanorum* (London: Wynkyn de Worde, 1510), image 10, story VI.

[45] Williams, *Gesta Romanorum*, 2; NLW 13076 B 8r.

> And after the emperor died, the son went to travel to many islands and he <u>saw</u> many foolish things.

> Anone this yonge lorde after the dethe of his fader wente and sought in many realmes and founde many foles rycheles.[46]

An interesting example contradicting this tendency is found in Story XI. Here the situation described is a repeated one: the girl has the shirt of a dead knight in her room and repeatedly looks at it:

> (Ex. 26) *A phan <u>welai</u> hi y krys, hi a wylai yn chwerw.*[47]

> And when she <u>saw/could see</u> the shirt, she would weep bitterly.

> and as oftentymes as she behelde it she wepte bytterly.[48]

This is an example of the meaning for imperfect described by Evans as "consuetudinal past, expressing repeated or customary action".[49]

The verb *clywed* 'to hear'

We have already discussed some examples of the verb *clywed* above, but this section is specifically dedicated to this verb. The distribution of clywed shows that this verb behaves similarly to *gweled*. In *PKM, Peredur*, and *Breuddwyd Rhonabwy*, that is, the so-called 'native' prose tales, almost all the tokens found are imperfect forms of clywed in main clauses, as the table below shows (*Breuddwyd Macsen* furnishes no instances of this verb).

	Main clause	Subordinate clause	Total
imperfect	18	2	20
preterite	2	2	4
Total	20	4	24

Table 9: Distribution for *clywed* in native texts

---

[46] *Gesta Romanorum*, image 7, story V.
[47] Williams, *Gesta Romanorum*, 14; NLW 13076 B: 19v.
[48] *Gesta Romanorum*, image 16, story XI.
[49] Evans, *A Grammar of Middle Welsh*, 110.

337

Translated texts provide significantly fewer examples of the imperfect form in main clauses but many more instances of the preterite in subordinate clauses, once again 'triggered' by the conjunction *pan* 'when' (28 out of 30 tokens).

	Main clause	Subordinate clause	Total
imperfect	8	2	10
preterite	3	30	33
Total	11	32	43

Table 10: Distribution for *clywed* in translated texts

Although this sample is definitely too small to draw definitive conclusions, we can claim that the main tendency that we saw for gweled also applies to clywed, i.e. the preference for imperfect forms in main clauses, and preterite forms in subordinate clauses. As for the differences between the 'native' and translated texts, a larger corpus needs to be analysed.

Interpretation

An inviting explanation for the observed difference in the distribution of imperfect and preterite forms in 'native' and translated prose is interference from source texts.[50] One could suggest that the more frequent use of the preterite of gweled in main clauses in translated texts is triggered by the differences in the tense system of the language of the source texts: the same Latin form, *vidit* in both main and subordinate clauses, might have an influence on the choice of the preterite in the Welsh target text. Thus, as noted by Parina, the "very fine semantic distinction between *gwelei/gwelas* forms"[51] that we find in native texts could have been lost in translation, since perhaps "translators were influenced by Latin which did not have such a fine distinction between the meanings as *gwelei* vs. *gwelas*." [52] However, using preterite forms in main clauses should not be seen as

---

[50] As suggested in Elena Parina, "Multiple Versions of *Breuddwyd Pawl* as a Source to Study the Work of Welsh Translators," in *Studia Celto-Slavica* 9 (2018): 79-100.

[51] Parina, "Multiple Versions of *Breuddwyd Pawl*," 89.

[52] Parina, "Multiple Versions of *Breuddwyd Pawl*," 90.

a fault or a feature of bad style, but rather as a variant that is less frequent in native prose.[53]

Theoretical works on modality help us to understand why perception verbs exhibit peculiar tense marking. Nicholas Gisborne explains why modalities work in a specific way with *see* and the like:

> [. . .] if *I could see you* is true at a given past point in time, then *I saw you* is true at that same time. This entailment does not follow with other verbs. If *I could play the piano* is true at a given point in the past, it does not follow that I was actually playing at that point in the past.[54]

This semantic property of perception verbs explains why in English *he saw* and *he could see* are often interchangeable. In many contexts both forms are equally possible, although there is a fine semantic difference between them. A search through a definitely idiosyncratic selection of works of British prose shows the distribution of the forms (see table below).[55] In the nineteenth century 'could see' is used rather rarely, while in the twentieth century we get more instances of this phrase. However, the simple past form 'saw' is still used three times more often at its highest point in our sample.

---

[53] This feature is, therefore, parallel to the distribution of word-order patterns analysed by Meelen, *Why Jesus and Job spoke bad Welsh*, see above, note 15.

[54] Nikolas Gisborne, "Dynamic Modality," The Slovak Association for the Study of English (*SKASE) Journal of Theoretical Linguistics* 4.2 (2007): 44-61, at 54, http://www.skase.sk/Volumes/JTL09/pdf_doc/4.pdf.

[55] The data for *Pride and Prejudice, Ivanhoe, The Two Towers*, and *Harry Potter and the Philosopher's Stone* are taken from the English subcorpus of The Russian National Corpus (ruscorpora.ru); the data for *A Christmas Carol* and *Adventures of Sherlock Holmes* are based on searching eBooks from the Project Gutenberg. We have not discarded the few homonyms, such as saw "the instrument," which however does not affect the general distribution of the forms. Similar tendencies are seen by using Google Books Ngram Viewer, subcorpus English fiction, search terms "he saw, he could see," retrieved 4.01.2022.

DISTRIBUTION PATTERNS

	1813	1820	1843	1892	1954	1997
	Jane Austen *Pride and Prejudice*	Walter Scott *Ivanhoe*	Charles Dickens *A Christmas Carol*	A. Conan Doyle *Adventures of Sherlock Holmes*	J.R.R. Tolkien *LotR The Two Towers*	J.K. Rowling *Harry Potter and the Philosopher's Stone*
saw	103	39	23	93	163	63
could see	7	3	6	30	42	20
total	110	42	29	123	205	83
%						
saw	93.6	92.9	79.3	75.6	79.5	75.9
could see	6.4	7.1	20.7	24.4	20.5	24.1

Table 11: 'Saw' vs 'could see' in English fiction

The exact semantic difference between the forms is beyond the scope of this article. Some authors characterize the use of simple forms as "somewhat more dramatic."[56] This observation, however, contradicts the distribution of the forms we see in English fiction. It is unlikely that a "more dramatic" form is used more frequently. The difference between *saw* and *could see* has also been analysed in terms of "marking durative or continuative aspect."[57] In their interesting discussion of equivalence between English and Welsh tense forms, Rottet and Morris suggest that "while the preterites *gwelodd* and *clywodd* have "saw" and "heard" as their usual translation equivalents, the imperfect forms *gwelai* and *clywai* are equivalent to "could see" and "could hear," but they also show examples with different equivalence."[58]

It would be highly interesting to study the distribution of gwelodd and gwelai in Modern Welsh texts. In this respect, the data from the one-million-word Cronfa Electroneg o Gymraeg shows that gwelodd

---

[56] Rodney Huddleston and Geoffrey Pullum, *The Cambridge Grammar of English* (Cambridge: Cambridge University Press, 2002), 169. Note that the authors discuss the present forms, but this observation applies to the past forms as well.

[57] Kevin Rottet and Steve Morris, *Comparative Stylistics of Welsh and English* (Cardiff: University of Wales Press, 2018), 206.

[58] Rottet and Morris, *Comparative Stylistics*, 206.

is more frequently used than gwelai (231 vs. 107), [59] i.e. the distribution (68.3% vs. 31.7%) is similar to the more modern English texts, but we would need to analyse the type of clauses in which these verb forms occur to establish whether we see a system similar to that of the native Middle Welsh texts.

The data from English fiction allows us to assess the usage of the same tokens in two translations of the *Mabinogion*. The distribution of 'saw' vs. 'could see' in the text published under the name of Lady Charlotte Guest between 1838 and 1845 and the latest translation by Sioned Davies (2007)[60] are the following:

	Guest	Davies
Saw	200	152
could see	15	151
Total	215	303
%		
saw	93.02	50.17
could see	6.98	49.83

Table 12: 'Saw' vs 'could see' in the translations of Guest and Davies

The translation of Lady Guest fits linguistically into the norms of her contemporary target language: almost every gwelei that we find in the Middle Welsh text is translated by 'saw' or its synonyms in Guest's version, the proportion is very similar to that found in *Pride and Prejudice* or *Ivanhoe*. Sioned Davies's translation is different from the norms of her contemporary prose since she brings into her English text the norms of the Welsh text, rendering many of the gwelei forms by "could see," so that this construction is used in her text more frequently than in contemporary English fiction.

---

[59] Cronfa Electroneg o Gymraeg (CEG): A 1 million word lexical database and frequency count for Welsh, accessed January 5, 2022, http://www.bangor.ac.uk/canolfanbedwyr/ceg.php.en.

[60] We used the Project Gutenberg eBook of Lady Charlotte Guest, trans., *The Mabinogion,* https://www.gutenberg.org/files/5160/5160-h/5160-h.htm; Davies, *The Mabinogion.* We are aware that these works do not intersect fully, but we still find the relation between the forms *saw* and *could see* in the two works informative for our study.

341

DISTRIBUTION PATTERNS

Conclusion

The different options that we see in these two English translations of the *Mabinogion* tales can be used as a parallel to what we observe in the translations into Welsh which we study: some follow strictly the stylistic norms of the target language, and some keep more of the norms of the source language. The employment of both imperfect and preterite forms in main clauses is grammatically correct in 'native' Welsh prose, but the use of the imperfect tends to be the default option. In some translated texts, possibly in connection with their Latin or French source texts, preterite forms are used more frequently than imperfect ones. This tendency does not get grammaticalized, as we see almost the same distribution of imperfect and preterite forms in *PKM* as in the sixteenth-century Welsh version of the *Gesta Romanorum* translated from English. The deviation from this distribution in some Middle Welsh translated texts may be interpreted along with other traces of translation features as part of a special register, within a wide range of possibilities available to translators. In this regard, the study of a grammatical feature, such as the one undertaken here, casts new light on issues of translation strategies.

Acknowledgements

This research stems from a number of projects on translations into Welsh which have been, or are being, undertaken at the University of Marburg, namely: "Early Modern cultures of translation in Wales: innovations and continuities" (10.2021-09.2024) and "The Welsh contribution to the cultures of translation of the Early Modern period: Strategies of translating into Welsh in the sixteenth century" (10.2018-09.2021), Co-PIs Dr. Elena Parina and Prof. Dr. Erich Poppe, both funded by the DFG within priority programme SPP2130 "Early Modern Translation Cultures"; "Translations as language contact phenomena–studies in lexical, grammatical and stylistic interference in Middle Welsh religious texts" (10.2015-09.2017), PI Professor Dr. Erich Poppe, Researcher Dr. Elena Parina, funded by the Fritz Thyssen Foundation; and "The Matter of France in Medieval Wales: A Study of Otuel" (07.2019-01.2022), PI Dr. Luciana Cordo Russo, funded by the Alexander von Humboldt Foundation. We are grateful to these funding bodies for their generous support. Our gratitude also goes to Prof. Erich Poppe for inspiration, as well as the organisers and participants of the Harvard Celtic Colloquium for giving us the opportunity to present our study and for the thought-provoking discussion that ensued. A special thanks to the anonymous reviewer for their helpful suggestions.

Concepts of Law and Justice in Medieval Welsh Poetry: reflections on Dafydd ab Edmwnd's elegy to Siôn Eos

R. Gwynedd Parry

Introduction

There existed a close kinship between poets and lawyers in medieval Wales. Many of the poets were also lawyers, or were closely related to lawyers, and both poets and lawyers sat at the same high tables. It is little wonder that in the poetry of both the *gogynfeirdd*, the poets of the princes (pre-1282), and *beirdd yr uchelwyr*, the poets of the nobility (post-1282), we find a richness in legal imagery and terminology, and sometimes evidence of acute understanding of legal phenomena.[1] This paper's aim is to demonstrate the potential dividends of exploring this dynamic between law and poetry, specifically in the Welsh context, by focusing on a poem from the fifteenth century, that of Dafydd ab Edmwnd's elegy (which can also be appropriately described as a eulogy) to Siôn Eos. It offers a new interpretation of the poem and demonstrates its evidential value to both cultural and legal historians seeking to make sense of a period when a transition in legal culture was underway, a transition which highlighted complex clashes of both cultural norms and concepts of justice.

Context

Before turning to the poem, it may be helpful to put matters in context. According to the native Welsh laws, Cyfraith Hywel or the Law of Hywel Dda, the *taeog* (servile) class could not exercise the "honourable crafts of the poet and blacksmith," which were reserved for the nobility.[2] The poets were men of status, close to the centres of power and influence. The *bardd teulu* (family poet) served an important function in his lord's court, and the best poets were recognized as *penceirddiaid* (master poets) under a self-regulating

---

[1] See, further, R. Gwynedd Parry, *Y Gyfraith yn ein Llên* (Cardiff: University of Wales Press, 2019), chapters 2 and 3.

[2] Dafydd Jenkins, Cyfraith Hywel: *Rhagarweiniad i Gyfraith Gynhenid Cymru'r Oesau Canol* (Llandysul: Gwasg Gomer, 1970), 19.

poetic cadre which was independent of royal authority.[3] The Welsh laws stipulated the duties of the bardd teulu and the pencerdd, the difference between the two, and what was owed to them by the king and his court.[4] The *bardd teulu* would entertain the court during the feast, and he had certain privileges, such as the right to a gold ring from the Queen or to be gifted a cow from the spoils of war.[5] The *pencerdd* also enjoyed privileges according to the laws, and would sit alongside the judge at the King's court.[6] His privileges included the right to payment of *amobr* when a maiden married and lost her virginity.[7] And after the conquest of 1282, many of the poets of the nobility would come from the *uchelwyr* caste, which indicated the continuing esteem with which the craft of the bard was held.[8]

The penceirddiaid were not the itinerant minstrels, rhymers or wasters portrayed derogatorily by the English kings (although the lesser, unlicensed poets may have been fairly described as such).[9] On

---

[3] Dafydd Jenkins, "Pencerdd a Bardd Teilu," *Ysgrifau Beirniadol* XIV (1988), 19-46. Also T. M. Charles-Edwards, *Wales and the Britons 350-1064* (Oxford: Oxford University Press, 2013), 676.

[4] There is an interesting discussion on the differences between the family poet and the pencerdd by Tudur Hallam, "Croesholi Tystiolaeth y Llyfrau Cyfraith: Pencerdd a Bardd Teulu," *Llên Cymru*, 22 (1999), 1-11.

[5] Aled Rhys William, *Llyfr Iorwerth* (Cardiff: University of Wales Press, 1960), 10; also Dafydd Jenkins, *The Law of Hywel Dda* (Llandysul: Gomer, 2000), 20.

[6] William, *Llyfr Iorwerth*, 21-22; also see Jenkins, *The Law of Hywel Dda*, 38-39.

[7] Dafydd Jenkins, "Bardd Teulu and Pencerdd," in T. M. Charles-Edwards, Morfydd E. Owen and Paul Russell, eds., *The Welsh King and his Court* (Cardiff, University of Wales Press, 2000), 142-166.

[8] Comments on the craft requirements of the lawyer and poet under the Welsh laws can be found in Sara Elin Roberts, "Addysg Broffesiynol yng Nghymru yn yr Oesoedd Canol: y Beirdd a'r Cyfreithwyr," *Llên Cymru*, 26 (2003), 1-17.

[9] As represented in laws introduced by Henry IV in response to Owain Glyndŵr's rebellion. See 4 Henry 4, c. 27 (1402), *Act Against Wasters, Minstrels, &c., in Wales*: "Item, to eschew many diseases and mischiefs which have happened before this time in the Land of Wales by many Wasters, Rhymers, Minstrels and other Vagabonds; It is ordained and

the contrary, many were noblemen whose poems were addressed to other noblemen, almost in the spirit of an aristocratic-poetic dialogue. In addition, many of the poets were also lawyers or related closely to lawyers.[10] For example, in the age of the native princes, we find Einion ap Gwalchmai, a nobleman descended from Meilyr Brydydd (Meilyr the poet), who was a poet and lawyer, and who served as a court magistrate (*ynad llys*) in the court of Llywelyn ab Iorwerth (c. 1173-1240).[11] He was one of Llywelyn's most important counsellors, and there is evidence that he took a leading role in many of the most important constitutional events of the period. For instance, he is named as one of Llywelyn's *gwyrda* (counsellors) in the Treaty of Worcester of 1218.[12] Exchanging his lawyerly mantle for a poet's chair, he also crafted an awdl praising Llywelyn and hailing his virtues as a lion and an adversary of the English.[13]

Other poets who were of lawyerly stock were Einion ap Madog ap Rhahawd, and Gruffudd ab yr Ynad Coch. They were both distant cousins, descended from a famous breed of lawyers if not the dominant legal family of the Middle Ages, namely the tribe of Cilmin Droetu of Uwch Gwyrfai in Arfon.[14] One of Einion's brothers was

---

stablished that no Waster, Rhymer, Minstrel nor Vagabond be in any wise sustained in the Land of Wales to make Commorthies or gathering upon the Common people there." See, further, Ivor Bowen, *Statutes of Wales* (London: T. F. Unwin, 1908), 34.

[10] See Morfydd E. Owen, "Noddwyr a Beirdd," in Morfydd E. Owen and Brynley F. Roberts, eds., *Beirdd a Thywysogion: Barddoniaeth Llys yng Nghymru, Iwerddon a'r Alban* (Cardiff and Aberystwyth: University of Wales Press and National Library of Wales, 1996), 75-107, in particular 84-85.

[11] See Roberts, "Addysg Broffesiynol yng Nghymru yn yr Oesoedd Canol," 6.

[12] J. E. Caerwyn Williams and Peredur I. Lynch, eds., *Gwaith Meilyr Brydydd a'i Ddisgynyddion ynghyd â Dwy Awdl Ddi-enw o Ddeheubarth* (Cardiff: University of Wales Press, 1994) *Cyfres Beirdd y Tywysogion* I, 427-503, 429.

[13] Williams and Lynch, eds., *Gwaith Meilyr Brydydd a'i Ddisgynyddion,* 439-440, Poem 25, l. 7.

[14] See Dafydd Jenkins, "A family of Medieval Welsh Lawyers," in Dafydd Jenkins, ed., *Celtic Law Papers: Introductory to Welsh Medieval Law and Government* (Bruxelles: Librairie Encyclopédique, 1973), 121-34.

Iorwerth ap Madog, the purported author of the Llyfr Iorwerth manuscript, one of the most important extant law manuscripts of the thirteenth century.[15] Gruffudd's legal links as a son of Madog Goch Ynad are evident from the father's sobriquet (Madog the Red Judge, or, possibly, Red Madog the Judge), although it is as the author of the great elegy to Llywelyn ap Gruffudd (c. 1223-1282) that he is best remembered.[16]

The poet and the lawyer were thus closely linked as practitioners of noble crafts and, in some cases, the connections were tribal if not familial.[17] A few personified both lawyer and poet, and it is believed that some of the poet-lawyers authored the law books. Indeed, the literary styles of the law books betray the influences of the literary ideas and devices of the poets.[18] It is believed, for example, that the consistent use of the *trioedd* (triads), the grouping of threes, in the law books was inspired by their use in prose and poetry. This supports the theory that the lawyers, like the poets, relied on memory in exercising their craft.[19]

An awareness of the traditions associated with the person of Hywel Dda is much in evidence in the law books of the thirteenth century, which is indicative of the influence of culture and tradition, particularly ideas about the unity of the nation and the authority of the king, on the content and nature of the law books.[20] These close

---

[15] Dafydd Jenkins, "Iorwerth Ap Madog: Gŵr Cyfraith o'r Drydedd Ganrif Ar Ddeg," *National Library of Wales Journal*, 8 (1953), 164-70.

[16] Rhian M. Andrews et al., eds., *Gwaith Bleddyn Fardd a Beirdd Eraill Ail Hanner y Drydedd Ganrif ar Ddeg* (Cardiff: University of Wales Press, 1996), *Cyfres Beirdd y Tywysogion VII*, 414-33, Poem 36.

[17] See Sara Elin Roberts, "The Welsh Legal Triads," in Thomas Glyn Watkin, ed., *The Welsh Legal Triads and other Essays* (Bangor: Welsh Legal History Society, 2012), 1-22, especially 7-10.

[18] Discussed by Morfydd E. Owen, "Gwŷr Dysg yr Oesoedd Canol a'u Rhyddiaith," *Ysgrifau Beirniadol*, 17 (1990), 42-62.

[19] A detailed approach to the legal triads is provided by Sara Elin Roberts, *The Legal Triads of Medieval Wales* (Cardiff: University of Wales Press, 2007); see also Morfydd E. Owen, "Welsh Triads: An Overview," *Celtica*, 25 (2007), 225-50.

[20] See Robin Chapman Stacey, "Law and Literature in Medieval Ireland and Wales," in Helen Fulton, ed., *Medieval Celtic Literature and Society* (Dublin: Four Courts Press, 2005), 65-82.

associations between the lawyer and the poet continued after the conquest of 1282 and reforms brought about with the Statute of Rhuddlan (or Statute of Wales) of 1284. Cyfraith Hywel thereafter ceased to be the primary legal code, although it would take many centuries before it would be completely extinguished.[21] As a result of the Statute of Rhuddlan, the laws of the English were imposed on the principalities, and especially the criminal law.[22] However, Welsh laws were tolerated, at least to some degree. The constitutional settlement was summarised thus: "although many material alterations were at the same time made in the Welsh laws, the conquered people still retained several provincial immunities and disabilities."[23] And so certain Welsh laws relating to land and other property would endure for some time, as would elements of the Welsh laws on inheritance (*cyfran*) despite the increasingly hostile political climate.[24]

If there existed a degree of tolerance of Welsh laws and customs in the principalities, Welsh laws also survived in those regions where the Statute of Rhuddlan did not have jurisdiction, such as in the March of Wales. The March was a collection of semi- autonomous lordships which enjoyed greater autonomy from royal interference than the traditional strongholds of the native princes in the west. In these territories, a combination of legal codes, Welsh, English, and hybrid, were applied, usually dependant on the ethnicity of the litigating

---

[21] See, for example, R. R. Davies, "The Administration of Law in Medieval Wales: The Role of the Ynad Cwmwd (Judex Patrie), in T. M. Charles-Edwards, Morfydd E. Owen and D. B. Walters, eds., *Lawyers and Laymen* (Cardiff: University of Wales Press, 1986), 258-73, at 269.

[22] Llinos Beverley Smith, "The Statute of Wales, 1284," *Welsh History Review* 10 (2) (1980), 127-54; also Paul Brand, "An English Legal Historian Looks at the Statute of Wales," in T. G. Watkin, ed., *Y Cyfraniad Cymreig: Welsh Contributions to Legal Development* (Cardiff: Welsh Legal History Society, 2005), 20-56.

[23] Theodore F. T. Plucknett, *Taswell-Langmead's English Constitutional History* (London: Sweet & Maxwell, 1960), 235.

[24] R. R. Davies, *The Age of Conquest: Wales 1063-1415* (Oxford: Oxford University Press, 2000), 368; also See Dafydd Jenkins, "Law and Government in Wales before the Act of Union," in J. A. Andrews, ed., *Welsh Studies in Public Law* (Cardiff: University of Wales Press, 1970), 7-29.

parties.[25] Indeed, the legal code would often be applied according to whether the parties were English or Welsh, and separate procedures catered for the two.[26] Put simply, those who were ethnically Welsh could expect to be tried by Welsh law and custom, and those who were English would be tried by English law and custom. Matters were not that straightforward, of course, and the marcher lordships would, for want of a better phrase, do their own thing when it came to the administration of justice, combining elements of Welsh and English custom that best suited the needs of expediency.[27] Wales was thus a collection of separate or loosely connected legal jurisdictions, some under the direct authority of the crown, others subject to the jurisdiction of a marcher lord.[28] But native Welsh laws enjoyed a greater longevity in the March than that of the principalities subject to the jurisdiction of the Statute of Rhuddlan of 1284.

Although the demise of Llywelyn ap Gruffudd and the end of the native princely line was hailed as a disaster by some of the poets, in truth, the native minor Welsh gentry came quickly to terms with the new regime.[29] Many adapted and embraced the opportunities for self-advancement which arose, thereby becoming loyal servants of the crown. Simultaneously, they sought to preserve and patronise Welsh culture, maintaining many of the old practices of giving succour to the poets which they had inherited from their forefathers.[30]

Due to the willingness of the Crown to tolerate the continuation of some of the Welsh laws, and because of their longevity in the

---

[25] R. R. Davies, "The Law of the March," *Welsh History Review* 5 (1), (1970), 1-30.

[26] The position is summarised by Sir Goronwy Edwards in "The Language of the Law Courts in Wales: some Historical Enquiries," *Cambrian Law Review* 6, (1975), 5-9.

[27] For an interesting discussion on this, see Diane M. Korngiebel, "English Colonial Ethnic Discrimination in the Lordship of Dyffryn Clwyd: Segregation and Integration, 1282-c.1340," *Welsh History Review*, 23 (2), (2007), 1-24

[28] Owen Hood Phillips a Paul Jackson, *Constitutional and Administrative Law*, eighth edition (London: Sweet & Maxwell, 2001), 16.

[29] J. Beverley Smith, *Llywelyn ap Gruffudd: Prince of Wales* (Cardiff: University of Wales Press, 1998), 569-71.

[30] Dafydd Johnston, *Llên yr Uchelwyr: Hanes Beirniadol Llenyddiaeth Gymraeg 1300-1525* (Cardiff: University of Wales Press, 2005), 3.

March, the adaptation and copying of Welsh legal texts continued well until the sixteenth century.[31] As knowledge of the native laws remained important to the nobility who were the principal upholders of law and order, they continued to be versed in the Welsh legal tradition.[32] The traumas of disinheritance and the importation of English legal officers to implement English laws had taken their toll on the native Welsh nobility in the immediate aftermath of conquest, of course.[33] The native princes and their families had been substantially extinguished, as had happened in England after 1066.[34] But whereas hardly none of the English nobility in Norman and Plantagenet England traced their lineage to the Saxons, many of the Welsh nobility of the later middle-ages were descended from the pre-conquest noble tribes, such as those of Marchudd ap Cynan, Collwyn ap Tango or Hwfa ap Cynddelw.[35] A process of rehabilitation in the fourteenth century had restored many of the native nobility to positions of authority and influence, as they practised "the arts of coexistence" with their English overlords.[36]

It is arguable that this degree of continuity in the social order from the age of the princes to the age of the nobility was an important contributor to cultural continuity, including legal and poetic culture. As the Welsh nobility continued to take an interest in Cyfraith Hywel after the conquest of 1282, so they also took up the mantle of their forebears and gave patronage to the poets.[37] Those poets adapted successfully to the constitutional changes and found refuge in the halls of their new benefactors. The poem that is the focus of this paper belongs to the period after 1282, the age of beirdd yr uchelwyr, and it is to this period that we now turn our attention.

---

[31] See Huw Pryce, "Lawbooks and Literacy in Medieval Wales," *Speculum* 75 (2000), 29-67, at 40-47.

[32] Johnston, *Llên yr Uchelwyr,* 451.

[33] R. R. Davies, *The Age of Conquest: Wales 1063-1415,* 360-1.

[34] For an overview, see R. Allen Brown, "The Norman Conquest" *Transactions of the Royal Historical Society* 17 (1967), 109-30.

[35] It is indeed striking to note that the majority of the nobility of North Wales was descended from native pre-conquest nobility and even native royal stock: see, generally, J. E. Griffith, *Pedigrees of Anglesey and Caernarvonshire Families* (Horncastle: W. K. Morton, 1914).

[36] R. R. Davies, *The Age of Conquest: Wales 1063-1415,* 415.

[37] R. R. Davies, *The Age of Conquest: Wales 1063-1415,* 417-19.

R. GWYNEDD PARRY

Legal Poetry

This context is key to our appreciation of the nature of the legal references found within the works of beirdd yr uchelwyr, and of the interplay between *cyfraith* and *cynghanedd,* law and poetics, in the fourteenth and fifteenth centuries. Evidence of poetic legal literacy often appears in the context of praise singing, elegies or poetry seeking favour or patronage, where the patron has legal credentials which the poet is keen to glorify. This, of course, was the stock in trade of the professional Welsh bard. Llywelyn Goch ap Meurig Hen (fl. 1350-90), declared the importance of having an understanding the law for a gentleman of his era, as he described in a poem his functions as law tutor in his nephews' household.[38] Guto'r Glyn (c. 1435-c. 1493) was also prolific in his deployment of legal terms in his poetry. He would praise the nobility as upholders of law and order, such as in his poem to Siôn Hanmer, whom he hailed effusely as, *Sesar dadlau a sesiwn/Swydd Elsmer yw'r Hanmer hwn* ("A Caesar of pleading and session/ at Ellesmere's court is this Hanmer").[39] The surname Hanmer is highly significant for this paper, and will shall be returning to it shortly.

The greatest Welsh poet of the middle ages, Dafydd ap Gwilym (c. 1315-c. 1370), in a cywydd to his chief patron, Ifor Hael (Ifor the Generous), praises him as *ynad hoywfoes,* (a courteous judge.)[40] Dafydd ap Gwilym was closely associated with the law at a personal level, as his uncle, Llywelyn ap Gwilym, who may have been his tutor as a poet, was Constable of Newcastle Emlyn, and thereby responsible for the administration of the law in that region.[41] The Constable's many legal credentials are mentioned in both the praise poem and the

---

[38] Dafydd Johnston, ed., *Gwaith Llywelyn Goch ap Meurig Hen* (Aberystwyth: University of Wales Centre for Advanced Welsh and Celtic Studies, 1998) 1-11.
[39] J. Llywelyn Williams and Ifor Williams, eds., *Gwaith Guto'r Glyn* (Cardiff: University of Wales Press, 1939), 168; Poem LXIII, lines 9-10.
[40] Thomas Parry (ed.), *Gwaith Dafydd ap Gwilym* (Cardiff: University of Wales Press, 1952), 78, Poem 16, line 37; also notes at 28.
[41] Regarding Dafydd ap Gwilym's use of legal terminology, see R. Gwynedd Parry, *Y Gyfraith yn ein Llên,* 49-54; also, Dafydd Johnston, *Iaith Oleulawn: Geirfa Dafydd ap Gwilym* (Cardiff: University of Wales Press, 2020), chapter 8.

elegy which Dafydd crafted in his honour.[42] They are rich in Welsh legal terms, such as *brawdwr* (judge), *canllaw* (counsellor) and *penrhaith* (chief witness or judge). In an elegy to Llywelyn ap Gwilym in the form of englynion, we become aware that the Constable met his death in sinister circumstances. The suggestion is that he was murdered, or, as Dafydd put it in verse, *honni mawr alanas* ("a great murder is claimed").[43]

A mystery surrounded the identity of the person responsible for the murder and the motive for it, and the use of the word *dygngoll* twice in the elegy is significant, as it means a profound loss and is also a legal term.[44] In Cyfraith Hywel, reference is made to *dri dygngoll cenedl*, a legal principle that arose when a family member had killed another and the family had paid their share of what was owed in compensation to the victim's kindred, but the killer had paid compensation that was short of a penny. Because the compensation was not fully paid by the killer, the family of the victim could legally exact revenge and kill the perpetrator.[45] As such, the killer's family lost one of their members and, at the same time, lost the compensation they originally paid.[46] As the purpose of compensation under Cyfraith Hywel was to avoid reprisals, the family of the killed was allowed to take steps to retaliate for the murder where no compensation was paid in full.[47] In the elegy to Llywelyn ap Gwilym, what is meant is the double loss of death and the loss of compensation for the death. There is therefore a sense of injustice coupled with a threatening tone, with the extensive use of the legal vocabulary and a constant emphasis on retaliation for the murder.[48]

---

[42] Parry (ed.), *Gwaith Dafydd ap Gwilym*, 31-38; also Dafydd Johnston et al. (eds.), *Cerddi Dafydd ap Gwilym* (Cardiff: University of Wales Press, 2010), 24-37.

[43] Johnston, *Cerddi Dafydd ap Gwilym*, 32, Poem 6, line 74.

[44] Johnston, *Cerddi Dafydd ap Gwilym*, 30-32, Poem 6, lines 38, 70.

[45] Jenkins, *The Law of Hywel Dda*, 146, 339.

[46] Johnston, *Cerddi Dafydd ap Gwilym*, 596.

[47] Thomas Glyn Watkin, *The Legal History of Wales* (Cardiff: University of Wales Press, 2007), 67.

[48] For a detailed discussion, see Sara Elin Roberts, "Dafydd ap Gwilym, ei Ewythr a'r Gyfraith," *Llên Cymru* 28, (2005), 100-14.

Dafydd ap Gwilym is remembered chiefly for his love poems (and judging by their volume, he was indeed a prolific lover). In some of these love poems he employs the law's processes in a metaphorical sense when he, for example, pleads for reconciliation with the object of his desire and offers compensation for the wrongs that have been committed by him towards her, or vice versa, when he claims recompense in cases where he is the injured party. And in other poems he adopts a courtroom scene when he appeals for an advocate on his behalf to plead for his lover's forgiveness.[49]

Other legal references arise in what might be described as political poetry, where the bard is critiquing or commenting on the law and its administration, expressing opinions about the state of the legal order or the injustices of this world. Tudur Aled (c. 1465-1525) was taught his bardic craft by his uncle, Dafydd ab Edmwnd.[50] Tudur Aled presents a powerful critique of English law in a poem from the late fifteenth century. In it, he entreats Hwmffre ap Hywel ap Siencyn and his kindred to reconcile their differences and forgo litigation before the courts. This was a case of familial civil war. The source of the family feud was a will in which the *penteulu*, the head of the family, had left the family estate to the eldest male son in accordance with the increasingly fashionable practice of primogeniture. Tudur Aled was a poet acting as an arbitrator in his pleading for reconciliation and blamed the entire affair on the importation of English legal culture.

Here is an extract which illustrates vividly Tudur Aled's views on the matter:

> *Cymru'n waeth, caem, o'r noethi,*
> *Lloegr yn well o'n llygru ni.*
> *Can bil a roed acw'n bwn-*
> *Croes Iesu rhag rhyw sesiwn!*
> *Câr yn cyhuddo arall,*
> *Hawdd i'r llaw gyhuddo'r llall.*[51]

---

[49] See R. Geraint Gruffydd, "A Glimpse of Medieval Court Procedure in a Poem by Dafydd Ap Gwilym," in C. Richmond, and I. Harvey, eds., *Recognitions: Essays Presented to Edmund Fryde* (Aberystwyth: National Library of Wales, 1996), 165-76.

[50] T. Gwynn Jones, ed., *Gwaith Tudur Aled* (Cardiff: University of Wales Press, 1926), 282-83, Poem LXX, lines. 29-30.

[51] Jones, ed., *Gwaith Tudur Aled*, 267, Poem LXVI, lines. 77-82.

Wales is worse for this stripping,
England better from our shame.
A hundred bills heaped on us there;
Jesus' cross, shield us from sessions!
One kinsman blames another,
Easily this hand blames that. [52]

This was a conflict which had its roots in the contamination of Welsh customs by the increasing encroachment of English justice. Recourse to the English courts seemed to be commonplace among the Welsh gentry, and, for Tudur Aled, this was to the detriment of Welsh ways and traditions. The cost of litigation, especially where it is a case of brother against brother, and where only the lawyers at the sessions profit, clearly had animated the bard.[53]

It would be misleading to suggest that Tudur Aled's viewpoint represented the general consensus on the importation of English legal custom. Hywel Swrdwal (fl. 1430-70) was a poet who traced his ancestry to the Norman Surdeval family, who were among the earliest Norman settlers in Brycheiniog in the twelfth century.[54] Although Gwent and Glamorgan were his poetic hinterlands, there are legal references in his ode to Hywel ap Siancyn of Nanhyfer (Nevern in Pembrokeshire), when his benefactor's knowledge of the law is praised.[55] There is reference to two laws, which suggests that two legal codes were in force in this part of Dyfed: *Efô a fedrai dröi/Y ddwy gyfraith i'n iaith ni* ("He could apply/ both laws in our language").[56] It may refer to the common law or ecclesiastical law in addition to Cyfraith Hywel.

A call for retaliation is what we encounter in his elegy to Watcyn Fychan of Brodorddyn (Bredwardine), murdered by an Englishman in

---

[52] For the translation, see Joseph Clancy, *Medieval Welsh Poems* (Dublin: Four Courts Press, 2003), 355.

[53] For a detailed analysis of this poem, see Gruffydd Aled Williams, "Tudur Aled ai cant yn dda om barn i: Cywydd Cymod Wmffre ap Hywel ap Siancyn o Ynysymaengwyn a'i Geraint," *Llên Cymru* 30, (2007), 57-99.

[54] Dylan Foster Evans, ed., *Gwaith Hywel Swrdwal a'i Deulu* (Aberystwyth: University of Wales Centre for Advanced Welsh and Celtic Studies, 2000), 1-5.

[55] Evans, ed., *Gwaith Hywel Swrdwal a'i Deulu*, 174.

[56] Evans, ed., *Gwaith Hywel Swrdwal a'i Deulu*, 56; Poem 13, lines 43-44.

the city of Hereford in 1456.[57] There was considerable tension between the Welsh and English inhabitants of city during that period, linked to the conflict that later became known as the Wars of the Roses. Watcyn was killed by a stray arrow during the conflict, to which there was an immediate and violent response by William Herbert of Raglan, Earl of Pembroke and patron of bards (died 1469), who was also a kinsman of the deceased. The city's mayors and justices were threatened and forced to place the blame for the murder on an Englishman named John Glover, along with five of his friends, who were thereafter hanged at the scene. Legal processes were ignored as Herbert secured the verdict he sought, and the subsequent inquest was held in Bredwardine rather than in Hereford, which would have been expected under the normal procedure.[58] It was there that the coroner and jury were held captive in the church until they gave the verdict that Herbert expected.[59]

Grief along with hatred towards the murderer are the dominant themes of the poem, with the fact that an Englishman had committed the deed adding to the poet's anger. Although the poem does not offer much detail about the legal processes, the line *Aur am Watgyn nis myn merch* ("his widow did not wish gold for Watcyn's life") implies that the widow of the victim was not willing to accept gold as compensation for his killing.[60] This is not an appeal for Cyfraith Hywel with its emphasis on compensation, but a call for the punitive methods of English law.[61]

The Hanging of a Harpist

We now turn to the poem which is arguably the most striking in the canon of Beirdd yr Uchelwyr which critiques a legal subject. A Welsh harpist called Siôn Eos is sent to the gallows by the Constable of Chirk (Y Waun) after being found guilty by a jury of killing a man in brawl in one of the taverns in the town. All that we know of the fate

---

[57] Evans, ed., *Gwaith Hywel Swrdwal a'i Deulu*, 89; Poem 23.
[58] See Dylan Foster Evans, "Murder in the Marches: Poetry and the Legitimisation of Revenge in Fifteenth-Century Wales" *Proceedings of the Harvard Celtic Colloquium* 18/19, (1998-99), 42-72.
[59] Evans, ed., *Gwaith Hywel Swrdwal a'i Deulu*, 190-91.
[60] Evans, ed., *Gwaith Hywel Swrdwal a'i Deulu*, 89; Poem 23, line 61.
[61] Evans, ed., *Gwaith Hywel Swrdwal a'i Deulu*, 195.

of Siôn Eos is contained in a poetic elegy by Dafydd ab Edmwnd (fl. 1450-97), a doyen among the Welsh poets of the fifteenth century, and, as already mentioned, an uncle to Tudur Aled (whose mother was Dafydd's sister).[62] Besides his poetic credentials, Dafydd ab Edmwnd may also have been learned in the law, and was certainly a member of a renowned juristic dynasty, the Hanmers, a Norman family who had settled in north-east Wales in the thirteenth century.[63] An ancestral uncle, David or Dafydd Hanmer, was a lawyer of distinction, and became a justice at the King's Bench Court in 1383. Margaret, or Marred, one of Dafydd Hanmer's daughters, was married to Owain Glyndŵr, and his sons fought for Glyndŵr's during the struggle for independence.[64] He was also a patron of poets, as the many poems in his honour testify.[65]

In common with other English families that had settled in north Wales, such as the Pulestons of Hafod Wern and other seats, or the Salusbury family of Llyweni and its branches, the Hanmers were a new breed of Norman-Welsh in the immediate post-conquest period.[66] But by the time of Dafydd ab Edmwnd, many branches of this family were fully integrated and had even adopted the Welsh patronymic tradition of surnaming.[67] Paradoxically, Dafydd ab Edmwnd was directly descended in the male line from Sir Thomas de Macclesfield who was an officer in the service of Edward I, the English king who

---

[62] See his entry in Meic Stephens, *Cydymaith i Lenyddiaeth Cymru* (Cardiff: University of Wales Press, 1986), 28-29.

[63] See J. E. Griffith, *Pedigrees of Anglesey and Caernarvonshire Families* (Horncastle: W. K. Morton, 1914), 286.

[64] Davies, *The Revolt of Owain Glyndŵr*, 137-38; also Gruffydd Aled Williams, "More than 'skimble-skamble stuff": the Medieval Welsh Poetry Associated with Owain Glyndŵr," *Proceedings of the British Academy* 181 (2012), 1-33.

[65] See Bleddyn Owen Huws, "Rhan o Awdl Foliant Ddienw i Syr Dafydd Hanmer," *Dwned* 9, (2003), 43-64; also, Bleddyn Owen Huws, "Gramadeg Barddol Honedig Syr Dafydd Hanmer," *Llên Cymru* 28, (2005), 178-80.

[66] Their history is given account by John Lord Hanmer, *The Parish and Family of Hanmer* (London: Privately Printed at the Chiswick Press, 1876).

[67] The significance of Anglo-Welsh names and surnames in Wales during the Middle Ages is considered by Laura Radiker, "Observations on Cross-Cultural Names and Name Patterns in Medieval Wales and the March," *Proceedings of the Harvard Celtic Colloquium* 26/27, (2006/2007), 160-98.

put paid to Welsh independence.[68] Even so, the extent of Dafydd ab Edmwnd's earnest Welshness is seen most clearly in a poem where he entreats a nobleman from Anglesey not to take an English wife. In his "Cywydd i Rys Wyn ap Llywelyn ap Tudur o Fôn rhag Priodi Saesnes", he counsels against the marriage with a descendant of Hengist and Horsa, what he describes as a *Saesnes o ryw Seisnig* ("an English woman of English stock").[69] Indeed, it appears that this suspicion of mixed marriages was one commonly shared within the bardic fraternity.[70]

Dafydd ab Edmwnd was a landowner and the owner of Yr Owredd estate in Maelor Saesneg on the porous and somewhat ill-defined border of England and Wales (in what would later become a detached part of Flintshire).[71] He was sufficiently established to be able to craft poetry according to his personal inclinations and without that dependency on patronage which typified his contemporaries. His poetic repertoire was wide, and included elegies, eulogies, poems seeking favour (*canu gofyn*), love poems and religious poems. Dafydd ab Edmwnd, besides his personal output as a poet, would leave a permanent mark on the Welsh bardic tradition as the leading agent in standardising the bardic strict meter conventions at the Carmarthen Eisteddfod of 1451.[72]

Although the consensus among scholars is to place Dafydd ab Edmwnd in the second class of Welsh poets in what was a golden period, it is also recognised that he has work that reaches the highest peaks.[73] And the elegy to Siôn Eos, as Saunders Lewis acknowledged,

---

[68] See also the note on the Hanmer family in the *Dictionary of Welsh Biography* (online).

[69] Thomas Roberts, ed., *Gwaith Dafydd ab Edmwnd* (Bangor: Jarvis and Foster, 1914), 91-93 (poem XLVII).

[70] See Helen Fulton, "Class and Nation: Defining the English in Late-Medieval Welsh Poetry," in Ruth Kennedy and Simon Meecham-Jones, eds., *Authority and Subjugation in Writing of Medieval Wales* (New York: Palgrave Macmillan, 2008), 191-212, at 204.

[71] W. T. R. Pryce, "Migration and the Evolution of Culture Areas: Cultural and Linguistic Frontiers in North-East Wales, 1750 and 1851," *Transactions of the Institute of British Geographers* 65, (1975) 79-107.

[72] See Roberts, ed., *Gwaith Dafydd ab Edmwnd*, at vii-xvii.

[73] Johnston, *Llên yr Uchelwyr*, 252.

was among his finest works.[74] The poem is crafted in the *cywydd* strict meter and is a beautiful and personal lament for a master harpist. Corroborating the aptness of his sobriquet *"Eos,"* which is Welsh for nightingale, the cywydd claims that neither angel nor man could fail to weep at hearing Siôn's renditions. But in addition to its aesthetic virtues, the elegy also offers a pungent critique of a legal order which, it is claimed, facilitated a miscarriage of justice.

Chirk, the scene of the events, was a marcher lordship where the Welsh and English shared an uneasy coexistence in the years following the ill-fated Glyndŵr rebellion. Due to the uncertainty about the precise date of the events concerned, we cannot be certain as to who was the Constable of Chirk who condemned the harpist to his fate. Authority in the March of Wales was in a state of constant flux, made worse by the attrition caused by the dynastic struggle that became later known as the war of the roses, a struggle in which the Welsh had more than a passing interest.[75] There is evidence to suggest that Thomas Strange was Constable of Chirk at the time of Henry V's death in 1422.[76] He was a member of the Lestrange family who had been prominent marcher lords in the area in question since soon after the Norman conquest. But Thomas Strange was dead by 1436, well before the events in question. A more likely candidate is Sir Otewell Worsley, an Englishman who married the daughter of Edward ap Dafydd Trevor of one of the native noble families of the Welsh borders.[77] One source suggests that he was appointed Constable of Chirk in 1445, but another source states that the date of appointment was 24 June 1461.[78] Worsley held the post before the time of Wiliam ap Siôn Edwart, the constable on whom Tudur Aled lavished praise.[79]

---

[74] See Saunders Lewis, *Meistri a'u Crefft* (Cardiff: University of Wales Press, 1981), 124.

[75] Victoria Flood, "Henry Tudor and Lancastrian Prophecy in Wales," *Proceedings of the Harvard Celtic Colloquium* 34 (2014), 67-86.

[76] Margaret Mahler, *A History of Chirk Castle and Chirkland* (London: G. Bell & Sons Ltd., 1912), 85, 87.

[77] Douglas Richardson and Kimball G. Everingham, *Magna Carta Ancestry: A Study in Colonial and Medieval Families* IV, second ed. (Salt Lake City: Genealogical Publishing Company, 2011), 107.

[78] Nathen Amin, *The House of Beaufort: The Bastard Line that Captured the Crown* (Stroud: Amberley Publishing Limited, 2017), chapter 24.

[79] Jones, ed., *Gwaith Tudur Aled*, Poem LXIII, 253-56.

Thomas Roberts recounted the tradition that the Constable of Chirk may have executed the harpist as an act of revenge on the Constable of Oswestry, who had earlier executed one of the servants of the Constable of Chirk for some unknown offence. As the Constable of Oswestry was a known benefactor and friend of Siôn Eos, the driving motivation behind his hanging, according to this theory, was pure revenge.[80]

The poem can be best analysed as an epic in three parts. The first part is that which provides us with an account of the circumstances that led to the execution. The poet's grievance is that the hanging was an unduly harsh and futile penalty for what had been an unintentional killing in the heat of the moment because of a 'petty cause.' From the outset, we are told that the harpist was hanged for killing another in a 'chance brawl.' This is a crucial point to which we shall return. No good could come from executing the perpetrator, the poet claims, and the hanging risked escalation and creating an appetite for revenge and blood feud.[81]

> *Drwg i neb a drigo 'n ôl*
> *Dau am un cas damweiniol.*
> *Y drwg lleiaf o 'r drygwaith*
> *Yn orau oll yn yr iaith.*
> *O wŷr, pam na bai orau,*
> *O lleddid un na lladd dau?*
> *Dwyn, un gelynwaed, a wnaeth*
> *Dial ein dwy elyniaeth.*
> *Oedd oer ladd y ddeuwr lân*
> *Heb achos ond un bychan.*[82]

Wrong for one who remains after
To stay mum about a chance brawl,

---

80 Roberts, ed., *Gwaith Dafydd ab Edmwnd*, 155.
81 The version studied here is as it appears in contemporary orthography in Thomas Parry, ed., *Oxford Book of Welsh Verse* (Oxford: Oxford University Press, 1962), thereafter OBWV, 138-41, Poem 75. See also Roberts, ed., *Gwaith Dafydd ab Edmwnd*, 78-81. The poem survives in several manuscripts, including Cardiff MS 7 and MS 19, and the British Museum MS 31 and MS 48.
82 OBWV, Poem 75, lines 1-10.

The least wrong of wrongdoings
By the best of all in our tongue.
Oh men, were it not better,
If one's slain, not to slay two?
Avenging one enemy's blood
Has made the enmity double.
Sad was two good men's slaying
For naught but a petty cause. [83]

Dafydd ab Edmwnd then presents us with his first ground of
appeal, which is that the condemned was tried and punished according
to English law, although he was, ethnically, a Welshman, and should
therefore have been availed of the principles of Cyfraith Hywel:

Sorrais wrth gyfraith sarrug
Swydd y Waun, Eos a ddug.
Y Swydd, pam na roit dan sêl
I'th Eos gyfraith Hywel?
Ar hwn wedi cael o'r rhain
Wrth lawnder, cyfraith Lundain,
Ni mynnent am ei einioes
Noethi crair na thorri croes.
Y gŵr oedd dad y gerdd dant,
Yn oeswr ni barnasant
Deuddeg, yn un oeddyn',
Duw deg, ar fywyd y dyn, [84]

I was angered by Y Waun's
Surly law, it took Eos.
Y Waun, why not under seal
Apply Hywel's law to your Eos?
When these imposed upon him,
In its fullness, London's law,
They would not, for his life's sake,

---

[83] Joseph Clancy, *Medieval Welsh Poems* (Dublin: Four Courts Press,
2003), 332-34, at 332.
[84] OBWV, Poem 75, lines 23-34.

Cut a cross or bare a relic.[85]
The man who was music's father,
They'd judged that he should not live,
The twelve, they were united,
Dear God, on taking his life. [86]

Dafydd ab Edmwnd may have had a valid legal point, as it was likely that the laws applied in the lordship of Chirk were dependant on the ethnicity of the accused. The execution of Siôn Eos came about because the laws of England, or the laws of London as they are described in the poem, were applied rather than the native Welsh laws. Had the Welsh laws, or the laws of Hywel, been applied in this case, the outcome would have led to compensation for the victim's family rather than punishing the perpetrator. Accordingly, the accused's life would have been spared. This is not merely a legal point, but an appeal to fairness and rationality.

We are also informed that the harpist was tried by a jury of twelve, the great English legal innovation that had been imported to Wales, and that no mercy was shown towards him.[87] This poetic reference to the jury is reminiscent of the cywydd crafted by Gruffudd Llwyd ap Dafydd ab Einion Llygliw (c. 1380-1420), towards the end of the fourteenth century, which also mentions the jury. His "Cywydd y Cwest ar Forgan ap Dafydd o Rydodyn" lists the names of twelve poets who could be summoned to serve on a jury in an inquest. That poem was a response to the case of Morgan ap Dafydd, who was accused of killing a legal officer somewhere between Cardigan and Carmarthen, and subsequently brought before the judge Sir David Hanmer (Dafydd ab Edmwnd's great uncle) in Carmarthen.[88]

---

[85] The translation of this line is not faithful to the Welsh original, and a more accurate version would be "to lay bare a relic nor to make the sign of the cross," both being indicative of forgiveness.
[86] Clancy, *Medieval Welsh Poems*, 332-33.
[87] See Dafydd Jenkins, "Towards the Jury in Medieval Wales," in John W. Cairns and John McLeod, eds., *'The Dearest Birth Right of the People of England': The Jury in the History of the Common Law* (Oxford: Hart, 2002), 17-46.
[88] See Thomas Roberts, "Cywydd y Cwest ar Forgan ap Dafydd o Rydodyn gan Ruffudd Llwyd ap Dafydd ab Einion," *Bulletin of the Board of Celtic Studies*, 1 (1921-23), 237-40.

The mention here of the refusal to *noethi crair* and *torri croes* (not to bare a relic nor to make the sign of a cross) to save the accused's life adds an apparently religious dimension to the poet's complaint, and it is a detail which has legal significance. An ideological retreat from employing divine intervention in English legal process had followed the Lateran Council of 1215, which prohibited priests from consecrating or otherwise blessing various forms of trial by ordeal, thereby rendering the process obsolete.[89] In fact, it has been a matter of debate and speculation as to the extent to which trial by water or by hot iron were in common use prior to this.[90] Moreover, there is a consensus among scholars that trial by ordeal, whether by water, fire or by battle, does not appear in any of the Welsh legal manuscripts.[91] Trial by ordeal is not mentioned in the practitioner's manual, *Llyfr Cynghawsedd*, and only in a few texts belonging to the Marcher regions is there any mention of trial by ordeal in legal process. Indeed, trial by compurgation and pleading, *rhwym dadl*, has been hailed as one of the great qualities of Welsh legal custom. [92]

Yet the absence of trial by ordeal did not preclude the invocation of divine intercession from the precepts of Cyfraith Hywel, as the use of the cross and/or a holy relic appears repeatedly in the manuscripts.[93] Indeed, in the Welsh law of homicide, there is explicit reference to the use of a relic and the swearing of oaths in order to establish the

---

[89] H. L. Ho, "The Legitimacy of Medieval Proof," *Journal of Law and Religion* 19(2), (2003-04), 259-98.

[90] See Margaret H. Kerr, Richard D. Forsyth and Michael J. Plyley, "Cold Water and Hot Iron: Trial by Ordeal in England," *Journal of Interdisciplinary History*, 22 (4), (1992), 573-95, at 581.

[91] As Dafydd Jenkins stated: "In Wales the classical and earlier lawbooks do not mention ordeal or battle: in a land which was never pagan, perhaps it was never thought proper to tempt God by asking for a miraculous vindication of the accused innocent. But the Welsh methods were objective: they depended on oaths sworn by the parties or by witnesses of various kinds, and the lawbooks tell the judge what oaths are required in the different kinds of case." Jenkins, *The Law of Hywel Dda*, xxxii

[92] See, for example, Watkin, *The Legal History of Wales*, 73; Jenkins, "Towards the Jury in Medieval Wales," 26-28.

[93] For references to the Holy Cross, see Jenkins, *The Law of Hywel Dda*, 123, 159 and 207.

liabilities of the killer's kindred for the compensation due to the victim and his kin.[94] Also, of passing interest, is Sara Elin Roberts's study of a religious custom in fifteenth century Brycheiniog in connection with a land action described as *dadl croes* (pleading the cross).[95] The action as described involved the use of the cross, which would have been placed on the disputed land or given to the defendant to "register that a legal action over the land had been initiated."[96] The defendant might then break the cross to indicate his disputing the claim. The cross was thus a device used to initiate proceedings, and to engage the defendant in the dispute.

This ritual gives some support to the belief that in the borderlands where a combination of Welsh and English customs co-existed, the holy cross and religious relics continued to play a vital part in legal process. Indeed, customs which appealed for divine guidance involving the use of a relic or cross may have originated in Cyfraith Hywel and continued to be in circulation in the Welsh borders into the fifteenth century. In this case, Dafydd ab Edmwnd's complaint was that the symbols of Christian mercy were not invoked to the detriment of his executed friend.

But the poet's principal argument was that compensation, which would have been paid in accordance with Cyfraith Hywel, would have been of more benefit than the execution, and that Siôn Eos's weight in gold would have been paid to circumvent the taking of the harpist's life *("er byw Siôn.")*

> *Y corff dros y corff pes caid,*
> *Yr iawn oedd well i'r enaid.*
> *Oedd, wedi addewidion*
> *Ei bwys o aur er byw Siôn.*[97]

> If body paid for body,
> Better's recompense for the soul.

---

[94] Jenkins, *The Law of Hywel Dda*, 145.
[95] Sara Elin Roberts, "Legal Practice in Fifteenth-century Brycheiniog," *Studia Celtica*, 35, (2001), 307-23.
[96] Roberts, "Legal Practice in Fifteenth-century Brycheiniog," 311.
[97] OBWV, Poem 75, lines 19-22.

Afterwards there were pledges
Of his weight in gold for Siôn's life.[98]

What is the significance of these pledges of gold, and how exactly might the application of Cyfraith Hywel have secured a different outcome? At the heart of the native Welsh law of homicide was the custom of *galanas*, which is referred to as one of the three columns of the law in the lawbooks.[99] *Galanas* was a term which represented both a vendetta or blood feud between the family of the victim and that of the perpetrator of a wrong (the Welsh word *gelyn*, meaning enemy, derives from the same root), but also the compensation designed to avoid such a vendetta.[100] The practical application of *galanas* required the kin of the wrongdoer to pay compensation to the kin of the victim, in accordance with rules laid out which took into account the degree of relationship, and which involved kindred up to the seventh degree of relationship (descendants of a common great grandfather, i.e. four generations, were thus involved).[101] It had similar counterparts in Anglo-Saxon, Irish and Icelandic legal codes.[102]

The custom of galanas, already on the wane in thirteenth century Gwynedd, would suffer a decline in the principalities with the introduction of English criminal law following the conquest of 1282, and the constitutional settlement in the Statute of Rhuddlan (Wales) 1284.[103] By then, the English had come to the view that the idea of

---

[98] Clancy, *Medieval Welsh Poems*, 332.

[99] For a discussion on how *galanas* is treated in the lawbooks, see Robin Chapman Stacey, *Law and the Imagination in Medieval Wales* (Philadelphia: University of Pennsylvania Press, 2018), 185-96; also see Dafydd Jenkins, "Towards the Jury in Medieval Wales" in J. W. Cairns and G. McLeod, eds., *The Dearest Birth Right of the People of England: The Jury in the History of the Common Law* (Oxford: Oxford University Press, 2002), 17-46, at 22-24.

[100] See R. R. Davies, "The Survival of the Bloodfeud in Medieval Wales," *History* 54, (1969), 338-57, at 344.

[101] Jenkins, *The Law of Hywel Dda,* 144-45.

[102] See Richard Ireland, *Land of White Gloves? A History of Crime and Punishment in Wales* (London: Routledge, 2015), 12-13.

[103] See W. H. Waters, *The Edwardian Settlement of North Wales in its Administrative and Legal Aspects* (Cardiff: University of Wales Press, 1935), 135-37.

paying compensation for a killing was not entirely palatable.[104] Yet, galanas endured longer in the march of Wales, where recourse to compensation rather than punishment continued as an alternative means of legal remedy.[105] Indeed, as Sir Rees Davies remarked, "in the march of Wales, *galanas* in the fourteenth and fifteenth centuries was still a recognized action at law and a means of terminating a case of homicide."[106] This was due partly to its deep roots within the Welsh cultural psyche, but also because the marcher lords, with their proverbial eyes for the main chance, would often personally benefit from many of the Welsh customs as they also required a tax or payment to the local magnate. It was a clear example of tolerating continuation in the interests of mutual convenience.[107]

The poet's grievance was that the accused was not tried in accordance with the native Welsh laws, which would have spared his life. Was there another ground of appeal? The constant reference in the poem to an unintentional killing may have alerted the reader to the possibility that this was a less culpable form of killing. But the poet offers us something more specific. In this extract, the poet turns his thoughts to the compatibility of the harpist's execution with English Law:

> *Er briwio'r gŵr, heb air gwad,*
> *O bu farw, ni bu fwriad.*
> *Yr oedd y diffyg ar rai*
> *Am adladd mewn* **siawns medlai.**
> *Ymryson am yr oesau,*
> *Rhyw yng a ddaeth rhwng y ddau;*
> *Oddyna lladd y naill ŵr,*
> *A'i ddial, lladd y ddeuwr.*[108]

---

[104] R. R. Davies, "The Twilight of Welsh Law, 1284–1536" *History* 51 (172), (1966), 143-64, at 143.

[105] For a case-study from Dyffryn Clwyd of the 1430s, see Llinos Beverley Smith, "A Contribution to the History of 'Galanas' in Late-Medieval Wales," *Studia Celtica*, 43 (2009), 87-94.

[106] Davies, "The Survival of the Bloodfeud in Medieval Wales," 344.

[107] Davies, "The Survival of the Bloodfeud in Medieval Wales," 353; also Davies, "The Twilight of Welsh Law, 1284-1536," 161.

[108] OBWV, Poem 75, lines 11-18; Emphasis added.

Though he stabbed the man, no denial,
If he died, there was no intent.
The fault was with some of them
Striking back in a chance mingling.
Disputing family lines,
Some trouble came between them;
From that, the one man's slaying,
And avenging him, both men slain.[109]

Joseph Clancy's translation does not alert us to the fact that the original Welsh version refers to *siawns medlai*.[110] *Siawns medlai*, a legal term, is a Welsh form of the Anglo-French phrase, *chance-medlee*, or *chaude mêlée*, which would later be Anglicised and evolve into the legal expression, chance medley. The phrased is derived from the French expression, hot fight, which became an English legal term meaning a sudden and unexpected killing during a violent struggle or affray. The essence of the chance medley was a killing without any premeditation or planning, or any malice aforethought. Chance medley thus became a shorthand phrase to mean a killing in the heat of the moment.

The legal distinction between a reckless killing, and killing by conspiracy or with malicious intent, was becoming firmly rooted in English law by the sixteenth century, and the outcome for the perpetrator would be radically different.[111] For the killer who acted in the course of an affray, and who successfully pleaded the partial defence of chance medley, would have his property forfeited, but, crucially, his life would be spared.[112] Later, the lesser killing would evolve into what would become known as *voluntary manslaughter*, a

---

[109] Clancy, *Medieval Welsh Poems*, 332.
[110] Neither is it to be found in the authoritative University of Wales Welsh language dictionary, *Geiriadur Prifysgol Cymru/ A Dictionary of the Welsh Language*: https://geiriadur.ac.uk/gpc/gpc.html.
[111] Joshua Dressler, "Rethinking Heat of Passion: A Defense in Search of a Rationale," *The Journal of Criminal Law & Criminology* 73, no. 2, (1982), 421-70, at 426.
[112] J. H. Baker, *An Introduction to English Legal History*, fifth ed. (Oxford: Oxford University Press, 2019), 571.

less culpable homicide than murder.[113] These evolving concepts of the criminal law represented a gradual shift of emphasis from measuring culpability on the basis of the injury caused to the victim, to that of the offender's state of mind and moral responsibility (known to common lawyers as the *mens rea*). Kamali's recent work has shown that even as early as the thirteenth and fourteenth centuries, the concept of *mens rea* and the role of the accused's intentions was discernible in English criminal law and a determinative factor for juries when assessing moral culpability. As she remarks, "mens rea played a crucial role in jury considerations from the earliest days of the criminal trial jury."[114]

However, there was a consensus among legal historians that the chance medley defence only came of age and became established as a recognised partial defence in English law during the mid to late sixteenth century. By then the defence, if established, meant that the accused was not found guilty of murder but of manslaughter.[115] Later, elements of the chance medley would be incorporated into the defence of provocation.[116] But the chronology in relation to the development of the chance medley defence, and its mentioning in this poem, is significant. For a considerable time, the belief was that the defence of chance medley could only be traced back as far as 1532, when a statute of Henry VIII explicitly mentioned it. Indeed, it was generally believed that the defence only emerged as a "term of record" in the reign of the second Tudor monarch.[117] However, Thomas Green's painstaking research proved that the expression 'chance melée' was in legal usage by the end of the fourteenth century, and was also

---

[113] As explained by Bernard J. Brown, "The Demise of Chance Medley and the Recognition of Provocation as a Defence to Murder in English Law," *The American Journal of Legal History* 7 no. 4, (1963), 310-18.

[114] Elizabeth Papp Kamali, *Felony and the Guilty Mind in Medieval England* (Cambridge: Cambridge University Press, 2019), 40-43.

[115] See Rollin M. Perkins, "A Re-Examination of Malice Aforethought," *Yale Law Journal* 43, (1934), 537-70, at 544; also Laurie J Taylor, "Provoked Reason in Men and Women: Heat-of-Passion Manslaughter and Imperfect Self-Defense," *UCLA Law Review* 33, (1986), 1679-735, at 1684.

[116] See Thomas Glyn Watkin, "Hamlet and the Law of Homicide," *Law Quarterly Review* 100, (1984), 282-310.

[117] See John R. Gillespie, "The Origin and Development of Chance-Medley in the Law of Manslaughter," *Kentucky Law Journal* 37 no. 1, (1948), 86-90, at 86.

mentioned in legal treatise at the beginning of the sixteenth century, well before the statute aforementioned.[118] Dafydd ab Edmwnd's claim that the killing occurred in in a chance medley is therefore highly significant, and not merely to the student of medieval Welsh poetry. It at least suggests that the phrase and its meaning had already gained general currency among lawyers and those with lay interests in the law by the middle of the fifteenth century, almost a century before it was mentioned in the statute of Henry VIII. Its appearance in this poem therefore gives further support to the belief that the chance medley defence had origins and common usage in English law far earlier than previously believed.

For the poet, it gave further grounds for arguing that the verdict and execution were inappropriate, and that the punishment did not fit the crime. Indeed, the compensation to the victim's kindred that might have resulted from the application of Cyfraith Hywel mirrored that of the power to forfeit the property of a person convicted of killing in a 'chance melée' that was to be found in English Law. In other words, and by way of a pleading in the further or alternative, Dafydd ab Edmwnd's poem is an argument to the effect that, even if Cyfraith Hywel was not the appropriate legal code in this case, neither was the hanging compliant with the emerging principles of the English common law. This was surely Dafydd ab Edmwnd's legal flair applied with poetical prowess.

The second and middle section of the poem is a lament for the lost harpist. It is more conventional in terms of its tone, although the detail is remarkable and provides a vivid portrait of the executed man:

> *Aeth y gerdd a'i thai gwyrddion*
> *A'i da'n sied wedi dwyn Siôn,*
> *A llef o nef yn ei ôl,*
> *A'i ddisgybl yn ddiysgol.*
> *Llyna ddysg! I'r llan ydd aeth;*
> *Lle ni chair lluniwch hiraeth.*
> *Wedi Siôn nid oes synnwyr*
> *Da'n y gerdd, na dyn a'i gŵyr.*
> *Torres braich tŵr Eos brig,*

---

[118] Thomas A. Green, "The Jury and the English Law of Homicide, 1200-1600," *Michigan Law Review* 74, (1976), 413-99, at 467-68.

Torred mesur troed musig;
Torred ysgol tŷ'r desgant,
Torred dysg fal torri tant.
Oes mwy rhwng Euas a Môn
O'r dysg abl i'r disgyblion?
Rheinallt nis gŵyr ei hunan,
Rhan gŵr er hynny a gân.
Ef aeth ei gymar yn fud,
Yn dortwll delyn Deirtud.[119]

Music and its green mansion
And its wealth's forfeit, Siôn gone,
And a cry from heaven follows him,
And schoolless is his disciple.
Behold learning: gone to the grave;
Where it's lacked, fashion longing.
After Siôn there's no fine art
In song, nor man who knows it.
An arm broke Eos' tree-top tower:
Broken the beat of music's foot,
Broken was descant's schoolroom,
Broken learning, like breaking a string.
Is there from Euas to Môn
Sufficient learning for students?
Rheinallt himself doesn't know it;
Despite that, he plays a man's part.
His fellow has been struck dumb,
Shattered the harp of Teirtud. [120]

The loss of the talented harpist who was also an accomplished tutor is the refrain. With his death, no one between Anglesey and Ewyas, the entire length of Wales in other words, could replace him. Mention is made of Rheinallt, another fine harpist from Dolgellau who had learnt his craft under the tuition of Siôn Eos.[121] Lloyd, in his *History of Powys Fadog*, mentions both in these terms: "At Dolgelley was born Reinallt, a clever harper, who contended with Sion Eos for

---

[119] OBWV, Poem 75, lines 35-52.
[120] Clancy, *Medieval Welsh Poems*, 333.
[121] Roberts, ed., *Gwaith Dafydd ab Edmwnd*, 155.

the laurel, about 1450, but was unsuccessful."[122] This along with what we know of Dafydd ab Edmwnd's career, would date the execution of Siôn Eos, and Dafydd ab Edmwnd's elegy, sometime during the second half of the fifteenth century.

In this and the subsequent sections of the elegy we are introduced to Welsh musical terminology, such as the word *desgant*, which is a borrowing from the English musical term, descant.[123] The repeated reference to *torri, torred/torres*, meaning to break, deepens the sense of irreplaceable and permanent loss. The harp of Teirtu, mentioned in this extract, is also mentioned in the legend of Culhwch ac Olwen as a magical instrument which could play itself or stop when requested: *Telyn Teirtu y'm didanu y nos honno. Pan uo da gan dyn, canu a wna e hunan; pan uynher idi, tewi a wna* ("Teritu's harp entertained me that night. If it pleased anyone, it would play itself; if desired, it would become silent").[124] Here, the poets laments that the legendary harp has been shattered by Siôn's death, a metaphor which further emphasises the extent of the loss.[125]

Other legal references are also significant in this section of the poem. In the lines "aeth y gerdd a'i thai gwyrddion/ a'i da'n sied wedi dwyn Siôn," the use of the word "sied" has a legal implication. It is translated by Clancy as "forfeit," but perhaps the more technically accurate translation would be escheated, which derives from the Middle English word, *chete*. To escheat was to invoke a process in English Law that resulted in a dispossession and transfer of ownership from the estate of a deceased person to another, usually higher authority such as the king, upon certain conditions being met.[126] One of those conditions was if the landholder committed a felony. In those

---

[122] See J. Y. W. Lloyd, *History of Powys Fadog* Vol. VI (London: Whiting and Co., 1887), at 402.

[123] For further guidance on this reference, see Sally Harper, *Music in Welsh Culture before 1650: A Study of the Principal Sources* (London: Routledge, 2016), at 131.

[124] Idris Foster, Rachel Bromwich and D. Simon Evans, eds., *Culhwch ac Olwen* (Cardiff: University of Wales Press, 1988), 23, lines 627-29.

[125] Peter Crossley-Holland, *"Telyn Teirtu": Myth and Magic in Medieval Wales* (Bangor: Canolfan Uwch-Astudiaethau Cerddoriaeth Cymru, 1997).

[126] See Notes, "Origins and Development of Modern Escheat," *Columbia Law Review* 61 no.7, (1961), 1319-40, at 1322.

circumstances, the legal reasoning was that "the felony so corrupted his blood that he could have no heirs."[127] The consequence was that the land would be forfeited by the Crown, and the heirs would be dispossessed of their patrimony.[128]

The deployment of the legal term, to escheat, had a literal meaning, as the executed felon's land would be forfeited to the Crown because of his conviction and execution (although we have no evidence that this happened in this specific case). But was the forfeiture legal? The poet makes a significant claim in the line, "*A 'i da'n sied wedi **dwyn** Siôn*." It seems that the Clancy translation overlooks the added significance of the word "*dwyn*" as the legal term "to steal" or "to thieve."[129] The use of the word "dwyn" has heightened significance because the poet is saying that Sion's life was stolen or taken illegally, and that, accordingly, the forfeiture was not lawful. We are therefore presented with potentially two unlawful takings, that of the life of the harpist and his patrimony. And even if we should not read this phrase too literally, the use of the term escheat had an added metaphorical meaning in this context. It arguably conveys a sense that Siôn had no worthy heirs in his craftsmanship as a harpist, nobody who could inherit his great talent, and that a great cultural asset had been lost with his execution. For the poet, Sion's death led to the dispossession of music and its mansions, which might also be interpreted as the venues where the harpist would perform being at least culturally escheated by a foreign authority.

The poem thereafter continues in an elegiac tone as it eulogises Siôn Eos's musical talent, a talent which the poet claims would cause an angel to weep. The harpist's technical skill as a harpist is described in detail and his fingering technique is given careful attention, such as in this couplet, *Myfyrdawd rhwng bawd a bys/Mên a threbl mwyn â*

---

[127] See S. F. C. Milsom, *Historical Foundations of the Common Law*, second edition (London: Butterworths, 1981), 109.

[128] Baker, *An Introduction to English Legal History*, 260.

[129] For comment on *dwyn* meaning *dwgyd*, that is, to steal, in the fifteenth century, see *Geiriadur Prifysgol Cymru/ A Dictionary of the Welsh Language*: https://geiriadur.ac.uk/gpc/gpc.html.

thribys ("A musing between finger and thumb/Mean (inner part) and sweet treble, three-fingered.)"[130]

> *Ti sydd yn tewi â sôn,*
> *Telyn aur telynorion.*
> *Bu'n dwyn dan bob ewin dant,*
> *Bysedd llef gŵr neu basant;*
> *Myfyrdawd rhwng bawd a bys,*
> *Mên a threbl mwyn â thribys.*
> *Oes dyn wedi'r Eos deg*
> *Yn gystal a gân gosteg*
> *A phrofiad neu ganiad gŵr*
> *A chwlm ger bron uchelwr?*
> *Pwy'r awran mewn puroriaeth,*
> *Pe na bai, a wnâi a wnaeth?*
> *Nid oes nac angel na dyn*
> *Nad ŵyl pan gano delyn.*
> *Och heno rhag ei chanu,*
> *Wedi'r farn ar awdur fu!*[131]

You are silent, not a sound,
Golden harp of the harpists.
He'd hold a string under each nail,
Fingers for man's voice or solo,
A musing between finger and thumb,
Mean and sweet treble, three-fingered.
Is there one with fair Eos gone
His equal for a prelude,
Invention, or men's music,
And twined tune before a lord?
Who now in sweet harmony,
Without him, could do what he did?
There's not a man or angel
Would not weep when he played the harp.

---

[130] For further guidance on *cerdd dant* and medieval Welsh musical terminology, see Harper, *Music in Welsh Culture before 1650: A Study of the Principal Sources*, 7-159.

[131] OBWV, Poem 75, lines 53- 68.

R. GWYNEDD PARRY

Ah do not play it tonight
After the master's judgment![132]

In the final section, the elegy reaches a crescendo, and becomes much more than a critique of temporal legal processes. The concluding part reminds us of a further, higher jurisdiction to whom all, including the Constable of Chirk and his legal consorts, is answerable. Heaven's jurisdiction is thus the third jurisdiction to whom the poet turns. Drawing upon the familiar verses in chapter seven of Matthew's Gospel, it also it reminds us that both bardic and legal culture were anchored in the mores of Christendom.[133]

Eu barn ym mhorth nef ni bydd,
Wŷr y Waun, ar awenydd.
A farno, ef a fernir
O'r byd hwn i'r bywyd hir,
A'r un drugaredd a ro
A rydd Duw farnwr iddo.
Os iawn farn a fu arno,
Yr un farn arnyn' a fo.
Efô a gaiff ei fywyd,
Ond o'u barn newidio byd.
Oes y nyn y sy yn nos,
Oes yn Nuw i Siôn Eos.[134]

The musician won't bear their judgement,
Y Waun's men, at heaven's gate.
Who judges, he will have judgment
From this world to long-lasting life,
And the same mercy he shows
God as a judge will show him.
If on him just was the judgment,
Be the same judgement on them the same..
He will still possess his life,

---

[132] Clancy, *Medieval Welsh Poems*, 333.
[133] See Matthew 7, 1-3.
[134] OBWV, Poem 75, lines 69-80.

Just changing worlds, by their judgment
Life for man is in the night,
Life in God for Siôn Eos.[135]

Conclusions

Dafydd ab Edmwnd's elegy to Siôn Eos is a potent combination of a powerful lament, a social and legal critique and an expression of faith and hope in divine justice. In its rich detail we find layers of meaning which, at first glance, can easily escape our attention. This is partly due to the beauty of the poetry and the sureness of the poet's craft, as we are effortlessly absorbed by the tragedy and the poet's grief. But when read carefully in the original, the poem discloses nuanced messages about the precarious state of law and order in what was a volatile border province where English, Welsh and Marcher laws were in a state of perpetual struggle for dominance and survival, and where, at times, none were appropriately applied.

Moreover, and with the benefit of legal historical understanding, we can see how the poetic tradition offers added insights into a period when Wales was experiencing what was often a traumatic conflict of legal culture and social values. It is a tradition that can bear vivid testimony of native responses to the importation of alien legal values. In this instance, where no official records of the specific episode survive, poetry fills the gap and serves as an unofficial source of reaction and response to a legal event. And with the benefit of hindsight, the fate of Siôn Eos can also be seen as a metaphor for the fate of the native Welsh laws. In some prophetic way, the execution of the harpist, as told by Dafydd ab Edmwnd, also foretold the end of the remaining vestiges of the native Welsh laws in the century that followed.

There are also some universal conclusions that might be drawn. In addition to a general appreciation of the value of literature as a medium for understanding the impact of law and legal phenomena, literature has an added important function among conquered peoples whose experiences, historically, have been suppressed.[136] The

---

[135] Clancy, *Medieval Welsh Poems*, 333-34.
[136] See James Seaton, "Law and Literature: Works, Criticism, and Theory," *Yale Journal of Law & Humanities* 11 (1999), 479-507; Richard Weisberg,

perspectives of such peoples are only rarely preserved in the official annals.[137] Where the legal chronicles are silent, literature takes an invaluable function upon itself. It provides testimony that is otherwise hidden, including marginalized impressions of justice and authority and minoritized challenges to the validity and legitimacy of the legal order. It was the poetic tradition and, later, the folk culture that gave the Welsh people their voices throughout the centuries, and those same media gave them the means of recording their experiences of the law. Literature and other forms of popular culture, in these circumstances, become the main evidential sources of people's responses to the law. This insight is surely relevant to the legal experiences of suppressed peoples throughout the world and throughout history.

Poethics and Other Strategies of Law and Literature (Columbia: Columbia University Press, 1992), 3-47.

[137] In the example of Wales, see the valuable discussion of Catrin Fflur Huws, "Law, Literature, Language and the Construction of Welsh Identity," in Thomas Glyn Watkin, ed., *The Carno Poisonings and other Essays* (Bangor: Welsh Legal History Society, 2010), 99-120.

St. Tysilio in Medieval Welsh and Breton Hagiography

Amy Reynolds

Cynddelw Brydydd Mawr, in the opening caniad of his twelfth-century poem "Canu Tysilio", introduced St. Tysilio's Welsh cult centre as *breinawg log* ("a privileged monastery") . . . *Meifod wen* ("blessed Meifod") and declared *caraf-i lan a'r llên gan gadredd* ("I love a church and the splendid clerics").[1] There are limited references to Tysilio in Welsh hagiography, Cynddelw's poem being the most detailed surviving Welsh source. Other surviving Welsh references suggest that Tysilio's cult was well-established and widely understood in the context of medieval mid-Wales, as he appears as a geographical and historical marker in other Welsh saint's lives. Most notably, Tysilio appears in traditions relating to St. Beuno during that saint's time in mid-Wales. Beuno's Welsh life survives in the various texts of Buchedd Beuno, fourteenth-century Middle Welsh adaptations of Latin traditions from the late eleventh and early twelfth centuries.[2]

---

[1] Lines 51-52 and 45, Cynddelw Brydydd Mawr, *Canu Tysilio*. English translations adapted by author from Professor Ann Parry Owen, "Canu Tysilio", *Seintiau*, Centre for Advanced Welsh and Celtic Studies (CAWCS), Aberystwyth, https://saint2.llgc.org.uk/texts/verse/TysilioCBM/edited-text.eng.html accessed 3/12/2021. My thanks to Prof. Owen for a draft copy of the translations before online publication. Sections of the poem have also been discussed and translated in Nerys Ann Jones and Ann Parry Owen ed., *Gwaith Cynddelw Brydydd Mawr* (Cardiff: University of Wales Press, 1991), vol.1, pp. 15-18, pp. 28-40, and Nerys Ann Jones and Morfydd E. Owen, "Twelfth Century Welsh Hagiography: the *Gogynfeirdd* poems to saints", in Jane Cartwright ed., *Celtic Hagiography and Saint's Cults* (Cardiff: University of Wales Press, 2003), pp. 45-75. See also the chapter on Gwyddfarch and Tysilio in Patrick Thomas, *Celtic Earth, Celtic Heaven: Saints and Heroes of the Powys Borderland* (Llandysul: Gomer Press, 2003), pp. 13-38.

[2] §9 *Beuno a deuth, ef a'e disgyblonn, hyt ym Meivot, ac yno y trigyawd ef y gyt a Thyssyliaw sant deugein nieu a deugein nos* ("Beuno came, he and his disciples, as far as Meifod, and there he stayed with saint Tysilio forty days and forty nights"). Patrick Sims Williams, ed., *Buchedd Beuno: The Middle Welsh Life of St Beuno* (Dublin: Dublin Institute for Advanced Studies,

Beyond Wales, Tysilio's cult has survived in a composite life of St. Suliau in Brittany, compiled in the diocese of Saint Malo for the church of Saint-Suliac in the fifteenth century.[3] This essay aims to provide a contextual analysis of two hagiographical texts, one of Welsh origin, Cynddelw's poem "Canu Tysilio", and one of Breton origin, the composite life of St. Suliau as described in Albert Le Grand's 1637 compilation of saint's lives, *Les Vies des Saints de la Bretagne Armorique*.[4] According to the postscript of Le Grand's narrative, his text of "La Vie de Saint Suliau" was compiled from "ancient manuscript legendaries of the cathedral church of Léon and the collegiate church of Le Folgoët . . . agreeing with the original of his [Suliau's] Life, kept in his church of Saint-Suliau-Sur-Rance".[5] A further copy of "La Vie de Saint Suliau" was produced from the Lections of the Breviary of St. Malo and reprinted in the Bollandist Society's *Acta Sanctorum* in the late seventeenth century.[6] G.H. Doble argued that a Latin life of Tysilio reached Brittany in the fifteenth century, based on the emergence of Welsh material in the legends of Suliau, but it remains possible that a Life of Tysilio was already at Brittany before the fifteenth century and incorporated into Breton material later. [7]

2018), p. 145. For further discussion of the transference of texts relating to Buchedd Beuno, see Sims Williams' introductory chapter in Sims Williams, *Buchedd Beuno,* pp. 1-89.

For further discussion of Tysilio's cult in Wales see Peter C. Bartrum, *A Welsh Classical Dictionary: People in History and Legend up to about A.D. 1000* (Aberystwyth: The National Library of Wales, 1993), pp. 628-629. S. Baring-Gould and J. Fisher, *The Lives of the British Saints: The Saints of Wales and Cornwall* (London: The Honourable Society of Cymmrodorion, 1913), vol. 4, pp. 296-305.

[3] G.H. Doble, *Saints of Cornwall: Part Five Saints of Mid-Cornwall* (Truro: Dean and Chapter of Truro, 1970, reprinted Felinfach: Llanerch, 1998), p. 119.

[4] Albert Le Grand, *Les Vies des Saintes de la Bretagne Armorique* (Nantes, 1637), several of Suliau's traditions translated and edited in Doble, *The Saints of Cornwall,* pp. 104-126.

[5] Doble, *Saints of Cornwall,* p. 119.

[6] Doble, *Saints of Cornwall,* pp. 119-120. Baring-Gould and Fisher, *Lives of the British Saints,* vol. 4, p. 296.

[7] Doble, *Saints of Cornwall,* p. 111.

The following discussion has developed from research into the importance of Meifod church in the twelfth century. As such it will focus primarily on the significance of "Canu Tysilio" in Welsh hagiography, and the role the text played in emphasising the importance of Meifod church in response to ecclesiastical change in Wales. Comparison with the Breton texts is intended to further illuminate the Welsh source material and provide context for the development and transference of Tysilio's cult in the twelfth century. Given the paucity of surviving medieval references to Tysilio in Wales, the Breton hagiography offers an insight into Tysilio's traditions in medieval literature and fills some gaps in understanding the extent of Tysilio's cult in Wales and wider Europe.

"Canu Tysilio" formed part of the Centre for Advanced Welsh and Celtic Studies "Seintiau" project on Welsh Saint's Cults, a multi-disciplinary research project into the saints of Wales, which began in 2013 and included separate projects concentrated on vernacular and Latin saint's traditions.[8] The poem has been published online as part of the project from a linguistic perspective, with extensive notations and a translation by Professor Ann Parry Owen, accompanied by a useful discussion of the manuscript tradition of "Canu Tysilio".[9] Ann Parry Owen's translation and notes are a useful resource to understanding the linguistic and cultural development of the poem, and offer insight into twelfth-century gogynfeirdd poetry addressed to saints, especially when compared with "Canu Dewi" and "Canu Cadfan". The poems "Canu Tysilio", "Canu Dewi" and "Canu Cadfan" are the only surviving extensive twelfth-century gogynfeirdd hagiography and offer an interesting insight into the relationship between Welsh poetry and the promotion of saint's cults in twelfth-century Wales.[10] The "Seintiau" project has offered the opportunity to

---

[8] Centre for Advanced Welsh and Celtic Studies (CAWCS), "Seintiau: The Cult of Saints in Wales", https://saints.wales/. Accessed 20/12/2021. The projects were funded by the UK Arts and Humanities Research Council, https://saints.wales/projects/. Accessed 06/03/2022.

[9] Parry Owen, "Canu Tysilio", CAWCS, https://saint2.llgc.org.uk/texts/verse/TysilioCBM/introduction.eng.html. Accessed 21/12/2021.

[10] Nerys Ann Jones and Morfydd E. Owen compared these three poems in their article on twelfth-century *gogynfeirdd* (Welsh poets of the twelfth to

make important, culturally significant, sources more accessible for wider dissemination and will no doubt result in further study of the saints in Wales within different contexts. The aim of this essay is to provide one such study. It is a discussion to accompany Ann Parry Owen's online publication of "Canu Tysilio" and to provide ecclesiastical context for the development and spread of Tysilio's cult. Particularly it will emphasise the role of the community of Meifod in the promotion of Tysilio's cult, highlight the significance of saint's cults in the twelfth-century Welsh church and provide a context for the compilation of "Canu Tysilio" and the Cambro-Latin *Vita* that both Cynddelw and the Breton compilers appear to have drawn from. Cynddelw's poem is as much a panegyric for Meifod church, and its superiority as a *clas* (religious community) church, as it is for Tysilio himself.[11] Ecclesiastical context is a key factor in understanding the significance of Tysilio in Welsh and Breton hagiography.

By comparing the themes in "Canu Tysilio" and "La Vie de Saint Suliau", this paper will argue both texts shared a common written source, suggesting the existence of a, now lost, twelfth-century Cambro-Latin *Vita* of St. Tysilio from which both Cynddelw and the Breton compilers adapted for their own texts. While an orthographic analysis between the texts would help to suggest more firmly the language of the shared text, this paper is intended as a contextual comparative. Without further linguistic study, it is not possible to establish the shared source was definitively Cambro-Latin: it is possible the Breton compilers were working from a Middle Welsh source. Proper nouns in the Breton text are based on Old Welsh orthography, as noted by Ann Parry Owen, evidencing an early Welsh written account of Tysilio.[12] Other evidence for the composition of Latin *Vitae* of Welsh saints in the late eleventh and twelfth century, such as Rhygyfarch's *Vita* of St. David, or Robert of Shrewsbury's *Vita* of St. Winifred, implies a Cambro-Latin written account of Tysilio would be more consistent with twelfth-century Welsh

---

fourteenth century) poetry. Jones and Owen, "Twelfth-century Welsh hagiography", in Cartwright ed., *Celtic Hagiography*, pp. 45-75.

[11] Jones and Owen, "Twelfth-century Welsh Hagiography", pp. 59-60.

[12] Introduction, Parry Owen ed., "Canu Tysilio", CAWCS, https://saint2. llgc.org.uk/texts/verse/TysilioCBM/introduction.eng.html. Accessed 14/12/2021.

hagiography. Patrick Sims-Williams, in his edition of *Buchedd Beuno*, discussed the transference of Latin and Welsh texts of Winifred and Beuno and compared the development of those texts with Tysilio, noting "the Welsh *Vita* of Tysilio, which the Bretons adapted to fit St. Sulian, is lost, but Cynddelw's poem in praise of Tysilio and Meifod leaves no doubt that such a *Vita* existed by c.1160".[13]

To understand the significance of "Canu Tysilio" in relation to the church at Meifod, it is worth understanding the context in which the poem was composed, by highlighting the importance of Meifod church in the twelfth century. Meifod is located in eastern Wales, in the kingdom of Powys near the Welsh/English border, in a landscape steeped in local political and spiritual significance, a mile north-east of Mathrafal believed by the thirteenth century to have been the *llys* (court) of the princes of Powys. D.R. Thomas, in his history of the Diocese of St. Asaph, put the earliest ecclesiastical site at Meifod to pre-seventh century, when he noted "eglwys Gwyddfarch", "the oratory of that ancient anchorite, a primitive structure, until it was superseded by the more substantial edifice which Tysilio built in the seventh century". According to Thomas, eglwys Gwyddfarch was still visible in the seventeenth century.[14] Both Tysilio and Gwyddfarch hold dedications at Meifod, alongside a twelfth-century dedication to St. Mary.[15]

In the twelfth century, the community enjoyed close relations with the political regime governing Powys, under Madog ap Maredudd (d. 1160), a dynasty re-established a generation earlier after

---

[13] Sims-Williams, *Buchedd Beuno*, p. 50. Introduction, Parry Owen ed., "Canu Tysilio", CAWCS, https://saint2.llgc.org.uk/texts/verse/TysilioCBM/introduction.eng.html. Accessed 10/12/2021

[14] D.R. Thomas, *The History of the Diocese of St. Asaph* (Oswestry: Caxton Press, 1906), vol.1, pp. 496-497.

[15] K. Steele, Royal Commission for Ancient and Historic Monuments Wales Coflein, https://coflein.gov.uk/en/site/163220. Accessed 8/12/2021.
Thomas, *History of the Diocese of St. Asaph*, pp. 496-497. A.W. Wade Evans, *Parochiale Wallicanum: the Names of Churches and Chapels within the Dioceses of St. David's, Llandaff, Bangor and St. Asaph* (Stow-on-the-Wold, 1911, Reprinted by Alpha Edition: Indianapolis, 2019), p. 90.

two centuries of Gwynedd overlordship.[16] Meifod was a *clas* church, home to a community of religious, with a series of dependent daughter chapels ranging from Llanfair Caereinion in the south-west to Alberbury in the Shropshire March.[17]

By the 1150s, the spiritual supremacy at Meifod was increasingly threatened. Norman conquest and settlement in Wales had an impact on ecclesiastical organisation in Wales, accompanied by efforts to subject the Welsh bishops to the authority of the archbishop of Canterbury and to centralise church administration through the development of territorial dioceses, deaneries and parishes.[18] The community at Meifod was not only threatened in supremacy by other secular churches, but also by the spread of reformed European monasticism. While the Cistercian order, arguably the most successful monastic order in Wales, was yet to be firmly established in central Wales by the mid-twelfth-century, houses were being founded in the southeast, northeast and in the March.[19] This is the context in which we find the composition of "Canu Tysilio". The text forms part of a programme of promotion, where the community members at Meifod found themselves adapting to external pressure.

"Canu Tysilio" thus formed part of a larger programme of change and modernisation at Meifod in the twelfth century. Under the patronage of local ruler Madog ap Maredudd, Meifod underwent a process of 'Europeanisation' while retaining elements that promoted its superiority as a native Welsh church. A rededication of the church

---

[16] For the significance of Madog's llys and the re-emergence of Powys in the twelfth century see, David Stephenson, *Medieval Powys: Kingdom, Principality and Lordships, 1132-1293* (Woodbridge: Boydell Press, 2016), pp. 23-57.

[17] For a discussion on Meifod's ecclesiastical supremacy in the twelfth century, see Stephenson, *Medieval Powys*, pp. 248-252.

[18] For an overview on the Norman influence on the Welsh church see R.R. Davies, *The Age of Conquest: Wales 1063-1415* (Oxford: Oxford University Press, 2000), pp. 172-212. Glanmor Williams, *The Welsh Church from Conquest to Reformation* (Cardiff: University of Wales Press, 1962), pp. 1-35. For the role of Welsh clergyman see, John Reuben Davies, "Aspects of Church Reform in Wales", *Anglo-Norman Studies*, 30 (2008), pp. 85-99.

[19] "Powysian polities III: the ecclesiastical dimension", in Stephenson, *Medieval Powys*, pp. 248-274.

to the Virgin Mary in 1156 accompanied, and possibly signalled the completion of, an ambitious rebuilding project of the church in the fashionable Romanesque style of architecture, including the surviving twelfth century arches and Westwerk, characteristic of northern European churches of the time.[20]

Alongside these European style additions, the community promoted its native importance, retaining the earlier dedications to the Welsh saints Gwyddfarch and Tysilio. When Madog was buried at Meifod in 1160, the Welsh chronicle Brut y Tywysogion specified it was in the church of Tysilio, *"eglwys Tissilaw sant"*, suggesting that the Marian dedication of 1156 was in addition to, not in replacement of, the native dedications.[21] This suggests that European and Welsh elements complemented each other, creating a juxtaposition of local and international where Meifod church acknowledged the universal cult of Mary, but the primary dedication remained Tysilio's.

The earliest copies of the poem "Canu Tysilio" survive in two manuscripts, Llawsygrif Hendregadredd in the National Library of Wales, and Llyfr Coch Hergest in Jesus College Oxford, both manuscripts contain important versions of the text and provide a compendium of medieval Welsh poetry and prose.[22] "Canu Tysilio" was later copied into the manuscript NLW 4973B in 1634 by John Davies of Mallwyd, apparently copied from the now lost pages of the manuscript Peniarth 118 copied by Siôn Dafydd Rhys earlier in the seventeenth century.[23] Cynddelw's poetry in the Hendregadredd manuscript features in five quires, the first of which, containing

---

[20] Brut y Tywysogion, Thomas Jones ed. and trans., *Brut y Tywysogyon or The Chronicle of the Princes: Peniarth MS. 20 Version* (Cardiff: University of Wales Press, 1952), 1155-56, pp. 58-59. Malcolm Thurlby, Romanesque Architecture and Sculpture in Wales (Herefordshire: Logaston Press, 2006), pp. 264-265.

[21] Jones ed., *Brut y Tywysogion*, 1159-60, p, 61.

[22] National Library of Wales, Llwysgrif Hendregadredd, NLW MS 6680B, f32-33. Oxford University, Celtic Manuscripts, Llyfr Coch Hergest, Jesus College MS111, f.291r-292r.

[23] For a discussion of the relationship between the various manuscripts containing "Canu Tysilio," see Manuscripts, Parry Owen ed., "Canu Tysilio", CAWCS, https://saint2.llgc.org.uk/texts/verse/TysilioCBM/mss.eng.html. Accessed 11/03/2022.

Cynddelw's religious poetry, is lost. "Canu Tysilio" comes at the end of this first quire and as such the first 100 lines are missing. The section containing "Canu Tysilio" is also irreparably damaged and in parts illegible. "Canu Tysilio" in Llyfr Coch is more legible and it is possible to read the title, "canu tyssilyaw yw hwn, kyndelw ae cant" near the top of column 1165 on 291r.[24]

The Hendregadredd and Llyfr Coch versions of "Canu Tysilio" are in themselves later medieval versions of the original poem. Cynddelw flourished in the mid-twelfth century and the content and themes of "Canu Tysilio" are in line with other twelfth-century gogynfeirdd poems.[25] The patron of "Canu Tysilio" is a controversial topic debated by scholars, with compelling arguments put forward for a place of composition either within Madog ap Maredudd's llys in Powys in the mid-twelfth-century, or at the court of Owain Gwynedd in the later twelfth-century.[26] The argument for a place of composition in Gwynedd is mainly based on scattered references to Gwynedd throughout "Canu Tysilio". Tysilio is described as *periglawr periglus Wyndyd,* "confessional priest to the people of Gwynedd," with further references to Penmynydd and Anglesey.[27] Meifod is introduced to the

---

[24] For detailed discussion of the manuscripts see section on Manuscripts, Parry Owen ed., "Canu Tysilio", CAWCS, https://saint2.llgc.org.uk/ texts/verse/TysilioCBM/mss.eng.html. Accessed 14/12/21. See also National Library of Wales, Hendregadredd Manuscript, https://www.library.wales/discover/digital-gallery/manuscripts/the-middle-ages/hendregadredd-manuscript. Accessed 8/12/2021. See also, Daniel Huws, *Medieval Welsh Manuscripts* (Cardiff: University of Wales Press, 2000), pp. 193-226.
[25] As highlighted in Jones and Owen's article comparing "Canu Tysilio", "Canu Dewi" and "Canu Cadfan*",* Jones and Owen, "Twelfth Century Welsh Hagiography", in Cartwright ed., *Celtic Hagiography,* pp. 45-75.
[26] Jones and Owen ed., *Gwaith Cynddelw Brydydd Mawr (GCBM),* p. 18. Jones and Owen, "Twelfth Century Welsh Hagiography", in Cartwright ed., *Celtic Hagiography,* pp. 59-61. Stephenson, *Medieval Powys,* pp. 66-67. Ann Parry Owen summarises these arguments in her introduction, Parry Owen ed., "Canu Tysilio", CAWCS, https://saint2.llgc.org.uk/texts/verse/ TysilioCBM/introduction.eng.html.
[27] Lines 173, 196, 138, Parry Owen ed., "Canu Tysilio", CAWCS, https://saint2.llgc.org.uk/texts/verse/TysilioCBM/edited-text.eng.html. Jones and Owen, *GCBM,* pp. 32-33.

poem as "near the place where Gwyddfarch is beyond Gwynedd".[28] David Stephenson, Nerys Ann Jones and Morfydd Owen have argued that these references to Gwynedd suggest that Cynddelw composed "Canu Tysilio" at the court of Owain Gwynedd, reflecting the political desires of Owain Gwynedd to authority over Powys, which became politically splintered following the death of Madog ap Maredudd in 1160.[29]

Given the focus on legitimising the rights of Powys, and descriptions of people and events key in the early development of a kingdom of Powys, the performance of "Canu Tysilio" would have had a more significant impact on a Powys audience, than Gwynedd. The church of Meifod features prominently throughout the poem and the final caniad provides a description of the communal hierarchy, strongly suggesting that the community had significant influence in the composition. Given the rededication of Meifod in 1156 and the ambitious rebuilding programme at the church in the mid-twelfth century under Madog's patronage, it could be suggested that this programme of promotion would provide a suitable context for Cynddelw's composition of "Canu Tysilio", dating the poem to circa 1156-60. The references to Gwynedd throughout "Canu Tysilio" more likely reflect a perceived extended superiority of Meifod and Powys, beyond the real border of the principality, by demonstrating Tysilio's significance as a saint within a Gwynedd context. Line 46, where Meifod is described as "the place where Gwyddfarch is beyond Gwynedd", could be explained as Tysilio lamenting his time away from Meifod and his tutor Gwyddfarch while in "confinement" in north Wales, as has been suggested by Ann Parry Owen.[30] Whether of Powys or Gwynedd origin, what is certain is that the poem was composed with considerable input from the community at Meifod. The poem contains contemporary descriptions of the church and community, the inclusion of such detailed knowledge of twelfth-

---

[28] Line 46, Parry Owen ed., "Canu Tysilio", CAWCS, https://saint2.llgc.org.uk/texts/verse/TysilioCBM/edited-text.eng.html. Jones and Owen, *GCBM*, p. 30.
[29] See above n. 24.
[30] Introduction in Parry Owen ed., "Canu Tysilio", CAWCS, https://saint2.llgc.org.uk/texts/verse/TysilioCBM/introduction.eng.html. Accessed 21/12/2021.

century Meifod implies a close connection between the church and poet.

The poem consists of nine sections (*caniadau, caniad, sg.*) in Middle Welsh and was likely composed to be performed orally in front of both lay and religious audiences, given the lively rhetoric of the poem and focus on motifs important in Welsh secular society. Warfare and lineage are emphasised throughout the poem and frequent references to the early history of an independent Powys would resonate in the llys of the rulers of Powys, particularly Madog ap Maredudd's llys, Powys had re-emerged as an independent polity under Madog's father after a long period of Gwynedd overlordship.[31] The whole poem weaves together religious and secular aspects, reflecting both the importance of the dynasty and early history of Powys, and the role of Meifod church as the predominant clas church of the region.

The opening caniadau focus on kinship and lineage, Tysilio's lineage is highlighted as the descendant of Brochwel Ysgithrog and Cadell ap Brochwel, two important early medieval rulers of Powys, both attested in early medieval Welsh historic sources.[32] Meifod church is introduced and described as a "privileged monastery", "burial-place of Kings" and "the dwelling place of three saints."[33] Meifod's privileges and rights are emphasised in phrases paralleled in twelfth-century Welsh law books. [34] The middle section of the poem further ties Tysilio to Powys, caniad four identifies Tysilio as the protector of the men of Powys at the Battle of Maes Cogwy (Maserfield), an important battle that developed the early territorial kingdom of Powys. [35] Throughout the Welsh hagiography, the main

---

[31] For the significance of Madog's llys and the re-emergence of Powys in the twelfth century see, Stephenson, *Medieval Powys,* pp. 23-57.

[32] For a political overview of the Cadelling rulers see Owain Wyn Jones, "*Hereditas Pouisi:* The Pillar of Eliseg and the History of Early Powys", *The Welsh History Review*, vol. 24, 4 (2009), pp. 45-56.

[33] Lines 51, 48 and 54, Parry Owen ed., "Canu Tysilio", CAWCS. Jones and Owen, *GCBM*, p. 30.

[34] Huw Pryce, "A New Edition of the *Historia Divae Monacellae"*, *Archaeologia Cambrensis*, 82 (1994), p. 31.

[35] Lines 111-134 Parry Owen ed., "Canu Tysilio", CAWCS, notes 48-55. Jones and Owen, *GCBM*, p. 31.

themes include focus on Tysilio's lineage and emphasis on strong military leadership, reflecting the importance of kinship and warfare in medieval Welsh society.

In the following caniad, Tysilio's importance as the founder of a range of churches is emphasised, implying that the churches listed, as later foundations by Tysilio, were subordinate to Meifod, Tysilio's cult centre. The churches include "a church beyond the tide, beyond Dinorben", which has been identified as Llandysilio on the Menai Straits, *"llan Bengwern"*, a reference to Powys Pengwern, which Gerald of Wales identified as Shrewsbury, and "the church of Llydaw".[36] There have been attempts to identify Llydaw as somewhere in Wales or Cornwall, but it could as easily refer to some Breton traditions with which Cynddelw or the Meifod community were familiar.[37]

"Canu Tysilio" includes several miracles associated with Tysilio, interestingly often without much context, suggesting the details of the miracles were expected to be understood by Cynddelw's audience. Cynddelw refers to a herd of cattle unable to move "held fast to the ground", and a "fiery torch" made from Tysilio's hand.[38] The most notable miracle mentioned in the poem is Tysilio and Gwyddfarch's vision of Rome. Interestingly, Cynddelw doesn't specify where or to whom this vision takes place, but the Breton texts detail it was a shared vision of Rome between Tysilio and Gwyddfarch, atop a hill within Meifod's monastic enclosure, a setting which is supported by Welsh toponymics at Meifod where the hill behind the village is named Gallt yr Ancr with a rocky outcrop called Gwely Gwyddfarch.[39] Cynddelw's poem begins with a description of Meifod and the church's enclosure, before moving on to detail the outline of Rome and declares it "a shining city, an everlasting city that cannot be

---

[36] See Parry Owen, "Canu Tysilio", CAWCS, notes 63, 64, 65. Lewis Thorpe ed., *Gerald of Wales: The Journey Through Wales and The Description of Wales* (London: Penguin Books, 2004), p. 223.

[37] Lines 135-154, Parry Owen ed., "Canu Tysilio", CAWCS. Jones and Owen, *GCBM*, p. 32.

[38] Lines 189-192 and 185-188, Parry Owen ed., "Canu Tysilio", CAWCS. Jones and Owen, *GCBM*, p. 33.

[39] Doble, *Saints of Cornwall*, p. 108.

destroyed", "created for pilgrimage".[40] By flowing from a description of Meifod to a description of Rome, Cynddelw implies that Meifod and Rome are comparable as places of pilgrimage, that both sites are a "renowned dwelling place", "always prepared [for visitors]".[41]

The final caniad of the poem further implies the role of the community of Meifod in the compilation of "Canu Tysilio", as it gives detailed description of the hierarchy of the community at Meifod, providing an invaluable insight into the relationship between members of clergy within a twelfth-century clas church. Cynddelw describes the church's "courageous prior" and "its leader", who "springs from its territory which is free between its two rivers", possibly a reference to the commote of Deuddwr (two waters), a region of mid-Powys. The poem names the archdeacon of Powys as "privileged Caradog", "a priest of extensive provision for the people of Powys". Cynddelw praises the hospitality of Meifod, describing the audience set "around lamps, around drinking horns, around an honourable drink", and describes the community as "the company of merciful and gentle virgins . . . of a bright crowd of angels." [42] The description of the community and the hospitable setting imply that Cynddelw's poem was performed with members of the clergy of Meifod as part of the audience; given the extensive material descriptions of Meifod, presumably at the church itself.

A number of events and names from "Canu Tysilio" also appear beyond the Welsh hagiography and feature in the Breton material, although there are thematic differences reflecting the difference of audience and period of composition. In his accompanying notes in *Les Vies des Saints de la Bretagne Armorique,* Le Grand states his sources included material from the dioceses of Léon and St. Malo, the latter

---

[40] Lines 159-170, Parry Owen ed., "Canu Tysilio", CAWCS. Jones and Owen, *GCBM,* p. 32.
[41] Lines 159-170, Parry Owen ed., "Canu Tysilio", CAWCS. Jones and Owen, *GCBM,* p. 32.
[42] Lines 225-239, Parry Owen ed., "Canu Tysilio", CAWCS. Jones and Owen, *GCBM,* p. 34.

which includes the church of St. Suliac-sur-la-Rance the original source of the Suliau text.[43]

"La Vie de Suliau" can be broadly separated into two sections: a Welsh prologue and a Breton narrative. The opening of the text focuses on Suliau's life in Wales, his early career and move into the community of *Meibot* under the direction of *Guymarcus*, against the wishes of his father *Brocmail*, evidently variations of the Welsh names Meifod, Gwyddfarch and Brochwel. There is mention of Suliau's lineage as the eldest son, not to highlight Suliau's kin group as is reflected in the Welsh material, but to emphasise Suliau's decision to pursue a religious lifestyle instead of materialistic gain.[44] The opening section also includes an account of a miracle where Suliau and Guymarch have a shared vision of Rome upon a hill within the monastic enclosure, comparable to Cynddelw's description of Rome.[45]

Following Guymarcus' death, Suliau is elected the head of the community but soon has to leave Meibot after being persecuted by his newly widowed sister-in-law for refusing her marriage proposal. Suliau first flees to *enez Suliau*, a dependent of Meibot in the river Mené, a reference to Ynys Tysilio in the Menai Straits, before crossing to Brittany. From here on emphasis on Suliau's connections with Meifod and Wales are replaced by Suliau's life in Brittany.[46]

At the start of Suliau's life in Brittany, he meets with St. Malo at the monastery of St. Aaron, creating a sense of place and embedding Suliau in the Breton religious traditions, before Suliau moves further inland to build a monastery on the river Rance. The story of the cattle sticking to the ground that is referred to in "Canu Tysilio" also appears in the Breton material in the context of the church of Saint-Suliac receiving local patronage, legitimising the ecclesiastical rights of the church, in the same way "Canu Tysilio" emphasises Meifod's.[47]

---

[43] Albert Le Grand, *Les Vies des Saintes de la Bretagne Armorique* (Nantes, 1637), several of Suliau's traditions translated and edited in Doble, *The Saints of Cornwall*, pp. 111-112.

[44] Doble, *Saints of Cornwall*, pp. 106-108.

[45] Doble, *Saints of Cornwall*, p.108.

[46] Doble, *Saints of Cornwall*, pp. 108-109.

[47] Doble, *Saints of Cornwall*, pp. 109-110.

The final section lays out the end of Suliau's life. Suliau refuses an invitation to return to Wales, bequeathing to the community at Meifod his staff and a book of gospels. Suliau dies in Brittany and is buried at Saint-Suliac-sur-la-Rance, his abbatial church, reinforcing the church as the cult centre of Suliau in Brittany and raising its importance as the burial place of saints.[48]

Comparing both pieces of hagiography, there is important overlap between the two narratives, but also there are significant differences that reflect the difference between Welsh and Breton audiences. That the Breton material derives from a Welsh written source is evident in the proper names of places and people in Wales. Meifod and Meibot; Guymarcus and Gwyddfarch; Mené and Menai; the Breton names are a variation of the old Welsh orthography, as noted by Ann Parry Owen in her comparison of proper nouns between Cynddelw and le Grand.[49] It is accepted that Tysilio never travelled to Brittany, but the similarities in orthography suggest that a written account of his traditions did.[50] The vision of Rome and the miracle of the cattle sticking to the ground also appear in both narratives, though with differing contexts.

Where the narratives differ, it is so that the Breton and Welsh compilers can emphasise themes that are important to their different audiences, picking and choosing the aspects that reflect the cultures of their respective societies. The Welsh material, compiled in Welsh, focuses on kinship and the ecclesiastical rights of Meifod church. The Breton material, compiled by Le Grand in French, introduces Suliau's life in Wales, but focuses on his Breton traditions to emphasise the legitimacy of the church of Saint-Suliac-sur-la-Rance. Another noticeable difference is the feast days of Tysilio, 8th of November, and Suliau 1st of October.[51]

---

[48] Doble, *Saints of Cornwall*, pp. 110-111.
[49] Introduction to Parry Owen ed., "Canu Tysilio", CAWCS, https://saint2.llgc.org.uk/texts/verse/TysilioCBM/introduction.eng.html. Accessed 15/3/2022.
[50] Note 64, Parry Owen ed., "Canu Tysilio", CAWCS.
[51] Baring-Gould and Fisher list two feast days for Tysilio, 8th of November as recorded in the majority of manuscript calendars, and 9th of November as listed in a Dementian calendar of three manuscript copies, cwrtmware MS.

ST. TYSILIO

That the Breton compilers were working from a Welsh source, rather than copying from Cynddelw's poem, can be ascertained by the narratives that are different in both texts. Most prominently, the Breton material contains a detailed description of Gwyddfarch and Tysilio's shared vision of Rome atop a hill within the monastic enclosure. That the location of this miracle was known in Wales is evident in the surviving toponymics, the hill of Gallt yr Ancr in Meifod and Gwely Gwyddfarch.[52] Cynddelw describes what the vision of Rome entailed, he gives details about the architecture of Rome, but doesn't specify where the vision takes place, presumably because his audience at Meifod would already be familiar with the locality. The Breton material, therefore, must derive from a Welsh source separate to "Canu Tysilio".

These similarities and differences suggest a common source both compilers worked from, rather than a direct copy of "Canu Tysilio" by the Breton compilers. The Breton narrative has a sharp break between Suliau's life in Wales and Brittany, implying that the Breton material Le Grand was working from was a combination of Welsh and Breton traditions, where the Welsh material had been added as a prologue to Suliau's life in Brittany. The orthography suggests the Welsh traditions come from a written source so it can be speculated that the *Vie* at Saint-Suliac was a composite of local Breton traditions of Suliau conflated with Welsh material to add authenticity. This is not necessarily a rare phenomenon, there are other saints with Welsh and Breton traditions which just further highlights the significance of cross-Celtic saint cults.[53] In his edition of Le Grand's work, Louis

---

44 and Panton MSS. 10 and 66. See Baring-Gould and Fisher, *Lives of the British Saints*, p. 67 and p. 75.

[52] For further discussion on the significance of Gwyddfarch and Tysilio's vision of Rome see, "Gwyddfarch and Tysilio: Seeing the Holy City", Thomas, *Celtic Earth, Celtic Heaven*, pp. 26-38.

[53] Examples include St. Non and St. Samson, see chapter 6, "Saints and Seaways: The Cult of Saints in Brittany and Its Archepelagic Links", in the section on Saints Names and Insular Links, in Caroline Brett, et al., *Brittany and the Atlantic Archipelago 450-1200: Contact, Myth and History* (Cambridge: Cambridge University Press, 2021), 231-291 at 256-276.

Kerdanet suggested the presence of a Welsh manuscript in Brittany when he referred in passing to a "légendaire galloise".[54]

Therefore, it can be speculated that there existed a Welsh, or more appropriately Cambro-Latin, *Vita* of Tysilio which has since been lost, that both Cynddelw and the Breton compilers were working from. Tysilio appears in other Welsh hagiography as a geographical marker, for example when St. Beuno stays at Meifod with Tysilio,[55] so it can be assumed that Tysilio's traditions were widely understood by medieval Welsh society, more widely understood than the scattered surviving Welsh sources relating to Tysilio suggest. As Cynddelw flourished in the mid-twelfth century the *Vita* must predate this. Ann Parry Owen and Patrick Sims-Williams have both argued for existence of a Cambro-Latin *Vita* of Tysilio in the mid-twelfth century.[56]

There's evidence of literary activity at Meifod in the early twelfth century, which may provide the context for a *Vita* of Tysilio. Evidence suggests a close ecclesiastical connection between mid-Wales, and St. Davids in the early twelfth century.[57] Before the creation of the diocese of St. Asaph in 1143, Powys was part of the diocese of St. Davids. In 1127, *Brut y Tywysogion* records the death of Daniel ap Sulien, archdeacon of Powys. The archdeacon of Powys was a position associated with Meifod church, evidenced in the final caniad of "Canu Tysilio" where Cynddelw refers to the archdeacon of Powys, Caradog, alongside the community at Meifod.[58]

Daniel's brother Rhygyfarch composed the late eleventh-century Latin Life of St. David, while another of Rhygyfarch's manuscripts, a

---

[54] Daniel Louis Miorcec de Kerdanet ed. Albert le Grand, *Les Vies des Saintes de la Bretagne Armorique* (Paris, 1837). Doble, *Saints of Cornwall*, p. 112. Jones and Owen, "Twelfth-century Welsh Hagiography", in Cartwright ed., *Celtic Hagiography*, p. 51.

[55] See n. 2 above.

[56] Sims-Williams, *Buchedd Beuno*, p50. Introduction, Parry Owen ed., "Canu Tysilio", CAWCS, https://saint2.llgc.org.uk/texts/verse/ TysilioCBM/introduction.eng.html. Accessed 10/12/2021.

[57] David Stephenson, "The 'Resurgence' of Powys in the late Eleventh and early Twelfth Centuries", *Anglo-Norman Studies*, 30 (2008), pp. 182-95 and David Stephenson, "Entries relating to Arwystli and Powys in the Welsh Chronicles, 1128-32", *Montgomeryshire Collections*, 99 (2011), p. 47.

[58] Jones ed., *Brut y Tywysogion*, 1124-27, p. 50.

copy of the Psalter, was illuminated by another of his brothers, Ieuan.[59] The illuminations in Ieuan's manuscript resembles motifs on the early twelfth century cross-slab at Meifod, which itself closely resembles a contemporary stone slab from St. Davids.[60] Though speculative, the Meifod-Sulien connection provides a possible context for a composition of a Latin life of Tysilio in the early twelfth century.

To conclude, close analysis of hagiographical literature like "Canu Tysilio", taking into consideration their specific historical contexts, can give scholars an insight into the extent of shared literary traditions in the Middle Ages. Here we have a localised saint's cult expressed in three languages, Welsh, French and Latin, over two separate countries. The Breton and Welsh traditions further emphasise the extent of shared linguistic and spiritual culture across Brythonic nations and highlight the ways in which communities on both sides of the channel applied literature relating to the cult of Tysilio to promote their own importance and agendas.

---

[59] Ricemarch Psalter, Trinity College Dublin MS.50. H. Jackson Lawlor ed., *The Psalter and Martyrology of Ricemarch* (London: Henry Bradshaw Society, 1914), 2 vols. Gillian Conway, "Towards a Cultural Context for the Eleventh-Century Llanbadarn Manuscripts", *Ceredigion*, 13:1 (1997), pp. 9-28. N. Edwards, "11th-century Welsh Illuminated Manuscripts: the Nature of the Irish Connection", in *From the Isles of the North: Early Medieval Art in Ireland and Britain* (Belfast: HMSO, 1995), pp. 147-55.

[60] For a full description and image see David Stephenson, "The Meifod Cross-slab: Origins and Context", *Montgomeryshire Collections*, 103 (2015), pp. 2-3 and Nancy Edwards, *A Corpus of Early Medieval Inscribed Stones and Stone Sculptures in Wales*, vol. 3 (North Wales: University of Wales, 2013), pp. 443-445.

Appendix 1: Flowchart demonstrating the transference of Tysilio's written traditions in Welsh and Breton texts.

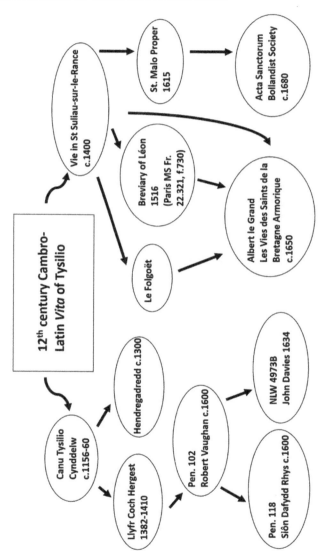

Patrons of Gaelic Manuscripts: Connections between the Roches, Fitzgeralds and the Mac Carthaigh Riabhach

Tatiana Shingurova

Introduction

The Book of Fermoy and the Book of Lismore are two manuscripts from late medieval Munster written for two local families: the Anglo-Norman Roches, the Lords of Fermoy, and the Gaelic Mac Carthaigh Riabhach (Mac Carthy Reagh), the Lords of Desmond. Both manuscripts were written at approximately the same time in Munster and share a relatively large number of texts in common.[1] Therefore, the idea that both manuscripts share some common sources and history has occupied the scholarship since the nineteenth century.

Previous discussions have been primarily focused on the scripts of the manuscripts and the question of whether the same scribe could have contributed to both codices. It all started in 1838 when Todd presented a letter from Colonel Currey of Lismore who quoted the historian O'Reilly, saying that both volumes were probably the work of the same scribe.[2] Later in the twentieth century, Murphy, in his catalogue, wrote in his entry on the Book of Fermoy that one of the scribes of the Book of Fermoy wrote in a very similar hand to one of the scribes of the Book of Lismore.[3] Most recently Ó Cuív, in his article, added the final point in this discussion so far, saying, "While it is neither impossible nor unlikely that the same scribe, working in

---

[1] It should be noted that even though the manuscripts share texts, most of the texts are preserved in different copies in these two manuscripts, see Brian Ó Cuív, "Observations on the Book of Lismore," *Proceedings of the Royal Irish Academy: Archaeology, Culture, History, Literature*, 83 C (1983): 269-92, at 284-5.

[2] Ó Cuív, "Observations," 282. See also Kevin Murray, "The Book of Lismore: Manuscript and Contents," *The Journal of the Cork Historical and Archaeological* Society, 126 (2021): 4-22.

[3] Elizabeth Fitzpatrick, Gerald Murphy and Kathleen Mulchrone, "1134: Book of Fermoy (23 E 29)," in *Catalogue of Irish Manuscripts in the Royal Irish Academy, Fasciculus XXIV-XXVII* (Dublin, 1928): 3091-3125, at 3095.

Cork in the second half of the fifteenth century, wrote for both Roches and Mac Carthaigh, I am not convinced that we can establish that from the manuscripts themselves."[4]

Following Ó Cuív's point, I would like to elaborate on the possibility that the same scribe(s) worked for patrons of both manuscripts. I will investigate potential family connections between the patrons of both manuscripts which may have enabled the communication between scholars and scribes in the area, which in turn may have influenced the content of both manuscripts.

I will investigate the family connections between the Roches, the FitzGeralds and, where possible, the Mac Carthaigh Riabhach via the FitzGeralds, since the latter had family connections with both the Mac Carthaigh Riabhach and the Roches. The present research is based mainly on the genealogies and the poem-book of the Roches in the Book of Fermoy. Unfortunately, there are no contemporary fifteenth and sixteenth century genealogies of the Roches, the Lords of Fermoy, which have survived; the earliest date to the seventeenth century.[5] I also use the genealogies of the FitzGeralds and the Mac Carthaigh. Below is a list of the primary sources used:

1. The Great Book of Genealogies by Dubhaltach Mac Fhirbhisigh (University College Dublin, Add. Irish MS 14, p. 825) from Alexander Roche to David, seventh Viscount of Fermoy (1600-35). Only the male line of the Roches is covered.[6]

2. The pedigrees of the Roches, Lords of Fermoy by George Carew, The Lord President of Munster (Lambeth Library, London, Carew MS 635, f. 34). Donnelly noted that this is one of the best authorities, since it is based on official information.[7] As noted in the manuscript itself, the

---

[4] Ó Cuív, "Observations," 282.
[5] Eithne Donnelly, "The Roches, Lords of Fermoy," *Journal of the Cork Historical and Archaeological Society*, 38 (1933): 86-91, at 86-7.
[6] *Dubhaltach Mac Fhirbhisigh. Leabhar Mór na nGenealach: The Great Book of Irish Genealogies*, ed. Nollaig Ó Muraíle, 5 vols (Dublin, 2003-2004), vol. 3 (2003), 154 (825.4), 747 (1400.1).
[7] Ibid., 86.

pedigree was recorded to attest the Roches' claims to certain lands.[8]

3. The Trinity College Pedigree (TCD F. IV. 18) for the sixteenth and seventeenth century genealogies.[9]

4. British Library, London, Harley MS 1425. This manuscript, written in different hands, includes the genealogies of Irish nobility and gentry. For the present article I use genealogies of the Roches, Lords of Fermoy (ff. 165-67), the Earls of Desmond (ff. 42-3), Barry (f. 32), O'Brian [sic] (ff. 2-8), and the Mac Carthaigh Riabhach and the Mac Carthaigh Mór (ff. 9-10, 21-2).

5. Genealogical sketches by Sir William Betham (for the Roches NLI G.O. 292 and the FitzGeralds G.O. 294 and G.O. 270).[10]

6. Genealogies of the Roches and the FitzGeralds by Bernard Burke.[11] Burke succeeded Sir William Betham as Ulster King of Arms. In his work he mentions that he used all sources available to him: "Public Documents and Records, Heralds' Visitations, Post Mortem Inquisitions, Patent Rolls, Lord's Entries and Funeral Certificates as

---

[8] Ibid., 86.

[9] Because of the lack of access to the manuscript, a secondary account was used instead, i.e., the articles on the Roches' family history by Eithne Donnelly. Eithne Donnelly, "The Roches, Lords of Fermoy," *Journal of the Cork Historical and Archaeological Society*, 38, 39, 41, 42, 50 (1933-37): (38) 86-91; (39) 38-40, 57-68; (41) 20-8, 78-84; (42) 40-52; (50) 63-75

[10] Because of the lack of access to the manuscript, secondary accounts (such as genealogical accounts by James Graves and Sainthill) were used instead. James Graves, "No. 2. The Earls of Desmond," *The Journal of the Historical and Archaeological Association of Ireland* 1.2 (1869): 459-98, at 460 (enclosed pedigree A); Richard Sainthill, *The Old Countess of Desmond: An Inquiry (Concluded): When Was She Married? with Numismatic Crumbs* (Dublin, 1863).

[11] Bernard Burke, *A Genealogical History of the Dormant, Abeyant, Forfeited, and Extinct Peerages of the British Empire* (London, 1866), 454-5.

well as various printed authorities."[12] Despite this, since he does not mention specific sources used for genealogies of each family, it is difficult to judge the reliability of his accounts.

7. The Complete Peerage of England, Scotland, Ireland, Great Britain, and the United Kingdom Extant, Extinct, or Dormant, compiled by George Edward Cokayne, Clarenceux King of Arms.[13]

In addition to genealogical accounts, the colophons in the Book of Fermoy and the poems from the poem-book of the Roches are used for evidence concerning the patrons of the manuscript.[14]

---

[12] Burke, *Genealogies*, ix.

[13] George Edward Cokayne, *The Complete Peerage of England, Scotland, Ireland, Great Britain and the United Kingdom*, 8 vols (London, 1887-98), vol. 3 (London, 1890), 297-303.

[14] 1) *Mise [a Aimi] ar h'inchaibh fein* (O Amy, I am Face to Face with Yourself) (poem 1360 in Katharine Simms and Mícheál Hoyne, *Bardic Poetry Database*, (2010a) <https://bardic.celt.dias.ie> [accessed 21 March 2022]), 2) *Formad ag cach re clu Muiris* (Everyone is Jealous to the Fame of Maurice) (poem 962 in *Bardic Poetry Database*), 3) *Gach fonn gu Feruibh Muighe* (All Lands Are Good Until Fermoy) (poem 1030 in *Bardic Poetry Database*), 4) *Gearr o dob inghill mna Mumhain* (It Is a Short Time Since the Women of Munster Were Pledged) (poem 1065 in *Bardic Poetry Database*), 5) *Dleaghar cundradh do chomhall* (A Covenant Must Be Fulfilled) (poem 717 in *Bardic Poetry Database*. The poem was also edited by Pádraig Ó Macháin in Pádraig Ó Macháin, *Téacs agus Údar i bhFilíocht na Scol* (Dublin, 1998), pp. 36-42), 6) *Teach da righan ráith Caisil* (The Rath of Cashel Is a House of Two Fortresses) (poem 1796 in *Bardic Poetry Database*), 7) *Néal ríoghna ós ráith Iughaine* (The Vision of the Queen Above the Rath of Iughaine) (poem 1482 in *Bardic Poetry Database*). Dublin, Royal Irish Academy, MS 23 E 29, The Book of Fermoy, at 1) p. 146, 2) p. 202, 3) p. 197, 4) p. 27, 5) p. 81, 6) p. 165, 7) p. 166. Damian McManus discussed patronesses of the poem-book of the Roches in his as yet unpublished work, Damian McManus, "Celebrating the Female: Eulogies, Elegies and Addresses to Noblewomen in Late Medieval Ireland" (forthcoming). See also a brief discussion about the poem-book of the Roches in Pádraig Ó Macháin, "Bardic Poetry in the Academy's Collection of Irish Manuscripts", in *Treasures of the Royal Irish Academy*, ed.

PATRONS OF GAELIC MANUSCRIPTS

Difficulties for which to account

The compilers of the *Complete Peerage* noticed in the entry on the genealogies of the Roches that "the pedigrees of these Lords are extremely obscure."[15] There are indeed many contradictory accounts of members of the family, discussed below. The fact that the poems from the poem-book of the Roches sometimes give completely different origins based upon the existing genealogical accounts, makes the research even more problematic.

The consistency in the names of heirs among the Viscounts of Fermoy also makes the research complicated. During the investigated period, we must face the fact that there were three persons styled "David, son of Maurice," and two persons styled "Maurice, son of David" in the Roche family.[16] The same could be said about the names of their daughters, who are frequently named either Ellen or Joan (also in Gaelic, Siuán, or sometimes written in English as Jane). The name Joan was also a common name among the wives of the Lords of Fermoy. Therefore, identifying and verifying some connections between investigated dynasties is a difficult task, and judging from the entry in the *Complete Peerage* mentioned above, 'confusion' is a faithful companion of historians who embraced the genealogies of the Roches, the Lords of Fermoy.

Two Munster codices: the place, the time of the compilation and the patrons

The places where the Book of Fermoy and the Book of Lismore were written are important to identify the potential influence upon each other. However, we can only suggest approximate places. In the case of the Book of Lismore, Macalister suggested that the manuscript was prepared in the Franciscan Friary in Timoleague as an offering to its patron.[17] However, Ó Cuív argued that the only certain evidence to claim that are colophons in Brussels MS written by Mícheál Ó Cléirigh, in which he said that he copied certain items "in the Friary

---

Bernadette Cunningham and Siobhán FitzPatrick (Dublin, 2009): 57-68, at 65-6.

[15] Cokayne, *The Complete Peerage*, 297.

[16] See Appendix.

[17] Robert Macalister, *The Book of Mac Carthaigh Riabhach, Otherwise the Book of Lismore* (Dublin, 1950), xii.

in Timoleague from the Book of Mac Carthaigh Riabhach."[18] This is insufficient evidence to identify where the manuscript was written. Another version is that the Book of Lismore may have been written in the Mac Carthaigh Riabhach's house at Kilbrittain, Co. Cork, which is based on a letter from 1642 in which an ally of Cromwell tells his father that he acquired a manuscript in the Mac Carthaigh Riabhach castle in Kilbrittain.[19]

Regarding where the Book of Fermoy was written, we know from the colophon in the manuscript by Torna Ó Maolchonaire that at least some items written for David, fifth Viscount (before 1561 X 1583) were added to the manuscript in Castletownroche, the dwelling of the Roche family in the sixteenth century.[20] There is no other place mentioned in the manuscript. It is likely that the entire work was written in and around Fermoy, in north Co. Cork. [21]

The Book of Fermoy was written in approximately 1457-1561 as is known from the colophons in the manuscripts which mention two patrons of the Book, David Mór (1448-88) and his great-great grandson, also called David, son of Maurice (d. 1583).[22]

There is a colophon by scribe William O'Hickey on page 55 at the end of the *Life of St George*, saying that he copied the text for his patron "Daibith mac Muiris meic hSeáin Do Róitsi" (David Mór

---

[18] Ó Cuív, "Observations," 271.

[19] John Collins, "Notes: The Book of Lismore," *Journal of the Cork Historical and Archaeological Society* 52:175 (1947): 88-90, at 89; Ó Cuív, "Observations", 271.

[20] RIA, MS D ii 1, at 153. Murphy, "1134: Book of Fermoy (23 E 29)", 3094. See more on the Book of Fermoy in Cathinka Dahl Hambro, "Hiberniores Ipsis Hibernis: The Book of Fermoy as Text-Carrier of Anglo-Irish Identity?" *Nordic Irish Studies*, 14 (2015): 95-110; John Carey, "Compilations of Lore and Legend: Leabhar na hUidhre and the Books of Uí Mhaine, Ballymote, Lecan and Fermoy", in *Treasures of the Royal Irish Academy*, ed. Bernadette Cunningham and Siobhán FitzPatrick (Dublin, 2009): 17-32, at 28-30; Tatiana Shingurova, "A Millennium with the Druid: The Mog Ruith Legend from the Seventh to the Seventeenth Century" (unpublished thesis, University of Aberdeen, United Kingdom, 2022), 126-204.

[21] Ibid., 3094.

[22] See Appendix.

Roche) in 1457.[23] Another scribe of the Book of Fermoy, Torna Ó Maoilchonaire, gives us the date 1561 on page 153 and provides us with the name of his patrons: "Daibith mac Muiris meic Daibith meic Muiris meic Daibith Mór ocus d'Oilen ingen Semuis meic Semuis meic Emain Meig Piarois" (who can be identified as David Roche, fifth Viscount and his wife Ellen Butler).[24]

The fact that only two patrons are mentioned with a gap of about one hundred years between them, does not mean that there were no contributions added to the manuscript in the intervening period. The way the poem-book of the Roches is laid out in the manuscript (poems dedicated to different generations are in different sections in the manuscript, written by different hands) allows for the possibility that some items may have been added during the time of Maurice, second Viscount, his wives (Joan and Mór) and his son David, third Viscount.[25]

As for the Book of Lismore, we know that the work was completed by the end of the fifteenth century since the patrons of the manuscript, Fínghin Mac Carthaigh Riabhach, Lord of Cairbre, and his wife, Caitilín (née FitzGerald) died at the beginning of the sixteenth century (d. 1505 and 1506, respectively).[26] Caitilín was a

---

[23] RIA, 23 E 29, at 55.

[24] James Henthorn Todd, *A Descriptive Catalogue of the Contents of the Irish Manuscript commonly called 'The Book of Fermoy'* (Dublin, 1868), 42.

[25] Poems on behalf of Joan, Mór, David and Cait(h)lín were added by one hand, whilst the poems attributed to David, fifth Viscount, and his mother Grainne were written by different hands and located in a different section of the manuscript. The poems mentioning Joan (possibly Joan the first wife of Maurice, second Viscount) are on pages 27-8, 81, 165-6, 194 in the Book of Fermoy; the poems dedicated to David, third Viscount and his wife Cait(h)lin are on pages 199-205; and poems dedicated to Grainne, wife to Maurice "Mad", fourth Viscount, and their son David, fifth Viscount are on pages 147-51. For the content of the manuscript and its scribes see Shingurova, "A Millennium with the Druid: the Mog Ruith Legend," 126-204.

[26]*Annala Rioghachta Eireann: Annals of the Kingdom of Ireland, By the Four Masters, From the Earliest Period to the Year 1616*, ed. and tr. John O'Donovan, 7 vols, second ed., vol. 5 (Dublin, 1856), 1289; Ó Cuív, "Observations," 269.

daughter of Thomas FitzJames FitzGerald, eighth (also accounted for as the seventh)[27] earl of Desmond and Ellice de Barry.[28] Caitilín FitzGerald's origins are crucial here because some patrons of the Book of Fermoy were also related to the FitzGeralds and to Caitilín herself. Caitilín's two brothers: James FitzThomas, ninth (eighth) earl of Desmond and Maurice FitzThomas, tenth (ninth) earl of Desmond, are also very important to the present story.

Caitilín, who died in 1506, was the contemporary of David Mór, the first patron of the Book of Fermoy, who died c. 1490, and his son Maurice, second viscount. Moreover, Caitilín was related to David Mór via his mother Emma Roche (née FitzGerald), sister of the famous Gerald FitzMaurice FitzGerald ("the Poet").

Although Maurice, second viscount is not mentioned as a patron of the Book of Fermoy, he seems to have been a patron of the poem *Formad ag cach re clu Muiris* in the poem-book of the Roches, included in the Book of Fermoy. Moreover, Maurice had a wife named Joan, the patroness of a few poems in the manuscript.[29] This Joan may have been of the FitzGeralds and possibly was a niece to Caitilín. The daughter of Maurice, second viscount and Joan, was Ellen Roche who was married to Caitilín's brother Maurice, tenth (ninth) Earl of Desmond, thus being Caitilín's sister-in-law.[30]

This brief overview shows that there were strong family connections between the Roches, the FitzGeralds and the Mac Carthaigh. This may have allowed and encouraged the networking between learned families working on their behalf. However, it is worth mentioning that the links between these three families neither started nor finished with Caitilín's generation.

---

[27] The confusion with the numerations of the Earls of Desmond comes from the elder brother of Gerald FitzMaurice FitzGerald, Nicholas who was called "an idiot" and who was superseded by his brother Gerald. James Grave, with a reference to Lynch's "Feudal Dignities" mentions that King Edward III granted the custody of Nicholas' estates to Gerald which would mean that Nicholas should be recognised as third Earl of Desmond, which makes his brother Gerald fourth Earl, etc. Graves, "The Earls of Desmond," 460 (enclosed genealogy, pedigree A).

[28] Harley MS 1425, f. 42. Graves, "The Earls of Desmond," 460 (enclosed genealogy, pedigree A).

[29] See discussion below.

[30] Harley MS 1425, ff. 42 and 167.

PATRONS OF GAELIC MANUSCRIPTS

The ancestry of David Mór: Maurice, son of John de la Roche and Emma FitzGerald

I start my story with the grandfather of David Mór, John, son of David Roche, second lord of Fermoy, who died in approximately 1386.[31] John is important for the present story for two reasons. Firstly, John was the last head of the family for two centuries who did not carry either the name David, son of Maurice or Maurice, son of David, and therefore his name is convenient to use as a starting point in genealogies.[32] Secondly, we know that John died leaving his young heir Maurice behind who was not of age.[33] Therefore, according to the Calendar of Patent Rolls, the custody of the Roches' land in Fermoy and Muskerry was given to Gerald FitzMaurice, fourth (third) earl of Desmond.[34]

Gerald FitzMaurice was renowned as a patron of bards and was a prolific composer of Irish verse himself.[35] He is known as the author of the *Gearóid Iarla* series, the book of poems which is partly preserved in the Book of Fermoy and partly in the Book of Dean of Lismore.[36] His teacher of bardic art was likely the poet Gofraid Fionn Ó Dálaigh, who refers to himself as such in the poem *A Ghearóid déana mo dháil*.[37] Simms describes him as "the most distinguished practitioner of the bardic art in the Ireland of his day".[38]

It is difficult to judge how much influence Gerald and his attitude towards bardic art had on the young heir of the Roches during the custody, but we know that Maurice Roche (1387-1448)[39] married

---

[31] Harley MS 1425, f. 166 suggests "1386" as the year of death.
[32] See figure 1.
[33] Donnelly, "the Roches", 50 (1935), 38.
[34] "The Calendar of Patent Rolls. 10. Ric. II. 92," quoted from Donnelly, "the Roches", 50 (1935), 38.
[35] Katharine, Simms, "The Geraldines and Gaelic Culture", in *Geraldines and Medieval Ireland,* ed. Peter Crooks, and Sean Duffy (Dublin, 2017): 264-277, at 265.
[36] Gerald FitzMaurice FitzGerald's *duanaire* (poem collections) have been edited by Gearóid Mac Niocaill in Gearóid Mac Niocaill, "Duanaire Ghearóid Iarla", *Studia Hibernica*, 3 (1963): 7-53.
[37] Ibid., 265.
[38] Ibid., 265.
[39] Donnelly, "The Roches," 50 (1935), 42.

Gerald's stepsister Emma, the daughter of Maurice, first earl of Desmond and his wife Margaret, the daughter of Richard de Burgh (the Red Earl of Ulster).[40] As with the rest of her family,[41] Emma acted as a patron to the poets, and there is a panegyric about her (*Mise [a Aimi] ar h'inchaibh fein*) by Maolmhuire Mac Craith in the Book of Fermoy.[42] This panegyric was probably added during the time of Emma's son, David Mór, who became first viscount of Fermoy and the first patron of the Book of Fermoy, as may be seen from the colophon by O'Hickey mentioned above.

Being raised within families who patronised Gaelic culture and poetry probably affected David Mór's attitude towards it. Moreover, his links to the Earls of Desmond would have furnished him with access to a network of learned families, which may have helped to initiate the compilation of the Book of Fermoy. A few personas who worked for him and/or for his parents were the scribes William O'Hickey, Domhnall Ó Leighinn and possibly the poet Seaán Óg Mag Raith who composed *Gach fonn gu Feruibh Muighe* for one David Roche.[43]

Mystery of Joan

The strong connection to the Earls of Desmond did not stop with David Mór, but continued during the lordship of his son, Maurice, second viscount. According to genealogies David Mór was married to Joan, daughter of Walter Burke MacWilliam Uachtar.[44] It is likely that the poem *Gach fonn gu Feruibh Muighe* was composed for this couple. The confusion with identifying patrons of this poem, and many others from the poem-book of the Roches, comes from the fact that a few of them are dedicated to another David, who was third viscount

---

[40] Account of his marriage to Emma can be found in Harley MS 1425, f. 166. Also see Donnelly, "The Roches," 50 (1935), 38.

[41] Richard de Burgh employed a personal bardic poet, Maurice Fitz Thomas; the first Earl of Desmond was a patron of the poem (together with his son Gerald) *A Ghearóid déana mo dháil.* Simms, "FitzGeralds," 274.

[42] Murphy, "1134: Book of Fermoy (23E 29)," 3108; Simms and Hoyne, *Bardic Poetry Database*, poem 1360.

[43] Simms and Hoyne, *Bardic Poetry Database*, poem 1030.

[44] Harley MS 1425, f. 166; Cockayne, *Complete Peerage*, 298; and Burke, *Genealogies*, 454.

of Fermoy (and the grandson of David Mór), and his mother Joan, who was the first wife of Maurice, second viscount of Fermoy. As the genealogies show, the name "David, son of Maurice" applied to both. Moreover, both were related to a woman named Joan.

Maurice, second viscount, son of David Mór was married first to a woman named Joan. However, the sources provide conflicting evidence as to the origins of this Joan. In the poems from the Book of Fermoy she is mentioned as a daughter of Aibhlín and Cormac, presumably the Mac Carthaigh, since they are descended from Eogan Mór according to the poem.[45] In the various Roche genealogies, however, Joan appears as a daughter of James FitzThomas FitzGerald, ninth (eighth) Earl of Desmond and his wife Margaret, the daughter of Tadhg Ó Briain of Thomond. [46] This would make Joan a niece to Caitilín, the patroness of the Book of Lismore.

The following poems in the Book of Fermoy mention Joan as a daughter of Cormac and Aibhlín:[47]

- *Gearr o dob inghill mna Mumhain*
- *Dleaghar cundradh do chomhall*
- *Teach da righan ráith Caisil*
- *Néal ríoghna ós ráith Iughaine*

If Joan (Siuán), as the poems claim, was of the Mac Carthaigh then the question is to which branch she belonged. 'Cormac' was as popular a name among Mac Carthaigh, as 'David' or 'Maurice' was among the Roches. However, we know that Joan's mother was Aibhlín. Since Joan was the first wife of Maurice, son of David Mór Roche, then she was living at the end of the fifteenth century, and her father should have been a contemporary of David Mór Roche (c. 1448-before 1488).[48] So far, I have not found in the genealogies of the Mac

---

[45] "*Teach (d)a righan ráith Caisil*," in Simms and Hoyne, *Bardic Poetry Database* (poem 1796).
[46] Harley MS 1425, f. 167.
[47] For translation of the titles and the references to the editions see footnote 13.
[48] Donnelly, "The Roches," 50 (1935), 68.

Carthaigh any Cormac Mac Carthaigh who might match this description.[49]

There are a few sources which associate Joan, the first wife of Maurice, second viscount, with the Geraldines. She is mentioned as a daughter of James FitzThomas, ninth (eighth) earl in the Trinity College pedigrees (TCD F. IV. 18), Harley MS 1425, ff. 166-67, the *Complete Peerage*, and the genealogies by Burke.[50] The same sources also mention the second wife of Maurice, second viscount as Mór, the daughter of Mathgamain O'Brien. Carew's pedigree gives a daughter of Theobald Burke of Castletown as the wife of Maurice, son of David Mór.[51]

The key to understanding the origins of Joan may lie in later connections between the Roches and the FitzGeralds. In the sixteenth century one Joan (Jane)[52] Roche, daughter of an unnamed lord of Fermoy[53] married James FitzJohn FitzGerald, fourteenth (thirteenth) earl of Desmond (d. 1558). The earl attempted to dissolve the marriage on the grounds of close affinity.[54] The name of Joan's father can be found in Harley MS 1425 f. 167, where it is given as David, third viscount Roche. This makes her the granddaughter of Maurice, second viscount and his first wife Joan, and a sister to Maurice "the Mad,"

---

[49] Harley MS 1425, ff. 9-10 (Mac Carthaigh Mór and Mac Carthaigh Riabhach), ff. 21-2 (Mac Carthaigh Riabhach), ff. 14-15 (Mac Carthaigh Muskerry). O'Hart, John, *Irish Pedigrees; or, The Origin and Stem of the Irish Nation*, 2 vols, fifth edition (Dublin, 1892), vol. 1, at 105-13 (Mac Carthaigh Mór), 118-20 (Mac Carthaigh Riabhach), 118-20 (Mac Carthaigh Muskerry). However, the difficulty is that frequently the names of wives are omitted in genealogical records.

[50] For Trinity College pedigrees see Donnelly, "The Roches," 50 (1935), 69; Cokayne, *The Complete Peerage*, 297; Burke, *Genealogies*, 454.

[51] Lambeth Library, London, Carew MS 635, f. 34. Donnelly, "The Roches," 50 (1935), 69.

[52] Sainthill in his work *Old Countess* with a reference to Sir Betham's papers refer to her as Jane: Sainthill, *Old Countess*, 64; Graves, "The Earls of Desmond," 460 (enclosed genealogy, pedigree A). It must be mentioned here that Sainthill refers to James FitzJohn as the fifteenth earl of Desmond. Sainthill, *Old Countess*, 68.

[53] The name is not given, but probably, considering the period we speak about, the daughter of "Mad" Maurice, fourth viscount.

[54] Sainthill, *Old Countess*, 64.

fourth viscount. If her grandmother Joan was a daughter of James, ninth (eighth) earl of Desmond, that would make the younger Joan (the daughter of David, third viscount) a grandniece to her husband James FitzJohn FitzGerald, and therefore explain his claim to divorce due to close affinity.

It is worth mentioning that Sainthill, who had access to Carew's genealogy but not to Harley MS 1425, was the first to suggest that Jane may have been "Mad" Maurice's sister and the daughter of David, third viscount, although he accepts that Carew's records do not list any of David's (third viscount) offspring apart from "Mad" Maurice.[55] Graves, in turn, who based his account of the FitzGeralds on a range of sources, including Sir Betham's and Carew's papers, as well as Sainthill's reconstruction of the Roches' genealogies, concluded that Joan (Jane) was a granddaughter to "Mad" Maurice, and, erroneously, a daughter of Maurice, Lord of Fermoy and his first wife, being thus a grandniece to her husband. Graves demonstrates a mistake in his records, since the successor to "Mad" Maurice was his son David, fifth viscount of Fermoy, who became viscount at some point before 1561. This dating is predicated on the colophon in the Book of Fermoy (page 153) of the same year which describes him as the one in charge of the Roches' land. Therefore, Joan could only have been a grandniece to James FitzJohn FitzGerald if she was a daughter of David, third viscount, who in turn was a son of Maurice, second viscount and Joan FitzGerald the daughter of James, ninth (eighth) earl of Desmond. Therefore, Graves was correct to say that Joan Roche, the abandoned wife of James, fourteenth (thirteenth) earl of Desmond, was the granddaughter of Maurice Roche, but he seems to confuse Maurice, second viscount with "Mad" Maurice, fourth viscount.[56]

As already described, both wives of Maurice, second viscount, Joan and Mór were patronesses of men of learning and bardic lore, as we can judge from the multiple poems dedicated to them in the Book of Fermoy. It would not come as a surprise if Joan was either of Mac Carthaigh or of Geraldine origins. It is worth mentioning that James, ninth (eighth) earl, as many of the FitzGeralds before him, had a place for bards at his court. There is a poem dedicated to him beginning *Gá*

---

[55] Ibid. See also Carew 635, f. 34.
[56] Graves calls him "Duff" in his genealogical records. Graves, "The Earls of Desmond," 460 (enclosed genealogy, pedigree A). See figure 1.

mhéid ngabáil fuair Éire (How Many Times was Ireland Conquered?) which is preserved in a number of manuscripts.[57] The poet is identified as Torna Ó Maolchonaire, who, considering the time the poem was composed (before 1487) was likely either the head of the family Torna Mór (d. 1468) or his son Torna Óg (d. 1532).[58] The colophon on page 153 of the Book of Fermoy shows that some Torna, son of Torna Ó Maolchonaire was working in 1561 for David, fifth viscount of Fermoy, the great-grandson of Maurice, second viscount.

Ellen Roche and Maurice FitzThomas, tenth earl of Desmond

Another connection between Caitilín and the Roches was via Ellen Roche, the daughter of Maurice, second viscount and Joan. Genealogies mention her marriage with Maurice FitzThomas, tenth (ninth) earl of Desmond, the brother of James, ninth (eighth) earl of Desmond, and Caitilín. This marriage is noted in Harley MS 1425, f. 167, and late genealogies by Burke and Graves (who based his account on Sir Betham's genealogical sketches).[59] Therefore, Caitilín was a sister-in-law to Ellen Roche. It is difficult to estimate when the marriage occurred, but according to Burke's genealogies, Maurice, tenth (ninth) earl married twice, with Ellen as his first wife, and he died in 1519.[60] Therefore, we can conclude that Ellen died some time before 1519 leaving behind four offspring, the eldest of whom, James FitzMaurice (d. 1529), became eleventh (tenth) earl of Desmond.[61]

Conclusion

In this article I looked at the family connections between the Geraldines, the Roches and the Mac Carthaigh Riabhach which may have had an impact on the creation of the Book of Fermoy and/or the Book of Lismore. The evidence shows that the patrons of these

---

[57] Simms and Hoyne, *Bardic Poetry Database* (poem 378).
[58] For Ó Maolchonaire's pedigree see Bernadette Cunningham and Raymond Gillespie, "Muirgheas Ó Maoilchonaire of Cluain Plocáin: An Early Sixteenth-Century Connacht Scribe at Work,"*Studia Hibernica*, 35 (2008): 17-43, at 19; for Torna Óg see Brian Ó Dálaigh, "The Uí Mhaoilchonaire of Thomond,"*Studia Hibernica*, 35 (2008): 45-68.
[59] Burke, *Genealogies*, 454. Graves, "The Earls of Desmond", 460 (enclosed genealogy, pedigree A).
[60] Graves, "The Earls of Desmond," 465.
[61] Graves, "The Earls of Desmond," 460 (enclosed genealogy, pedigree A).

manuscripts were related to each other by marriage. Those family connections, especially between the Roches and the FitzGeralds extended beyond the fifteenth and sixteenth centuries. As the study above has shown, the following people should be considered in any discussion of these connections:

The FitzGeralds

Thomas, eighth (seventh) earl of Desmond, his children:

- James, ninth (eighth) earl of Desmond
- (a putative daughter Joan (née FitzGerald) who married Maurice, second viscount of Fermoy)
- Maurice, tenth (ninth) earl of Desmond
- Caitilín (née FitzGerald) who married Fínghin Mac Carthaigh Riabhach.

James FitzJohn FitzGerald, fourteenth (thirteenth) earl of Desmond who married and later divorced Joan Roche, his grandniece.

The Roches

David Mór, first viscount of Fermoy
Maurice second viscount of Fermoy

- his daughter Ellen Roche who married Maurice, tenth (ninth) earl of Desmond.

David, third viscount of Fermoy

- his daughter Joan (Jane) Roche who married James FitzJohn FitzGerald, fourteenth (thirteenth) earl of Desmond.

The Mac Carthaigh Riabhach

Caitilín (née FitzGerald) who married Fínghin Mac Carthaigh Riabhach.

This purely genealogical research cannot establish the impact which those dynastical relations may have had on the construction and content of the Book of Fermoy and the Book of Lismore. However, we know that the FitzGeralds of Desmond and the Roches were famous for supporting Gaelic culture and acting as patrons to poets, scholars, and scribes. We know that some learned families, such as the

Ó Maolchonaire worked for both families. Women of the time played an important role in patronising scholars, and as McManus emphasises in his as yet unpublished work, almost half of the poems in the poem-book of the Roches are dedicated to women. Women from Anglo-Norman nobility were highly engaged in cultural life supporting scholarly networking at the time. Therefore, the stories of the women discussed in this article may shed some new light on the history of the Book of Fermoy and the Book of Lismore.

PATRONS OF GAELIC MANUSCRIPTS

Appendix: The genealogies of the Roches and the FitzGeralds connections illustrating the discussed

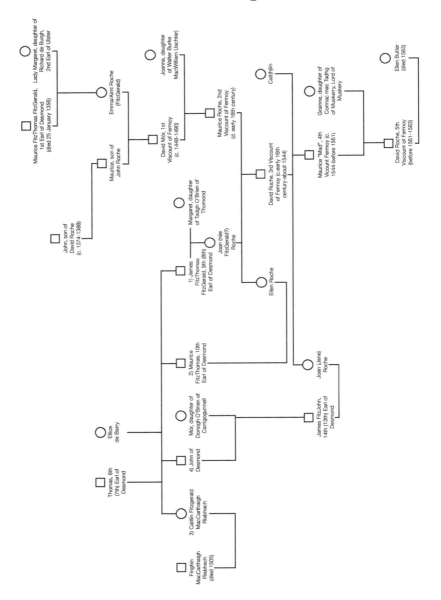

Translating Treachery: Representations of Aeneas in Medieval Irish and Welsh Literature

Susannah L. Wright

A mere ten lines into Virgil's *Aeneid*, the narrator announces that his main character is a man *insignis pietate*, 'renowned for his *pietas*' (*Aen.* 1.10). The Latin word *pietas*, known for being notoriously difficult to translate,[1] is defined by the *Oxford Latin Dictionary* as "an attitude of dutiful respect towards those to whom one is bound by ties of religion, consanguinity, etc."[2] This Roman concept might be described somewhat more fully as a sense of duty that can encompass righteous conduct not only toward the gods–its closest point of contact with the English derivative 'piety'–but also toward one's family, country, and, in Aeneas's case, followers and fellow Trojans. Aeneas is identified about twenty times in his eponymous epic with the related adjective *pius*, 'dutiful,'[3] and this signature attribute becomes one of his defining characteristics in Virgil's poem and elsewhere.[4] In later

---

[1] For the challenges presented by *pietas*, see Barbara Cassin, ed., *Dictionary of Untranslatables: A Philosophical Lexicon* (Princeton, NJ: Princeton University Press, 2014), s.v. "*pietas.*"

[2] P. G. W. Glare, ed., *Oxford Latin Dictionary*, second ed. (Oxford: Oxford University Press, 2012), s.v. "*pietās*," 1. Further sections of the definition outline cases where *pietas* is applied to relationships between mortals and gods (2); between children and parents (3a), and *vice versa* (3b); between spouses (3c); between citizens and the state, and *vice versa* (4a); and between troops and their commander (4b).

[3] J. D. Noonan, "*Sum Pius Aeneas*: Aeneas and the Leader as *Conservator*/Σωτήρ," *Classical Bulletin* 83.1 (2007): 65-91 at 67. The adjective *pius* is used of Aeneas at *Aen.* 1.220, 1.305, 1.378, 4.393, 5.26, 5.286, 5.418, 5.685, 6.9, 6.176, 6.232, 7.5, 8.84, 9.255, 10.591, 10.783, 10.826, 11.170, 12.175, and 12.311; it directly precedes his name in all cases but two (*Aen.* 5.418, where *pio* and *Aeneae* are separated by *sedet*, and *Aen.* 7.5, where *exsequiis* divides *pius* and *Aeneas*).

[4] The body of scholarship on *pietas* as Aeneas's defining characteristic is extensive. Notable treatments include W. R. Johnson, "Aeneas and the Ironies of *Pietas*," *Classical Journal* 60.8 (1965): 360-64; Karl Galinsky, *Aeneas, Sicily, and Rome* (1969; reprint, Princeton, NJ: Princeton

Latin texts, the notion of *pietas* remained proverbially associated with Aeneas, despite questions about the morality of his behavior and, importantly, despite alternative ancient traditions–some even predating Virgil–that suggested he had escaped from Troy by an act of betrayal.[5]

In medieval Irish and Welsh literature, the peripheral tale of Aeneas's treachery gains new prominence. The Middle Irish *Imtheachta Aeniasa* (*IA*),[6] an adaptation of the *Aeneid* (*Aen.*), opens with a scene involving Aeneas's and Antenor's betrayal of the Trojans, and both *Togail Troí* (*TTr*) and *Ystorya Dared* (*YD*), the Middle Irish and Welsh reworkings of Dares Phrygius, likewise refer to the treachery motif. This article will consider medieval Celtic representations of the treasonous Aeneas with an eye toward the reshaping of this theme for Irish and Welsh audiences. The

University Press, 2015), 3-61; Michael C. J. Putnam, "*Pius* Aeneas and the Metamorphosis of Lausus," *Arethusa* 14.1 (1981): 139-56; and Noonan, "*Sum Pius Aeneas.*"

[5] As Galinsky has observed, "although some later authors disagreed sharply with [the characterization of Aeneas as pious and dutiful], his *pietas* was that quality for which he was known best and which came to overshadow all his other traits" (*Aeneas, Sicily, and Rome*, 4). Aeneas's ongoing association with *pietas* can be demonstrated by figures like Lactantius-who acknowledges Aeneas's reputation as "the greatest example of *pietas*" (*maximum pietatis exemplum, Divine Institutes* 5.10) while disparaging him as a false representative of the virtue-and Augustine, who describes Aeneas as "so often called *pius*" in the opening paragraphs of the *City of God* (*Aeneas ipse, pius totiens appellatus*, 1.3). For the interplay between classical and Christian ideas of *pietas*, see James D. Garrison, *Pietas from Vergil to Dryden* (University Park, PA: Pennsylvania State University Press, 1992), 9-60. Summaries of the ancient evidence involving Aeneas's treachery can be found in Sergio Casali, "*Facta impia* (Virgil, *Aeneid* 4.596-9)," *Classical Quarterly* 49.1 (1999): 203-11 at 206 n.6, and "The Development of the Aeneas Legend," in *A Companion to Vergil's* Aeneid *and its Tradition,* ed. Joseph Farrell and Michael C. J. Putnam (Malden, MA: Blackwell, 2010), 37-51 at 41-43, as well as Giampiero Scafoglio, "The Betrayal of Aeneas," *Greek, Roman, and Byzantine Studies* 53 (2013): 1-14.

[6] Though the *Dictionary of the Irish Language* uses "*Aen.*" as an abbreviation for *Imtheachta Aeniasa*, I reserve that abbreviation for the Latin text and instead use *IA* for the Irish adaptation.

prominence of the treacherous Aeneas in these traditions is made all the more fascinating by the significant role they grant to his offspring; as we will see, the final lines of *IA* frame Aeneas as the ancestor of future world rulers, and Brutus, the traditional founder of Britain, was one of his descendants (as described in the *Lebor Bretnach, Brut y Brenhinedd,* and elsewhere).[7] The question of how Aeneas is portrayed in these texts therefore has relevance not only to the reception of classical epic, but also to our understanding of medieval Irish and Welsh views on genealogy, group identity, and self-representation.

A traitor is born: Virgil, Dares, and Dictys

In order to explore the manifestations of this treachery motif in medieval Irish and Welsh literature, we will need to begin by considering classical treatments of Aeneas's departure from Troy. The best-known version today comes from *Aen.* 2, where Aeneas himself tells Dido, the queen of Carthage, the harrowing tale of his escape. In his account, the Trojans are tricked into believing that the Greeks have

---

[7] The identification of Aeneas as a founding ancestor goes far beyond the texts considered in this paper and their places of production. For the genealogical prominence of Aeneas and the Trojans in medieval Europe and beyond, see Richard Waswo, "Our Ancestors, the Trojans: Inventing Cultural Identity in the Middle Ages," *Exemplaria* 7.2 (1995): 269-90; Nicholas Birns, "The Trojan Myth: Postmodern Reverberations," *Exemplaria* 5.1 (1993): 45-78; Marie Tanner, *The Last Descendant of Aeneas: The Hapsburgs and the Mythic Image of the Emperor* (New Haven, CT: Yale University Press, 1993); and Joseph Bowling, "Famed Communities: Trojan Origins, Nationalism, and the Question of Europe in Early Modern England," Ph.D. diss. (City University of New York, 2018), 31-73. Medieval and Renaissance traditions associating the Trojans with the Turks are discussed in Margaret Meserve, *Empires of Islam in Renaissance Historical Thought* (Cambridge, MA: Harvard University Press, 2008), 22-64; Thomas J. MacMaster, "The Origin of Origins: Trojans, Turks and the Birth of the Myth of Trojan Origins in the Medieval World," *Atlantide* 2 (2014): 1-12; and James G. Harper, "Turks as Trojans, Trojans as Turks: Visual Imagery of the Trojan War and the Politics of Cultural Identity in Fifteenth-Century Europe," in *Postcolonial Approaches to the European Middle Ages: Translating Cultures,* ed. Ananya Jahanara Kabir and Deanne Williams, Cambridge Studies in Medieval Literature 54 (Cambridge: Cambridge University Press, 2005), 151-79.

sailed away and are convinced to bring the Trojan horse–which, unbeknownst to them, is teeming with Greek warriors–inside the walls of Troy. That night, as Troy sleeps after celebrating what its inhabitants believe to be the unexpectedly auspicious end of the Trojan War, the Greeks pour forth from the Trojan Horse, open the gates to their comrades outside the walls, and take the city by storm. Following a night of desperate fighting, fear, and carnage–during which Virgil's Aeneas says he was frightened by every breeze and noise (*Aen.* 2.725-29)–the hero manages to escape the city of Troy with his son Ascanius at his side and his father Anchises upon his shoulders, carrying the rescued household gods of Troy (known as the *penates*). Though he loses his wife Creusa along the way, Aeneas gathers a group of Trojan stragglers on Mount Ida, who will follow under his leadership to seek out a new home after the fall of the city.[8]

Virgil's version of the story gained widespread acceptance in his own day and thereafter, and the image of Aeneas escaping with father, son, and *penates* has spawned countless artistic representations.[9] But though Virgil's account is the most famous today, it describes only one of the many ways Aeneas might somehow have survived the fall of Troy, as Poseidon's prophecy in the *Iliad* had made clear he would (*Il.* 20.300-8).[10] Already by the time the *Aeneid* was composed, there were multiple strains of thought regarding Aeneas's escape. Some historians, like Xenophon and Diodorus Siculus, had suggested that Aeneas survived because of his *pietas*; but another version, articulated

---

[8] For an appraisal of Virgil's handling of earlier traditions in Aeneas's narrative, see Frederick Ahl, "Homer, Vergil, and Complex Narrative Structures in Latin Epic: An Essay," *Illinois Classical Studies* 14 (1989): 1-31 at 24-30.

[9] For the popularity of this theme in black figure vase painting, see Susan Woodford and Margot Loudon, "Two Trojan Themes: The Iconography of Ajax Carrying the Body of Achilles and of Aeneas Carrying Anchises in Black Figure Vase Painting," *American Journal of Archaeology* 84.1 (1980): 25-40 at 30-36. Ancient visual representations of Aeneas's *pietas* have also been treated by Galinsky (*Aeneas, Sicily, and Rome*, 4-35), while a helpful survey of the continued prominence of scenes from the *Aeneid* in European art through the nineteenth century has been provided by Philip Hardie (*The Last Trojan Hero: A Cultural History of Virgil's* Aeneid [London: I. B. Tauris, 2014], 189-208).

[10] Casali, "Development," 40-41.

by Menecrates of Xanthos in perhaps the fourth century BCE, put forth a more shameful story, in which Aeneas betrayed his fatherland due to his hatred for Paris.[11] Even in the *Iliad*, there are signs of tension between Aeneas and the ruling dynasty of Priam and his sons (*Il.* 13.458-61, 20.178-83), which may have prompted some of these variant versions.[12] By betraying Troy to the Greeks, the stories go, Aeneas had bought the chance for himself and his family to escape the city's fall.

As has been noted by Casali, Ussani, and others, this alternate version of the story–which I will call the "traitor tradition"–may have left traces even in Virgil's *pietas*-oriented portrayal of the hero.[13] After Aeneas leaves Carthage in *Aen.* 4, the abandoned Dido rebukes herself for not being affected sooner by what she calls *facta impia*, 'wicked' or 'impious deeds' (4.596). The Latin does not state whose *facta impia* these are, prompting many scholars to propose that the phrase refers to Dido's betrayal of her oath to her dead husband; conversely, Casali has suggested that it serves as an allusion to Aeneas's possible betrayal

---

[11] Casali, "Development," 42-43 and Scafoglio, "Betrayal," 3-5. Xenophon refers to Aeneas's reputation for εὐσέβεια, the Greek equivalent of *pietas* (*Cynegeticus* 1.15), while Diodorus Siculus describes a display of Aeneas's character during a truce between the victorious Greeks and remaining Trojans (*Bibliotheca* 7.4 Vogel-Fischer). When the Greeks offer the Trojan survivors a chance to leave the city with whatever they can carry, Aeneas selects his own father; upon being offered a second opportunity to choose by the admiring Greeks, he takes up his household gods, reinforcing his perceived εὐσέβεια. An entirely different picture, however, is presented by the fragmentary evidence from Menecrates of Xanthos (preserved at Dionysius of Halicarnassus, *Roman Antiquities* 1.49.3-4): in his account, Aeneas overthrows Priam due to his resentment for the ruling house and gives the city over to the Greeks, becoming "one of the Achaeans" (εἰς Ἀχαιῶν) in the process. Further ancient evidence concerning Aeneas's departure is detailed in Vincenzo Ussani, Jr., "Enea traditore," *Studi italiani di filologia classica* 22 (1947): 109-23 at 109-13.

[12] Scafoglio, "Betrayal," 8.

[13] Casali, "*Facta impia*," 206-11. See also Nicholas Horsfall, "The Aeneas-Legend and the *Aeneid*," *Vergilius* 32 (1986): 8-17 at 16-17; Ahl, "Complex Narrative Structures," 24-31; Galinsky, *Aeneas, Sicily, and Rome*, 46-51; and Ussani, "Enea traditore," 116-23.

of Troy.[14] According to this interpretation, rumors of the treacherous Aeneas seem to have reached Dido even before the hero himself washes up on her shores. The description of Aeneas in the frieze on the Carthaginian temple of Juno, where he is said to be *principibus permixtum* . . . *Achiuis*, "thoroughly intermingled with the Greek leaders" (1.488), may likewise hint at the ambiguous circumstances of his escape.[15]

Though there are traces of the treasonous Aeneas before and in Virgil, the two most prominent and extensive surviving accounts of Aeneas's betrayal of Troy are the much later *De excidio Troiae historia* attributed to Dares Phrygius and the *Ephemeris belli Troiani* ascribed to Dictys Cretensis.[16] These texts–which, for the sake of convenience, I will refer to by the names of their purported authors from here on out–frame themselves as eyewitness reports of the events of the Trojan War, with Dares ostensibly writing from the Trojan perspective and Dictys from the Greek. Though now widely identified as late-antique in origin, they gained broad acceptance in the Middle

---

[14] Casali, "*Facta impia*," 203-6. The potential attribution of *facta impia* to Aeneas is rendered even more incriminating for the hero by the fact that *impius* represents a direct negation of his characteristic adjective *pius* (see note 3 above).

[15] Casali, "*Facta impia*," 208 and Ahl, "Complex Narrative Structures," 26-29.

[16] Ferdinand Meister, ed., *Daretis Phrygii de excidio Troiae historia* (Leipzig: Teubner, 1873); Werner Eisenhut, ed., *Dictyis Cretensis ephemeridos belli Troiani libri* (Leipzig: Teubner, 1958). References to both texts will follow the paragraph numbering of these editions. The standard translation is R. M. Frazer, Jr., *The Trojan War: The Chronicles of Dictys of Crete and Dares the Phrygian* (1966; reprint, Bloomington, IN: Indiana University Press, 2019). Several pieces by Stefan Merkle can help set these perplexing works in context: "News from the Past: Dictys and Dares on the Trojan War," in *Latin Fiction: The Latin Novel in Context*, ed. Heinz Hofmann (London: Routledge, 1999), 155-66; "The Truth and Nothing but the Truth: Dictys and Dares," in *The Novel in the Ancient World*, ed. Gareth Schmeling, rev. ed. (Boston: Brill, 2003), 563-80; and, on Dictys specifically, "Telling the True Story of the Trojan War: The Eyewitness Account of Dictys of Crete," in *The Search for the Ancient Novel*, ed. James Tatum (Baltimore, MD: Johns Hopkins University Press, 1994), 183-96.

Ages as seemingly authentic firsthand reports of the events that happened at Troy.[17]

Both texts present a much less flattering vision of Aeneas than the one we see in Virgil. In Dares's version, which I will summarize in somewhat more detail, the prominent Trojans Antenor, Aeneas, and Polydamas unsuccessfully encourage Priam and his remaining sons to seek peace with the Greeks late in the war (37); in response, Priam rebukes Antenor and Aeneas, blames them for the conflict, and even plans to have them killed, thinking they might betray the city (38). Later, Antenor meets secretly with other Trojan leaders and formulates a plan to do exactly what Priam fears, then invites Aeneas to participate in their plot (39). Polydamas brings word to the Greek leaders, who eventually agree to trust the traitors but still try to assess their faithfulness by demanding a password that they can test with Aeneas, his father Anchises, and Antenor (40). Once this test is passed, the members of the Greek council swear no harm will come to the traitors and their families or possessions if Troy is handed over to them the following night. Antenor and Aeneas are designated to lead the guard at the gates—which Dares describes as carved with a horse's head, a clever way of accounting for the tale of the Trojan Horse—and to lay the city open to the Greeks (40).

On the assigned night, Antenor and Aeneas let Achilles's bloodthirsty son Neoptolemus (also known as Pyrrhus) into Troy and then immediately begin trying to secure a safe path out of the city for themselves and their families (41). After the initial chaos of Troy's fall subsides, Agamemnon summons the Greek leaders to a meeting and asks how they should deal with the Trojan traitors; the Greeks unanimously agree to honor their pact (42). Once Neoptolemus realizes, however, that no one has found Priam's daughter Polyxena, it is discovered that Aeneas has sheltered the maiden. She is brought forth and sacrificed upon Achilles's grave, and Agamemnon angrily

---

[17] Medieval authors who relied on the accounts of Dares and Dictys, either directly or through an intermediate source, include Benoît de Saint-Maure, Guido delle Colonne, Boccaccio, and Chaucer. For the relevance of Dares and Dictys to a number of medieval texts, including the *Chanson de Roland*, see Sarah Spence, "*Felix Casus*: The Dares and Dictys Legends of Aeneas," in Farrell and Putnam, ed., *A Companion to Vergil's* Aeneid *and its Tradition*, 133-46.

orders Aeneas and his followers to leave the land at once (43). The text closes as Aeneas sets sail for unknown shores with 3,400 followers of different ages (44).

In the extended version of the treachery episode in Dictys (4.18– 5.17), Aeneas likewise participates in the betrayal of Troy, though Antenor is characterized there as the primary actor driving the proceedings. Following the city's destruction, the leaders of the Greeks encourage Aeneas to sail with them to Greece, offering him a kingdom as powerful as their own (5.16). He chooses instead to remain at Troy, but his stay winds up being more short-lived than he expects: according to Dictys, Aeneas tries to drive Antenor out of the kingdom shortly after the Greeks depart, but fails to drum up sufficient support from the neighboring areas. Once Antenor learns of his plan, he refuses to let Aeneas back into the city and forces him to leave by sea with all he owns (5.17).

These two accounts of the traitorous Aeneas formed the core of many later medieval representations, which tend to treat their narratives as definitive and factual descriptions of the events that unfolded at Troy.[18] Dares's version receives particular emphasis in the medieval Irish and Welsh texts to which we will now turn.

Beginning with betrayal: Aeneas in *Imtheachta Aeniasa*

We will consider first the Middle Irish *Imtheachta Aeniasa,* which adapts the *Aeneid* while also exemplifying an engagement with the traitor tradition that goes far beyond the disputed references we find in Virgil. Next, we will examine two very different reworkings of Dares, the Middle Irish *Togail Troí* and Middle Welsh *Ystorya Dared.* It is worth noting at the outset that these texts are generally best treated as reworkings or adaptations of their classical predecessors, rather than 'translations'; even the most 'faithful' among them still

---

[18] Spence, "*Felix Casus,*" 134-36. Speaking specifically of fourteenth-century English readers, C. David Benson has noted that Dares and Dictys would have seemed to their medieval audiences like "eyewitness reporters who preserved the truth of their own time just as contemporary clerical chroniclers were preserving the present" (*The History of Troy in Middle English Literature: Guido delle Colonne's* Historia Destructionis Troiae *in Medieval England* [Woodbridge, UK: D. S. Brewer, 1980], 11).

demonstrate significant modification of their sources on both structural and stylistic levels.[19]

Imtheachta Aeniasa,[20] likely written in the twelfth century (or perhaps eleventh), demonstrates a high level of familiarity with the Virgilian text, but nonetheless makes alterations that result in a work very different from its Latin model. The most prominent of these

---

[19] Barbara Hillers, "The Odyssey of a Folktale: *Merugud Uilix Meic Leirtis,*" *Proceedings of the Harvard Celtic Colloquium* 12 (1992): 63-79 at 63. For a helpful overview of medieval Irish classical adaptations and their literary and historical contexts, see Ralph O'Connor, "Irish Narrative Literature and the Classical Tradition, 900-1300," in *Classical Literature and Learning in Medieval Irish Narrative,* ed. Ralph O'Connor, Studies in Celtic History 34 (Cambridge: D. S. Brewer, 2014), 1-22 at 13-22.

[20] George Calder, ed. and trans., *Imtheachta Æniasa: The Irish Æneid* (London: Irish Texts Society, [1907] 1995). For the date and transmission history of the text, see Erich Poppe, "A New Introduction to *Imtheachta Aeniasa,* the Irish *Aeneid*: The Classical Epic from an Irish Perspective," in Calder, *Imtheachta Æniasa,* 1-40 at 30-33, and Diego Poli, "L'*Eneide* nella cultura irlandese antica," in *Letterature comparate: Problemi e metodo. Studi in onore di Ettore Paratore* (Bologna: Pàtron, 1981), 997-1012 at 1001-2. Several other illuminating examinations of *IA* have been undertaken by Poppe, which include "*Imtheachta Aeniasa*: Virgil's *Aeneid* in Medieval Ireland," *Classics Ireland* 11 (2004): 74-94; "A Virgilian Model for Lúirech Thredúalach?," *Ériu* 54 (2004): 171-77; and "*Imtheachta Aeniasa* and its Place in Medieval Irish Textual History," in O'Connor, ed., *Classical Literature and Learning,* 25-39. Further key treatments of the text include Robert T. Meyer, "The Middle-Irish Version of the *Æneid,*" *Tennessee Studies in Literature* 11 (1966): 97-108; Robert J. Rowland, Jr., "Aeneas as a Hero in Twelfth-Century Ireland," *Vergilius* 16 (1970): 29-32; John R. Harris, "Aeneas's Treason and Narrative Consistency in the Mediaeval Irish *Imtheachta Aeniasa,*" *Florilegium* 10 (1988-91), and *Adaptations of Roman Epic in Medieval Ireland: Three Studies in the Interplay of Erudition and Oral Tradition,* Studies in Epic and Romance Literature 5 (Lewiston, NY: Edwin Mellen Press, 1998), 81-117 (on which see also the review of Uáitéar Mac Gearailt at *Éigse* 34 [2004]: 220-24); Isabel Kobus, "*Imtheachta Aeniasa: Aeneis*-Rezeption im irischen Mittelalter," *Zeitschrift für celtische Philologie* 47 (1995): 76-86; and Julie LeBlanc, "Heroic Traditions in Dialogue: The *Imtheachta Aeniasa,*" in *Crossing Borders in the Insular Middle Ages,* ed. Aisling Byrne and Victoria Flood, Medieval Texts and Cultures of Northern Europe 30 (Turnhout: Brepols, 2019), 203-25.

modifications involve the plot: rather than mirroring the complex shape of Virgil's opening books, the Irish adapter creates an entirely new narrative structure, representing events as they actually might have happened instead of beginning *in medias res* and relying extensively on inset narrative to tell the full story.[21]

Most importantly for the purposes of this paper, the text opens not with a Virgilian invocation of the Muse, but instead with a scene derived from the narrative of Dares. We begin the morning after the fall of Troy, as Agamemnon and the other Greek leaders consider what should become of Antenor, Aeneas, and their fellow Trojan traitors. In Dares's version of the same episode, the Greek leaders unanimously agree to let the Trojan traitors go free before eventually forcing Aeneas to leave after they learn he has concealed Polyxena (42-43). The Greeks of *Imtheachta Aeniasa*, however, are even less forgiving: after Nestor describes Trojan treacheries of the past in a characteristically lengthy fashion (*IA* 10-41), he identifies Aeneas as a perpetual enemy of the Greeks and convinces the others to banish him from Troy outright.[22] The closing words of his speech are as follows:

> *Is demin daibsi, dono, ni ba ferr cairrdius Ænias ribsi dia facbaithi isin Trai, inas in cairdis [s]in Priaim fri Grecu. Is mairg Greca dobera tairisim fair; ar is nama Grec dogress Ainias. Sochaidi do curadaib ⁊ do caithmiledaib ⁊ d' anrudaib Grec torchair lais dia laim fen isna VII cathaib LX ar C dochuiredh rinde oc diden na Trae.*

> It is certain to you, then, that if you leave Aeneas in Troy his friendship with you will be no better than was that of Priam with Greeks. Woe to Greek that will put confidence in him, for Aeneas is ever an enemy to

---

[21] For the many modifications made by the Irish adapter to the text of the *Aeneid*, see Poppe, "New Introduction," especially 1-30.

[22] Though Nestor's closing words regarding Aeneas appear to be independent, the opening portions of his speech seem to reflect engagement with *TTr* and have been identified by Brent Miles as providing a summary of that text (*Don Tres Troí: The Middle Irish History of the Third Troy* [Dublin: Irish Texts Society, 2020], 46-47).

Greeks. A multitude of heroes and battle-soldiers and champions of the Greeks fell by him by his own hand in the hundred and sixty-seven battles that were fought against us in defense of Troy.[23]

The text then treats Aeneas's journey in a revised version of Virgil's narrative structure, chronicling the travels of Aeneas and his men at length (*IA* 49-302) before permitting them to reach Carthage and the court of Dido (302-407). There, Aeneas does tell a modified and abbreviated version of his story (408-668), particularly the fall of Troy, but readers reach that moment with a different perspective in mind: already from the opening lines of the text, we are primed to think that Aeneas left Troy as a traitor who helped to bring the city down, rather than a refugee driven from his homeland and deserving Dido's pity.[24]

Though we hear the Irish Aeneas tell of the Trojan Horse, his valiant deeds on Troy's last night, and his desperate and fearful attempts to save his family and the city's household gods, the specter of the opening scene looms large throughout the text. Even seemingly benign moments like Ilioneus's speech to Dido on Aeneas's behalf–where he speaks of the piety of the Trojan race and of their leader (*IA* 330-41)–gain new significance in light of the betrayal lurking in the background. Perhaps some of Virgil's earliest readers, who could have had the accounts of Menecrates and others in mind when encountering the text of the *Aeneid* for the first time, might have had a similar reaction to the emphasis placed there on Aeneas's reputation for righteous behavior. In *Imtheachta Aeniasa*, however, the effect is especially prominent, with the treachery theme appearing right at the beginning of the text as the preamble to an otherwise fairly Virgilian representation of events.

---

[23] Calder, ed. and trans., *IA* 41-46.

[24] As in the *Aeneid*, the Trojan refugees' arrival in Carthage is followed in *IA* by the ill-starred love story of Aeneas and Dido (668-931). For the Irish redactor's treatment of this episode, see Hannah Zdansky, "Love in Translation: The Irish Vernacularization of the *Aeneid*," in *The Language of Gender, Power and Agency in Celtic Studies*, ed. Amber Handy and Brian Ó Conchubhair (Dublin: Arlen House, 2014), 43-58, as well as T. Hudson Williams, "Cairdius Aenias ocus Didaine (The Love of Aeneas and Dido)," *Zeitschrift für celtische Philologie* 2 (1899): 419-72 at 419-23.

TRANSLATING TREACHERY

Treachery on Troy's last night: Aeneas in *Togail Troí*

The theme of Aeneas's betrayal appears also in the Middle Irish *Togail Troí* (The Destruction of Troy) and the Middle Welsh *Ystorya Dared* (The History of Dares), which both adapt Dares's *De excidio Troiae historia*. Both texts exist in multiple versions, complicating the picture considerably in terms of their analysis; for the purposes of this paper, I will focus primarily on the first recension of *Togail Troí*[25] and the text of *Ystorya Dared* found in the Red Book of Hergest.[26] As we will soon see, these texts take very different approaches to Dares, with *Togail Troí* presenting a significantly expanded and enhanced version of the narrative, while *Ystorya Dared* hews much closer to the Latin original. Importantly, however, both texts have been classified as predominantly historical.[27] Helen Fulton has connected them

---

[25] Whitley Stokes, ed. and trans., "The Destruction of Troy," in *Irische Texte mit Übersetzungen und Wörterbuch*, ed. Whitley Stokes and Ernst Windisch, series 2:1 (Leipzig: S. Hirzel, 1884), 1-142. The surviving copies of *Togail Troí* are customarily divided into three recensions; for an overview, see Olivier Szerwiniack, "Le mythe de Troie en Irlande au Moyen Âge: *Togail Troí* et ses recensions," *Troianalexandrina* 18 (2018): 101-25 at 105-9. Editions of the second recension include Whitley Stokes, ed. and trans., *Togail Troí: The Destruction of Troy from the Facsimile of the Book of Leinster* (Calcutta, 1881), and R. I. Best and M. A. O'Brien, eds., *Togail Troí, from the Book of Leinster, Vol. IV* (Dublin: Dublin Institute for Advanced Studies, 1966). An edition of the third recension is in preparation by Michael Clarke. Regarding the date of the text, see Gearóid Mac Eoin, "Das Verbalsystem von Togail Troí (H.2.17)," *Zeitschrift für celtische Philologie* 28 (1960-61), 73-136 and 149-223 (especially 193-202), along with Uáitéar Mac Gearailt, "Change and Innovation in Eleventh-Century Prose Narrative in Irish," in *(Re)Oralisierung*, ed. Hildegard L. C. Tristram, ScriptOralia 84 (Tübingen: G. Narr, 1996), 443-96, and "Issues in the Transmission of Middle and Early Modern Irish Translation Prose: *Togail Troí* and *Scéla Alaxandair*," in *Adapting Texts and Styles in a Celtic Context: Interdisciplinary Perspectives on Processes of Literary Transfer in the Middle Ages. Studies in Honour of Erich Poppe*, ed. Axel Harlos and Neele Harlos, Studien und Texte zur Keltologie 13 (Münster: Nodus Publikationen, 2016), 103-34 at 103-25.

[26] See note 45 below.

[27] Erich Poppe, "The Matter of Troy and Insular Versions of Dares's *De Excidio Troiae Historia*: An Exercise in Textual Typology," *Beiträge zur Geschichte der Sprachwissenschaft* 19.2 (2009): 253-98 at 278-82.

specifically with the model of Christian historiography exemplified by the arguments of Boethius, in which world events are seen to occur in repeating cycles;[28] as she puts it, "for Boethius, . . . history moves in cycles of collapse and restoration, in which kings and heroes are fated to choose, by free will, the destiny already laid down for them."[29] In this model, the fall of one great civilization, like Troy, can be seen as prefiguring the rise and eventual fall of another.

The version of Aeneas's betrayal presented in *Togail Troí* expands considerably on the relatively sparse description of Troy's last night found in Dares, including a few key modifications that have intriguing implications for the resulting characterization of Aeneas.[30] In Dares, the primary emphasis falls on the planning of the betrayal and its aftermath days later; its immediate consequences, though mentioned, are treated in a rather bland manner unlikely to provoke much of an emotional reaction from readers. In *Togail Troí*, however, the devastation of Troy brought about through the schemes of Antenor, Aeneas, and their fellow traitors is depicted in a vivid and

---

[28] Helen Fulton, "History and *historia*: Uses of the Troy Story in Medieval Ireland and Wales," in O'Connor, ed., *Classical Literature and Learning*, 40-57 at 47-49 and 52-53.

[29] Fulton, "History and *historia*," 48.

[30] In-depth treatment of the relationship between *TTr* and the Latin text of Dares can be found in Leslie Diane Myrick, *From the* De Excidio Troiae Historia *to the* Togail Troí: *Literary-Cultural Synthesis in a Medieval Irish Adaptation of Dares' Troy Tale*, Anglistische Forschungen 223 (Heidelberg: Universitätsverlag Winter, 1993). Other significant examinations of *TTr* include Robert T. Meyer, "The Middle-Irish Version of the Story of Troy," *Études celtiques* 17 (1980): 205-18; Uáitéar Mac Gearailt, "*Togail Troí*: Ein Vorbild für spätmittelirische *catha*?," in *Übersetzung, Adaptation, und Akkulturation im insularen Mittelalter*, ed. Erich Poppe and Hildegard L. C. Tristram, Studien und Texte zur Keltologie 4 (Münster: Nodus Publikationen, 1999), 123-29, as well as "*Togail Troí*: An Example of Translating and Editing in Medieval Ireland," *Studia Hibernica* 31 (2000-1): 71-85; Poppe, "Matter of Troy"; Brent Miles, *Heroic Saga and Classical Epic in Medieval Ireland*, Studies in Celtic History 30 (Cambridge: D. S. Brewer, 2011), 66-144; and Michael Clarke, "The Extended Prologue of *Togail Troí*: From Adam to the Wars of Troy," *Ériu* 64 (2014): 23-106, along with "International Influences on the Later Medieval Development of *Togail Troí*," in Harlos and Harlos, ed., *Adapting Texts and Styles*, 75-102.

visceral fashion that substantially elaborates on what we find in Dares. In one case, a single sentence from the Latin text is amplified into an extensive and graphic description in the Irish version, occupying over ten lines in Stokes's edition:

> *tota nocte non cessant Argiui deuastare praedasque facere.*[31]

For the whole night the Argives do not cease from devastation and the taking of plunder.

> *Ní rabi cumsanadh ann, tra, co find na matne for indriud ⁊ orcain na cathrach. Roloisced an chathir coraibe tría chorthair tenedh ⁊ fo smúit dethcha. Robúrestar ⁊ robécestar Badb úasv. R[o]gáirset demna aéoir úasv chind, ar rop aitt léo martad mar sin do thabhairt for síl n-Ádhaim, fobíth rop fórmach muinntire dóib sin. Mór, trá, an t-anféth ⁊ in míchostadh robói 'sin Trói in n-aidchi sin. Robói crith ar détaib na lobar. Rotódáiled fuil nam-míled: roíachtset na senóre: roscretsat na nóidein: roéighset na hingena macdacht. Romiimrit, trá, sochaide do mnáibh sáerv sochenívl andsin ocus rothaithmigit trílse na fedb, ⁊ romarbait na slúaigh. Rohinred ⁊ rohaircedh ⁊ rodéláraighed an chathir.*

Now until the white of the morning, there was no pause to the devastation and the ruin of the city. The city was burnt, so that it was in (?)[32] a fringe of fire[33]

---

[31] Meister, ed., *De excidio* 41.

[32] The preposition used here (*tre*, 'through') is somewhat surprising. See Electronic Dictionary of the Irish Language (*eDIL*) , s.v. "tre," Ib for senses "implying mixture, mingling, etc."; of particular relevance are the three instances listed as corresponding to the Modern Irish *tré theine*, 'on fire.' The last of these involves the same preposition and noun pair found here in *TTr*, tre and cor(r)thar: *tré choirthir smáil teineadh ⁊ tennáil*, "within a fringe of smoke and fire and flame" (Lucius Gwynn, ed. and trans., "The Life of St. Lasair," *Ériu* 5 [1911]: 73-109 at 76, line 24 and 77).

[33] As noted in *eDIL*, the noun *cor(r)thar*, 'fringe, edging, border,' can be paired

and under vapour of smoke. Badb bellowed and roared above it. Demons of the air shouted above . . . ;[34] for pleasant it was to them that slaughter should befall Adam's seed, because that was an increase to their (the demons') household. Great then were the turmoil and the . . .[35] that were in Troy on that night. There was trembling on the teeth of the weak. The blood of the soldiers was poured forth. The old men wailed, the infants cried, the grown-up girls lamented. Multitudes of noble, well-born women were misused there, and the widows' tresses were loosened, and the hosts were slain. The city was devastated and ruined and swept away.[36]

Where Dares's version of Troy's last night is characteristically compressed and pays little attention to the human cost of the city's betrayal, the Irish redactor has emphasized its horrific implications for people at many different levels of society: soldiers, old men, infants, grown-up girls, well-born women, and widows (*TTr* 1902–5). And, as the city falls, a uniquely Irish touch embellishes the dire and desperate scene: the description of *Badb* bellowing and roaring above the city, accompanied by the "demons of the air" (*demna aéoir*, 1898).[37] The atrocities of the fall of Troy, when expressed this way, cannot help but demand the reader's shock and horror.

---

with the genitive singular of *teine*, 'fire,' to mean 'fringe of fire, conflagration, blaze.' The phrase appears in the late Middle Irish "Life of St. Lasair" as quoted in note 32, as well as at *TTr* 156 (in reference to Hercules' earlier sack of Troy) and in a text from the *Book of Leinster* (Whitley Stokes, ed. and trans., "The Violent Deaths of Goll and Garb," *Revue Celtique* 14 [1893]: 396-449 at 418, section 34).

[34] The sense is presumably 'overhead.'

[35] Stokes's translation marks the noun *míchostadh* as a crux. Following *eDIL* (s.v. "mí-chostud)", it can be understood here as 'turbulence,' a synonym of the preceding *anféth* ('turmoil, unrest').

[36] Stokes, ed. and trans., *TTr* 1895–1906. As noted in Stokes's preface (*Irische Texte,* second series, part 1: 2), his text retains instances of *v* for *u* in accordance with the manuscript.

[37] For this and other instances of *Badb* in medieval Irish classical adaptations, see LeBlanc, "Heroic Traditions," 217-219.

One of the most appalling events of Troy's fall as told by Virgil in *Aen.* 2–where it is part of Aeneas's inset narration to Dido–is the murder of the elderly king Priam, who has uselessly strapped armor on his feeble shoulders one last time. As Priam takes shelter before the altar, Aeneas sees him slain by Achilles's son Neoptolemus in a brutal and sacrilegious fashion (*Aen.* 2.506–58). In contrast, Dares mentions the death of Priam–who is represented much less favorably in that text and had already been making plans to have the traitors killed–in rather dispassionate terms, dispatching him in a single terse sentence: *Neoptolemus in regiam inruptionem facit, Troianos caedit, Priamum persequitur, quem ante aram Iovis obtruncat* ("Neoptolemus makes an attack on the palace, kills Trojans, [and] chases Priam, whom he slaughters before the altar of Jove," 41).

But it is here that *Togail Troí* makes a particularly intriguing choice, one with significant bearing on the reader's impression of Aeneas: the text strays from its typical reliance on Dares to describe the attack on Priam's palace and the murder of the king in thoroughly Virgilian terms instead. Though *TTr* does not present the events from Aeneas's perspective, many prominent details from his account in *Aen.* 2 are incorporated to augment Dares's succinct description of the Trojan ruler's demise. Among others, these include the death of one of Priam's sons before his eyes (in Virgil Polites, in *TTr* unnamed);[38] Priam's final failed attempt to cast a spear at Neoptolemus;[39] and the old king's death before the altar (in Virgil of the household gods, in Dares of Jove, in *TTr* of Minerva).[40] All the while, the Irish Aeneas is entirely absent from the events his Virgilian counterpart had so movingly recounted. The fight for the palace is described much more vividly in the Irish text than in Dares, drawing directly on Aeneas's narration from Book 2 of the *Aeneid*–but in a way that removes the hero himself, erasing the role he claims to have played on that final night. The story that Virgil's Aeneas tells Dido is rewritten and reframed, leaving its narrator out of the picture.

Other examples of this tactic are plentiful. One striking case concerns the Trojan defense of Priam's palace, where Virgil's Aeneas

---

[38] *Aen.* 2.526-32, *TTr* 1884-86.
[39] *Aen.* 2.544-46, *TTr* 1886-88.
[40] *Aen.* 2.550-53, *TTr* 1888-89.

describes the Trojans hurling roof-tiles and any projectiles they can find at the approaching Greeks to slow their onslaught:

> *Dardanidae contra turris ac tota domorum*
> *culmina conuellunt; his se, quando ultima cernunt,*
> *extrema iam in morte parant defendere telis,*
> *auratasque trabes, ueterum decora alta parentum,*
> *deuoluunt; alii strictis mucronibus imas*
> *obsedere fores, has seruant agmine denso.*[41]

> In turn the Trojans ripped apart the towers
> and roof-tiles–seeing that the end was near,
> they readied these as weapons for defense
> while on the very brink of death–and toppled
> the gilded beams that were their fathers' pride.
> Others, swords drawn, stood at the doors below
> and guarded them in thick and ready lines.[42]

Togail Troí, too, mentions these various projectiles (notably not found in Dares), but with an expanded list of makeshift weapons and the erstwhile narrator Aeneas nowhere to be found:

> *In fairend aile immorro dochótar side for sonnachaib*
> *7 dvmaib 7 chnoccaib togla an denna, corgabsat ic*
> *tréndíbricud na slógh, conid immaille notheilgidís*
> *forru na gae 7 na claidbe 7 na sciathu 7 na saigte 7*
> *bairne na cloch fo chossa 7 sailge 7 cláradv 7 dromclai*
> *7 ochtaige na ngríanán 7 na taige cláraidh.*
> *Robrissiset dano benna na stúagdorus, 7 rochuirset i*
> *cenn na ńGréc, co rothascairset ilmíli dona slúagaib*
> *fón innas[s]in.*

---

[41] *Aen.* 2.445-50. Latin text quoted from R. A. B. Mynors, ed., *P. Vergili Maronis Opera* (Oxford: Clarendon Press, 1969).

[42] These lines are drawn from an in-progress verse translation of the *Aeneid* (under contract with Norton) that I am developing jointly with Scott McGill.

The others, however, went on the palisades and mounds and sconces(?)[43] of the citadel, and began to cast mightily at the hosts in such wise that they hurled together on them the spears and the swords and the shields and the arrows and the rocks of the stones under foot, and the beams and planks and roofs and poles of the balconies and the plank-houses. Then they broke the pinnacles of the archways and flung them against the Greeks, so that in that wise they laid low many thousands of the hosts.[44]

While Virgil's Aeneas mentions these desperate defense efforts shortly before describing how he himself joined the Trojans on the roof to launch a tower down upon the advancing Greeks (*Aen.* 2.458-68), the Aeneas of *Togail Troí* has already been identified as one of the leading traitors at this point in the narrative. In fact, when the traitors go to meet the Greeks, Aeneas's name is unexpectedly listed before Antenor's (*TTr* 1831), making it seem as if he might even be a more central figure in the plot than his counterpart, who is typically shown as the instigator elsewhere. The two of them let Neoptolemus through the gates together before Antenor himself, as in Dares (41), leads him directly to the palace (1843-46).

When the destruction of the royal household and the brutal murder of the king occur, readers can thus link them directly to the act of betrayal committed by Antenor and Aeneas. Where, in Dares's Latin text, the events are described matter-of-factly and without much room to feel emotion or sympathy for the Trojans, the visceral picture of the carnage we see in *Togail Troí* reframes the deeds of the traitors in a still more critical light. This Aeneas is not a hero who seems to

---

[43] The phrase translated here, *chnoccaib togla*, seems literally to mean 'siege-mounds' (from *cnocc*, 'lump, mound,' and the genitive singular of *togail*, 'siege'). As *eDIL* indicates (s.v. "cnocc "), a similar phrase is found at line 1748 of *In Cath Catharda* (the Irish adaptation of Lucan's *Bellum Ciuile*), where the earthworks erected by Caesar's men in his siege of Massilia are described as *cnuic debhtha*, 'fighting mounds.' For a text and translation of *In Cath Catharda*, see Whitley Stokes, ed. and trans., "*In Cath Catharda*, The Civil War of the Romans: An Irish Version of Lucan's *Pharsalia*," in Stokes and Windisch, ed., *Irische Texte*, series 4, part 2: 2 (1909), 1-581.

[44] Stokes, ed. and trans., *TTr* 1863-70.

have given all he could to save his city, but a different kind of figure entirely–one whom readers would be justified to hold morally responsible for all the horrors of Troy's fall, including the slaughter of the pitiable elderly king. While Virgil's Aeneas begins his story by claiming that he played a substantial part in the events of Troy's fall (*Aen.* 2.5-6) and frames himself as one of the city's final and most stalwart defenders, the Aeneas of *Togail Troí* is shown to play a major role of a very different kind: the blood of Troy's last night is on his hands.

History, genealogy, and treason: Aeneas in *Ystorya Dared*

Where *Togail Troí* amplifies and intensifies the account of Troy's betrayal and fall from Dares's version, the Welsh *Ystorya Dared*[45]

---

[45] John Rhys and J. Gwenogvryn Evans, eds., *The Text of the Bruts from the Red Book of Hergest* (Oxford: Clarendon Press, 1890), 1-39. This remains the only published text of *YD*, which lacks a standard edition or English translation (though one is currently in preparation by Helen Fulton). Like *TTr*, *YD* exists in multiple recensions; roughly forty-five copies of the text survive, which have been listed in full by B. G. Owens, "Y Fersiynau Cymraeg o *Dares Phrygius* (*Ystorya Dared*), eu Tarddiad, eu Nodweddion, a'u Cydberthynas" (unpublished M.A. thesis, University of Wales, 1951). More recently, a concise account of the text's transmission and an overview of its editing difficulties has been offered by Helen Fulton, "A Medieval Welsh Version of the Troy Story: Editing *Ystorya Dared*," in *Probable Truth: Editing Medieval Texts from Britain in the Twenty-First Century*, ed. Vincent Gillespie and Anne Hudson, Texts and Transitions 5 (Turnhout: Brepols, 2013), 355-72 at 364-70. Though Owens identified six principal categories of manuscripts (IA, IB, IIA, IIB, III, and IV), Fulton has reclassified them into two main types: Version A and Version B, which align with Owens's Versions IA and IB and IIA and IIB, respectively ("Medieval Welsh Version," 365 and n. 28). The text found in the Red Book of Hergest is grouped by Fulton into Version A, with two different translations of Dares likely lying behind the discrepancies between her Versions A and B (Fulton, "Medieval Welsh Version," 365). Owens similarly suggested that his Versions IA and IIA reflect independent translations of two distinct Latin sources ("Y Fersiynau Cymraeg," clxxxiii). Erich Poppe has also proposed a relationship between the second recension of *TTr* and the version of *YD* that Owens calls IA ("Personal Names and an Insular Tradition of Pseudo-Dares," *Ériu* 53 [2003]: 53-59),

proceeds along different lines. In general, its representation aligns rather more closely with what we find in the Latin text; though much could be said about its handling of Dares, this paper will focus instead on its place among the Welsh chronicles.[46] As Fulton has argued, *Ystorya Dared* held a unique historical relevance for its Welsh audience on the basis of the tradition by which Brutus, the legendary founder of Britain, was descended directly from Aeneas; through this connection, the events of the Trojan War become a sort of prequel to the ultimate founding of Britain and, therefore, to the rise of the Welsh people themselves as descendants of noble Trojan ancestors.[47] The prominence of the figure of Brutus in the genre of Welsh historiography is illustrated well by the usage of the related term *brut* for vernacular works that trace the early history of the British people, such as *Brut y Brenhinedd* (The Chronicle of the Kings)[48] and *Brut y Tywysogyon* (The Chronicle of the Princes).[49]

---

and Anja Jäcke has identified connections between versions IA and III and a surviving Latin text of Dares ("Auf den Spuren des insularen Dares," in *Allerlei Keltisches: Studien zu Ehren von Erich Poppe*, ed. Franziska Bock, Dagmar Bronner, and Dagmar Schlüter [Berlin: Curach Bhán, 2011], 29-44).

[46] The models of historiography represented by *YD* and *TTr* have been discussed by Fulton ("History and *historia*"), as has the relationship of *YD* with the Welsh historical chronicles ("Troy Story: The Medieval Welsh *Ystorya Dared* and the *Brut* Tradition of British History," *Medieval Chronicle* 7 [2011]: 137-50). For a detailed study of the Welsh historical chronicles, see Owain Wyn Jones, "Historical Writing in Medieval Wales," Ph.D. diss. (Bangor University, 2013). Of particular relevance to the present paper is Chapter 1, "The Manuscript Context of Medieval Welsh Historical Texts" (30-70).

[47] Fulton, "Medieval Welsh Version," 358.

[48] For *Brut y Brenhinedd*, see Brynley F. Roberts, ed., *Brut y Brenhinedd: Llanstephan MS. 1 Version*, Medieval and Modern Welsh Series 5 (Dublin: Dublin Institute for Advanced Studies, 1971) and John Jay Parry, ed. and trans., *Brut y Brenhinedd: Cotton Cleopatra Version* (Cambridge, MA: Medieval Academy of America, 1937).

[49] Fulton, "Medieval Welsh Version," 357. For *Brut y Tywysogyon,* see Thomas Jones, ed. and trans., *Brut y Tywysogyon, or The Chronicle of the Princes: Red Book of Hergest Version*, second ed., History and Law Series

In terms of genre, *Ystorya Dared* aligns very closely with this *brut* tradition; like its source text, the work is historicizing and presents a seemingly realistic and factual version of the events of the Trojan War. The classification of *Ystorya Dared* as a historical work is supported not only by its content and overall approach, but by its context in the manuscript tradition: the text is invariably accompanied in medieval manuscripts by other works from the *brut* tradition, either *Brut y Brenhinedd* (the Welsh adaptation of Geoffrey of Monmouth) or one or both of the native Welsh chronicles, *Brut y Tywysogyon* and *Brenhinedd y Saesson* (The Kings of the English).[50] *Ystorya Dared* is thus regularly positioned as something of a preface to the Welsh chronicles, which typically begin with Brutus material drawn from Geoffrey.[51] Even so, it is striking that this historicizing text leaves no room for doubt about the role of the traitorous Aeneas; it is at once an accurate representation of Dares's version of events and, simultaneously, a work taken seriously as a description of the prehistory of the Welsh people. According to Fulton, it is not until Brutus—whose story often immediately follows *Ystorya Dared* in the manuscripts—that the stigma attached to Aeneas's line can be fully canceled out.[52] Even then, however, his betrayal may still cast a shadow on subsequent generations: as inconvenient a founding ancestor as the treacherous Aeneas might seem, he makes a surprisingly suitable predecessor for traitors yet to rise in the later legendary history of Britain.[53]

---

16 (Cardiff: University of Wales Press, 1973) and *Brut y Tywysogyon, or The Chronicle of the Princes: Peniarth MS. 20 Version*, History and Law Series 11 (Cardiff: University of Wales Press, 1952).

[50] Fulton, "Medieval Welsh Version," 357-58 and 364. For *Brenhinedd y Saesson*, see Thomas Jones, ed. and trans., *Brenhinedd y Saesson, or The Kings of the Saxons: BM Cotton MS. Cleopatra B v and the Black Book of Basingwerk, NLW MS. 7006*, History and Law Series 25 (Cardiff: University of Wales Press, 1971).

[51] Fulton, "Troy Story," 138.

[52] Fulton, "History and *historia*," 56.

[53] I am grateful to Catherine McKenna and Paul Russell for the suggestion that Aeneas's act of betrayal might prefigure the deeds of later traitors portrayed in Geoffrey's history (among whom especially Mordred comes to mind).

In direct genealogical terms, the Trojans held much more perceived relevance to the Welsh than to the Irish, who attributed their own origins to both Europe and Asia (as the *Lebor Gabála* can be seen to demonstrate).[54] Nevertheless, however, Aeneas is granted prominence in Irish literature as the ancestor of future peoples and world rulers. The *Lebor Bretnach*, the Irish translation of the *Historia Brittonum* attributed to Nennius, acknowledges his place as the ancestor of Brutus, and, through Brutus, of the early Britons.[55] In a similar vein, readers who travel with Aeneas to the conclusion of his journey in *Imtheachta Aeniasa* are left with the observation that numerous future lines of world rulers will be drawn from him, his son Ascanius, and his wife Lavinia:

> ⁊ *is do shil Æni[a]sa* ⁊ *Asgain* ⁊ *Lauina rogenetar flaithi* ⁊ *rigraidh Roman* ⁊ *oirigh in domuin o sin riam co ti in brath.*

> And from the seed of Aeneas, Ascanius, and Lavinia have sprung Roman lords, and king-folk, and rulers of the world from thenceforward till the judgment-day shall come.[56]

---

[54] Fulton, "History and *historia*," 50-51. For the *Lebor Gabála*, see R. A. Stewart Macalister, ed. and trans., *Lebor Gabála Érenn: The Book of the Taking of Ireland*, 5 vols. (Dublin: Irish Texts Society, 1938-56).

[55] *Lebor Bretnach* 8-10. Paragraph numbers are drawn from A. G. van Hamel, ed., *Lebor Bretnach: The Irish Version of the Historia Britonum Ascribed to Nennius* (Dublin: Stationery Office, 1932). A text accompanied by an English translation can be found at James Henthorn Todd, ed. and trans., *Leabhar Breathnach annso sis: The Irish Version of the Historia Britonum of Nennius* (Dublin: Irish Archaeological Society, 1848); the passage in question appears in paragraphs 5-7 there.

[56] Calder, ed. and trans., *IA* 3213-15. As Poppe has observed ("New Introduction," 8), the summary of Aeneas's descendants provided in the short epilogue to *IA* (3206-15) aligns closely with a historical text about Silvius from the Yellow Book of Lecan (for which see Kuno Meyer, "Silvius, Stammvater der Britten," *Zeitschrift für celtische Philologie* 12 [1918]: 376). The Silvius tract or a related account is likely to have served as a source for the final section of *IA* (Poppe, "Introduction," 8). See Miles, *Don Tres Troí*, 47 n. 52 for the possibility that the concluding lines of *IA* lie

For someone reading the text the whole way through, the effect might be rather jarring: it begins with Aeneas being expelled from Troy along with his fellow traitors, and by the end, he and his family members are acknowledged as founding ancestors of countless royal dynasties yet to come.

As we examine the place of Aeneas's treachery in medieval Irish and Welsh literature, we find a number of striking differences from ancient approaches to the same topic. In Greek and Latin texts from Homer to Virgil, the possibility that Aeneas's escape from Troy occurred through suspicious means was seemingly more of a fringe idea than a mainstream one. Once the *Aeneid* brings the hero's *pietas* to the forefront, his possible treachery is relegated even further to the margin; following the supposedly 'eyewitness' accounts of Dares and Dictys in late antiquity, however, the idea of Aeneas's treachery seems to become much more widespread. By the time of the Irish and Welsh texts considered in this paper, it is treated as a central and consistent element of the character's story. *Pius Aeneas* has been replaced, by and large, by a shadowy and somewhat more questionable character—one who might well be to blame for all the atrocities committed in the final agonies of Troy. Nowhere is this contrast more apparent than at the start of *Imtheachta Aeniasa*, which does not begin, as Virgil's version does, with a man *insignis pietate*, but instead with one being expelled from the homeland he has helped destroy.

Alongside the growing prominence of the traitor tradition, Aeneas is singled out as the ancestor of future peoples descended from the Trojans and, through them, the Romans. Like his descendant Brutus—who, as the legend goes, would be banished himself after accidentally killing his father with an arrow[57]—Aeneas is driven from

---

behind references to the *rígrad Roman*, 'family line of Roman kings,' at the end of *Togail Troí* as transmitted in Royal Irish Academy MS D iv 2 (1223) and the Book of Ballymote (Royal Irish Academy MS 23 P 12 [536]).

[57] This account of Brutus's fate occurs in both *Lebor Bretnach* (§5 in van Hamel's edition and §7 in Todd's) and in *Brut y Brenhinedd* (pages 9-10 of Parry's text); the former adapts in Irish the *Historia Brittonum* attributed to Nennius, while the latter reworks in Welsh the *Historia regum Britanniae* of Geoffrey of Monmouth. For the episode as it appears in *Historia Brittonum*, see David Dumville, ed., *The Historia Brittonum, 3: The 'Vatican' Recension*

his homeland by an act that ultimately sets him up to serve as the founder of a new civilization. His divine destiny and the workings of the Fates seem rather subordinate to the practical reality that he cannot stay to govern the civilization ruined by his betrayal.

These two key themes–Aeneas as traitor and Aeneas as founding ancestor–seem on the surface to be in conflict, and further investigation is warranted to evaluate their uneasy coexistence not only in medieval Celtic literature, but also in other medieval vernacular literatures where the two seemingly contradictory representations appear together. Though the character of Aeneas in Virgil has prompted numerous scholarly investigations and has been at the center of major debates concerning the morality of his actions, the Aeneas who turned on Troy and fled to found the line that would lead to Rome seems much more complicated still. Is this Aeneas a refugee or a renegade, and what place did his supposed treachery occupy in the minds of the medieval Irish and Welsh?

Perhaps, in the cyclical or Boethian model of history that has been associated with texts like *Togail Troí* and *Ystorya Dared*, the *impius* Aeneas is merely a required step in the progression of history– something that must happen for Troy to fall and Rome to rise, and then for Rome to fall and its successors to rise in turn. As the story of the Trojan traitors grew in prominence, Aeneas's divine mandate to sail to Italy may have faded into the background for Irish and Welsh audiences; but the fact remains that, one way or another, Aeneas had to be forced from Troy to establish the line of Rome and, with it, the line of Brutus. The story of Virgil's Aeneas, singled out for his exceptional *pietas* despite his sometimes dubious deeds, becomes reshaped as it is retold. In medieval Ireland and Wales, a profoundly different picture emerges, a new Aeneas molded by engagement with the traitor tradition no less than with Virgil himself. This Aeneas

---

(Cambridge: D. S. Brewer, 1985), §5 and John Morris, ed. and trans., *British History and the Welsh Annals*, Arthurian Period Sources 8 (London: Phillimore, 1980), §10; for Geoffrey's rendering, see Michael D. Reeve, ed., and Neil Wright, trans., *The History of the Kings of Britain* (Woodbridge: Boydell, 2007), 1.6-7. Early versions of the Brutus tale and the modifications made by Geoffrey are discussed in Thea Sommerfield, "Filling the Gap: Brutus in the *Historia Brittonum*, *Anglo-Saxon Chronicle* MS F, and Geoffrey of Monmouth," *Medieval Chronicle* 7 (2011): 85-102.

becomes a fascinating and complex figure pushed on toward his destiny not by righteous behavior and the will of Fate, but instead by betrayal and banishment. Aeneas does not look quite so *pius* anymore—but perhaps that makes him all the more intriguing.

Acknowledgments

Many thanks are owed to the anonymous reviewer at PHCC and to the editors for their thoughtful feedback and support in bringing this article to completion. I am also grateful to Joseph Nagy for his helpful comments on a draft of the paper and to Richard Thomas for encouragement of the project, as well as to the attendees of HCC 40 for their questions, insights, and suggestions.

Abstracts of Papers Presented at the Fortieth Harvard Celtic Colloquium

Not that informal: Social Practice of Scottish Gaelic and non-formality

Fañch Bihan-Gallic

The paper explores the social use of Scottish Gaelic by adult learners of the language outside formal classes. It highlights the difference between language practices in non-formal and informal situations, revealing that Gaelic is, more often than not, absent from the latter. The analysis is based on a year of ethnographic research conducted in Scotland as part of a broader project aiming at a better understanding of linguistic practices amongst learners.

One of the key aspects of second language acquisition (SLA) is social practice of the target language in various contexts, both formal and informal. Theories of SLA have complexified these contexts by distinguishing between informal and non-formal practices, the latter being a more structured environment. Non-formal interactions tend to be particularly prominent for adult learners of Scottish Gaelic, many of whom spend more time in conversation circles and Gaelic-related clubs than using Gaelic in shops, in the street or within their family and friend groups.

My research led me to notice a clear gap between informality and non-formality, with what could be seen as a form of diglossia: while non-formal contexts tend to be strongly Gaelic-speaking, informal ones are often English-speaking–even amongst the same people, and within the same social groups. This is a problem that can thwart efforts to revitalise and revernacularise Scottish Gaelic. Understanding these social and linguistic practices better may inform activists and policy-makers, both in Scotland and in other endangered language areas.

FORTIETH CELTIC COLLOQUIUM

Remarks on pragmatic fronting and poetic overdetermination in Middle Cornish

Benjamin Bruch and Joe Eska

As a verb-second language, one expects Middle Cornish to allow only a single argument/complement to appear in the Left Periphery of affirmative main clauses. But one finds a significant number of examples in which both a subject and a full non-adjunct XP co-öccur in the Left Periphery, presumably owing to poetic overdetermination, which alters the surface configuration in order to enable the required syllable-count or rhyme in the verse line. Object personal pronouns never occur in the Left Periphery, but a full non-adjunct XP and subject personal pronoun co-öccur in a significant number of clauses, in that order, in all but a single token. George 1990 & 1991, based upon an analysis of *Beunans Meriasek*, finds five examples of full object DP and subject personal pronoun which coöccur in the Left Periphery, which, he states, are not motivated by poetic overdetermination. He concludes, on that basis, that the construction is generated by the grammar. In this paper, we examine the entire verse corpus of Middle Cornish and argue that all examples are, ultimately, motivated by poetic overdetermination, not only in order to enable the required syllable-count or rhyme, but–crucially–usually also to encode pragmatic information.

Editor's Note: The authors published this paper with this title in the *North Amercan Journal of Celtic Studies*, vol. 5 no. 2 (2021) 131-193.

'Till the brink of Doom and the end of the world': History and Eschatology in the Irish version of Lucan's *Pharsalia*

Brigid Ehrmantraut

Multiple works of Classical epic were translated and adapted in medieval Ireland, including Vergil's *Aeneid*, Statius's *Thebaid*, and Lucan's *De Bello Civili (Pharsalia)*. These medieval Irish versions are more creative adaptations than word-for-word translations, but the twelfth-century text *In Cath Catharda* (The Civil War), the Irish version of Lucan, is particularly interesting for remaining closer to its source material in both phrasing and plot than many other medieval Irish Classical adaptations. At the same time, *In Cath Catharda* subtly incorporates Lucan's epic into medieval pseudohistorical frameworks of world history, placing the work in dialogue with earlier Christian commentators as well as with a growing twelfth-century interest in synchronism and world history. This paper will examine how, through biblical allusions, apocalyptic imagery, narrative reorganization, and the addition of a pseudohistorical prologue, *In Cath Catharda* ties Lucan's underlying narrative into a larger Christian model of *historia*, and elevates the Battle of Pharsalia to a cataclysm on par with the Flood or Judgment Day. As I will discuss, the Irish text also identifies and magnifies aspects of Lucan's anti-imperialism in the service of its new Christian framework: the civil war which Lucan treats as an unnatural agent of social breakdown becomes in Irish an eschatologically-oriented conflict. *In Cath Catharda* is an excellent example of how Classical literature can contribute to the writing of medieval historiography, while remaining true to a Classical work's original themes and style.

One Thing Leads to Another: An Old Irish dialogue between Cormac and Coirpre on the legal consequences of seduction

Charlene Eska

This paper concerns a dialogue between the mythical king, Cormac, and his son, Coirpre. In the first part, Coirpre confesses to raping a woman. Cormac asks why he did such a thing, and Coirpre's excuses for his actions follow in a series of repetitive questions and answers. The second part of the dialogue is ascribed entirely to Cormac, and it forms his 'instructions' to his son. The instructions describe the steps from flirtation to kissing to seduction to conception without resorting to violence. Cormac's 'instructions' also touch upon the real legal consequences of begetting a child, whether by rape or consent.

FORTIETH CELTIC COLLOQUIUM

Editor's note: A later version of this presentation was published by the author with this title in the *North American Journal of Celtic Studies*, vol. 5 no. 2: 242-250.

Strategies and influences: text creation and text reproduction by Irish schoolchildren in the National Folklore Collection of Ireland

Nikita Koptev

The Schools' Scheme of 1937/8, initiated by the Irish Folklore Commission, was an almost unprecedented experiment. Not only did it contribute to one of the biggest collections of folklore in Europe, but it also arguably boosted the cultural development of children and created a catalyst for the intergenerational transmission of tales. Children from 26 counties collected folk materials on 55 topics indicated in the booklet *Irish Folklore and Tradition* (1937). While the majority of the texts in the Schools' Collection of the National Folklore Collection of Ireland were collected from adults, some, arguably, were produced by the children themselves. The fact that the texts in the Schools' Collection were created in the school context as part of the Composition lessons predetermined several crucial features. Moreover, the way the collection process was organised by the Folklore Commission influenced the outcome as well. This paper will examine prominent features of the texts, strategies employed by children and influential factors that could have changed the outcome of the Schools' Scheme of 1937/8.

Editors' Note: We hope to publish a revised article by this author in a future issue of *PHCC*.

Editing Welsh folk poetry: international influences on T. H. Parry-Williams

E. Wyn James

One of the most brilliant Welsh scholars of the twentieth century was Sir T. H. Parry-Williams (1887-1975). He was also an outstanding poet and prose writer. Folk poetry is central to his work. It was a key influence on his creative writing: among his main modes of literary expression was the *rhigwm* (rhyming couplet), an adaptation of 'light-hearted ballad-type versifying'. Furthermore, one of his chief contributions to Welsh scholarship was the series of four edited volumes of popular free-metre verse of the early modern period which he published between 1931 and 1940: *Carolau Richard White* (1931), *Llawysgrif Richard Morris o Gerddi* (1931), *Canu Rhydd Cynnar* (1932) and *Hen Benillion* (1940).

This paper will draw attention to the 'dualities' in Parry-Williams's life and work, examine his work as editor of folk poetry and explore the reasons why so much of his energy focussed on such poetry. There were indigenous Welsh influences which may well have kindled his interest in folk poetry, not least perhaps his predecessors in the Chair of Welsh at Aberystwyth, Daniel Silvan Evans and Sir Edward Anwyl, and his teacher and mentor at Oxford, Sir John Rhŷs. Another factor may have been his strong links with several German academics, including studying under Rudolf Thurneysen at Freiburg between 1911 and 1913. Then there were Irish influences; and he was certainly familiar with the work of Child and Kittredge at Harvard.

Geoffrey Keating's *Forsa Feasa ar Éirinn*: Between Senchas and New History

Feliks Levin

The objective of this paper is to reconsider the debate about the nature of Geoffrey Keating's *Foras Feasa ar Éirinn* as a product of history-writing. B.Ó Cuív and D. Ó Corráin place *Foras Feasa ar Éirinn* in the context of Gaelic historical tradition of *senchas*, whereas B. Ó Buachalla, B. Bradshaw, and B. Cunningham point out its close connection with Renaissance historicism. The former address *Foras Feasa ar Éirinn* from the perspective of the categories of modern historiograhy while the latter exaggerate the extent of the revolutionary character of historiographic change in early modern European history-writing.

The paper will suggest a more balanced approach to Keating's text which takes into account the arguments of the critics of the concept of 'historiographical revolution'. They highlighted that 'the history of history is not a neat progression from one mode of thought to another' and that in early modern history writing the old and the new co-existed.

The paper will examine the influence of Irish and non-Irish discursive strategies on the style of Geoffrey Keating's history-writing in *Foras Feasa ar Éirinn*. It will examine elements of continuity with native historical tradition; influence of English history-writing and Keating's clerical experience on authorial engagement with the text, ways of argumentation, and strategies of authentication of the presented material in *Foras Feasa ar Éirinn*.

More than just fire and brimstone:
Manx manuscript sermons, 1696–1863

Christopher Lewin and Peadar Ó Muircheartaigh

The volume of extant manuscript sermons in the Manx language is remarkable by any measure. Over 700 manuscript sermons written in Manx survive from the period between 1696 and 1863, exceeding the number found in Irish and Scottish Gaelic combined. Most of the manuscripts have identifiable authors and contain precise details of dates and places of preaching, as well as re-use and adaptation, and are thus a rich source of information on the social, religious and linguistic history of the Isle of Man.

In linguistic terms, the texts are particularly valuable for shedding light on the evolution and standardization of Manx orthography, and on phonological and morphosyntactic variation. The corpus is also an important testing ground for questions of linguistic variation and change in the Gaelic languages more generally. Despite their value to scholarship, Manx sermons have been little-studied and only three manuscript sermons have been edited to date (Morrison 1906; Kavanagh 1947; Lewin 2015).

This paper will outline the extent of the corpus and place it in the broader context of contemporary British and Irish sermon writing and preaching, as well as examining questions of transmission, composition, translation and preservation. The potential of the material to inform our understanding of the social and linguistic history of the Isle of Man will be demonstrated.

ABSTRACTS

'He himself tempts no one': Breandán Ó hEithir's novels *Lig Sinn i gCathú* and *Sionnach ar mo Dhuán*

Brian Ó Conchubhair

Born in 1930, on Inishmore, the Aran Islands, Breandán Ó hEithir, a nephew of Liam O'Flaherty, garnered attention and no little notoriety as a journalist, broadcaster, poet, and author who wrote in both Irish and English. On the occasion of his death in 1990, the *New York Times* described Ó hEithir as "a social critic and author of the first Irish-language novel to lead the country's best-seller list." That book, *Lig Sinn i gCathú* (1976) appeared in English as *Lead us Into Temptation* (1978) and both editions led to controversies and a series of letters in national newspapers. A second novel entitled *Sionnach ar mo Dhuán* followed in 1988 and earned a controversial review in the *Irish Times* and a slew of letters. Liam Mac Con Iomaire published a biography, entitled *Breandán Ó hEithir: Iomramh Aonair* in 2000. This paper focuses on the two published novels and discusses Ó hEithir's merits as a novelist, how his style and technique developed between the two books, and argues that the latter work reveals a more nuanced, sophisticated literary understanding of form, metafiction, structuring, and plot development.

Popular Beliefs, the Native Literary Tradition, and Medieval Saints' Cults: St. Derfel and the Reformation

Katharine Olson

This interdisciplinary paper examines a wide variety of evidence drawn from Middle/Early Modern Welsh poetry and prose, historical records, landscape studies, and folklore regarding the medieval cult of the saint Derfel Gadarn and its fate (including that of sacred objects associated with it) during the 'Long Reformation' of the seventeenth and eighteenth centuries.

Derfel Gadarn (Derfel the Strong, or Mighty), was reputedly a late fifth or early sixth-century warrior saint. In life, he was said to have fought as one of Arthur's knights at the Battle of Camlan. His genealogy is uncertain, but some later versions of the *Bonedd y Saint* record him as a descendant of Hywel ab Emyr Llydaw. Indeed, one remarkable and celebrated survival of the Reformation to the present day is part of a wooden figure of Derfel Gadarn: his stag or horse (*Ceffyl Gadarn*) and his staff (*Ffon Gadarn*). While much has been written of the destruction of the wooden image of St. Derfel himself in the fire at Smithfield in 1538, there has been far less written on the medieval cult and the fate of his stag/horse and staff in the seventeenth and eighteenth centuries.

This paper offers a more in-depth examination of his principal church of Llandderfel (Merioneth), cult, and popular beliefs during this period. It demonstrates both the slow pace of change in terms of the implementation of reform as well as the nature of Protestant iconoclasm and attempts to regulate the use of sacred space and objects on a local basis. Lastly, it assesses the complex nature and development of religious identities, sacred space, saints' cults, and popular beliefs and practices in sixteenth-, seventeenth-, and eighteenth-century Wales and places these within a wider British, Irish, and European context.

'Ablach–Parcels of a Carion, &c.' to 'Rudha–A Point of Land': A Newly Discovered Scottish Gaelic Dictionary by Alasdair mac Mhaighstir Alasdair?

Domhnall Uilleam Stiùbhart

Over the past three decades the life and work of the major Scottish Gaelic poet Alexander MacDonald or Alasdair mac Mhaighstir Alasdair (c. 1700-c. 1770) has been the focus of increasing scholarly attention. A volume of conference proceedings (*Alexander MacDonald: Bard of the Gaelic Enlightenment*) was published in 2012, and in a series of exceptionally significant articles Ronald Black has demonstrated the poet's foundational rôle both in codifying modern Scottish Gaelic and in advocating its specifically Scottish, national identity. In this paper I shall offer a modest contribution to Mac Mhaighstir Alasdair scholarship by examining a 27-page manuscript dictionary or word list preserved in Edinburgh University Library Special Collections among the papers of Donald Mackinnon

ABSTRACTS

(1839–1914), the first Professor of Celtic in Scotland. I shall discuss the volume's provenance, and, by comparing the scribal hand with documents written by Alasdair mac Mhaighstir Alasdair, raise the question as to whether it may have been compiled by the poet himself. I shall consider various possible contexts for the dictionary's creation, situating it in the framework of other early modern lexicographical activities in Scottish Gaelic. Finally, I shall discuss in what ways the volume might throw further light on the life and work of Alasdair mac Mhaighstir Alasdair, not only as a major poet, but also as a lexicographer, song-collector, cultural broker, and cultural entrepreneur.

Editor's Note: We hope to publish a version of this paper in a future volume of *PHCC*.

Earthly and Paradisal Modes of Empire
in *Suidiugud Tellaig Temra*

Daniel Watson

Recent scholarship has shown that Ireland was increasingly imagined as an empire throughout the Middle Irish period, and that the reception of Orosius' *Historiae adversus paganos* played a crucial role in this development. According to Orosius, there had been a providential translation of the seat of world empire from place to place since the time of its first emergence. The argument is that this historiographical framework provided a decisive means of conceptualising Ireland as the legitimate imperial successor to Rome. If the true seat of empire had moved in the past, it was then comprehensible that it would move again. This conclusion seems to be correct. However, the extant scholarship has yet to deal with the problem of how Orosius' idea of the *translatio imperii* could be successfully repurposed in this way. Orosius did not conceive of there being any further translations of empire before the end of the world following its translation to Rome. Thus, the application of this idea to a political order that was not conceived to be a continuation of Rome, or a reinstantiation of it, but its successor, is far from straightforward. This paper will look at the way in which the Middle Irish text, *Suidiugud Tellaig Temra* (The Settling of the Manor of Tara), repurposes Orosian historiography, so that Ireland, rather than Rome, comes to be its natural conclusion on this side of the Apocalypse.

Owain in the Desert: Reading
Chwedl Iarlles y Ffynnon in Its Manuscript Context

Hannah Zdansky

Studies of the *Chwedl Iarlles y Ffynnon*, or *Owain*, have focused on comparing the text to the closely related work of Chrétien de Troyes or have sought to examine the narrative in light of traditions common in Celtic literature more broadly. For instance, the experience that the protagonist undergoes can easily be viewed as an example of the "Wild Man in the Woods" motif. And it is certainly true that the text fits comfortably alongside the *Four Branches of the Mabinogi*, with the Four Branches being considered didactic in intent, representing in Welsh literature the European tradition of "mirrors for princes." While such studies furnish us with important lenses through which to view the text, little work has been done on situating *Owain* within its manuscript contexts, which present other possible hermeneutics. In this paper, I will examine the Middle Welsh *Chwedl Iarlles y Ffynnon* in its earliest manuscript context: the Llyfr Gwyn Rhydderch. *Owain* bears remarkable similarity in a number of details to both the lives of Mary of Egypt (*Buchedd Mair o'r Aifft*) and Mary Magdalene (*Buchedd Mair Fadlen*) found in the same manuscript, suggesting that readers should have, and likely did, make comparisons between them. What this does, then, is hold up a penitential lens to the text. Owain fails to live up to the standards of both a husband and a ruler, takes off into the wilderness and becomes bestial (hairy) while undergoing spiritual reflection and renewal, and comes out on the other side a reformed man.